THE OXFORD HANDBOOK OF

DANCE AND COMPETITION

THE OXFORD HANDBOOK OF

DANCE AND COMPETITION

Edited by

SHERRIL DODDS

OXFORD

UNIVERSITY PRESS

Oxford University Press is a department of the University of Oxford. It furthers
the University's objective of excellence in research, scholarship, and education
by publishing worldwide. Oxford is a registered trade mark of Oxford University
Press in the UK and certain other countries.

Published in the United States of America by Oxford University Press
198 Madison Avenue, New York, NY 10016, United States of America.

Library of Congress Cataloging-in-Publication Data
Names: Dodds, Sherril, 1967– editor.
Title: The Oxford handbook of dance and competition / edited by Sherril Dodds.
Other titles: Handbook of dance and competition
Description: New York, NY : Oxford University Press, 2019. |
Includes bibliographical references and index.
Identifiers: LCCN 2018005395 | ISBN 9780190639082 (cloth : acid-free paper) |
ISBN 9780190639112 (Oxford handbooks online)
Subjects: LCSH: Dance—Social aspects. | Dance—Competitions.
Classification: LCC GV1588.6 .O84 2019 | DDC 792.8—dc23
LC record available at https://lccn.loc.gov/2018005395

1 3 5 7 9 8 6 4 2

Printed by Sheridan Books, Inc., United States of America

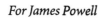

For James Powell

CONTENTS

PART I ECONOMIC AND SOCIAL CURRENCIES OF COMPETITION

PART II RE-CHOREOGRAPHING AND RE-PRESENTATION FOR THE COMPETITION FRAME

PART III WINNING, PARTICIPATION, AND THE NEGOTIATION OF MEANING

PART IV JUDGING, SPECTATORSHIP, AND THE VALUES OF MOVEMENT

PART V LOSING, FAILING, AND AUTO-CRITIQUE

PART VI HIDDEN AGENDAS AND UNSPOKEN RULES

Illustrations

Acknowledgments

THE opportunity to thank a range of wonderful individuals is perhaps my favorite moment in bringing a book project to a close. First I must thank Norm Hirschy, Senior Editor at Oxford University Press, whose enthusiasm and expertise have been generous in equal measure at each stage of publication. Indeed, his energetic embrace of dance publishing overall has ensured that we are a visible and robust field of study. I have also deeply appreciated my regular interactions with Editorial Assistant Lauralee Yeary, whose patience, knowledge, and good cheer have been extremely helpful in guiding me through various publishing technicalities. I would like to acknowledge the support of Boyer College of Music and Dance at Temple University, and specifically Dean Robert Stroker, who generously granted me course release, which enabled completion of the book in a timely manner. Further thanks must go to the Dance Department at Temple University, where I was able to work with two outstanding students in support of this project. Cindy Paul, an undergraduate BFA Dance major, kindly volunteered to assist during the summer break and I must thank her for all of the facts and figures about dance competition that she uncovered. A huge debt of gratitude goes to PhD Dance student Elizabeth Bergman, who worked as a Research Assistant over the past year. I cannot thank her enough for her sharp attention to detail and charming communications as she took care of all of the citations and bibliographic referencing. It was a pleasure to share an obsessive desire to make everything as perfect as possible, and I would have seriously struggled without her. She is a jewel. I feel incredibly fortunate to have worked with such a diverse range of bright and committed authors whose thinking on competition has certainly shaped mine. I appreciate the care and insight that they have brought to this collective work. And I particularly want to thank Susan Leigh Foster, who willingly agreed to write the Afterword, and cheerfully thanked me, even when I dropped all twenty-seven chapters in her in-box just before the winter break. Finally, I want to thank my lovely family, James, Billy, and Dylan, who find me skipping out to do research at all kinds of anti-social hours or staring at my computer screen for a little longer than they might like. Thank you for helping me do what I love.

Contributors

Daniel Belgrad is Associate Professor of Humanities and Cultural Studies at the University of South Florida. He is the author of *The Culture of Spontaneity: Improvisation and the Arts in Postwar America* (1998) and is currently writing a book on the influence of ecological thinking in American culture since 1960.

Elena Benthaus has a PhD in Dance Studies from the School of Culture and Communication at the University of Melbourne, an MA in English/American Studies and Theatre Studies, and a degree in Modern and Contemporary Dance. Her research focuses on the production, circulation, and transmission of affect in popular screendance works.

Melissa Blanco Borelli is Senior Lecturer in Dance in the Drama, Theatre and Dance Department at Royal Holloway, University of London. She is the editor of *The Oxford Handbook of Dance and the Popular Screen* (OUP, 2014) and author of *She Is Cuba: A Genealogy of the Mulata Body* (OUP, 2015), winner of the 2016 SDHS de la Torre Bueno Prize for best book in dance studies.

Erin Brannigan (PhD) is Senior Lecturer in Dance at the University of New South Wales and works in the fields of dance and film as an academic and curator. Her recent publications include *Dancefilm: Choreography and the Moving Image* (2011) and *Bodies of Thought: 12 Australian Choreographers*, co-edited with Virginia Baxter (2014).

Rachel Carrico is a scholar, artist, and educator whose research explores the aesthetic, social, and political dimensions of dance in the New Orleans second line tradition. She holds a PhD in Critical Dance Studies from the University of California, Riverside, and parades annually with the Ice Divas Social Aid and Pleasure Club.

Jeremy Carter-Gordon is a teacher, performer, and scholar of traditional music and dance. In 2011 he was awarded a year-long Thomas J. Watson Fellowship to learn, record, and document European hilt-and-point sword dances. He holds an MA in Dance Knowledge, Practice, and Heritage from Choreomundus.

Pallabi Chakravorty is Associate Professor and Director in the Department of Music and Dance at Swarthmore College. Her most recent books are *Dance Matters: Performing India on Local and Global Stages* (2010, co-editor), *This Is How We Dance Now: Performance in the Age of Bollywood and Reality Shows* (2017), and *Dance Matters Too: Markets, Memories, Identities* (2017, co-editor). She is artistic director of Courtyard Dancers, a nonprofit dance company based in Philadelphia and Kolkata.

Sally Crawford-Shepherd is a dance practitioner, choreographer, and lecturer. She achieved a BFA in Dance at University of Missouri-Kansas City, an MA in Choreography at Trinity Laban, and her PhD in Dance Ethnography at De Montfort University. She is currently the Coordinator of Dance at the University of the West Indies, St Augustine Campus, Trinidad.

Sherril Dodds is Professor of Dance and Director of the Institute of Dance Scholarship at Temple University. Her research focuses on popular dance, screen dance, and cultural theory, and her publications include *Dance on Screen* (2001), *Dancing on the Canon* (2011) and *Bodies of Sound* (2013). She was a cofounder of the international research network PoP MOVES.

Mary Fogarty is Associate Professor of Dance at York University, Toronto, Canada. She is a co-editor of *Movies, Moves and Music: The Sonic World of Dance Films* (2016) with Mark Evans, and *The Oxford Handbook of Hip-Hop Dance Studies* with Imani Kai Johnson (OUP, forthcoming). She teaches breaking classes locally for the Toronto B-Girl Movement.

Catherine E. Foley is Senior Lecturer in Ethnochoreology at the University of Limerick, Ireland. She is Founding Chair Emerita of the international society, Dance Research Forum Ireland; Founding Director of the National Dance Archive of Ireland; and is the elected Chair of the International Council for Traditional Music's Study Group on Ethnochoreology. Catherine has published widely and is a dancer and musician.

Susan Leigh Foster, choreographer and scholar, is Distinguished Professor in the Department of World Arts and Cultures at University of California, Los Angeles. She is currently at work on a book entitled *Valuing Dance: Commodities and Gifts in Motion*. Three of her danced lectures can be found at the Pew Center for Arts and Heritage website, http://danceworkbook.pcah.us/susan-foster/index.html.

Nadine George-Graves is Professor of Theater and Dance at University of California, San Diego, and past president of the Congress on Research in Dance. She is the author of *The Royalty of Negro Vaudeville: The Whitman Sisters and the Negotiation of Race, Gender, and Class in African American Theater, 1900–1940* (2000) and *Urban Bush Women: Twenty Years of Dance Theater, Community Engagement and Working It Out* (2010). She is the editor of *The Oxford Handbook of Dance and Theater* (2015).

Ruth Hellier-Tinoco (PhD) is a scholar–creative artist and Associate Professor at the University of California, Santa Barbara. Her research and teaching focus on experimental performance-making; community arts and eco-activism; sport and music; and the politics and poetics of performance, theater, music, and dance in Mexico. Publications include *Embodying Mexico: Tourism, Nationalism and Performance* (2011) and *Women Singers in Global Contexts* (2013).

April F. Masten is Associate Professor of American History at Stony Brook University. She studies the convergence of ideas and events that built structures of opportunity for cultural producers in the nineteenth century. Her first book looked at female visual artists. Her current project is a double biography of rival challenge dancers, Irish American John Diamond and African American "Juba."

Rowan McLelland is a Lecturer in the Dance Department at the University of Roehampton, London. She was a professional ballet and contemporary dancer, and now practices vintage swing dances. She was an AHRC fellow at the Shanghai Theatre Academy in 2016.

Juliet McMains (PhD) is author of *Spinning Mambo into Salsa: Caribbean Dance in Global Commerce* (OUP 2015) and *Glamour Addiction: Inside the American Ballroom Dance Industry* (2006). She is a Professor in the Dance Program at the University of Washington.

Liz Mellish is an independent researcher who completed her PhD at University College London in 2014. Her current research focuses on social dance, cultural events, and choreographic practices in Southwest Romania, and the history of the Balkan dance scene in the United Kingdom. She is Secretary of the International Council of Traditional Music study group on Music and Dance in Southeastern Europe.

Kathy Milazzo is an Adjunct Professor in Writing in Clovis, New Mexico. She received her PhD in Dance Studies from the University of Surrey, focusing on sub-Saharan African/Africanist influences on flamenco and Spanish dance. Her publications on Spanish dance and culture range from historical inquiries to anthropological explorations.

Celena Monteiro is a PhD candidate and Associate Lecturer in Dance at the University of Chichester. The working title for her current research is *European Dancehall Queen Competitions in the Digital Age: Transcultural Feminine Identity Production in Performance*. She holds an MA in Dance Anthropology (University of Roehampton).

Janet O'Shea is Professor of World Arts and Cultures/Dance at University of California, Los Angeles. She is author of *At Home in the World: Bharata Natyam on the Global Stage* (2007) and co-editor of the *Routledge Dance Studies Reader* (second edition, 2010). She is currently completing a manuscript entitled *Risk, Failure, Play: What Martial Arts Training Reveals about Proficiency, Competition, and Cooperation*.

Meghan Quinlan is a Lecturer in Dance at Kennesaw State University. She holds a PhD in Critical Dance Studies from University of California, Riverside, and a BA in Dance and English from Marymount Manhattan College. Her current research uses Gaga, Ohad Naharin's movement language, as a case study to explore politics of technique, nationalism, neoliberalism, and gender in international contemporary concert dance trends.

Kaitlyn Regehr (PhD) is an ethnographer and documentarian. Her work has appeared internationally in academic and popular print outlets, including *Variety Magazine* and the *Los Angeles Times*. In addition to serving as a topic specialist for *BBC World*, Regehr has created documentary content for networks such as Super Channel (CA), SWR (DE), and ARTE (FR).

Laura Robinson (PhD) is a popular dance scholar and Lecturer in Dance: Urban Practices at the University of East London. Her doctoral research focused on the construction and performance of spectacle in male street dance crew performances on British television talent shows. Publications include chapters in *Bodies of Sound* (2013) and *The Oxford Handbook of Dance and the Popular Screen* (2014).

Karen Schupp is Assistant Professor in Arizona State University's School of Film, Dance, and Theatre. She is the author of *Studying Dance: A Guide for Campus and Beyond* (2014), the book chapter "Sassy Girls and Hard-Hitting Boys: Dance Competition Culture and Gender," in *Dance and Gender: An Evidence-Based Approach* (2017) and numerous scholarly articles examining innovative pedagogical approaches.

Nalina Wait is a dance artist, dance lecturer at Australian College of Physical Education, and PhD candidate at the University of New South Wales, researching improvised composition. Her professional performing credits include award-winning works by Sue Healey, Rosalind Crisp, Dance Works, Hans Van Den Broeck, and Marina Abramović. She has presented at Ecole des Hautes études en Sciences Sociales, UNSW, and *ASDA* Sydney University.

Sarah Wilbur (MFA, PhD) is a choreographer, dance scholar, and the Mellon Postdoctoral Fellow in Dance Studies at Brown University. Her current book project analyzes institution building through a dance lens, using as her case study the fifty-year struggle to uphold norms of dance production and professionalization in the Dance Program at the US National Endowment for the Arts (NEA).

Emily Winerock is a visiting Assistant Professor in History at the University of Pittsburgh. Her research focuses on the politics and practices of dancing in sixteenth- and seventeenth-century Europe. A scholar-practitioner, she also teaches Renaissance dance workshops and is a cofounder of The Shakespeare and Dance Project.

Yutian Wong is Associate Professor in the School of Theatre and Dance at San Francisco State University, where she teaches courses in dance history and theory, composition, and writing in the discipline. She is the author of *Choreographing Asian America* (2010) and the editor of *Contemporary Directions in Asian American Dance* (2016).

Ying Zhu is Assistant Professor of Dance at the University of South Florida. She holds a PhD in Critical Dance Studies from the University of California Riverside. She is presently at work on a book project using the Vietnam Veterans Memorial as a case study to consider the body, as a complicating factor, in processes of national, collective memorialization.

THE OXFORD HANDBOOK OF

DANCE AND
COMPETITION

INTRODUCTION

Competition Culture: Winning and Losing at Dance

SHERRIL DODDS

WHILE we might commonly conceive of dance either as a creative, artistic practice, or as a recreational, community activity, we would not necessarily jump to the idea of dance as competition. Of course, in recent years the popularity of television shows that feature competitive dance or high-profile studio dance competitions come to mind, but to think of all dance as subject to the values and structures of competition may require a little more work. Indeed, I hope to show that a competition paradigm frames twenty-first-century life, and that its narratives of winning, achievement, and success have shaped how and why we dance. Within the global economy, free-market trading is organized around a framework of competition, which creates powerful monopolies of wealth and political control. In the realm of the social, consumer capitalism ensures that people compete for jobs, education, and lifestyle. And at the level of cultural expression, competition touches upon creative choices, artistic practice, and their circulating values. Consequently, dance does not exist as an autonomous art form, but instead moves through and in response to this framework of aspiration, judgment, and worth. *The Oxford Handbook of Dance and Competition* therefore sets out to interrogate the complex interactions between dance and competition, and how dancing bodies both create and respond to opportunities to compete.

DANCE AS A COMPETITIVE PRACTICE

Aside from formal competition events, we might be tempted to think of dance as untouched by competition. Certainly, the bourgeois conception of art views it as separate from the vulgar realm of commerce and contest (Storey 2003), although there are multiple instances in which the elite world of art dance comes into contact with a competition paradigm. In an editorial on competition and dance education, Janice

LaPointe-Crump (2007) observes how renowned concert dancer Mikhail Baryshnikov was the proud recipient of a gold medal at the International Ballet Competition in Varna, Bulgaria, and that art choreographer Kurt Jooss gained prominence when his expressionist ballet, *The Green Table* (1932), won the *Concours International de Chorégraphie*. Indeed, international dance competitions attract illustrious judges with prestigious concert dance careers. For instance, the jury for the inaugural edition of the Korea International Modern Dance Competition included Mark Baldwin, artistic director of Rambert Dance Company in the United Kingdom, and Bruce Marks, a former dancer with American Ballet Theater and jury chairperson of the USA International Ballet Competition (Lee 2010).

In addition to official competition events, professional dancers engaged in art dance must also compete in other ways, which clearly impacts their identity as performers. Dancers compete to win places at distinguished training academies, to gain positions in professional companies, and to secure the most coveted roles. Consequently, these demanding career goals can foster tendencies toward perfectionism and performance anxiety. In an anthology on elite performance across athletics, the performing arts, and business, sports psychologist Gloria Balague (2009) describes how performance involves comparison to others, which creates a competitive ethos that propels individuals to win or outdo fellow participants. She notes that competition, as a Western norm, can motivate performers to excel, but it also can lead to negative attributes such as envy and self-centeredness. The need to compete against others, and even against one's previous performance, becomes enmeshed with feelings of success and failure. Performance psychologist Lynda M. Mainwaring (2009) also suggests that perfectionism can produce maladaptive behaviors such as deep anxiety and fear of failure.

While dancers enter into competition as workers, choreographers must also compete to ensure that their dances gain prominence. In a climate of economic scarcity for the arts, choreographers rival for funding to produce dance, and negotiate with curators and presenters to show their work. As diverse funding models exist across different nation-states, this requires choreographers to compete in a variety of ways. For instance, in the United States, the arts have a history of private sponsorship; therefore choreographers are required to attract wealthy arts patrons or executive officers of major corporations who might take an interest in their work. Meanwhile, in the United Kingdom, choreographers typically apply to funding bodies, such as the national Arts Council and the regional dance agencies, to acquire economic support.[1] Consequently, choreographers work hard to interpret the rules and tastes of these awarding organizations, and to win the attention of the dance representatives employed by the funding bodies, who develop high levels of social capital as a result. Indeed, the dance works themselves are propelled into competition as companies feverishly market and promote them to solicit audience interest, and this same idea can extend to entire dance genres.

In a critique of the colonizing discourses that place some dance (specifically those perceived as non-Western) within the category of "world dance," dance scholar Marta Savigliano (2009) observes how the institutionalizing practice of "worlding" dance has created a climate of competition. She specifically uses the example of UNESCO's collection of dances that fall under the category of "intangible cultural heritage," stating that this project "places these allegedly 'vulnerable' practices into a framework of competition—for survival, for appreciation, for conservation through documentation and research, for preservation through education, and for dissemination through sponsored national and international tours and presentations" (Savigliano 2009, 175). A similar example arises with the Dance Heritage Coalition's list of America's Irreplaceable Dance Treasures in which 900 nominations were submitted and then judged to secure a position in the top 100.[2] In this instance the winning collection includes dancers, choreographers, dance venues, dance organizations, and dance companies.

In the same way that the creative endeavor of art dance is assumed to remain separate from the tawdry practices of economic and social competition, vernacular dances, those that we do in recreational spaces for enjoyment, interaction, and relaxation, also might appear at a safe distance from the language of competition. Yet a little further probing suggests otherwise. Of course many vernacular dances are reframed as competition forms, such as the foxtrot, waltz, rumba, and tango, which have their roots in a localized social dance practice, but are now performed within a transnational competition circuit. Even in the context of recreational settings, however, social dance traditions display elements of contest in their structure and organization. While this type of informal competition might appear to be relaxed and good-natured in its approach, the desire to attain social kudos, bragging rights, and small prizes or cash reward has the potential for hotly contested dance interactions. Dance scholar Barbara Glass (2007) identifies how competition in dance pervades West and Central Africa, and how these displays of virtuosic one-upmanship have also come to characterize African American social dance forms. The link between competition and community emerged in the earliest examples of African American dance during the era of slavery. The Ring Shout, which Glass (2007, 32) suggests is the "oldest continuously practiced African-derived dance in the United States," frequently included a contest between two singers and then extended into improvised movements. Continuing through to the US Declaration of Independence in 1776, and the period of emancipation that followed, a number of African American festivals and social gatherings emerged, such as General Training Day,[3] the corn shucking,[4] and Congo Square;[5] dancing was a major feature of these community events, and inevitably dancers would enter into a competitive, improvised exchange (Glass 2007). Opportunity to engage in "challenge dances" also came about with the arrival of European migrants in the 1700s and early 1800s, who brought their own traditions of dance contest, such as Irish jig dancing; dance-offs quickly sprang up as they came into contact with African American dancers willing and able to participate (Glass 2007). In the context of African American social dance, competition contributed to engendering community spirit and showcasing black achievement. Indeed, Glass (2007) details a vast range of African American dance traditions in which contest forms a key component of the form: buck dancing, cakewalk, jitterbug, tap, breaking, and stepping, to name a few. Throughout the collection, several chapters address the competitive challenge that characterizes the dances of the African diaspora.

Competition as an Economic
and Cultural Dominant

That dance has been subject to the values and structure of competition across multiple styles and genres is perhaps no surprise given the interest in competition at a global level. While I do not suggest that all cultures and nations treat competition in the same way, several scholars observe how competition has emerged as an economic and cultural dominant. Specifically, the politico-economic tenets of neoliberalism have ensured that competition reigns as a global value system. Anthropologist David Harvey (2005) asserts that the theory of neoliberalism rests upon ideas of individual freedom, free-market trading, and minimal state intervention. Rooted in classic Western liberal thinking, which was founded on the enlightenment philosophy of the individual capacity to think freely, rationally, and independently of government and authority, and which underpins a liberalist economic paradigm that supports a trading market free to operate without government intervention, neoliberalism reworks classic liberalism within a framework of globalization (Steger and Roy 2010). Globalization describes the rapid expansion and escalation of economic networks across the world, facilitated by the high-speed creation and exchange of information through digital technologies, and resulting in vast multinational corporations (Steger and Roy 2010). Consequently, the neoliberalist paradigm not only supports the deregulation of the economy and the privatization of state operations, it demands that all human actions are steered by the marketplace (Harvey 2005). Furthermore, competition has become the modus operandi of the neoliberal ethos: "Competition—between individuals, between firms, between territorial entities (cities, regions, nations, regional groupings) is held to be a primary virtue" (Harvey 2005, 65). Global studies scholars Manfred B. Steger and Ravi K. Roy state that neoliberalism and its philosophy of competition have impacted almost all nations. Yet Harvey (2005) argues that, in spite of its ideological claims of freedom and common sense, neoliberalism demonstrates a poor record of achievement both in relation to capital accumulation and quality of life. Notably, Steger and Roy (2010) show how neoliberalism is often interlinked with neoconservative values, such as extreme militarism and patriotism, old-fashioned family values, and a lack of engagement in multiculturalism and environmental issues.[6] Therefore neoliberalism extends beyond an economic system into an entire worldview.

The grip of neoliberalism on social and cultural life has been felt across the globe, although its belief systems have been embraced by some nations more than others. Several scholars observe how the United States has demonstrated a commitment to competition unparalleled by any other country (Duina 2011; Rosenau 2003). This indicates an American exceptionalism based on the belief that the United States is a greater and more knowledgeable nation that any other. In her book, *The Competition Paradigm: America's Romance with Conflict, Contest and Commerce*, public health scholar Pauline Rosenau describes how competition is perceived as essential for character building and social interactions: "Competition is said to be in some way unqualifiedly superior to other forms of social motivation. It makes demands of self-discipline, toughness, courage, and sacrifice" (2003, 2). She goes on to suggest that competition has become a universal value, a taken-for-granted ideology that assumes individuals operate as self-interested social actors, and divides people into winners and losers.

In his book, simply titled *Winning* (2011), sociologist Francesco Duina draws on a range of theorists to think through the place of competition as a social phenomenon and how this invites certain modes of behavior. He calls upon psychoanalyst Sigmund Freud's belief that humans possess a strong desire to kill or destroy, therefore competition acts as a safety valve through which these urges can be played out in a controlled environment. Moving on to sociologist Pierre Bourdieu's ideas of distinction, Duina (2011) argues that competition allows individuals to distinguish themselves from their peers; whereas a winner enters into a selective space or elite group, losers are left behind.[7] While victory provides certainty about success, loss prompts us to question our skills and selfhood, and indicates that we have misjudged to some extent. Yet winning cannot be assumed an end in itself. As Duina (2011) shows, winners need to continue to work to maintain their position, and losers must address their shortcomings. Rosenau (2003) also observes that competitors rarely start from equal positions given that an imbalance of resources, skill, and wealth can impact on performance, which undermines winning as an absolute marker of success.

I would further argue that competition does not always prioritize pitting oneself against and at the expense of others. LaPointe-Crump (2007, 4) invokes the Latin root of compete, *competere*, meaning "to seek or strive together," which emphasizes a collective effort or, as LaPointe-Crump asserts, working to perform beyond expectations. Although the discourse of competition as an economic and cultural dominant has become deeply pervasive, some scholars have attempted to reclaim failure as a philosophical alternative (Gross and Alexander 2016; Halberstam 2011; Petroski 2001). And while the Western neoliberalist paradigm has extended to multiple nations, other belief systems regarding the purpose and value of competition continue to exist. As I have highlighted in the previous section, Africanist ideas of contest as a means to organize community and showcase achievement also circulate globally. In this volume, several authors address questions of success and failure, and winning and losing at dance, although we are collectively interested in the ways in which dance is bound up with competition of varying forms, and how specific frameworks of competition shape dance practice.

What Competition Does to Dance

Within a social, political, and economic landscape that privileges competition, it bears little surprise that dance becomes enmeshed within the values and structures of contest. Across a range of film and television, we see a fascination with dance competition and how it inserts bodies into narratives of rivalry and one-upmanship. The contest be-tween individual dancers, dance groups, and dance genres offers a common plot struc-ture within popular dance film, such as *Saturday Night Fever* (1977), *Strictly Ballroom* (1992), *You Got Served* (2004), *Stomp the Yard* (2007), and the *Step Up* (2006, 2008, 2010, 2012, 2015) and *StreetDance* (2010, 2012) series, to name but a few. The desire to see dancing bodies set in competition with each other also extends to documentary films, such as *Mad Hot Ballroom* (2005), which follows a public school ballroom dance competition; *First Position* (2011), which focuses on the Youth America Grand Prix; and *Jig* (2011), which centers on the Irish Dancing World Championships. Furthermore, dance competitions feature in multiple television entertainment shows, such as *Come Dancing* (1949–1998), *Strictly Come Dancing* (2004), *So You Think You Can Dance* (2005–present),[8] *Dancing with the Stars* (2005), *America's Ballroom Challenge* (2006), *America's Best Dance Crew* (2008), *Dance India Dance* (2009), and *Got to Dance* (2009).[9] On screen, competition dance serves the purpose of spectacle and drama, as it must vis-ually captivate film and television audiences, and hook into spectators' desire to follow the successes and failures that play out as dancers move through each round.

Beyond screen representations, formalized dance competitions are a global phenom-enon, across a multitude of styles and genres, which are staged as regional, national, and international events.[10] Undoubtedly, the reframing of dance as a formal competi-tion changes the practice. In a study of competitive Irish dance, anthropologist Frank Hall (2008) asserts that competition homogenizes the movement according to adjudi-cation standards, and in so doing provokes issues of authenticity, authority, and control of the culture. Thus competition potentially fixes dance as judges maintain agreed-upon competencies that construct a version of the dance considered to be correct or true to its purported origin. Within the competition framework, preservation and reproduc-tion frequently curb adaptation or innovation. Several authors in this volume also focus on the interests, priorities, and impact of officially sanctioned competitions on dance, although I pause here to consider the breadth of children's dance competitions in the United States, which are dependent upon and closely aligned to the multitude of dance studios throughout the country that children attend as a recreational activity. Notably, these local studios are typically a feeder to university dance programs; therefore the aes-thetic values that underpin dance studio training and its close relationship to competi-tion culture influence how and why dancers move as they enter higher education.

The Association of Dance Conventions and Competitions (ADCC) operates in the United States as a nonprofit organization and seeks "to promote quality, integrity, and op-portunity within the dance competition and convention industry."[11] The extent of dance competition culture is evident from its website, which states, "[the ADCC] was founded in 2014 to support the 300+ dance competition and convention owners, 40,000+ dance studios, and hundreds of dance merchants across the country as we work together to expand and professionalize our industry."[12] On an ADCC Affiliate Membership form, it suggests that dollar revenue for the dance competition industry in 2012 stood at $486.6 million.[13] Clearly, dance competition is big business. Dance scholar Susan Leigh Foster (2017) traces how private dance studios have transformed dance from a leisure pursuit to a competition framework; therefore student dancers have little opportunity to train and perform outside this competition ethos. Through a Marxist lens, Foster (2017) observes the shift in dance from a use-value, invested in meaningful personal expression and creativity, to an exchange-value as dance enters a marketplace designed for high levels of social and economic return for the people and institutions involved. Foster (2017) views competition as a neoliberal endeavor as dance studios participate in training students for the labor force, thus replacing community values with market values.

The economic and social impact that dance competition places on its young participants should not be underestimated. In a *New York Times* article on dance competition, journalist Debra West (2004, 4) relays how families must provide significant financial support for children who are eager to enter: "'She dances to the bathroom, she dances to breakfast,' said her father, who estimated that it costs $15,000 a year for Jordan and her sister, Rachel, to compete. That includes eight or nine hours of lessons a week, rehearsal time, choreography fees, travel expenses, entrance fees and costumes." Yet this also comes with an emotional cost, as parents must bear the brunt of devastated children who fail to win (West 2004). In a later article, also in the *New York Times*, journalist Erika Kinetz (2005) describes how these competitions, which attract thousands of participants primarily between the ages of ten and sixteen, have bolstered dance studios, raised dance standards, and attracted talent scouts and other industry professionals; yet ethical questions have emerged regarding both the emphasis on competition over other values, and how these young people are represented on stage.[14] While I do not intend here to tangle over the question of whether such competitions are inherently good or bad for their child participants,[15] competition seems to be intrinsically bound up with questions of moral value.

In line with a neoliberal rhetoric, Foster (2017) identifies a pervasive belief that competition is good for dance. LaPoint Crump (2007) meanwhile sets up the argument that dance and competition are grounded in antithetical belief systems, although she plays this as a ruse as she goes on to demonstrate how competitions are commonplace in American arts education. Notably, her bait concerning the relationship between dance and competition motivated several readers to respond outlining both the ills and benefits of competition in dance.[16] Indeed, several scholars attempt to address the complexity of what competition brings to dance and how this shapes both individual and community behavior. In a study of the National Student Dance Competition in Taiwan, using Bourdieu's ideas of habitus and cultural reproduction, dance scholar JuanAnn Tai (2014) argues that, on the one hand, these competitions play a significant role in the socialization of young dance students; yet, on the other, they restrict opportunities for individual creativity and agency. And anthropologist Meena Khandewal and communications scholar Chitra Akkoor (2014, 278) focus on Indian dance competitions in collegial settings to demonstrate how these highly professional public performances stage a "confident hybrid American-Indian identity," which nevertheless masks the complex lived experience of immigrant communities.[17]

I am therefore less interested in absolute values of competition regarding its capacity to be intrinsically good or bad for dance. Instead, I have asked the authors in this collection to think about what competition does to dance, and how dance responds to and negotiates ideas of competition. As this volume shows, there are multiple ways in which dancers resist, critique, and provide alternative choreographies and discourses in response to the way competition might seek to contain and control bodies. Only by looking at the detailed contexts in which competition happens, and suspending value judgments about the relative merits or dangers of competition, can we begin to think through the nuanced relationship between dance and competition and what it means for those involved.

What Dance Does to Competition

The Oxford Handbook of Dance and Competition examines dance practices across a diversity of settings to consider how dance both produces and engenders the values of competition. The dances under discussion span social dance from late sixteenth- and early seventeenth-century England, and early twentieth-century American vaudeville, through to twenty-first-century dance on the global screen. The performance contexts in which these competition dances arise encompass the concert and commercial stage, the recreational spaces of sports, folk, and popular dance, and the film and television media. And the international reach of the volume attends to dancing in China, India, North and South America, the Caribbean, Australia, and Europe. Although the collection includes dances that have attracted substantial scholarly interest, it also introduces movement genres that are new or emergent topics within dance studies, such as Gaga, martial arts, Romanian folk dance, *Sean Nós*, British rapper dance, Jamaican dancehall, and New Orleans second line.

The book is organized in six parts, and each takes a different perspective on dance and competition. As always in an edited collection, the content of each chapter might belong to more than one part; therefore the reader is welcome to reflect on how each chapter can be placed in conversation with others. *Part I: Economic and Social Currencies of Competition* examines competition as a means of economic survival and social standing. In Chapter 1, "Taking the Cake: Black Dance, Competition, and Value," Nadine George-Graves traces the cakewalk as it moves across several performance contexts to illustrate how it engenders African American values of accomplishment and visibility while being subject to social and monetized economies of race and racism. In Chapter 2, "You've Got to Sell It! Performing on the Dance Competition Stage," Karen Schupp considers the values that are sold through studio dance competitions, in relationship to how young girls choose to invest in these competitions to create their own meanings and sense of achievement. In Chapter 3, "Competitive Capers: Gender, Gentility, and Dancing in Early Modern England," Emily Winerock turns to dance manuals and the English literature of the late Renaissance to show how the galliard offered a competitive opportunity to showcase individual standing in relation to masculinity and gentility. In Chapter 4, "Endangered Strangers: Tracking Competition in US Federal Dance

Funding," Sarah Wilbur observes not only how the federal funding organization, the National Endowment for the Arts, has placed dance-makers and dance in competition with each other, but also how its early philanthropic mission protected Euro-American concert dance, while its later strategy supported a neoliberalist agenda that served to support the US economy. And in Chapter 5, "Marking Your Territory: The Struggle to Work in Flamenco," Kathy Milazzo tackles how five flamenco dancers working outside Spain have been prompted to find creative solutions to sustain their professional practice in a depressed marketplace fixated on a Romantic flamenco past.

Part II: Re-Choreographing and Re-Presentation for the Competition Frame addresses how dancing bodies and movement aesthetics are re-choreographed in response to a competition format, and how this changes the meanings and values associated with the dance. In Chapter 6, "Reappropriating Choreographies of Authenticity in Mexico: Competitions and the Dance of the Old Men," Ruth Hellier-Tinoco explores five case study examples of the Dance of the Old Men to show how competition sets in motion concepts of authenticity, appropriation, and control at both local and state level. In Chapter 7, "Above and Beyond the Battle: Virtuosity and Excess within Televised Street Dance Crew Competitions," Laura Robinson focuses on how street dance competitions on television construct virtuosic and corporeally enhanced super-bodies, but which favor the choreography of the collective over the neoliberal obsession with the individual. In Chapter 8, "Shifting Dynamics: *Sean Nós* Dancing, Vernacular Expression, and the Competitive Arena of the *Oireachtas*," Catherine E. Foley discusses how the vernacular practice of *sean nós* dancing in Ireland rethinks issues of performance, identity, place, and authenticity as it enters a competition arena. And in Chapter 9, "Visible Rhythms: Competition in English Tap Practice," Sally Crawford-Shepherd reflects on how success is re-evaluated as tap dance shifts from a live improvised challenge dance that foregrounds auditory rhythms, to a televised competition form, via theatrical performances and examination syllabi, to place increasing emphasis on set choreography and visual spectacle.

Part III: Winning, Participation, and the Negotiation of Meaning concerns how dancers approach competition, and the strategies they use to negotiate and challenge the dominant rhetoric of the competitions in which they are involved. In Chapter 10, "The International Dancehall Queen Competition: A Discursive Space for Competing Images of Femininity," Celena Monteiro argues that Jamaican dancehall queen competitions offer a site for women to simultaneously embody and critique dominant discourses across the intersections of gender, race, and sexuality. In Chapter 11, "Congratulations, We Wish You Success: Competition and Community Participation in Romanian Dance Festivals," Liz Mellish reveals the contradictions that coexist across Romanian dance competitions in which the formal competition downplays rivalry in favor of community participation and a desire to sustain the dance, yet a healthy sense of competition plays out informally between local dancers, choreographers, and group leaders. In Chapter 12, "Non-Competitive Body States: Corporeal Freedom and Innovation in Contemporary Dance," through a Foucauldian analysis of the disciplinary power effects that shape the body, Nalina Wait and Erin Brannigan assert that whereas codified forms of contemporary dance place dancers' bodies in competition with an ideal, the "(un) disciplined" field of somatic practices engenders a non-competitive ethos. In Chapter 13, "Reclaiming Competitive Tango: The Rise of Argentina's *Campeonato Mundial*," Juliet McMains contends that, in light of the Europeanist appropriation of tango into formal competition events, Argentinean dancers have sought to reclaim and redefine tango on their own terms; this project nevertheless remains entangled with biases and values that have emerged through locating tango in a competition frame. And in Chapter 14, "Dance-Off, or a Battle for the Future: Dance Reality Shows in India," Pallabi Chakravorty addresses the complex articulations of desire in television dance competitions in India through the consumerist desires of a remix aesthetic, the eroticization of the female body, and the desire to win as a means to secure social mobility.

Part V: Judging, Spectatorship and the Values of Movement attends to the values and criteria that underpin frameworks of judgment and experiences of spectatorship in the competition realm. In Chapter 15, "Miss Exotic World: Judging the Neo-Burlesque Movement," Kaitlyn Regehr posits that judging and evaluating neo-burlesque artists within a national competition, which appears to uphold dominant standards of beauty and femininity, stands in contrast to the neo-burlesque commitment to body positivism, social inclusivity, and a progressive feminist politics. In Chapter 16, "Rapper Dance Adjudication: Aesthetics, Discourse, and Decision-Making," Jeremy Carter-Gordon turns to English rapper dancer competition to illustrate the different kinds of criteria that inform judges' processes of evaluation, and the various ways in which they transform their perceptions into a ranking. In Chapter 17, "Dismantling the Genre: Reality Dance Competitions and Layers of Affective Intensification," Elena Benthaus identifies the generic and intertextual cues, specifically in relation to American vaudeville and melodrama, to show how they create an affective spectatorship experience for viewers of the reality television dance competition *So You Think You Can Dance*. In Chapter 18, "Why Are Breaking Battles Judged? The Rise of International Competitions," Mary Fogarty looks at the contentions that underpin judging practices in international breaking competitions, and how such "taste-making" is concomitantly influenced by the promoters who organize these events. And in Chapter 19, "Not Another Don Quixote! Negotiating China's Position on the International Ballet Stage," Rowan McLelland establishes that while ballet competitions in China position its dancers, teachers, and training institutions at a standard of excellence on the global stage, its lesser investment in Chinese ballet companies results in the best competition dancers leaving to work outside China.

Part V: Losing, Failing, and Auto-Critique takes up an antithetical position to suggest that failure, loss, and a resistance to structures of winning can be a welcome or celebrated position, and one that is embodied within danced attitudes to competition. In Chapter 20, "Dancing with the Asian American Stars: Margaret Cho and the Failure to Win," Yutian Wong considers how actress and comedian Margaret Cho's failure to win *Dancing with the Stars* seeks to critique tropes of Asian American contest and ideas of belonging, but ultimately fails to destabilize the restricted paradigm that delimits Asian American success. In Chapter 21, "Loss of Face: Intimidation, Derision, and Failure in the Hip-Hop Battle," Sherril Dodds examines how facial choreography is part of a strategic play in hip-hop battles that both provokes and reveals failure, but which also privileges values other than winning and success. In Chapter 22, "Making Play Work: Competition, Spectacle, and Intersubjectivity in Hybrid Martial Arts," Janet O'Shea looks to the language of sports and games to move martial arts sparring outside an outcome-oriented model of winning and losing, toward a process-driven interest in creativity and play. And in Chapter 23, "You Can't Outdo Black People: *Soul Train*, Queer Witnessing, and Pleasurable Competition," Melissa Blanco Borelli presents an intervention against the neoliberal belief in competition and individualism to assert that a viral YouTube commentary on the dancers from the *Soul Train* line offers a collective queer black pleasure that "out-does" the deleterious effects of capitalism on black social life.

Finally, *Part VI: Hidden Agendas and Unspoken Rules* exposes some of the veiled ideas and strategic agendas that underpin dance competition. In Chapter 24, "Freedom to Compete: Neoliberal Contradictions in Gaga Intensives," Meghan Quinlan focuses on a Gaga dance intensive to assert that, although the experience emphasizes personal growth and individual pleasure, this training opportunity places dancers in competition with one another as they seek to pursue career opportunities within the neoliberal marketplace. In Chapter 25, "'We'll Rumble 'em Right': Aggression and Play in the Dance-Offs of *West Side Story*," Ying Zhu and Daniel Belgrad contend that while the film is frequently read as an interethnic contest between the Puerto Rican Sharks and the white-ethnic Jets, the choreography reveals a broader competition between the values of youth and the constraints of adulthood. In Chapter 26, "Dancing like a Man: Competition and Gender in the New Orleans Second Line," Rachel Carrico attends to the gendered outcomes of second line footwork competitions that typically privilege a masculinist frame, yet provide opportunity for women to critique such criteria and evaluations through engaging the perspective of a "badass femininity." And in Chapter 27, "Man and Money Ready: Challenge Dancing in Antebellum North America," April F. Masten elaborates on the social and economic conditions of mid-nineteenth-century American life to show how male and female dancers earned a viable living through challenge dances that were strategically promoted through social interactions and the popular media. The collection ends with an Afterword by Susan Leigh Foster, whose recent work has also turned to productive questions concerning the relationship between dance and competition (Foster 2017).

As a final thought, I hope that *The Oxford Handbook of Dance and Competition* encapsulates and contributes to ongoing debates over competition as a deeply embedded social and economic practice, which often seeks to fix bodies according to normative concepts or to create marked indicators of inequality. More important, however, my aim with this collection is less concerned with showing how dance perpetuates a competition paradigm, than with how it employs a tactics of resistance or critique through moving in ways that reveal and undermine the power structures of competition. Dance not only enters into challenges, contests and competitions, but in doing so its embodied actions also do the work of contesting, challenging, and offering competing or alternative ideas. In this sense, dance wins every time.

NOTES

1. Further information about these funding bodies can be found at http://www.artscouncil.org.uk/ and https://www.danceuk.org/resources/navigating-dance-world/agencies/ (accessed January 13, 2017).
2. See http://www.danceheritage.org/treasures.html (accessed January 19, 2017).
3. General Training Day was a military holiday across the seventeenth, eighteenth, and early nineteenth centuries, and became an important African American holiday for socializing and dancing (Glass 2007).
4. The corn shucking is a harvest festival from the slavery period, but which continued into the twentieth century, whereby African Americans came together to husk corn, and would end with a supper for the workers, along with music and dancing (Glass 2007).
5. Congo Square was part of the French Quarter in New Orleans, and would feature a rich mix of "African-based and Afro-Caribbean dance" (Glass 2007, 93).
6. Although the authors exemplify these values in the 1980s neoliberal policies of former US president Ronald Reagan and British prime minister Margaret Thatcher, the 2016 US presidential election campaign of Donald Trump was founded on these same neoconservative beliefs.
7. Duina (2011) provides an extensive study of winning and losing, and the traits and values that underpin them.
8. Originally a US production, *So You Think You Can Dance* has been franchised in thirty-seven countries.
9. Versions of the British *Got to Dance* have been exported to eight other countries.
10. For dance competitions outside Europe and North America, the following articles reference contests in Korea (Jin 2005; Kim 2014), India (Fernandez and Reyes 2008), Taiwan (Tai 2004), and Australia (Russo 2010).
11. https://www.theadcc.org/ (accessed January 27, 2017).
12. https://www.theadcc.org/about-the-adcc/history/ (accessed January 27, 2017).
13. http://www.dancecompgenie.com/ClientData/pdf/ADCC_Studio_Affiliate_Membership.pdf (accessed January 27, 2017).
14. Although Kinetz (2005, 1) specifically references "midriff-baring outfits," other concerns might be directed at the extensive use of adult makeup and costuming, and the sexualized, racialized, and gendered dimensions of the choreography.
15. In this volume, Karen Schupp offers a nuanced reading of the stakes involved in studio dance competition specifically from the perspective of the young girls involved.
16. LaPointe-Crump's (2007) ideas featured in an editorial from the *Journal of Physical Education, Recreation & Dance*, and several readers directly responded to her assertions in the January 2008 issue.
17. On a similar topic, geographer Elizabeth Chacko and English scholar Rajiv Menon (2013) focus on second-generation South Asian students in the United States and their performances within collegiate *bhangra* and *raas garba* song and dance competitions. Chacko and Menon (2013) detail how the element of contest places greater emphasis on displays of cultural authenticity as performers seek to appeal to first-generation South Asian judges; yet their dance performances are full of references to US and other national cultural practices that reveal the complex hybrid position they inhabit with their contemporary lives.

REFERENCES

Balague, Gloria. 2009. "Competition." In *Performance Psychology in Action: A Casebook for Working with Athletes, Performing Artists, Business Leaders and Professionals in High-Risk Occupations*, edited by Kate F. Hays, 161–187. Washington, DC: American Psychological Association.

Chacko, Elizabeth, and Rajiv Menon. 2013. "Longings and Belongings: Indian American Youth Identity, Folk Dance Competitions, and the Construction of 'Tradition.'" *Ethnic and Racial Studies* 36(1): 97–116.

Duina, Francesco. 2011. *Winning*. Princeton, NJ: Princeton University Press.

Fernandez, Lisa, and Gary Reyes. 2008. "Biggest Indian Dance Festival to Feature 500 Performers." *San Jose Mercury News*, April 26, 3B.

Foster, Susan Leigh. 2017. "Dance and/as Competition in the U.S. Privately Owned Studio." In *The Oxford Handbook of Dance and Politics*, edited by Rebekah J. Kowal, Gerald Siegmund, and Randy Martin, 53–76. Oxford: Oxford University Press.

Glass, Barbara S. 2007. *African-American Dance: An Illustrated History*. Jefferson, NC: McFarland.

Gross, Daniel, M., and Jonathan Alexander. 2016. "Frameworks for Failure." *Pedagogy* 16(2): 273–295.

Halbertstam, Judith. 2011. *The Queer Art of Failure*. Durham, NC: Duke University Press.

Hall, Frank. 2008. *Competitive Irish Dance: Art, Sport, Duty*. Madison, WI: Macater.

Harvey, David. 2005. *A Brief History of Neoliberalism*. Oxford: Oxford University Press.

Jin, Dae-woong. 2005. "Ethnic Dancers Compete in Soeul." *The Korea Herald*, September 2.

Khandewal, Meena, and Chitra Akkoor. 2014. "Dance On!: Inter-Collegiate Indian Dance Competitions as a New Cultural Form." *Cultural Dynamics* 26(3): 277–298.

Kim, Joohee. 2014. "Class Reproduction and Korean Male Dancers Receiving Exemption from Military Service through Dance Competitions." *Journal of Global Scholars of Marketing Science* 24(4): 453–460.

Kinetz, Erika. 2005. "Budding Dancers Compete, Seriously." *New York Times*, July 7, https://www.nytimes.com/2005/07/07/arts/dance/budding-dancers-compete-seriously.html.

LaPointe-Crump, Janice. 2007. "Competition and Dance Education." *Journal of Physical Education, Recreation & Dance* 78(7): 4–5, 9.

Lee, Hyo-won. 2010. "Korea's First Modern Dance Competition Opens in Soeul." *Korea Times*, August 2, http://www.koreatimes.co.kr/www/news/art/2011/06/145_70648.html.

Mainwaring, Lynda M. 2009. "Working with Perfection." In *Performance Psychology in Action: A Casebook for Working with Athletes, Performing Artists, Business Leaders and Professionals in High-Risk Occupations*, edited by Kate F. Hays, 139–159. Washington, DC: American Psychological Association.

Petroski, Henry. 2001. "The Success of Failure." *Technology and Culture* 42(2): 321–328.

Rosenau, Pauline V. 2003. *The Competition Paradigm: America's Romance with Conflict, Contest and Commerce*. Lanham, MD: Rowman & Littlefield.

Russo, Frank. 2010. "Dance Contest Returns to Its Former Home." *Innisfail Advocate*, February 6, 4.

Savigliano, Marta E. 2009. "Worlding Dance and Dancing Out There in the World." In *Worlding Dance*, edited by Susan Leigh Foster, 163–190. Basingstoke, UK: Palgrave Macmillan.

Steger, Manfred B., and Ravi K. Roy. 2010. *Neoliberalism: A Very Short Introduction.* Oxford: Oxford University Press.

Storey, John. 2003. *Inventing Popular Culture.* Oxford: Blackwell.

Tai, JuanAnn. 2014. "Identities and Dance Competition: Re/Discovering the Force from Within." *Research in Dance Education* 15(3): 303–315.

West, Debra. 2004. "Young Dancers Compete to Earn and to Learn." *The New York Times,* March 9.

PART I

ECONOMIC AND SOCIAL CURRENCIES OF COMPETITION

CHAPTER 1

....

TAKING THE CAKE

Black Dance, Competition, and Value

....

NADINE GEORGE-GRAVES

FOR WHAT IT'S WORTH

....

LEGEND has it that, as a teenager, the light-complexioned Leonard Reed won an all-white Charleston dance contest at the Orpheum Theater in Kansas City. Before he could officially collect his prize, two black usherettes exposed him as actually being black. Outed, Reed grabbed the money and ran before the owner could take the money back and kick him out. The owner called out, "Catch the nigger!" and a mob ensued. In the melee, Reed managed to get himself lost in the crowd, pulled up his collar, and joined in the cry in pursuit of the "black man," also yelling "Catch the nigger!" Eventually, he slipped away with his cash.[1]

This anecdote indicates a number of salient issues at the convergence of competition, race, identity, value, and dance (Figure 1.1). Reed moved from white to black to white again within a matter of moments. But he was only in peril when he was black or at the verge of being found out. One wonders what the mob was chasing: a rumor, a mirage, a fiction? A threat? To what? Dancing? Winning? Occupying the same space and perhaps touching? One might argue that they were not even chasing Reed (although I am sure he would beg to differ) or his audacity in passing. Rather, they were chasing fear. Reed exposed the precariousness of identity as read on the body, and dance became a vital link in the process of racism. Who owned that prize money? It is too simple to argue that Reed won fair and square, and the prize should be his regardless of race. That was not what was at stake. What *was* at stake were the foundations of identity that the owners and patrons of the establishment held fast. The mob was literally chasing nothing, nobody. The mob was chasing itself. Reed understood. He played the game and, fortunately, escaped and won. And when he slipped away, the white mob was left playing a game with absurd rules meant only to breed privilege.

FIGURE 1.1. The cakewalk became America's first dance craze, ushering in a new era of social and stage dance.

Imagine the people next to Reed looking at him as another white person in pursuit of the very person they were looking at in solidarity. Imagine the emotional and cognitive swings they would have experienced if they had learned the truth at that moment. Was Reed bemused? Terrified? A bit of both? Had he passed so often that he knew he could get away with the performance? Did he have an escape plan? Was the prize money worth the risk?

At the turn of the nineteenth to the twentieth century, the stakes around the negotiations of race and value in black dance (a site that blurred the lines between the amateur and the professional) were high—a matter of life and death in some cases. In the preceding example, the Charleston, a black dance, was co-opted, monetized, and located in an all-white performance space. Black bodies were banned on stage, though the black aesthetic was celebrated, and black people were allowed to serve the patrons. (Black people are always allowed to serve patrons.) Reed's transgression was "worth" more than just "getting away with" something. His actions reveal the hypocrisy and anxiety around the rules of identity. His body moving in space was doing more than dancing. He threatened to trouble the shaky ground supporting racist practices and racism itself. And he called to question the "ownership" of black dance moves (a call that echoes throughout African American dance history). Reed's racial ambiguity (to some contemporaneous eyes) allowed him to compete in both white and black competitions and win prizes at both sites. He was also able to perform professionally on both black and white circuits. But there were limits: he could not become too big on white circuits lest he be found out. He earned more money performing white, of course, though he likely performed the same material. And when he did perform as an African American, he had to reckon with the fact that less talented white dancers were earning more wages, though the differences between him and them could not be read on the body. The traditional optic excuse for racism, visible physical markers, could not be deployed. For our purposes, Reed's negotiations allow us entry into the interrogation of the meaning behind blackness, movement, and competition.

Competition has been instrumental in the development of African American dance at a number of historical sites. The creation of American tap dance, particularly at the meeting of African and Irish traditions, is probably the most commonly discussed site of black dance, competition, and race relations. In early American dance history, the birth of American tap dance tells a story of aesthetics through competition and race. Images abound of black and Irish dancers competing in the Five Points neighborhood of Manhattan to prove not only individual prowess, but also ethnic subaltern hierarchy. Competition among black dancers was also a way for performers to gain professional traction. The spirit of competition permeates the history of tap, and the spirit of out-dancing a rival directly led to the creation of an aesthetic built on displays of crowd-pleasing virtuosity.[2] For example, even though others performed stair dances before Bill "Bojangles" Robinson, his performative skills and showmanship led him to "win" it as his signature move.

In addition to tap, a host of other black dance genres, including ragtime dance, swing dance, 1950s rock and roll dancing, *Soul Train* disco dancing, and breaking, were built on competition. Throughout American history, black dancers engaged in one-upmanship to gain popularity, created signature styles when no copyright law would protect their intellectual property, and played up rivalries to increase the dramatic stakes behind dance battles. In doing so, these artists pushed and continue to push the boundaries of concepts like "compensation," "value," "worth," and "stakes."

Though it is important to understand this broader history, it is beyond the scope of this chapter to do that kind of investigation justice.[3] Also, it is important to hone in on the nuances of these negotiations at any specific site. The cakewalk is a particularly rich genre for this analysis.[4] Focusing on cakewalks as sites of black/white competition, black/black competition, and even white/white competition (in the case of slave masters betting against each other on the dexterity of their property), helps to examine the significant social negotiations underlying contests at these important junctures. In this chapter, I interrogate the sites of competition in the early plantation cakewalk, postwar public and professional cakewalk settings, and in a number of theatrical stage examples of cakewalk dancing, and ultimately argue that the real stakes of competition are not always what one might expect.

THE EARLY CAKEWALK

The cakewalk traveled from the plantations of the South, where slaves developed the high-prancing dance to both emulate and mock those dances rooted in European ballroom that were performed in the big house by the white masters, to a social event (danced by African Americans sometimes without the "white gaze"), to professional performances (on the minstrel stage into early musical comedies and film), to a blending of amateur and professional (minstrel finales where audience members joined in the last promenade, and cakewalk contests sponsored by musical performances), to a business most lucrative for white dance instructors, and to contests for any dancers who performed for black or white judges. In all of these spaces, the meanings behind these movements changed significantly, and competition (and the stakes therein) reveals the ways in which America holds race dear.

The term "cakewalk" has come to mean many things over the years, but the general sense is that of something easily achieved. This may seem to suggest that winning cakewalk contests was easy. On the contrary, the "ease" of the cakewalk cited in the etymology of the term with contemporary vestiges is an aesthetic ease, a performative ease. Linked to the aesthetic of the cool, as articulated by Robert Farris-Thompson (1973) and Brenda Dixon-Gottschild (1996), this is the ease of appearance while displaying virtuosity. This is the icing on the cake (so to speak), that on top of impressive technique, remarkable displays of talent were performed "effortlessly," with a smile and sometimes feigned ignorance at one's own skill. "What, this old move? Can't you do it?"

Though I have known the cakewalk for many decades, I was recently introduced to a new use of the term. Imagine my surprise when, as a new parent in the local elementary school (my son had just started kindergarten), I was asked to volunteer to run the cake-walk as part of the school's annual fundraising carnival. The school—in the middle of the suburban master-planned community of cookie-cutter beige houses of Irvine, California, with a population that is 45.75% white, 38.2% Asian, 9.8% Hispanic, and only 1.7% black—was the last place that I expected to hear the word "cakewalk." My response, in shock, was "Excuse me?!" After a moment of excitement that this fundraising event might connect to my research, I learned of the way the school was actually using the term. It turns out that their definition of a cakewalk meant a contest that consisted of walking around in a circle to music, and when the music stops, whoever is standing next to the spot with a cake on it gets to take that cake home. Quite possibly, the easiest "dance" contest ever: a literal cakewalk! Walk and get a cake. Dancing was not even required: the ease without the virtuosity. There was no performing, no judging, no competition. It was basically musical chairs without the fighting to get to the right spot. It was random. If you happened to be standing next to the cake when the music stopped, the prize was yours. Quick internet research led me to see that Irvine is not alone in this practice. The term "cakewalk" has had a long journey, and my moment of cognitive dissonance highlights the importance of attending to the history and meanings behind movements. It also indicates the importance of attending to details and focusing on particular moments to understand how a slave means of support, pride, training, and aesthetic development in the Antebellum South and a practice by a group of mainly white and Asian five-year-olds walking around in a circle in twenty-first-century suburbia could share the same name.

The history of the development of the cakewalk style is complicated and wrapped in narratives of not only race and competition, but also gender, ability, upward mobility, and national identity, among other concepts. These shift over time from when black people were slaves in America to their entrée into the entertainment industry through the crack in the barriers to professionalism. One of the practices that greatly influenced the movement quality was the "chalk line walk" of the 1850s. Here, slaves moved smoothly (without staccato prancing) on a line with straight and curvy sections while balancing a bucket of water on their heads. Prizes were awarded to dancers who walked the most erect and spilled the least amount (preferably none) of water. The lessons of this movement went beyond the practical skills of transporting items on one's head without dropping them. Like the sentiment of staying on the "straight and narrow path" of ethical conduct (rooted in the New Testament and no doubt part of the Christianizing of slave populations) and walking the line of balance between extremes, the movement corporealized the attitude of behaving with propriety and decorum. Winning a competition with these underlying meanings likely also pointed to moral as well as physical uprightness.

The circular pattern (also later found in the "walk around" of minstrel shows), as well as the fervor and seriousness of the "ring shout," likely influenced the cakewalk, although the rhythms differ. The graceful shuffling of the feet along a circular path in the ring shout while the shoulders remained rigid was also probably borrowed by the cakewalk. As in the cakewalk, the lower half of the body demonstrated isolated movements while the upper half remained relatively stable. Hips would sway, feet would tap, stamp, and stomp, while the torso stayed unyielding. At various points, individuals might break away (sometimes to the center of the ring) to do solo improvisations and then return to the group. Clapping and stomping provided contrasting staccato to the gliding shuffles. This embrace of contradictory impulses is also evident in the cakewalk. It is not a stretch to recognize the metaphor of holding contradictory impulses within one body as significant. Rooted in West African polyrhythms and taking on new meaning in slavery, it bespoke the value of the skill of moving in two different ways at once and navigating multiple spaces. Whereas the objective of the ring shout was to praise God, there seemed to be a hidden secret behind the cakewalk. Is the couple being serious or mocking? Both at the same time? The useful skills of dancing around laws against dancing in order to praise God (while retaining African ways) that were contained in the ring shout are echoed in the cakewalk and the social navigations of later eras. The embrace of contradictions here was the serious and playful, the mastery and mockery, the held and released, all of which were advantageous post-reconstruction skills for African Americans.

It is important to note that a number of sources also point to Seminole roots of the cakewalk, though this genealogy is less supported by some accounts than others.[5] The claim is that black people in Florida witnessed war dances of the Seminoles that alternated between energetic displays of power and virility, and slow, solemn partnered processions, and that either they borrowed the movement or there was a cross-cultural influence and blending of styles. This movement style developed into an aestheticized style of walking among African Americans in Florida. Classes then developed among the black population, and the teaching of the dance and correct way to promenade became a business in the 1880s. The development of Florida into a winter holiday resort area contributed to the development and dissemination of the movement to Georgia, the Carolinas, and further northward to Virginia and eventually New York.

In plantation settings, masters took notice of their slaves dancing and began wagering with other masters over the dancing prowess of their property. Though the slaves danced, it was the owners who competed, betting against each other to see who had the best dancers. They would provide hand-me-down clothes from their own closets to their best walkers and bring them to other plantations to compete. Women might wear dresses with ruffles and hoops, and men might sport high hats, long split-tailed coats, and walking sticks. In thinking through the stakes of competition, these might be considered "remuneration" for their skills when they were allowed to keep the clothes, but the real prize money went to the masters. Whites would arrive in carriages at neighboring plantations to witness the challenge. These competitions usually happened on Sundays or Saturday nights, lest plantation labor be disturbed. Whether or not the slaves had "fun" is an impossible question, though it is important to note that they were required to perform this dance work for their masters' financial gain and entertainment under the constant threat of slavery. In the winter (again when the demand for field labor was reduced) the competitions happened on other nights as well. Banjos, fiddles, and Jew's harps accompanied cakewalks and Irish Sunday jig dance contests. While owners won money, cakes were most often the prize awarded to the performers. These cakes varied from a hoecake wrapped in a cabbage leaf to a tall extra-sweet coconut or plum cake. It is from here that we develop phrases like "that takes the cake" to indicate any given nonpareil. Other prizes included cornmeal baked in ashes, molasses pulled candy, and other kinds of small cakes. Again, whether or not these prizes were "worth" their dancing labor also presents a false question. It did not matter. The slaves had no choice—though, undoubtedly, the prizes were incentives for improving skills and developing craft. Surely, winning these competitions for the slaves was better than not winning them, and there are accounts of the material benefits afforded the winners. However, we cannot truly know by what yardstick we should measure the stakes of competition or judge the dancers from our twenty-first-century perch. In the perverted plantation setting, slaves became performers and the cakewalk became entertainment and commerce (though dance had been so since slaves were forced to dance on the decks of slave ships to increase their value).[6] Monetary value as well as self-worth shifted their attachments to performative skill. In other words, we can and should speculate about how slaves valued themselves vis-à-vis their dancing. How might senses of self-worth shift as the competitive stakes of cakewalk dancing increased, and how did this forum present and foreclose opportunities? Of course, slaves had capacity for joy despite their nonhuman status, and no doubt it felt good to be valued as a dancer. Though we must keep trying to understand all of the particulars that fed and continue to feed such systems, we should not presume that we will ever truly know what it felt like to compete under those circumstances. On the other hand, neither should we be cold and calculating in our analysis, forgetting that these were people with names, families, lives, and lives that could have been.

Though our empathy for and understanding of what it *felt* like is limited, we can recognize that the rise in value of the reward (sometimes measurable in monetary terms, sometimes in terms of pride) led to the further development of intricacies and virtuosities in performative styles. Remaining composed while balancing a jug of water on the head or hand later led to displays of percussive breakdowns during breakaways from the decorous promenade. For example, waiters entertained guests by dancing while balancing cups and glasses at restaurants and hotel ballrooms. The increase in the spectacle, virtuosity, and competitions of cakewalk dancing spread the form into more public settings as the cakewalk grew in popularity on stage and screen. Performing the cakewalk became even more theatrical as it reached more of the population (for audience members as well as for professional and amateur participants). The possibilities for commercial and personal gain increased, as well as the stakes of competition.

COMPETITION IN PUBLIC AND PROFESSIONAL CAKEWALK SETTINGS

Indicative of the worth of the cakewalk for African Americans was its continued popularity even after the Civil War. Away from the plantation, the cakewalk became even grander in style. The performers wore fancier clothes and the choreography became more elaborate. The demand for the dance increased from 1876, hit its peak from 1895 to 1905, and briefly resurged around 1915. Over these nearly forty years, the competitive ventures shifted significantly. At a time when the United States was divided into white public spheres and black public spheres (with transgressions being noteworthy), the performance of the cakewalk, and the competitive stakes that surrounded it, can be divided likewise along black/white color lines.

Though a detailed examination of the history of the cakewalk is beyond the scope of this chapter, we can further look to the aesthetic itself and the particulars of competition in a number of select contexts to deepen our assessment of the stakes of these performances, especially as the narrative of cakewalk dance competitions moves into public and professional settings. The unspoken messages behind the bodily command and control, the grace under pressure, the fluidity of gliding or prancing with a bucket on the head, even the imitation of white definitions of decorum and elegance were that these black male and female bodies were to be respected. The erect dignified walking, flirtatiousness and high kicking, as well as the costuming with gowns, suits, bows, canes, and hats, were an argument for inclusion in the realm of humanity. Their uprightness indicated their *uprightness*. In other words, physical stance was a clue to social standing. And the ease with which they displayed virtuosity ("It's a cakewalk!") meant that this was inalienably so. The corporeal argument was less that class, respect, and morality are solely performative, but that these black bodies are equal to white bodies. From the parity of physicality, it is not too far of a stretch to conclude that the rights afforded white bodies likewise belong to black bodies. At the same time, the playfulness of the dance indicated that the black dancers did not take these notions too seriously, acknowledged the performativity therein, had a healthy amount of disrespect for the underlying beliefs, and knew well what lay behind these beliefs.

The cakewalk appeared in both serious and comedic forms in public forums. Where the serious cakewalk maintained a sober air, the comedy cakewalk pushed the rules with choreographic jocularity. The serious cakewalk emphasized an upright torso, with tilts forward and backward from the waist. This was perhaps in reference to palm trees being able to shift with the wind far forward and far backward without breaking, a symbolism within parts of Africa to convey resilience and flexibility. Another interpretation was leaning forward to protect the present and future, and leaning back to protect the past. Dancers would gracefully hop from one leg to the other, quickly kicking out the free leg from the knee in a prancing manner. Top hats and skirts would be raised, along with considerable greeting and bowing (as literal and figurative nods and winks to white upper-class mannered pretentions). Occasionally a dancer would perform an individualized feat to show off and then would return to the rhythm of the group.

The comedy cakewalk exaggerated this grace and allowed more room for play. In a recording from May 11, 1903, by the American Mutoscope & Biograph Company, five dancers (two couples and a solo man) perform a comedy cakewalk. The men wear top hats and coattails, and carry canes. The women wear elaborate hats and long dresses that they hike up in order to kick their legs. The movements here are playful. The clip begins with the dancers in a straight line along the back. A man shuffles his legs side to side moving forward, cane in both hands, moving side to side. He then crisscrosses his legs and waddles back to the line bowlegged. He picks up the couples, and they promenade around in a tight circle, with the men lifting their hats high above their heads, turning around themselves, smiling and appearing to have a great time. One man twirls his cane several times, and more bowlegged waddling and tipping of hats ends the clip.[7]

Sometimes the lines between serious and comedic cakewalks were blurred. Furthermore, the same movement might hold different meanings in different bodies, and there were sometimes disconnects regarding expectations. For example, when vaudeville performer Aida Overton Walker taught white women the dance, she emphasized respectability and dignity, whereas the women were looking for transgression. Like the Reed anecdote, this example allows us to dig deeper into an interracial encounter through dance. Whereas the Reed example lends insight into racial negotiations around passing, Walker's interactions with upper-class white women at the site of a dance lesson no doubt created possibilities for complicated negotiations of gender and class as well as race. All of the iterations and contexts for the cakewalk emphasized the "proper" ways for ladies and gentlemen to move *as* ladies and gentlemen, even when the choreography undermined these mores. The stakes of movement for Walker were much different than the stakes for the white women she taught. The white female project of easing Victorian-era constraints (rooted in the principles of true womanhood) and the black female project of rights of virtue and propriety (when these and other similar attributes were actively denied them) met at the site of the cakewalk.

This goes to show that there are many possible ways of understanding the politics of performance. Since the basic steps are easy (fancy walking), the meanings behind the movements (transgression, respectability, mockery, and so on) were born from the attitude of the performers. Competition in terms of virtuosity led to one set of results, and competition in terms of subtext, coding, manner, and attitude led to others. This allowed all dancers to participate bodily in psychic culture. In other words, the cakewalk might be a perfect medium for the dancer who was less interested in performing impressive tricks but able to display the elegant comportment conducive to respect.

For most of the nineteenth century, mainstream American social dances were dances imported from Europe (such as the waltz, polka, and quadrille). Though the cakewalk has European roots, it was the slave influences that made it distinctly American. The loosening of the stiff European dancing body (especially in the comedic cakewalk), the playfulness, sass, mockery, virtuosity, and competitiveness all signaled slave and American attitudes. Cultural critic Megan Pugh (2015) argues that the cakewalk was America's first national dance.[8] Despite formal efforts by professional dance educators in the United States to create a national dance to match the French minuet, the Spanish flamenco, or the Dutch chain dance, nothing they devised became a trend or an evocation of American identity and national pride. Meanwhile, the dance that began in mockery on plantations transitioned into posh dancehalls and created the first dance "craze." The resistance of white dance masters to the popularity of the cakewalk is not surprising. The play between serious and silly did not fit the idea of national pride; the development of the dance from the people (bottom up) and not from the dance masters (top down) was perhaps too democratic, the origins from slavery were unthinkable, and the roots in mockery indicated a mockery of the hypocrisy of America's founding principles. The desire to create a national dance speaks to the push for "America" to define itself not in the context of its European roots. The resistance to the cakewalk being a mechanism in that project speaks to continued racism at the root of the national project.

Nevertheless, the cakewalk (along with ragtime music and ragtime animal dances) became an unofficial national dance, and the United States' cultural "identity" as a nation of innovation and high standards, as well as fun and playful transgression, was furthered. This resurfaces later in cultural modes like rock and roll and hip-hop. Of course, money is often an important part of the equation in the popularization of any aesthetic style, and the cakewalk became a lucrative business as the music publisher Tin Pan Alley amassed a fortune from the dance music. To make money on the music, however, it had to stay popular (Figure 1.2). And in order to stay popular, it had to be danceable. Pugh describes the fervor with which America embraced the cakewalk:

FIGURE 1.2. Together with the dance, the rhythms of the cakewalk moved from plantation to stage and ballroom.

Across the country hundreds of black churches and social clubs organized cakewalks as fundraisers. Whites cakewalked at parties and hired black cakewalkers to perform at the festivities. Giant cakewalking competitions took place annually at Madison Square Garden, and a touring production of the cakewalk in San Francisco sold over ten thousand tickets in just two nights. After the white millionaire William K. Vanderbilt won a cakewalk competition at a friend's house, Bert Williams and George Walker took out an advertisement in the paper betting fifty dollars that they could beat him in a competition. Walter Gray, an African American cakewalk champion from Kansas, went for even higher stakes: a group of businessmen agreed to back "their saddle-colored champion" against Vanderbilt to the tune of five thousand dollars. Vanderbilt didn't take the bait, but the message was clear: these were challenges of black against white, working men against the elite, originators against imitators. And everyone knew who would have come out ahead. When two white couples competed against black cakewalkers in Hartford, Connecticut, the *Courant* reported that "as was to be expected, they had no chance for the prize." Black superiority was a foregone conclusion. (Pugh 2015, 20–21)

Although Pugh fails to acknowledge and trouble the term "black superiority," it is important to recognize that the belief in the superior dancing skills of African Americans was a double-edged sword loaded with biologically based false notions of natural ability versus skill and hard work at developing technique. Also, those accolades about superiority extended no further than the dance floor, while white superiority in nearly all other realms was assumed. No doubt, the white contenders were not actually offended. The inability of this couple to beat the black dancers was likely a good-natured joke, as nothing of consequence was actually at stake for them. Of course, the whole dance is built on a mockery of white superiority, but ultimately there was no real shift in power in acknowledging this superior status. There was not even the threat of a shift. The cakewalk was a safe practice for whites to permit and concede a position of inferiority.

Several national and international events helped to popularize the dance in the mainstream public. The 1876 Centennial Exposition in Philadelphia final capstone events featured a romanticized antebellum plantation scene, the end of which was a cakewalk contest, replete with a large cake as the prize to the winning couple. The following year, proto-musical theater entrepreneurs Harrigan and Hart produced "Walking for Dat Cake, An Exquisite Picture of Negro Life and Customs" as a sketch in a comedy routine at New York's Theater Comique on lower Broadway (Figure 1.3).

Coney Island had cakewalk contests on Saturday nights and paid $6 a couple. Professional dancers would show up to make extra money on the weekends. If venues at Coney Island paid dancers to participate, it meant that they were a draw that produced greater profit. The dance became popular in Europe, especially England, and in 1900 it was featured at the Paris World's Fair, ushering in a craze in France.[9]

The Creole Show (1890–1897) was a black burlesque (in the sense of variety, not striptease) featuring beautiful black dancing girls and pioneering a number of performance ventures. Although technically a minstrel show, it got rid of blackface and the

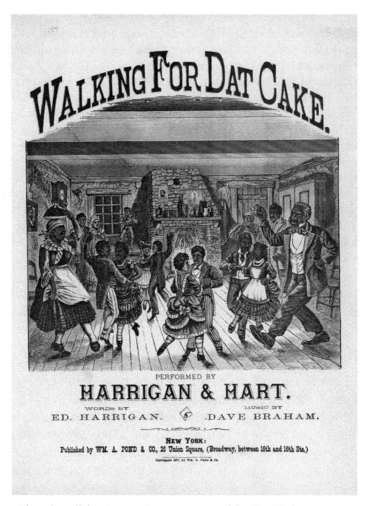

FIGURE 1.3. The cakewalk becomes an important part of the New York stage.

all-male cast, which allowed partner dancing without the derogatory blacking up, therefore lending new meaning to dances like the cakewalk. In 1893 the dance team of Charles E. Johnson and Dora Dean popularized elegant dancing styles within the show, emphasizing a simple, dignified, and well-dressed style. Johnson added fancy stepping and became known as the "Cakewalk King."

Madison Square Garden[10] also became an important site for the cakewalk (Figure 1.4). The original caption accompanying this image indicates that Madison Square Garden's cakewalk contest was a weekly event performed by African Americans and judged by whites. Vaudevillian, actor, and writer Tom Fletcher describes a typical event:

> The Madison Square Garden competition was always a sell-out . . . [t]he judges, including many of New York's prominent brokers, sportsmen and athletes, especially

FIGURE 1.4. Madison Square Garden held regular cakewalk contests.

prize fighters, would take their places on the stage. Walter F. Craig and his orchestra of fifty pieces would be seated on the stage to provide the music. . . . When the contest music started, first would appear a drum major who would go through a routine with his baton then return to his place as leader. Then the curtain would part and 50 or 60 couples would come from behind the stage on to the floor, prancing and dancing to the tempo of the music. It was very reminiscent of the grand entry at a circus. The girls' dresses were of all colors. The men wore full dress, clown clothes or comedy costumes with the big checks. When all the walkers were on the floor, then the 50 or 60 couples could all be seen doing different prances and dance steps ranging from buck-and-wing to toe dancing and, in fact, everything known to the terpsichorean art. (Fletcher 1954, 105)

The winning walkers, judged according to timing, style, and execution, not only won the night's prize, but also often formed professional acts and went into vaudeville and musical theater. A number of performers became well known as cakewalkers, including Bert Williams, Aida Overton Walker, George Walker, and Ernest Hogan. Many of these artists also made money instructing white society folk on the latest dances. Madison Square Garden also hosted the national championships in a three-night event that culminated in a contest in which winners from small-town contests competed against each other. Here competition led to improvisation and innovation as new steps were designed to impress judges and win prizes (with stakes raised from hoecakes to gold belts and diamond rings).

By 1908, when the first International Conference of Dancing Masters met in Berlin and held a March of Nations performance, the cakewalk mixed with the two-step was selected to represent the United States. By some measurements, the rise of the cakewalk as a national American dance in this international setting suggests that it "won" the competition for American pride and status. But the contradictory entanglements of race, status, aesthetics, virtuosity, and worth move to complicate this notion of competition and winning. Although the popularity of this black art form led to monetary success, this was not entirely the case for black artists. The competitive stakes for white America and black America around these dances were different.

Again, mockery plays a significant role here. As stated earlier, the cakewalk is a dance steeped in sarcasm and the ridicule of master society, white America's performance and pretentions of class, and American ideals. Yet at the same time, it demonstrates a mastery of those performative ideals, a claim to the rights of status, and a forcing of the national aesthetics away from stuffy Victorian/Anglophile restraint and toward the free-spirited looseness that would define the ragtime and jazz eras. The "looseness" of the dance across social groups and aesthetic tastes allowed for multiple performances and spectatorships. That this embodied freedom was playing out at the same time that questions about the implementation of the Reconstruction amendments were debated is not a coincidence. The struggle to control black bodies unfolded both on the national stage and on the ballroom stage.

Minstrelsy became the most important stage genre for the cakewalk. On the minstrel stage, the cakewalk was performed by white men in blackface (and some in drag as well), with comic and derisive intentions.[11] A cakewalk that included audience members became the favored ending of minstrel shows. It was an embodied way for audiences to, on the one hand, sanction the minstrel performance they had just witnessed and, on the other, become implicated in the complex negotiations therein. By participating bodily in a competition or merely as a fun finale, complicity in the raced and gendered negotiations of minstrelsy must be extended to audiences (black and white). The fun of parading provided value in a political economy that did not necessarily need financial remuneration. In other words, whether or not audience members got "prizes," they were nonetheless "rewarded," and "skill" played less of a role in the competition than what really mattered: the battle for social status.

I am unconvinced by arguments that suggest white Americans were ignorant of the injurious representations of minstrelsy, simply shrugging it off as harmless fun. It is too convenient to argue for such a naïve position. Perhaps they did not care about affording black Americans full human status, but enough bourgeois African American public figures decried minstrelsy that it was a willful ignorance, if ignorance at all. Rather, I maintain that the hegemonic workings of an art form deemed harmless were a cogent part of racial negotiations, and the moment African Americans gained voices through social and political means, the debates gained wider, national attention. And not surprisingly, black artists, when given limited access to professional entertainment, worked those images to their financial advantage (even if not always for the greater good of social status). The cakewalk in minstrel settings is an important example for understanding the complex intertwining of race and performance in the United States. White people putting on a minstrel mask in these settings (whether or not they blacked-up) and black people exaggerating their performances into what was or would become a stereotype further indicate the different stakes at play around the cakewalking body based on race. While white cakewalkers delighted in the fun of the cakewalk, black cakewalkers navigated a line between delighting in that fun and risking the perpetuation of demeaning stereotypes.

Clorindy and *Color Struck*

Beyond minstrelsy, the cakewalk also featured in other African American stage genres. For example, the dance became so essential to African American performance that it needed to be added to the musical theater production of *In Dahomey* in response to the number of letters requesting the dance (Glass 2007).

In 1898, *Clorindy: or the Origins of the Cake Walk* (arguably the first Broadway musical with an all-black cast) presented the titular cakewalk as an elegant affair with well-dressed black men and women moving gracefully to ragtime music. The status of this show further solidified the argument that African Americans have rights to high-class status, grace, and propriety. No longer mocking white worth, but rather asserting the right to it, this choreographic move reflects broader social moves. It is not only meaningful that the creative team thought it possible and necessary to stake these corporeal claims, they also devoted one-third of the musical to the cakewalk.

However, the show was not entirely progressive (Figure 1.5). For example, the dialogue and plot were mainly erased from the performance, as the first showing was at the outdoor Casino Theatre Roof Garden, and the performers' voices could not compete with street noise. What remained was a variety show that lacked the structuring plot that would help to support a serious aesthetic claim. On the other hand, twenty-six performers got bragging rights for being the first African Americans on Broadway, and African Americans could claim the status of artist. Indeed, African American participation in American musical theater increased after this performance, and old minstrel formats waned. Yet stereotyping did not die with minstrelsy and coon songs (including the ones popularized in *Clorindy*) that accompanied cakewalks, which created new barriers for serious black performers. For example, Hogan had to sing ten encores of the stereotypical "Who Dat Say Chicken in Dis Crowd," demonstrating the cost and demands of success. Thus, although the cakewalk enjoyed a competitive "win" with *Clorindy*, we must again trouble what was at stake in this performance.

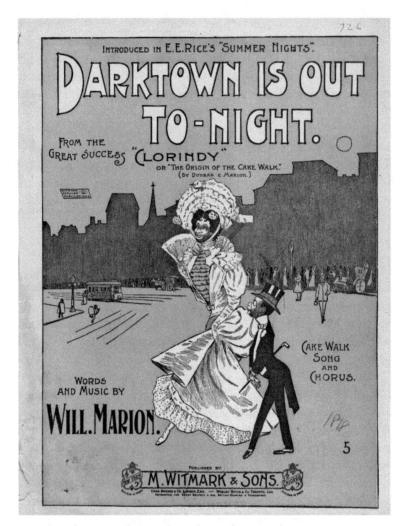

FIGURE 1.5. *Clorindy* presented a complicated mix of grace and stereotype.

A close reading of some of the lyrics in the show allow for attention to the complexities of the negotiations. Ernest Hogan, who was criticized for composing coon songs with derogatory images of African Americans, sang "The Hottest Coon in Dixie" in *Clorindy* (lyrics by Paul Laurence Dunbar and music by Will Marion Cook). Within the lyrics, the singer boasts of being fashionable and drawing everyone's attention when he goes out. He sings about performing respectability, wearing a suit, silk plug hat, gloves, and cane, and the key to his success (wins) as behaving properly:

> When e'er I meet some merry beaux,
> Here's what the darkies say.
> *Chorus:*

Behold the hottest coon,
Your eyes e'er lit on,
Velvet ain't good enough,
For him to sit on,
When he goes down the street,
Folks yell like sixty,
Behold the hottest coon in Dixie.
The reason why I always win,
My manners are complete,
It's not because I've got the tin,
But then I am so sweet,
The ladies cannot pass me by,
I've always got a girl,
And this is just the proper cry,
They give me, with a whirl. (Martin and Primeau 2002, 160)

Dunbar was embarrassed by the lyrics to the songs in *Clorindy* and vowed never to write another coon show. He understood the damage that the derogatory name did, even if the songs themselves were innocuous. Black artists navigated a line between resisting stereotypical images in order to redress social consequences and reproducing them because they were marketable. On the one hand, perpetuating these images were what the market demanded, and many black artists were faced with the choice of performing according to these desires or not earning a living. On the other hand, as more and more black artists and audience members became aware of the consequences of these portrayals, they pushed the aesthetics away from these images, sometimes subtly (like dampening exaggerated facial expressions) and sometimes by offering more interesting alternatives that were less damaging. Attending to the nuances of meaning in "coon" songs in this light is necessary. For example, in the songs for *Clorindy* there is a disconnect between the sentiment and the word "coon." "Coon" undermines the work of the songs, but one must ask to what extent was this a necessary move? To what extent did audience members (even black audience members) expect or demand such lyrics? Was the cakewalk able to skirt the stereotypical line of the "Zip Coon/Black Dandy" image? To what degree did this image do more harm than good? And could these contradictions (the stereotypical image of a coon in contrast to the image of a proud young man) exist in the same performance? The song troubles racial meaning, currency, and power only through the use of the terms "coon" and "darkies." In fact, if these words were substituted with "man" and "people," the song would be perfectly acceptable; the song refers not only to the key to success in a cakewalk, but also in life. If an accompanying cakewalk is performed in a serious manner, it could help elevate the race; if performed in a comedic or "low" manner, it could potentially have the opposite effect. Importantly, money is not the key to winning these competitions, nor is it the prize. Like the cakewalk, the song argues for the weight of performance and the value of respect as award over money ("tin"). The fact that so much of the meaning here depends upon how one reads performative choices indicates the fluidity of value in these negotiations. The meaning and impact of these images and contradictory messages shifted over time. It also shifted among audience members at the same performance, as one person's laughter at a performer's dandyism might lead to different judgments about the race than another person's laughter. In other words, the danger of an audience member judging the entire race on one dandy performance was not equal. Performance also allowed for poking at the social fabric. At one point in the show, right before a big cakewalk, the chorus sings, "White fo'ks yo' / Got no sho'! Dis huh's Darktown night." The same atmosphere that allowed subversion under the laughable auspices of a "coon" show allowed performers to safely cast such aspersions.

The cakewalk also became an important device in writer and anthropologist Zora Neale Hurston's straight play *Color Struck* (1925). Set in 1900, the play primarily addresses intra-racial colorism and the crippling psychological effects of internalized racism. But the way in which Hurston sets up the conflict is salient to this discussion. The play opens with the members of a Jacksonville, Florida, community boarding a train in the Jim Crow coach, bound for St. Augustine to compete in a cakewalk competition against other area towns. The mood of anticipatory joy indicates the significance of the event. It offers an opportunity not only to compete, but also to gather as a community, travel, perform in a dancehall, and test one's mettle against community-defined standards. The entire town is rooting for its dancers, and the competition, like a sporting event, creates hometown loyalties and good-natured rivalries. Importantly, these are African American towns (or "colored," to use the preferred contemporaneous term). This is a black world, with its own rules, talent, and prizes. Like a trophy, the dancers who bring the cake home to their town also will bring home pride and bragging rights. The prize for the warm-up dance, the pas-me-la, is a fascinator (an adorned hair or hat clip), but the cake for the final event is the grand prize. Though the prize is not cash, the cake carries value, and to emphasize its importance, the announcer grandiosely states that the couples will compete, "fuh de biggest cake ever baked in dis state. Ten dozen eggs—ten pounds of flour—ten pounds of butter, and so on and so forth." Later, we see the impressive cake as part of the cakewalk. "*Four men come out from behind the platform bearing a huge chocolate cake. The couples are 'prancing' in their tracks. The men lead off the procession with the cake—the contestants make a grand slam around the hall*" (Hurston 2008, 44). Everyone in town has a stake in the event. Even the conductor comments on the prize:

> RAILWAY CONDUCTOR: I hope somebody from Jacksonville wins this cake.
> JOHN: You live in the "Big Jack?"
> RAILWAY CONDUCTOR: Sure do. And I wanta taste a piece of that cake on the way back tonight.
> JOHN: Jes rest easy—them Augustiners ain't gonna smell it. (Hurston 2008, 37)

Thirty-five years after the Emancipation Proclamation began a process of freeing slaves in the American South, the kids imagined by Hurston on this train (among the first African Americans born free in the South) would have had a sense of freedom unknown before them. Surely, not ignorant of the continued brutalities of the Jim Crow era, the possibilities underlining the trip to St. Augustine are significant nonetheless.

The description of the opening scene provides clues into the image of the prospect for this generation and demographic:

> Before the curtain goes up there is the sound of a locomotive whistle and a stopping engine, loud laughter, many people speaking at once, good-natured shrieks, strumming of stringed instruments, etc. The ascending curtain discovers a happy lot of Negroes boarding the train dressed in the gaudy, tawdry best of 1900.
> (Hurston 2008, 35)

Hurston's fashion commentary notwithstanding, she sets an uplifted, jovial scene. That a cakewalk competition is the source of this verve is not incidental. These young adults are proud. They are proud of making it to the contest, and they are proud of making it to the twentieth century. Effie, a young and attractive woman, tells a potential suitor that she is on the outs with her boyfriend because "[a] man dat don't buy me nothin tuh put in *mah* basket, ain't goin' wid *me* tuh no cake walk." Part and parcel of her haughty attitude is the fact that this trip is an occasion, an event that warrants excess.

The central plot hinges on the fact that one of the couples, Emma and John, are having a spat because Emma thinks John was smiling at Effie. Effie has lighter-colored skin than Emma, and Emma is jealous. This eventually undoes the couple. More salient to this discussion are the consequences this has on the cakewalk contest. Emma and John are agreed to be Jacksonville's best cakewalkers and, without them, St. Augustine might win the competition. Their argument almost caused them to miss the train, and one dancer remarks, "Don't y'all skeer us no mo' lake dat! There couldn't be no cake walk thout y'all. Dem shad-mouf St. Augustine coons would win dat cake and we would have tuh kill 'em all bodaciously." Another states, " 'Walkers' never walked till John and Emmaline prance out." We get to see a demonstration of John and Emma dancing in the train aisle to much applause, and Effie then dances down the aisle alone.

WESLEY: Come on out, Effie! Sam aint heah so you got to hold up his side too. Step on out.(*There is a murmur of applause as she steps into the aisle. Wesley strikes up* "I'm gointer live anyhow till I die." *It is played quite spiritedly as Effie swings into the pas-me-la—*)

WESLEY: (*in ecstasy*) Hot stuff I reckon! Hot stuff I reckon!(*The musicians are stamping. Great enthusiasm. Some clap time with hands and feet. She hurls herself into a modified Hoochy Koochy, and finishes up with an ecstatic yell.*)(*There is a babble of talk and laughter and exultation.*)

JOHN: (*applauding loudly*) If dat Effie can't step nobody can.

EMMALINE: Course you'd say so cause it's her. Everything she do is pretty to you.

JOHN: (*caressing her*) Now don't say that, Honey. Dancing is dancing no matter who is doing it. But nobody can hold a candle to you in nothing. (Hurston 2008, 38)

This should be a light happy story about a young happy couple dancing and winning a contest. But Hurston argues through her characters that, even though this is a black world, the effects of white oppression in the form of colorism and internalized racism are borne on these young people. With Sam and Effie fighting (Sam does not come to the competition), along with John's insensitive attention to Effie, and Emma's jealousy over the color of Effie's skin, John and Emma break up, and John and Effie compete for Jacksonville and win. The cake as the prize is central and part and parcel of the movement: "*The cake is set down in the center of the floor and the winning couple parade around it arm in arm. John and Effie circle the cake happily and triumphantly. The other contestants, and then the entire assembly fall in behind and circle the cake, singing and clapping*" (Hurston 2008, 44).

Though Jacksonville wins the competition, Emma loses her chance at happiness. Like the cakewalk itself, colorism presents a convoluted entanglement of meaning around whiteness and blackness that is not easily understood. Was John more attracted to Effie because of her lighter skin tone or was he innocent? Probably both. Was Emma justified in her jealousy or blinded by her own colorism? Probably both. Was the cakewalk positive about blackness/whiteness or negative? Probably both. And a simple binary solution is inadequate. More useful is taking a step (specifically a cakewalk step) back, as this chapter attempts, to examine the roots of racial entanglements. The historical causes of colorism, like the historical influences of the cakewalk, are uniquely American. The bringing together of these races under the white supremacist system of slavery and the subsequent events necessarily brought about both.

Who Won?

This chapter peels back the layers of meaning behind the different stakes of cakewalk competition, the hidden secrets behind the prancing, and the multiple meanings in the confident attitude. Achieving virtuosity within plantation confrontations, walking the straight and narrow line of moral fortitude while dancing around the letter of some laws, these dancers embraced contradictory impulses, navigated multiple spaces, and demanded that black male and female bodies be respected. With resilience and flexibility, cakewalkers bent forward into the future and bent back to remember the past. They created a dance craze that helped define a nation like no other dance before. They used their bodies to wage battles over representation, and their performative choices indicated the fluidity of identity. They tapped into the possibilities of mobility and the bodily ties to progress and hope for individuals and larger communities, despite continuing struggles. Ultimately, cakewalk dancers highlighted a demand to reinterpret definitions of our notions of value, worth, currency, and stakes. Competition was at the heart of all of these meanings.

The multiple sites of analysis examined in this chapter all point to the important ways in which competition, value, and identity take form in cakewalk dance settings.

The Reed example opens the conversation by exposing the tenuous racial logics that supported discrimination in dance competitions and black bodies. Reed's refusal to be a fixed raced identity supports the claim that we need to reimagine the stakes at play and value of the prizes in these settings. Rooted in complicated African, European, and Native American traditions, the cakewalk on antebellum Southern plantations were competitions between masters affording slaves a modicum of respite and prizes in the shape of food and clothing, at the same time that it allowed for small but significant transgressions through coded movement. As the cakewalk grew in popularity off the plantation in public and professional settings, the wagers shifted. Monetary remuneration and the cultural capital of dignity and respectability increased in value. When factoring in gender, the cakewalk meant different things for black and white women and the ways in which they wanted society to view them. While official bragging rights for the status of "the national dance" were withheld from the cakewalk, the dance craze became an important component in what distinguished America from other nations and helped solidify a distinctly popular "American" identity, despite resistance from the upper echelons of the professional dance world. Dance contests and the increasingly lucrative cakewalk sheet music business expanded the value of the cakewalk in the mainstream economic marketplace. On stage, in minstrelsy, musical theater, and "straight" dramas, artists used the cakewalk as entertainment and metaphor to capitalize on the dance's popularity and negotiate and make arguments about raced bodies in America. External and internal arguments about the value of black skin were played out on these stages as rehearsals for real life. Serious aesthetic, mockery, popular fun, comic genre, elegant, dignified, stereotypical, low-, medium-, and high-stakes competition all described the cakewalk at one time or another. Virtuosic performances rooted in ironic mimicry pushed to help define a nation at these cakewalk sites.

But who won? And by what yardstick do we measure? In some respects, we are still in a corporeal and psychic competition that we term "race relations." It is beyond the scope of this chapter to debate the "progress" America has made in terms of the grand racial reckoning, but it is important to comprehend that dance will always be a significant part of those negotiations and a site for productive investigation because of the possibilities afforded by layers of meaning coded in the moving body. The cakewalk provides a rich and complex example of this.[12]

Notes

1. This story is cited in many biographical accounts of Reed. For one, see the Library of Congress webpage on Reed: http://memory.loc.gov/diglib/ihas/loc.music.tdabio.160/default.html (accessed January 10, 2017).
2. For a list of important tap dance challenges, see Hill (2010).
3. For good comprehensive studies of early black dance, see Stearns and Stearns (1994), Emery (1988), Malone (1996), Hazzard-Gordon (1990), Dixon-Gottschild (2002), Glass (2007), and Valis Hill (2010).

4. It is also beyond the scope of this chapter to analyze more recent intercultural competitions in historically black dance forms, such as global hip-hop dance competitions.

5. See Urlin (1912), Butler and Butler (1967), Evan and Evans (1931).

6. As a historian, I find it necessary to remind readers of the global catastrophe that was the transatlantic slave trade system to combat contemporary racist moves (like the Texas High School history books that referred to slaves as "workers") to water down the devastating effects of slavery.

7. https://www.youtube.com/watch?v=8jXJcw_ORP8 (accessed September 19, 2016).

8. The idea of any one dance (or set of dances) representing a nation or national pride is complicated and beyond the scope of this chapter. Rather, it is important to examine this historical moment and the factors that went into the *desire* to create or declare a dance corporeally emblematic of the nation. The cakewalk operates in two senses here. One might think about the cakewalk as a contender for this official title, and one might think about the large influence the dance was having regardless of official status. Even though the dance could not be an official contender, it is important to recognize that it tapped into the ethos of many people in the United States at the turn of the nineteenth into the twentieth century.

9. For more on the cakewalk's influence in France, see Whiting (1999).

10. The current Madison Square Garden (the fourth with the title) opened in 1968. In 1892, at the time of Figure 1.4, when the cakewalk appeared at Madison Square Garden the likely venue was the second one bearing the name, which opened on Madison Square at East 26th street and Madison Avenue in 1890. At the time it was the largest commercial presenting venue in New York.

11. Offstage, white society members also blacked up to cakewalk for charity events.

12. Many thanks to Jon Reimer for research assistance.

References

Butler, Albert, and Josephine Butler. 1967. *The Encyclopedia of Social Dance*. New York: Albert Butler Ballroom Dance Service.

Dixon-Gottschild, Brenda. 1996. *Digging the Africanist Presence in American Performance: Dance and Other Contexts*. Westport, CT: Greenwood Press.

Dixon-Gottschild, Brenda. 2002. *Waltzing in the Dance: African American Vaudeville and Race Politics in the Swing Era*. New York: St. Martin's Press.

Emery, Lynn Fauley. 1988. *Black Dance from 1619 to Today*. Princeton, NJ: Princeton Book.

Evans, Bessie, and May G. Evans. 1931. *Native American Dance Steps*. New York: A. S. Barnes.

Farris-Thompson, Robert. 1973. "An Aesthetic of the Cool." *African Arts* 7(1): 41–91.

Fletcher, Tom. 1954. *One Hundred Years of the Negro in Show Business*. Boston: Da Capo Press.

Glass, Barbara S. 2007. *African-American Dance: An Illustrated History*. Jefferson, NC: McFarland.

Hazzard-Gordon, Katrina. 1990. *Jookin': The Rise of Social Dance Formations in African-American Culture*. Philadelphia: Temple University Press.

Hill, Constance Vallis. 2010. *Tap Dancing America: A Cultural History*. New York: Oxford University Press.

Hurston, Zora Neale. 2008. "Colorstruck (1926)." In *Zora Neale Hurston: Collected Plays*, edited by Jean L. Cole and Charles Mitchell, 33–50. New Brunswick, NJ: Rutgers University Press.

Library of Congress. "Leonard Reed [biography]." In *Performing Arts Encyclopedia*. www. memory.loc.gov/diglib/ihas/loc.music.tdabio.160/default.html.   Accessed   January 10, 2017.

Malone, Jacqui. 1996. *Steppin' on the Blues: The Visible Rhythms of African American Dance.* Urbana; Chicago: University of Illinois Press.

Martin, Herbert Woodward, and Ronald Primeau, eds. 2002. *In His Own Voice: The Dramatic and Other Uncollected Works of Lawrence Dunbar.* Athens: Ohio University Press.

Pugh, Megan. 2015. *American Dancing: From the Cakewalk to the Moonwalk.* New Haven, CT: Yale University Press.

Stearns, Marshall, and Jean Stearns. 1994. *Jazz Dance: The Story of African American Vernacular Dance.* New York: DaCapo.

Urlin, Ethel L. 1912. *Dancing, Ancient and Modern.* New York: Appleton.

Whiting, Steven Moore. 1999. *Satie the Bohemian: From Cabaret to Concert Hall.* New York: Oxford University Press.

Audiovisual Sources

comedy cakewalk mpeg. 2010. YouTube video, 0:30. Posted by "Dance Scholar," January 26, www.youtube.com/watch?v=8jXJcw_ORP8. Accessed September 19, 2016.

CHAPTER 2

YOU'VE GOT TO SELL IT!

Performing on the Dance Competition Stage

KAREN SCHUPP

As a competitive dancer in the 1980s and early 1990s, my teachers encouraged me to "sell it!" The phrase "sell it" was their way of emphasizing the importance of creating an entertaining performance for the audience and, by default in dance competitions, the judges. Successfully "selling a dance" entices an audience into watching what a performer has to offer, "buying into" his or her distinctive strengths, and engaging with the themes or narrative of the performance. To sell a dance, performers need confidence as technicians, presence as artists, and the wherewithal to persevere, set and attain goals, handle stress, and work well with others. Selling the dance is not easy, yet the sense of personal accomplishment that comes from engaging an audience through performance is incredibly rewarding.

Although the idea of selling the dance applies to a wide range of dance contexts, the phrase takes on a dual meaning in dance competition culture. Dance competitions, which focus on contemporary, jazz, tap, hip-hop, and ballet, and attract thousands of competitors, most of whom are adolescent girls, play a central role in private-sector dance training, and operate on a "pay to dance" system. Entry fees are required to participate, which raises complex questions about what exactly is sold, bought, and invested in as young people enter into dance competition culture. First, dance competitions sell a performance slot that provides dancers an opportunity to perform for a panel of judges on a professionally lit and dressed stage while competing among their peers. Second, competitors receive constructive criticism from a panel of judges, the opportunity to spectate, if they wish, as an audience member, and a souvenir for their participation, such as lapel pins indicating award status or large trophies indicating high overall scores.

Yet beyond buying into an opportunity to perform, to be evaluated, and to spectate, competitors' level of investment far surpasses these simple transactions. Dance competitions give young dancers a place to express and test themselves through performance. By performing on stage with the intent of receiving feedback and recognition from the judges, competitors demonstrate and self-assess their dance capabilities. The rush of engaging a large audience that is familiar with competitive dance and the thrill of being with peers who are passionate about dance clearly contribute to the appeal of dance competitions. Through observing peers from other studios, competitors develop increased awareness of dance competition culture, which drives their desire to improve. Through the judges' critiques, competitors gain an outsider's perspective on their dancing, which carries greater value than the day-to-day feedback supplied by their dance studio teachers. The multilayered experience of watching peers, performing before knowledgeable audiences, and receiving evaluative feedback connects competitors to a large dance community and may lead to new opportunities within dance competition culture.[1] Training for and performing in dance competitions cultivates and calls for transferable proficiencies—skills that are not necessarily artistic or technical, but are needed to successfully perform. Through the physical and emotional labor invested in their training and performance, competitors acquire resiliency, perseverance, time management, self-efficacy, and interpersonal awareness. Although the joy of performing, development of community, and acquisition of transferable proficiencies are not directly bought or sold, competitors' commitment to these intangible qualities underscores their motivation to participate in dance competitions.

To better understand what motivates adolescents to invest in dance competition culture, in this chapter I explore the interplay between what is sold, bought, and invested in at dance competition events. The research for this qualitative study comes from four key areas: my memories of dance competition culture as a dancer, teacher/choreographer, and judge in the 1980s and 1990s; semi-structured interviews with seven adolescent girls who currently participate in dance competitions;[2] attendance at dance competitions as an audience member, and observing dance competition performance footage on social media; and examining dance competition websites. My theoretical framework is rooted in literature on the construction of bodily ideals both within dance and Western culture (Foster 1997), the dancer's contributions to contemporary dance practices (Roche 2015), the formation of dancing communities (Hamera 2007), and dance learning in relation to ideas of conspicuous consumption (Carolan 2005) and the experience economy (Pine and Gilmore 1998). From this, I argue that dance competitions offer adolescents a meaningful venue through which to perform, build community, and nurture transferable proficiencies. Although not explicitly "for sale," these qualities provide an understanding of why competitors "pay to dance."

I begin with a brief history and overview of dance competition, before examining the experiences of the seven adolescent girls and my observations of dance competition events to illustrate how "selling" the dance operates in the pursuit of performance, the cultivation of community, and the refinement of transferable proficiencies. I conclude by demonstrating how dance competitions highlight the implicit and positive experiential components, and downplay the explicit and competitive elements of these events, to promote a sense of personal investment and achievement from competitors that stems from selling a dance on the competition stage.

Constructing a Stage Where Everyone Wins: A Brief History

> Step into the spotlight! The stage is yours!
>
> —Showstopper (2016)

As videos of young people performing dances, celebrating wins, and mugging for the camera play, the preceding quote flashes across Showstopper's website (www.goshowstopper.com). Showstopper, one of the oldest corporate competitions in the United States, started in 1978 when founder Debbie Roberts realized that "dancers needed an exciting stage where they could do what they love, while also receiving feedback that pushed them to be their best" (Showstopper 2016, n.p.). For almost forty years, Showstopper has "watched incredible dancers work the spotlight, become part of their family, and dance their way to success" (2016, n.p.). Showstopper was one of the first corporate competitions to offer competitors a place to "sell their dance" on a highly produced, spotlit stage.

The image of stepping into the spotlight alludes to glamor, which is markedly different from the humble beginnings of dance competitions in the early 1970s. At first, dance competitions were primarily run by local business or nonprofit organizations (Guarino 2014). Competitors were supposed to watch their entire category, after which one adjudicator publicly shared feedback before awarding first, second, and third place; there was no guarantee that each competitor would receive an award. In this model, competitors publicly received knowledgeable advice for improvement and learned what an adjudicator valued in a performance. Furthermore, in the 1970s and 1980s, competitors frequently performed in "low-tech" settings with little stage lighting, no special effects, and a simple sound system; videos, photographs, and souvenirs were rarely sold.

As I was leaving the competition world in the mid-1990s, dance competitions were becoming multi-day events where competitors perform in professional performance settings, sometimes specifically (although temporarily) built for the occasion. For example, Showstopper now decorates the stage space with an LED cyclorama that provides different background images for each dance, close-up real-time video projections that flank the stage, and logo-adorned wings with ample sidelights. Competitors are not mandated to watch other performances,[3] although several do, and audio-recorded feedback is given to teachers after the event (which may mean that competitors do not hear the judges' critiques). The removal of the public adjudication from the daily schedule created more performance opportunities, which translates to greater revenue for dance competition organizations. In most dance competitions today, every entry receives an award based on a predetermined score rubric (Figure 2.1). For example, at Showstopper, all dances that score in the specific point range receive a "Double Platinum" award, which means that multiple "Double

Platinum" awards may be conferred in one category. At regional events, all dances that achieve a certain minimum score qualify for the organization's national dance competition, where the entry fees are higher. Additionally, a plethora of souvenir items, including performance videos and photographs, dancewear with motivational quotes, concessions, and programs are sold.

Since my participation in dance competitions, the costs have drastically changed. The entry fee for my first solo in the mid-1980s would be roughly US$15 today when adjusted for inflation; to perform the same solo today would cost about US$105. Although this increase is due to the profitability of dance competitions, it is also partially due to the cost of administering dance competitions. When dance competitions moved out of low-tech facilities, expanded to offer multiple regional and national competitions, and started to use three or more judges instead of one adjudicator per competition, they needed to pay for venue rental, employee travel and salaries, administrative costs, insurance, and liability fees (Weisbrod 2010). Professionalizing the dance competition experience came at a cost for both organizers and competitors.

FIGURE 2.1. A competitive dancer poses with her awards at a regional competition.

Photography by Melissa Fincher Mergi. Used with Permission.

BUYING AND SELLING: DANCE COMPETITION FRAMEWORKS AND STAKEHOLDERS

> The Starpower Family could not be more excited to offer another year of enthusiasm, energy, and professionalism! Starpower thrives on its relationships and support from studio directors, teachers, performers, and parents over the past two decades. We want to express our deepest thanks to all of you who have helped to make us number one in the industry!
>
> —Star Dance Alliance (n.d.b.)

Dance competition culture's symbiotic relationships are exemplified in the preceding quote from Star Dance Alliance, an organization that owns and operates nine distinct dance competition and convention circuits, including Starpower (Figure 2.2). The network of stakeholders who buy, sell, and invest in dance competitions includes the following: organizations that operate the contests; dance studio owners and teachers who train dancers for these events and broker financial transactions between dance competition competitors and dance competition organizers; young people who train at dance studios and represent them through participation in the competition events; and guardians who furnish logistical and financial support to the participating dancers.

FIGURE 2.2. Competitors crowd the stage for an awards ceremony.

On average, dance competition organizations host between twenty-two and twenty-five regional competitions and one to three national events per year (Guarino 2014; LaRocco 2012; Schupp 2006). Competition fees do not vary much from competition to competition. For regional events, solos cost approximately US$100–110 per entry, duos and trios cost US$50–55 per person per entry, and groups cost US$40–50 per person per entry. For competitors who are deeply involved in dance competitions, the costs can easily top US$1,000 per month (LaRocco 2012), and "Dance Dad Tim" Colley, author of the autobiography *All In: My Amazing Journey as a Dance Dad* (2014), admits that his family spends around US$35,000 each year to finance his daughter's dance training and participation.

At dance competitions, competitors perform short choreographed dances. Competitive categories are organized around the dance style, average age of the competitors in a dance, number of dancers, and, occasionally, the amount of training the dancers possess.[4] A panel of expert judges, usually seated in the front row of the audience, evaluates each dance by providing a numerical score and, in most cases, audio-recorded feedback. While the judging is typically guided by a subjective four-part rubric that evaluates performance, choreography, technique, and overall appearance, judges tend to look for "quality technique," performance quality, clear lines and transitions, musicality, personal style, professional overall appearance, appropriate costume choices, and memorability (Wollins 2014), as exemplified in the professional commercial dance venues that feature these dance styles. The criteria are extremely vague, and there seems to be an unstated standard about what constitutes a good dancer. The archetypal competition dancer is young, long and lean, hyper mobile yet toned; performs movements that demand great power and flexibility, primarily in the lower body, and a sense of muscular control; uses dance movements that are a combination of jazzy moves, balletic vocabulary, and acrobatic tricks; is able to convey a story primarily through facial expressions and musicality that mirrors the rhythmic structure of the music; and wears a dazzling costume that accentuates the body's performance of gender and uniformity (Schupp 2017; Weisbrod 2010). These ideas are central to how dancers "sell it" on stage and how dance competitions sell events to competitors.

The competition dance aesthetic aligns with the dance styles and expectations of the "commercial dance world" where many judges perform and choreograph, and dance competition competitors may seek future careers. Although a spectrum of dance exists within a space of commercial transaction, I refer here to dance that seeks to sell a tangible product, such as dance in advertising commercials or backup dancing to promote a celebrity pop star's music. Because its goal is to sell a commodity for profit, commercial dance is highly visible within North American culture and therefore recognizable to US consumers. As such, it is not surprising that the evolution of dance competitions coincides with the rise of dance studios in the United States. As founder of the National Registry of Dance Educators Elsa Posey (2002) articulates, the amount of dance schools across the United States grew tremendously from the 1970s to the 1990s, perhaps due to the growth of the middle class, which led to increased leisure time and disposable income, and the increased presence of media featuring dance during this era. The teaching methods and dance styles taught in dance studios are strongly tethered to the ethos of dance competitions (Guarino 2014; Schupp 2006, 2017; Weisbrod 2010). Dance studio owners stay in business by responding to the demands of local communities (Posey 2002; Risner, Godfrey, and Simmons 2004); hence the majority of US dance studios offer tap, jazz, lyrical or contemporary, hip-hop, and ballet. Not surprisingly, these dance forms dominate the entertainment industry and are regularly featured in dance competitions and dance studios (Posey 2002; Weisbrod 2010). Dance competitions implicitly determine, in relationship to commercial dance, the technical and artistic standards that guide dance studios' teaching practices in these styles. Dance competition competitors are then affected by the broader values of the commercial dance arena, which in turn shapes their ideas about the role of dance performance in a larger cultural context and reinforces the privileging of commercial dance values and practices in competition settings.

INVESTING IN EXCELLENCE: EXPERIENCING PERFORMANCE, COMMUNITY, AND TRANSFERABLE SKILLS

Star Dance Alliance is an alliance of top international dance competitions committed to bringing you the greatest dance competition experience of your life. Each of our participating competitions holds the highest standards in competitions and we are reaching ahead into the future every season to provide a power packed competition line up.

—Star Dance Alliance (n.d.a.).

Dance competition organizations endeavor to offer positive experiences and high standards, and contribute to the future of dance. These values are reflected in dance competition culture's marketing materials and business practices, and competitors' motivations to partake in dance competitions. For example, Starpower's home page prominently features four images: one of young dancers wearing identical warm-up jackets, triumphantly embracing a trophy as confetti flutters around them; a second image featuring a close-up on two adolescent girls' jubilant expressions as they hold a trophy; one of an adolescent girl darting in a fully extended *grand jeté* toward her audience with a huge smile and arms extended triumphantly; and an image of an adolescent girl performing a layout exposing her heart to the space above her (Star Dance Alliance n.d.c.). Each of the images includes smiling faces and trained bodies that allude to hard work and accomplishment. Promotional images such as these are often captured during actual competitions and thereby reflect the competitors' experiences performing, forming communities, and fostering transferable proficiencies. Examining the presence of these aspects in dance competition culture uncovers the symbiotic relationships between competitors' motivations and dance competition frameworks.

TAKING THE STAGE: PERFORMANCE
EXPERIENCES AND EXCHANGES

> That was probably the hardest thing for me to do when I was younger,
> that leg-spin. And I remember doing *relevé* turns in the dance, like twice
> I think in that dance . . . it was a lot of hard work to do. And I always would
> be like, "Okay, you can do this." And then when I would get it, I would just
> be like so happy with myself, when I could actually do it, and be like, "Oh,
> I worked so hard for this; now I actually have it."

This quote comes from Suzi,[5] a thirteen-year-old who trains over twelve hours a week
and competes "just about every weekend in the spring," as she described her most
memorable dance competition experience. Suzi's intense enthusiasm for dance shone
through as she recalled performing her first competitive solo at the age of eight. Her
reflection is significant because it sharply demonstrates the significance of working toward a performance. The pursuit to perfect choreography, both technically and artistically, and the gratification of demonstrating the accomplishment of personal goals in
performance drives many in competitive dance.

Although performing is perhaps the most memorable part of dance competitions,
participating as an engaged audience member is a critical component of the experience. Elizabeth, a bubbly seventeen-year-old who talked excitedly about her involvement with dance competitions, and Suzi both spoke to how competitive dancers learn
from watching their peers at dance competitions (Figure 2.3). Elizabeth shared that
dance competitions are "a good way to grow and to learn a lot, and to get other people's
perspective. Everyone is so amazing with dance that it's really hard to keep up and be
above." Suzi echoed this as she conveyed her excitement for watching "all the other girls
and guys perform their competition dances, and to see how good they are, and like what
we can improve on to go against them."

In dance competition culture, most of the explicit dance learning takes place in
students' dance studios as they sweat through technique classes, grapple with learning
choreography, and vigorously rehearse under the guidance of their dance teachers.
However, what competitors observe on the competition stage and what is reinforced
by the judges' rankings, competition advertisements, and trends in commercial dance
drive their performance aesthetics; competitors want to execute or surpass what their
peers perform on stage.

Although each dance and dancer is unique, there is a common aesthetic in dance competition culture, as exemplified by the performance of a fifteen-year-old soloist at the
Kids Artistic Review Dance Finals (*Juliette Roberts* 2015). When it is her turn to perform,
the music that plays between entries fades as the emcee announces her entry number
and title of the dance. As she struts on stage to perform her lyrical solo, "Bang Bang,"
using her gaze, she acknowledges the judges as the audience cheers. She takes the stage

FIGURE 2.3. A soloist waits in the wings for her turn to take the stage while watching her competitors.

Photography by Melissa Fincher Mergi. Used with Permission.

in a costume designed to emphasize the "dancerly" nature of her body: a rhinestone-adorned bikini with fabric panels on the front and back of the lower body. Within the first five seconds of her short dance, she instantly "sells it" to the judges by confidently executing two *développé à la seconde* that extend to a full 180 degrees. She goes on to perform fifteen variations on *développés* and *grand battements*, four turn sequences that involve multiple variations on *fouetté* turns and *en dehors pirouettes à la seconde*, and five large leaps, the biggest one being a center switch split leap performed at the musical climax. These "technical" movements are punctuated with sensual movements where she caresses her head and neck, contracts her middle, and arches her back to portray angst and vulnerability; isolations such as head rolls and hip thrusts to highlight musical accents; and movements that directly mimic the song's lyrics, such as leaping to the floor on the words "hit the ground." Her movement is bound yet expansive and comes from a "pulled up" posture that resists gravity, quickly initiated with a sustained follow through, tempered with acrobatic elements without being gymnastic, and accompanied by dramatic pantomimes. When she finishes, she quickly bows and exits, in a pedestrian manner, while the audience applauds. The cycle starts anew as the next soloist waits in the wings.

While competitors perform, judges record real-time audio critiques. In addition to judges, fellow competitors observe, from the wings and the audience, and consider each performance in relation to their own capabilities and aspirations; competitors see other young people performing, with various success, similar turn sequences, explosive leaps, expansive leg extensions, and other sharply executed movements. Additionally, performers assess their own performances. Competitors eagerly discuss what stands out in their own performances and those of others throughout the competition event.

The performance content results from the intertwined influences of the competition judges, dance studio teachers, and the competitors themselves. The choreography, movement vocabulary, technical understanding, and dancing bodies that the judges reward through high scores implicitly set the standards for dance competitions. Yet, because objective technical and artistic criteria do not exist for most dance competitions, these standards stem from what competitors offer judges in performance. Because these events are competitions, teachers often strategize on how to highlight students' strengths in competition routines, which perhaps explains the prevalence of "tricks" within competitive dance choreography. Although dance studio teachers or guest choreographers create the dances, and the judges' rankings influence choreographic and performance trends, dancers actively contribute to performance standards in dance competitions as they prepare for and perform at competitive events and watch their peers.

The importance of learning performance standards from peers and near peers was reinforced as the interviewees described either the best solo they have seen in a dance competition or their favorite dancers. For example, when Joy, a sixteen-year-old with an outgoing personality who offered concise yet detailed information about her experiences, described the best solo she has seen, she readily recalled the name of a solo dancer who was only slightly older than she. I was struck by the sincere admiration Joy has for this performer as she described how the dancer "went up there, and she had this strength behind her and just this power and demanded everyone's attention to watch her on stage. And it just took my breath away, and I was like 'Wow, I want to have that demand on stage from now on.'" For Joy, as well as the other interviewees, observing her peers solidified her ideas about what constitutes a good competitive performance and gave her an aesthetic ideal to work toward.

Looking to peers to determine what is considered to be an ideal dancer is an opportunity that the competitive framework of these events provides without directly selling it. Dance competitions bring together different studios and, in doing so, adolescents can see "what else is out there." Through this comparison, they push themselves to accomplish more, which deepens the skills teachers can call upon in choreography, thus advancing the performance level presented on the competition stage, which raises the judges' performance standards, which then reinitiates this cycle. In her research that situates dancers as active contributors to contemporary dance culture, dance scholar Jennifer Roche (2015) explains how contemporary dancers are more than passive recipients of choreographers' material. Roche demonstrates, both through recounting her own experiences and interviews, how dancers actively bring dance to life and shape choreographic practices. Through Roche's work, dancers' agency in shaping dance practices—specifically in contemporary dance culture, where dancers are expected to be proficient in numerous styles and ways of working—is validated. Although Roche examines postmodern concert dance practices and adult dancers, her argument applies to adolescents in the competitive dance scene. Competitive dancers frequently train in "all styles" represented in dance competition culture, and are able to quickly adapt to and transfer skills between these styles. As teachers seek to feature dancers' performance and movement strengths in their choreography, the skills of competition dancers determine the movement vocabulary of a dance routine; the choreography stems from what the dancer brings to the rehearsal and performance process. Finally, since the adolescents pay for their lessons, their ideas about what they would like to work on and include in their routines will be carefully considered through the teacher's expert lens. In these ways, adolescents actively contribute to the advancement of performance standards in competition dance culture.

Another way that adolescents feed off each other to advance performance standards in dance competition culture is best explained in relationship to Susan Foster's (1997) theorization of the demonstrative body. In her work on how dance training shapes bodily perception, Foster names three types of bodies that dancers encounter in their training: the perceived body, the body that sweats, feels, and executes movement; the ideal body, the body that epitomizes the aesthetics of a given dance style; and the demonstrative body, the body that demonstrates what dancers need to achieve and work on in order to attain perfection in a given dance style. Unlike other dance styles where students may encounter a demonstrative body that is significantly older or does not embody the ideal dancing body in his or her demonstration, the demonstrative body in competition dance is a young, active body (Weisbrod 2010). At the competition event, students encounter on stage the body that best demonstrates the skills that adolescents need and want to acquire in order to advance. By observing peers who are slightly or significantly better than themselves, competitive dancers become aware of and contribute to emerging performance standards.

Ideas about performance and the dancing body are underscored by dance competition's marketing. Websites, print material, and logos tend to feature young people in expansive body positions with smiling facial expressions. The quintessential body in these advertisements depicts the "fit body" of an actual dance competition competitor. Sociologist Michael S. Carolan (2005) argues that the United States has entered a new phase of conspicuous consumption in which the accumulation of "nice things" is no longer a satisfying way to present a person's wealth and power. He asserts that people are embodying conspicuous consumption by striving to *be* "the nice thing." Carolan (2005, 96–97) states that "a muscular worked-out body . . . implies a well worked-out wallet. . . . It embodies our cultural ethic regarding the importance of hard work, dedication, and perseverance, without upsetting our equally embedded proclivities toward consumption." Although not specifically addressing dance, the correlation between Carolan's observations of the embodiment of conspicuous consumption and the body's role in dance competitions is clear. In dance competition, the ideal dancer embodies a combination of "long and lean" and "athletic and toned," and moves in a "controlled way" for girls; it is "athletic and toned" and moves in a "powerful and athletic way" for boys (Schupp 2017). Because dance competitions and the training required to successfully participate in these events implicitly sell contemporary ideas about how the bodies of a given economic status should look and move, Carolan's ideas about the conspicuous body are certainly at play. This is turn raises questions about what is being purchased: Is it the joy of learning and performing dance, or the chance to attain the body acquired through this training and the privileges that body signifies?

As participation in dance competition culture is relatively expensive, conspicuous consumption and ideas about class mobility and status in relation to the purpose of dance and dancing may indirectly influence parents' and guardians' decision to enroll children in competitive dance lessons. Participating in dance competition culture is a significant financial investment with little to no direct financial return. Yet most parents have a strong desire to provide the best life possible for their children, including activities that bring joy in the present and contribute to a successful future. Often, the relevance of arts education is tied to promoting student success in disciplines such as math, reading, and writing. Under this rhetoric, the rationale for arts education is grounded in improved academic achievement outside the arts, which is quite different from engaging in an art form purely to learn more about it. Given that academic success in traditional school subjects is viewed as a gateway to prosperity, parents may be conspicuously consuming dance competition culture to demonstrate their investment in their children's futures.

The constant yearning to accomplish higher performance standards influences the dance studios' business structures. For contemporary adolescents, dance studio training geared toward dance competitions is steadily becoming the primarily location to study dance (Weisbrod 2010), perhaps because dance studios' teaching practices are well aligned with adolescents' need for constant feedback. The Cassandra Report (2015), a research-based study that examines the ethos of contemporary youth, suggests that Generation Z, those born between the mid-1990s and the early 2010s, have a strong desire to be part of a feedback loop in which they seek genuine criticism and view failure as a chance to learn more. This speaks to their eagerness to buy into dance competition events where they learn from their peers and expert judges, and to intensely prepare for these events in their dance studios.

Successfully participating in dance competitions entails additional classes and rehearsals and, as a result, some dance studios can financially benefit through participating in dance competitions. For example, many dance studios have a competition team or company composed of the most advanced students of a given age group, often selected through an audition process, who are required to take a minimum number of classes per week at the dance studio. Special privileges, which demand additional fees, are extended to team members, such as performing solos, duets, or trios, and working with guest choreographers. Competition team members are typically obliged to pay coach's fees, buy specific logo-adorned warm-up clothing, and purchase or rent props or scenery for their dances. Notably, these additional fees are not included in the regular tuition structure. Families who can afford multiple classes per week per child, the extra expenses of costumes and guest choreographers, and competition fees (as well as the additional time required for these extra opportunities) can wield greater influence over the atmosphere in a competitive dance studio. This creates a financial and social hierarchy that excludes those without financial capital from the elusive, yet enjoyable, pursuit of performance. In other words, it takes a significant commitment of time and money to acquire the technical and artistic confidence to "buy" a dance on the competition stage.

Building Families: Community and Positive Experiences

> In [the] competition world, I feel like most competition teams are like one big family because we all just get along, because we do the same things and we like the same things. It just depends on what the teacher has taught the students and how they teach [the students] to treat other people in dance.

Mary, a mature fifteen-year-old, described the formation and vitality of community, both within studios and within competition events. She was soft spoken but commanding, and is a dedicated dancer with a strong sense of responsibility to herself and others. In addition to the joy of performing, "being a team" is another appealing quality of competitive dance for Mary.

It makes sense that Mary views her fellow dancers and studio community as a family. Although Mary did not offer information about her teammates, it is likely that they dance together on an almost daily basis. To many competitive dancers, the dance studio is a second home where they eat meals, complete homework, and converse with peers between classes. At a competition, competitors may spend two to four days dancing with, performing for, and observing the same competitive teams (Figure 2.4). For regional competitions, competitive teams will likely encounter the same dance studios every year. As these events aggregate over time, dancers start to view themselves as a part of a "dance family" and the larger competition experience as a community.

A feeling of community is frequently present as competitors prepare to perform at dance competitions. At a national competition, I observed a group of five dancers, wearing matching forest-green, glittering biketards, thick buns in their hair, and large rhinestone earrings, assemble backstage. Although their height and complexions varied, they had a similar muscularity: strong thighs, flat midsections, and toned arms. They looked and interacted like a family. They were able to individually situate themselves while maintaining a connection to the group: two dancers discussed the dance onstage while stretching, two rehearsed choreography, and one performed a series of abdominal exercises. As their performance neared, they formed a tight circle by each standing in

FIGURE 2.4. Teammates in warm-up jackets watch the competition.

first position, draping their arms around each other's shoulders, and bowing their heads. Huddled, they took turns quietly speaking and breathed together. Their teacher was not present; they performed this ritual on their own. After about two minutes, they quietly left the circle to take their spots in the wings.

They went on to perform a well-rehearsed and synchronized contemporary dance to a popular song, with choreography including partnering where one dancer manipulates her partner's leg into a high extension; unison *pirouettes, grand jetés,* and acrobatic movements; and weight-sharing movements, such as vaulting a dancer to a tremendous height as she leaps. When the dance was complete, they exited the stage as a group. Back in the wings, breathless, they smiled and congratulated each other. Their competitors said "good job" to them as they exited the backstage area and they politely responded. As they made their way to the dressing rooms, they smiled and nodded as people, including strangers, inquired about how the performance went. They were still out of breath and could not say more than "good," but their body postures and smiling faces exuded confidence and pride. Upon entering the dressing room, their parents followed close behind with congratulations, hugs, and reports of the audience's reactions. Their parents congratulated not only their own child, but also the other dancers with comments like, "good job Morgan, that was beautiful."

Interviewees echoed the experience I observed. Joy described a pre-performance team ritual she participated in that speaks to the bonds established through training and performing with a group: "[B]efore we went onstage, we held hands, and we just talked about how we were feeling. And the energy we got before that, and when we went on-stage, was a really memorable experience for me because it wasn't just my feelings; it was the entire group's. . . . [I]f we hadn't come together as a group, the dance could've gone totally different." What Joy described speaks to social and psychological relationships that she believes the group possessed, which are requisite relationships for a successful performance. Dance competitions provide a venue for competitors to showcase their aesthetic understanding of dance that is symbiotic with the development of a studio community.

Community is further created between and among dance studios participating in a competition. Leah, a soft-spoken sixteen-year-old, expressed that, for her, attending dance competitions is "more for the experience, and just being with other studios, and being friendly to them and everything." Here, Leah indirectly addresses the importance of connecting to a larger community within the dance competition framework. Community continues to grow as dancers develop social relationships outside their studios and witness their peers' dancing. Mary recalled how a competing dance studio "took me into the dressing room and was friendly with me. And they got me ready for my performance" during a competition that her teachers were unable to attend. Mary acknowledged that there is the occasional "snobby" dancer, but she qualified that dancers' behavior "depends on the studio and . . . how they've interpreted the dance competitions." The emphasis on community and "sportsman-like" conduct is encouraged by dance competitions, which occasionally commend the best backstage behavior with an award according to how "nice [studios] were being to other studios," according to Leah.

While the enjoyment of performing brings together dancers, their collective practice in the studio forms the strong sense of community evidenced in these settings. In her study of dance in Los Angeles, performance studies scholar Judith Hamera (2007) argues that dance practices are sites for reconceiving intricate sociopolitical intersections. Hamera looks at the value of dance for the dancers, the ones doing the dancing, to suggest that analyzing dance from this perspective demonstrates how the capacity of dance communities to bringing individuals toward a common goal can be a model for revolutionizing a sense of intimacy in the "global city." Hamera discusses how dancers, both professional and amateur, use the pursuit of technique to build communities. Hamera asserts that the labor required to gain technique in any dance form is relational; the acquisition of technique inherently brings one dancing body into dialogue with other dancing bodies and, through this interchange, community is built. In this way, dancing and all the actions related to dancing create solidarity for a group; working together to learn and perform dance "provides social bedrock for imagining new ways of being together and being oneself" (Hamera 2007, 13). Although the competitive dance community was not included in Hamera's (2007, 2) analysis, her assertion that dance communities are "constituted by doing dance: making it, seeing it, learning it, talking, writing and fantasizing about it" pertains to the competitive dance experience. There are numerous social, economic, political, and perhaps psychological relationships formed as individual bodies train for and perform together in dance competitions, as seen in the interviewees' recollections and my observations of dance competition events.

Over time, the US economy has shifted from an economy based in manufacturing to a service economy, to an economic paradigm that now includes the sale of experiences. In the experience economy model, which emerged in the 1990s, businesses create memorable experiences for their consumers, and the memories and feelings related to and the transformative characteristics of the experience are thought to be the "product" (Pine and Gilmore 1998). The heart of the experience may be an event, like a dance competition performance, but the experience goes beyond what is actually purchased. For instance, dance competition entry fees provide the chance to compete, but also include the location, atmosphere, and setting of the event, who else participates, and the affinity for the experience as a whole (Sunbo and Darmer 2008). These elements combine to allow consumers to "[perform] their own experiences" (Sunbo and Darmer 2008, 176). Creative industries, including the performing arts, have adapted within the experience economy. While the arts have always valued the experiential nature of both making and participating in art, the economic emphasis of "selling" that experience has led to a greater emphasis toward creative entrepreneurship and away from an artisan model (Deresiewicz 2015). In this framework, making art or performing dance, as in the case of dance competition culture, is viewed as "something that can be packaged as an experience, . . . that is networked, curated, publicized, fetishized, tweeted, catered, and anything but solitary" (Deresiewicz 2015, n.p.).

Essentially, dance competitions package and sell the experience of performing and being a part of a dance community. Through paying an entry fee to perform on the competitive stage, adolescents purchase the chance to surround themselves with other young people who are passionate about performing dance. Adolescent dance competition competitors pay entry fees to perform and, through the act of performing, they bond with their teammates and other adolescent dancers. This experience and the resultant memories of coming together for and through the dance competition event are appealing to adolescent dance competitors. Arguably, each competitor has an experience that is unique from her or his peers. The experience of an immersive dance experience in which adolescents test themselves through performance as they share the stage with, observe, and meet their regional or national peers is a significant and memorable investment within dance competitions.

Fostering positive feelings and memories is promoted through the practice of granting each entry an award based on a predetermined score rubric instead of solely ranking first, second, and third place in each category, as this practice increases the likelihood that all competitors will leave feeling good about their performance and place in the dance competition community. Rhee Gold (quoted in Falker, 2013), an established entrepreneur in dance competition culture and private-sector dance education, observes that as the number of dance competitions rapidly increased throughout the 1990s, they began competing for consumer-competitors. From Gold's perspective, the best way to attract and retain competitors was to make everyone feel proud of his or her performance and participation in the event, which led to giving an award to every contestant. This practice coincides with the rise of the experience economy in the late 1990s. As dance competitions evolved, organizers started selling the positive experience of a successful performance with and for people with similar dance interests. In this way, competition organizers either capitalized on or encouraged competitors' desire to showcase their talent and connect to a larger community. By framing dance competitions as an "experience," dance competitions produced a venue where the cycle of advancing performance skills and developing communities exists outside the dance studio. In doing so, dance competitions are able to commodify the joy of performing and the resultant establishment of community by offering regional and national exchanges of information and interactions with other dancers. In this way, adolescent dance competitors can sense the exhilaration of performing and acknowledge the relational attributes they develop on the competition stage.

LEARNING BEHIND THE SCENES: TRANSFERABLE PROFICIENCIES

> I want people to know that what they see onstage is so much work and takes so long to get to that point to where we can step on that stage and do what we do for everyone. . . . [S]tanding on that stage is so terrifying, and at the same time so exhilarating.

Elizabeth, quoted here, participates in six dance competitions a year as a member of her studio's competition team. Unlike the other interviewees, she does not compete as a soloist, yet being on stage and performing is perhaps the most memorable part of Elizabeth's dance competition experiences. I was struck by and empathized with the amount of resilience, tenacity, self-assessment, and goal setting that Elizabeth's dance training and competition experience both cultivate and mandate. These attributes are present in each young woman's recollections of her dance competition experiences and are vital to creating successful performances and building a sense of community.

The occasion to perform for a larger audience is exhilarating for most performers, such as Joy, who explained that she "loves performing [for the] bigger audience" and "just expressing all my feelings out on the stage for the audience." When dancers arrive at a competition, they have already dedicated a great deal of physical and emotional labor, time, and money not only advancing their technique and artistry, but also perfecting their dances in anticipation of performing for a large audience. Furthermore, competitors arrive at the competition wanting to do their best, which necessitates negotiating the pressures of performing for a large audience in addition to the judges, preparing prior to performing, navigating the performance itself, and reflecting post performance.

On the second afternoon of a national competition, I noticed a hip-hop group rehearsing in a busy corridor. The purpose for the rehearsal seemed twofold; it was a pre-performance ritual and a time to navigate some of the unknowns that arise when performing at a competition. In this particular group, there were six dancers wearing a variety of black and white costumes portraying a generic representation of hip-hop culture: baseball hats, baggy pants, tank tops, and sneakers. Two female teachers played music from an iPhone, and gently encouraged the dancers as they rehearsed by saying things like "Do what you need to do, but do it on the right count," "You've got to focus," and "Nice! That was perfect!" The dancers were unwavering in their rehearsal ethic, despite the distractions in the hallway; numerous conversations occurred in the space, people literally walked through the rehearsal to get to the dressing rooms, and the music from the auditorium was audible. The dancers' ability to listen to their teachers and continuously dance indicated that they are comfortable concentrating in chaotic situations.

Once finished with the run-through of their dance, they discussed whether or not the blackout provided at the end of each dance would work for their performance (the blackout was critical to the dance's ending, which is choreographed to give the illusion of fading away). One teacher explained, although the dancers already seemed to know this, that they have no control over when and how the blackout will occur. Unprompted, the dancers offered ways to adapt to the indeterminate conditions. One dancer volunteered, "we can follow your lead, Tim, and keep moving until you stop." Another suggested, "We can turn this part upstage so that we can see the lights actually go out." Their adeptness at offering suggestions and talking through possible solutions, with very little input from the teachers, points to their interpersonal intelligence and abilities to adapt and problem-solve.

Before dancers can take the stage, they need to prepare themselves, mentally and physically, for their dances (Figure 2.5). While some teachers offer a ballet barre or warm-up class or run rehearsals in the venue's hallway, some competitors, especially soloists, such as Natalia, a pragmatic fourteen-year-old, have their own ways of preparing, which point to the fundamental nature of responsibility and the ability to handle stress at dance competitions. Natalia explained how at a particularly stressful competition, she "put on my headphones, went to the barre, and did what I wanted to do" instead of observing and getting intimidated by her competitors, which would cause her to "be a hot mess the whole rest of the day."

For several of the interviewees, the act of performing presents a means of self-assessment. Ideas about "rising to the occasion" and performance as a "learning experience" surfaced in many interviews. Cami, a reflective and seemingly introverted fourteen-year-old, described a type of instant self-critique that occurs immediately after she performs: "Um, when I get done, like, if I'm really like happy with how I did, I'll be like, 'Okay, whew! That was cool.' Or like if I'm not, then it's just like another learning experience. It's not like I'm going to go like cry or like be upset." Natalia conveyed how participating in a prestigious dance competition increased her self-confidence. She shared that, prior to that event, she did not do "good like under pressure, but like that time, like, I really rose to the occasion." For the interviewees, the learning that occurs at dance competitions not only happens through watching other performances, preparing to compete, and the judges' critiques, but also occurs through performing.

FIGURE 2.5. A soloist receives last-minute advice and encouragement from her teacher and a peer.

Photography by Hannah Mergi, Kaitlyn Principe, and Melissa Erla. Used with Permission.

Implicit in the interviewees' descriptions and my observations of the dancers at the national competition are the transferable proficiencies that dance competition culture requires and develops, skills that are gained both in the dance studio and on the competition stage. Both dance competition studios and dance competition owners leverage the entrepreneurial potential of these transferable proficiencies by providing a place where the aptitudes needed to succeed in many disciplines are acquired through preparing to participate and performing in dance competition events. In other words, the development of these skills is implicitly sold in dance competition culture and, for some parents and participants, may be of greater importance than gaining expertise within the field of dance. These skills grow as competitors acquire techniques and prepare to perform as part of a community. Faithfully completing the daily repetition of warm-up exercises and drills calls for tenacity and grit. Carving out time from school and social activities to dance ten to twelve hours a week is dependent on time management. Continual progress as a dancer requires the facilities to self-assess, hear and apply criticism, and set goals. Interpersonal intelligence is needed to dance as part of a group. The successful embodiment of dance competition movement fosters proficiencies that are required for competitive dance, yet are applicable to other areas of the competitors' lives.

Each young woman recounted the perseverance, ability to handle subjective assessment, and self-composure required to perform within a competition framework. Their dedication is reared through learning and practicing their competition dances, which involves a significant investment of time and energy. Mary frankly stated, "If you don't put the time and effort into what you want to do, and you don't have the dedication, there's no point in doing anything with [your dancing]." Once at dance competitions, competitors must focus under pressure and navigate the subjective nature of the judges' critiques. Natalia described her mental state while warming up for a solo competition event when she said, "I learned that intimidation can't be anything against you; only if you let it be against you." Joy articulated how she handles the subjective nature of the judges' criticism by explaining, "some days, judges are just going to have bad days, and you're going to get scored lower, and you have to learn how to recover from your loss and be able to snap right back up into full force at the next competition." Cami talked about pre-performance anxiety that dissipates once she starts a solo performance. She explained, "Like you're out there by yourself. You don't want to like mess up or anything. . . . But like I'm not nervous until right before I go onstage. So I'm like, 'Okay, here it goes,' so then I go on, and I'm like, 'Okay, here I am,' and then I just do it." This switch from nerves to confidence was echoed by Leah, who stated, "I learned that it's really important to—like it's really important to know your dance. But like once you know your dance, you don't have to like think about it . . . [and you can have] fun while doing it." For competitors, the hard work pays off in the moment of performance, their chance to sell their dancing to the audience and themselves, and that moment is perhaps the emotional axis around which the acquisition of performance abilities, transferable proficiencies, and community revolve.

SELLING IT!

> At NYCDA, the dancer always comes first! We proudly create a positive, nurturing environment. Come experience it all for yourself. Each year, NYCDA provides more and more incredible experiences, opportunities, and professional resources. NYCDA is your investment in the future—for yourself, your studio and your dancers.
>
> —Lanteri (2014, n.p.).

In the succinct "Personal Message from Joe Lanteri" (the founder and director of New York City Dance Alliance [NYCDA], a highly reputable competition and convention established in 1994), excerpted in the preceding and featured on NYCDA's website, Lanteri celebrates the importance of dancers; a sense of evolution or legacy; the "NYCDA family" that includes teachers, studios, and parents in addition to dancers; and the opportunities for growth that NYCDA delivers. In his positive, informally penned, yet respectful letter, his passion for NYCDA is perceptible; however, the word "competition" is never mentioned. This omission reinforces the idea that dance competitions are aware that the experience of participating in competitions transcends the competitive

nature of the event; what is bought, sold, and invested in, as money is exchanged between competitors and organizers, proves more complex than simply purchasing
a chance to compete. Lanteri's letter encapsulates numerous values of the experience
economy by balancing attention on the individual dancer's experience and the creation
of a community to create a packaged experience that is easily sold and purchased. Dance
competition organizations are cognizant of the experiential component that they sell as
part of their competitions, just as competitors recognize that they invest in an experience beyond the purchase of a performance opportunity.

Just as teachers encourage dancers to "sell the dance" to engage an audience, dance
competitions "sell the dance" by shining the spotlight on the positive attributes that
can be obtained from full immersion in the dance competition experience. As Lanteri's
(2014) letter illustrates, dance competition organizations explicitly point to the positive characteristics of the experience in vague and open-ended ways. Lanteri prioritizes
the "passion, commitment and enthusiasm" that the organizers bring to the event,
emphasizes the idea of "Nationals" as a celebration, uses the word "family" and the
thrill of "re-uniting" to allude to the multiple layers of stakeholders in dance competition culture, and highlights the "nurturing environment" and "incredible experiences"
that NYCDA provides. The letter prompts dancers to get excited about the energy,
opportunities, and professionalism that NYCDA is known for and encourages dancers
to imagine performing amidst others who love dance. Significantly, as noted earlier,
Lanteri's letter does not use the word "competition"; as well as evoking ideas regarding
the thrill of winning, competition potentially highlights the discomfort of defeat and
draws attention to the core commodity at stake: the chance to compete. Lanteri's letter
clearly sells the positive experiential aspects of dance competition without mentioning
the financial demands or negative associations of loss.

The adolescent girls interviewed for this chapter and observed at dance competitions,
like my younger self, participate in dance competitions because they are driven to
improve their dancing, value being a part of a community, and love performing;
competitions, affiliated performances, and dance classes provide a place for them to en-
rich their passion. In this way, competitors actively and positively engage with dance
through dance competition culture, and their pride stems from their commitment to
themselves, their communities, dance, and competition culture. The symbiotic nature of competitors' motivation to advance as dancers and the competitive frameworks
and business practices of dance competition creates a continuous feedback loop that
promotes performance mastery, the development of a community, and the cultivation of transferable proficiencies. In this way, the chance to "sell it" to a larger audience,
while engaging in a contest against one's peers and challenging oneself in performance,
represents a "soft sell" in dance competition culture.[6] The motivation to participate in
dance competitions stems from competitors' investment in dance; their experience of
participation, which is shaped by the competitive framework, moves beyond what is
simply bought and sold.

The triangulated, participatory investment in today's dance competition culture, where advancing performance skills, building a community, and developing

transferable proficiencies are intertwined, mirrors my own experiences as a competitor over twenty years ago. In 1994, I was crowned Miss New York State Dance Olympics; this was the most significant award of my dance competition career. Although I admit that winning the title was a great accomplishment, what I remember most about the competition goes beyond vying for first place. I still vividly recall the joy of the performance. The support I felt from my "studio family" formed relationships that are still part of my life today. The transferable proficiencies I gained from participating in that and other competitions have been tremendously valuable throughout my career on and off stage. So although the financial and administrative structures have shifted as competitions have become more "professional" and the movement vocabulary, costumes, and choreographic structures used to "sell it" have changed, the root of the experience has remained the same.

In closing, dance competition events "sell it" well, yet the "it" shifts depending on how the experience is viewed. Dancers sell their dance ability on stage by proving themselves not only to themselves but also to peers through developing and using transferable proficiencies to advance as dancers. Dance studios sell the opportunity of continued growth in dance, a connection to a likeminded group of dancers, and the assumption that engaging with dance indicates a certain class status and investment in a child's future. Dance competition organizations have packaged the experience of performing dance into a commodity. Included in this package, disguised as a pre-professional performance experience, is the conspicuous consumption of dance in which dance is entertainment oriented and values a competitive spirit. Participants invest in an individualized experience grounded in the joy of performance, connecting with a community, and developing transferable proficiencies through performing dance. As such, "selling it" on the competition stage remains a worthy investment for adolescents passionate about dance.

Notes

1. Such opportunities include convention scholarships, acceptance to summer programs, and the chance to work for dance competition conventions.
2. The interview data in this project originated from a mixed-method research study using a sequential explanatory strategy (Creswell 2009), which I conducted to examine gender in dance competition. The first part of the project consisted of a cross-sectional survey that was completed by 111 people. When the quantitative portion of the research was complete, survey competitors were invited to participate in interviews about their experiences with dance competitions. The seven adolescent female dancers included in this chapter completed interviews as part of the gender and dance competition culture project. In addition to asking about their experiences related to gender in dance competitions, interviewees were asked about their general experiences of dance competition culture.
3. In some cases, competitors within the same category may perform outside their category's assigned time to keep events from running behind, making it especially difficult to gauge who competitors are directly competing against.

4. Showstopper, for example, includes three competition levels: "Performance" for dancers who train less than three hours a week; "Advanced" for dancers who have limited competition experience and dance up to five hours a week; and "Competitive" for dancers with competition experience who dance more than five hours a week.

5. For anonymity purposes, pseudonyms are employed in the chapter.

6. "Soft sell" refers to a sales approach that identifies customers' unstated needs and wants and uses a friendly and subtle sales message to sell a product.

REFERENCES

Carolan, Michael S. 2005. "The Conspicuous Body: Capitalism, Consumerism, Class and Consumption." *Worldviews: Environment, Culture, Religion* 9(1): 82–111.

Cassandra Report. 2015. "Winter/Spring 2015 Cassandra Report: Gen Z." http://cassandradaily.com/life/now-available-the-winterspring-2015-cassandra-report/. Accessed April 15, 2015.

Colley, Tim. 2014. *All In: My Amazing Journey as a Dance Dad*. Bradenton, FL: BookLocker.com.

Creswell, John W. 2009. *Research Design: Qualitative, Quantitative, and Mixed Method Approaches*. Thousand Oaks, CA: Sage.

Deresiewicz, William. 2015. "The Death of the Artist—and the Birth of the Creative Entrepreneur." *The Atlantic*, January/February. https://www.theatlantic.com/magazine/archive/2015/01/the-death-of-the-artist-and-the-birth-of-the-creative-entrepreneur/383497/. Accessed September 22, 2017.

Falker, Kimberly. 2013. "Rhee Gold, Dance Studio Life Magazine, and Motivational Speaker." *Ballet Uncovered: Balancing Pointe Podcast*. Podcast audio, December 12.

Foster, Susan Leigh. 1997. "Dancing Bodies." In *Meaning in Motion: New Cultural Studies of Dance*, edited by Jane C. Desmond, 235–257. Durham, NC: Duke University Press.

Guarino, Lindsey. 2014. "Jazz Dance Training via Private Studios, Competitions, and Conventions." In *Jazz Dance: A History of the Roots and Branches*, edited by Lindsey Guarino and Wendy Oliver, 197–206. Gainesville, FL: University Press of Florida.

Hamera, Judith. 2007. *Dancing Communities: Performance, Difference and Connection in the Global City*. London: Palgrave Macmillan.

Lanteri, Joe. 2014. "Personal Message from Joe Lanteri." http://www.nycdance.com/uploadedFiles/Landing_Pages/2014-2015%20Website%20Letter.pdf. Accessed July 22, 2016.

LaRocco, Claudia. 2012. "Dance Competitions for Youngsters. Tap-Tap-Tapping into a National Obsession." *New York Times*, September 2. http://www.nytimes.com/2012/09/03/arts/dance/dance-competitions-for-youngsters.html. Accessed February 20, 2014.

Pine, B. Joseph, II, and James H. Gilmore. 1998. "Welcome to the Experience Economy." *Harvard Business Review*, July–August. https://hbr.org/1998/07/welcome-to-the-experience-economy. Accessed May 27, 2015.

Posey, Elsa. 2002. "Dance Education in Dance Schools in the Private Sector: Meeting the Demands of the Marketplace." *Journal of Dance Education* 2(2): 43–49.

Roche, Jennifer. 2015. *Multiplicity, Embodiment and the Contemporary Dancer: Moving Identities*. London: Palgrave Macmillan.

Risner, Doug, Heidi Godfrey, and Linda C. Simmons. 2004. "The Impact of Sexuality in Contemporary Culture: An Interpretive Study of Perceptions and Choices in Private Sector Dance Education." *Journal of Dance Education* 4(10): 23–32.

Schupp, Karen. 2006. "The Culture of Dance Competitions." Paper presented at the International Conference of the Congress of Research in Dance, Tempe, Arizona, November 2–5.

Schupp, Karen. 2017. "Sassy Girls and Hard-Hitting Boys: Dance Competitions and Gender." In *Dance and Gender: An Evidence-Based Approach*, edited by Wendy Oliver and Doug Risner, 76–96. Gainesville: University Press of Florida.

Showstopper. 2016. "Home." http://www.goshowstopper.com. Accessed March 15, 2016.

Star Dance Alliance. n.d.a. "Home." http://www.stardancealliance.com. Accessed November 23, 2015.

Star Dance Alliance. n.d.b. "Starpower, About Us." http://www.starpowertalent.com/aboutus.html. Accessed April 25, 2016.

Star Dance Alliance. n.d.c. "Starpower, Home." http://www.starpowertalent.com. Accessed June 15, 2016.

Sundbo, Jon, and Per Darmer, eds. 2008. *Creating Experiences in the Experience Economy.* Cheltenham, UK: Edward Elgar.

Weisbrod, Alexis A. 2010. "Competition Dance: Redefining Dance in the United States." PhD diss., University of California Riverside.

Wollins, Jill. 2014. *Dance Competitions: Are You Ready?* Waldorf, MD: Starpower Talent Competition.

Audiovisual Sources

Juliette Roberts—Bang Bang. 2015. YouTube video, 2:31. Posted by "DancingWithYT," January 6, https://www.youtube.com/watch?v=bUQqpFHVUzA. Accessed June 1, 2016.

CHAPTER 3

···

COMPETITIVE CAPERS

Gender, Gentility, and Dancing in Early Modern England

···

EMILY WINEROCK

IN his dance instruction and etiquette manual *Discursos Sobre el Arte del Danzado* (1642), Spanish dancing master Juan de Esquivel Navarro describes the rules and ritual of *retos*, or the dance challenge. He explains that if a rival disparages a man's dancing skills, the man should publicly confront him in his dancing school. First he must call for and dance an *Alta*, "the Dance by which the others are drawn forth to Dance" (Brooks 2003, 289). Then he should declare,

> I challenge and dare so-and-so, student of so-and-so, to dance and perform four variations of *Pavana*, six Passages of *Gallarda*, two variations of *Folías*, two of *Rey*, two of *Villano*, *Chacona*, *Carnario* and *Rastro*, to do more and look better than I, with good musical accompaniment. (Brooks 2003, 298)

The challenger then puts down money, half of which will go to "him who plays the music" and the other half to the winner of the challenge or dance duel (Brooks 2003, 298). Dance scholar Lynn Matluck Brooks (2003) notes in her commentary on the manual that the language of the *reto* closely followed that of fencing challenges of the period, including the dancers naming seconds. She also clarifies that the series of dances specified were a standard sequence taught in the Spanish dancing schools and would be known to all the young men likely to end up challenging or being challenged to a dance duel.

The recipient likewise follows a script to accept a challenge. Esquivel explains that the recipient should go to the challenger's dancing school, call for and dance an *Alta*, and then state,

"It has come to my notice, that so-and-so, student of Master So-and-so, has challenged me to dance and perform" (all this with his hat in his hand). On finishing what
he has said, he puts the hat on with all the arrogance he can muster and continues,
saying: "I accept the Challenge, according to the form in which he has stated it, and
I deposit the same quantity that he deposited, and name so-and-so and so-and-so as
my Seconds." (Brooks 2003, 299)

The dancers set a time and place for the duel and, when the day comes, they perform
their variations. The spectators vote on the winner, who, his reputation vindicated,
receives honor and fame, as well as the prize money.[1]

Esquivel's manual is the earliest surviving book-length publication on Spanish
dancing, and his description of the dance duel offers a fascinating picture of how
Spanish gentlemen used dance to contest and confirm their reputations on and off the
dance floor. Certain details even give a glimpse of the tone of these encounters: "he puts
the hat on with all the arrogance he can muster" (Brooks 2003, 299). However, what is
perhaps most interesting about Esquivel's description of the dance challenge is its singu-
larity. There are no dance duels mentioned in the other surviving Spanish dance texts,
nor do they appear in Spanish dramatic literature, although many plays and interludes
feature other types of dancing. This leads Brooks (2003, 63) to conclude that "[t]his is
not to say that the *reto* was entirely an imaginative creation of Esquivel's—although it
may have been—but rather that, if it was a known phenomenon, its practice was far
from widespread."

This chapter examines descriptions of competitive dancing in English literature of
the late Renaissance. While only one text describes a dance duel similar to Esquivel's
reto, English sources include several instances of clearly competitive dancing. These
examples show that competitive dancing was certainly known in late Renaissance
Europe, even if it was not common.

Much of the scholarly discourse on dancing in the early modern period has focused
on dance as a metaphor for, and an embodied representation of, order and harmony.
Both seventeenth-century masque authors and modern scholars have observed that early
modern performers and spectators "read" the carefully executed choreographies in court
masques as the physical embodiment of cosmic motion and a visualization of the well-
ordered state (Daye 2008; Jonson 1979 [1618]; Franko 1993; Orgel 1975; Ravelhofer 2006).
In the countryside, dancing at religious, seasonal, and life-cycle celebrations brought
people together literally and figuratively, fostering neighborliness and helping to resolve
community conflicts (Forrest 1999; Hutton 1994; Winerock 2012). Conversely, when
dancing was not orderly, it represented a threat to the harmonious motions of the cosmos
and the peaceful functioning of the community. Both secular and religious authorities
condemned drunken, riotous, licentious, and irreverent dancing (Goring 1983; Pennino-
Baskerville 1991; Wagner 1997), while playwrights and masque writers staged "disorderly"
dances to foreshadow disruption and tragedy (Brissenden 1981; Howard 1993).

Dance scenes in English plays of the late sixteenth and early seventeenth centuries,
however, point to another function of dancing that does not fit neatly into the preceding

categories: to distinguish individuals rather than illustrate the cohesion or harmoni-ousness of the group. Indeed, these depictions of dancing provide counterexamples to dance scholar Mark Franko's (1993, 33) observation that "theatrical dancing originally appeared as a visual manifestation and physical embodiment of social, political, and cosmic theories of order to the virtual exclusion of individual expressivity." The clearest examples occur in staged dance competitions, but more informal dancing can also mo-tivate comments from spectators within the play that highlight the excellence, grace, or notable skills of a particular dancer. Moreover, since play texts depict dancing in con-text, dramatic dance scenes can shed light on references to and descriptions of competi-tive dancing in instructional manuals, conduct guides, and other sources.

To broaden understanding of the multiple roles and complex significance of dancing in late sixteenth- and early seventeenth-century England, I examine compet-itive dancing in four literary works: Thomas Middleton, William Rowley, and Philip Massinger's *The Old Law*; William Shakespeare's *Twelfth Night*; William Kemp's *Nine Daies Wonder*; and an anonymous song from the "Blundell Family Hodgepodge Book." These case studies follow an overview of the galliard, the preferred dance type for com-petitive dancing in the Renaissance. The intention is not to invalidate readings of dance's cosmic or communal significance, but rather to complement them, demonstrating how early modern playwrights employed competitive dancing to convey nuances of char-acter, especially those pertaining to the gender and gentility of a particular dancer.

The Galliard

Stage directions for dances in early modern plays rarely specify the choreography or dance type to be performed. The surrounding dialogue sometimes contains hints, how-ever, as to what the playwright might have envisioned. These textual clues indicate that the dance English playwrights most frequently intended for scenes featuring compet-itive and distinguishing dancing was the galliard. The galliard was ubiquitous in early modern Europe. Every Italian dance treatise and dance music collection published or republished between 1560–1630 included at least one galliard, all the extant French and Spanish dancing manuals featured it, and there were even manuals dedicated entirely to the galliard and its variations (Brooks 2003; Compasso 1560; Nevile 2008). The galliard was similarly popular in England, and printed sources mention it more frequently than any other dance type (Winerock 2012).

Dancing manuals like Lutio Compasso's *Ballo Della Gagliarda* (1560), Thoinot Arbeau's *Orchésographie* (1589), Fabritio Caroso's *Nobiltà di Dame* (1600), and Cesare Negri's *Le Gratie d'Amore* (1602) provided detailed instructions for how to perform the galliard.[2] The basic step-pattern consisted of four kicks and a *cadenza*, or closing jump. These five steps gave the galliard its nickname: *cinq-pas* in French, *cinque passi* in Italian, and "sinkapace" in English (Berger 1982; Compasso 1560). The basic step-pattern's kicks and jumps required some athletic skill, but it was the numerous variations and embellishments that made the dance truly challenging. The best galliard dancers added caprioles or capers (jumps with multiple beats or quick switching of the feet in the air) as well as turning jumps, spins, and other impressive ornamentations.[3] "Some in their cinqueapase did nimbly bound, / Some did the Cros-point, some high Capers cut, / And on the toe some other turned round," writes the Welsh poet Hugh Holland in *Pancharis* (Holland 1603, sig. C10v).

To help the reader and would-be dancer, Thoinot Arbeau includes several simple illustrations of galliard steps and embellishments in *Orchésographie*, including a crossing step and a caper (see Figures 3.1–3.4).

Dancers would combine these steps to create complex variations, sometimes choreographing them in advance, sometimes improvising them on the spot. The convention of repeating on the right foot what one performed on the left made improvised sequences particularly challenging. The dancer instantly had to memorize the steps he had just executed, and then perform them in reverse without rehearsal. Galliard-specific manuals like *Ballo Della Gagliarda* provided choreographies that dancers could learn in advance and rules for putting together new step combinations. While not everyone appreciated courtiers' "lofty galliards, which alter every day with new devises," for the most part, spectators and fellow dancers appreciated innovation and improvisation, especially when the galliard was danced as a male solo or as part of a competition or challenge (Colse 1596, sig. A4v). Those participating in galliard competitions needed to have a ready supply of "trickes" or variations: "happye was he that before his Ladye coulde do the lustiest tricke" (McGee 2003; Rich 1574, sig. J2).

To invent new galliard step variations and to execute them smoothly and gracefully required a substantial amount of study and practice. Students at the universities of Cambridge and Oxford attended dancing schools in town, young men in London studied dancing at schools or privately, and country elites learned the latest dances from traveling instructors (Winerock 2012). George Villiers, the Duke of Buckingham, employed two French dancing masters, and all of the Tudor and Stuart monarchs had dance instructors at their courts and in their households (Montagut 1619; Ravelhofer 2006).

Yet mastery in dancing required practice as well as knowledge. Future barrister Justin Pagitt wrote in his notes on the art of dancing that it was necessary to "ffollow yr dauncing hard till you have gott a habit of dauncing neately" (quoted from Walls 1996, 114). Instructors and fellow dancers might offer tips and tricks for the more difficult steps as well. Cesare Negri recommended practicing caprioles and other high jumps while holding onto a table and chair (see Figure 3.5).

In his essay "Of Nature in Men," politician and philosopher Francis Bacon mentions dancers who wear thick shoes while practicing, because "it breeds great Perfection, if the Practise be harder then the use" (Bacon 1625, 227). This method seems particularly suited to the galliard: the noticeable difference in weight between thick practice shoes and lightweight dancing slippers would help one jump higher and with greater precision, benefits that would be particularly welcome in competition or performance.

GREVE DROITE
OR
PIED EN L'AIR DROIT

FIGURE 3.1. Galliard steps from *Orchésographie* (1589, 45v, 43v, 46, 48): front kick right.

PIED CROISÉ GAUCHE

FIGURE 3.2. Galliard steps from *Orchésographie* (1589, 45v, 43v, 46, 48): cross-step left.

RUADE DROITE

FIGURE 3.3. Galliard steps from *Orchésographie* (1589, 45v, 43v, 46, 48): back kick right.

CAPRIOLE

FIGURE 3.4. Galliard steps from *Orchésographie* (1589, 45v, 43v, 46, 48): capriole or caper.

FIGURE 3.5. Practicing caprioles from Cesare Negri, *Le Gratie d'Amore* (Negri 1602, 80).

The galliard was the dance preferred by young male courtiers for displaying masculine agility and virility (Sutton 1998). In his poem *Orchestra* (1596), lawyer and poet Sir John Davies describes the galliard as having "[a] spirit and a vertue Masculine," due to its "loftie turnes and capriols in the ayre" (Davies 1596, stanza 68).[4] However, it could also be performed as a male–female couple dance and was the favorite dance of Queen Elizabeth (Ravelhofer 2004; Sutton 1998). This variety and flexibility made the galliard perfect for conveying, or complicating, a dancer's gender on the stage. When performed, a galliard could match the style one would expect from that dancer in that situation, or could present a telling alternative. For example, if a young man danced the galliard with a partner in the flashy, technically demanding style suitable for a solo piece, rather than in the more moderate and elegant style appropriate for a man and woman dancing together, that might indicate that he was more interested in showing off for the spectators than in honoring the woman with whom he danced. Because audiences knew the galliard quite well, playwrights could rely on spectators recognizing unusual as well as conventional depictions.

Similarly, as a courtly dance, the galliard lent itself to displaying, and disputing, a dancer's social status. Dancers executing intricate footwork with effortless grace conveyed their nobility, while those who showed obvious effort or awkwardness caused spectators on and off the stage to question their elite status. Further complicating these distinctions was the difficulty in recognizing and negotiating the mutable boundaries between admirable and excessive proficiency. The "loftie turnes" and capers lauded by Sir John Davies as the essence of the galliard's masculinity were precisely the steps educators and conduct writers warned against unless a gentleman were in private or masked (Castiglione 1561; Winerock 2011).

Spectacular leaps and turns were impressive and displayed masculine traits, but they were the province of the professional, not the gentleman. Only the most talented amateurs could perform capers and leaps with the requisite *sprezzatura*, or nonchalance, demanded by Baldesar Castiglione in *The Book of the Courtier* (1561). Otherwise, as conduct guides and dancing manuals like James Cleland's *Institution of a Young Noble Man* (1607) and Barthélemy de Montagut's "Louange de la Danse" (1619) warned, one might be mistaken for a lowly dancing instructor. A gentleman had to find the "golden mean" between dancing like an awkward, amateur novice and a "low status, if high capering, professional dancing master," balancing expectations for both vigorous, masculine athleticism and understated, genteel elegance (Winerock 2011, 461).

One context in which a gentleman could display the greatest mastery of dancing possible was the male-only galliard competition. Although there was potentially an element of male–female competition in alternating solos in courtly couple dances, and some women may have behaved competitively toward each other on the dance floor, for elite dancers there is only evidence of men participating in the more formal dance competitions such as the tassel contest and the galliard "dance-off."

In the tassel game, gentlemen took turns trying to elegantly kick a tassel hung above the ground. In *Nobiltà di Dame*, Caroso describes "The Jump to the Tassel," or *salto del fiocco*:

> Have the tassel held as high as a man—more or less, as one pleases—stand with your side turned toward the tassel; then raise your left foot somewhat (simultaneously lifting your right), and turning your entire body to the left, while jumping as high as you can, crossing your right leg over your left, raising your [right] toe high enough to touch the tassel, and landing on the ground on the same spot as when you began, still with your right foot. (Caroso 1600, 119)

After each dancer had taken his turn kicking the tassel, the tassel was raised higher, and all the participants again attempted to kick the tassel. Those who failed or fell were disqualified, and the competition continued until only one dancer, the winner, remained.

But being able to kick the tassel at any height was only one aspect of the competition; spectators also expected the participants to impress and entertain them with a pleasing variety of jumps. Negri lists thirteen different "jumps of the tassel" of varying difficulty in *Le Gratie d'Amore* (Negri 1602; Kendall 1985). He explains that all of his variations can be divided into two jump types. In the first type, the dancer faces the tassel head on (see

FIGURE 3.6. Jumps of the tassel from Cesare Negri, *Le Gratie d'Dmore* (1602): jump facing toward tassel.

FIGURE 3.7. Jumps of the tassel from Cesare Negri, *Le Gratie d'Dmore* (1602): jump facing away from tassel.

Figure 3.6). In the second type, the dancer begins the jump facing away from the tassel but turns to face it during the jump (see Figure 3.7).

Some of the variations are quite distinctive, such as the twelfth jump, in which the dancer lands with the "right knee on the ground" (Kendall 1985, 124a). Others incorporate supplemental galliard steps, such as the eleventh jump, which adds a half capriole and one and a half turns in the air. To master even one of these jumps was impressive, but to win praise in a competition, one needed to execute several variations flawlessly. Dance scholar Nathan Kronenfeld, who has reconstructed Negri's jumps of the tassel, notes that the height of the kicks is not the real challenge, since kicking higher merely requires flexibility, which can be achieved by stretching. Rather, acquiring (and then displaying) the "virtuosity inherent in being able to do these steps *at all* is the main goal"; if one can jump into the air, turn at least one full circle, and kick a target accurately before landing neatly, the height of the target is almost negligible (Kronenfeld 1999). Kronenfeld (1999) also observes that there is little concrete evidence that jumps to the tassel were generally danced within the context of a competition. While this is obviously an important qualifier, I argue that enough evidence of competitive galliard dancing in general exists to make it likely that a subset of the galliard, such·as jumps to the tassel, might also be competitive.

Jumping for the tassel and official galliard competitions were only done by men, but all the component steps (the kicks, turns, and jumps) were danced by women when the galliard was performed as a duet for a couple. In Caroso's *Gagliarda di Spagna* (Spanish Galliard), for example, the men and women begin and end dancing together, with the middle of the dance containing two sets of solos (Caroso 1600). In each set, the man performs a complex galliard variation, and then the woman "repeats what the gentleman has just done" (Caroso 1600, 197). Having the man dance his solo first each time might be a nod to patriarchy, and the styling of the moves could be gendered, but the galliard steps themselves and the combinations called for in choreographies were egalitarian (Winerock 2011).

This formulation leads to a certain competitive dynamic. Through his solos, the man challenged the woman to observe, memorize, and replicate his improvisations accurately. If she did so successfully, she showed herself to be his equal, which in early modern Europe was to defy the accepted narratives of women's inferiority. Moreover, one might imagine a powerful woman and expert dancer like Elizabeth I adding embellishments to the repetition of her partner's solo, symbolically winning the round by demonstrating not just equal, but superior, dancing skills.

Another convention arose when performing galliard duets and other couple dances that similarly fostered a competitive element. During the partner's solo, the other dancer watched but did not stay so still as to "resemble a statue," but was supposed to take a few steps, adjust his gloves, or fan herself in order to "appear most graceful" (Caroso 1600, 163). The choreographic sanction for one partner to move about while the other performed a solo challenged the soloist to catch and hold the partner's (and the rest of the audience's) attention, whether by inventing complex, intricate sequences or displaying noteworthy skill and grace.

The galliard was not the only early modern dance that could be competitive, but it was certainly the most prominently featured. References to dancing galliards are frequent in English and European writings of the late sixteenth and early seventeenth centuries, but they are often brief, tangential, or decontextualized. As we have seen, dancing manuals, conduct writings, and poems sometimes allude to the situations and scenarios in which galliards, specifically, and competitive dancing, more generally, occurred. It is in play texts, however, that we find the richest and most illuminating descriptions of competitive and distinctive dancing.

The Old Law

Several early modern plays contain dances featuring galliards performed by one or more dancers, but only one extant play stages a galliard competition. In Thomas Middleton, Philip Massinger, and William Rowley's *The Old Law, or A New Way to Please You*, an elderly husband, Lisander, challenges three young courtiers and would-be suitors of his young wife to a competition in the "feats of youth":[5]

> Bring forth the weapons, we shall find you play!
> All feats of youth too, jack-boys, feats of youth,
> And these weapons: drinking, fencing, dancing,
> Your own roadways, you glisterpipes! (Middleton et al. 1656, II.ii.107–110)

Much to the surprise and embarrassment of the young men (and the amusement of the audience), Lisander out-dances, out-fences, and out-drinks them, "What! Shall we put down youth at her own virtues? / Beat folly in her own ground?" (Middleton et al. 1656, III.ii.197–198)

We can assume that the weapon for the dance contest is the galliard, as this is the dance Lisander had been practicing in an earlier scene and on which the Dancing Master compliments him:

> For your galliard, sir,
> You are complete enough, ay, and may challenge
> The proudest coxcomb of 'em all, I'll stand to it. (Middleton et al. 1656, III.ii. 99–101)

This mastery of the galliard is especially impressive for Lisander, a man of seventy-nine, since even the basic galliard steps involve athletic kicks and leaps, while more advanced variations, such as those presumably performed by Lisander, might include multiple turns and extra switches of the feet in the air. While the exact galliard steps danced by the first courtier and Lisander are lost to time, the surrounding text makes clear that Lisander's performance is unquestionably superior; "I have hit you soundly," Lisander exclaims after his competitor concedes defeat (Middleton et al. 1656, III.ii.43). The young courtier's response, "You've done well, i'faith, sir," is quite possibly a genuine compliment, the "sir" suggesting that Lisander has earned his respect (Middleton et al. 1656, III.ii.41; Griffiths 1996). Lisander's comment at the beginning of the dance-off that he will "observe Court Rules" and have his (hopefully) less skilled opponent dance first, may even be evidence that galliard competitions occurred frequently enough to have known rules (Middleton et al. 1656, III.ii.33).

By associating dancing with drinking and dueling, the authors of the play suggest that dancing provides a similar display of young male bravado. By winning the three contests, Lisander proves himself the better man and best deserving of his wife. Moreover, his mastery of youthful activities insinuates that despite his age, he is still virile enough to beget children:

> Why may not we be held as full sufficient
> To love our own wives then, get our own children,
> And live in free peace till we be dissolved? (Middleton et al. 1656, III.ii.200–202)

In addition, he has revealed the three courtiers as shams. By outperforming them in dancing, fencing, and drinking, Lisander calls into question their entitlement to be called gentlemen, courtiers, or even men, "you are all but maggots / For all your beamy outsides!" he exclaims (Middleton et al. 1656, III.ii.205–206).[6]

But is not Lisander himself a sham? Dance scholar Skiles Howard writes that "the dancing duel that [Lisander] foolishly provokes ridicules the deadly competitiveness of courtly self-fashioning," but Lisander's inclusion of dancing in his arsenal is hardly foolish; even his rivals must admit his superior skills (Howard 1998, 137). What is foolish is Lisander's desire to prove himself by competing with young men in the arts of youth in the first place. The playwrights suggest that dancing is an appropriate, even admirable, activity for a young man, but they call into question its propriety for an older gentleman.

This age-based distinction appears in a number of other sources. For example, Thoinot Arbeau (1589, 129) notes in *Orchésographie* that "every dancer acquits himself to the best of his ability, each according to his years and his degree of skill." Young people who could "nimbly trip" were supposed to dance the most energetic and athletic dances, while less physically demanding, more sedate dances were appropriate for older dancers (Arbeau 1589, 129).[7] The processional pavane, for example, could be done with grace and decorum by even the most elderly dancers, but the galliard should only be danced by the young and fit (Winerock 2012). In this regard, Lisander's dancing in *The Old Law* is both impressive and ridiculous. His skill is noteworthy, and he wins the contest, but his participation in the contest, as well as his choice of dance, reveals a lack of propriety. Lisander is like Master Morello in Castiglione's *The Courtier*, an old man who, instead of accepting his age, dyes his hair and dances with young women (Castiglione 1528). While Master Morello may enjoy these antics, they cost him the respect of his peers. Lisander's reputation is similarly threatened.

An anonymous dialogue printed by Richard Jones under the title *The English Courtier, and the Cuntrey Gentleman* (1586) also examines the age-appropriateness of dancing. The work, in which two gentlemen discuss how best to serve one's prince, borrows heavily from *The Courtier*, but goes into greater detail than Castiglione does regarding precisely what sort of dancing is suitable at what age. In the dialogue, the character Valentine specifies that a man should only "take upon him to daunce" until the age of thirty-five; after age thirty-five, "hee is rather to be imploied in serious services, then left at leysure, to entertayne Ladies, or daunce a Galliard" (Anon. 1586, sigs. L2r–L2v). This age restriction even applies to professional dancers. Valentine notes that "even in those that make profession of daunsing, unlesse their yeares be fit for the use therof, they doo rather instruct others, then use it them selves" (Anon. 1586, sig. L2r).

Valentine also conceives of dancing, not as an effeminate or effeminizing frivolity, but as one of the "lusty exercises" that befits the gentleman soldier, "it shall well become his age and profession, to handle all sorts of armes, both on horseback and foote, leape, daunce, runne, ride" (Anon. 1586, sig. L1v). Although he does not say so explicitly, it seems likely that the type of dancing Valentine had in mind for a young gentleman was an athletically demanding dance, like the galliard, that could showcase the man's strength, agility, and dexterity while demonstrating his skill and prowess in general and in relation to his fellows.

While authorial intent is rarely transparent, in this scene, one can reasonably conclude that Thomas Middleton, William Rowley, and Philip Massinger staged the dance competition between Lisander and the young courtiers to clearly demonstrate Lisander's surprising youthfulness, both his genuine skill in the youthful art of dancing, and his juvenile lack of discretion and propriety, of which audience members might have been skeptical without the evidence of their own eyes. The competition format juxtaposes the performance skills of Lisander and the courtiers, fostering comparisons not just of their dancing, but of their actions and characters.

Twelfth Night

Formal, scripted dance competitions may be rare in early modern English plays, but examples of dancing with a competitive flavor abound. Even among friends, words and actions could easily become competitive. British historian Elizabeth Foyster's (1999, 130) explanation that "[i]nstead of seeking mutuality, men's talk is often featured in the records left to us as highly competitive and concerned with one-upmanship," also applies to men's dancing. A dance-based "one-upmanship" of this type occurs in William Shakespeare's *Twelfth Night, or What You Will* (1602). In their first scene together, Sir Toby Belch demands of Sir Andrew Aguecheek, "Art thou good at these kickshawses, knight?" (Shakespeare 1974, I.iii.115–116). "What is thy excellence in a galliard, knight?" (Shakespeare 1974, I.iii.120). On the one hand, Sir Toby acknowledges and complements Sir Andrew on his social position by stressing his title and assuming that he is familiar with the galliard and its steps, as was required for a proper courtier and gentleman. On the other hand, stressing the word "knight" is a challenge; if Sir Andrew cannot dance well, he is not living up to his title.

Sir Andrew rises to the bait, claiming, "Faith, I can cut a caper," which he then proceeds to demonstrate (Shakespeare 1974, I.iii.121). The quality of his performance is suspect, however. As Arbeau explains in his dancing manual, "there are many dancers so agile that while executing the *saut majeur* [large jump] they move their feet in the air and such capering is called *capriole*" or a caper, but it is not clear that Sir Andrew can be counted among them (Arbeau 1589, 91). The caper is difficult even for the sober and physically fit, and Sir Andrew is certainly not the former in this scene, and probably not the latter either.

The amount of actual dancing in this scene is minimal, but its performance matters a great deal to our understanding of these men's characters and their relationship. If Sir Andrew's demonstration is anything less than impressive, Sir Toby's response, "Ha, higher! Ha ha, excellent!" is mocking and ironic, or if read as sincere, reveals Sir Toby's own ignorance (Shakespeare 1974, I.iii.141). According to Skiles Howard, "As the breathless boasts of the two seedy courtiers in *Twelfth Night* suggest, the measure of a man was the height and amplitude of his 'kickshawses'" (Howard 1993, 334). Yet, while Sir Andrew's boasts may be breathless, Sir Toby's responses are clever and mocking. He successfully goads Sir Andrew into further embarrassing himself, "Wherefore are these things hid? . . . I would not so much as make water but in a sink-a-pace. . . . Let me see thee caper" (Shakespeare 1602, I.iii.126–141).[8] Howard's contention that the excellence of a man's galliard reflected the excellence of the man is more easily supported. In both *Twelfth Night* and Middleton et al.'s *The Old Law*, the galliard is used to question and prove (or disprove) manliness.

But these galliard displays do not unequivocally confirm the dancer's masculinity or courtier qualifications. Instead, they highlight the ambiguity and complexity of contemporary debates surrounding dancing, gender, and gentility. An older married man would ordinarily have a higher status than a young unmarried man, but Lisander's proficiency at dancing, the art of young men, compromises his social status at the same time as it suggests his virility. Does he still deserve the respect due to an elder and head of household if he associates himself with the lifestyle of a young man about town? Likewise, Sir Andrew must strike a balance in his galliard steps. A certain proficiency in dancing is expected of a courtier, but if Sir Andrew's capers are too good, he risks being mistaken for a professional dancing master instead of a gentleman. In *The Old Law* and in *Twelfth Night*, Middleton et al. and Shakespeare exploit the nuances of early modern dance etiquette and expectations for comic effect, but they also record for posterity the difficulties encountered by those who attempted to assert their gender and status through dance.

Kemps Nine Daies Wonder

Early modern plays and dancing manuals offer few detailed descriptions of overtly competitive dancing. However, other literary sources from the period do contain examples of clearly competitive dances. Descriptions of dancing in works such as the boastful, exaggerated, but nevertheless informative tract *Kemps Nine Daies Wonder* (1600) complement depictions in plays like *The Old Law* and *Twelfth Night*, helping to paint a richer and fuller picture of early modern English dancing.

In 1600, soon after leaving the Chamberlain's Men, William Kemp, one of the Shakespearean theater's most famous clowns and master of the jig, performed the impressive feat of dancing a morris dance all the way from London to Norwich (Wiles 2004). Shortly thereafter, Kemp published an autobiographical pamphlet about the venture entitled *Kemps Nine Daies Wonder*. The morris was an active, vigorous dance with technically demanding jumps, kicks, and stamps. Morris dancers wore bells on their legs and coats with special long, sleeves. A musician playing a pipe and tabor, a small drum, usually provided accompaniment (see Figure 3.8).

Usually a small group of men performed the morris, dancing well-rehearsed, choreographed figures, but Kemp's version of the morris was apparently a solo dance and did not involve the choreographed figures for multiple dancers common to the genre.[9] Nevertheless, *Kemps Nine Daies Wonder* notes several men and women who joined Kemp in dancing. The account is of general interest to dance and theater historians, but the descriptions of these amateur dancers are particularly relevant to a discussion of competitive dance, status, and gender.

In his account, Kemp describes various people who danced with him for part of his journey. One of the people who joined Kemp was a butcher, "a lusty, tall fellow" (Kemp 1600, sigs. B3r–B3v). The butcher pronounced that he "would in a Morrice keepe mee

FIGURE 3.8. Detail from title page of William Kemp, *Kemps Nine Daies Wonder* (1600).

company" from Sudbury to Bury, a distance of around fifteen miles (Kemp 1600, sig. B3v). [10] After a short distance, however, the butcher quit:

> Ere wee had measur'd halfe a mile of our way, he gave me over in the plain field, protesting, that if he might get a 100. pound, he would not hold out with me; for indeed my pace in dauncing is not ordinary. (Kemp 1600, sig. B3v)

The butcher might have been a stout, energetic fellow, and a proficient dancer, but he could not keep pace with a professional performer like Kemp.

Yet Kemp writes, "a lusty Country lasse" from among the spectators, calling the butcher a "faint hearted lout," said she herself could dance a mile (Kemp 1600, sig. B3v). Tucking up her russet petticoat, she "garnisht her thicke short legs" with some of Kemp's morris bells, and alongside Kemp "shooke her fat sides: and footed it merrily to Melfoord, being a long myle" (Kemp 1600, sig. B3v). Kemp's description of the woman, with her "thicke short legs" and "fat sides" is not complimentary, but he readily acknowledges that her ability to keep up with him was impressive. He also praises her dancing skills, saying, "she had a good eare," and that she "daunst truely" (Kemp 1600, sig. B3v).

That a woman could out-dance a "lusty tall fellow" called the butcher's strength, courage, and masculinity into question. Less physically "lusty" than a woman, Kemp mocks the butcher as a "faint hearted lout" and his perpetual shame is ensured by Kemp's printing of the account. At the same time, the impressive dancing of the country lass does not entirely fall within the boundaries of acceptable feminine behavior, especially since she was "ready to tucke up her russet petticoat" in order to dance, revealing her legs to all in a most indecorous manner.

THE BLUNDELL FAMILY
HODGEPODGE HORNPIPE

Literary references to the hornpipe suggest that it was also an athletically demanding dance associated with country lads, but offering country lasses the opportunity to tuck up their petticoats. There are no known choreographies from before
the second half of the seventeenth century, although a number of early hornpipe
tunes survive.[11] In addition, a handful of literary and archival sources mention the
dance in passing. Taken together, they provide sufficient evidence for a general
consensus that the hornpipe was rustic in character, energetic, and associated
with northern England, especially Derbyshire, Nottinghamshire, Lancashire, and
Scotland (Pforsich 1998).

One of the longer and more colorful references to the hornpipe dance occurs in
a song recorded by royalist soldier and topographer William Blundell in 1641 in the
"Blundell Family Hodgepodge Book."[12] The hornpipe takes place in Little Crosby
in Lancashire. Blundell owned Crosby Hall in Little Crosby; therefore, his perspective is that of a gentleman describing the festive practices of his lower-status
neighbors. David George, editor of the Lancashire volume of the *Records of Early
English Drama*, notes that the song may describe the celebrations in honor of May
Day and the dancing that often accompanied the decking of the maypole (George
1991, 321 n. 32–35).

The details in the song confirm the preceding description of the hornpipe as upbeat and energetic, but they also stress the element of competition as well as "harmless mirth" (quoted in George 1991, 32). Some of the hornpipes mentioned in the
song are danced by male-female couples who "tooke sydes" against each other for
the prize of a wheat cake. Others are danced by groups of young men from different
villages, likewise competing for wagers and prizes. Throughout the song, one finds
lyrics describing the hornpipe dancers' competitiveness. The hornpipe of the "ladds
of Latham" was formerly "held to have bene the best / and far to exceede all the rest,"
but was now thought to be "to[o] sober" causing the Latham lads to have to "give it
over" (quoted in George 1991, 33). On the other hand, two of the couples, "Rowland
and Nelly / with Susan and Billie / Gott all the glory" and reportedly won the wager
(quoted in George 1991, 35).

While the song does not give many choreographic details, the lyrics provide some
choreographic clues. The dancers "tripped and skipped," and they "did hopp," with the
result that "loose legs shaked," and "the maydes buttocks quaked" (quoted in George
1991, 32–35). Clearly, the hornpipe was energetic, the dancers "did swett them selves
into a Jelly" dancing it, but most of the descriptors are quite generic and could apply to
most high-energy dances (quoted in George 1991, 33). Still, they are sufficient to create
an overall impression of energetic movement, general merriment, and friendly competition. The vigorous nature of the dance suggests that the couples as well as the "ladds"
who dance the hornpipe are young and fit.

Interestingly, although the hornpipes in the song are clearly competitive, and the lyrics name quite a few of the dancers, the dancing is nevertheless more communal than individualistic. There is no distinction made between the two couples who win the wheat cake, while for the group dances, the dancers' shared identity as villagers trumps individual recognition. The hornpipe song thus offers examples of dancing that are both competitive and communal.

DANCE AND CHARACTERIZATION

In *The Meanings of Manhood in Early Modern England*, British historian Alexandra Shepard (2003, 135) observes, "Male preoccupations in slanderous exchanges were often a direct product of contests over rank and status, to which patriarchal concepts of manhood were firmly harnessed." Dramatic representations indicate that in late sixteenth- and early seventeenth-century England, another popular means of manifesting the "competitive assertion of position" was through dance (Shepard 2003, 135). On occasion, early modern plays depict formal dance competitions, such as the galliard competition in *The Old Law*, but in the majority of early modern dance scenes, the competitive component is subtler and less official. In these scenes, the comments of spectators within the play and the performance itself direct the audience's attention to one particular dancer. This distinction is always purposeful.

Indeed, upon further reflection, one might argue that depictions of dancing that highlight the individual, rather than the group, challenge us to consider the extent to which nonfictional theatrical and social dancing, both in the past and today, are similarly competitive, with audiences inclined to notice or distinguish the individual, even during ensemble dances, while individual dancers are aware of and strive to attract that notice.

Regardless, exploring scenes of competitive dancing demonstrates the utility and importance of dancing as a characterization tool. This is because the stakes in dancing before an audience are higher than simply demonstrating one's terpsichorean competence. The implication in early modern literature is that competence in dancing signifies competence in general, while lack of facility in dancing symbolizes other, more profound inabilities or impairments. Thus, an author can show a character dancing well or poorly to indicate that person's overall excellence or lack thereof and through competitive dancing, can rank characters in comparison to each other, as well. Furthermore, in plays with dance scenes, having characters dance on stage *demonstrates* rather than merely *describes* their personal characteristics, creating a more convincing, as well as more entertaining, portrayal. Nevertheless, as the nondramatic works examined here reveal, vivid descriptions of dancing can be almost as informative as embodied performances. In all of the sources examined, dancing (or failing to dance) in a manner appropriate for one's gender, social rank, age, and circumstances suggests the dancer's ability and inclination (or inability and disinclination) to meet and conform to societal expectations more generally.

This chapter opened with a rare description of the Spanish *retos*, or dance challenge. My research suggests that dancing duels were rare in England, not just in Spain, both in literature and in real life. Yet, at the same time, this chapter also vindicates Esquivel. In English dramatic literature of the late Renaissance, there is at least one dance duel between two men in which honor and reputation are at stake, and there are several descriptions of dancing that is not structured as a duel but that is definitely competitive. While he may have exaggerated the importance and prevalence of the dance duel, it seems unlikely that Esquivel invented it. Rather, the Spanish dancing schools may simply have provided a formal structure and script for a type of competitive dancing that had occurred throughout Europe in a more ad hoc, informal fashion for decades.

NOTES

1. Nadine George-Graves's examination of the cakewalk (in Chapter 1 of this volume) reminds us that not all participants in competitive dancing were willing competitors. While the examples discussed in this chapter primarily feature enthusiastic participants, one can easily imagine situations with reluctant competitors. It is clear from Esquivel's manual that not only would losing a dance duel entail a loss of honor and reputation, but so too would refusing a challenge. There were likely many recipients of challenges who wished they could decline but felt bound by honor to accept.

2. Several scholars have carefully considered the question of the relevance of European Continental dancing manuals for English dancing, arguing convincingly that contemporary references to foreign dances in England suggest widespread, personal knowledge. Scholars have also found enough evidence of traveling dancing masters, musicians, and courtiers teaching, learning, and disseminating dances to hypothesize that this was a common occurrence, at least at court (see Nevile 1998; Ravelhofer 2006).

3. The modern equivalent of the caper would be the scissor kick or the ballet step, the *entrechat*.

4. In the first edition, stanza 67 was mislabeled 70, and stanza 68, the one cited here, was mislabeled 71, although on the following page stanzas 70 and 71 were correctly labeled.

5. The play's main author is likely Thomas Middleton, with Rowley contributing the comic subplot including Act III, and Massinger adding some later revisions. Although published in 1656, the play was probably written ca. 1614–1618 and revised by Massinger ca. 1626 (Lake 1975, 206–211; Logan 1975, 70, 265).

6. While it is not one of the official "weapons" in the battle, Lisander's colorful oaths and inventive insults throughout the scene also demonstrate his mastery of youthful language.

7. Arbeau mentions age appropriateness for different varieties of branles, but his comments are applicable to most dance types.

8. See, for example, the comic effect in performance of Sir Andrew's attempts at galliard capers in the *Twelfth Night* scene in *The Bard's Galliard . . . or How to Party like an Elizabethan*, a performance of dance scenes from Shakespeare plays that I directed and choreographed as an undergraduate student at Princeton University in 1999 (0:48). Archival footage of the scene can be viewed at https://www.youtube.com/watch?v=9iwMT8t6ono.

9. John Forrest (1999) also points out that unlike most dances, Kemp's morris had no definite beginning or end and no set length. He dances for different amounts of time each day, and other dancers join him for variable lengths of time and at different points in his dance, not necessarily from the beginning.

10. Google maps estimates that, today, walking from Sudbury to Bury St. Edmunds would take approximately five and a quarter hours.

11. Because the dance styles of the early and late seventeenth century vary so drastically, it is unlikely that late seventeenth-century hornpipe choreographies bear much resemblance to early seventeenth-century hornpipes. This is also true for the Baroque *gigue* versus the Renaissance jig, *courante* versus *coranto, alemande* versus almain, and so on (Brainard 1998; Pforsich 1998).

12. A hodgepodge book is a miscellany, a motley assortment of quotations and excerpts, un-attributed songs and poems, and observations by the collection's author or authors. Some miscellanies were the product of several generations of family members.

References

Anon. 1586. *The English courtier, and the Cuntrey Gentleman*. London.

Arbeau, Thoinot. 1967. *Orchesography*, translated by Mary S. Evans and edited by Julia Sutton. New York: Dover. (Originally published as *Orchésographie*, Langres, 1589).

Bacon, Francis. 1625. *The essayes or counsels, ciuill and morall, of Francis Lo. Verulam, Viscount St. Alban*. London.

Berger, Harry, Jr. 1982. "Against the Sink-a-Pace: Sexual and Family Politics in *Much Ado About Nothing*." *Shakespeare Quarterly* 33(3): 302–313.

Brainard, Ingrid. 1998. "Social Dance: Court and Social Dance before 1800." In *International Encyclopedia of Dance: A Project of Dance Perspectives Foundation, Inc.*, edited by Selma J. Cohen, vol. 5, 620–621. New York: Oxford University Press.

Brissenden, Alan. 1981. *Shakespeare and the Dance*. Atlantic Highlands, NJ: Humanities.

Brooks, Lynn Matluck. 2003. *The Art of Dancing in Seventeenth-Century Spain: Juan de Esquivel Navarro and His World*. London: Associated University Presses.

Caroso, Fabritio. [1986] 1995. *Courtly Dance of the Renaissance: A New Translation and Edition of the "Nobiltà di Dame"(1600)*, edited and translated by Julia Sutton. Reprint, New York: Dover.

Castiglione, Baldesar. 1561. *The courtyer of Count Baldessar Castilio diuided into foure bookes. Very necessary and profitable for yonge gentilmen and gentilwomen abiding in court, palaice or place, done into English by Thomas Hoby*. Translated by Sir Thomas Hoby. London.

Castiglione, Baldesar. 2000. *The Book of the Courtier*, edited and translated by Leonard Eckstein Opdycke. Ware, Hertfordshire: Wordsworth. (Originally published as *Il Cortegiano*, Venice, 1528.)

Cleland, James. 1607. *ΠΡΩΠΑΙΔΕΙΑ, or The institution of a young noble man*. Oxford.

Colse, Peter. 1596. *Penelopes complaint: or, A mirrour for wanton minions. Taken out of Homers Odissea, and written in English verse*. London.

Compasso, Lutio. 1995. *Ballo della gagliarda*. Edited by Barbara Sparti. Freiburg: fa-gisis. (Originally published in 1560.)

Davies, John. 1596. *Orchestra or A poeme of dauncing Iudicially proouing the true obseruation of time and measure, in the authenticall and laudable vse of dauncing*. London.

Daye, Anne. 2008. "The Jacobean Antimasque within the Masque Context: A Dance Perspective." PhD diss., Roehampton University.

Esquivel Navarro, Juan de. 1642. *Discursos sobre el Arte del Dançado, y sus Excelencias y Primer Origen, Reprobando las Acciones Deshonestas*. Sevilla.

Forrest, John. 1999. *The History of Morris Dancing, 1458–1750*. Toronto: University of Toronto Press.

Foyster, Elizabeth A. 1999. *Manhood in Early Modern England: Honour, Sex and Marriage*. New York: Longman.

Franko, Mark. 1993. *Dance as Text: Ideologies of the Baroque Body*. Cambridge, UK: Cambridge University Press.

George, David, ed. 1991. *Records of Early English Drama: Lancashire*. Toronto: University of Toronto Press.

Goring, Jeremy. 1983. *Godly Exercises or the Devil's Dance? Puritanism and Popular Culture in Pre-Civil War England*. London: Dr. William's Trust.

Griffiths, Paul. 1996. *Youth and Authority: Formative Experiences in England 1560–1640*. Oxford: Clarendon.

Holland, Hugh. 1603. *Pancharis the first booke. Containing the preparation of the loue betweene Ovven Tudyr, and the Queene*. London.

Howard, Skiles. 1993. "Hands, Feet and Bottoms: Decentering the Cosmic Dance in *A Midsummer Night's Dream*." *Shakespeare Quarterly* 44(3): 325–342.

Howard, Skiles. 1998. *The Politics of Courtly Dancing in Early Modern England*. Amherst: University of Massachusetts Press.

Hutton, Ronald. 1994. *The Rise and Fall of Merry England: The Ritual Year, 1400–1700*. Oxford: Oxford University Press.

Jonson, Ben. 1979. *Pleasure Reconciled to Virtue*. In *Ben Jonson's Plays and Masques*, edited by Robert M. Adams. New York: W. W. Norton. (First performed in 1618, and first published in 1641.)

Kemp, William. 1600. *Kemps nine daies wonder, performed in a daunce from London to Norwich*. London.

Kendall, G. Yvonne. 1985. "*Le Gratie d'Amore* 1602 by Cesare Negri: Translation and Commentary." PhD diss., Stanford University.

Kronenfeld, Nathan. 1999. "Cesare Negri's *Salti del Fiocco*." *Tassel Reconstruction*. http://www3.sympatico.ca/kronenfeld/Negri/tassel-reconstruction.html.

Lake, David J. 1975. *The Canon of Thomas Middleton's Plays*. Cambridge, UK: Cambridge University Press.

Logan, Terence P., and Denzell S. Smith, eds. 1975. *The Popular School: A Survey and Bibliography of Recent Studies in English Renaissance Drama*. Lincoln: University of Nebraska Press.

McGee, Timothy J., ed. 2003. *Improvisation in the Arts of the Middle Ages and Renaissance*. Early Drama, Art, and Music Monograph Series 30. Kalamazoo: Medieval Institute Publications, Western Michigan University.

Middleton, Thomas, William Rowley, and Philip Massinger. 1656. *The excellent comedy called, The old law, or, A new way to please you*. London.

Montagut, Barthélemy de. 2000. *Louange de la danse*. Edited by Barbara Ravelhofer. Cambridge, UK: RTM. (Originally written circa 1619.)

Negri, Cesare. 1602. *Le gratie d'amore*. Milan.

Nevile, Jennifer. 1998. "Dance in Early Tudor England: An Italian Connection?" *Early Music* 26(2): 230–234, 237–242, 244.

Nevile, Jennifer, ed. 2008. *Dance, Spectacle, and the Body Politick, 1250–1750*. Bloomington: Indiana University Press.

Orgel, Stephen. 1975. *The Illusion of Power: Political Theater in the English Renaissance*. Berkeley: University of California Press.

Pennino-Baskerville, Mary. 1991. "Terpsichore Reviled: Antidance Tracts in Elizabethan England." *Sixteenth Century Journal* 22(3): 475–494.

Pforsich, Janis. 1998. "Hornpipe." In *International Encyclopedia of Dance: A Project of Dance Perspectives Foundation, Inc.*, edited by Selma J. Cohen, vol. 3, 375–377. New York: Oxford University Press.

Ravelhofer, Barbara. 2004. "Dancing at the Court of Queen Elizabeth." In *Queen Elizabeth I: Past and Present*, edited by Christa Jansohn, 101–115. Münster: Lit Verlag.

Ravelhofer, Barbara. 2006. *The Early Stuart Masque: Dance, Costume, and Music*. Oxford: Oxford University Press.

Rich, Barnaby. 1574. *A right exelent and pleasaunt dialogue, betwene Mercury and an English souldier contayning his supplication to Mars*. London.

Shakespeare, William. 1623. *Mr. VVilliam Shakespeares comedies, histories, & tragedies*. London.

Shakespeare, William. 1974. *Twelfth Night, or What You Will*. In *The Riverside Shakespeare*, edited by G. Blakemore Evans. Boston: Houghton Mifflin. (First performed in 1602, and first published in 1623.)

Shakespeare, William. 1988. *The Winter's Tale*, edited by Frank Kermode. New York: Signet Classics. (First published in 1623.)

Shepard, Alexandra. 2003. *Meanings of Manhood in Early Modern England*. Oxford: Oxford University Press.

Sutton, Julia. 1998. "Galliard." In *International Encyclopedia of Dance: A Project of Dance Perspectives Foundation, Inc.*, edited by Selma J. Cohen, vol. 3, 107–108. New York: Oxford University Press.

Wagner, Ann. 1997. *Adversaries of Dance: From the Puritans to the Present*. Urbana: University of Illinois Press.

Walls, Peter. 1996. *Music in the English Courtly Masque 1604–1640*. Oxford: Clarendon.

Wiles, D. 2004. "Kemp, William (d. in or after 1610?)." In *Oxford Dictionary of National Biography*, online edition, edited by Lawrence Goldman. Oxford: Oxford University Press. http://www.oxforddnb.com/view/article/15334.

Winerock, Emily F. 2011. "'Performing' Gender and Status on the Dance Floor in Early Modern England." In *Worth and Repute: Valuing Gender in Late Medieval and Early Modern Europe*, edited by Kim Kippen and Lori Woods, 449–472. Toronto: Centre for Reformation and Renaissance Studies.

Winerock, Emily F. 2012. "Reformation and Revelry: The Practices and Politics of Dancing in Early Modern England, c.1550–c.1640." PhD diss., University of Toronto.

Audiovisual Sources

Winerock, Emily. 1999. *The Bard's Galliard . . . or How to Party like an Elizabethan.* Directed by Emily Winerock. The production is posted in twelve segments on YouTube. Posted by "Winerock," September 1, 2015. https://www.youtube.com/watch?v=SxghDXniq2c&list=PLwVD9pPtQwPsrif3UPaOErybONPCzCYK3. Accessed January 15, 2017.

Winerock, Emily. 2015. *The Bard's Galliard 7 12th Night.* YouTube video, 1:33. Posted by "Winerock," September 1. https://youtu.be/9iwMT8t6ono?t=46s. Accessed January 15, 2017.

....

CHAPTER 4

ENDANGERED STRANGERS

Tracking Competition in US Federal Dance Funding

....

SARAH WILBUR

The National Endowment for the Arts at Fifty

....

On September 29, 2015, the current chair of the National Endowment for the Arts (NEA), Jane Chu, announced a series of funding initiatives to commemorate the agency's fifty-year history of granting federal taxpayer subsidies to nonprofit artists and organizers (see Figure 4.1).[1] On this monumental occasion, Chu detailed a string of additions to the NEA's ever-expanding portfolio of national-scale grant programs. Notably, these new competitive funds do not mention dance or cultural traditions explicitly. Grant criteria instead emphasize the agency's growing interest in supporting artists who can deploy "creativity" to produce various human and economic deliverables. The economic rationales at play at the NEA today stand in sharp contrast to its inaugural approach to domestic arts subsidy, which dedicated taxpayer funds to preserving artistic "excellence" and through programs privileging Euro-American "high art" traditions (principally ballet and modern dance). In contrast, a new grant competitor is emerging through contests like the NEA's fiftieth anniversary leadership initiative *Creativity Connects*. This new funding program rewards grant competitors who can work with non-arts partners to grow non-arts sectors of the US economy.[2] And, while the notion that arts engagement produces returns in areas such as business, education, and the environment is both interesting and debatable, what concerns me in this chapter is how the NEA's engineering of federal funding contests today makes a nominal purchase on dance.

Saying that NEA grant competitions exclude dance is, of course, not the same as showing how. When I suggest that federal dance funders today have disinvested in dance, I do not mean to infer that dance performances are no longer resourced by the state. Instead, I examine the radical structural differences between the NEA's inaugural

FIGURE 4.1. The National Endowment for the Arts at fifty image, *NEA Magazine* (2), 2015.

Photo courtesy of the National Endowment for the Arts.

(1965–1980) and millennial (2000–present) approaches to engineering dance grant competitions. From this, I show how instruments of dance recognition and resourcing install different competitive ideals. As a political institution, the NEA is certainly not alone in granting legitimacy to nonprofit dance organizers. But, as the lone federal arts philanthropic arm of the US federal government, the agency's ideological obligation to recognize the cultural expression of the broad and diverse US citizenry makes it an important case study through which dance researchers can see how institutionally imposed competition (de)legitimizes dance "makers."[3]

Debates about competition in US dance funding too often collapse into discussions of "winners" and "losers," leaving aside questions about the politics of institutional engineering and fail to show how grant-making processes function as dynamic contests in their own right. While the economic exclusions in federal dance funding form part of my discussion, my main focus concerns how the NEA's inaugural and millennial funding regimes discursively establish competitive ideals in dance.[4] In analyzing two diverse historical approaches to grant seeking and grant making, I will, thus, consider how key institutional players, such as NEA senior leadership, staff, and citizen advisors, formed and reformed dance funding mechanisms in response to external political pressures, including the people to whom they were answerable.

The chapter is organized in two parts. After offering a brief overview of the historical conditions of the NEA's emergence and its basic framework as a funding body, I undertake a comparative analysis of the agency's ever-changing instruments of dance funding, specifically its narrative rationales for arts subsidy and grant criteria. In terms of scope, I have elected to hurdle the period known as the "Culture Wars" (1980–1996)[5] to focus attention on structural divergences between what I conceive as the NEA's *preservationist* (1965–1980) and *investment* (2000–present) funding regimes. I ask how NEA funding mechanisms construct an ideal grant competitor and situate this study between two periods of relative institutional stability, when grant programs ran multiple years without major changes. My purpose is to show how, under pressure from US legislators and excluded publics, NEA decision-makers instituted radical overhauls that shifted the agency's early rhetorical promotion of dance "excellence," a regime that *preserved* concert dance production curricula, toward an *investment* approach that sought to protect the "health" of the US cultural economy.

Methodologically, I evidence these political pressures and institutional restructurings by drawing from archival accounts of NEA history and program criteria (agency publications and internal documents secured through Freedom of Information Act request) and interviews that I have been conducting since 2013 with past and present NEA dance leadership, staff, and citizen panel reviewers who experienced these pressures and policy changes firsthand. These data highlight the NEA's position within a broader neoliberal economic streamlining of the federal government bureaucracy.

Political theorist Wendy Brown (2015) shows how neoliberal reason operates in governmental bodies to redistribute expense and accountability to nonfederal bodies. Her notion of "responsibilization" aptly describes the difference between the two funding regimes that I address here. Whereas inaugural NEA grant competitors were expected to preserve or advance specific dance traditions and supply the nation with "great art," millennial competitors are expected to use dance and art to deliver beneficial returns in social or economic policy areas that the state once protected. Following my comparison of the paternalisms and capitalisms that undergird these disparate regimes of federal dance support, I close by suggesting that dance researchers dedicate greater energy to elucidating the choreographic function of institutional tools, the ways in which policies shape the comportment of dance artists and the many people who organize on their behalf. By maintaining critical and reflexive awareness of institutionally imposed constraints, dance scholars might move with renewed purpose within the institutions that they are privileged to inhabit.

THE US MODEL OF FEDERAL DANCE
FUNDING: DECENTRALIZED BY DESIGN

As a nation, the United States was relatively late in the game to establish federal domestic funding for the arts and for artists. After decades of supporting artists through non-arts policy programs within the US Departments of Labor[6] and State,[7] President Lyndon B. Johnson signed an official domestic arts policy agency into existence on September 29, 1965, with the National Foundation on the Arts and Humanities Act. Johnson's signature on the Act was a performative gesture that established institutional umbrellas for the National Endowments for the Arts (NEA) and the Humanities (NEH), respectively. The conjoinder legislation authorizing both Endowments suggested that the US government would bolster its status as a world power through federally subsidized funds to art and culture. As NEA historian Donna Binkiewicz (2004) has shown, the agency's institutional origins were a political byproduct of Cold War efforts by networked legislators who ran in elite intellectual, artistic, and philanthropic circles. As I will show, political connections between elected officials and arts patrons strongly influenced the agency's early dance grant-making infrastructure, as did strategic alignments with Johnson's "Great Society" initiative, a domestic policy platform that sought to eliminate poverty and racial injustice and that pushed a historically unprecedented number of social policy proposals through Congress, which included Medicare, The Immigration and Nationality Services Act, and the Civil and Voting Rights Acts (Binkiewicz 2004, 76). The authors of the NEA's enabling legislation leveraged the successful advancement of federal funds for science research and funds for competition at the National Science Foundation (NSF) in the early 1960s. This also served to push the federal government to take up domestic funding for US cultural advancement as central to citizen betterment and to improved perceptions of the United States abroad. Lack of legislative expertise in scientific inquiry had been part of the rationale for the NSF's institutional annexation and citizen-run infrastructure; as with the NSF, the NEA's institutionalization as an independent agency run by employees and governed by peer experts was envisioned to achieve more effective distribution of taxpayer resourcing in domestic art and culture.

I rehearse these precedents to press the point that institutions and their policies do not emerge "from scratch." The NSF's overarching rationale and institutional blueprints strongly informed the NEA's inauguration and its decentralized chain of command. While I do not want to suggest that the NEA's institutional infrastructure has remained static, I flag attention to how the early governmental engineering of the NEA reflected the political strategies of its legislative advocates and also was structurally informed by grant contests in areas like science and education. Inside the agency, the NEA's decentralized chain of command also reflects the structural contours of the larger federal bureaucracy of which it is a part.[8]

As an independent agency of the executive branch, the NEA lacks the political authority of a US State Department or cultural ministry wherein elected officials directly control the allocation of funds and govern arts resourcing. The agency's annual budget is introduced first by the US president, is debated in congressional subcommittees in the House and Senate, and frequently is amended before receiving a full congressional vote. Internal to the agency, macro-policy decisions are made by a presidentially appointed NEA chair and the National Council on the Arts (NCA), whose terms of service are limited. Daily operations and grant competitions are administered by citizen employees and interns who work within the agency's discipline-specific divisions (today called "artistic fields"). Dance grant contests are governed by panels of citizen peer experts who are selected by Dance Program directors on the basis of their knowledge of nonprofit dance. Notably, NEA staff do not hold term limits. The temporally unrestricted character of staff hiring has historically lent significant control to discipline-specific directors. Especially during the agency's first three decades of grant making, NEA Dance Program directors held considerable power and influence through their capacity to nominate citizen reviewers and to structure and recommend changes to grant programs, which were then organized by discipline.[9] Prior to 1995, NEA citizen panelists were responsible for evaluating applicants and deciding on allocation amounts. Since 1996, panels have been reduced in size, and final allocation decisions have rested with the NCA and the NEA chair. Simply speaking, NEA funds are indirectly granted to arts organizers by the citizens who run the agency, not by elected officials. This dizzying chain of NEA command aligns with the tripartite structure of US governmental mechanisms, a structure advanced by settler colonialists out of a libertarian suspicion of centralized state power and intervention (Toepler 2010).

Anxiety over direct or total state control by federal legislators also informs the US nonprofit infrastructure and the public–private leveraging model of fund eligibility that undergirds NEA support for the arts. To impose what policy scholars describe as an "arms-length" relationship between legislators and grant winners, the NEA employs the institutional technology of the matching arts grant. The NEA has administered funds through matching grants throughout its history; these awards require grantees to secure equivalent nonfederal cost share and also to set expiration dates as a condition of winning support. This uniquely American model of contingent state arts funding connects with capitalist expansion as a uniquely American policy priority; the NEA's matching funding model took its historical cue from private-sector advancements that preceded the NEA's 1965 inauguration, including the Ford Foundation's multifarious arts initiatives in the late 1950s (Kreidler 1996; Wyszomirski and Cherbo 2000). Matching grants appealed to philanthropists and elected officials for the distance that they inscribed between artists and funding bodies; the practice of awarding small, partial NEA "seed funds" was thought to attract additional nonpublic investors. This so-called multiplier effect structurally de-obligated the funding body (in our case, the state) from being the lone supporter of a group or proposed project (Lowry 1978). To this date, and with few exceptions, NEA funds cannot comprise more than 50% of a grantee's proposed project budget. Federal grants are also time-stamped, engineered to expire within one to two years of an award. To maintain this "arm's length" relation, NEA grant winners are not generally allowed to apply for repeat support for a project without significant revision or expansion.

These institutionally allocated contingencies suggest that, despite the symbolic and economic gains at play when an artist "wins" NEA funding, the exercise of securing federal funding requires significant time and money for grant competitors. Material and temporal contingencies have been historically braided into NEA funding criteria that categorically exclude dance organizers who lack a strong administrative support system, who work in socioeconomically marginalized communities, or who lack proximity to wealthy patrons, earned income, or hereditary wealth. The fluctuating character of NEA annual appropriations and regulations imposed by the president and Congress add to these burdens and make the shape and direction of NEA fund competition in dance difficult to track. Rather than tracking who wins or what winning means to NEA dance grantees,[10] I now turn to the political architectures of the NEA's inaugural and millennial regimes to show how changing patterns of recognition and resourcing have placed dance works, workers, and ways of working in different kinds of competition.

THE NEA'S INAUGURAL APPROACH TO FUNDING CONCERT DANCE PRESERVATION (1965–1980)

> While no government can call a great artist or scholar into existence, it is necessary and appropriate for the Federal Government to help create and sustain not only a climate encouraging freedom of thought, imagination, and inquiry but also the material conditions facilitating the release of this creative talent. . . . The world leadership which has come to the United States cannot rest solely upon superior power, wealth, and technology, but must be solidly founded upon worldwide respect and admiration for the Nation's high qualities as a leader in the realm of ideas and of the spirit. . . . To fulfill its educational mission, achieve an orderly continuation of free society, and provide models of excellence to the American people, the Federal Government must transmit the achievement and values of civilization from the past via the present to the future, and make widely available the greatest achievements of art.
>
> —National Foundation for the Arts and Humanities Act (1965)

The preceding excerpts from the NEA's enabling legislation evidence the extent to which the agency's inauguration was justified as part of the state's responsibility to advance exceptional US creative talent, excellence, and achievement. Using domestic cultural subsidies (competitive grant programs) as tools, the state could more effectively regulate and reinforce US superiority in the realms of "the ideas and spirit." Livingston Biddle, the NEA's third chairman (1977–1981) and one of the draftsmen of the enabling legislation (who worked then under Rhode Island senator and NEA proponent Claiborne Pell), opens his historical account of the NEA by describing Pell's early request for statistical data on annual and per-capita expenditures by European countries on art. Biddle's mission, then, as the author of the NEA's enabling legislation was to bolster Pell's case for a dedicated agency for arts funding comparable to those of European countries, the Soviet Union, and Canada (Biddle 1988). Pell and Biddle depended on these data and testimony from wealthy New York arts patrons like John D. Rockefeller III to convince doubtful legislators that dedicating federal funding to art was critical to matching European advancements in areas like science, technology, military, and commerce (Biddle 1988). Where skeptical elected officials saw federal promotion of art as a frivolity, early NEA proponents saw federal grants to the "Greatest Achievements" in art as instruments that might persuade US citizens and the world that the United States could match and surpass developed nations in "encouraging freedom of thought, imagination, and inquiry." Rhetorically at least, the NEA's early justifications for arts subsidy imagined an ideal artist as one whose "superior" creative talent modeled "excellence" for citizens and the world, and who warranted preservation on the grounds of the work's sheer merit.

It was one thing to verbally espouse merit-based rationales for federal grant making, and another to structurally engineer grant programs to fulfill this charge economically and practically. To answer this call for cultural *preservationism*, early NEA leadership established philanthropic programs that drew structural influence from funding models that were already proliferating in the private sector. As cultural sociologist Paul DiMaggio (1986) and dance historian Linda Tomko (1999) have shown, US industrial capitalists in the early twentieth century were immersed in the project of dedicating surplus wealth to support Eurocentric art and artists through formal and informal associations. In other words, US private philanthropic support for concert dance predated NEA/NEH conjoinder by a number of decades.[11] By casting high-profile ballet and modern dance patrons, producers, and artists as early NEA dance advisors, the agency's institutional influence grew through forklifted programs and the networked connections of concert dance advocates from large cities like New York, Boston, and San Francisco. By connecting early federal grant contests to existing philanthropic efforts, NEA decision-makers could demonstrate maximum symbolic impact to legislators who were still resistant to the concept of national arts funding. Early NEA dance grants to already high-profile artists and dance companies proved to skeptics that minimal federal funds could be leveraged to maximum economic and symbolic reach.[12]

Significantly, the first two years of NEA funding allocations were, literally, no contest. NEA advisors brought lists of worthy candidates to the NCA for a vote. Not surprisingly, the experts in dance that were invited to sit on the inaugural NCA were among the strongest proponents of American ballet and modern dance in New York City. Early dance awards certainly reflected these cultural values and connections. The presence of American Ballet Theatre's (ABT) principal choreographer Agnes De Mille and co-director/designer Oliver Smith on the inaugural NCA influenced the NEA's first dance grant: an unrestricted $100,000 bailout to their nonprofit dance company. A grant of this scale, to a company of this magnitude, simultaneously launched the NEA's reputation as an institutional protector of American ballet. Critics lauded the ABT bailout in the popular press as a triumph, while sidestepping the fact that 25 percent of the agency's entire fiscal allocation for 1965 went to a single dance company (NEA Annual Report #1, 1966, 16).[13] In the absence of any significant opposition, the NCA approved additional grants of $250,000 to ABT just two months later to support a domestic tour of the United States. Another large sum of $394,830 was awarded to ABT in 1967, a grant that constituted 63 percent of the entire budget allotted to dance in that year (Straight 1988). While these disproportionate economic figures are indeed staggering, I want to examine how ballet production models were hard wired into NEA eligibility criteria and funding competitions from 1967 to 1980.

In the first fifteen years of federal dance fund competition, NEA dance grants were structured to support incorporated dance artists who organized production through training-to-performance models of dance repertory creation and touring. Incorporated dance makers were organized groups who had established 501c-3 charitable organizational status; nonprofit organization made grant distribution easier to account for and to track. Companies with schools appealed to funders as a sign of an intent to maximize earned income, disseminate codified techniques, and build audiences. Dance organizations like ABT that were engaged in producing and touring catalogues of short "repertory" works appealed as a way to regionally distribute "excellent" choreographies to proscenium performance venues that had been newly established, not by the NEA, but in the mid-1950s through the Ford Foundation's regional arts initiatives. Ford's investment in preserving ballet and proscenial dance training-to-performance models and the state-funded cultural diplomacy tours by concert dance artists during the Cold War are worth detailing here as structural precedents that shaped grant criteria that the Dance Program would uphold well into the 1980s.

In 1957, the Ford Foundation had instituted a series of programs under the leadership of W. McNeill Lowry that had dedicated an unprecedented $29.8 million in private grants to be distributed to regional ballet organizations. Between 1963 and 1973, ballet regionalization boomed across the United States and built on the Foundation's previous urban-planning initiatives that had enabled the construction of civic performing arts centers in major US cities. The fabrication of proscenium "houses" to shelter concert works sparked an exodus of ABT, New York City Ballet, and San Francisco Ballet artists, whose anchoring presence as heads of regional ballet companies provided regional rest stops for these dominant institutions and for the growing cadre of largely New York–based modern dance artists who were eager to tour work to concert venues. While conflict of interest prevented Ford's principal fund architect "Mac" Lowry from serving on NEA advisory boards, he was an invited attendee for the first round of NCA deliberations, where his opinions buttressed those of long-standing ballet institutionalizers like De Mille and Smith (Lowry 1978). This history helps us to see how none of the NEA's inaugural dance advisors were strangers to each other, or to the project of engineering concert dance "Excellence."

In addition to resourcing New York–based American ballet in its early round of dance grants, the inaugural NCA also distributed awards to members of the US modern dance vanguard who had links to private patrons and who had participated in State

Department–sponsored foreign diplomacy tours during the Cold War.[14] Choreographers like Martha Graham won multiple NEA grants during the late 1960s that re-routed her work from foreign to US domestic stages. Graham's fifteen-year stint as a featured artist on diplomacy tours convinced NEA advisors of her capacity to disseminate performances and classes in her codified dance technique to a growing US domestic leisure class.[15] That Graham's concert dance repertoires had played to an unprecedented international audience between 1950 and 1965 clearly bolstered her appeal to advisors weary of the expense of funding dance, a cultural form that struggled with a so-called "cost disease" saddling the performing arts generally. As defined by cultural economists William Baumol and William Bowen (1966), dance's "cost disease" reflected its incapacity to generate earned income and its material costs as a high-labor cultural product with low reproducibility. So, while Graham's concert dance works lacked a dependable "script" or "score" that could enable reproduction on par with theater and music, for example, her ability to deploy dancers to teach hundreds of tuition-paying dance students and re-stage her choreography on regional repertory companies rendered her a strong competitor in a system established to preserve "excellent" art. I point to these early philanthropic blueprints to insist that NEA grant infrastructures are never politically neutral; they follow the cultural biases and strategies of the people who set these mechanisms in motion. Specific to dance, the competitive ideal of the training-to-concert-performance models that grew over the NEA's first fifteen years of federal dance grant making was shaped by the interests of dance advisors. The fact that former American National Theater Association members who had awarded Graham state diplomacy funding sat on the inaugural NCA clearly conditioned her 1966 award of $124,250, which enabled her ensemble's first domestic tour in fifteen years to thirty-two US cities. Having demonstrated how early philanthropic blueprints follow the political strategies of key decision-makers in dance, I want to conclude my discussion by following these patterns and pathways from 1967 to 1980, once a formalized Dance Program was put in place.

While the portfolio of grant programs implemented by inaugural Dance Program director June Batten Arey underwent subtle changes across this fifteen-year period, grant competitions continuously hailed a trio of ideal competitors: regional and local arts agencies capable of networking touring engagements; concert dance presenters who sought to bring dance to their venues; and dance companies invested in creating and regularly touring ballet and modern dance repertoires to regional concert stages. It is also important to note that this infrastructural triad of (regional and state) *funders, presenters*, and *companies* were allowed to apply for multiple forms of support in the agency's early years. Such grants included the Coordinated Dance Residency and Touring Program; Dance Touring Program for Large Companies; Commissioning/ Production Challenge Grants; and the Individual Artist Fellowships in Dance. Notably, the NEA's annual reports expose the regularity with which concert dance artists, presenters, and regional mediators secured federal funding from more than one grant program during the inaugural regime.[16] A closer look at each of these grant programs reveals how each bolstered concert dance creation and repertory touring as federal arts policy priorities through a range of notable incentives.

Economically and structurally, the Coordinated Residency Touring Program principally benefitted state arts agencies (SAAs) by providing matching funds to be leveraged with state tax levies for the explicit purpose of increasing multi-state coordination of concert residencies and touring.[17] By doubling federal dollars with state support, public funders in each state were encouraged to take a chance on dance. The presence of matching NEA funds multiplied the number of performances in a given region and demonstrated sought-after returns on public dollars to state legislators, at once. Dance presenters, the second leg of the infrastructural triad, were empowered to produce concert dance performances through the Dance Touring Program for Large Companies, a program that provided matching support for concert venues committed to bringing the "best major American dance companies" to new audiences (Associated Councils of the Arts 1971, 10).[18] Of the funding mechanisms that directly targeted nonprofit dance companies the Dance Commissioning and Production Challenge Grants offered independent professional choreographers (artists without permanent association with nonprofit dance ensembles)resources to travel to cities outside their home residence to create or restage a concert work for new audiences. Through the administration of NEA touring grants, a directory of agency-sanctioned performers and groups began to circulate, from which managers of proscenium houses could cooperatively enlist touring companies for longer periods in a given region. Though this idealized "list" was geographically diverse in its inclusion of dance organizers from all fifty US states, the NEA's narrowing of grant criteria to the production of concert dance traditions (ballet and modern dance) installed EuroAmerican aesthetic guided production curricula that clearly excluded artists working outside of the realm of quote-unquote "fine art." In response to these newly available institutional resources, the number of nonprofit concert dance companies grew and sought entry into budding networks of funders, presenters, and organizers working to distribute ballet and modern dance to uninitiated publics across the United States. With federal appropriations to the NEA consistently on the rise from 1965 to 1980, this period has often been referred to by dance historians as a "dance boom." Structurally, however, these historical precedents and programmatic contingencies together suggest that this period of expansion was a contingent one at best.

Whereas the previously listed programs hailed grant seekers who could organize their dance operations through a 501c-3 nonprofit charter (a legal charitable status and standard of eligibility for federal subsidies in many areas), the NEA Fellowships to Individual Artists in Dance (hereafter Fellowships) were among the most flexible and sought-after funding instruments to emerge in the history of the agency.[19] The only source of unincorporated dance support directly awarded to individuals, the Fellowships offered ease of access and minimal constraints in terms of production and administration (they were initially two-page applications). Eliminated in 1995 by congressional mandate,[20] Fellowship funds were earmarked for artistic development and research as an end in itself no final production was required. While the less-restricted character of this non-matching award for dance research and development support benefited hundreds of dance artists across the career continuum over the NEA's first thirty years of grant making, the program's Western-aesthetic-guided assumptions of the choreographer as lone agent of dance production drew disproportionate interest from artists whose work was culturally aligned with dance modernism and oriented toward the concert stage.[21]

People make policies. And NEA grant mechanisms and the ideal competitors that they inscribe do not emerge "from scratch." By following preexisting institutional blueprints, inaugural dance decision-makers joined public resources to private philanthropic efforts that sought to promote the national profile of ballet and modern dance as culturally exceptional domains of dance production. Over time, some artists working outside Euro-American dance traditions would begin to restructure production operations to align with this *preservationist* approach, but many others working in indigenous or tribal communities, rural areas, and vernacular dance forms remained politically ineligible for federal grant contests.[22] Turning now toward the current century, I want to consider the institutional pressures and political accountabilities that conditioned a structural overhaul of the agency's inaugural approach to funding concert dance "Excellence." Competitive ideals in NEA grant programs post-millennium prioritize artists who are capable of using dance as an instrument of various forms of capital development.

THE NEA'S MILLENNIAL APPROACH TO FEDERAL DANCE FUNDING AS FINANCIAL INVESTMENT (2000–PRESENT)

As I have argued thus far, any debate on competition in federal dance funding must necessarily account for the shaping influence of NEA decision-makers and the people to whom they are answerable. I have also insisted that NEA grant criteria have choreographically shaped artists' comportment and aspirations in different ways throughout US history. Whereas the NEA's early approach was collectively authorized by legislators and allied arts philanthropists who shared the paternalistic mission to protect concert dance traditions and logics of production as barometers of "excellence," increased legislative pressures into the twenty-first century conditioned a significant shift away from the so-called supply side of dance production (funding artists and presenters) and toward the economic gains that dance can "deliver" as a stipulation of funding. Through grant contests that swap out cultural gains for economic ones, it remains clear that the preservation of specific dance traditions is no longer an NEA policy priority.

Today, when would-be competitors log in to the NEA website to search for grant opportunities, they no longer see programs organized by arts disciplines. Catch-all terms like "creativity" abound and de-emphasize medium specificity. Programs have been engineered from the top down by NEA senior leadership, based on what creative expression, participation, production, or consumption ostensibly adds to the US cultural economy. Staff within the agency's discipline-specific divisions continue to administer grant applications and panel governance, but citizen dance advisors no longer weigh in on policy decisions or control grant amounts as they once did. Staff members today spend much of their workday translating the agency's complex online application process and articulating its broad-based goals to aspiring grantees. As with the *preservationist* regime, this outcome-oriented shift toward dance as a tool of non-arts policy *investment* did not unfold accidentally. The NEA's institutional re-engineering of narrative justifications for federal arts spending and grant criteria was conditioned, in part, by executive branch mandates to streamline government operations that commenced under President Ronald Reagan (1981–1990) and that has been continued under the Clinton, Bush, and Obama administrations.

One of the key narrative strategies central to the *investment* turn has been the NEA's rhetorical promotion of art "work" as a reward in itself. A rationale aligned with social welfare policy restructurings by millennial President William Jefferson "Bill" Clinton (1993–2001), the discourse of "hard work" was then coupled with labor program funds structured to turn federally dependent citizens into financially independent workers. While Clinton's welfare reforms invoked moral arguments for putting low-income citizens to work and championed welfare as a federal obligation, his policies rewired existing programs in ways that simultaneously drained fiscal entitlements and shifted the burden of labor policy resourcing increasingly to the nonprofit sector. Through what Brown (2015) describes as the neoliberal process of "braiding" democratic and moral arguments together to defend decimated fund infrastructures, Clinton's programs put five-year lifetime limits on welfare for single parents and denied food stamp provisions for legal immigrants for ten years or until citizenship (O'Connor 2002).[23] I mention the Clinton administration's strategic de-evolution of welfare to flag attention to the unstable state of federally funded social, economic, and cultural infrastructures postmillennium; the NEA and nonprofit arts organizers were not immune from feeling the effects of this shift.

Since the turn of the twenty-first century, the NEA has increasingly justified federal arts spending as a tool for social and economic policy development in non-arts sectors. Millennial publications issued by the agency championed the NEA's value as a funding body by swiftly and strategically joining Clinton's call to put the nation (and its art and artists) to work. The *American Canvas* monograph (Larson 1997) was the first of subsequent reports that aggressively lobbied for NEA-funded art as a tool for community growth and development, using populist language that cast artists as purveyors of a healthy and more sustainable arts "ecology."[24] The idea of artists as productive workers capable of producing human and economic returns gained significant political force between 2009 and 2013, when former Broadway producer and entrepreneurial NEA chair Rocco Landesman took the helm. Landesman rebranded agency operations through the slogan "Art Works," and through publications that promoted the tripartite value of art "works" themselves; of art as a method of transforming ("working on") audiences and communities; and of federal investment in artists as "workers" and significant contributors to the US gross domestic product. Such economic rationales for federal investment in art and artists gained political force through new grant programs instituted by Landesman and his successor (and current chair) Jane Chu. Both of these highly entrepreneurial leaders have introduced new grant contests that take advantage of executive branch budgetary incentives to extend the NEA's programmatic reach in the absence of increased appropriations from Congress. These incentives and programmatic offshoots require federal institutions to share costs with nonfederal "partners" and are worth contextualizing further to reinforce the new competitive ideals that NEA's millennial grant logics inscribe.

Under the administration of President Barack Obama (2004–2012), federal agents and agencies won significant points for "partnering," for finding ways for previously estranged federal bureaucrats to share responsibility and cost. Obama's Office of Management and Budget (OMB) promoted Interagency Partnership Incentives that awarded increased appropriations points to federal departments and agencies that could share service delivery and de-isolate previously siloed areas of federal governance. NEA chairs Landesman and Chu (both Obama NEA appointees) took advantage of these gains to rewrite grant programs in ways that actively connected the arts to non-arts areas of federal policy. These leaders also commissioned research studies and released marketing materials spotlighting NEA connections to agents at the US Departments of Health and Human Services (NEA 2013), Education (NEA 2011), Housing and Urban Development (NEA 2010), and Defense (Americans for the Arts 2010).[25] Through reports that invoke quantitative data to reinforce the value of art and of the NEA to non-arts policy issues, millennial NEA leadership cast ideal NEA grant competitors as artists capable of using cultural work to address issues of greater interest to the legislators who control the NEA's budget and livelihood. And, while cost sharing across federal agencies is certainly not a new concept,[26] *investment*-era grant programs like Art Works and Our Town merit closer examination for the kinds of partnering, sharing, and maneuvering that they impose on today's nonprofit dance makers.

Two current NEA funding mechanisms, Art Works and Our Town, structurally replace NEA's earlier emphasis on the cultural "who," "what," and "how" of dance production with evidence of tangible deliverables that art contributes to the US economy as a criteria for federal support. The agency's flagship grant category, developed under Landesman, Art Works canvases a broad swath of activity, including "artistic creation, public engagement, lifelong learning, and community vitalization through the arts" (NEA website). This catchall cultural clustering blurs one underlying goal, articulated in grant guidelines: funded projects must improve access to and consumption of art among under-initiated demographics. Winning projects in the Art Works category are quite diverse in terms of content, but project descriptions offered by recent dance grantees overwhelmingly champion increased arts engagement as central to project aspirations. No longer institutionally oriented toward the preservation and pursuit of concert dance "excellence" as an instrument of US cultural exceptionalism, NEA grantees today use dance to expand citizen consumption, productivity, and participation in measurable ways. Whether a "winning" program extends the distribution of dance to previously restricted publics, enhances the professional development and skilling of a nondance group, or provides a template for a "scalable" program that furthers dance participation in any form, Art Works prioritizes citizen production and awards funds based on the extent to which a project framework can be forklifted and applied in new contexts. Simply put, the NEA's *investment* regime is structurally hardwired to produce maximum economic growth through cross-sector "partnerships" and minimal federal "seeds."

A glance at a recent roster of Art Works dance grantees exposes some of the ways that artists today are organizing production to answer the NEA's call. In round two of the 2016 grant cycle, sixty-eight projects won funds through the NEA Dance Program. Awarded projects include those proposed by nonprofit dance companies, service organizations, foundations, preservation institutes, and festivals that mention dance.[27] Again, the question of who "won" is less important to me than the strategies that lent their dance projects a competitive edge. Funded programs here included the Guest Choreography Project by grantee Alonzo King (LINES Ballet, San Francisco), which leveraged federal funds ($20,000) for use of the organization's long-standing dance training center to give students opportunities to study and perform with guest artists as part of their pre-professional training.[28] Projects like choreographer David Dorfman's concert piece, *Aroundtown*,[29] took a scaled-down approach to dance engagement, by using funds ($10,000) to stage audience participation within the production itself. While the economically nominal size of Art Works grants come nowhere near to covering the cost of these enterprises, project descriptions dutifully foreground the social and economic deliverables that the NEA champions as its raison d'être.[30] Dance, in these grant-winning examples, is valued as a social adhesive or method of workforce development, a far cry from dance's inaugural function as an instrument to secure the "Nation's high qualities as a leader in the realm of ideas and of the spirit" (National Foundation for the Arts and Humanities Act, 1965).

In 2010, a programmatic counterpoint to Art Works emerged and took flight as Landesman introduced the Our Town grant program and its adjacent philanthropic discourse of Creative Placemaking.[31] Another effort instituted by NEA senior leadership to inspire cooperation between artists, municipal government institutions, and non-arts investors, Our Town grants are notably larger than Art Works ($75,000–$200,000), and require significant leveraging (funds and labor) on the part of all partners. Critics of this program have suggested that its rationale strategically conflates what policy scholars call the "creative continuum" approach to community development (an approach honoring the indigenous cultural expression of local communities) with the "creative industries/ creative cities" approach to economic development (an approach that conflates economic deficits with cultural ones and favors outsourcing artists to fill in perceived gaps).[32] This strategically "fuzzy" language allows the NEA to canvass the broadest possible swath of cultural workers, tools, and methods, despite consistent challenges to this discursive flattening (Gadwa 2013; Markusen 2013). Such pushback has not quelled the success of Our Town/Creative Placemaking in expanding the involvement of urban planners, architects, social service agents, and health and environmental bureaucrats on NEA advisory boards. Whereas dance and "fine arts" advocates once regularly sat on panels, today non-arts investors frequently perform roles as panelists and coauthors of agency research publications. These newly sanctioned arts experts, in turn, have assisted senior leadership in rewriting arts production criteria and curricula in language and data-driven figures that US bureaucrats use and understand.

In case of any confusion about the economic motivations that undergird interagency grant programs and contests, current NEA chair Chu has defended Our Town's programmatic design as an explicit strategy to better align the Arts Endowment with the economic policy agendas of the executive branch. She explains that

> [t]he NEA created Our Town as a catalytic investment tool. It has served as the Obama Administration's signature place-based arts program. . . . As part of President Obama's "Ladders of Opportunity" agenda, and in strategic partnership with sister federal agencies, the NEA makes Our Town grants as anchor investments. (Schupbach 2014, 65)

In addition to structurally tethering art and creativity to non-arts development agendas, Our Town's programmatic infrastructure demands complex contracts that are beyond the reach of many nonprofit dance artists. Funded projects in this category average upward of fifteen partners, including a mandatory municipal agency. It is not uncommon to see artists partnering with social service organizations, botanical gardens, religious institutions, science institutions, local retailers, banks, farms, educational institutions, and even land trusts (Markusen and Gadwa 2010). While support for artists working in dance has not disappeared entirely during what many call the NEA's "place-based" turn, Our Town's programmatic emphasis on economic values and institutional connections exposes dance's weak networks and lack of physical real estate as factors that alienate many aspiring grantees. Such dangerous estrangement can be seen in the narrow number of funded projects that feature dance in the Our Town grantee portfolio.

Of the 382 grants given through the NEA Our Town grant program at the time of writing, just twenty explicitly include dance. Again, I am less concerned with "who won" and more interested in the way in which funding criteria force artists to organize and produce work. I am interested in how, for example, Alison Orr's $100,000 grant to engage residents of Austin Texas's Eastern Crescent neighborhood explicitly deploys dance as a tool in public parks, pools, and spaces to attract tourists and residents to places that are underutilized. I am equally curious about how American Dance Institute's 2016 grant for $75,000 uses dance (culturally undefined) to animate and renovate a formerly deserted lumberyard. In the case of the Good Works Network's Our Town award in 2015, I wonder how dance artists specifically use $75,000 in federal funds to impose arts, marketing, and management skills on underemployed citizens in the city of New Orleans. While these projects undeniably provide employment and recognition for dance artists and organizers, and may provide value to local project participants, this hyper-instrumental emphasis on economic outcomes masks the cultural "what" of dance and leaves little room to account for less tangible (or economically wasteful) dimensions of dance work. By requiring grant competitors to seek and secure economic partnerships and to steer production toward economic and social gains, millennial funding guidelines de-historicize and de-discipline dance. To compete for dance support in a system that equates "sustainability" with financial independence, NEA arts *workers* exhibit economic savvy and strongly networked connections to investors beyond the conventional "arts" realm. While this last claim may, at this point, be quite obvious, the ideal competitors for the NEA's investment regime are not artists first: they are entrepreneurs.

NEA grant competitions today have traveled a long way away from early efforts to preserve Eurocentric aesthetic values and production traditions by artists with established critical track records in large cities like New York. For today's dance organizers who seek legibility at the level of the state, the question remains as to whether they can handle the funder-allocated burden of multi-sector project coordination that the NEA's current infrastructure demands. The grant guidelines for Art Works and Our Town warn would-be grantees that the administrative burden for collecting required information and reporting on the outcomes of a single award is estimated at an average of 29.5 hours per project. Millennial NEA dance grantees will undoubtedly dedicate copious energies to dance; they will also spend time conducting market research, data collection, and evaluating the outcome of federal taxpayer dollars spent. Such administrative burdens are hardly exclusive to the NEA or arts subsidy, but the additional labor of tailoring products and services toward economic endgames reinforces the argument that I make throughout this comparison: funding policies shape dominant perceptions of what dance is and does in US culture. Today, and in past decades, the embodied exercise of gaining political legibility in dance at the level of the state has its costs.

The absence of dance organizers and artists from *Our Town* grant rosters is alarming in that it further alienates dance, an already estranged US cultural field. By de-disciplining dance, the millennial approach to dance fund competition allows economic interests to supplant cultural ones, and rewards administrative capacities and networked relations of artists over their aesthetic skills and methods. Democratic in form, competition for NEA Our Town grants does not guarantee democratic participation, in practice. I conclude by considering what dance researchers can do to nuance debate about institutional gatekeeping and the problem of funder-imposed estrangement.

CONTESTING FUNDER-IMPOSED ESTRANGEMENT

Whereas federal dance funders in the NEA's inaugural years structured competition around the ideological project of preserving and professionalizing ballet and modern dance, those responsible for engineering the millennial approach have replaced cultural preservationism with market growth as a funder-designated endgame. By shifting from a *preservationist* to an *investment* approach, NEA key players have rerouted management of larger social policy issues to artists and non-arts partners. The present appeal to non-arts investors as arbiters of art and culture has certainly yielded new opportunities for US arts organizers. But, at the same time, the economic rationales underpinning the present regime force artists to dedicate their energies toward outcomes beyond the people, place, and practice of dance itself. Two competing strains of capitalist paternalism are at play, here. During the first fifteen years of NEA operation, grant mechanisms coaxed aspiring grantees to align their operations with EuroAmerican concert dance aesthetics and production norms valued by elite arts patrons and organizers who sat on then-powerful NEA grant panels. Over the last fifteen years, dance's cultural specificity has been structurally dismantled and replaced by grant contests that emphasize the development of human capital as a desirable outcome of federal arts investment. Taken together, these historical tensions and answerabilities reinforce how people in power make policy through their daily participation in government institutions. And, while I have labored here to consider the structural constraints imposed by NEA funding blueprints, this chapter says nothing about how NEA grantees have exercised their obligation to the state, in practice. There is still work to be done to credit the many people whose committed enactments authorize nonprofit dance practice and production in US culture. Local analyses that unpack the infrastructural maneuvers of dance organizers could do much to reveal the disciplinary force of the NEA and many other consecrating institutional bodies that merit closer examination in dance scholarship.

Despite the many political estrangements articulated in the preceding, dance's survival has not been my principal preoccupation here. What I hope to have theorized, through this historical comparison of NEA grant mechanics, is a choreographic relation between the cultural values and political rationales of NEA key players and the institutional infrastructures that uphold dance's competitive ideals at the level of the state. When one remembers the historically partial and contingent character of US federal arts funding, it seems unlikely that aspiring grantees own enough political pull to challenge these instabilities directly. Stuck in the cycle of leveraging federal and nonfederal supports and meeting criteria, dance artists are often forced to focus myopically on their own survival as a first order of business. Wary of biting the hand that feeds them, dance artists and organizers today can benefit from institutional inquiries that evidence why they can no longer look to the past models of production as viable blueprints for future success.

Postscript/Provocation

Whenever I mention my study of NEA institution building in arts and humanities circles, I encounter many who cite the agency's redistributive framework and/or stagnant economic appropriations as evidence of its lost power as a funding body. This ambivalence is not unfounded, but it risks alienating leagues of committed arts researchers from actively joining US arts policy debates. By examining this dynamic, I have exposed how such political disappointment functions as a symptom and strategy of neoliberal governmentality, a political regime choreographically configured to silence opposition and mask the decimation of public infrastructures that its logics tacitly uphold. Such dismissiveness does not immobilize me. It inspires and moves me to continue to research people who make policies through a choreographic lens, to show how institutional instruments shape artists' work, and to evidence how institutions function as human infrastructures. The NEA is not an abstract power center; it is a dance support system upheld by people with differential power and competing investments in dance recognition and resourcing. At a historical moment when threats to public infrastructures are widespread,[33] the NEA's paradoxical charge to recognize and resource the cultural expression of a broad and diverse US citizenry demands ongoing body-level attention. Institutional tools only gain power when people put them to use.

NOTES

1. This motion graphic outlines the agency's outlook and fiftieth anniversary campaign: https://www.youtube.com/watch?v=acxQcMwQpoI (accessed April 26, 2016).
2. The first round of Creativity Connects grantees was granted in FY2017. For a list of recent grantees see: https://apps.nea.gov/grantsearch/ (accessed May 4, 2018).
3. My effort here to expand the number of "makers"—or achieved standpoints that authorize dance, follows Paul Bonin-Rodriguez's (2015) discussion of policy cooperation between artists and arts intermediaries post-1997.
4. I am less concerned here with connecting the neoliberalization of dance funding to broader US economic policies; such a perspective would align with contemporary Marxist theoretical frameworks that parse the deleterious effects of the government deregulation, de-unionization, downsizing, redistribution, privatization, and defunding, such that unfold in David Harvey's (2005) brief history of the topic. My work, thus, aligns more directly with Michel Foucault's (1978–1979) questions about how neoliberal governmentality reshapes notions of subjectivity, in this case artistic identity. Wendy Brown's (2003, 2015) discussion of neoliberal instrumental reason and expansion of Foucault's investigation also strongly influence this project.
5. As I discuss elsewhere, Dance Program directors and staff spent the 1980s experimenting with various changes to presenting and touring programs in, part, as a response to Executive Branch mandates to trim cost-heavy areas of NEA administration. The infrastructure for funding dance touring was reorganized four times during 1983–1996, and the NEA Dance Program also saw the loss of individual fellowships in dance in December 1995, when the 104th Congress enacted a 39% decrease in federal appropriations that forced the agency to lose half its staff overnight. For more on these changes, see Wilbur (2017).
6. For dance histories of Progressive-era labor initiatives during the Great Depression, see Prickett (1989), Graff (1997), and Franko (2002).
7. For more on the political influence of Cold-War dance-export programs by the US State Department, see Prevots (1998), Kowal, (2010) and Croft (2015).
8. This chapter will not delve into the myriad indirect ways in which the government has resourced the arts through non-arts departments and agencies, nor will it attempt to weigh

the influence of private-sector contributions by individual, foundations, and corporations. These tenets are addressed in *How the US Funds the Arts,* (NEA, 2012): https://www.arts.gov/sites/default/files/how-the-us-funds-the-arts.pdf (accessed July 18, 2016).

9. After 1995, and as this structural analysis will show, congressional mandates rerouted 40% of the agency's annual appropriations to regional, state, and local arts agencies for redistribution, a move that shifted the political sway of NEA peer reviewers.

10. Annual reports from 1965 to 1997 list NEA dance grantees: https://www.arts.gov/about/annual-reports (accessed August 28, 2017). Readers seeking information on grantees from 1998 to the present can conduct a database search here: https://apps.nea.gov/grantsearch/ (accessed August 18, 2016).

11. DiMaggio's (1986) work on the historical evolution of the nonprofit organization in the late nineteenth to mid-twentieth centuries convincingly demonstrates how "cultural capitalists" in Boston formed voluntary associations of cultural patrons, many of which grew into prominence as philanthropic institutions by combining consolidated wealth and political sway with municipal governments. Whereas DiMaggio attends principally to urban elites who invested in the advancement of artistic enterprises including state theaters, museums, and symphonies, dance historian Linda Tomko (1999) has tracked arts patronage and philanthropy from a dance and gender studies perspective to link domestic philanthropic efforts by wealthy wives and daughters of US industrialists during the Progressive era to various forms of theatrical, social, and folk dance patronage. Following these preceding studies, one might conclude that the NEA early citizen advisors were, by and large, the precise kinds of "cultural capitalists" (DiMaggio's term) or "cultural custodians" (Tomko's term) that had advanced dance through private channels.

12. This kind of partial or contingent economic interdependence between state and private patrons was integral to early staff and advocates in the US legislature, alike. In the NEA's 1965 year-end report to Congress, members of the National Council on the Arts reinforced these goals by framing the purpose of domestic federal funding as a project of "help(ing) existing organizations which have, through notable achievement, established standards of recognized worth, and which are in acknowledged need of financial help in order to continue functioning, to expand, and to develop" (NEA Annual Report #1, 1965, 31).

13. For a list of the first NCA members see: https://www.arts.gov/sites/default/files/NEA-Annual-Report-1964-1965.pdf (accessed September 5, 2016).

14. It is worth mentioning here that the inaugural NCA funds were not competitive awards; advisors issued a slate of recommended winners to the chair for approval, based on their "expert" knowledge of the field and networked connections.

15. At the time of the NEA's inauguration, the Graham Company had been touring abroad for fifteen straight seasons. The NCA saw this gap as an area of high-profile philanthropic investment, leveraging the occasion of the first round of federal dance grants in 1966 to fund Graham's first domestic tour in fifteen seasons (Bauerlin and Grantham 2008).

16. Comprehensive lists of inaugural NEA dance grantees and grantees from the late twentieth century (1966–1996) are embedded in the agency's annual reports, available in digital form here: https://www.arts.gov/about/annual-reports (accessed September 4, 2017).

17. A "residency" was defined by mainstream dance presenters as a longer-term stay by a dance company in a single community, with contracted ancillary activities such as classes, lecture-demonstrations, public appearances, and post-performance talkbacks (Shagan 1977).

18. The "large" stipulation in the program's title referenced both scale of production and geo-graphical locus. NEA grantee rosters from this period also reveal a disproportionate edge held by organizations that were geographically anchored in major US urban epicenters like San Francisco and New York (NEA Annual Reports, 1965–1980).

19. In their 1965 inaugural list of recommendations to Congress, the NCA signaled an urgent need for federal arts philanthropists to counterbalance federal philanthropic support for established arts organizations with programmatic alliances with individual artists. As unique purveyors of the creative pulse of the United States, the NCA argued that individual artists merited federal recognition for "their profound contribution of the creative artist to American Life, and to the future goals of our society" (NEA Annual Report #1, 1965, 9).

20. The NEA's first roster of grantees in this category reinforced modern dance professionalization as an NEA priority through $103,000 in independent artist allocations to Alvin Ailey, Merce Cunningham, Graham, Jose Limón, Alwin Nikolais, Anna Sokolow, Paul Taylor, and Antony Tudor (Bauerlin and Grantham 2008, 42).

21. During 1966–1996, NEA dance grantees were listed in the agency's annual reports, archived here: https://www.arts.gov/about/annual-reports (accessed September 22, 2017).

22. Artists working outside the concert dance realm gained eligibility for single sources of funding starting in 1971 with the annexation of the NEA Expansion Arts Program, and in 1974 through the adjacent formation of the NEA Folk Arts Program, under then NEA chair Nancy Hanks. These important categorical annexations grew in terms of appropriations in subsequent years but lacked multiple inroads. Thus the institutional expansion of non-concert dance "makers" abided contingent directions when compared to concert dance counterparts.

23. Clinton's welfare restructuring is a classic example of bipartisan political structuring aimed at the neoliberal project of turning welfare-dependent citizens into responsible citizens and productive workers. His programmatic advances did so by combining political conservative mechanisms aimed at market growth (for example, compulsory work requirements) with liberal mechanisms aimed at resourcing US citizens (such as job training programs), and by offering economic incentives to nonprofit agencies to pick up labor skilling and social service as part of their missions. For more on the infrastructural politics of Clintonian welfare reforms, see O'Connor (2002).

24. Artists and former staffers publicly convened, wrote, and resisted the 190-page report's narrative on the grounds that the agency was turning its back on art and artists, capitulating squarely to legislative interests, and refusing to take responsibility or to hold conservative politicians accountable for the attacks and draconian cuts of the 1990s. For more on this resistance, see Brenson et al. (1998).

25. Additionally, the NEA works with more than twenty other federal agencies, state and local governments, state and regional arts agencies, and private nonprofits: https://www.arts.gov/partnerships#sthash.8HBQnTYM.dpuf (accessed May 22, 2016).

26. As early as the early 1970s, cultural directories were published by the NEA and federal councils to elucidate the breadth of direct (NEA) and indirect (non-NEA) subsidies operating to support cultural production, expression, and participation across the US federal government (Associated Councils of Arts 1975).

27. A complete list of grantees in round two of *Art Works* allocations for 2016 is available here: https://www.arts.gov/sites/default/files/Spring_2016_Artistic_Discipline_Grant_List_FINAL_FINAL3.pdf (accessed August 1, 2016).

28. Organizations like LINES that have long-standing commitments to professional and community dance education carry particular appeal in the present paradigm because they stand equipped to expand dance services in plural directions. For more on the company, see: https://www.linesballet.org/ (accessed August 18, 2016).

29. Artists like Dorfman, who have historically labored to introduce the practice of modern dance to uninitiated populations and whose connection to dance university presenters, including those at his home institution (Connecticut College), are rewarded for demonstrating choreographic ingenuity and fund adaptability. For more on the company, see: http://www.daviddorfmandance.org/ (accessed August 18, 2016).

30. Additional Art Works–funded projects that deploy dance for human capital development and neighborhood revitalization in 2016 to include a grant of $30,000 for Ballet Hispanico (New York) for *Coreográfico*, a new choreography institute targeting emerging and under-recognized Latino choreographers. Spaceworks NYC's Dance Lit program won funds to house artists-in-residence at the Williamsburg Library to serve as "proactive partners" producing performances, educational offerings, and discussions that contribute to the "long-term stability and vibrancy of the neighborhood" (NEA ArtWorks Grant List Final 2016, 40)

31. Considered by policy experts to the signature programmatic advancement of NEA chair Rocco Landesman (2009–2013), Creative Placemaking privileges arts interventions whereby "partners from public, private, non-profit, and community sectors strategically shape the physical and social character of a neighborhood, town, city, or region around arts and cultural activities. Creative Placemaking animates public and private spaces, rejuvenates structures and streetscapes, improves local business viability and public safety, and brings diverse people together to celebrate, inspire, and be inspired" (Markusen and Gadwa 2010, 1).

32. Emblematic publications on the "creative economy" side of the debate include Putnam (2000) and Florida (2002). Publications touting the "creative continuum" approach include Wali et al. (2002) and Jackson et al. (2003).

33. On March 16, 2017, current president Donald J. Trump's OMB released his budget blueprint calling for the massive and historically unprecedented defunding of government departments, agencies, and programs, including the NEA and NEH. Trump's comprehensive budget made the same moves, and constitute the first time that a US president has used the instrument of the budget proposal to explicitly call for the NEA's elimination outright. At the time of this writing the NEA's budgetary fate has been at least partly assuaged through amendments offered by the Subcommittee on the Interior and Appropriations, which leave the budgets of both Endowments relatively intact with $5 million appropriations cuts. I discuss the question of the agency's preservation under Trump in Wilbur (2017).

References

Americans for the Arts. 2010. *Arts, Health and Well-Being across the Military Continuum: White Paper and Framing a National Plan for Action*, edited by Judy Rollins. National Initiative on Arts & Health in the Military. www.americansforthearts.org/sites/default/files/pdf/2013/by_program/legislation_and_policy/art_and_military/ArtsHealthwellbeingWhitePaper.pdf. Accessed January 8, 2017.

Associated Councils of the Arts. 1971. *Washington and the Arts: A Guide and Directory to Federal Programs and Dollars for the Arts.* Washington, DC: ACA Publications.

Associated Councils of the Arts. 1975. *Cultural Directory: Guide to Federal Funds and Services for Cultural Activities.* New York: ACA Publications..

Bauerlin, Mark, and Ellen Grantham, eds. 2008. *NEA: A History: 1965–2008.* Washington, DC: National Endowment for the Arts.

Baumol, William J., and William G. Bowen. 1966. *Performing Arts—The Economic Dilemma: A Study of Problems Common to Theater, Opera, Music, and Dance.* Hartford, CT: Twentieth Century Fund.

Biddle, Livingston. 1988. *Our Government and the Arts: A Perspective from the Inside.* Washington, DC: Americans for the Arts.

Binkiewicz, Donna. 2004. *Federalizing the Muse: United States Arts Policy and the National Endowment for the Arts 1965–80.* Chapel Hill: University of North Carolina Press.

Bonin-Rodriguez, Paul. 2015. *Performing Policy: How Contemporary Politics and Cultural Programs Redefined US Artists for the 21st Century.* New York: Palgrave Macmillian.

Brenson, Michael, Alejandro Diaz, Judy Kim, Malgorzata Lisiewicz, and Jessica Murray. 1998. "American Canvas: A Roundtable on the 1997 NEA Report." *Art Journal* 57(3): 69–76.

Brown, Wendy. 2003. "Neo-liberalism and the End of Liberal Democracy." *Theory & Event* 7(1). https://muse.jhu.edu/. Accessed January 8, 2017.

Brown, Wendy. 2015. *Undoing the Demos: Neoliberalism's Stealth Revolution.* New York: Zone; Cambridge, MA: MIT Press.

Croft, Clare. 2015. *Dancers as Diplomats: American Choreography in Cultural Exchange.* New York: Oxford University Press.

DiMaggio, Paul, ed. 1986. *Nonprofit Enterprise in the Arts: Studies in Mission and Constraint.* New York: Oxford University Press.

Florida, Richard. 2002. *The Rise of the Creative Class and How It's Transforming Work, Leisure, Community, and Everyday Life.* New York: Basic Books.

Foucault, Michel. 2004. *The Birth of Biopolitics: Lectures at the Collége de France, 1978–79*, edited by Michel Senellart, translated by Graham Burchell. New York: Picador.

Franko, Mark. 2002. *The Work of Dance: Labor, Movement, and Identity in the 1930s.* Middleton, CT: Wesleyan University Press.

Graff, Ellen. 1997. *Stepping Left: Radical Dance in New York City, 1928–1942.* Durham, NC: Duke University Press.

Harvey, David. 2005. *A Brief History of Neoliberalism.* New York; Oxford: Oxford University Press.

Jackson, Maria Rosario, Joaquín Herranz, and Florence Kabwasa-Green. 2003. *Art and Culture in Communities: A Framework for Measurement.* Washington DC: Urban Institute.

Kowal, Rebekah J. 2010. *How to Do Things with Dance: Performing Change in Postwar America.* Middleton, CT: Wesleyan University Press.

Kreidler, John. 1996. "Leverage Lost: The Nonprofit Arts in the Post-Ford Era." *The Journal of Arts Management, Law, and Society* 26(2): 79–100.

Larson, Gary. 1997. *American Canvas.* National Endowment for the Arts. https://www.arts.gov/sites/default/files/AmericanCanvas.pdf. Accessed May 23, 2016.

Lowry, W. McNeil. 1978. *The Performing Arts and American Society.* London: Prentice Hall.

Markusen, Ann. 2013. "Fuzzy Concepts, Proxy Data: Why Indicators Would Not Track Creative Placemaking Success." *International Journal of Urban Sciences* Volume 17(3): 291–303.

Markusen, Ann, and Ann Gadwa. 2010. *Creative Placemaking*. Washington, DC: National Endowment for the Arts.

National Endowment for the Arts. *Annual Reports #1–49 (1965–2015)*. http://arts.gov/about/annual-reports\. Accessed April 23, 2016.

National Endowment for the Arts. Grant Database. https://apps.nea.gov/grantsearch/. Accessed August 7, 2016.

National Endowment for the Arts. 2011. *The Arts and Human Development: Framing a National Research Agenda for the Arts, Lifelong Learning, and Individual Well-Being*. November. White paper. National Endowment for the Arts. https://www.arts.gov/publications/arts-and-human-development-framing-national-research-agenda-forthe-arts-lifelong. Accessed January 15, 2017.

National Endowment for the Arts. 2012. *How the United States Funds the Arts*, 3rd edition. Washington, DC: National Endowment for the Arts.

National Endowment for the Arts. 2013. *The Arts and Aging: Building the Science: Summary of a National Academies Workshop*. National Endowment for the Arts. February. https://www.arts.gov/publications/arts-and-human-development-framing-national-research-agenda-forthe-arts-lifelong. Accessed January 15, 2017.

National Endowment for the Arts. 2016. *Art Works*. Round Two Grant Database (Final). https://apps.nea.gov/grantsearch/SearchResults.aspx. Accessed January 15, 2017.

National Endowment for the Arts Dance Program. *Year End Overview Reports 1981–1995*. (Archive courtesy of Sali Ann Kreigsman.)

Gadwa, Anne Nicodemus. 2013. "Fuzzy Vibrancy: Creative Placemaking as Ascendant US Cultural Policy." *Cultural Trends* 22(3–4): 213–222.

O'Connor, Brennan. 2002. "Policies, Principles, and Polls: Bill Clinton's Third Way Welfare Politics (1992–1996)." *Australian Journal of Politics and History* 48(2): 396–411.

Prevots, Naima. 1998. *Dance for Export: Cultural Diplomacy and the Cold War*. Middletown, CT: Wesleyan University Press.

Prickett, Stacey. 1989. "From Workers' Dance to New Dance." *Dance Research: The Journal of the Society for Dance Research* 7(1): 47–64.

Putnam, Robert. 2000. *Bowling Alone: America's Declining Social Capital*. New York: Palgrave Macmillian.

Schupbach, Jason. 2014. "The Next 50 Years of Creative Placemaking, Some Thoughts." *Art Works Blog*, January 14. National Endowment for the Arts. https://www.arts.gov/art-works/2015/next-50-years-creative-placemaking-some-new-thoughts. Accessed May 22, 2016.

Shagan, Rena. 1977. *A Blueprint for Booking and Tour Management*. Washington, DC: National Endowment for the Arts.

Straight, Michael. 1988. *Nancy Hanks: An Intimate Portrait*. Durham, NC: Duke University Press.

Toepler, Stefan. 2010. "Roles of Foundations and Their Impact in the Arts." In *American Foundations*, edited by Helmut Anheier and David Hammack, 283–304. Washington, DC: Brookings Institution.

Tomko, Linda. 1999. *Dancing Class: Gender Ethnicity and Social Divides in American Dance 1890–1920*. Bloomington: Indiana University Press.

Wali, Alaka, Rebecca Severson, and Mario Longoni. 2002. *Informal Arts: Finding Cohesion, Capacity and Other Cultural Benefits in Unexpected Places*. Chicago: Chicago Center for Arts Policy.

Wilbur, Sarah. 2017. "Does the NEA Need Saving?" *TDR/The Drama Review*. 61(3): 96–106.

Wyszomirski, Margaret J., and Joni Maya Cherbo, eds. 2000. *The Public Life of the Arts in America.* New Brunswick, NJ: Rutgers University Press.

Audiovisual Sources

The National Endowment for the Arts: About Us. 2016. YouTube video, 1:48. Posted by "National Endowment for the Arts," January 19. https://www.youtube.com/watch?v=acxQcMwQpoI. Accessed January 8, 2017.

CHAPTER 5

···

MARKING YOUR TERRITORY

The Struggle to Work in Flamenco

···

KATHY MILAZZO

FLAMENCO's popularity reaches across the globe and, while it might appear to be a profitable transnational practice, several factors profoundly affect professional flamenco dancers in their search for work. As with the rest of the performing arts, the economic downturn, one of the leading obstacles hindering employment in recent decades, has significantly impacted flamenco. A decline in available arts funding has directly affected dancers everywhere and has influenced what producers consider lucrative. For flamenco, the need to fill theaters with dancers direct from Spain takes precedence over supporting local companies, a marketing strategy compounded by the limitations of what audiences frequently expect in flamenco performances. Even though flamenco continues to evolve, this latter issue affects employment because the art form is still defined by deeply rooted Romantic narratives.

As a performance art, flamenco crystallized in the commercial marketplace of nineteenth-century Andalusia in southern Spain as a tourist commodity for audiences titillated by vivid accounts of voluptuous dancers as painted by Richard Ford in his travel diary, *A Handbook for Travellers in Spain*. Ford, an English author, wrote his work based on his travels between 1830 and 1833 (Centro Cultural el Monte 2007). This colorful work is thought to have inspired the most famous fictitious Spaniard of the last 200 years: Merimée's Carmen, clenching a rose in her teeth as she moves her supple torso and honeyed hips, allowing her observers to feast their eyes and dream of passion, adventure, and forbidden love (Centro Cultural el Monte 2007, 23). Even to this day, the link between Carmen and flamenco shapes flamenco's image.

If competing with Carmen is daunting, dancers searching for work also contend with the idea that the Romantic flamenco world should be populated ideally by ethnic Spanish Gypsies, or, second, by dancers of southern Spanish extraction. The Spanish Gypsies who comprise the old flamenco families are dynastic; therefore companies are typically composed of family members or close friends. The *gitano* (southern Spanish Gypsy) hierarchy decided by blood was noted as far back as Demófilo's 1881 compilation of Andalusian songs (Machado y Álvarez 1881). Many important authors, including the renowned Spanish poet, playwright, and essayist Federico García Lorca, continued this theme in subsequent publications, like his essay on Deep Song in the 1920s (Lorca 1975). Furthermore, American author Donn Pohren (1962, 82), in his seminal book on flamenco written during the waning years of Francoism,[1] blatantly states that "non-Spanish *aficionado* should be warned of one thing—regardless of his proficiency in performing flamenco, or his accumulation of knowledge about flamenco, he will always be thought of, and referred to, as that fellow who performs well, or knows a lot, *considering* he is a foreigner." This Spanish Gypsy narrative has dominated flamenco for over one hundred years.

The struggle to procure work in flamenco affects all practitioners, regardless of nationality. At the time of this writing, Spain's unemployment rate hovers around 20 percent (Trading Economics 2016). Dwindling performing spaces also impact the viability of flamenco in Spain. In the geographical triangle of flamenco's birth, situated among Seville (the city of Carmen), Jerez (the home of many great Gypsy artists), and Cádiz (the ancient port city dating back to the Phoenicians), the few flamenco *tablaos* that remain cater primarily to tourists.[2] Many Andalusian cities host a flamenco festival during the year, but the pool of performers is often limited to international headliners and/or local performers. While flamenco *peñas*, or private clubs, still exist, they only present performances sporadically or during the festivals. Because performance opportunities are restrictive, many Spanish flamenco artists actively seek work outside the country. Fortunately, flamenco has never been more popular globally (Aoyama 2007), and flamenco festivals now appear across Europe, North and South America, Japan, and Africa.[3] Students of flamenco everywhere continually discover the aesthetics, discipline, and power of flamenco, but this means that more dancers find themselves competing for work.

I therefore set out to explore the coping strategies and struggles that dancers face on a quotidian basis through a series of interviews with working dancers from a range of geographical locations and nationalities. Specifically, this study addresses European and American dancers who seek employment opportunities both at home and abroad in order to ascertain circum-Atlantic flamenco trends. All of the dancers interviewed have devoted decades to their pursuit of flamenco and are committed to its preservation and growth. Martine Haesen is a Belgian dancer, resident within her home country, who runs her own dance studio but is developing opportunities for dancers to study in Spain. Nélida Tirado is a dancer from the Bronx in New York who has worked with flamenco luminaries from both the United States and Spain. Esther Weekes is British, but became so enamored of flamenco that she left her life in the United Kingdom to live and perform in Spain. Antonio Granjero hails from the flamenco center of Jerez, yet he found more opportunities working in Santa Fe, New Mexico. And, finally, Eva Encinias Sandoval established a heart for flamenco in Albuquerque, New Mexico, first through the University of New Mexico, before expanding her reach to establish a flamenco conservatory and, most recently, a *tablao*. Even though Spanish nationals face many of the issues addressed in this chapter, I specifically focus on European and American dancers because the struggle to work outside flamenco's homeland adds to the complexity of the stories presented by these dancers.

Like all performing arts, flamenco faces new challenges in the shifting trends of audiences and funding. Working dancers increasingly search for new ways to engage audiences, locate funding sources, and educate their viewers in order to compete in the public marketplace. Material gathered in the five interviews informs the four themes explored in this chapter. First I examine flamenco as a cultural industry to recognize an indisputable bond with its country of origin in spite of globalization trends that attract practitioners from all corners of the planet. Second, I explore how economic obstacles arose in the career paths of Tirado and Granjero, presenting both stumbling blocks and detours in their pursuit of employment. Third, I show how Weekes and Haesen creatively explore flamenco fusions with jazz idioms, which brings into question how broadly flamenco can be defined. And finally, I trace Encinias's prodigious grassroots efforts to develop flamenco in the outposts of New Mexico as a means to embed it firmly within Albuquerque culture.

FLAMENCO AS A CULTURAL INDUSTRY

Flamenco was born in Spain and became a recognized art form in the mid-nineteenth century, although its antecedents can and should be traced back to the previous century in order to understand why it looks like it does. In 1700, the Bourbon regime in Spain brought French fashions to the Spanish court when the grandson of Louis XIV came to the throne (Kamen 2005). Regional movements responded to the centralization of government in Madrid, and one of the most influential protests occurred when an Andalusian identity emerged to contest the Bourbon culture proliferating in central Spain. Exemplified through a subcultural expression of bohemianism, the resultant anti-Bourbon sensibilities were symbolized by the *majismo* movement that emerged in the latter half of the 1700s out of Seville, and spread to other urban areas (Steingress 1998). Costumes, gestures, and dances forged in lower class urban settings were transformed into symbols of insurgency to challenge the cultural and political control of the Spanish Bourbon regime. French influence ended during the Napoleonic Wars in the early 1800s when the Spanish, who had risen up in defiance, staged one of the first guerrilla wars in modern Western history. The heroics of their daring subversive maneuvers captured the imagination of the Western world, propelling Spain to become a popular tourist destination for European and American travelers, especially Romantic authors. As a staggering number of travel writers wrote about Spain, their Orientalist perceptions of Spain as an exotic location peopled by *majos* and *majas* were reinforced and reiterated continually in print (Mitchell 1994).[4] Significantly, several studies point to the emergence of flamenco as a distinct art form resulting from this lucrative tourism industry (Aoyama 2007; Navarro García 2002; Orellana 2015; Ortiz et al. 1998; Steingress 1998).

Perceptions of Spain as a land of Gypsies who swaggered and danced through the streets emanated from the imagination of the Romantic age and created new narratives that, through widespread distribution, engendered repercussions that affected the burgeoning Spanish nationalism. Because the *majismo* movement emphasized Spanishness over French influences, Andalusian culture became a symbolic representation of all Spanish nationalism. This action affected flamenco by elevating its position from a low-class art form to a national icon. The criteria for this action depended, in part, on what the market considered a lucrative commodity, which was dance, as depicted through the Romantic trope by Romantic travel writers. Sociologist Gerhard Steingress (1998, 95) avers that "[e]l romanticismo se convirtió en el mecanismo tanto del desarrollo cultural del país como de la formación y el arraigo de una identidad nacional genuina [Romanticism converted itself through the mechanics of the developing cultural movement of the country into a formation and rooting of a genuine national identity]." In other words, Romanticism converted a developing art form into a national representation of all things Spanish. Although not all Spanish people prefer to be symbolized by flamenco, it is deeply rooted in Spanish consciousness and remains one of Spain's most recognizable exports.

Until the early twentieth century, the practice and teaching of flamenco were limited to Spanish and/or Gypsy performers. In the 1920s, American dancers, such as Ted Shawn and La Meri, traveled to Spain to study with teachers like José Otero, a second-generation professional flamenco and Spanish dancer who was born in Seville in 1860 and learned his craft from the first professional flamenco dancers. One dancer of Austrian extraction living in California made the mistake of moving to Spain in 1936 when the Spanish Civil War broke out. She remained stranded in the midst of the turmoil for a year before she could return to California where she subsequently starred in several movies (Riesenfeld 1938). The work of these non-Spanish dancers in the early twentieth century served to expand awareness of Spanish culture across the globe.

A good example of the spread of flamenco in the United States is the arrival of the first teachers of significance from Spain in 1915. The Cansino family was brought over by socialite Mrs. Stuyvesant Fish to dance at social functions in New York. The six siblings were trained in Madrid by their father Antonio Cansino, and as dance writer and critic Ann Barzel (1944, 94) describes,

> [The Cansino siblings] launched on the Keith Orpheum Circuit, and danced in cinema house prologues. . . . When the Cansinos settled down to teach in America, Eduardo, José and Elisa lived on the West Coast and Angel and his American ballet wife, Suzita, in New York. That range of Spanish dances, flamenco, peasant and classical, as taught by the Cansinos was a revelation to most Americans, as were the intricacies of the *zapateado*, the art of playing the castanets, and the finger cymbals.

As Spanish dance became more familiar to American audiences, it was featured in many Hollywood movies and theaters across the country, prompting the need for wider access to its techniques. Eduardo Cansino's daughter, Margarita Carmen Cansino, became the famous American actress Rita Hayworth. Several of her films feature dance segments, including a Spanish dance in *The Loves of Carmen* (1948) in which Hayworth's Carmen seduces actor Glenn Ford with her castanet playing, swirling hips, and flashing eyes. Spanish dance was easily recognized in old movies through culturally identifiable costuming, music, Gypsy associations, and heel stamps; the women typically wore flowers in their hair and the men sported short jackets and high-waisted trousers.

Geographer Yuko Aoyama's (2007) study on consumption and globalization in flamenco identifies the impact of culturally embedded industries as a source of employment. She defines flamenco as a cultural industry that relies upon the pedagogy, display, and commodification of the arts as established in Spain. Regardless of nationality, all performers speak Spanish in their *jaleo*, the encouraging shouts that raise the energy of live performances, and singers utilize unique modalities inherent in the music that reflect Arab melodies from Islamic Spain. Importantly, dancers move in ways that are culturally specific to people from Spain.[5] Because cultural industries are largely grounded in place-specific cultural heritages, Aoyama (2007) posits that they are not usually subject to "offshoring." Flamenco is alluring, however, and draws many non-Spaniards to seek out teachers and performing opportunities throughout the world. Foreign dancers do so by immersing themselves in the culture that gave birth to flamenco. It is almost impossible to separate the art form from the culture, even for dancers living outside Spain.

The United States is not the only country that appreciates Spanish dance: flamenco is hugely popular in Japan. Aoyama (2007, 109) notes that as "an indicator of its popularity, the number of flamenco classes offered in the US is far lower than those in Japan; there is estimated one flamenco instructor per 1.7 million people in the United States, whereas in Japan the same estimate ranges between one instructor per 440,000 (low estimate) to 200,000 (high estimate)." Although the United States and Japan contain the most aficionados, dancers from all over the world flock to Spain to study, either at annual events like the Festival de Jerez, which offers two intense weeks of classes punctuated by three flamenco performances nightly, or for longer durations of time in order to be immersed in flamenco culture. In these economically depressed times, Spain embraces the commercialization of flamenco as an integral aspect of Spanish tourism through energetic marketing of the major flamenco festivals.

Since flamenco has assumed its position as a world dance form enjoyed by dancers and audiences all over the globe, it is no longer exclusive to dancers from Spain and has endured much "offshoring" in recent decades. The staggering number of well-trained flamenco dancers now creates more competition among job seekers. So how does this affect flamenco as a cultural industry? While hundreds of dancers spend years plunging into Spanish culture to understand and present a flamenco that honors its Spanish roots, many working dancers find that the general public is often woefully uneducated as to what constitutes good flamenco. Or, even worse, many people who hire dancers do not know what flamenco is and how it differs from other Latin dance forms.

Globalization has homogenized flamenco through the ossification of the Carmen trope while diversifying its articulations, as evidenced by the array of choreography found on the Internet.[6] The tragic, seductive character of Carmen is particularly suited for consistent renewal, as noted by literature and performance scholar Evlyn Gould (1996, 3), because she appeals to "bohemian" communities "ready to be critical of and even to lobby against the unspoken pressures on the formation of identity." Dance scholar Ninotchka Bennahum (2013, 142) explains that, with Merimée's novella, the Carmen figure "took on colossal and mythic form in the European collective consciousness" so that all Gypsy dancers were identified as Spanish. *Carmen*, the story, is an anarchical narrative that empowers feminists and condones ideations of freedom, in spite of the heroine's eventual death. Because Carmen resonates on many levels, she continues to offer an escape, a fantasy to viewers, and, unfortunately, she became the iconic image of all Spanish dancers because of her huge popularity.

Belgian dancer Martine Haesen became smitten by flamenco while working for the 1992 Exposition in Seville when the great flamenco singer Camarón de la Isla died. Equating the reaction to his death to that of Elvis Presley because Spaniards were crying in the streets, she felt motivated to learn more about the art form that clearly affected so many people.[7] She searched for someone to teach her, but found her first attempts thwarted because many flamenco teachers did not make the material easily accessible to students. For instance, they might not use counts, thus forcing dancers to figure out how movements fit into the feel of the rhythmic cycles, or *compases*, which can be accented in a seemingly infinite variety of ways. A common *compás* of 12 can be counted as two threes and three twos, or accents might fall on counts 12, 3, 7, 8, and 10. Indeed, a joke describes flamenco as an art form that takes a lifetime to learn to count to 12. Decisively, Haesen went back to Belgium to learn the basics and then returned to Spain to study at Amor de Dios, the legendary dance school and center of flamenco in Madrid. To finance her education, she worked eight months of the year at the Spanish tourist office in Antwerp, and then danced four months in Madrid. The hardest challenge she faced in pursuing her dream was the frustration of the learning process. Not only is flamenco a difficult language to master, but also, as she progressed, she was increasingly daunted by the sheer number of good dancers around her.

I met Haesen in 2007 in Maastricht in the Netherlands when I took her classes at studios organized by the city. In Maastricht, a medium-sized city with a population of 120,000, flamenco was popular and the program supported two flamenco teachers. Haesen began her dance training in ballet and was greatly influenced by innovative flamenco dancers like Andrés Marín; I found that her style covered much space and utilized the entire body, rather than focusing on heelwork. After teaching in Maastricht for a few years, she clashed with the new directors who took over the performing arts program. They chose to change the direction of the program to appeal to a wider range of city residents, rather than continue to invest in the art form. In short, Haesen was offered a position teaching salsa instead of flamenco, an action that indicated a profound lack of knowledge regarding the aesthetic differences between the two styles.

Haesen now lives in Belgium and teaches flamenco in her own dance studio, where she works to build a clientele. For her, delving into flamenco requires experiencing Spain and Spanish culture because practitioners need to understand where it came from and why it remains a vital part of Spanish life. To this end, she organizes two-week tours for dancers to attend flamenco festivals or special programs of study. Since the 1990s, Haesen has noticed an opening in Spanish attitudes toward foreign dancers. When she first started, she was admonished for trying to play *palmas* (rhythmic hand claps) during a performance and was told to be quiet and listen. Now, she sees her students being invited to dance the Sevillanas by other women at the Féria in Seville.[8] After dancing herself, she is often asked where she is from. She recalls that one woman simultaneously insulted and complimented her for saying she danced well in spite of not being Spanish. Haesen noted that "she simply didn't believe I was not Spanish—how about that—meaning I was either lying or/and foreigners are not capable to dance."[9] Although the woman's comment reflects Pohren's observation that foreigners are demoted in the flamenco hierarchy, in general Haesen usually feels accepted in Spain.

Esther Weekes, also a non-Spaniard working in Spain, sees more foreign dancers attaining a level of success there. She senses that if a dancer works hard and has the time and money to devote to learning flamenco, he or she can find work in companies in Spain. In her interview, she mentioned other dancers she has encountered in Spain, such as Cristina Hall, an American from San Francisco, who danced with modern flamenco artist Israel Galván and now has her own company, and Chloé Brûlé-Dauphin, a French Canadian, who together with Spanish dancer Marco Vargas were met with accolades at the recent Bienal de Flamenco in Seville for their innovative choreography. It seems apparent, therefore, that, as a cultural industry, the professional flamenco world accepts non-Spanish dancers who attain a level of mastery or who contribute to the business of the art form.

Economic Obstacles

Outside Spain, flamenco is undergoing a transition in places where it has long flourished, such as New York. Nélida Tirado, a flamenco dancer of Puerto Rican descent, comes from the Bronx and has achieved a formidable level of success in her professional career. She started her studies at Ballet Hispanico, where the curriculum includes a rigorous Spanish dance and flamenco component. While apprenticing with the ballet company, she was invited to tour with José Molina's flamenco troupe in the United States. She continued her flamenco career performing as a soloist in Carlota Santana's New York–based company, Vivo Flamenco Carlota Santana, and then was invited to appear with Sevillian artist María Pagés in her troupe touring Spain. For four years she traveled back and forth across the Atlantic working with the Maria Pagés Company, making many connections, and enjoying rich performance experiences as she performed with some of flamenco's best artists. During the times she was in the United States, she supplemented her income with work in *Riverdance* productions.[10] In 2007, *Dance Magazine* named Tirado one of its "25 Dancers to Watch," the magazine's prestigious yearly compilation of "who's new and who's breaking through" (Schwab 2016). When Antonio El Pipa, from Jerez, Spain, needed another dancer for the flamenco segment of Gypsy Caravan, a touring company that covered the United States, he called Tirado out of the blue because of her reputation. El Pipa typically employs his own family first, so this was both a great accolade and a prestigious opportunity for her. Tirado admits that "finding work for the first decade of her professional career was relatively easy."[11]

Now she speaks of struggles that she never faced when she was younger. The flamenco scene in New York City is changing. Fifteen years ago, good flamenco *tablaos* could be found in Greenwich Village and Brooklyn Heights, and the owners were avid aficionados. Yet Tirado observes that there are no *tablaos* in New York now. Since those halcyon days, real estate in New York has escalated to such a degree that the arts and artists have fewer affordable venues. One ticket for a Broadway show now costs over $300, a single flamenco class costs $25, and a New York City studio apartment is over $3,000 in monthly rental. Dance productions are beholden to the economy, and shows simply must fill theaters to turn a profit. In spite of her profound experience, local dancers, like Tirado, do not represent the commercially lucrative "authentic" dancing from Spain, which leaves her in the position of competing with markets that prefer profitable superstars. Tirado observes that the most effective advertisements must declare, "Direct from Spain."

Unfortunately, theaters emphasizing productions featuring major stars offer tickets that are too expensive for many potential audiences; and smaller venues, which could support local talent and reach a less wealthy public, no longer exist. Flamenco developed in intimate performing spaces that not only facilitated emotional bonds between performers and their public, but provided forums where uneducated audiences could gain an understanding and love of the art form. With the loss of smaller venues, the demand for flamenco is threatened because audiences are neither cultivated nor invested in learning what makes good flamenco. Tirado states that she no longer sees discerning audiences, educated fans who understand the nuances of a carefully crafted piece of choreography. In her opinion, New York audiences prefer flashy performances like the rhythmically accessible four-count rumbas of the Gypsy Kings and dancers wearing lots of flounces who move about energetically.[12] In short, audiences now look for spectacle and no longer take the time to educate themselves on the subtleties and variations of the art form. In support of this observation, Aoyama's (2007) research found that the demand for cultural commodities that involve a level of exoticism typically show an element of distancing by audiences seeking both a nostalgia for the past and a romanticism of the culture. Flamenco represents an Oriental expression in this regard, in that the public considers it to be an anachronistic signifier of the Rita Hayworth and José Greco days. Therefore, the typical viewer reverts to the Romantic expectations of earlier times and often eschews explorative interpretations like those of Rocío Molina, an innovator from Spain. Molina is a young dancer in her early thirties who is both an intrepid choreographer and a virtuosic dancer. Because of her explorations into diverse worlds like hip-hop, art, and philosophy, her ambitious ideas have resulted in accusations of "killing flamenco" (Mackrell 2014). Even at a recent Festival Flamenco in Albuquerque, New Mexico, this major flamenco star did not receive the same positive reactions awarded to more traditional performers, despite her impeccable technique and refreshing perspectives. Most flamenco audiences seem to prefer explosive representations of the dusty tourist fare.

Tirado states that the biggest challenge of work in the United States is this lack of understanding. She finds "restaurant owners who offer flamenco shows typically do not know good flamenco and many do not even like it." They struggle to pay exorbitant rents; therefore if a casual acquaintance can execute the Sevillanas or a dance learned in a workshop, she will be hired before a seasoned performer. Drawing in clientele takes precedence over quality. In restaurant settings, it is not unknown for some customers to complain about the "noise" of heelwork and castanets interrupting their conversations.[13] Tirado's choreography includes slow movements with graceful, high *braceo* (arm work) that gives space to the singers and musicians. Her dancing is strong, her heelwork powerful, as she deliberately draws the discerning eye to admire distinctions like her carefully articulated arms and fingers, rather than peruse her body as another manifestation of a seductive Carmen. Although Tirado's work is intense and artfully articulated, a lay audience might no longer have the patience or the knowledge to appreciate a thirteen-minute piece of choreography like her Alegrías during dinner.[14]

The transformation of the New York City performing arts scene began in the late 1990s. In 2001, under the auspices of the RAND Enterprise Analysts, a group of scholars undertook a study that identified a fundamental shift emerging in the performing arts system in the United States. Although the percentage of patrons attending live performances has increased due to an overall growth in population numbers, audiences are not sustainable because younger generations are "more comfortable with entertainment provided through the Internet and other emerging technologies" (RAND 2001, 2). As pressures mount to produce programming that appeals to mass audiences, market strategies increasingly control the selection of what is performed. Innovation is harder to sell, and companies must increasingly find new methods of diversification to "deal with financial demands in an increasingly competitive leisure market" (RAND 2001, 6). These prescient observations from 2001 are reflected in New York's relentless gentrification that has escalated since the economic downturn beginning in 2005. In that year, the National Housing Institute noted that reinvestment in gentrifying neighborhoods in New York occurred at an unprecedented "scale and pace that is unmatched historically" (Newman and Wyly 2005). Although gentrification is equated with neighborhood improvement, in reality, through a process of class transformations, it remakes the lower, "working-class space to serve the needs of middle- and upper-class people" (Newman and Wyly 2005). Two *New York Times* articles a decade later debate the pros of keeping some spaces affordable against the cons of greedy landlords forcing tenants out through lucrative sales in the city's new comprehensive rezoning laws (Alberts 2014; Editor 2016). Performing and practice spaces for small dance companies and independent dancers are reduced in this transformative gentrification process.

A blatant example of this debacle is marked by the destruction of flamenco's home in New York. Fazil's was a run-down rabbit warren of dance studios situated between a strip club and a long-distance telephone business on Eighth Avenue in Manhattan. There were holes in the walls, missing floorboards, heating problems, and empty wine bottles and cigarette butts littering the studios on Saturday mornings. For seventy-three years, Fazil's was the spiritual home of tap dancers, belly dancers, and flamenco artists (Dunning 2008). Supposedly film star and tap dancer Fred Astaire used to rehearse there during his vaudeville days, and it was never refurbished after that. Because flamenco, with its nailed shoes, is notoriously hard on floors, Fazil's was like the social pariah of the dance world in New York. In 2008, with rezoning and development, that entire block of buildings was razed and luxury high-rise apartments replaced Fazil's. Now there is no single place for flamenco performers to congregate in the city, and dancers are scattered about.

Concurrently, in Spain, after enjoying rapid growth in the European Union, the economic crisis deeply affected Spanish dancers. Those who made good work connections in other parts of the world took the opportunity to leave Spain. One such dancer is Antonio Granjero from Jerez de la Frontera, who was performing in Madrid when María Benitez saw him dance and invited him to join the María Benítez Company out of Santa Fe, New Mexico. Benitez, with her high Native American cheekbones and proud comportment, began her flamenco studies with a student of the Cansino family in Taos, New Mexico. After studying and performing in Spain for a number of years, she returned to New Mexico with her Spanish husband in 1966 and established a highly successful company that lasted until 2007. Granjero joined Benitez in the 1990s, establishing roots in Santa Fe. While dancing with Benitez's company, he also started his own company, Entreflamenco, in 1998, which performed on both sides of the Atlantic. After Benitez retired, Granjero moved to San Antonio, Texas, creating a nonprofit organization for his company whereby its mission "is to preserve, disseminate and create awareness of our diverse artistic Spanish traditions . . . and bridging the culture and art of Spain to the USA" (Entreflamenco program, Summer 2016). Although there was interest in his work in San Antonio, he laments that the city concentrates its resources on tourism, sports, and food. After struggling for a few years in Texas, he and his family returned to Santa Fe, where they are presently building their own *tablao* a few blocks from the venerable old Spanish plaza. New Mexico, with its population of less than two million people, proudly supports flamenco and is home to several professional flamenco companies.[15] Granjero notes that financial contributions to his company from the city of Santa Fe for one year matched the amount that San Antonio offered in seven years, and the latter is the seventh largest city in the United States. His frustration with funding sources is apparent when he states that "as an artist, I don't mind giving and investing everything I have to my work, but I would like politicians to see and appreciate what I do."[16]

His life in Santa Fe is still not easy, however, even though his outreach efforts are prodigious. In the past year, he opened the Santa Fe School of Flamenco; donated time and effort to Arts in Education and Community Outreach programming serving over 6,000 individuals; taught flamenco in physical education programs in local high schools; and offered classes free of charge to local dancers—all for instilling the love of flamenco in his chosen city. At the same time, he performs nightly in the María Benítez room in one of Santa Fe's luxury hotels while building his own *tablao*, which opened in September 2016. Granjero confided that only two types of people do what he does: impresarios who have money to invest, and crazy artists like him who, instead of going to Cancun for vacation, spend their time and money investing in their dreams. Nevertheless, Granjero's mission to educate his public about the art form will require persistence because Santa Fe is a major tourist city in New Mexico, and audiences attending performances, especially during the summer months, are not always knowledgeable about the intricacies of the art form.

I attended two performed by Entreflamenco in Santa Fe in the summer of 2016. Estefania Ramirez, Granjero's wife and business partner, is an impressive dancer in her own right (Figure 5.1). I have rarely seen so much grace and femininity in a Spanish dancer. While she can sharply execute her movements with precision, her dancing is

FIGURE 5.1. Estefania Ramirez and Antonio Granjero.

Photo courtesy of Morgan Smith.

composed and organic. Her lithe body carves high arches with her upper back and her serpentine arms caress and accent flamenco's intricate rhythms as she moves through harmoniously placed torqued positions. There is intensity in her dancing, but no stress. Heelwork phrases, a percussive component of flamenco that divides notes into several beats, have increased in speed over the decades. Some dancers pound out rhythms with ferocity. Ramirez, on the other hand, articulates her feet rendering the distinctions between *tacones* (heel sounds) and *plantas* (ball of the foot) clearly audible. She even manipulates the ruffles and weight of flamenco's costumes with ease and aplomb, and does not throw the fabric in fits of fury. When her speed and energy reached a crescendo, the audience, composed mostly of tourists, ebulliently jumped to their feet to give her a standing ovation.

Granjero, as the company's headliner, takes the position of honor as the final performer. His dancing leaves me speechless. He is presently at his peak and dances with all of the control, spontaneity, skill, and finesse of the world's top dancers. While other company members presented the same perfectly crafted choreography in both shows I saw, Granjero danced two dissimilar pieces, both with nuanced shades of tone in his heelwork, space for the musicians, impeccable timing, and his own personal styling. In the first show, he incorporated angularity reminiscent of shapes influenced by cubism as he bent his elbows in ninety-degree angles, creating a curious displacement of common flamenco anatomy. His refreshing modern approach explores ways of expanding flamenco's body positions, lending credence to his observations that flamenco is a living art form. In the second performance, he was cat-like, springing from heelwork to dance steps, never losing his intensity, completely focused and immersed in the music, singing, and complex rhythms swirling around him. Keeping the rhythmic cycle, the *compás*, is one of flamenco's biggest challenges, and to be able to intricately improvise complex choreography to reflect the moment's inspiration reflects a master of his craft. Granjero is presently one of flamenco's best interpreters of the art form. Yet, in spite of his striking performance, the audience did not spring to their feet when he concluded, suggesting they were more impressed with the familiarity of Ramírez's female body as a Carmen surrogate. Their applause was polite.

In talking with Granjero, I was curious about how he views flamenco and the contestations between the supposed old and new schools proliferating in the flamenco world. Old school is exemplified by Antonio Mercé, "La Argentina," in the early twentieth century. Her life and lasting influence made Spanish dance a viable concert dance form. As she progressed through her career, "Argentina's solos became longer, with fewer danced each night, as each dance began to contain a more sophisticated narrative. Slowly, Argentina began to mount full-evening ballets with libretti and orchestration" (Bennahum 2000, 11). Although she died when Franco came to power in 1936, her theatrical style of flamenco dance was the standard for decades. A new school emerged in the later Franco years, led by strong, powerful dancers like El Farruco, who was from an old Sevillian gypsy family. His dancing appeared more introverted as he gazed downward, seeming to dance for himself and not for an audience. El Farruco utilized speedy heelwork, punctuating it with individualized movements of kicks and twists that defied conventional flamenco body positions. Between explosive phrases, he stopped and paced the dance space, listening to the music and softly playing *palmas* while awaiting his next inspiration. Interestingly, this latter style reflects the present-day tourist preference for explosive energy, passion, and Gypsy associations. Granjero shifts between flamenco schools, and he forges ahead with new inspirations. While not taking the long pauses between outbursts like some dancers do, he nonetheless has El Farruco's spark of spontaneity. Granjero considers flamenco to be still alive and evolving, an observation reflected in his choreographic explorations. He states that the most important thing in cultivating this art is not to lose the essence of flamenco, and he defines this essence as the culture and daily living of flamenco. Even in an outpost far from Spain like Santa Fe, Granjero, as a choreographer, maintains ideations of flamenco's Spanish culture by working in the flamenco idiom, engaging musicians, and teaching the dance. Santa Fe's weather and old Spanish culture have many similarities with his home of Jerez, which helps Granjero maintain his Spanish identity. In spite of working in the United States since the 1990s, he is still much more comfortable speaking Spanish.

Granjero's major concern in today's flamenco world is the manifestation of stereotypical representations. The Romantic trope, symbolized by Carmen, hinders flamenco's continued development by limiting its expansion beyond the embedded longings for escapism that her character personifies. Entreflamenco serves a niche market that must negotiate "popular" with "high" art and attract audiences outside specific ethno cultural communities to remain commercially viable. Granjero must continually maintain his outreach efforts to attract both consumers and patrons so that their understanding of flamenco can move past archaic ideas.

FLAMENCO FUSION

As flamenco continues to thrive as a theatrical art form, its choreography inevitability transforms and expands through global contemporary articulations, despite being associated with Spanish tradition. Granjero states that, as long as an artist maintains the essence of Spanish philosophy, customs, and sensibilities, flamenco can and should be influenced by other forms of dance, music, and art. Indeed, some artists find such paths open before them in spite of their original intentions. In 2002, Esther Weekes (Figure 5.2) became so enamored of flamenco after attending a performance in London, she moved to Spain to immerse herself in the dance. She began in Madrid, renting a small room, and studying at Amor de Dios. The studios at Amor de Dios attract the highest caliber of teachers, but students pay by the week and drop in and out of classes; therefore continuity of learning can be difficult. Weekes felt that she needed something more immersive, so she auditioned for Mario Maya, a renowned flamenco choreographer and *bailor* (male dancer), who was teaching an intensive six-month course in Granada at el Centro Internacional de Estudios Gitanos. Afterward, she relocated to Seville, where she currently lives, studies, and performs.

FIGURE 5.2. Esther Weekes.

Photo courtesy of Daniel Pérez Galisteo

At the intensive program in Granada, Weekes was overheard singing in the restroom. Because of her good voice, she was invited to participate in a jazz jam. It was a pleasurable experience and inspired her to seek out some jazz musicians when she moved to Seville. In spite of her intentions to be a flamenco dancer, she found opportunities to work as a jazz singer who enhances the music with flamenco heelwork and movements. Her first group, Yacara, consisted of Weekes and three other jazz musicians. Yacara worked in Seville performing in places like the Museo del Baile Flamenco, flamenco's museum of music and dance, which features a stage in the building's covered courtyard. As a jazz singer, she found other noteworthy work accompanying a popular dancer from Jerez, Andres Peña, in his choreography for the Flamenco Festival de Jerez, one of flamenco's most eminent yearly events. Concurrently, Yacara underwent changes when new musicians who could add flamenco rhythms and singing to the jazz base joined the group, which then was renamed Jazzoleá. Weekes does not sing flamenco, too, but continues as the group's lead jazz and blues singer and flamenco dancer. She has performed in London, the jazz festival in Cádiz, and has toured Belgium. Weekes finds that she enjoys the fusion because "singing helps her hear what she wants to dance to."[17] Phrasing from both jazz and flamenco informs the music she articulates vocally and physically.

To reach this level of success, Weekes made some hard choices. Her first apartment in Madrid was a room in a house. It was so small that when her mother came to visit her, she commented with obvious dismay, "I didn't know you are living like this." But Weekes found that if she lived frugally, she could afford to live her dreams. Her rental house in London supplies most of her income, but she has supplemented it occasionally by teaching English. She learned that someone who wants to move forward in flamenco in Spain "needs to be able to study over a long period of time," so she stresses the importance of having a long-term plan before pursuing a career in another country. And she learned the importance of budgeting. When she first began studying in Madrid, if she could only afford one class a week, she made that class valuable by going over the material time and again. Spanish dancers can and often do live at home to save on rent, but foreign dancers need support. Altogether, Weekes notes that the worst thing she has faced in her quest to perfect the practice is loneliness. To some extent, she reflects that this isolation was self-inflicted because she did not seek out other dancers or musicians with whom she could practice. Now, after fourteen years, she finally feels she is reaching a level of competence. One of her objectives was to gain the approval of peers in Spain before venturing outside the country. She reasoned that "I like the competition. I want to know I am doing it right."

I was surprised that Weekes, as a foreign dancer trying to make a life and career in flamenco in Spain, did not experience competition from other dancers, as Martine Haesen did. Weekes attributes this to "keeping her head down" and just getting on with it. She has probably been harder on herself in her desire to achieve. Now that she has worked with a group, she finds fair treatment because, through her endeavors, she brings more professional opportunities to her fellow musicians. She states that "creating work for Spaniards and not taking away from anyone else makes me feel more accepted." While she did not expect her career path, she remained open to unusual opportunities, which ultimately led her away from competing with other flamenco dancers in Spain.

Flamenco remains her true passion, and she positions herself at a curious crossroad. One of her concerns about singing jazz and blues in a group is that she does not want to be pigeon-holed as a Josephine Baker figure.[18] As a black British woman, it is all too easy to fall into the stereotype of the "dark" chanteuse fronting the male musicians. Initially, I was reluctant to identify Weekes as black British because the label redirects her story to a focus other than her struggle to pursue her art. Whereas Baker was a headliner, a star, supported by musicians and other dancers, Jazzoleá is a performing ensemble. Weekes integrates her singing and heelwork sequences into the melodies and percussion of the music as an equal member of the group. She strives to obtain work through talent and to not use her body as both a marked subject and a marketing ploy. First impressions of Weekes reveal an attractive black woman, but once she starts singing and dancing, her artistry directs the viewers' attention to the quality of the performance. Like most jazz ensembles, Jazzoleá's musicians all take their individual solos, and Weekes is no exception. As a striking black woman, her look is inevitably a selling point. Although Weekes identifies as black British, she does not want that classification to define her art.

While Jazzoleá complicates the boundaries of traditional jazz and flamenco, its music is still rooted in Spanish culture through the dance, musical phrasing, and rhythms, in spite of its jazz orientation. It took the collaboration of Spanish musicians and a British jazz and blues singer/flamenco dancer to create this unique, progressive sound. Jazzoleá performs jazz standards like "Night and Day" with jazz piano and drum, and flamenco elements like guitar *rasguedos* (strumming) and *falsetas* (melodic phrases), dance movements, and *palmas*. Some pieces are straight jazz punctuated by tap-like heelwork, or feature Weekes's skat singing. The group is gaining more employment, not only in Spain, but also throughout Europe. Jazzoleá exemplifies globalization with the melding of musical styles, yet remains deeply influenced by the local flamenco culture through the abilities of its performers.

The mixture of styles inherent in Jazzoleá's music can be labeled as fusion, which raises the question of how broadly flamenco can be defined. Instead of creating a homogenous articulation, fusion serves as a collage in which its individual elements remain ascertainable. Cultural studies scholar Jorge Pérez (2015, 252) engages in a lively debate on flamenco fusion, arguing that "a strictly formal scrutiny of flamenco fusion in terms of its faithfulness to or its deviation from a pure form misses some of the contributions of these innovative practices." He notes that flamenco has always relied on tourism for its financial viability, but the "geographic paradox" that cultural industries face strive to balance "the desire to maintain a 'place-based identity' with the need for 'export markets for their survival'" (Pérez 2015, 253). Fusion ensembles like Jazzoleá contribute to flamenco's growth by raising awareness of its existence and by creating possibilities both artistically and as a commercial enterprise. They depart from images of flamenco *puro*, as exemplified in spontaneous performances such as those of El Farruco, as they strive to create new modes of expression that are artistically fulfilling. Jazzoleá advertises itself as a jazz ensemble, but flamenco is a medium that expands the group's artistic expression.

Haesen also dabbles in the jazz idiom, but not with the same intent. Weekes shapes her flamenco movements as visual and percussive elements within the jazz format, inspired by jazz and flamenco phrasing emerging from the songs. Haesen dances to straight jazz music in the flamenco idiom, using flamenco rhythms and swing.[19] None of the other musicians with whom she works is trained in flamenco. Her objective is to expose and educate audiences in the Low Countries to flamenco, showing that it is a progressive art form signifying more than an anachronism from Romantic literature. She finds audiences in Amsterdam more informed than other local areas because they are receptive to innovative flamenco styles, which allows the city to present many experimental flamenco performers. In general, however, she finds that the Low Countries are not familiar with flamenco, a problem she is striving to address.

Dance scholar Michelle Heffner Hayes (2015, 283) discusses experimental flamenco styles as displayed by contemporary artists like Israel Galván who "deconstructs the flamenco vocabulary at such a high level of sophistication in so many implicit, coded references to the form's history . . . that his departure from the traditional framework of understanding . . . flamenco dance challenges our ability to comprehend what is happening on stage." Audiences expecting traditional expressions of the art form are often dismayed or disoriented by innovations, as was made apparent in the receptions between Granjero's and Ramirez's solos in the hotel in Santa Fe. Arguably, an objective of sustainable performing arts is to provoke reaction and not remain relegated to an ossified past. As artists, flamenco dancers should have space to challenge their audiences with thought-provoking choreography and skill.

Creating obvious fusion articulations clarifies intent, and Haesen's aim to promote the artistry, rhythms, and postures of flamenco to reach a wider public is an illustration of its versatility. She greatly enjoys the challenges and exposure of performing with a jazz group because it inspires her, like Weekes, to pursue different patterns and phrasing. Haesen's approach exhibits innovative stylizations, and she uses flamenco moves in a variety of musical genres. Dancers like Weekes and Haesen work in a cultural industry outside the perimeters of its base by branching out in endeavors that ultimately bring more visibility to flamenco on a wider scale.

Forging New Territories

The more dancers network, the better chances they will have to find employment, such as when Weekes was overheard singing in the restroom in Granada or Granjero was dancing in Madrid when María Benitez happened to be in search of a male dancer. One of the most formidable success stories in flamenco in the United States is that of Eva Encinias Sandoval, the head of the University of New Mexico's (UNM) flamenco division in Albuquerque, and also the matriarch of a flamenco dynasty spanning four generations of dancers. Her impressive networking skills create an exemplary methodology for establishing a flamenco organization.

Encinias grew up in Albuquerque dancing and teaching at her mother's studio before she entered UNM as a dance major. Like many dance programs in the 1970s, universities primarily focused on modern and ballet curricula, but because Encinias had experience teaching flamenco, the Dance Program in the Theatre and Dance Department asked if she would create a class. She was intrigued because, having completed the program at UNM, she knew that the modern and ballet classes were structured differently from the typical flamenco paradigm. Ballet and modern classes begin at the barre, or with slow movements that warm up the body in preparation for combinations of floor work, jumps, and turns. Flamenco classes, both within and outside Spain, often begin with little or no warm-up before learning set dances. I studied with Mariquita Flores from 1986 to 1996. Born in 1916 in the province of Cádiz in southwest Spain, she was one of the first flamenco teachers in New York and had an illustrious career in movies and in theatrical productions. Her classes exemplified traditional flamenco methodology, and her style was Old School theatrical. We frequently warmed up with a dance we knew well, like the Sevillanas, before she launched into new choreographies. Technique was addressed in the confines of the dances themselves, not in separate exercises or combinations. Flores would stop a dance and have us repeat a certain movement or step until we could do it, but not in a different manner from the arranged choreography. Only in the last thirty years have issues of dance injuries and dancers' health changed the way many flamenco instructors teach; they now incorporate short warm-ups before plunging into repertoire. Flamenco pedagogy still mostly relies on choreography; therefore when dancers attend festivals in Spain, they essentially purchase a dance by signing up for classes that offer a dance form they are interested in acquiring.[20]

Encinias was truly a pioneer when she decided to break with the flamenco methodology and organize her classes differently, beginning with a warm-up before moving on to center work, arm- and heel-work sequences, turning exercises, and then finishing with a variation. Her goal was to keep the class moving and engage the students so that flamenco did not feel overly static, sticking on some of the tedious minutiae inherent in the execution of a movement. In short, she did not want the class to be "detail heavy."[21] She needed to sell it. Ballet and modern dancers were extremely receptive and, slowly, interest at the university and in the city of Albuquerque grew as well. Encinias's classes are vibrant and driven with compelling momentum. They have frequently been voted the most popular classes on campus, according to the UNM newspaper, and Encinias is grateful for the teaching opportunities in the university setting (which additionally offered her a neutrality in the dance community that removed her from rivalry among local dance studios). After ten years of growth, Encinias was able to expand the Department's offerings to three levels of flamenco technique.

UNM's dance majors with a flamenco concentration attend a four-year program consisting of at least three technique classes a week and courses in dance history, dance analysis, kinesiology, and choreography. For those entering at the beginning level of flamenco, four years do not necessarily give a dancer the chance to fully develop, especially if a dancer is new to the form. Because flamenco cannot and should not be defined solely as a technique and requires an understanding of the culture to capture the artistry, Encinias struggled with how to add weight to the program to increase the experience for her students. While pondering this dilemma, she was approached by the dean of the College of Fine Arts to present a flamenco performance for the fiftieth anniversary of the College. She countered that, with funding, she could provide two performances and some workshops for the UNM students. In 1987, with a budget of $3,000, Albuquerque's first Festival Flamenco presented American dancers Teo Morca, Lydia Torea, and Vincente Romero in two sold-out performances, supplemented by Eva's own company, Ritmo Flamenco. The Flamenco Festival of 1987 was hugely successful for the income it generated through ticket sales and for the recognition it brought to the college. It validated Encinias and her efforts to further flamenco in Albuquerque and New Mexico. The dean of the College of Fine Arts subsequently provided funding through 1991 for four more festivals, allowing Encinias to continue to invite celebrated dancers from across the United States.

After this success, Encinias again looked for ways to expand. She wanted to add an international direction to the annual event, but the university backed out financially. The College of Fine Arts agreed to support her with space for workshops and performances, but it could no longer supply funding. New Mexico is the second poorest state in the country (DePersio 2015), but that did not hinder Encinias from turning her own dance company into a nonprofit organization so that she could apply for funding and grants to fulfill her vision. By scrambling hard for new revenue sources,[22] in 1992 the fifth Festival Flamenco brought in luminaries La Tati from Spain and the American dancer and movie star José Greco as the headliners. The Festival Flamenco continued to expand and peaked at two weeks of classes and performances in 2007 before economic difficulties cut it down to ten days. It remains one of the most important flamenco festivals in the country and attracts the world's most prominent flamenco stars. Interestingly, Encinias is finding it easier to employ dancers from Spain since the economic downturn because she can offer competitive wages in a reputable festival. Spain's flamenco artists are more eager to work and no longer present problems that caused late changes in programming at some of the past festivals.

Encinias is a strong woman and an excellent entrepreneur. As a mother, however, she exhibits vulnerability and is greatly concerned that her family's future remains secure. Dynastic impulses have ruled the flamenco world since its inception, as noted by Leblon's (1995) observation of the existence of twenty-five Spanish Gypsy flamenco families from sixteen towns in Andalusia. Indeed, most of these flamenco families are related, and companies are often identified through the family name, like El Farruco's progeny, Los Farrucos, comprising El Farruquito, La Farruca, and several other relatives. Therefore, it is no surprise that Encinias's two children, Marisol and Joaquin, attended the UNM dance program and became flamenco artists. The Encinias family founded the National Institute of Flamenco in 1999 as a conservatory training school and home to the flamenco repertory company Yjastros, directed by Joaquin. It provided another forum for Encinias to develop Albuquerque's flamenco future through the opportunity to teach children. Marisol pursued her master of fine arts degree at UNM, where she is presently a lecturer of dance as she continues to perform with Yjasteros. Joaquin carries on the family expansion and now heads a charter school for the arts for students in grades 7–12, Tierra Adentro New Mexico (TANM), where students take daily classes in dance, art, and music. Joaquin's three children have also studied at the Institute, attended the Dance Program at UNM, and now dance with Yjastros. The Encinias dynasty in Albuquerque plans for the future.

One of the criticisms leveled against Encinas is her preference to elevate family members. Some dancers in the UNM Dance Program, Institute students, and former Yjastros members with whom I have spoken over the years felt slighted because they thought they were not treated equally. Although there is an artistic vision of solid technique for

Yjastros dancers, the family's dynastic impulses have led some outsiders to seek work elsewhere, often for financial reasons. While it can be difficult to obtain employment in family companies, as Tirado did with El Pipa's company, nepotism is accepted because of the marketability of flamenco family names and the prestige of performing with them. Indeed, the recognition of superstar names like Los Farrucos attracts art marketers focusing on procuring the most lucrative productions. There is no doubt that Encinias has created a formidable flamenco scene through hard work, but she admits there have been special opportunities for family members. It seems apparent that the Encinias brand name is being nurtured and protected in Albuquerque's flamenco community, but there is a concerted effort to offer as many performing opportunities as the local market will sustain, albeit on the nonprofessional level for most of the Institute's students. It must also be said that family members aspiring to join Yjastros go through the same rigorous process of training, and all must attain a credible level before being permitted to perform or teach. Or, as Encinias states, "everyone pays the price."

Encinias succeeds in the competitive flamenco scene by continuing to knock on doors to look for new ways to keep her flamenco empire viable. She collaborated with the Cervantes Spanish Institute in Albuquerque to offer a guitar certification program so the hundreds of local dancers being trained can have live accompaniment. A continual rotation of world-class guest teachers in the UNM flamenco program has raised the level of dancing substantially so that five graduates joined Yjastros as apprentices in 2016.

Tending the Flame

After 2005, flamenco around the world faced the economic downturn. On one side of the Atlantic, Spanish dancers scrambled to find work outside their home country; while on the other, New York dancers lost their home studio and saw the closure of *tablaos*. At the same time, lay audiences did not keep up with changing trends of the art form, preferring instead to consider it an ossified relic from the Romantic age. Even Encinias's empire in New Mexico was affected by the economic crisis, and no festival was held in 2009, for the first time since its creation in 1987.

Since the first decade of the 2000s, flamenco has found itself at the mercy of a public that prefers spectacle, to the detriment of dancers without superstar status. Yet, the quest these five dancers have to present credible flamenco that expresses their individual lives pushes them to stay true to their visions. Or, as Tirado says, "I don't want to just shake my butt in a pretty dress." Encinias's answer to keeping flamenco alive is to find new ways to sell it. To this end, she encourages students to attend college to attain degrees and become smarter people. Weekes thinks the key is to not wait to be chosen for a job, but to find ways to create new opportunities and remain open to chances that she never before considered.

All of the interviewees are first and foremost artists. They all strive to present highly articulated, well-crafted flamenco that reflects them as individual spirited human beings. They also exhibit the hunger that drives dancers to pursue their dreams in spite of persistent obstacles. Granjero firmly believes that life experience must influence flamenco to capture its essence and its culture, and that this must be done with knowledge and credibility. When asked to define flamenco *puro* (pure flamenco), he answered, "For me, it's my life." Tirado admits that dancing sustains her psychologically. "It's everything," she says. Her son, who is now a dancer, performs with her, which has elevated their experience by sharing heightened energy, thus making the performances more about life. Tirado states that for her, "flamenco is honest; your personal everything, everything you have lived. It cannot be faked with a pasted on smile and a flower in the hair." Haesen opines that "flamenco is like the Bermuda Triangle—it pulls you in so hard, you cannot get out." For these artists, no other life could possibly compare.

All five of the interviewed dancers find themselves frequently competing with Carmen and facing economic obstacles as they strive to convey the function of Spanish culture in flamenco to students as well as fickle, uneducated audiences. Tirado and Granjero compete with major stars in Spain as they strive to establish a viable base for their own companies. Haesen and Weekes explore new ways of using the language of flamenco to increase performance opportunities. While the commercial tendencies of marketplaces might be formidable, all these performers feel that not dancing flamenco would be worse. These five dancers persist in spite of obstructions, detours, and scarce opportunities. To succeed, they must constantly seek out new and unusual paths to carve inroads into the unstable art world. Furthermore, they must continually educate the public to maintain a market that will support new and innovative work. Those who reside outside of flamenco communities, like Haesen, also struggle to find other flamenco musicians and singers with whom to perform. Or, if a dancer can build a strong base, as Encinias did with her impressive ability to create a flamenco empire, then, Encinias said with a gleam in her eye, an artist can be optimistic and plot to train guitarists to "accompany the 50 million dancers emerging from the Albuquerque schools and then look for ways to educate flamenco singers."

NOTES

1. Francisco Franco was the conservative, military dictator of Spain from 1936 until his death in 1975. His fascist rule repressed Spain's growth in the twentieth century and his iron-fisted rule was greatly feared.
2. *Tablaos* are bars/restaurants that feature flamenco shows and typically have a raised wooden platform for the performers. In the traditional setting of *tablaos*, the dancers, singers, and musicians are seated on chairs arranged at the back of the stage. Everyone supports those taking a solo through rhythmic hand clapping, or *palmas*, and *jaleo*, encouraging shouts that increase the energy of the shows.
3. For example, flamenco festivals appear in Bolivia (http://www.la-razon.com/index.php?_url=/la_revista/flamenco-festival-bolivia_0_2385361504.html); in Tokyo (http://www.

flamencofestival.org/eng/noticias/flamenco-festival-tokio-115/); in Vancouver, Canada (http://www.vancouverflamencofestival.org/); and in Morocco (http://www.africanindy.com/chillout/top-10-festivals-that-move-africa-5187773), where flamenco singer Diego el Cigala was featured in the Fez Festival of World Sacred Music.

4. Mitchell cites Manuel Bernal Rodriguez's statistics that there are more than eight hundred travel narratives written by foreign tourists.

5. From living and traveling in Europe for several decades, I observed cultural differences in the way people move. Spanish people do not move expansively; the angle at which women hold their fans is a distinctive extension of their arms, their posture is erect, and their heads are usually held high.

6. In addition to the thousands of interpretations of Bizet's opera performed since its debut in 1875, ballet choreographers who have tacked the Carmen theme include Roland Petit of France (https://www.youtube.com/watch?v=dwZkITTBTtU) and Carlos Acosta from Cuba (https://www.youtube.com/watch?v=6gxAoknp7HM). Other dance styles tackled this story as well: a hip-hop version by Annemarieke Moes was presented in the Netherlands (https://www.youtube.com/watch?v=IUQZOfFSsHQ); a Bollywood spectacle was choreographed by Honey Kalaria (https://www.youtube.com/watch?v=MfxyQpiAGFA); and numerous flamenco productions such as Carlos Saura's 1983 movie, choreographed by Antonio Gades (https://www.youtube.com/watch?v=c3IDqF27ues), which was my personal catalyst into the flamenco world.

7. Elvis Presley, who died August 16, 1977, made rock and roll's African American roots palpable for white audiences with his unique style of singing with gyrating hips. He was extremely popular from the 1950s until his death and was dubbed "the King." The Western world went into mourning when he died. Radio stations across the United States immediately began playing his songs. Thousands of weeping fans from around the world descended on his home in Memphis, Tennessee, necessitating a call for control by the local police. It is estimated that over 80,000 people attended his funeral while millions more watched the events on television (http://entertainment.howstuffworks.com/elvis-presley-biography36.htm).

8. The Sevillanas is the national dance of Spain and is widely danced at *férias* (fairs) and in clubs. It is a dance for couples and is often one of the first dances students learn. Typically, it is composed of four short choreographies known as *coplas*.

9. I interviewed Martine Haesen on July 20, 2016. In this case and with quotations from other dancers whom I interviewed, to avoid repetition I will only provide the interview date with the first quotation.

10. *Riverdance* is an international production based on traditional Irish dance and music. It debuted in 1994 and became a worldwide phenomenon by 1995. Incorporating related dance forms like flamenco and tap dance, *Riverdance* appeared on the David Letterman show in 1996 and had a run on Broadway in 2000. *Riverdance*, September 30, 2016 (http://riverdance.com/historical-cast-list-1995-to-date/).

11. I interviewed Nélida Tirado on July 30, 2016.

12. Flamenco dresses typically feature many layers of ruffles and ruffled underskirts. These costumes have undergone changes in style throughout the years, from floor length to knee height in the 1960s, to skirts that fit tightly across the hips and thighs. In spite of the length, most flamenco skirts have some ruffles or flounces. Skirt work is considered a marked characteristic of flamenco dance, as female *bailarinas* will sinuously move the ruffles in serpentine patterns around their bodies. One of the most recognized skirts is the *bata*

de cola, the dress with the long train covered in ruffles on both top and bottom. It might be anywhere from two to eight feet long and requires much practice to avoid tripping or getting it caught on the heel of the shoe.

13. This is one of my personal experiences while performing in a restaurant in Albany, New York, in the late 1990s.

14. The Alegrías is considered a light (as opposed to deep or heavy) flamenco *palo*, or form. It is one of the most highly structured *palos*, consisting of long, sung verses, a substantial heelwork section, and a *silencio*, or adagio section where the guitarist might insert complicated melodies.

15. As of October 2016, the companies in New Mexico include Granjero's Entreflamenco, Juan Siddi Flamenco Santa Fe, Jesús Muñoz Flamenco, and the National Institute of Flamenco, which supports five flamenco companies including Yjastros, a professional company currently (October 2016) employing nine full-time dancers and five apprentices.

16. I interviewed Antonio Granjero and his wife, Estefania Ramirez, at their as yet unopened *tablao* in Santa Fe on July 14, 2016.

17. I interviewed Esther Weekes on July 6, 2016.

18. Josephine Baker was a black American singer/dancer from St. Louis who achieved fame and fortune in the jazz scene of Paris in the 1920s. While she faced less racial prejudice in France than in the United States, she was positioned by the public as an exotic figure, made popular through her banana dance, performed topless with a belt of cloth bananas around her hips. Baker spent most of her life in France and served in the French underground fighting against the Nazi occupation of France.

19. *Soniquete*, or swing, is a quality in flamenco that propels the rhythms with identifiable impulses on specific beats of the music. It influences where a dancer places his or her emphases in the movements.

20. Flamenco forms cover a spectrum of light dances (*chico*) like tangos and rumbas, deep forms (*jondo*) like Soleares, Siguiriyas, and Peteneras, and Gypsy styles like Bulerías and Alegrías. The names of the forms (*palos*) are plural because they are typically composed of unrelated sung verses. Each form has its own rhythmic emphasis and sound.

21. I interviewed Eva Encinias on July 11, 2016, at the National Institute of Flamenco in Albuquerque, New Mexico.

22. Encinias literally knocked on doors all over Albuquerque and located funding sources from a variety of city offices, including Albuquerque's Chamber of Commerce, the city's Hispanic Chamber of Commerce, and from many local businesses and patrons.

References

Alberts, Hana R. 2014. "Illuminating New York City's Gentrification One Story at a Time." *New York Times*, November 5. http://ny.curbed.com/2014/11/5/10026820/illuminating-new-york-citys-gentrification-one-story-at-a-time. Accessed October 13, 2016.

Aoyama, Yuko. 2007. "The Role of Consumption and Globalization in a Cultural Industry: The Case of Flamenco." *Geoforum* 38(1): 103–113. https://www.researchgate.net/publication/222613105_The_Role_of_Consumption_and_Globalization_in_a_Cultural_Industry_The_Case_of_Flamenco. Accessed August 12, 2016.

Barzel, Ann. 1944. "European Dance Teachers in the United States." *Dance Index* 3(4–6): 56–100.

Bennahum, Ninotchka Devorah. 2000. *Antonia Mercé "La Argentina": Flamenco and the Spanish Avant Garde*. Hanover, NH: University Press of New England.

Bennahum, Ninotchka Devorah. 2013. *Carmen: A Gypsy Geography*. Middletown, CT: Wesleyan University Press.

Centro Cultural el Monte. 2007. *La Sevilla de Richard Ford 1830–1833*, edited by Fundación el Monte. Seville: Pinelo Talleres Gráficos.

DePersio, Greg. 2015. "America's Poorest States in 2015." *Investopedia*, August 6. http://www.investopedia.com/articles/investing/080615/americas-poorest-states-2015.asp?ad=dirN&q o=investopediaSiteSearch&qsrc=0&o=40186. Accessed October 18, 2016.

Dunning, Jennifer. 2008. "Last Dance: A Studio Tears up Its Floors." *New York Times*, February 8. http://www.nytimes.com/2008/02/09/arts/dance/09fazi.html. Accessed August 16, 2016.

Editorial Board. 2016. "Saving a New York Neighborhood from Gentrification." *New York Times*, April 23. http://www.nytimes.com/2016/04/23/opinion/saving-a-new-york-neighborhood-from-gentrification.html?_r=1. Accessed October 13, 2016.

Entreflamenco. 2016. Program for Summer Season. *Flamenco*. Santa Fe, NM: Spanish Danzart Society.

Flamenco Vivo Carlota Santana. http://www.flamenco-vivo.org/carlota-santana. Accessed October 2, 2016.

Gould, Evlyn. 1996. *The Fate of Carmen*. Baltimore, MD: Johns Hopkins University Press.

Hayes, Michelle Hefner. 2015. "Choreographing Contemporaneity: Cultural Legacy and Experimental Imperative." In *Flamenco on the Global Stage: Historical, Critical and Theoretical Perspectives*, edited by K. Meira Goldberg, Ninotchka Devorah Bennahum, and Michelle Heffner Hayes, 280–291. Jefferson, NC: McFarland.

Kamen, Henry. 2005. *Spain 1469–1714: A Society of Conflict*, 3rd edition. Harlow, UK: Pearson Longman.

Leblon, Bernard. 1995. *Gypsies and Flamenco*. Hatfield, UK: Gypsy Research Center; University of Hertfordshire Press.

Lorca, Federico García. [1975] 1998. *In Search of Duende*, translated by Christopher Maurer. New York: New Directions.

Machado y Álvarez, Antonio "Demófilo." 1881. *Colección de cantes flamencos*, 3rd edition. Madrid: Ediciones Demófilo.

Mackrell, Judith. 2014. "Rocío Molina: Flamenco and Beyond." *The Guardian*, October 15. https://www.theguardian.com/stage/2014/oct/15/rocio-molina-flamenco-bosque-ardora. Accessed September 11, 2017.

Mitchell, Timothy. 1994. *Flamenco Deep Song*. New Haven, CT: Yale University Press.

Navarro García, José Luis. 2002. *De Telethusa á La Macarrona: Bailes andaluces y flamencos*. Seville: Portada Editorial.

Newman, Kathe, and Elvin Wyly. 2005. "Gentrification and Resistance in New York City." *NHI Shelterforce Online* 142. http://nhi.org/online/issues/142/gentrification.html. Accessed October 13, 2016.

Orellana, Rocío Plaza. 2015. "Spanish Dance in Europe: From the Late Eighteenth Century to Its Consolidation on the European Stage." In *Flamenco on the Global Stage: Historical, Critical and Theoretical Perspectives*, edited by K. Meira Goldberg, Ninotchka Devorah Bennahum, and Michelle Heffner Hayes, 71–80. Jefferson, NC: McFarland.

Ortiz Nuevo, José Luis, and Núñez, Faustino. 1998. *La Rabia del Placer: El origen cubano del tango y su desembarco in España (1823–1923)*. Seville: Diputación de Sevilla, Área de cultura.

Pérez, Jorge. 2015. "Flamenco Fusion: Cross-Cultural Conditions and the Art of Raising Consciousness." In *Flamenco on the Global Stage: Historical, Critical and Theoretical Perspectives*, edited by K. Meira Goldberg, Ninotchka Devorah Bennahum, and Michelle Heffner Hayes, 252–259. Jefferson, NC: McFarland.

Pohren, Donn. [1962] 1990. *The Art of Flamenco.* Madrid: Society of Spanish Studies.

RAND Corporation. 2001. *The Performing Arts in a New Era.* Full report by Kevin F. McCarthy, Arthur Brooks, Julia Lowell, and Laura Zakaras. Santa Monica, CA: RAND. http://www.rand.org/pubs/monograph_reports/MR1367.html. Accessed September 30, 2106.

Riesenfeld, Janet. 1938. *Dancer in Madrid.* New York: Funk & Wagnalls.

Steingress, Gerhard. 1998. *Sobre flamenco y flamencología.* Seville: Signature Ediciones de Andalucía.

Schwab, Kristin. 2016. "How We Choose Our 25 to Watch." *Dance Magazine,* December 30. http://dancemagazine.com/views/how-we-choose-our-25-to-watch/. Accessed October 12, 2016.

Trading Economics. 2016. "Spain Unemployment Rate." Last modified September 2016. http://www.tradingeconomics.com/spain/unemployment-rate.

Audiovisual Sources

BBC 3: Bollywood Carmen: Honey Kalaria and Stars in Bradford. 2013. YouTube video, 12:26. Posted by "Honey Kalaria," September 9. https://www.youtube.com/watch?v=MfxyQpiAGFA. Accessed January 27, 2017.

"Carmen" Hiphop Choreography by Annemarieke Moes. 2011. YouTube video, 2:34. Posted by "Annemarieke Moes," July 7. https://www.youtube.com/watch?v=IUQZOfFSsHQ. Accessed January 27, 2017.

Carmen Trailer 1983. 2014. YouTube video, 1:41. Posted by "Video Detective," October 8. https://www.youtube.com/watch?v=c3IDqF27ues. Accessed January 27, 2017.

An Introduction to Carlos Acosta's Carmen (The Royal Ballet). 2015. YouTube video, 5:43. Posted by "Royal Opera House," November 12. https://www.youtube.com/watch?v=6gxAoknp7HM. Accessed January 27, 2017.

Laurent Hilaire and Alessandra Ferri: George Bizet—Carmen (choreography Roland Petit). 2013. YouTube video, 6:13. Posted by "Lila," April 7. https://www.youtube.com/watch?v=dwZkITTBTtU. Accessed January 27, 2017.

PART II

RE-CHOREOGRAPHING AND RE-PRESENTATION FOR THE COMPETITION FRAME

CHAPTER 6

···

REAPPROPRIATING CHOREOGRAPHIES OF AUTHENTICITY IN MEXICO
Competitions and the Dance of the Old Men

···

RUTH HELLIER-TINOCO

ZACÁN ARTISTIC CONTEST OF THE P'URHÉPECHA PEOPLE

···

IN the highlands of the state of Michoacán, Mexico, in the village of Zacán, a large, covered auditorium reverberates with the buzz of laughter, music, and rhythmic foot-stamping. Several thousand audience members are gathered, wrapped in thick jackets to resist the cold night air. On stage a straggly line of four masked old men stumble and shuffle into the performance space. With backs curved, they support themselves on roughly hewn walking sticks sculpted from upturned roots. Their toothy grins light up their rosy faces, as their long white hair hangs over their shoulders. Costumed in white shirts and baggy trousers, neatly embroidered in geometric cross-stitch around wrists and ankles, each wears a matching bright woolen *gabán* (poncho).[1] Their heads are topped with large straw hats covered in rainbow-colored ribbons tumbling over their faces. With faltering steps, the men stagger to the center of the platform. Each dancer wears leather sandals with thick wooden soles that clatter noisily and unevenly, accentuating each footfall. A hush of anticipation descends over the expectant crowd.

A strident chord on violin, vihuela, and bass shatters the muted silence and the old men begin to dance, the vigorous rhythm of their footwork equal to that of the music. Stamping, hopping, and creating complex figures, they display a remarkable degree of energy for such seemingly elderly men.[2] After vigorously dancing for two minutes, the piece comes to a distinctive end: close, open, close. The dancers' knees apparently give way under their weight and they stagger about, barely able to stand, in a display of exhaustion and heavy breathing. A ripple of laughter and clapping flows through the audience. After gathering their strength, the dancers begin again, breaking into frenetic, rhythmic, and precise footwork. They execute two more set pieces and, to tumultuous applause, the dancers raise their hats above their heads and stumble off stage.[3] In the center of the auditorium just in front of the stage, a line of judges makes notes and confers. Members of the crowd stand, move around, talk loudly, purchase snacks, and then settle back in their seats.

The contest performance re-commences: a straggly line of four masked old men stumble and shuffle into the performance space. With backs curved, they support themselves on roughly hewn walking sticks sculpted from upturned roots. Their toothy grins light up their rosy faces, as their long white hair hangs over their shoulders. This scenario is repeated each year as part of the two-day Artistic Contest of the P'urhépecha People (El Concurso Artístico del Pueblo P'urhépecha) in Zacán (Figure 6.1).[4] This event, which serves as a festival, contest, and fiesta, includes dance groups, music ensembles and singers, athletes, food, fireworks, stalls, fun-fair rides, and Roman Catholic masses.

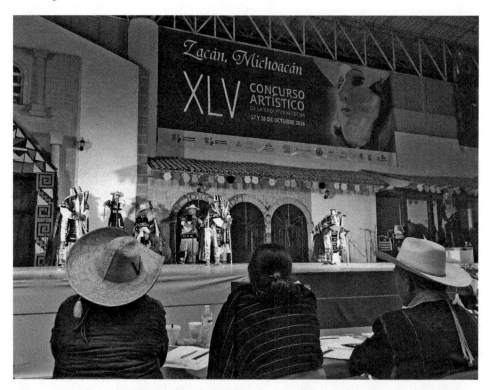

FIGURE 6.1. The ensemble Tzipikua, Los Viejos Alegres, performing the Dance of the Old Men at the Zacán Artistic Contest of the P'urhépecha People, 18 October, 2016, Zacán, Michoacán, México. Tzipikua is led by Procopio Patricio Cázares from the Island of Jarácuaro, Lake Pátzcuaro. They were the winners of the 2016 Tata Gervasio López prize.

Control through Competitions

The opening description centers on the Dance of the Old Men of Jarácuaro: *la Danza de los Viejitos de Jarácuaro*. It is performed by different groups during the course of the contest, forming a key part of the dance repertoire classified as "authentic P'urhépecha dance."[5] In this chapter I focus my attention on issues that arise through this and other competition contexts incorporating the Dance of the Old Men. I specifically discuss the operation of state and local power; appropriation and reappropriation; authority and authorship; and processes of authentication and authenticity.

Throughout the twentieth century and into the twenty-first, dance competitions have been an indispensable element in multiple Mexican contexts. They encompass a range of dance genres, including modern, folkloric, and ballet, and take place through local village socio-religious fiestas, governmental tourist displays, school exhibitions, and nationally televised contests.[6] Dance competitions serve as choreographic archival repertoires, and they exercise control over tradition versus innovation. Although they generate visibility and dissemination of the dance, they also perform a substantial fixing and perpetuation of a set repertoire. The circulation of a *convocatoria*, a call for contestants, which stipulates judging and contestant criteria, is a ubiquitous element in all competitions. By setting out criteria, these *convocatorias* enable dancers and choreographers to enter a competition knowing the specific requirements, rules, objectives, prizes, and rewards. Convocatorias are used by most dance organizations, institutes, and cultural governmental agencies. They provide clear guidelines, including overt calls for what should be danced (from new choreography to explicit demands for traditional practice) and definitions of who is eligible to dance.

Although dance contests generally have explicit financial reward through prize monies, the economic consequences are multiple and diverse. While I do not overtly deal with economics in this chapter, I draw attention to financial factors inherent in competitions involving the Dance of the Old Men (see Hellier-Tinoco 2011). As cultural theorist Néstor García Canclini (1993, 11) notes, separating areas of culture and economics is a false divide, for "in reality, economy and culture march along intertwined with one another . . . any cultural fact . . . always leads to an implicit socioeconomic level . . . [and] any practice is simultaneously economic and symbolic." As the Dance of the Old Men closely intersects with the tourist industry, incorporating competitions as tourist display, the financial implications are considerable.

Within these competition frameworks, issues of appropriation, authority, and authenticity are multifaceted, intersected, and contradictory, particularly when issues of ethnicity and race are involved. Appropriation is a common strategy in the construction of national repertories and tourist attractions, with the exhibition and display of dance as key to these processes (see Kirshenblatt-Gimblet 1998). Authenticity is a socially constructed category, the meanings of which are negotiable. Where dance is concerned, costumes, music, and choreography can serve as markers of the "authentic," yet, as anthropologist Jane Desmond (1999, xix) has noted, "it is the physical presence of *some* bodies, not others, which functions as the ultimate grounding for these notions of the 'authentic.'"[7] Within the competition frame, the historical foundation of movement practices classified as "Indigenous" is crucial to authentication, and ownership of movement effectively passes from individual bodies to a "nation." In this chapter, however, I discuss how these dancing bodies create opportunities for revitalization, self-legitimation, and resistance.

THE MOST REPRESENTATIVE DANCE

The P'urhépecha peoples are one of over sixty Indigenous societies living in present-day Mexico, with a population of about 130,000, many of whom speak the P'urhépecha language. The P'urhépecha region lies some 230 miles west of Mexico City (see Figure 6.2); it comprises four zones that include the Lake Pátzcuaro area (with six inhabited islands, of which the Island of Jarácuaro is one) and the highlands (which embrace the

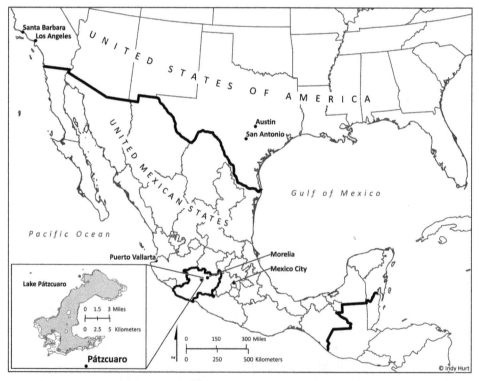

FIGURE 6.2. Map of Mexico and the southern United States, with inset of Lake Pátzcuaro.

Map by Indy Hurt. Used with permission.

FIGURE 6.3. Map of the State of Michoacán, Mexico, marking Lake Pátzcuaro, Zacán, and other communities in the P'urhépecha region.

Map by Indy Hurt. Used with permission.

village of Zacán) (Figure 6.3). Prior to the Spanish incursion in the sixteenth century, the mighty P'urhépecha empire covered a much larger landmass, with the grand capital city of Tzintzuntzan located on the edge of Lake Pátzcuaro. In 1530, even though the civilization was decimated, the P'urhépecha peoples survived, albeit under colonial rule from the Iberian Peninsula, followed by national rule after independence. Since the last decades of the twentieth century, a movement for the autonomy of the P'urhépecha nation has grown in strength and numbers, with its four-color flag (green, blue, purple, yellow) and insignia much in evidence.[8] The ritual ceremony of the P'urhépecha New Year, reintroduced in 1984, has become a potent performance of autonomous self-identification.

In the twenty-first century, multiple dance and musical practices are embedded in village life. Yet despite this diversity, only one "representative" dance is associated with the P'urhépecha peoples and indeed the whole state of Michoacán: the Dance of the Old Men of Jarácuaro. In the early 1920s, in the aftermath of the Mexican Revolution, a *dance of old men* was appropriated and utilized by centralized government officials as part of nation-building processes for the repertoire of national dances. A version of the dance from the Island of Jarácuaro was fixed and disseminated through state-controlled processes as a potent icon of *mexicanidad* and *lo mexicano*: that which is deemed to be wholly and authentically Mexican. Simultaneously, the Dance of the Old Men was promoted as an icon of Mexico for the burgeoning tourist industry, with the goal of attracting both national and international tourists. In serving these aims, the Dance of the Old Men usefully embodied notions of Indigenousness, authenticity, rurality, folklore, and "the past." Importantly, the lattice of significations generated in the early 1920s is still in place today.[9] Through the ninety-year trajectory as a nationalist and touristic dance, both state and local competitions have played a strategic role in shaping and perpetuating choreographic, performative, and signifying elements of the Dance of the Old Men.

For my discussion in this chapter, I draw on my long-term research examining contexts and processes of nationalism and tourism, specifically in relation to the Dance of the Old Men of the Island of Jarácuaro and the celebration of Night of the Dead of the Island of Janitzio.[10] I employ participant-observation methods (including playing the violin with an ensemble from the Island of Jarácuaro),[11] interviews, article and object analysis (tourist paraphernalia, films, brochures), and documental archival work (news media, audio recordings, and government documents).

To explore the ramifications of dance and competition, I discuss five case studies of contests involving the Dance of the Old Men, moving chronologically from the 1930s to the present day. The first example was organized in 1931 by the Cultural Missions of the Ministry of Education, in which local P'urhépecha groups from the Lake Pátzcuaro area competed in the village of Tzintzuntzan. This case study reveals a nationalizing framework in operation. The second case examines contest publications produced in the 1950s (which include choreographic notation and documentation) for national school contests of regional dance. Examples three and four are both located in the Pátzcuaro area. The third looks at contests as performative exhibitions for national and international tourists to the Lake Pátzcuaro region for the festivities of Night of the Dead from the 1960s onward. And the fourth case study focuses on contests for P'urhépecha peoples (rather than tourists) as performers and audience, but these are organized by the National Indigenist Institute. In the fifth example, I return to the Zacán Artistic Contest of the P'urhépecha People.

APPROPRIATION AND RIVALRY

Before turning to the five case studies, I briefly provide two contextualizing frameworks: first, the national processes of appropriation in Mexico; and second, competitive elements of local P'urhépecha fiestas. The first offers insights into the long-term trajectory of nationalizing processes and shaping of this dance within macro political and ideological contexts. The second gives an explanation of ways in which competitiveness and rivalry are inherently part of local P'urhépecha fiesta environments, rather than being a model imposed during nationalizing processes.

Appropriation: Inculcating National Identity and Tourist Attractions through Dance

The nationalistic role of the Dance of the Old Men was initiated in the post-revolutionary years of the 1920s. Following the Mexican Revolution, a period of intense nation-building ensued, with governmental agents shaping a sense of "authentic Mexicanness." Tangible manifestations of Mexicanness were necessary to inculcate unity and patriotism as Mexico was (and remains) a country of great diversity. Given the multiplicity of peoples, issues of race, ethnicity, and class were at the heart of nationalist agendas. Paradoxical positions regarded Indigenous peoples as holding back the country, while also being the future of the country through their link with the prehispanic past. Indigenous peoples were incorporated into the nation (for progress, modernization, and economic advancement), even as the ideology of *mestizaje* promoted a mixed nation of mestizo peoples.[12]

As attributes for Mexicanness emphasized Indigenous and rural forms, so the notion of authenticity was a key element. A set of cultural artifacts (music, dance, food, clothes) was ascribed authenticity through governmental processes of authentication, labeling, and framing what should be read as authentic or not (García Canclini 1993; González 2010; Gutiérrez 2010; Hellier-Tinoco 2011; Vaughan 1997; Vaughan and Lewis 2006). Appropriating and disseminating dance practices as authentically Mexican was an important element in constructing national identity. The shaping of a national repertoire of dances in part took place through festivals, displays, and contests. These processes of appropriation and dissemination in the 1920s and 1930s were so successful that the repertoire of folkloric dances performed in the twenty-first century by multiple folklórico ensembles[13] was already established and fixed by the end of the 1930s.[14] For example, in 1937 and 1939, a series of theatricalized performances titled *Danzas Auténticas Mexicanas* (Authentic Mexican Dances), staged in the governmental Palacio de Bellas Artes (Palace of Fine Arts) in Mexico City, included the Dance of the Old Men (Hellier-Tinoco 2011).

For the purposes of Mexican nationalism, the practices of the P'urhépecha peoples served as an ideal model of authentic indigeneity, even though they were viewed as in need of incorporation, assimilation, and modernization. As far as dance practices were concerned, although a great variety existed throughout the P'urhépecha region (mostly performed for socio-religious celebrations), one specific version of one dance became the most representative. In 1923, musician, dancer, and teacher Nicolás Bartolo Juárez of the Island of Jarácuaro came to the attention of governmental musicologist Rubén M. Campos through his local fame as a member of the family string quartet (Campos 1928). Campos visited Jarácuaro and witnessed a dance of old men led by Bartolo Juárez being danced in the streets. Subsequently, Bartolo Juárez was taken to Mexico City by state officials to teach the dance to a group of student teachers, who then performed for an audience of foreign dignitaries. Through these processes, *a* dance of old men became *the* Dance of the Old Men. With this event, a dance and music practice framed as

Indigenous was displayed on a stage as a representation of authentic Mexicanness for an outsider audience. Hence the dance became fixed, and a specific choreography was created, which transformed a free-form durational and processional dance into a temporally and spatially limited set of short pieces, each with their own defined patterns. This form became the model for future performances by multiple groups, ranging from folkloric ensembles to local P'urhépecha groups in the Lake Pátzcuaro region.

In the ensuing years, many activities, including contests, were organized that promoted and disseminated the Dance of the Old Men of Jarácuaro, particularly through governmental frameworks, including the Secretariat of Education (Secretaría de Educación Pública; SEP) and the Secretariat of Tourism. Therefore, contests were partly responsible for molding and legitimizing notions of authenticity by acting as value-laden and pedagogical frameworks for codifying the dance. Specific dance elements and aesthetics were promoted as more or less authentic in relation to Mexicanness and Indigenousness. For instance, most contests exercise control through precise criteria that construct and perpetuate those elements considered to be "valuable." Those specific elements receive higher marks in adjudication and, through these processes, reification takes place.

Competitiveness: Dance and Music in Local P'urhépecha Fiestas

While twentieth-century nationalistic and touristic contexts are one essential element for my discussion, a second framework is competitiveness in local P'urhépecha socio-religious fiestas. In particular, this overview provides a key for understanding both state-sanctioned dance contests and the Zacán Concurso in relation to the criteria for dance and music. Each village celebrates many special dates throughout the year, marking the major feast days of the Roman Catholic calendar. Dance and music form an integral part of these fiestas, which also usually encompass a Mass, feasting, and fireworks over the course of three days. The dances, performed by a group of villagers, serve as a religious fulfillment or promise (*una manda*), demonstrating gratitude through movement.[15] Music, on the other hand, is contracted out to P'urhépecha ensembles from the nearby region. One neighborhood (*barrio*) aims to demonstrate superiority over another through music. Perhaps the most intense example of this is the celebration of Corpus Christi, when as many as eight neighborhoods each contract a band, all of which play simultaneously in the village square after processing round the village. The musical repertoire includes three elements: new P'urhépecha compositions, classic P'urhépecha pieces, and other genres such as opera overtures and military band classics.

In less formal settings, music contests have also taken the form of *serenatas*, night-time events in which contracted musical ensembles from local villages compete for prestige, with judgment awarded by the villagers through applause. Again, the repertoire includes new and classic P'urhépecha compositions, along with many other genres.[16] In even more informal contexts, young men might while away the nights by singing *pirekuas* (songs in the P'urhépecha language) to the accompaniment of a guitar, with small groups or individuals standing on different corners, effectively competing with each other for recognition (Chamorro 1994).[17] Therefore both organized and informal contests have played, and continue to play, prominent roles in the cultural life of P'urhépecha communities. These local rivalries perpetuate, conserve, and modify dance practices, serving as a catalyst for change and a driving force for continuation and transmission.

From these two contextual frameworks that outline the nationalist and touristic agenda of the state to fix the Dance of the Old Men as authentic and Indigenous, along-side the local community interest in embracing the continuation and adaptation of the dance, I turn to five competition case studies to examine how different processes contributed to the construction of the Dance of the Old Men.

Five Competitions: From Local to Transnational, 1931–2016

One: Local Rivalries and the Educational Cultural Missions (1931)

In October 1931, a Dance Competition (*Concurso de Danza*) took place in the lakeside village of Tzintzuntzan, former capital of the P'urhépecha empire, where stone ruins of the vast ceremonial structures still remain. It was organized by the Cultural Missions (*Misiones Culturales*), an important strategic constituent of the nationalizing government under the auspices of the SEP.[18] With an almost religious fervor, the task of each team of teachers from the Cultural Missions was to provide practical, vocational, artistic, and general education to all inhabitants of a village over a three-year period. The overarching goals of the program were to reach every small community in Mexico and to bring about social change through pedagogic practice. During the Dance Competition, P'urhépecha villagers from local communities performed various dances, including the dance that had been appropriated by the government in 1923: the Dance of the Old Men. Indeed, the ensemble of Nicolás Bartolo Juárez won first place, with a group from the nearby village of Cucuchucho awarded second (Bartolo Juárez 1937). Therefore, this dance contest provided a seal of authentication to the person who first had been used to transmit the dance outside a socio-religious context. Notably, the SEP, one of the most powerful and important state institutions in the 1920s and 1930s, overtly controlled the context.

At this event, three of the teachers (Fernando Gamboa, Luis Felipe Obregón, and Santiago Arias Navarro) made detailed records and notation of the Dance of the Old Men as performed by Bartolo Juárez and his ensemble (Gamboa et al. n.d.). They documented the choreography (including floor patterns, steps, and figures) and costume, and wrote a brief narrative history of the dance. Significantly, this document was subsequently used as a resource by other teachers of the SEP, particularly through the General Directorate of Indigenous Affairs.[19]

Through this local yet government-organized contest, the dance and P'urhépecha village dancers from Lake Pátzcuaro were officially incorporated into national processes in their own locality. Although the dancers were not required to compete, local processes of rivalry ensured that the villagers demonstrated their own prowess. Yet, the presence of governmental representatives (the teachers) within the framework of a national pedagogical institution and their role in notating the Dance of the Old Men led directly to fixing and disseminating the dance for national educational competitions, as I describe in my second example.

Two: Didactic Publications and Boarding Schools, 1950s

From the 1930s onward, dance publications and contests fulfilled a symbiotic relationship, particularly concerning the Dance of the Old Men and the national folkloric dance repertoire. Through multiple didactic and populist publications, the Dance of the Old Men was fixed choreographically and was given a permanent place in the repertoire of representative Mexican dances. Each publication and contest contributed to the processes of essentialization and authentication by defining the origins, meanings, and choreographic notations of the dance. This consolidated the dance as an efficacious corporeal medium for creating a shared sense of belonging and for shaping a notion of Mexicanness in national and international contexts.[20]

Renowned dancer Josefina Lavalle observed that dance and music were taught in schools as an integral element of the nationalization processes (Lavalle 1988). The SEP instigated many processes to disseminate and inculcate officially sanctioned ideas (Lavalle 2002; Ramos Villalobos 2011). Throughout Mexico, school festivals of regional dance, summer courses, and diplomas in folkloric dance, all of which included competitive elements, promoted the importance of the Dance of the Old Men as representative of Michoacán. Indeed, when Amalia Hernández created the Ballet Folklórico de México in the late 1950s, the choreography for the Dance of the Old Men drew directly on a version danced in the 1920s and 1930s by Bartolo Juárez and the Orozcos of Jarácuaro, and by Antonio Pablo and his family of Cucuchucho, as danced and documented in the Lake Pátzcuaro Cultural Missions contests and as theatricalized in Mexico City events.[21]

This second example illustrates the importance of notation and documentation in relation to dance contests and the Dance of the Old Men. In 1958, the SEP published a book encompassing narrative descriptions, musical notation, and drawings of a selection of regional dances performed for national cultural and sporting contests in state-run boarding schools between 1953 and 1958 (Castro Agúndez 1958). All schools and pedagogical institutions directed through the SEP were instrumental in organizing contests and festivals of so-called regional dances, which included the Dance of the

Old Men. Boarding schools were particularly important in the transmission process, through the staging of contests and the production of audio recordings and descriptive documentation.

The published account of "The Old Men" (*Los Viejitos*) disseminated this dance as a key part of the national dance repertoire. The dance was labeled as P'urhépecha and, on the one hand, it was acknowledged as having a prominent place in programs of *costumbrista* exhibitions from the 1920s. This recognized its performance within theatricalized displays of local customs in Mexico City (Hellier-Tinoco 2011; Ortiz Bullé Goyri 2003, 2005). Yet, on the other hand, the description of the Dance of the Old Men referred to dance contexts relating to Roman Catholic celebratory days and seasons (Castro Agúndez 1958). Consequently, this reveals and perpetuates a partly invented history, which is promulgated to this day, particularly in *ballet folklórico* displays and contests in Mexico and the United States. The dissemination of notation and descriptions for use in competition contexts in schools therefore extended the notion of the "correct" way to execute the dance, ensuring that particular criteria were met, and circulating this fixed version in state schools throughout Mexico. As such, the Dance of the Old Men, as form and context, was increasingly recognized by a broader range of Mexican citizens, with further repercussions for the national tourist industry, as evidenced in my third example.[22]

Three: Lake Pátzcuaro for Tourists

The Dance of the Old Men as representative of the state of Michoacán and the P'urhépecha peoples continued to proliferate, and my third example considers the dance contests designed to engage tourists. Such performances of the dance function not only to attract international tourists, but also to lead Mexican visitors to iconic areas publicized as authentically Mexican. Dance can provide visitors with experiences of authenticity and "otherness" (Desmond 1997), and dance competitions can afford tourist audiences a contained and overt space of easy gratification, through strategic terms such as "traditional," "original," "ritual," and "local." Significantly, dance contests can also act as a form of mutual cultural affirmation, simultaneously generating income for the dancers, while providing the tourists with their preconceived display of the local spectacle.

From the 1920s onward, the Mexican nationalist processes for shaping an authentically Mexican dance repertoire intersected, and at times merged, with a state-driven tourism trajectory through the development and dissemination of tourist attractions for national and international visitors. The Dance of the Old Men of Jarácuaro, as part of the repertoire of national dances, was of key importance in entertaining tourists and providing an overtly authenticated Indigenous dance. Crucially, the Lake Pátzcuaro region itself, specifically the tiny Island of Janitzio, was promoted as a tourist destination. During the 1920s, the celebration of the Night of the Dead on the Island of Janitzio was strategically appropriated by state processes and transformed into an icon of folkloric nationalism.[23] The island itself, as site and sight, was developed as a tourist attraction from the 1930s onward through the building of a huge statue in its center (Hellier-Tinoco 2011). Over the decades, visitor numbers to the island for Night of the Dead increased, reaching tens of thousands in the 1960s. This triggered the instigation of an official, government-funded Festival and Contest of Music and Dance to provide entertainment for the sightseers. As the years passed, the locations of the Festival and Contest were augmented to include Pátzcuaro, Tzintzuntzan, and other islands.

Although the contests continue in the twenty-first century, my examples are from the decade of the 1990s. As with all dance contests, *convocatorias* were circulated and panels of judges selected. Contests included traditional dances (*danzas tradicionales*) and P'urhépecha songs and ensembles (*pirekuas y orquestas*).[24] P'urhépecha villagers from many of the islands, as well as lakeside and lake-region communities, presented dance and music performances. Some ensembles existed prior to the event, whereas others were formed specifically for the contest. These contests encouraged and supported creativity through the composition of new dances and music expressly for the occasion, particularly based on using local work activities as the movement vocabulary. For example, the Dance of the *Huacaleros* simulated the transportation of *huacales*, or wooden crates, containing heavy pottery items made in the lakeside village of Santa Fe. Fishing activities were featured in dances of The Fish (*Pescado*), Traveling Fisherman (*Pescador Navegante*), and *Chinchorros* and *Mariposas* (types of fishing nets).[25] One P'urhépecha man from the Island of Jarácuaro, Gervasio López, who was well known and who appeared in official governmental events as a representative of the Dance of the Old Men, created and choreographed the Dance of the Sowers (*La Danza de los Sembradores*) with his sons, performing the family agricultural activity through dance.[26] Other dances drew on existing socio-religious dances, such as those danced for Carnival.

Through the interface of real life and the re-enactment of work activities in dance, the visitors' experience centered on a complex and contradictory mix of overt and covert display and exhibition. This relied on a network of associations that engaged notions of Indigenousness, ancient tradition, authenticity, mysticism, pre-Catholicism, and pre-modern activities (MacCannell 1973, 1999, 2001). This touristic dance competition provided an environment for the local population to generate new choreographies specifically for the event, and even encouraged villagers who had previously not performed beyond village contexts to dance for unknown visitor audiences. The reward of prize money formed a particularly important incentive to participate, and the openness of the judging enabled a wide range of choreographies. Yet, despite the variety of dances presented, the Dance of the Old Men was already deeply embedded in the visitor consciousness as *the* most representative, authentic, and traditional dance, and thus performances of this dance received the most attention and applause. In this case, the dance competition context enabled creativity, but did not alter the predominance of the Dance of the Old Men. This sits in contrast with a series of local contests in the town of Pátzcuaro, held during the same decade but for local audiences only, which serves as my next case study.

Four: Lake Pátzcuaro for Locals

While large tourist-oriented contests were held during the Night of the Dead, another series of contests was organized in the 1990s through a different governmental body, the National Indigenist Institute (Instituto Nacional Indigenista; INI).[27] These local contests took place in the town of Pátzcuaro; however, in contrast to the touristic competitions, the INI contest was specifically organized for P'urhépecha dancers, musicians, and audiences. Held in the grounds of the INI premises in Pátzcuaro, the dance and music contests took place on the basketball court, the usual location for village socio-religious dances. The space was transformed with a painted backcloth that depicted a scenario of Lake Pátzcuaro, showing local men and women fishing and dancing (Figure 6.4). Stalls serving food and displaying craftwork from many areas of the P'urhépecha region were set out nearby.

As usual, a *convocatoria* was circulated throughout the P'urhépecha region, setting out the categories for contestants, the judging criteria, and the money prizes. On the day of the contest, dance groups and musical ensembles performed and competed

FIGURE 6.4. The Genaro Camilo family of the Island of Urandén perform the Dance of the Old Men in 1997 in Pátzcuaro. The occasion was an all-day competition event for P'urhépecha contestants and audiences, organized by, and held in the grounds of the National Indigenist Institute (INI), Pátzcuaro. A *chinchorro* fishing net, usually deployed on the nearby lake, was strung up over the basketball court, with a painted backdrop depicting the Island of Janitzio and the Dance of the Fish (*Pescado*) acting as scene-setter.

Photography by Ruth Hellier-Tinoco. Used with permission.

within formal categories: traditional dances (*danzas tradicionales*); brass and wind bands (*bandas*); mixed string, wind, and brass ensembles (*orquestas*); string groups (*conjuntos*); and singers of P'urhépecha songs (*pireris*). A panel of judges sat at a table at one end of the basketball court, facing the performers and the backdrop. Informal rows of chairs were set out around three sides of the court, and audience members came and went throughout the day. The master of ceremonies introduced each group in the P'urhépecha language, with translations provided in Spanish, thereby establishing this as a contest for and with P'urhépecha people. Contestants traveled not only from the local P'urhépecha Lake Pátzcuaro region, but also from the P'urhépecha highlands. Dances therefore included those often presented for the touristic Night of the Dead contests, and also dances from the highlands, including the Kurpitis, which are significant in the Zacán Contest. Various ensembles performed the Dance of the Old Men and, in a context reminiscent of the early 1930s, ensembles from the Islands of Urandén and Jarácuaro competed against each other. Despite the close proximity to the tourists visiting Pátzcuaro and Janitzio, within the privacy of the INI compound the Dance of the Old Men functioned as an activity entirely for local P'urhépecha spectators and participants, yet still functioning within a governmental framework. The competition context provided an incentive to participate (and to gain prestige and a win a small monetary prize), although the environment was low key and informal, and the judging criteria somewhat hazy. The Dance of the Old Men was present, but was simply one among many dances, thereby providing a sense of re-signification. As I come to my final example, I show how these processes are fulfilled in the Zacán Contest.

Five: Zacán Artistic Contest of the P'urhépecha People

Returning now to the dance competition mentioned in the opening vignette, I describe how the Zacán Artistic Contest of the P'urhépecha People provides evidence of reappropriation and self-designation. This happens through the unique nature of this community contest within the socio-religious fiesta framework. Zacán is a small village in the P'urhépecha sierra (west of Uruapan), located in the folds of the volcano Paricutín, which erupted in 1943.[28] As a result of the eruption, local people lost terrain, and traditional village fiestas in the vicinity were affected when people moved away from the area to look for land and work elsewhere.[29] In 1971, a group of professional P'urhépecha men from Zacán, all of whom had left the region at a young age, instigated the Zacán event after sensing an uncertainty of identity among the young P'urhépecha people and perceiving that their traditions were being replaced by non-P'urhépecha dance and music. They therefore decided to rescue and re-cultivate certain customs through reinstating a traditional fiesta (Aguilera Ortiz 1985). Through the celebration of the patron saint of the village, Saint Lucas (October 17–18), they established the Artistic

Festival of the P'urhépecha People and modeled the event on the usual practices for Saints' Days.

At first it was to be an occasion solely for the people of Zacán and other local communities in the P'urhépecha highlands. Transport and roads in the region made travel extremely difficult; therefore any expectation of wider participation was unlikely. Music, dance, food, and fireworks were all important elements of the festivities and, as with most traditional fiestas, a dance and music *concurso* (contest) also featured, with participants competing for prestige and prize money. Local groups performed one after the other in front of a small community audience on the basketball court. The competition element enabled many groups to perform, offering a forum for comparison and exhibition, and serving as a point of reunion and cohesion for the local community members. One particular masked dance from this area of the P'urhépecha highlands, the Kurpitis, became a core element.[30] Although not the focus of this chapter, the characterizations, choreographies, and costumes for this dance are highly distinctive.[31]

By the mid-1980s, the number of people attending the event had increased to such an extent that a stage and auditorium were erected for the contest, and in the first decade of the 2000s this was expanded to a large stage within a specially constructed auditorium that was capable of accommodating a crowd of thousands. During the contest, groups performed a series of pieces according to certain categories. A panel of judges awarded marks and, as with most competitions, the power to judge and control criteria was, and remains, a central component. In order to explore the significance of this contest for the P'urhépecha people, I consider four important aspects of the dance event.

First I look to "Tata" Gervasio López and the naming of a contest prize.[32] The Dance of the Old Men of Jarácuaro was danced in the Zacán Contest from the 1980s onward (Figure 6.5). Significantly, the ensemble of "Tata" Gervasio López from Jarácuaro was one of the main groups competing with this dance initially (Figure 6.6). López was the man most represented as synonymous with the Dance of the Old Men of Jarácuaro from the mid-1950s until his death in November 1999. López grew up on the Island of Jarácuaro where, under the tutelage of Bartolo Juárez, he was involved with the Dance of the Old Men from an early age. He formed his own ensemble in the 1950s, particularly incorporating his sons and other family members. He was frequently promoted through governmental agencies as an authentic representative of the P'urhépecha people, and he and his ensemble performed in countless venues throughout Mexico, and also in Europe and the United States. He received little financial remuneration and, according to his sons, felt taken advantage of by the various agencies (Hellier-Tinoco 2011). Yet his participation in the Zacán Contest with the Dance of the Old Men provided López with a potential income and further circulation within P'urhépecha, rather than outsider, contexts. The version of the Dance of the Old Men he performed was judged as the most authentic, and was less "spectacular" and showy than other ensembles, with precise footwork that was low to the ground.

By the late 1990s, a major modification took place in the Zacán Contest, with the inclusion and involvement of non-P'urhépecha *ballet folklórico* ensembles. Therefore, the Dance of the Old Men was performed numerous times during the course of the event by

FIGURE 6.5. The Dance of the Old Men at the Zacán Artistic Contest of the P'urhépecha People in the 1980s.

Photography by Jesús Bugarini. Used with permission.

FIGURE 6.6. The Dance of the Old Men at the Zacán Artistic Contest of the P'urhépecha People, performed by Gervasio López and family of the Island of Jarácuaro, 1998.

Photography by Ruth Hellier-Tinoco. Used with permission.

both P'urhépecha and non-P'urhépecha groups. Thus, the judging processes began to consider the authenticity of the body, where previously such notions had been irrelevant. The inclusion of non-P'urhépecha contestants also altered the nature of the event considerably, transforming it from an occasion with, by, and for local P'urhépecha peoples to one of a folkloric show. Although community cohesion and the sharing of practices was still important, this was somewhat dissipated by the presence of other concerns. This also set up other anomalous juxtapositions. For example, in 1998, when López and his ensemble from Jarácuaro performed the Dance of the Old Men, the Ballet Folklórico of Michoacán, a non-P'urhépecha group from the town of Uruapan, performed a dance created in the 1980s in the village of Jarácuaro, La Danza de los Enguangochados.

In competition contexts, naming a prize in memory of an individual performs a fixing role. Such is the case with López. In 2000, after López's death in 1999, a special prize was established, "in memory of the illustrious master Tata Gervasio López from the Community of Jarácuaro,"[33] named "La Danza de Los Viejitos, de Jarácuaro." Although López had attempted to make the most of opportunities that were presented to him in relation to performing the dance, he was frequently caught in a context of constructed authenticity that required a utilitarian response. As López was represented as an artifact of cultural patrimony and public property that belonged to the nation, the prize performed the role of honoring López's memory, and commemorating his lifelong role in promoting the Dance of the Old Men and acting as representative of Indigenous peoples. Yet the named prize also acts to reclaim his name and the Dance of the Old Men from national constructs through acknowledging López's role in relation to this dance and providing a marker of P'urhépecha self-designated authenticity.

The second issue that emerges from the Zacán Contest concerns its media circulation and the drama of the contest. By 2005 there were one thousand contestants participating, including P'urhépecha and non-P'urhépecha ensembles: sixty dance groups, forty-five *bandas*, thirty *orquestas*, and ninety *pireris*. The contest was promoted heavily through television and other media, and the event itself was also broadcast on television. As noted in 2008, "In the Press Briefing . . . the director of the Commission for Fairs, Expositions and Events . . . recognized the significance of this cultural event which each year manages to attraction national and foreign tourism" ("Listo" 2008). The last few years have also seen the introduction of a Facebook page and blogspots (Facebook Zacán Michoacán de Ocampo; concursozacan.blogspot.mx; Zacan-mich. blogspot.com). Not only has media involvement increased, but also governmental interest, with state and national representatives attending the live event. On October 18, 2016, a carefully choreographed line of officials took their places across the performance stage, with the governor of the State of Michoacán standing in the center.

The value of this event as a formal competition (rather than a festival), with criteria and adjudicators, evidently plays a role in the increased media attention and the type of reporting that occurs. Short articles are published before and after the contest, functioning to publicize the event and to define the competition as an important framework for reviving and strengthening traditional P'urhépecha dance.[34] In a 2015 article announcing the circulation of the convocatoria, one reporter noted how local government official Roberto Maldonado Hinojosa "considers the competition to be a highly important event in crossing state and national borders to showcase P'urhépecha culture and language to other states" ("Emiten convocatoria" 2015). On September 22, 2016, the announcement of the judges for the 45th Contest circulated in state media, and after the contest the winners were reported.[35] Thus the framework of both announcing the criteria and judges, and of reporting on the tension of a contest and the winners, provides media outlets with a dramatic element suitable for engaging audiences and readers.

The third issue relates to the presence of "different" bodies and the control of tradition. The *convocatoria* is produced in both the P'urhépecha and Spanish language, side by side, and includes an opening call that describes the organizational bodies involved with the contest; to whom the contest is open; and a set of judging criteria. The published wording acts as a core activator and controller of meaning and authority. The wording and framing are important because the shifts and changes over the last few years indicate subtle but significant ways in which the perception of dance forms and bodies have been shaped and controlled. For instance, these competition contexts enable the control of who may compete. As I noted earlier, as non-local performers from folkloric dance ensembles participated alongside Indigenous P'urhépecha performers, often enacting the same dance form, such as the Dance of the Old Men, notions of corporeal authenticity were brought into sharp juxtaposition. For many years the Zacán Contest was open to anyone who wanted to enter: "Any singer of pirekuas, orquestas, dance ensembles or bandas can enter" (Convocatoria 2012). By 2013 this changed, limiting the participants to only P'urhépecha people: "Any singer of pirekuas, orquestas, danzas and bandas *of P'urhépecha people* can enter" (Convocatoria 2013, my emphasis added).[36] In 2016, contestants had to show a form of identification to establish themselves as authentically P'urhépecha.

Along with the change in regulations concerning *who* may compete in the Zacán Contest, the role of judges in controlling notions of "tradition" has been made more overt. In 2011, point thirteen in the long list of instructions and criteria stated, "The decisions of the Judges will be final, in terms of the level of adherence to tradition of the diverse performances" (No. 13, 2011).[37] This was repeated again as point sixteen, specifically in relation to dance performances: "The decisions of the Judges will be final, in terms of adherence to the tradition of the diverse performances and the accompaniment of the dances by musical pieces from the P'urhépecha repertoire" (No. 16, 2011).[38] A further addition in 2013 demonstrated even greater control of elements in relation to the notion of authenticity: "there will be special attention paid to identify elements, in the orchestral and dance performances, that are *not part of the P'urhépecha culture*" (Convocatoria 2013, my emphasis added) (Figures 6.7 and 6.8). Emphasizing the role of dance and tradition, in 2011 a Special Prize for Dance was created and awarded, "for the dance that represents the best demonstration of revival" (Convocatoria 2011).[39] This action reinforced the role of dance in the Zacán Contest as one of looking to the past to generate the future.

FIGURE 6.7.   Poster for the Zacán Artistic Contest of the P'urhépecha People, 2014.

Used with permission.

The fourth issue I describe concerns the question of judging authenticity. By naming the criteria of "tradition" and "part of the P'urhépecha culture," which can be understood as constructs of authenticity, the Zacán judges are able to demonstrate their power and authority in relation these notions. The self-framing of these concepts is particularly striking considering the overt difference used for dance and for music practices. For dance, the emphasis is on the reification of tradition over new creation and the transmission of this movement between bodies. For music, new creation is one of the criteria for excellence and authenticity.

FIGURE 6.8. Poster for the Zacán Artistic Contest of the P'urhépecha People, 2014, showing the *convocatoria*, or call for contestants.

The convocatoria for dance states the following:
For each dance that is entered the entry must include

(a) the place of origin of the dance;
(b) the motive for dancing the dance;
(c) dates on which it is danced;
(d) to whom [the saint or divinity] the dance is dedicated (Convocatoria 2013).

By referring to "place of origin," "motive," and "date," each dance is firmly placed in a traditional village setting. Within this framework, authentic dance is regarded as serving a function only within a socio-religious context, in relation to a specific date and saint or divinity. Dance is clearly given the role of rescue and revival in which notions of "tradition" are firmly entrenched; thus opportunities for choreographic innovation are restricted. On the one hand, the Dance of the Old Men of Jarácuaro does not fit the criteria because it was developed through governmental nationalistic and tourist contexts. Yet, on the other hand, the dance is judged as the "most authentic." Conversely, many dances created by P'urhépecha villagers from the Lake Pátzcuaro region for the tourist-oriented contests for Night of the Dead are considered not "traditional" because they are newly created, and therefore are unsuitable for the Zacán Contest (including the Dance of the Sowers created by Gervasio López).

In contrast to the dance criteria, a key criterion for musical ensembles involves new composition. Indeed, all the musical categories include a requirement for newly created P'urhépecha works, thereby continuing the usual practice of *serenatas* of village fiestas from decades earlier:

> Orquestas will play a highland son and an abajeño, *one of which must have been composed recently by a member of the Orquesta*;
>   Musical bandas will play three pieces: an overture and a regional highland *son* and an *abajeño*, and *one of the latter two must have been composed recently by a member of the Banda*;
>   Pireris will sing two songs [in P'urhépecha language], a *son* and an *abajeño, one of which should be composed by the singer* ("de inspiración propia"), and the lyrics in P'urhépecha must be submitted. (Convocatoria 2013, emphasis added)

Although there are many discrepancies and the judges are not necessarily unified, processes that provide for their own frameworks are clear. This competition context therefore clearly enables those creating the criteria to self-define.

To some degree, the role of the Dance of the Old Men in the Zacán Contest perpetuates notions of danced authenticity initiated in the 1920s by the governmental institutions in the aftermath of the revolution, when dances labeled as Indigenous were a useful element in fervent nation-building and cultural patrimony, and in which the Dance of the Old Men was sanctioned through governmental events. Another perspective offers a more complex interpretation in which processes of reappropriation and of self-authentication complicate a simplistic framework through the politics of autonomy. These processes are crucial to recognition and Indigenous rights, through decentering, self-legitimation, and self-assertion.

In an article in *Xiranhua*, a website and newspaper in P'urhépecha and Spanish, under the title "Zacán: More Than an Expressive Forum," the president of the Zacán organizing committee in 2008, Jorge Morales Campos, described how the event enabled "the strengthening of the creation, performance and dissemination of the cultural richness of the diverse expressions of the P'urhépecha people . . . maintaining the identity and tradition of P'urhépecha people alive" ("XXXVII Concurso Artístico" 2008). Engaging the very categories of authenticity and essentialist classification instigated by official processes, these Zacán strategies prove efficacious for establishing rights, presence, and territory (including ideological territory) through self-representation. The bodies that dance choreographic forms labeled as "traditional" by the communities dancing them counter and resist the ideologically constructed notions of *indigenismo* of the 1920s. The contest allows the P'urhépecha organizers to reclaim the definitions and their own bodies. Transmission through the contest framework is more potent than a festival because there is more at stake and because the criteria can be overtly demonstrated and controlled. However, even as processes of local reclamation have continued apace, so too have developments that would place the Zacán Contest into a global framework, through the UNESCO designation on the Representative List as an Intangible Cultural Heritage of Humanity. Even now, the Zacán Contest features on the official UNESCO website on the video for the *pirekua*, which received the designation in 2010, with heavy promotion by the state tourist board ("Pirekua" www.unesco.org).[40]

SELF-POWER AND CONTEST

Through my five examples of the Dance of the Old Men in different competition contexts, I have discussed the operation of state and local power; appropriation and reappropriation; authority and authorship; and processes of authentication and authenticity. I have shown how issues of control and decision-making are significant: the 1931 Cultural Missions competition involved local rivalries, a national pedagogical framework, and teachers as documenters; the 1950s contests in state-run boarding schools created publications that fixed and disseminated one form of the Dance of the Old Men; the 1990s Lake Pátzcuaro competitions were organized as entertainment for national and international tourists, and enabled new creations; the 1990s National Indigenist Institute contest focused specifically on local P'urhépecha groups; and finally, the Zacán Contest stages both notions of control and self-determination.

In terms of questions concerning how the competition context impacts the dance as practice, answers coalesce around the idea of perpetuating an unchanged choreographic practice. The choreographic practices remain very similar, but the framework is changed through the context of contest enabling a performance of power. Appropriation is countered through the contest criteria and the self-naming of the criteria of tradition and authenticity. In response to the question of how the competition impacts the dancers, here the answers lie in notions of control and power relations. The dancers are still being judged and evaluated, and there are contentions, rivalries, and assessment of judges, but those in control are the P'urhépecha community, in all its diversity and complexity. That the Dance of the Old Men plays a significant part in these processes is crucial, enacting a provocative role that obfuscates and complicates issues of the designation and practice of Indigenous peoples and *indigenismo* in twenty-first century Mexico. Ninety years after the Dance of Old Men was appropriated by the nationalist government, the Zacán Contest decenters and brings power to a periphery—a periphery struggling for rights and self-governance. It is fitting that, on October 18, 2016, the dance group that was awarded the Tata Gervasio López prize was an ensemble from the Island of Jarácuaro: Tzipikua, Los Viejos Alegres, led by Procopio Patricio Cázares. As the straggly line of masked old men stumbled and shuffled across the stage, and then burst into expertly executed footwork, they were performing a moving choreography of reappropriation and power.

Notes

I gratefully acknowledge the extraordinary hospitality of many friends, musicians, and dancers in the P'urhépecha region, particularly the families in the Islands of Jarácuaro, Urandén, and Pacanda, and elsewhere in Mexico. For their support and feedback I thank many colleagues in the Dance Ethnography Forum, the British Forum for Ethnomusicology, the Congress on Research in Dance, the Society for Dance History Scholars, the Society for Ethnomusicology, the International Council for Traditional Music, la Asociación Latinoamericana de Antropología, and the Musée d'ethnographie de Neuchâtel and Institut d'ethnologie, Switzerland. I acknowledge the support of the Academic Senate of the University of California, Santa Barbara, for providing funds to attend the 2016 Zacán Concurso. For their inspiring and insightful discussions, I thank the UCSB undergraduate students of fall 2016 who took my course *Politics and Poetics of Musics and Dance in Mexico*.

1. All translations are mine, unless otherwise stated.
2. The footwork is known as *zapateado* or *zapateo*, a generic term used in Spain and Latin America for a range of movements executed by the feet.
3. One of the set pieces is named *La Competencia*, the Contest, and encompasses a solo by each dancer in turn, in which they demonstrate their most sophisticated footwork.
4. In the last few years the title has alternated between *pueblo* and *raza*. *Raza* is generally translated as "race," but also as "peoples."
5. During the 2016 contest, the Dance of the Old Men was performed only a couple of times, although many other masked dances of old men and young men were performed by adults and children.
6. At the highest institutional and governmental levels, dance competitions facilitate the most creative and experimental choreography that easily holds its own alongside top choreographers in major global contexts, and disseminate conventional practices to a wide

audience. For example, in 2011, a reality television show titled *Ópera Prima en Movimiento* featured a competition for ballet dancers to enter the prestigious company of the national Palace of Fine Arts (*Ópera Prima en Movimiento* 2011: Alejandro Cruz Atienza, Mexico City: INBA, CONACULTA, SEP, Canal 22).

7. See also Buckland (2001).
8. The movement is particularly active through the Supreme Council of the Indigenous of Michoacán (el Consejo Supremo Indígena de Michoacán). (See the Facebook page Consejo Supremo Indígena Michoacán).
9. See Hellier-Tinoco (2011) for a full historiography and analysis. For many video clips of the Dance of the Old Men, see my companion website: www.oup.com/us/embodyingmexico.
10. See Hellier-Tinoco (2004, 2010a and b, 2011, 2014).
11. I attended the 45th Zacán Contest of the P'urhépecha People on October 17–18, 2016, enabling me to be cognizant of the most recent changes in this event.
12. Although independence from Spanish rule in 1821 signaled "Mexico" as a nation, European forms, particularly ballet and opera, were promoted during the French intervention (1862–1867), and later by President Porfirio Díaz, against whom the revolutionary wars were instigated. It is important also to recognize the African presence in Mexico. In the seventeenth century, African bodies (enslaved and free) were part of a complex caste system in the mixing of Indigenous and European, and hierarchies were based on racial combinations and perceptions of "purity" through physiognomy.
13. These range from the most commercialized and professional Ballet Folklórico de México de Amalia Hernández in Mexico City to amateur ensembles throughout Mexico and the United States.
14. The *folklórico* repertoire known in the United States was shaped well before Amalia Hernández created her company and thus Hernández appropriated an already appropriated repertoire of dances (Hellier-Tinoco 2011).
15. As P'urhépecha migration, both inside the Republic and to the United States, is common in this region, villagers frequently include family members who do not live permanently in the village.
16. The string quartet and the *orquesta* (mixed strings and wind) of Nicolás Bartolo Juárez from the Island of Jarácuaro were particularly famous in the region (Campos 1928).
17. Mexican ethnomusicologist Arturo Chamorro (1992, 1994) has examined this phenomenon in relation to P'urhépecha *bandas*, or wind bands.
18. See Mendoza García (2016) for a discussion of the *jarabe tapatío* and the Cultural Missions.
19. Néstor García Canclini (1985, 39) has suggested that it was the action of the Cultural Missions that "gave this dance a clearly defined choreography for exhibiting it as a spectacle." However, although the choreography became fixed through activities instigated by the SEP, it was not under the auspices of the Cultural Missions, but rather prior to this through the theatricalized events in Mexico City (Cine Olímpia and Teatro Sintético). Significantly, Nicolás Bartolo Juárez was influenced by the staged events in Mexico City, for which he had been the original principal Indigenous teacher, which led to adjustments to his own performances in the Lake Pátzcuaro region when danced within the context of contests organized by the Cultural Missions.
20. See, for example, Dickens (1954).
21. In 1952 Hernández formed the Modern Ballet of Mexico (Ballet Modern de México), which transformed into the Ballet Folklórico of the Palace of Fine Arts (Ballet Folklórico

de Bellas Artes), and subsequently became the Ballet Folklórico de México (Lavalle 1988; Shay 2002; Tortajada Quiroz 1995).

22. Importantly, the Dance of the Old Men was also specifically used in the United States to inculcate Mexicanness in citizens living beyond the national border (see Hellier-Tinoco 2011).

23. This included being theatricalized on stage in Mexico City in 1930 (see Hellier-Tinoco 2011).

24. Other contests included Traditional Clothes and Costumes (Traje Tradicional) and Altars and Crafts (Ofrendas y Artesanias). The Contests of Traje Tradicional held in Tzintzuntzan and Pátzcuaro engendered a complex reception environment for audiences. Creating an overt and deliberate exhibition of P'urhépecha clothing worn by and modeled on *any body* placed the focus on the artifacts themselves as a form of cultural heritage. Clothing worn by local P'urhépecha Lake Pátzcuaro residents was placed into both an ethnographic and entertainment frame, performing as cultural heritage and as a referent of tradition and authenticity.

25. For a discussion of the performance of fishing using the butterfly net (*mariposa*), see Hellier-Tinoco (2011).

26. In the Dance of the Sowers, López and his sons presented a scenario of men sowing and plowing (as undertaken on the fertile soils of Jarácuaro) and women carrying food to the workers. The men were costumed in the *traje de manta* (as used for the Dance of the Old Men), while the women wore their everyday clothes. An image of this dance, depicting Pedro López holding a hoe in a Jarácuaro field, with hills and open sky in the background, was used as the cover for a cassette recording by López's ensemble, which included the music for the Dance of the Sowers (1989). Produced by the recording company Discos Alegría as part of their series entitled *Folklore Mexicano*, the image generated an association of nature, a preindustrial rural idyll, and folklore in terms of a contemporary life in Lake Pátzcuaro.

27. INI was replaced by the National Commission for the Development of Indigenous Peoples (Comisión Nacional para el Desarrollo de los Pueblos Indígenas, CDI) in 2003.

28. The name of the volcano in P'urépecha is Parhíkutini. The full name of the village is San Pedro Zacán, in the municipality of Los Reyes.

29. Los Reyes and San Juan Parangaricutiro were obliterated, and Zacán (pop. 876), Angahuan (pop. 1,314), and Zirosoto (pop. 1,314) were heavily affected.

30. This has various orthographies, including K'urpites and Curpites. The P'urhépecha name, from *kurpiticha*, means "those who get together." This masked dance is associated with nativity celebrations, encompassing the characters of a Wise Man/Joseph; a Maringuía/ Virgin Mary; and the Kurpitis/shepherds. In the village setting of Caltzontzin, the Kurpitis dance involves a competition element (*la competencia*), held on December 23, to decide which of two groups of young, single men will take on the dance. From early in the day the dancers and their supporters gather inside the designated room. The atmosphere is lively and even slightly dangerous, as the spectators passionately defend their chosen group. The chosen group, none of whom may have danced before, take on an official role for the year. A similar process takes place in San Juan Nuevo, with an atmosphere much like a boxing match or similar sporting contest (for an excellent video, see https://www.youtube.com/ watch?v=4U2UbKbB4Ko [accessed July 17, 2016]).

31. Many videos exist on YouTube and I urge readers to view this exquisite dance.

32. *Tata* (father) is a term of endearment and respect.

33. "En memoria del ilustre maestro Tata Gervasio López, oriundo de la Comunidad de Jarácuaro."

34. "En aras de recuperar y fortalecer elementos tradicionales" in "Convocatoria concurso" (2015). See "Emiten convocatoria" (2015).
35. For example, "Ganadores del concurso artístico de Zacán 2015." See also ""¡Estos son los ganadores..."
36. "Podrán inscribirse todos los Pireris, Orquestas, Grupos de Danza y Bandas" (Convocatoria 2012); "Podrán inscribirse todos los Pireris, Orquestas, Danzas y Bandas *del pueblo P'urhépecha*" (Convocatoria 2013) (emphasis added).
37. "Las decisions del Jurado serán inapelables, teniendo en cuenta el grado de apego a las tradiciones de las diversas ejecuciones" (Convocatoria 2011).
38. "Las decisions del Jurado serán inapelables, teniendo en cuenta el apego a las tradiciones de las diversas ejecuciones y el acompañamiento de las danzas con piezas musicales del repertorio p'urhépecha" (Convocatoria 2011).
39. "... para la Danza que represente la major expression de rescate" (Convocatoria 2011). The prize is the "Juan Manual Maldonado Valencia Prize."
40. See also Hellier-Tinoco (2016).

References

Aguilera Ortiz, Porfirio. 1985. "Antecedentes." In *Zacán: renacimiento de una tradición,* photo essay by Jesús Bugarini, 13–19. Morelia: Instituto Michoacano de Cultura, Gobierno del Estado de Michoacán.

Bartolo Juárez, Nicolás. 1937. *Sones isleños del Lago de Pátzcuaro.* Jarácuaro, México: Archivo Regional, DAPP.

Buckland, Theresa Jill. 2001. "Dance, Authenticity and Cultural Memory: The Politics of Embodiment." *Yearbook for Traditional Music* 33:1–16.

Campos, Rubén M. 1928. *El Folklore y la música mexicana: Investigación acerca de la cultura musical en México (1525–1925).* México: Secretaría de Educación Pública.

Castro Agúndez, Jesús. 1958. *Monografía y música de danzas y bailes regionales presentados en las jornadas nacionales deportivas y culturales llevadas a cabo en los años de 1953 a 1958.* México: Secretaría de Educación Pública, Dirección General de Internados de Enseñanza Primaria y Escuelas Asistenciales.

Chamorro Escalante, J. Arturo. 1992. *Universos de la música p'urhépecha.* Zamora: Centro de Estudios de las Tradiciones, El Colegio de Michoacán.

Chamorro Escalante, J. Arturo. 1994. *Sones de la guerra: rivalidad y emoción en la práctica de la música p'urhépecha.* Zamora: El Colegio de Michoacán.

Desmond, Jane C. 1997. "Embodying Difference: Issues in Dance and Cultural Studies." In *Meaning in Motion: New Cultural Studies of Dance,* edited by Jane C. Desmond, 29–53. Durham, NC: Duke University Press.

Desmond, Jane C. 1999. *Staging Tourism: Bodies on Display from Waikiki to Sea World.* Chicago; London: University of Chicago Press.

Dickens, Guillermina. 1954. *Dances of Mexico.* London: Max Parrish, Royal Academy of Dancing and the Ling Physical Education Academy.

Gamboa, Fernando, Luis Felipe Obregón, and Santiago Arias Navarro. n.d. *Los viejitos: danza del estado de Michoacán. Cucuchucho del lago de Pátzcuaro.* México: Secretaría de Educación Pública, Dirección General de Asuntos Indígenas.

García Canclini, Néstor. 1985. *Notas sobre las máscaras, danzas y fiestas de Michoacán.* Michoacán: Comité Editorial del Gobierno de Michoacán.

García Canclini, Néstor. 1993. *Transforming Modernity: Popular Culture in Mexico.* Austin: University of Texas Press.

González, Anita. 2010. *Afro-Mexico: Dancing between Myth and Reality.* Austin: University of Texas Press.

Gutiérrez, Laura G. 2010. *Performing Mexicanidad: Vendidas y Cabareteras on the Transnational Stage.* Austin: University of Texas Press.

Hellier-Tinoco, Ruth. 2004. "Power Needs Names: Hegemony, Folklorisation and the *Viejitos* Dance of Michoacán, Mexico." In *Music, Power and Politics,* edited by Annie J. Randall, 47–64. New York; London: Routledge.

Hellier-Tinoco, Ruth. 2010a. "Corpo/Reality, Voyeurs and the Responsibility of Seeing: Night of the Dead on the Island of Janitzio, Mexico." *Performance Research* 15(1): 23–31.

Hellier-Tinoco, Ruth. 2010b. "¡Saludos de México (el auténtico)!: Postales, anuncios espectaculares, turismo y cuerpos actuantes." *Fractal* 46: 79–98.

Hellier-Tinoco, Ruth. 2011. *Embodying Mexico: Tourism, Nationalism and Performance.* New York: Oxford University Press. Companion website: www.oup.com/us/embodyingmexico. 42 video resources recorded by Ruth Hellier-Tinoco.

Hellier-Tinoco, Ruth. 2014. "Embodying Touristic Mexico: Virtual and Erased Indigenous Bodies." In *Meet Me at the Fair: A World's Fair Reader,* edited by Laura Hollengreen, Celia Pearce, Rebecca Rouse, and Bobby Schweizer, 71–80. Pittsburgh: ETC and Carnegie Mellon Press.

Hellier-Tinoco, Ruth. 2016. ""Our Heritage?": Dancing Resistance, Creating Music—Transnational Tourism, UNESCO's Intangible Cultural Heritage, and Indigenous Autonomy in the P'urhépecha Region of Mexico." Paper presented at the IV Biennial Conference, International Association of Inter-American Studies (Human Rights in the Americas). University of California, Santa Barbara, October 4–6.

Kirshenblatt-Gimblett, Barbara. 1998. *Destination Culture: Tourism, Museums, and Heritage.* Berkeley; Los Angeles: University of California Press.

Lavalle, Josefina. 1988. *El Jarabe . . . el jarabe ranchero o jarabe de Jalisco.* México: Centro Nacional de Investigación, Documentación e Información de la Danza 'José Limón.'

Lavalle, Josefina. 2002. *En busca de la danza moderna mexicana. Dos ensayos.* México: INBA/CONACULTA/Ríos y Raíces.

MacCannell, Dean. 1973. "Staged Authenticity: Arrangements of Social Space in Tourist Settings." *American Journal of Sociology* 79(3): 589–603.

MacCannell, Dean. 1999. *The Tourist: A New Theory of the Leisure Class.* Berkeley: University of California Press.

MacCannell, Dean. 2001. "Remarks on the Commodification of Cultures." In *Hosts and Guests Revisited: Tourism Issues of the 21st Century,* edited by Valene L. Smith and Maryann Brent, 380–390. New York: Cognizant Communication Corporation.

Mendoza García, Gabriela. 2016. "The Jarabe Tapatío: Imagining Race, Nation, Class and Gender in 1920s Mexico." In *The Oxford Handbook of Dance and Ethnicity,* edited by Anthony Shay and Barbara Sellers-Young, 319–343. New York: Oxford University Press.

Ortiz Bullé Goyri, Alejandro. 2003. "El teatro indigenista mexicano de los años veinte: ¿Orígenes del teatro popular mexicano actual?" *Latin American Theatre Review* 37(1): 75–93.

Ortiz Bullé Goyri, Alejandro. 2005. *Teatro y vanguardia en el México posrevolucionario (1920–1940)*. México: Universidad Autónoma Metropolitana.
Ramos Villalobos, Roxana Guadalupe. 2011. "La formación dancística en México (1919–1932)." In *El Teatro de Ahora: un primer ensayo de teatro político en México*, edited by Israel Franco and Antonio Escobar Delgado, 243–263. México: Instituto Nacional de Bellas Artes.
Shay, Anthony. 2002. *Choreographic Politics: State Folk Dance Companies, Representation and Power*. Middletown, CT: Wesleyan University Press.
Tortajada Quiroz, Margarita. 1995. *Danza y poder*. México: INBA-CENIDI-Danza.
Vaughan, Mary Kay. 1997. *Cultural Politics in Revolution: Teachers, Peasants, and Schools in Mexico, 1930–40*. Tucson: University of Arizona Press.
Vaughan, Mary Kay, and Stephen Lewis. 2006. "Introduction." In *The Eagle and the Virgin: Nation and Cultural Revolution in Mexico, 1920–1940*, edited by Mary Kay Vaughan and Stephen Lewis, 1–20. Durham, NC; London: Duke University Press.

Other Sources

"XXXVII Concurso Artístico de la Raza p'urhépecha." 2008. http://www.xiranhua.com.mx/noticias/noticia221_1.html. Accessed December 2008.
Convocatoria 2011. XL concurso artístico de la raza p'urhépecha Zacán. Poster.
Convocatoria 2012. XLI concurso artístico de la raza p'urhépecha Zacán. Poster.
Convocatoria 2013. XLII concurso artístico del pueblo p'urhépecha Zacán. Poster.
Convocatoria 2014. XLIII concurso artístico de la raza p'urhépecha Zacán. Poster.
Convocatoria 2015. XLIV concurso artístico del pueblo p'urhépecha Zacán. Poster.
"Convocatoria concurso artístico de Zacán." *La Extra*. 2015. September 30.
"Dan a conocer la convocatoria del XLV concurso artístico de la raza p'urhépecha." Respuesta.com.mx. 2016. September 22.
"Emiten convocatoria del XLIV concurso artístico de la raza p'urhépecha." *La Jornada, Michoacán*. 2015. September 28.
"¡Estos son los ganadores del XLV Concurso de la Raza P'urhépecha!" MiMorelia.com. 2016. October 19.
"Ganadores del concurso artístico de Zacán 2015." MiMorelia.com. 2015. October 20.
"Listo, Festival de la Raza P'urhépecha de Zacán." 2008. http://www.cbtelevision.com.mx/cultura/listo-festival-de-la-raza-purhpecha-de-zacan/ 15 Oct 2008. Accessed October 2008.
"Pirekua, Traditional Song of the P'urhépecha." UNESCO. www.unesco.org/culture/ich/en/RL/pirekua-traditional-song-of-the-purhepecha-00398#video. Accessed October 2016.

CHAPTER 7

ABOVE AND BEYOND THE BATTLE

Virtuosity and Collectivity within Televised Street Dance Crew Competitions

LAURA ROBINSON

> If you believe in superheroes, we are those superheroes, in real life, on stage, right now.
>
> —Mark "Swarfe" Calape, A Team (2011)

In keeping with the dramatic trope of the television talent show, Calape's pre-performance interview hypes up the A Team's pending audition. Through his affinity with superhuman beings, Calape prepares the home television viewer for the extreme physical stunts they are about to witness and frames the crew's competitive performance through the idea of human bodies transcending their material capabilities. Calape does not disappoint. Eight males in trench coats curiously toy with playing cards, while a lone girl waits in the center, wearing an oversized T-shirt emblazoned with an *A*. To an atmospheric soundtrack, the crew executes tightly controlled floor slides, shifts in body weight, quick flexes of the arms, and slow and smooth turns in carbon-copy unison. The camera cuts between medium close-up shots of the individual dancers and wide group shots to capture both the intricate labor of each dancer and the perfectly timed group syncopation. A sharp change in tempo, accompaniment, and the removal of trench coats signals a harder dynamic. Two dancers perform identical aerial corkscrews downstage, and are quickly followed by all nine dancers executing an aerial backflip in precise unison. Stunt after stunt follows, leaving judge Adam Garcia holding his head in his hands, while judge Kimberley Wyatt stares open-mouthed, with hands dangling in disbelief. As a finale, one dancer performs over six identical "windmills" in time with the repetitive electronic soundtrack, while the rest of the crew encircles the lone performer.[1] The crew comes to a controlled finish in contrast with the previous corporeal pyrotechnics, slowly rising from a crouched position as the music fades. The judging panel jumps into a standing ovation and the studio audience screams with approval.

In the context of televised street dance crew competitions, the A Team is not alone in creating the illusion of enhanced corporeal beings through choreographic display. Through tightly controlled and highly labored performances, street dance crews on television talent shows, such as the British *Got to Dance* (*GTD*; 2009–2014) and *Britain's Got Talent* (*BGT*; 2007–present), and the US series *America's Best Dance Crew* (2008–2012, 2015), push the boundaries of the physically possible into the realm of fantasy.[2] Human attributes of pain and exhaustion are replaced by machine-like invincibility and, for two and a half minutes, dancers transform the constructed persona of the "ordinary" television talent show worker into the mythic, the invincible, and the virtuosic. These explosive performances provoke both physical and emotional affective reactions in the judging panel and studio audience, as bodies appear to defy gravitational limitations and execute strict uniformity, rapid speeds, and physical dexterity in a variety of hip-hop dance styles.[3]

With crews continuously testing the limitations of their corporeality through these competitions, these screen dance choreographies therefore raise three key questions that I explore within this chapter: First, how is virtuosity defined in the context of competitive televised street dance choreography? Second, what are the ways in which crews create the illusion of corporeal transcendence? And third, how does the collective virtuosity of the crew operate in relation to discourses of virtuosity as the epitome of individual excellence? To explore these questions, I provide a close analysis of five televised street dance crew performances featured on British television talent shows: Peridot's semi-final performance on *BGT* (Peridot 2010); Flawless's audition performance on *BGT* (Flawless 2009); Diversity's final performance on *BGT* (Diversity 2009); Ruff Diamond's semi-final performance on *GTD* (Ruff Diamond 2013; and the A Team's audition, as previously described. In conversation with interdisciplinary theoretical frameworks regarding virtuosity and excess, I consider these concepts in relation to the continued emphasis on technology and the street dance body, or, as I propose, the techno-corporeality of the choreography. In particular, I focus on the application of animation techniques, synchronicity, and the construction of "meta-bodies" within these choreographies, while also considering the televisual treatment of the crews within the neoliberal cultural economy of the competition. Prior to the dance analysis, I commence with a discussion of the relationship between dance and competition, followed by an exploration of virtuosity in relation to dance practice and, specifically, hip-hop dance culture.

DANCE AND COMPETITION

The placement of vernacular dance styles within sporting codes of competition and organization shifts both intention and reception. Ethnomusicologist Amy Stillman's (1996) and anthropologist Frank Hall's (2008) respective studies of hula dance and Irish dance competitions reveal a dynamic shift in the aesthetic of the style to achieve the associated commodities of trophies, prizes, and visual exposure. In hula dance competitions, greater emphasis is placed on visual display rather than the musical and poetic elements of the form, and dancers contend with "increased demands for physical fitness and body conditioning, even bodybuilding," due to the increased demand for physical feats and athletic displays in the competition (Stillman 1996, 373). Irish dance competitors aim to "outdo" previous years' winning routines with more complex footwork and elevation, while the embodiment of "Irishness" becomes secondary to visual spectacle (Hall 2008).

Similarly, the incorporation of hip-hop dance practices in the commercial competitive format of the television talent show shifts emphasis from the "corporeal orature" of the style, as described by dance scholar Thomas DeFrantz (2004, 76), to an emphasis on spatial formation and outward execution.[4] In its vernacular origins, the competitive nature of breaking fueled the virtuosic elements of the performance, creating multiple head spins, physically precarious power moves, such as the windmill or the suicide, and an ever-increasing velocity and ferociousness (Toop 2000).[5] This desire to defy the limitations of the body through physical skill and athletic prowess is further enhanced by the placement of the mediated street dance body in a crew format and competitive framework.

Despite the continued academic focus on solo hip-hop dance practice operating in the spatial construction of the group cypher (Banes 1985, 2004; DeFrantz, 2004; Hazzard-Gordon 1996; Rose 1994), hip-hop and funk dance styles have a strong history situated in group or crew formations. These groupings include the Lockers and the Electric Boogaloos performing on *Soul Train* (1971–2006) in the early 1970s, competitive b-boy crews such as the Rock Steady Crew and the New York City Breakers, and the geometric formations of Michael Jackson and Janet Jackson's back-up dancers (Lockerlegends 2011). In the context of reality television in the United Kingdom, the Kombat Breakers' appearance on *BGT* in 2007, followed by the high-profile win of Diversity on *BGT* in May 2009, led to street dance crews becoming part of the fabric of British television talent show competitions. Over fifty duet, trio, and group performances were recorded between 2008 and 2013, and crews such as Diversity, Flawless, Twist and Pulse, Chris and Wes, the A Team, Trinity Warriors, Kazzum, Antics, and Ruff Diamond have reached their respective finals.

Despite the preference toward the subjective opinion of a panel of judges rather than a reliance on codified rules and criteria, these competition structures have a direct effect on the crew choreography. In the example of the A Team on *GTD*, the crew is restricted to a one and a half–minute segment for its audition. The need to quickly attract the judges' and viewers' attention is paramount in the crew's progression in the competition; thus emphasis is placed on the rapid execution of gymnastic feats. As the edit frequently results in the omission of optimum angles for the reception of such showcase moments within the choreography, crews rely on the quantity of stunts.[6] The A Team additionally demonstrates its members' dexterity within the short time frame by appearing to defy the physical laws of gravity, force, and speed. The slow execution of turns and floor glides in the sustained and wistful dynamic of the opening section of their audition are juxtaposed against the sharp intricacy of arm tutting, with dancers continuously shifting the velocity of their grounded and aerial movement phrases. The time-bound structures of the competition therefore have a direct influence on these choreographies, placing greater emphasis on virtuosic acts and illusionary techniques that create visual impact through pushing the body to its physical limitations. But how does the classical concept of virtuosity as a notion of artistic excellence operate within competitive street dance performance?

Going beyond the Human

The term *virtuosity* refers to "going beyond" human excellence through "hyperdisciplined, hyperlabouring thus hypervisible" displays of skill (Hamera 2000, 147). While the term *virtuosity* is more often used to describe canonical Western art forms, such as ballet and opera, these displays of hyper-skill are historically situated at the border between popular culture and high art, embracing both Western concert dance and the theatrical spectacles on the popular stage (Osterweis 2013). In his study of the violinist Niccolò Paganini, communications scholar David Palmer (1998) situates the appeal of virtuosity in the revelation and transcendence of individual agency: the triumph of artistic prowess that emerged from the Renaissance era. In Western concert dance, dance scholar Ariel Osterweis (2013, 2014) reveals that the ballet soloist was revered for her levels of skill, her ability to replicate such performances night after night, and her capacity to visually distinguish herself from the *corps de ballet*. In terms of the popular dancing body, writings regarding virtuosity are predominantly situated in historically staged forms of entertainment, such as circus, cabaret, and magic (Darley 2000; Kershaw 2003). Theatrical spectacle thrived in the live popular entertainment forms of the late eighteenth century that were "designed to stimulate and capture the eye and, often the gut (viscera) as well, rather than the head or intellect" (Darley 2000, 40). Acts, such as circus acrobatics, conjurers, vaudeville performers, puppeteers, and burlesque performances, placed emphasis on high skill, elaborate props, special effects, tricks, and stage devices to produce "intense and instantaneous visual pleasure: the production of imagery and action which would excite, astound and astonish the audience" due to the implausibility of their performances (Darley 2000, 40).

Similar to these historically situated accounts of popular dance virtuosity, hip-hop dance offers distinctive aesthetics divergent from a comparison with the Western art canon's virtuosic aesthetic ideals of beauty, refinement, and grace. Virtuosity and dexterity can be viewed throughout African American social dance history, from slaves' circle dances of the 1840s to the block parties of the 1940s (Hazzard-Gordon 1990). In particular, the continued emphasis on high skill can be witnessed in the athleticism, versatility, and the velocity required in the execution of breaking, as evidenced by several dance scholars. In reporting on the breaking style, dance scholar Sally Banes emphasizes the "flamboyance" of the dance, likening the floor and aerial performances to those of gymnasts or circus entertainers ([1985] 2004, 18). Observing the bounce and physical recoil of the body, DeFrantz (2004, 78) situates hip-hop virtuosity in both the technical skill of the mixmaster and in the powerful "weightiness and aggressive physicality" of the body. In the hip-hop idiom, bodies emulate the sudden change in rhythms and accents of sampled music tracks through isolations and accenting polyrhythms with body parts, allowing dancers to visualize the beat through a variety of creative means. The hip-hop dancing body labors through its physical tightness, creating fragmented performances that mimic the rhythms and samples of the mixed tracks. De Frantz (2004, 78) states that

> [t]his is a virtuosity of precision and attack; of finish joined to flow. The movement startles the viewer with angularity and asymmetry; with an outwardly-explosive directness of precision unknown to earlier black American social dances.

In the case of street dance crew choreography, the grounded center of gravity derived from African diasporic practice is coupled with the polyrhythmic attack and flow of the body in motion. As witnessed in the A Team's audition, limbs slice and carve through the air as if expelled from the body. Dancers balance and topple from their heads, while chest cavities and arm joints appear dislocated and mutilated. Animation techniques give the illusion of the loss of skeletal limitations through liquid arm, leg, and torso waving. Gliding allows the feet to slip and slither fluidly across the floor with reptilian qualities, while popping electrifies and mechanizes the body. A tension of push and pull exists between symmetrical and asymmetrical design, as dancers play with angles and clean lines and then distort them through judders, pops, and gravity-defying freezes.

These performances thus produce spectacles of bodily control, efficiency, and precision, emulating and surpassing previous auditions and showcases, and often previous crews' attempts in the competition. The setting apart of bodies through high skill levels, achieved through intensive, repetitive labor and heightened by the dramatic rhetoric of the competition, results in the crews' ability to produce televised moments that amaze and astound the viewer. It is here, I argue, where the term *virtuosity* is aligned with concepts of transcendence and corporeal excess.

TRANSCENDENCE AND EXCESS

The term *excess* refers to a state of overindulgence, surplus, or exaggeration. It is subjectively loaded in its sense of reaching beyond permitted and conservative limitations, and in producing too much or going beyond rational need. Through the reimagining the body as a fluid and "excessive" entity with transgressive potential (Williams 1998, 2001), the term *virtuosity* can be further understood as a state of moving beyond the physical efforts of the artist. In particular, Osterweis (2013, 68) importantly highlights how the "highly kinetic choreography" witnessed within the African diaspora, including honed skill, execution, charisma, versatility, and velocity, draws traditions from the African diaspora's aesthetic resistance to "statis or capture." Complex histories of corporeal oppression have subsequently resulted in an excessive performance aesthetic that takes risks and places the agility and dexterity of the body at the center of the movement experience.

Dance scholar Gabriele Brandstetter (2007, 178) further explores the concept of virtuosic excess in her analysis of the solo performing artist in the eighteenth century, "whose actions . . . contravene the boundaries of the physically possible while at the same time concealing from delighted audiences the nature of his transgression." Brandstetter (2007, 185) links the implausibility and technical skill of the virtuoso with ideas of "the phantasm of the machine," in both the superhuman and repetitive execution of ability that reflected eighteenth-century engine technology. She captures this enacting of the machine in her description of the artist J. J. Grandville's illustrations of the Romantic ballerina:

> The sylphide ballerina of Romantic ballet whirls around en pointe in a pirouette. She is the flywheel of this great, general rotation. To her left, legs are moving in grotesque-arabesque poses, having gained their independence as a particularized bodily series. To her right, the human body is transformed into a doll and finally into a spinning top by the speedy mechanics of the turn. This scenario pushes the theatricality of movement, as a figure of virtuoso mechanics, in the sense of Blasis's body code, to the extreme—crossing the line of what is considered worthy of admiration and astonishment towards the grotesque. Grandville's picture stages a fascination with a uniform, inexhaustible and self-regulating mechanics. (Brandstetter 2007, 188)

Here, Brandstetter establishes the important distinction of the virtuosic body blurring the boundaries between artistic excellence and the grotesque in its reflection of the contemporary era of mechanical intervention, moving away from the aesthetically pleasing Renaissance ideal of artistic prowess. In a contemporary cinematic example, Osterweis's analysis of the film *Black Swan* (2010) depicts this crossing over between human and other, referencing the moment that the protagonist ballerina Nina grows wings during her *fouettés*.[7] She states that this moment marks "the point at which the pinnacle of her [Nina's] technical achievement coincides with raw animalistic attributes associated with the ecstatic" (Osterweis 2014, 74).

Virtuosity, as explored by Brandstetter and Osterweis, not only speaks to ideas of artistic excellence, but also to the transcendence from the human into a boundary figure. This reinterpretation of virtuosity results in a shift in aesthetic archetypes, and further demonstrates how corporeal excess can reflect and embody the contemporary moment. Returning to the choreographic displays of the street dance crew, the following analysis will thus explore this crossing into virtuosic excess, with particular attention to the physical negotiation between technology and the competitive body.

ANIMATING ILLUSION

Peridot's robot-inspired semi-final performance on *BGT* is brought to life through a mixture of muscle shudders, sharp starts and stops, leg pops, chest isolations, gliding of the feet, and angled arm lines. Bodily joints and bones appear to dissolve through waving, while fluid actions are transformed into static, mechanical shudders through body popping. Accompanied by the soundtrack of pistons and clouded in dry ice, movements suddenly stop and start as if being controlled by internal motors, or appear to break down and malfunction, with the upper arm taut while the lower arm dangles lifelessly. Dancers form a line across the stage, linking hands to elbows, and wave the lower arms inward toward a central dancer. Once the crew "plugs into" the central dancer, the eight-limbed waving creature leans back, and the *en masse* arm wave is replicated in the central dancer's dislocated isolation of his chest cavity.

Animation techniques, which include the stylistic practices of popping, waving, gliding, roboting, strutting, tutting, ticking, and boogalooing, originated in the mid-1960s in the Bay area of Los Angeles.[8] Crews, such as the Robot Brothers, were inspired by cartoons, science-fiction television programs, store mannequins, and martial arts films, and dancers attempted to physically recreate the actions of these mediated bodies (Lockerlegends 2011). These illusionary techniques tense, release, curve, and angle the body away from habitual pedestrian movement.[9] Gliding, for example, removes friction from the transference of foot to foot, with weight passing seamlessly, as if the feet were gliding across ice. Popping is the rapid tensing and relaxing of the muscles, creating a freeze-frame effect, while ticking speeds up this process, creating the effect of the body in a strobe light. Through the physical interpretation of science fiction characters and cartoons, these styles already allude to the transformation from the human into fantasy. For example, "the robot" came into public consciousness through the Jackson 5's televised performance of "Dancing Machines" on the Carol Burnett Show in 1974, creating the term "doing the robot" (MRDAVEYD 2013). In his historical populist account of animation techniques, filmmaker and hip-hop impresario Michael Holman states that for African American youth, the imitation of robots allowed them to "escape to a world where everything is perfect, sharp and in control" (Holman 1984). Animation techniques emulate a metaphorical body without biological or material limitations, achieving images usually only witnessed through the treatment of the television edit.

Peridot's mastery of corporeal illusion, framed in a technological narrative, is but one example where animation techniques are used to create the impression of technologically enhanced beings within crew performances.[10] In this example, the emphasis is firmly placed on the technological enhancement of the body through these techniques. Instead of displays of athletic flair, Peridot demonstrates the "going beyond" the body through the portrayal of micro-technologies: the corporeal control over the micro-circuitry and micro-isolation of the fast-twitch muscles and joints that create the illusion of technologically enhanced cyborgian beings.

Posthumanist and transhumanist discourse situate the relationship between the body and technology as seeking to reconceive the concept of the human (Badmington 2000; Gray 1995; Hayles 1999; Holland 1995; Shilling 2005; Tomas 1995). These discussions arise from an increased reliance on digital communication, a continued engagement with interactive digital environments, and the physical and abstract presence of the organic body in virtual spaces. Donna Haraway's 1985 seminal feminist essay, "A Manifesto for Cyborgs: Science, Technology, and Socialist Feminism in the 1980s," describes the fusion between human and machine as a cyborg: a hybrid that crosses between social reality and fiction (Haraway [1985] 2000).[11] Haraway argues that the physical distinction between reality and fiction has been blurred and demands a reconsideration of corporeal boundaries. In Western popular literature, science fiction, and Hollywood films, hyper-robotic and CGI (computer-generated imagery) manifestations are imagined through futuristic characters and have become the basis of a populist understanding of the cyborg. This cross between human and machine is visualized through contemporary film portrayals, including the *Terminator* series (1984, 1991, 2003, 2015), the *RoboCop* series (1987, 1990), *Blade Runner* (1982), and *The Matrix Trilogy* (1999–2003). Cultural studies theorists David Tomas (1995) and Samantha Holland (1995) argue that these mediated human–machine hybrids highlight the concern and fear surrounding the technological body. These technological manipulations put into question the status of the material body in this blurred space, and raise questions regarding the loss of the self and the departure of traditional dualisms, such as gender and the mind–body split.[12]

The technologically enhanced aesthetic of crew performances alludes to the relationship between technology and the corporeal, or the techno-corporeality of the body. Rather than reflecting the mechanical, as stated in Brandstetter's analysis of virtuosic excess, Peridot embodies the contemporary digital. The performance of micro actions, such as arm or leg pops, or the controlled isolation of small or complex body parts, including ribs, shoulders, and fingers, suggests a concealment and internalization of power, rather than an overt and aggressive display of machinic strength. In her research into technology and the body, film and gender theorist Claudia Springer (1996, 39) states that "mechanical technology, with its engines, gears, pistons, and shafts, has been joined and in many ways superseded by the increasingly miniaturized micro circuitry of electronic technology." Thus, street dance crews, such as Peridot, utilize animation techniques as a form of virtuosic excess, creating a fusion between the anatomical form of the body, the mechanical, and the digital.

SYNCHRONIZATION

Alongside the use of animation techniques, examples of this techno-corporeal fusion can also be observed in the continuous use of perfectly executed group synchronicity that creates the illusion of digitally produced duplicate bodies. Across all duet and crew choreographies in street dance crew competitions, emphasis is placed on the use of multiple bodies performing identical movement sequences. Crews face the studio audience and mirror the tempo and rhythmic structure of the accompaniment through their gestures and actions. These choreographies are rehearsed and refined through drill-like studio training to the extent that human error is removed and the crew members appear to be identical copies of each other. Such synchronicity holds currency in the televised talent show competition, as crews who do not achieve tight unison, precise stunts, and honed bodily technique will not achieve home viewers' votes and will be eliminated from the competition.[13]

Flawless, as implied by its name, achieves a "flawless" performance in their audition through the dancers' choreographic and spatial precision. Rather than the controlled gliding of the A Team, Flawless's accuracy lies in the speed of execution and the fact that every crew member's movement is identical, regardless of complexity or speed. From the beginning of the audition, a static fixed shot captures the nine dancers in their triangle formation as they perform a combination of arm pops and waves that spread out into various directions, while remaining perfectly synchronized in their timing. They gradually build up the texture of the choreography, with only three dancers performing in unison, and then introduce several others to join, with the same sequence. The equal spatial distance between each member in a symmetrical design creates the impression of one single body digitally duplicated several times in a kaleidoscopic pattern, while the filming of the crew from a wide shot and 45-degree angle masks any individual mistakes or differing facial expressions.

In anthropologist Marcel Mauss's ([1934] 2006) analysis of bodily techniques, he draws parallels between military organizational systems and the assembly of a machine to show how both systems strive to achieve efficiency. Additionally, Springer's (1996, 17) study of humans and machines also notes that Victorian industrialization saw the shift from an exploited human labor force to machines that "improved on what they saw as the deficiencies of human workers." In the example of the street dance crew, Flawless achieves such machine-like efficiency through the use of multiple dancers, physically multiplying the body across the stage. Dancers appear to embody the mechanisms of the machine to eradicate "human" deficiencies, achieving high levels of strength, speed, and endurance to simulate the gears, pistons, and motors of the crew "machine." While illusionary in quality, the multiplication of the body across the television screen amplifies both the number and the status of the crew. Bodies appear to exceed corporeal possibilities through their labor, and human attributes of pain and exhaustion are replaced by machine-like invincibility. These virtuosic performances of carbon-copy unison therefore conjure up representations of technologically enhanced beings, with the crew unit presented as the perfect machine, tirelessly working to create the overall product of the dance.

META-BODIES

In the opening to its final performance on *BGT*, Diversity uses fluid body waving and a shift in group formation to smoothly morph into a three-tier robot with claw-like legs and eight spider-like arms. Each dancer creates the legs, limbs, and/or heads of the creature/robot, accompanied by the sound of a whirling mechanical engine that mimics the transformational sound of robots from the children's cartoon series turned Hollywood blockbuster, *Transformers* (2007). The Diversity robot marches and strikes its arms out to the side, accompanied by five heavy, rhythmic mechanical beats. Later in the choreography, dancers stand behind each other with their arms overlapping the front dancer. As the soundtrack says "breathe," three six-limbed, armored aliens are revealed through claw-like hand movements, achieved through the opening and closing of each of the dancers' arms. These meta-bodied structures continue, with the crew playfully recreating the buzzers of the judges with dancers' heads, and finally creating the image of an airplane in flight, emphasized by the background digital screen effects of shooting images of light.

Through the manipulation of the human form and the morphing into mechanical and monstrous beings, crews such as Diversity appear to exceed the limitations of the corporeal form, transforming into helicopters, bicycles, racing cars, elevators, and telephones. Similar to the digital computer-generated creatures in live-action cinema, street dance crews create menacing and enhanced lifeforms through their embodied live-action performances. This is achieved without the aid of scaled-down models, computer scanning, 3D modeling, key frame animation, or animatronics (Whissel 2014).[14] I describe these figures as meta-bodies: mechanically and digitally enhanced lifeforms created through the careful layering of several dancers within a gymnastic stunt. Each dancer within the crew becomes the building block of a larger structure through the layering, balancing, and eventual abstraction of body parts. The results of these stunts are mechanical, monstrous and zoological beings that transform individual dancers into a single collective.

In her study of cinematic special effects and, more specifically, digitally enhanced lifeforms in cinema, film and media scholar Kristen Whissel (2014, 93) highlights the multiple definitions of the term *vital*. She associates the term with "organic life and death as well as the optimal functioning of technology" and describes digitally enhanced creatures on screen as holding "excessive . . . vitality" due to their surplus bodily excess and the vital spark or flame that brings them to life (Whissel 2014, 92). While already alive, crews exceed their humanity and their human form by reimagining this vitality through the careful composition of several bodies to create a hyper-body. Similar to the cinematic process of creating compelling digital beings through animation, crews "remediate embodied, live-action performances into persuasively vital digital beings," but achieve this through virtuosic excess, rather than through digital intervention (Whissel 2014, 91). The spectorial fascination with these figures lies in their ability to combine human performance with digital and mechanized movement qualities, blurring the line between the "animate and inanimate, organic and inorganic, material and code" (Whissel 2014, 92).

Diversity and fellow crews use the choreographic device of meta-bodies to go "above and beyond" the possibilities of the solo dancer through the distortion of the human form and forge an alliance with the technological through excessive vitality. This continuous staging of the techno-corporeal reflects the contemporary era of mechanical and digital intervention, and again demonstrates the crews' physical negotiation of human virtuosity within a heavily digitized age. Brandstetter (2007, 191–192) states that, in the context of the twentieth-century shift to image and sound, "one reads again and again that performing artists now find themselves competing with recordings, that they find themselves in the unfortunate situation of never being able to live up to their own 'ideal' productions." In her research on the competition body, dance scholar Alexis Weisbrod (2010, 98) also observes the rivalry between the stage body and the mediated body, stating that "audiences have a strong reverence for these extreme physical abilities, and anything the competition body can accomplish to meet similar superhuman criteria is met with acceptance and acclaim." By achieving the same feats as cinematic bodies, including the creation of cinematic style meta-bodies, these crew performances demonstrate physical prowess and the capabilities of the organic body in a competitive and mediated environment.

DIAMONDS IN THE RUFF

Alongside the street dance crews' affinity with technological enhancement, the exaggerated narrative of television talent shows allows further potential for performances of excess. These programs encourage viewers to engage with crew performances by voting for their favorite contestants to remain in the show. The panel of judges educates and guides the audience's decision, and doubles as a vital source of entertainment due to the opportunity for conflicting opinions. This potential for conflict ties in with the narration of the programs, which is purposefully structured to enhance the competitive themes of risk, opportunity, and chance. In the case of Saturday night peak-time talent shows, these programs become event television: "television that attracts huge audiences and becomes part of the popular discourse of everyday life. Like soap operas, the action . . . is contextualized and amplified by excessive media commentary including chat shows, interviews, tabloid newspaper coverage and the circulation of participants' images as celebrities" (Biressi and Nunn 2005, 11).

Unlike the big-budget production capabilities of Hollywood street dance films, such as the *Step Up* film series (2006, 2008, 2010, 2012, 2014), the lower budget international television franchise model cannot replicate the same level of digital intervention with regard to CGI and blue screen slow-motion capture. Despite these lower production values, the emphasis on special effects and the technological enhancement of the human body is still prevalent within these choreographies. The home viewer thus experiences crew performances through the design of the producer/editor, whereby the zooming and panning of the camera, as well as the post-production manipulation of live and pre-recorded footage, augments and amplifies the street dance body.[15]

In Ruff Diamond's semi-final performance on *GTD* series four, a low camera positioned at the foot of the stage creates the impression of a dancer's aerial routine almost flying into the camera lens. The close-up positioning of the camera at the foot of the circular stage captures one dancer executing a front flip over another dancer, and the camera angle amplifies the height of the drop to the floor. The camera cuts from a front-facing mid-shot that encases the entire crew and depicts one dancer preparing to perform a gymnastic sequence upstage. The camera then quickly cuts to a side camera and reveals the dancer in midair, then zooms out to reveal the same dancer completing another back flip over another dancer. Here, the fast cut between cameras provides multiple perspectives of the stunt in full flight, and the movement of both the camera and the dancer enhances the speed and dexterity of the stunt's execution.

Pre-recorded VT[16] segments additionally enable the amplification of crew performances. These pre-performance segments squeeze hours of raw footage of interviews, previous performances, and judges' comments into thirty-second sequences to quickly grab the viewer's gaze in a short space of allotted time. Prior to their semi-final performance, Ruff Diamond's VT segment is first introduced by rapid frames of motion spliced together, bombarding the viewer with pre-recorded aerial corkscrews, split leaps, falls, and the final image of the crew with fists in the air as the words "RUFF DIAMOND" shoot out from the screen. Using post-production digital editing techniques, including slow motion, rapid overlaying of footage, and high color saturation, producers construct the image of crews as superhuman beings.[17]

It is the narrative of ordinary versus extraordinary that feeds into the notion of excess and going above and beyond judges' and the public's expectations in the competition. In their interview prior to their semi-final performance, the members of Ruff Diamond are interviewed in their home town of Hartlepool, a coastal town in northeastern England. The crew describe themselves as "stranded from the rest of the street dance scene," with accompanying footage of them rehearsing at an unused pier and in a small apartment. The crew state that "because of where we're from, we have to work a lot harder than crews from, say, London" and "we've not got any teachers, we kind of have to figure it out for ourselves."

These interviews continue the reality television model that portrays popular dance as a means of transformation from the "ordinary," increasing the contestants' opportunities for fame and increased economic worth. In both *BGT* and *GTD*, the productions present crew members discussing their competition experience in a stationary interview or through the situation of the crew in everyday geographical environments, such as small terraced homes, street corners, or empty parking lots. Crews describe their experiences using colloquial language, and the everyday location of the interviews continues the working-class-based construction of the "ordinary." As highlighted in sociologist Jade Boyd's (2012, 264) analysis of *SYTYCD*, "the ordinariness of the extraordinary performer is emphasized through out-of-studio and backstage camera shots, the close 'capturing' of seemingly private moments of frustration, expectation, insecurity, joy, and failure through the fetishization of emotion." Through personal accounts and the selling of the self, televised references to the contestants' home life and their economic and cultural backgrounds situate the reality contestants as "ordinary" and ready to make the transition to the "better" life of celebrity.

These pre-recorded interviews are interwoven with the rapidly edited clips of digitally enhanced virtuosic stunts. Such prosaic "human" response, achieved through the close-up positioning of the camera, jars against the indestructible and machine-like images of the crew witnessed seconds earlier. Producers re-present these dancing bodies by editing together high-affect moments or "jolts" of previous performances, which include high kicks, spins, flips, and a series of aerial stunts (McMains 2010, 263). In the case of Ruff Diamond, a crew member discusses the town being stranded, while another member performs a backward somersault off the pier ledge in slow motion. High-affect moments from their audition, such as one dancer being hoisted horizontally into the air and caught by the feet of a supine dancer, are woven into images of the gray, drab background of the pier location. Additionally, the interview ends with slow-motion, high-color images of breaking power moves and a synchronized suicide drop. While ordinariness is conveyed through the crew's location, status, and content of their interviews, the viewer is continuously reminded of the crew members' extraordinary physical ability and their potential to transition to a new and improved self through their dancing talent. This post-production editing contrasts rhetorics of ordinary human struggle, as presented by the reality television competition, against the extraordinary, machine-like, and superhuman performances of these techno-corporeal bodies of excess.

INDIVIDUAL VERSUS COLLECTIVE

Within the analysis of synchronicity and the formation of meta-bodies in crew performances, the importance of the crew structure over the individual dancer becomes more apparent. In terms of virtuosic performance, Osterweis (2014, 71) observes that such an excessive performance quality originated through "the trope of the soloist," as witnessed in Western concert dance and the rise of the principal dancer. This was a virtuosity driven by individual capitalist ambition to surpass competitors and achieve uniqueness by being positioned in front of the *corps de ballet*. As witnessed in popular music concerts, music videos, and YouTube clips, the celebrity positioned at the front of the supporting back-up dancers continues to reaffirm this depiction of hierarchical status. Street crew dancers complement, mirror, and mimic their movements at the front of the apex triangle or crowd scene, duplicating the physical presence of the celebrity (Bench 2014). Even in cinematic portrayals of hip-hop dance, "dance crews exist only in the background [behind the leading actors], with uncertain and uninterrogated fates" (Arzumanova 2014, 178).

This strive for individual gain is replicated in the neoliberal capitalist format of the reality television show. Jen Harvie (2013, 12) describes neoliberalism as a political ideology that "recognizes and prioritizes the individual's right to seek self-fulfillment and to do so in conditions unrestricted by state-institution end regulations."[18] In neoliberal capitalism, the individual is free to generate self-reward, but this self-reward in turn produces and increases the profits of private organizations and governments through open market capital circulation (Harvie 2013). This right to self-fulfillment and reward lies at the core of reality television formats, with the individual striving to achieve fame, fortune, and social mobility. Participants endeavor to win the desired rewards and prize money offered by the competition, while also increasing their celebrity status through media coverage to ensure future employability after the competition. Yet these rewards are diminutive in comparison with the profits of the production companies.

In the context of street dance crew competitive performance, the concept of virtuosity as capitalist ambition moves away from the emphasis on the individual to one of coalition and partnership. The continued emphasis on the crew structure of the performances, or the collective identity of the group, challenges the "cult of individualism" that operates in the television talent show (Osterweis 2014, 71). In her study of the film *Save the Last* Dance (2001), communications scholar Inna Arzumanova (2014, 179) describes hip-hop dance crews as "the closest image of coalition politics, of collective mobilization and group identity enactment." This politics of cooperation emerges through the shared labor of the performance and, via rehearsal, repetition, and improvement, dancers achieve a collective synchronization in striving to construct a shared vision. Like cogs in a machine, each crew member is vital in creating the overall choreographic effect. The crew format in the television talent show places emphasis on no single dancer, achieving the visually spectacular aesthetic through collaboration, cooperation, and power in numbers.

Rhetorics of community and friendship are also emphasized verbally through VT segments and interviews with hosts and judges. Flawless presents the crew members as a close-knit unit by describing themselves as "a family with a passion for dance," stating after their audition that they are just "happy to be on the stage with my brothers and my friends" (2009). Diversity emphasizes the importance of community over the desire to win; one member states that "to be doing this with my brother and my best mates, it's just the best feeling in the world you know" (2009). When receiving their final comments from the judges, all crews hold on to each other, demonstrating a united front and conveying the message of "whatever happens, we've got each other." This emphasis on the cooperative community unit, as well as the brotherhood of the crew over the individual, jars against the reality television rhetoric of individual gain. Here, the experience of dancing with family and friends is depicted as holding higher value than that of the success of any particular member of the crew.

By performing complicated polyrhythmic sequences in tight unison, as well as reinforcing their collective identity in interviews, crew dancers thus present a strong community unit within the neoliberal capitalist agenda of the televised competition. These performances of virtuosic excess create not only powerful images of bodies moving in congruence, but also a collective whose economic success is only determined by the individual performances of its counterparts. In her recent study of gadgets, bodies, and advertisements, dance scholar Melissa Blanco Borelli (2016, 427) states that "the collective action of dancing together creates new communities that negotiate different ways of being autonomous in capitalism" forging a "politics of togetherness." This emphasis on the collective over the individual through the shared labor of the crew challenges and disrupts the construction of individual capitalist gain.

It should be noted that this choreographic "politics of togetherness" is still ultimately rooted in the desire to succeed, in terms of potential media exposure offered to the crews, as well as the opportunity to win the competitions' cash prizes. After judges have delivered their feedback to the crews in the semi-final and final performances, digital telephone numbers appear on screen next to the crews, enabling remote spectators to advance crews in the competitions through telephone, text, and web voting. The dancers enhance these sales pitches in order to increase their appeal to the home voter. Crews including the A Team, Flawless, and Diversity perform choreographed unison sequences of telephone gestures with their hands, nodding and smiling directly into the camera lens as the numbers and terms and conditions of the competition are read out by the television hosts. Self-fulfillment and financial reward continue to be linked to the neoliberal capitalist discourse of the reality television competition, but are masked by the performance of collectivity.

ASPIRATION THROUGH PERSPIRATION

The concept of transition and transformation from the ordinary to the extraordinary is at the heart of the reality television competition structure, and manifests within performances of virtuosic excess that create the illusion of transcending the corporeal. Through their need to achieve maximum exposure on the television screen, street dance crews physically contend and compete with cinematic digitally enhanced bodies through their performances of techno-corporeality. In order to be seen (and to compete within) the media spectacle of the competition and the context of the television show, street dance crews perform excess by way of their labor, technical aptitude, personality, and the reimagining of the corporeal form into machines, animals, and monstrous lifeforms. Crews labor beyond corporeal limitations and create the appearance of transcendence to a higher level of ability, despite the restrictions of the organic corporeal form and the television format of the competition.

Aspiration, as the corporeal struggle to achieve economic success, becomes an essential performance quality in a competition format. This ambition drives the crew to become more than just another reality television act, but rather to create a hybridity between human and machine. Through their emphasis on the collective, crew performances not only exceed corporeal limitations through a collegial choreographic approach, but at the same time challenge the reading of virtuosity as performances of individual excellence, putting into question the neoliberal strive for individual gain.

NOTES

1. The windmill is a breaking power move in which the dancer rotates the torso in a circular path on the floor, leveraging from the upper chest, shoulders, and back, while holding the legs in a V-position.
2. Herein, I use the following abbreviations: *BGT* (*Britain's Got Talent*), *GTD* (*Got To Dance*), and *SYTYCD* (*So You Think You Can Dance*).
3. In popular media, dance crew performances in television talent shows are labeled under various umbrella terms, including "street dance," "hip-hop," "urban," and "commercial." Such terms are problematic in their reduction of complex artistic forms to stereotypical sound bites. This varied lexicon is reflective of several areas of confusion: the unwritten and historical context of multiple forms, genres and subgenres of African-diasporic cultural practice; the cultural appropriation of these diverse practices; and the lack of research surrounding the transnational cultural flows of hip-hop culture. While the historical origins of breaking (sometimes known as "break dancing") and its early dissemination are prevalent subject matters in academic literature, contemporary UK hip-hop dance culture, the commercialization of hip-hop dance, and the emergence of the term "street dance" are all under-researched areas. In recognition of these fraught issues of classification, where possible, I use precise stylistic terminology in line with popular histories of their origins. These include locking, popping, roboting, and electric boogaloo (funk styles); breaking and hip-hop party dances (hip-hop); house, vogueing and waacking (club styles); nuskool hip-hop choreography, krump, and jerking. Where unavoidable, I refer to these vernacular practices through the umbrella term "hip-hop dance." This differentiation between street dance and hip-hop dance purposely removes the hierarchy that surrounds these performances in relation to their deemed inauthenticity in comparison with "authentic" vernacular practices of hip-hop dance.
4. DeFrantz's (2004) analysis of hip-hop dance practice in his article, "The Black Beat Made Visible: Hip Hop Dance and Body Power," also highlights the importance of black social dance as a form of identity construction due to its "corporeal orature": the production of meaning through the speech-like quality of the movement. Instead of inscribing meaning onto the dance from an outside perspective, DeFrantz discusses how black social dance requires a physical embodiment in order for the dance's full communicative meanings to be apparent.
5. The suicide drop is a power move in which the dancer suddenly drops on his or her back.
6. The preceding research findings are supported by informal conversations with dancers, crew members, and production editors between 2009 to the present. My position as a dancer, dance professor, and dance development manager has led to many discussions with dance artists who have been involved with reality television competitions, including *SYTYCD*, *BGT*, and *GTD*. During conversations with dancers involved in television talent shows, they revealed that in some cases the production team worked with the choreographer to select appropriate camera angles. In other instances this was decided purely by the television production team.
7. In the final scenes of the film, Nina physically transforms on stage by growing black wings instead of arms.
8. A detailed list of the varying techniques can be found at http://www.hiphopunite.com/index-styles.html.

9. Here I use the term *pedestrian* to describe everyday/ordinary movements as pioneered by the Judson Dance Theater (Burt 2006).

10. Other crew performances include Back2Back (Back2Back 2011), Bionik Funk (Bionik Funk 2011), Cerebro (Cerebro 2011), Legacy (Legacy 2012) and Antics (Antics 2012). In particular, popping duet Static Movement states in the VT segment prior to their audition that "we want [the audience] to question the reality of what they are actually seeing," making them question "what's going on and how did they do that" (Static Movement 2012). The duet draws upon the techniques of robotics, popping, ticking, waving, and extreme isolations of the head and chest cavity to create the illusion of cyborgian lifeforms.

11. She comments that "late twentieth century machines have made thoroughly ambiguous the difference between natural and artificial, mind and body, self-developing and eternally designed, and many other distinctions that used to apply to organisms and machines. Our machines are disturbingly lively, and we ourselves frighteningly inert" (Haraway [1985] 2000, 52).

12. The Cartesian split is developed from the work of René Descartes and describes a dualism between the mind and the body. Holland (1995) argues that cyborgs on film put into question this conceptual dualism, where hybrids take the form of humans but lose their human individuality, suggesting that the human mind equates to humanity.

13. In the case of Abyss on *BGT* series five (Abyss 2011), their audition fails to impress the judges due to the crew not demonstrating the same level of precision of other previous dance acts.

14. See Whissel (2014) for a full explanation of cinematic techniques.

15. In cinematography, zooming is the smooth transition between a long shot and a close-up shot in television. Panning refers to the horizontal rotation of the camera from a fixed position.

16. Despite the shift to digital recordings, the term *VT* stands for "videotape" and refers to pre-recorded and edited footage.

17. In particular, *Got to Dance*'s time-freeze technology, introduced in 2013, involves a hi-tech camera technique that captures spins, flips, and twists in 360-degree motion, creating the "so-called Matrix effect" (Fletcher 2013). These camera shots not only suspend the dancer, but reveal a 360-degree perspective of the stunt.

18. Harvie (2013) notes that neoliberalism has been cultivated by both the United Kingdom's New Labour and Coalition governments. She maintains that neoliberal capitalism was spurred on by mounting state debt and the British financial crisis in 2007.

References

Arzumanova, Inna. 2014. "'It's Sort of "Members Only'": Transgression and Body Politics in *Save the Last Dance*." In *The Oxford Handbook of Dance and the Popular Screen*, edited by Melissa Blanco Borelli, 166–181. Oxford: Oxford University Press.

Badmington, Neil. 2000. *Posthumanism*. Houndmills, Basingstoke: Palgrave.

Banes, Sally. [1985] 2004. "Breaking." In *That's The Joint!: The Hip-Hop Studies Reader*, 1st edition, edited by Murray Forman and Mark Anthony Neal, 14–20. London; New York: Routledge.

Bench, Harmony. 2014. "Monstrous Belongings: Performing 'Thriller' after 9/11." In *The Oxford Handbook of Dance and the Popular Screen*, edited by Melissa Blanco Borelli, 393–411. Oxford: Oxford University Press.

Biressi, Anita, and Heather Nunn. 2005. *Reality TV: Realism and Revelation.* New York: Columbia University Press.

Blanco Borelli, Melissa. 2016. "Gadgets, Bodies and Screens: Dance in Advertisements for New Technologies." In *The Oxford Handbook of Screendance Studies*, edited by Douglas Rosenberg, 421–438. Oxford: Oxford University Press.

Boyd, Jade. 2012. "Hey, We're from Canada but We're Diverse, Right?": Neoliberalism, Multiculturalism, and Identity on *So You Think You Can Dance Canada*." *Critical Studies in Media Communication* 29: 259–274. doi: 10.1080/15295036.2011.637222.

Brandstetter, Gabrielle. 2007. "The Virtuoso's Stage: A Theatrical Topos." *Theatre Research International* 32: 178–195. doi: 10.1017/S0307883307002829.

Burt, Ramsey. 2006. *Judson Dance Theater: Performative Traces.* Oxford; New York: Routledge.

Darley, Andrew. 2000. *Visual Digital Culture: Surface Play and Spectacle in New Media Genres.* London; New York: Routledge.

DeFrantz, Thomas, F. 2004. "The Black Beat Made Visible: Body Power in Hip Hop Dance." In *Of the Presence of the Body: Essays on Dance and Performance Theory*, edited by André Lepecki, 64–81. Middletown, CT: Wesleyan University Press.

Fletcher, Alex. 2013. "'Got to Dance' Introduces Groundbreaking 96 Cameras." *Digital Spy*, January 23. http://www.digitalspy.co.uk/tv/s112/got-to-dance/news/a453171/got-to-dance-introduces-groundbreaking-96-cameras-watch-video.html#ixzz3mH4bRh1p. Accessed May 4, 2014.

Gray, Chris Hables. 1995. *The Cyborg Handbook.* New York: Routledge.

Hall, Frank. 2008. *Competitive Irish Dance: Art, Sport, Duty.* : Macater.

Hamera, Judith. 2000. "The Romance of Monsters: Theorizing the Virtuoso Body." *Theatre Topics* 10(2): 144–153. doi: 10.1353/tt.2000.0013.

Haraway, Donna. [1985] 2000. "A Manifesto for Cyborgs: Science, Technology, and Socialist Feminism in the 1980s." In *The Gendered Cyborg: A Reader*, edited by Gill Kirkup, Linda James, Kath Woodward, and Fiona Hovenden, 50–57. London; New York: Routledge in association with the Open University.

Harvie, Jen. 2013. *Fair Play: Art, Performance and Neoliberalism.* Houndmills, Basingstoke: Palgrave Macmillan.

Hayles, N. Katherine. 1999. *How We Became Posthuman: Virtual Bodies in Cybernetics, Literature, and Informatics.* Chicago: University of Chicago Press.

Hazzard-Gordon, Katrina. 1990. *Jookin': The Rise of Social Dance Formations in African-American Culture.* Philadelphia: Temple University Press.

Hazzard-Gordon, Katrina. 1996. "Dance in Hip Hop Culture." In *Droppin' Science: Critical Essays on Rap Music and Hip Hop Culture*, edited by William Eric Perkins, 220–237. Philadelphia: Temple University Press.

Holland, Samantha. 1995. "Descartes Goes to Hollywood: Mind, Body and Gender in Contemporary Cyborg Cinema." In *Cyberspace Cyberbodies Cyberpunk: Cultures of Technological Embodiment*, edited by Mike Featherstone and Roger Burrows, 157–174. London: Sage.

Holman, Michael. 1984. "Locking and Popping (Electric Boogie)." *Hip Hop-Network.* http://www.hiphopnetwork.com/articles/bboyarticles/popinelectricboogie2.asp. Accessed April 10, 2014.

Kershaw, Baz. 2003. "Curiosity or Contempt: On Spectacle, the Human, and Activism." *Theatre Journal* 55(4): 591–611. doi: 10.1353/tj.2003.0170.

Lockerlegends. 2011. "History of Locking." *Lockerlegends.* http://lockerlegends.net/history-of-locking/. Accessed May 3, 2011.

Mauss, Marcel. [1934] 2006. "Techniques of the Body." In *Techniques, Technology and Civilisation*, edited by Nathan Schlanger, 77–96. New York: Berghahn Books and Durkheim.

MRDAVEYD. 2013. "The History of Bay Area Hip Hop Dance: Roboting, Strutting, Boogaloo & Funk." *Hip Hop and Politics*, December 16. http://hiphopandpolitics.com/2013/12/16/history-bay-area-hip-hop-dance-roboting-strutting-boogaloo-funk/. Accessed April 10, 2014.

McMains, Juliet. 2010. "Reality Check: *Dancing with the Stars* and the American Dream." In *The Routledge Dance Studies Reader*, 2nd edition, edited by Alexandra Carter and Janet O'Shea, 261–272. London; New York: Routledge.

Osterweis, Ariel. 2013. "The Muse of Virtuosity: Desmond Richardson, Race, and Choreographic Falsetto." *Dance Research Journal* 45(3): 53–74.

Osterweis, Ariel. 2014. "Disciplining *Black Swan*, Animalizing Ambition." In *The Oxford Handbook of Dance and the Popular Screen*, edited by Melissa Blanco Borelli, 68–82. Oxford: Oxford University Press.

Palmer, David. L. 1998. "Virtuosity as Rhetoric: Agency and Transformation in Paganini's Mastery of the Violin." *Quarterly Journal of Speech* 84: 341–357. doi: 10.1080/00335639809384223.

Rose, Tricia. 1994. *Black Noise: Rap Music and Black Culture in Contemporary America.* Hanover, NH: University Press of New England.

Shilling, Chris. 2005. *The Body in Culture, Technology and Society.* London; Thousand Oaks; New Delhi: Sage.

Springer, Claudia. 1996. *Electronic Eros: Bodies and Desire in the Postindustrial Age.* Austin: University of Texas Press.

Stillman, Amy. 1996. "Hawaiian Hula Competitions: Event, Repertoire, Performance, Tradition." *The Journal of American Folklore* 104(434): 357–380. doi: 10.2307/541181.

Tomas, David. 1995. "Feedback and Cybernetics: Reimaging the Body in the Age of the Cyborg." In *Cyberspace Cyberbodies Cyberpunk: Cultures of Technological Embodiment*, edited by Mike Featherstone and Roger Burrows, 21–44. London: Sage.

Toop, David. 2000. *Rap Attack 3: African Rap to Global Hip Hop.* 3rd revised edition. London: Serpent's Tail.

Weisbrod, Alexis. 2010. "Competition Dance: Redefining Dance in the United States." PhD diss., University of California, Riverside. http://escholarship.org/uc/item/6924g6c6. Accessed June 7, 2011.

Whissel, Kristen. 2014. *Spectacular Digital Effects: CGI and Contemporary Cinema.* Durham, NC; London: Duke University Press.

Williams, Simon. 1998. "Bodily Dys-order: Desire, Excess and the Transgression of Corporeal Boundaries." *Body and Society* 4(2): 59–82. doi: 10.1177/1357034X98004002004.

Williams, Simon. 2001. *Emotion and Social Theory: Corporeal Reflections on the (Ir) Rational.* London; Thousand Oaks, CA: Sage.

Audiovisual Sources

Please note: the following references replicate the formatting/spelling exactly as it appears on YouTube.

Abyss Street Dance Group Britains Got Talent 2011 HD. 2011. YouTube video, 1:30. Posted by "Megaroyalwedding2011," May 21. http://youtube.be/IM6uS_ASNmw. Accessed February 2, 2017.

Alien. 1979. Directed by Ridley Scott. USA: Brandywine Productions and Twentieth Century-Fox Productions, 2000. DVD.

America's Best Dance Crew. 2008–2015. Broadcast by MTV, directed by Ryan Polito.

Back2Back | Audition | Got To Dance Series 2. 2010. YouTube video, 1:19. Posted by "Got To Dance," December 17. http://youtube.be/q_Lj6cVlvDc. Accessed February 2, 2017.

BIONIK FUNK- Britain's Got Talent 2010. 2010. YouTube video, 00:55. Posted by "Gettoasted91," May 1. http://youtu.be/jhj7wsWXBOI. Accessed February 2, 2017.

Black Swan. 2010. Directed by Darren Aronofsky. 20th Century Fox Home Entertainment, 2011. DVD.

Blade Runner. 1982. Directed by Ridley Scott. The Ladd Company, The Shaw Brothers (in association with) (as Sir Run Run Shaw), Warner Bros. (through: A Warner Communications Company) (as Warner Bros.), Blade Runner Partnership (Jerry Perenchio and Bud Yorkin present), 2006. DVD.

Britains got talent- Abyss semi-finals. 2011. YouTube video, 5:43. Posted by "OurLennox," June 1. http://youtube.be/_AcsabhfD9Q. Accessed February 2, 2017.

Britain's got talent—Friday—Kombat Breakers. 2007. YouTube video, 4:25. Posted by "Leeurmston," June 15. https://youtu.be/L-B6gHuovS8. Accessed February 2, 2017.

Cerebro Audition- Got to Dance. 2011. YouTube video, 1:49. Posted by "Got To Dance," January 21. http://youtube.be/-He1UkiVjVg. Accessed February 2, 2017.

Diversity: Dance Group-Britain's Got Talent 2009- The Final. 2009. YouTube video, 4:57. Posted by "Britain's Got Talent," May 30. http://youtube.be/PtwVfJqBfms. Accessed March 13, 2017.

Flawless-Britains Got Talent 2009. 2009. YouTube video, 6:05. Posted by "BritainsSoTalented," April 11. http://youtube.be/6GrOMLylvhQ. Accessed February 2, 2017.

*Got to Dance 2012—Popping—Legacy Audition—@OfficialVM_*. 2011. YouTube video, 3:14. Posted by "Virtualmovementmo," February 13. https://youtu.be/eDFp1KBOByk. Accessed February 2, 2017.

Got to Dance 4 Live Final: Ruff Diamond Final 3. 2013. YouTube video, 1:06. Posted by "Got to Dance", March 17. https://youtu.be/YfVv8Y7Evqo. Accessed February 2, 2017.

Got to Dance Series 3: A-Team Audition.2011. YouTube video, 2:45. Posted by "Got to Dance," December 30. http://youtube.be/-6hW-TxN54M. Accessed February 2, 2017.

Got to Dance Series 3: Antics Final Performance. 2012. YouTube video, 1:16. Posted by "Got to Dance," March 4. http://youtu.be/e-uVSIDFI-E. Accessed February 2, 2017.

Got to Dance Series 3: Static Movement Audition. 2012. YouTube video, 3:41. Posted by "Hardcoreaaron," January 12. https://youtu.be/MMwHII5vTrw. Accessed February 2, 2017.

Peridot- Britain's Got Talent 2010- semi-final 3. 2010. YouTube video, 2:01. Posted by "Britain's Got Talent," June 2. http://youtu.be/K996V5v9uPQ. Accessed February 2, 2017.

Robocop. 1987. Directed by Paul Verhoeven. Orion Pictures, 2003. DVD.

Robocop 2. 1990. Directed by Irvin Kershner. Orion Pictures and Tobor Productions, 2007. DVD.

So You Think You Can Dance. 2010–2011. Broadcast by BBC1, directed by Don Weiner.

Step Up. 2006. Directed by Anna Fletcher. Touchstone Pictures, Summit Entertainment, Offspring Entertainment and Eketahuna LLC, 2007. DVD.

Step Up 2: The Streets. 2008. Directed by Jon. M Chu. Touchstone Pictures, Summit Entertainment and Offspring Entertainment, 2008. DVD.

Step Up 3D. 2010. Directed by Jon. M Chu. Touchstone Pictures, Summit Entertainment and Offspring Entertainment, 2010. DVD.

Step Up All In. 2014. Directed by Trish Sie. Summit Entertainment and Offspring Entertainment, 2014. DVD.

Step Up: Miami Heat. 2012. Directed by Scott Speer. Summit Entertainment and Offspring Entertainment, 2012. DVD.

Terminator 2: Judgement Day. 1991. Directed by James Cameron. Carolco Pictures, Pacific Western, Lightstorm Entertainment, Canal+ and T" Productions, 2008. DVD.

Terminator 3: Rise of the Machines. 2003. Directed by Jonathan Mostow. C-2 Pictures, Intermedia Films, IMF, Mostow/Lieberman Productions, Columbia Pictures and Warner Bros. 2010. DVD.

Terminator Genisys. 2015. Directed by Alan Taylor. Paramount Pictures and Skydance Productions, 2015. DVD.

Terminator Salvation. 2009. Directed by McG. Halcyon Company, Wonderland Sound and Vision, Columbia Pictures and Warner Bros, 2009. DVD.

The Matrix. 1999. Directed by the Wachowski Brothers. Warner Bros., Village Roadhsow Pictures, Groucho II Film Partnership and Silver Productions, 2011. DVD.

The Matrix Reloaded. 1999. Directed by the Wachowski Brothers. Warner Bros., Village Roadhsow Pictures, Silver Productions, NPV Entertainment and Heineken Branded Entertainment, 2003. DVD.

The Matrix Revolutions. 1999. Directed by the Wachowski Brothers. Warner Bros., Village Roadhsow Pictures, Silver Productions and NPV Entertainment, 2004. DVD.

The Terminator. 1984. Directed by James Cameron. Hemdale Film, Pacific Western, Euro Film Funding and Cinema 84, 2009. DVD.

Transformers. 2007. Directed by Michael Bay. DreamWorks SKG, Paramount Pictures, Hasbro, Di Bonaventura Pictures, Amblin Entertainment, SprocketHeads and thinkfilm, 2007. DVD.

CHAPTER 8

··

SHIFTING DYNAMICS

Sean Nós *Dancing, Vernacular Expression, and
the Competitive Arena of the* Oireachtas

··

CATHERINE E. FOLEY

Competitions have been central to the rise in both the interest and numbers (of all ages) in *sean nós* dancing. Many competitions . . . take place
on larger stages under glitzy lights in front of a static audience and *sean
nós* has a different appearance. . . . It becomes strained and unnatural and
leans more towards a show-style performance. . . . In competition on large
lit stages with cameras, many natural elements of the style are lost.[1]

FROM the 1970s, a solo, vernacular step-dance practice in Ireland called *sean nós* dancing
entered the arena of formal staged competitions. Although a competitive spirit and a
friendly rivalry had previously existed within the practice, the change of context from
informal intimate gatherings to staged competitive events gave rise to concerns around
issues of performance, identity, place, and authenticity. This chapter examines these issues in relation to one staged competition, the *Oireachtas*, considered to be the primary
national competition for *sean nós* dancers in Ireland. It also presents the voices of *sean
nós* dancers who express their views on these issues.

My research is framed within ethnochoreological discourse, and the *Oireachtas
sean nós* dance competitions are my fieldwork site. Methodologically, I utilize a
number of ethnographic research methods: my role as an adjudicator of *sean nós*
dancing competitions at many events, including the *Oireachtas* since 2003; ethnographic interviews with *sean nós* dancers; participant observations of *sean nós* dancing
workshops; questionnaires; and informal conversations with *sean nós* dancers,
adjudicators, and others who are interested in *sean nós* dancing. I have extensive experience of the indigenous performing arts in Ireland; this has given me access to the field
and has provided me with a cognitive and embodied pre-understanding of the activities
and social interactions that exist within it (Foley 2011, 2012, 2013, 2014).

Sean nós literally means "old style." The term was originally popularized in Ireland in relation to an unaccompanied singing style in the Irish language and was appropriated in the 1970s to refer to the semi-improvisatory, percussive, vernacular solo step-dance practice, found mainly in the predominantly Irish-speaking Conamara *Gaeltacht*[2] region on the west coast of Ireland. This style of dancing was originally practiced by step dancers, mostly male dancers, in rural communities of the region at local social events for entertainment purposes. Due, however, to political and identity mobility factors in the Conamara *Gaeltacht* in the early 1970s, which I will discuss shortly, this solo dance practice became an iconic audiovisual identity marker of the region and was introduced to the formal competitive arena of the *Oireachtas*. Although other regions of Ireland also have old style, traditional solo step-dance practices (Foley 2012, 2013), this chapter focuses only on the *sean nós* dancing practice of Conamara,[3] where it is perceived, for the most part, to embody sociocultural values relating to a rural, traditional way of life of the people of the region.

THEORIZING COMPETITION AS
PLATFORM AND PROMOTOR

It is generally understood by ethnochoreologists and dance anthropologists that when a dance practice is recontextualized outside its original context of practice, it not only is shaped by its new context, where new meaning is ascribed to it, but the dance practice itself may also assist in shaping the new context (Daniel 1995; Foley 2013; Ness 1992).

Competition as a field site has been explored by a number of scholars (Erlmann 1996; Foley 2013; Hall 2008; Larsen 2008; Ní Bhriain 2010; Turino 2000), and theories exist on the impact of this contextual frame on indigenous performing arts. Some scholars see competitions as a cosmopolitan framing of folklore, although "*competition* per se is not exclusively a cosmopolitan mode of performance" (Dudley 2003, 18). Indeed, the cosmopolitan framing of folklore through competition in Ireland can be traced back to the end of the nineteenth century, when mostly middle-class intellectuals in the cultural nationalist movement, the Gaelic League, framed folkloric indigenous performing arts within competitive contexts for preservation and cultural promotional purposes. Within this cosmopolitan framing, the indigenous performing arts shifted from intimate and participatory modes of practice to formal and presentational modes of performance. This does not imply, however, that intimate modes of practice disappeared, but rather that they declined. This general shift affected the presentation and aesthetic of performance of these practices (Foley 2013).

Some scholars propose that competition has a narrowing, homogenizing, and controlling effect on indigenous dance practices. For example, anthropologist Frank Hall (2008) and ethnochoreologist Catherine Foley (2012, 2013) argue that the competitive framing of Irish step dancing from the end of the nineteenth century was popular and effective for the ideological agenda of the Gaelic League. They note that, in this scenario, hegemonic structures generally prevailed, which had an homogenizing and controlling effect on the practice (Foley 2012, 2013; Hall 2008). Ethnomusicologist Thomas Turino (2000) likewise suggests that shifts in context to competitive arenas generally have an agenda of control, uniformity, and planning over individual spontaneity. Yet, competition continues to provide an important platform for the promotion of indigenous performings arts practices in many parts of the world. According to musicologist and sociologist Veit Erlmann, "competition is perhaps the predominant mode of social interaction in modern capitalist societies" (1996, 224). This is reinforced by anthropologist Sally Ann Ness (2008, 18), who states, "It is difficult to imagine a value more core in western cultures than the value placed on being able to achieve a single, identified goal." It is therefore not surprising to find indigenous performing arts within the competition-oriented contextual framework.

In this chapter, I examine *sean nós* dancing within the competition-oriented context of the *Oireachtas* festival, and consider the following issues: the role that the *Oireachtas sean nós* dance competitions play in defining and consolidating community identity; how the competitions function to control, preserve, promote, or change dance values and identities; the ways that they impact on creativity and the generally understood ethno-aesthetic of the practice; and how they affect the transmission of *sean nós* dancing. First, however, I provide a brief introduction to *sean nós* dancing as a practice within its rural contextual milieu of Conamara.

SEAN NÓS DANCING AS A VERNACULAR DANCE PRACTICE

In Conamara, *sean nós* dancing, with its semi-improvisatory nature, is understood to be different from Irish solo step dancing, known locally as *rince foghlamtha* (learned or trained dancing). The latter is formally taught in towns and cities of Ireland, and elsewhere, to young male and female dancers by qualified Irish dance teachers who are generally registered with Irish dance organizations such as *An Coimisiún, An Comhdháil*,[4] and others. The primary performance context for dancers in these organizations is competition, where a specific step-dance aesthetic is promoted (Foley 2013). This includes choreographed dances or "steps," restrained posture, a codified technique, and a rhythmical dexterity of the feet. Dances are generally choreographed to "hard shoe" percussive dances or "light shoe" dances; the latter require an aesthetic of airborne graceful movements. Some of the more advanced dancers within these organizations are regarded as virtuoso dancers. In *sean nós* dancing in Conamara, however, virtuosity is not an objective of the practice. Neither is one assessed on technique or on "set" choreographed dances. Instead, one is assessed on one's competence at combining elements and motifs from a percussive dance practice that advocates improvisation, individuality, personality, a musical sense, a tidy close-to-the-floor style of dancing, and a lightness and evenness of rhythm. One is also assessed on one's ability to creatively dialogue with the accompanying Irish traditional musician.

Although a rivalry existed within the vernacular practice of *sean nós* dancing in Conamara, there were no formally organized competitions prior to its inclusion in the *Oireachtas*. According to *sean nós* dancer and *Oireachtas* winner Páraic Ó Hoibicín,

> In my younger age . . . there were a good few *sean nós* dancers . . . around our place. You'd see a session in a pub or a party . . . and you'd see when they had a couple of drinks . . . they'd go on the floor. It was like a competition between themselves, thinking they might be better than the next person. . . . But there was no competition there, but they went on the floor. . . . That being in Caharoe and Spiddal and Carna and that area.[5]

In the 1970s there were not many *sean nós* dancers in Conamara. These were predominantly old men who danced socially and informally to Irish traditional music on melodeon or button accordion in pub sessions, at house dances or at parties. The house dances were locally called *times* and people would say, "*Tá times sa teach!*" ("There is times in the house!"). *Sean nós* dancers danced in between social dances, such as the Stack of Barley, the Johnny, the waltz, or the Conamara Half Set. Reels were the most popular music types to which to perform a *sean nós* dance, although a *sean nós* dancer might also dance to a jig (Foley 2008). These dancers percussively tapped or beat out the rhythm of the accompanying music with their feet and danced within a small confined space; some might dance on top of a barrel. According to Páraic Ó Hoibicín, the older dancers danced loosely and very close to the floor, and their taps had an evenness. The old saying was, "If he was a good *sean nós* dancer, he wouldn't break eggs under him," or "He'd dance on a plate."[6] This aesthetic emphasized a lightness and a tidyness in movement—an aesthetic that also prevailed in work and life.

Although declining as a vernacular dance practice in the 1970s, the *Oireachtas* festival assisted in reviving and popularizing it through the inclusion of *sean nós* dancing competitions in its festival programming, which I come to now.

The *Oireachtas*

The institution of the *Oireachtas* exists as the primary, national festival for *Gaeltacht* communities in Ireland. It is also historically enmeshed with Irish cultural politics. As part of an anti-colonial and de-Anglicization endeavor, the Gaelic League, a cultural nationalist movement, established the *Oireachtas* in 1897 as an Irish national festival of competitions and social events to promote the Irish language as the vernacular language of Ireland. The arts were incorporated into the *Oireachtas* festival to assist with this endeavor, and competitions in Irish step dancing were also included (Costello 2015; Foley 2013; Ó Laoire 1997, 2000).

Oireachtas means "assembly," and the *Oireachtas* festival comprises an assembly of people predominantly from the *Gaeltacht* regions of Ireland (Figure 8.1); others interested in the Irish language and Irish indigenous performing arts may also attend. The *Gaeltacht* regions were identified by the Irish state in 1926 to safeguard the Irish language as a vernacular language.

The establishment of the *Oireachtas* was "loosely based on the notion of the ancient Gaelic cultural festival" (Foley 2013, 139) and was also inspired by the Welsh *eisteddfod* festival. In the early decades of the *Oireachtas*, Western European arts were also represented, including competitions in choral singing; the latter emphasized an Anglo-Irish aesthetic. Today, however, the indigenous performing arts form the focus of the *Oireachtas*.

The *Oireachtas* constitutes an annual six-day festival of competitions in Irish-language poetry, storytelling, *agallamh beirte* (a rhymed spoken duet), *lúibíní* (another duet, but humorous and newly composed based on current issues), fiddle, uilleann pipes, harp, *sean nós* singing, and *sean nós* dancing. These competitions generally run from Tuesday to Sunday at the end of October/beginning of November and hence the official title of the festival, *Oireachtas na Samhna* (the November Assembly).

FIGURE 8.1.   Le caoinchead Údarás na Gaeltachta (Gaeltacht regions of Ireland).

Image courtesy of Údarás na Gaeltachta.

The competitions at the *Oireachtas* are organized according to categories of age, and in the *sean nós* singing competition they are also categorized according to gender. Competitions are held throughout the festival from early morning until late evening. Additionally, the festival hosts formal events, such as book and CD launches, debates, concerts, *céilís*, discos for young people, and *Club an Oireachas* (the *Oireachtas* Festival Club), which takes place every night of the festival. Within the context of this six-day festival, the *sean nós* dancing (*Rince Aonar ar an Sean Nós*) competitions occur on Friday and Saturday. Because of the increase in numbers for this competition, preliminary rounds are held on Fridays to select those dancers who are to go forward to the final rounds, held on the Saturdays; the final rounds are broadcast live on *Steip Beo* by the Irish-language television station, TG4, and can be accessed by people in Ireland and overseas.

The end of the festival is always celebrated with a Catholic mass in Irish on the Sunday morning. This reinforces a belief of some cultural nationalists that Catholicism is equated with Irishness and that Irishness might be best found in the rural communities on the west of Ireland. As Foley states,

> The rural West had long been recognized as a repository of the "purest" and most "authentic" folk culture. This [notion] resonated with the cultural nationalist programme of the Gaelic League earlier in the century, and indeed, the European romantic movement of the eighteenth and nineteenth centuries when intellectuals in Europe were preoccupied with the notion that "the peasant constituted the 'pure' repository of all that is good and authentic in the national ethos." (Foley 2013, 207)[7]

The *Oireachtas* festival represents an important event for the *Gaeltacht* communities in Ireland; each community has its own distinct dialect of Irish or Gaelic and is identified with a particular geographical region of Ireland, with it own landscapes, cultural specificities, and economic ways of life. The meeting together of these *Gaeltacht* communities therefore represents a meeting of the *Gaels* (the Irish); it is "the great national festival of Gaelic Ireland" (Foley 2013, 139). The Irish *sean nós* singer and scholar Lillis O'Laoire (1997, 167) interprets these *Gaeltacht* regional communities as "ethnicities" and, following the ethnomusicologist Martin Stokes (1994), states that they are to be

> understood in terms of the construction, maintenance and negotiation of boundaries and not in a putative social "essence" which fills gaps within them . . . such boundaries are in a process of continual contestation and renegotiation.

Local allegiances to a particular *Gaeltacht* community are present at the *Oireachtas* festival, where individuals hope for a "home" win. The *Oireachtas* event therefore assists in maintaining, contesting, and negotiating these different constructions of community, and the *sean nós* dancing competition is an important aspect of this process.

Gaeltacht communities look forward to this annual festival where individuals within each community and, indeed, those outside it, compete for recognition and reward.

The *Oireachtas* is, therefore, an important meeting place for people from all *Gaeltacht* communities and for those advocates of the Irish language and culture from outside the *Gaeltachts*. They gather to immerse themselves in an entertaining but serious Irish-language festival where young and old intermingle and socialize around both formal competitions and informal sessions of traditional music, *sean nós* singing, and dancing. The informal sessions are peppered throughout the event and generally occur in an impromptu manner in corners of rooms or foyers. Many attendees return year after year and book hotel rooms a year in advance.

The *Oireachtas* demands significant organization and full-time members of staff, including Director Liam Ó Maolaodha, who currently work in the *Oireachtas* office in Dublin. The *Gaeltacht* communities and others who attend the *Oireachtas* are aware of the ritualized program structures and the choreo-musical-scapes and sonic-scapes[8] that dominate throughout the festival. It is particularly important for *sean nós* dancers, as this event attracts fellow *sean nós* dancers, musicians, singers, and Irish-language speakers. For many attendees, including *sean nós* dancers, the presence of these indigenous practices with the Irish language locates this particular style of dancing in context in the Conamara *Gaeltacht*. In effect, the *Oireachtas* festival becomes a microcosm of an imagined ideal Gaelic Ireland, and *sean nós* dancing can be interpreted as an embodiment of this imagined ideal.

THE *RINCE AONAR AR AN SEAN NÓS* COMPETITION

The *Rince Aonar ar an Sean Nós* competition[9] entered the *Oireachtas* festival as a result of the *Gaeltacht* civil rights movement (*cearta shíbhialta na Gaeltachta*), established in the late 1960s in the Conamara *Gaeltacht* in County Galway, in western Ireland. In protest at the economic neglect of the *Gaeltacht* regions by the Irish government, unemployment, and emigration, the *Gaeltacht* civil rights movement held its own "protest" *Oireachtas* festival, known as *Oireachtas na nGael* (the Irish *Oireachtas*). This was held in Ros Muc in Conamara in November 1970, and was in opposition to the national *Oireachtas* festival. Up until this time, no national *Oireachtas* had been held in the Conamara *Gaeltacht* region. Dublin had been home to the festival until this time.

Considering that the rural west of Ireland had been identified as "authentic" Ireland within the folkloric imagination and cultural nationalist revival movements during the late nineteenth century and early decades of the twentieth century (Foley 1988, 2012, 2001, 2013; Ó Laoire 2000), the people of the Conamara *Gaeltacht* perceived it as a slight that the *Oireachtas* had not been held there; neither had the indigenous performing arts of the *Gaeltachts* been well represented within the *Oireachtas* (Costello 2015). Since the predominantly middle-class Gaelic League officials organized festivals and events in the larger centers in Ireland where the Gaelic League was more organized, the people in the

Gaeltacht regions saw themselves as simply resources for the Irish language. Two more *Oireachtas na nGael* festivals were held in 1971 and 1972. The 1971 festival took place in Kerry (another *Gaeltacht* area) and the 1972 festival was held again in Conamara. The success of these "protest" festivals prompted the national *Oireachtas* to give more emphasis to the *Gaeltacht* areas and their indigenous performing arts. In 1974, the national *Oireachtas* was held in Conamara, and a *Rince Aonar ar an Sean Nós*[10] competition was included, for the first time, in its program,[11] Thus, *sean nós* dancing and its aesthetic style of performance became an audiovisual and kinesthetic identity marker for the rural Conamara *Gaeltacht*. Indeed, it became a metaphor for the region, its cultural values, and its associated traditional rural way of life. From 1974, the national *Oireachtas* was held annually outside Dublin, but in 2015, it again relocated to Dublin. *Sean nós* dancing within the competitive framework of the *Oireachtas* has increased in popularity since 1974.

The indigenous performing arts, including *sean nós* dancing, have become central to programming at *Oireachtais* festivals. The *sean nós* dancing competition is today a highlight of the festival and draws hundreds of people to witness and to participate in this show of *sean nós* dancing selves. *Sean nós* dancers, however, have concerns that this formal competitive platform may transform the rural *sean nós* style of dancing and the values embodied in its practice.

THE COMPETITORS

Anybody who can dance solo step dances in an Irish traditional/regional style is eligible to enter the *sean nós* dancing competition at the *Oireachtas*, provided they pay a small entry fee. It is not a requirement to be able to speak the Irish language, the *lingua franca* of the festival. This is contrary to conditions of entry for step dancers to the *Oireachtas* and Gaelic League *feiseanna* during the turn of the twentieth century. According to Foley (2013, 139),

> Conditions for entry to the competitions included that professional dancers could not participate in Gaelic League step dancing competitions;[12] in some cases, step dancers had to pass an Irish language examination before being allowed to compete in step dancing competitions; and in the early years of step dance competitions at the *Oireachtas*, dancers would not be awarded a prize should their dance costume not be made from Irish fabrics and materials.

There is no qualifying round before the *Oireachtas* festival today and, hence, a wide range of dance competencies and different traditional regional styles can be observed. There are five competitions in *sean nós* dancing at the *Oireachtas*, and these are categorized according to age: under the age of nine (Figure 8.2), nine to twelve, twelve to fifteen, fifteen to eighteen, and the Senior *Rince Aonar ar an Sean Nós* competition for participants

FIGURE 8.2. *Rince Aonar ar an Sean Nós* competition for participants under the age of nine. *Oireachtas na Samhna* 2012. Le caoinchead Údarás na Gaeltachta.

Image courtesy of Údarás na Gaeltachta.

over 18. Dancers are not allowed to use any kind of props. Winners are rewarded by receiving first prize (the TG4 Trophy, a silver medal and €1,000) or second prize (a bronze medal and €500).

Both male and female dancers participate in the *sean nós* dancing competitions. Throughout the twentieth century, *sean nós* dancing within its rural vernacular context was dominated by male dancers; today there are many female *sean nós* dancers, and some of them have won the *Oireachtas*. In 2015, there were 180 competitors in the *sean nós* dancing competitions in total. The majority of these *sean nós* dancers had learned the dance style by attending formal *sean nós* dancing workshops; some had picked up *sean nós* dancing informally from observing older *sean nós* dancers in their localities; others had combined the two modes of transmission. The dancers are generally aware of the original informal context of the dance practice and, to develop their knowledge, skills, and practice, some have observed expert *sean nós* dancers and have danced socially with them at pub sessions and performed at concerts, festivals and so on. Again in 2015, all the competitors from under nine to eighteen years of age were Irish; the majority had addresses in the west of Ireland. The competitors in the senior competition came, for the most part, from the west of Ireland, but there were also participants from other counties in Ireland (Dublin, Derry, Kildare, Louth, Meath (Rathcairn) and from outside Ireland (the Czech Republic and the United States). For many of the adult dancers, *sean nós* dancing contributes to their sense of identity and their expression of that identity. Indeed, within a globalized world where access to different dance practices may be provided via technology and where mobility has exposed individuals to different means of self and cultural expression, individuals as cosmopolitan selves have opportunities to select from a broad palette of movement practices. *Sean nós* dancing is one of these practices.

Concerning the uptake of *sean nós* dancing by dancers from outside Conamara, Páraic Ó Hoibicín states,

> They wouldn't have the same feeling for it as the people who are representing the area . . . but I think if the dance and the music is in your heart, it will come out. It doesn't matter where you're from. They like the tune and they like the dance. If they don't dance to represent the area, they dance for the love of it. The people who are very rhythmy, they dance it out of respect for where the dance came from.[13]

Respect for "where the dance came from" is important to *sean nós* dancers in Conamara, but they are also happy to see others from outside Conamara perform it. However, some like to see a *sean nós* dancer from Conamara win the *Oireachtas*, as they believe that they best embody what it means to be a *sean nós* dancer; they are perceived as "the real thing." A sense of "authenticity" is therefore associated with not only the dance style itself, but also where the dancers come from. Although dancers from Conamara and Rathcairn have been the predominant winners at the *Oireachtas, sean nós* dancers from outside these areas have also won the *Oireachtas*.

Since 2004, the final rounds of the *sean nós* dance competitions have been broadcast live on national television. The program *Steip Beo* has had a huge impact on bringing a public awareness to *sean nós* dancing. Because of this media coverage, the competitions are generally held in big auditoriums in hotels, conference centers, or community centers. The stage is set with the symbolic backdrop of the *Oireachtas*, the *Oireachtas* crest, situated on a large white screen. A wooden portable platform is center stage. This mobile stage represents the spatial aesthetic of nineteenth- and twentieth-century spaces associated with rural kitchens where the *sean nós* dancer generally performed. A chair is provided for a solo accompanying musician, generally a button accordion player. A table sits to the left of the stage, where the trophies to be awarded are displayed, and a microphone is placed near it for the presenter or master of ceremonies of the event. TG4 has its camera personnel placed strategically around the auditorium; one camera spans the whole auditorium while another takes close-ups of the dancers' feet, which are shown on the backdrop throughout the competitions. The audience is seated on the tiered seating of the auditorium.

Presentation of self on stage is important to the *Oireachtas* personnel, particularly with the television broadcast in mind. Before the competitions, all dancers (and adjudicators) have make up applied for the cameras. Costumes are smart but informal; shoes are leather soled, and no taps are allowed. This has caused some unease with *sean nós* dancers, as some steel pieces were traditionally used by *sean nós* dancers in the Conamara region in the recent past.

All dancers are provided with a number and are introduced in Irish by the presenter according to his or her number. Before the dancer performs, details such as his or her name, regional address, where and from whom he or she learned *sean nós* dancing, and the competitions he or she has previously won are announced to the audience, television viewers, and adjudicators. Festival participants have questioned at times the appropriateness of announcing previous wins and where participants come from. This information, they feel, can be biased in favor of those who have won in the past and those who come from Conamara. However, to give some background on the dancers and to make the program entertaining for television audiences, the information continues to be provided.

Dancers take to the stage in turn and immediately speak with the musician, informing him or her of the music, and sometimes the specific tune, they may wish him or her to play, since they may feel they dance better to a favorite. Each performance lasts about three minutes, after which the dancer thanks the musician and shakes hands with him or her before leaving the stage to applause.

The *sean nós* dance competitions bring together dancers with different styles of dancing. This can be challenging for adjudicators, as some dancers perform in the *sean nós* style of Conamara and others perform in their own local traditional style or "old style" dancing based on set repertoire. According to one *sean nós* dancer, "An tOireachtas has given a platform to many people from many countries, many traditional styles, and has given dancers outside of Conamara an opportunity to showcase their styles."[14] However, because of different aesthetic values that prevail in specific traditional regional styles, some *sean nós* dancers express concern and argue for two *sean nós* dance competitions at the *Oireachtas*: one for the semi-improvisatory *sean nós* dancing style of Conamara; and another competition for the non-improvisatory *sean nós* dancing styles, which are based on set repertoire. Indeed, within the *sean nós* Conamara style, there are different styles based not only on individual competencies, understandings, and interpretations of the practice, but also on how people have been exposed to or been taught *sean nós* dancing, which I will come to shortly. However, despite concerns and challenges, the *Oireachtas* is perceived by *sean nós* dancers and others as the main national event of the year in the *sean nós* dancing calendar, and winning the *sean nós* dancing competition is a major achievement and honor.

THE ADJUDICATORS

Three adjudicators sit at three separate tables between the stage and the audience. The adjudicators observe and write comments on each individual performance during and immediately after each performance. No criteria are provided by the *Oireachtas* organization for adjudication; the criteria are decided upon by each individual adjudicator. This reflects the decision of the *Oireachtas* Office to rely on the knowledge and competencies of its adjudicators.

Competitors perform sequentially, and adjudicators do not generally confer with each other during the competitions; at the end of the competitions they discuss and agree on the *sean nós* dancers who they believe deserve to win the First and Second award in each competition. According to one *sean nós* dancer,

> Most dancers that win competitions in *sean nós* are stand out dancers, so I never really come across any backlash of how competitions are judged. Everyone understands that judging *sean nós* dancing is very personal and it very much depends on a judge's taste who comes first and who comes second. But always the top five dancers are very easy to pick, even from an audience's point of view.[15]

The adjudicators rotate throughout the festival. Six *sean nós* dance adjudicators are selected annually for an *Oireachtas* and are requested to adjudicate specific competitions for the preliminary and final round competitions. These adjudicators come from different backgrounds: *sean nós* dancing; Irish trained step dancing (Foley 2013); and the academic world of Irish dancing. Consequently, they bring different dance experiences that influence the decision-making process of adjudication. All adjudicators must be able to speak Irish, as this is the *lingua franca* of the festival; all communication, feedback to dancers, and commentaries on the competition sheets are in Irish.

THE AUDIENCE

The audience at the *Oireachtas sean nós* dancing competitions consist of competitors' family members, friends, and members of the public who are interested in *sean nós* dancing. Since the live television broadcasting of the competitions from 2004, the competitions are heavily supported by both *Gaeltacht* and non-*Gaeltacht* people. Young and old are present, all with different relationships to *sean nós* dancing. Some audience members are experienced *sean nós* dancers, others are experienced observers, others are researchers, while others are there for the first time. The presence of cameras for the live broadcast provides a sense of excitement and formality; the MC of the event enhances the sense of formality, control, and organization.

Audience members applaud after each performance, which again contributes to the formality and organization of the event. Family members and friends of competitors may applaud louder for the competitor in whom they have a special interest. Also, those dancers who are considered by the audience membership to have performed particularly well are generally applauded more loudly. Those members of the audience who are familiar with informal participatory *sean nós* dancing contexts may offer a shout of encouragement or support should the dancer on stage do something to invite this. For example, humor is valued in the *sean nós* dancer, and when dancers express that they are enjoying themselves through spontaneous leg or arm gestures, facial expressions, or smiles, the audience may respond to it with encouraging exclamations, remarks, or shouts. Also, very young or very old dancers generally receive supportive and encouraging applause. Overall, the atmosphere is full of excitement and anticipation about how competitors will dance and who will win the *Oireachtas* this year.

THE IMPACT OF COMPETITION ON *SEAN NÓS* DANCING AND *SEAN NÓS* DANCERS

According to folklorist and anthropologist Richard Bauman, ". . . all performance, like all communication, is situated, enacted, and rendered meaningful within socially defined situational contexts" (1992, 46). The practice of *sean nós* dancing has been adapted to suit the formally staged competitive context of the *Oireachtas*. This has been particularly so since the commencement of the live television broadcast of the *sean nós* dancing competition on *Steip Beo*. The *Oireachtas* sees this media platform as an important one to popularize the festival and to disseminate the Irish language and *sean nós* dancing. Consequently, much organization is involved in presenting the festival in a technical, professional, and slick manner. Also, since *Steip Beo* airs for only a set period of time, dancing and adjudication take place under time pressure. This presentational mode of performance is in line with Turino's (2000) argument that the shift from participatory to presentational formats has an agenda of control, uniformity, and planning over individual spontaneity. According to one anonymous *sean nós* dancer,

> Competitions have been central to the rise in both the interest and numbers (of all ages) in *sean nós* dancing. Many competitions . . . take place at local festivals on small stages or in bars in which the audience and the casual atmosphere can enhance the dancer but on larger stages under glitzy lights in front of a static audience *sean nós* has a different appearance. . . . It becomes strained and unnatural and leans more towards a show-style performance. . . . It's naturally a casual style and the setting of the competition plays a major role in how it's performed. I believe that through competition the style has been given recognition and is appreciated by those who seldom get the chance to see *sean nós*. The *Oireachtas* is watched by many overseas and such a wide selection of styles are viewed. However, my view is that in competition on large lit stages with cameras, many natural elements of the style are lost.

Furthermore, the excitement and strain of competing live in front of thousands of people have the potential to put pressure on *sean nós* dancers. Some are afraid to improvise during the competition in case they make a mistake or it does not work out for them; instead, they may learn their dance as a set piece and try to make it appear improvised. As one *sean nós* dancer and *Oireachtas* winner Liam Scanlon states in relation to *sean nós* dance competitions at the *Oireachtas*,

I can never be fully comfortable. In one way you're trying to remember all the things you want to do and show within two minutes, and you're trying to perform or act for the audience, and you're also trying to live in the moment. So, you're thinking of the next step ahead but you're also trying to live in the moment which is really difficult. . . . At the *Oireachtas* it's becoming a little bit more staged. The musician is behind you, you can't see them. You're facing out to a few hundred people sitting in the audience, and the cameras and the lights. It can be very daunting.[16]

Páraic O Hoibicín concurs:

I'll never dance my best in a competition. . . . But my best dancing was in a session in a pub and nobody would ask you to dance until you'd hear a tune and you couldn't stay on the chair yourself. You did not want anybody to ask you or request you to dance. You were there. You went on the floor because you did not want to let that tune go and it was a rhythmy tune and you loved it.[17]

The preceding interview excerpts indicate the pressure that *sean nós* dancers feel when dancing in formal competitions. However, winning the *Oireachtas sean nós* dancing competitions is prestigious, which is an incentive to enter. Senior *Oireachtas* winners have received invitations to perform at concerts in Ireland and abroad, feature on television programs, and give *sean nós* dance workshops. According to dancer and *Oireachtas* winner, Emma O'Sullivan,

A week after I won, I was contacted by lots of different groups to work at festivals, so I think the competition for me was a great way of being accepted into the *sean nós* dance community, having grown up outside of it and having only taken up the dance as an adult. I certainly found that it gave me more credibility as a dancer. Everyone in 2006, when I started, was working towards the *Oireachtas* competition.[18]

Today, in 2016, some *sean nós* dancers, who have won the *Oireachtas,* may also feel pressure when they re-enter it. According to Liam Scanlon,

Competition has become a little more pressurized. I've had people say to me afterwards that if they'd won again they wouldn't put themselves up there for fear of losing, which doesn't bother me but it goes to show that it's becoming something like that if you have reached a certain level, the only way is down afterwards. Whereas I see that if you've won, you've won. It's a brilliant honor.[19]

Therefore, dancers who have won the *Oireachtas* may feel pressure when re-entering it, as losing the *Oireachtas,* especially when it is broadcast live before thousands of people, may not assist in enhancing their reputations in the *sean nós* dancing world. Others, however, believe that winning or losing does not prevent them from competing or from attending the *Oireachtas,* because the *Oireachtas,* important as the competitions are, is more than the competitions.

The Social Dimension of the
Oireachtas: A Matter of Sharing

For many *sean nós* dancers, the *Oireachtas* may be the only time of the year when they get to meet so many other *sean nós* dancers. Therefore, for some dancers, the competitive dimension of the *Oireachtas* may not be the most important aspect of the event. For example, Liam Scanlon states,

> The competition isn't the main part. It's the entire festival. It's the celebration of the Irish language. It's the mixing of people you see once a year, through dance. . . . So [after the competitions], there would be sessions during the day. You'd be meeting people all day and then *Club na Féile* (Festival Club) would be on in the evening time and you'd have Paudie O'Shea playing music on stage—lively music and everybody would be up. You'd have your *sean nós* dancers on the floor and everyone would join in. . . . Sometimes the Hoibicíns would start off, or Labhrás Cholm Sonaí Learaí would be there and do a step, and you'd have a few hundred people in the room cheering them on, and just the energy that was there then. Everybody would join in.[20]

The informal, social, and participatory contexts of *sean nós* dancing define for many dancers what is considered to be the "real" context for *sean nós* dancing. The atmosphere is friendly, informal, and relaxed; alcohol may be available, and lively dance music is playing. Dancers spontaneously take to the floor and dance for themselves: they internalize the music and allow their bodies to express what they feel when they listen to the music. Within this informal context, they are not afraid to improvise. As Páraic O Hoibicín states, "To me, it's a gift that I got; that I'm able to step it out on a tune. . . . It's a gift that you can time it and it lifts your heart." Dancer after dancer takes to the floor with encouraging shouts, remarks, and cheers from observers, amidst chatter, laughter, and lively music. Here is the opportunity to join and share the space with other *sean nós* dancers, where participation contributes to and enhances the sharing of the performance and the continuity of the practice; the context also maintains and negotiates connections and relationships to this particular dance community.

The Issue of Transmission
in *Sean Nós* Dancing

The popularization of *sean nós* dancing, through *Steip Beo*, has produced an increase in the demand in formal *sean nós* dance workshops. Many winners and participants of the *Oireachtas* therefore find themselves in demand to teach *sean nós* dancing workshops at local events and festivals in Ireland and further afield. Some of the aspiring *sean nós* dancers may never have been to Conamara, but their exposure to the dance form is either through television (*Steip Beo*), concerts, workshops, or some tutorial DVDs that are available for purchase. Consequently, some *sean nós* dancers express concern that those learning formally at workshops or from DVDs may simply imitate the style of a teacher or dancer, thus contributing to homogenizing the style. Others may record and learn from performances of dancers on *Steip Beo*, and may again imitate particular dancers' styles. According to Páraic Ó Hoibicín,

> There are a lot of people in the competition . . . about 150 people. . . . They're all good dancers. And more or less when you see one, you've seen the whole lot of them.[21]

This supports ethnochoreologist Egil Bakka's contention that "[o]rganized teaching tends to systematize, place elements in fixed order, and standardize step patterns, while it discourages variation and individuality" (2002, 61). Imitations of particular individual styles go against the aesthetic of *sean nós* dancing, which is about individual personality, expression, and style. An ethnographic anecdote from my field notes supports this:

> One year when adjudicating the *Oireachtas Rince Aonar ar an Sean Nós* competitions and listening to the introductions of competitors, most of the younger dancers were introduced as having formally learned from older and particularly well known *sean nós* dancers. Then a young female dancer came on stage. She was from a well known *sean nós* dancing family and, although some of the other dancers competing had stated that they had learned from her father, Páraic Ó Hoibicín, the presenter stated that "she had not learned from Páraic Ó Hoibicín." In other words, she did not learn formally and was not imitating her father's style; she was going to dance in her own individual style.

Individual expression and style are important to *sean nós* dancers. No formal classes existed in *sean nós* dancing in Conamara during the 1950s and 1960s. Instead, aspiring *sean nós* dancers observed different individual styles performed informally in the area, and they constructed their own style of dancing based on local stylistic influences. Individualism, personality, and creativity are expected and valued in *sean nós* dancing, and individual *sean nós* dancers, such as Páraic Ó Hoibicín, Séamus Devaney, Seosamh Ó Neachtain, Róisín Ní Mhainnín, and Máirtín Mac Donnacha, have become equated with particular personal styles. Currently, *sean nós* dancers praise the *Oireachtas* for having assisted in popularizing the dance form, but they are also concerned that the *Oireachtas* competition, with its focus on televised performances, professional organization, and winners, may contribute to the decline in creativity, spontaneity, and individualism and, therefore, may increase the homogenization of its practice. Indeed, many of the dancers with individual styles who provide workshops find their own styles being imitated in competitions like the *Oireachtas*. As Liam Scanlon observes, younger children growing up watching it (*Steip Beo*), if they're not coming from a tradition where they see it in their area or in their environment, or have a history of it, the only experience they have of it is competitions. They see certain people winning it with a certain style and then they feel if they want to win they have to change their style to emulate a certain person and a certain way of dancing. I think that could be a big danger. . . . That it becomes taught, and then that this is what you have to do to win . . . it becomes then like a poorer cousin of Irish dancing.[22]

For *sean nós* dancers and for the *Oireachtas* Office, the challenge in the *sean nós* dance competitions is managing to support and promote the practice while allowing it to develop with integrity into the future; how it develops is a concern for all involved, particularly as those who have learned informally are on the decline. However, for the moment, *sean nós* dancing is alive and well, and the *Oireachtas* has contributed to popularizing it.

AGENCY AND NEGOTIATION WITHIN THE *SEAN NÓS* DANCING COMPETITIVE FRAMEWORK

> Competitions may be conceived to challenge musical [dance][23] hierarchies as well as social hierarchies, although the promotion of a given musical [dance] genre is often linked to the interests of a particular social group or ideological position. (Dudley 2004, 22)

Sean nós dancing is iconic of, and culturally affirms, the Conamara *Gaeltacht*. It provides a site for revisiting and reimagining this *Gaeltacht* visually, kinetically, and sonically. By providing a platform for *sean nós* dancing in the 1970s, the *Oireachtas* illustrated a positive response to the *Gaeltacht* civil rights movement in Conamara. This civil rights movement illustrated active agency on the part of the *Gaeltacht* community and a need for recognition; *sean nós* dancing assisted in providing this visual, kinetic, and sonic recognition and became an important identity signifier of the region. Thus, as an informal, solo vernacular dance practice, *sean nós* dancing was recontextualized and was reframed for formal presentation within a cosmopolitan competitive context at the *Oireachtas*. In this process, however, some *sean nós* dancers expressed concern that qualities such as spontaneity, individualism, and creative expression—viewed as important characteristics to holders of the tradition—were challenged. Turino (2000) argues that such reframings of indigenous practices may be a threat to participatory and community-based indigenous practices. Although this may be true, I would also suggest that the traditional rural way of life that supported *sean nós* dancing in the region of Conamara had, for the most part, been replaced by modernity by the 1980s and that today it is generally practiced by those who choose to dance it as a leisure-time activity; some of these dancers come from respected and well-known families of *sean nós* dancers. The *Oireachtas* festival, therefore, has assisted in reviving *sean nós* dancing by promoting and facilitating competitions in the practice and by encouraging social participation and sharing at informal sessions and the *Club na Féile* events at the festival. The *Oireachtas* has also exposed the practice to a broader national and international audience by annually broadcasting the *sean nós* dancing competitions on *Steip Beo*.

Many *sean nós* dancers state that *sean nós* dancing is changing, but, at least, it is still alive. The practice of *sean nós* dancing has been disseminated beyond Conamara. And, although some *sean nós* dancers may have concerns about the competitive reframing of *sean nós* dancing, they are also cognizant of the opportunity provided by this reframing for sharing, promoting, and disseminating this dance practice.

Dancers from both inside and outside Conamara perform *sean nós* dancing because they enjoy the experience of dancing it; they can express their love of Irish traditional music through their dancing; and they appreciate the sociality surrounding its practice. Some may dance to represent their people, their worldview, and their region; others, from outside the *Gaeltacht* region, may perform to represent their constructed multidimensional identity. Most *sean nós* dancers continue to dance on an amateur basis; however, others are attempting to make a professional living from it. All these dancers form the current community of *sean nós* dancers who engage in and share their practice by participation at local, national, and international events, including informal social events, workshops, competitions, festivals, and television broadcasts. The *Oireachtas*, as the primary *sean nós* dancing competitive event, assists in maintaining and negotiating relationships within this dance commuity. It also functions to promote and provide a platform for *sean nós* dancing where dancers can express and embody their cultural values, identity, and place in the world.

NOTES

1. Anonymous, interview with the author, August 24, 2015.
2. A *Gaeltacht* is a region in Ireland where the Irish language is the primary vernacular spoken language of the people living there.
3. In 1935, a new *Gaeltacht* was created in Rathcairn, County Meath, in the East of Ireland, when twenty-seven Irish-speaking families from Conamara were resettled there and given farms and houses by the Land Commission. The initiative was to help stop the decline of the Irish language by creating an Irish-speaking community in a new location in the East of Ireland. *Sean nós* dancers from Conamara were among those who went to Rathcairn, and consequently today a thriving community of *sean nós* dancers is located there.
4. *An Coimisiún* was established by the Gaelic League in 1930 (see Foley 2013); this is the largest Irish step-dance organization in the world and remains under the auspices of the Gaelic League. *An Comhdháil* was established in 1969 when teachers within *An Coimisiún* decided to leave the organization to establish their own separate organization, independent from the Gaelic League. Each organization holds separate step-dance competitions and separate teacher and adjudicator qualifying examinations.

5. Páraic Ó Hoibicín, interview with the author, February 6, 2015.
6. Ibid.
7. See also Shay (2008).
8. These "-scapes" build on anthropologist Arjun Appadurai's (1990) five-dimensional set of "-scapes".
9. Although the dance competition is officially called the *Rince Aonar ar an Sean Nós* competition (Solo *Sean Nós* Dancing competition), I will refer to it hereafter as the *sean nós* dancing competition.
10. The name *Rince Aonar ar an Sean Nós* was used by a *Raidio na Gaeltachta* (Irish radio) presenter named Mairtín Jamsie Ó Flatharta from the Aran Islands in Conamara and the name remained to allude to the local, solo, vernacular style of step dancing performed at the time, for the most part, by elderly men in the Conamara region (Brennan-Corcoran 1994; Costello 2015).
11. Personal communication with Séamus Ó Méalóid.
12. *An Claidheamh Soluis*, December 9, 1899, 622; August 11, 1900, 349.
13. Páraic Ó Hoibicín, interview with the author, February 6, 2015.
14. Anonymous, interview with the author, 2015.
15. Anonymous, 2015, author questionnaire.
16. Liam Scanlon, interview with the author, November 19, 2015.
17. Páraic Ó Hoibicín, interview with the author, February 6, 2015.
18. Emma O'Sullivan, questionnaire 2015.
19. Liam Scanlon, interview with author, November 19, 2015.
20. Ibid.
21. Páraic Ó Hoibicín, interview with the author, February 6, 2015.
22. Liam Scanlon, interview with author, November 19, 2015.
23. The addition of "[dance]" is mine.

References

Appadurai, Arjun. 1990. "Disjuncture and Difference in the Global Cultural Economy." *Public Culture* 2(2): 1–24.
Bakka, Egil. 2002. "Whose Dances, Whose Authenticity?" In *Authenticity: Whose Tradition?*, edited by Laszlo Felfoldi and Theresa J. Buckland, 60–69. Budapest: European Folklore Institute.
Baumann, Max Peter, Jonathan Stock, and Frank Gunderson. 2003. *The World of Music, Contesting Tradition: Cross-Cultural Studies of Musical Competition* 45(1). Berlin: VWB—Verlag fur Wissenschaft und Bildung.
Bauman, Richard. 1992. "Performance." In *Folklore, Cultural Performance, and Popular Entertainments: A Communications-Centered Handbook,* edited by Richard Bauman, 41–49. New York; Oxford: Oxford University Press.
Brennan-Corcoran, Helen. 1994. "Dancing on a Plate: The Sean Nós Dance Tradition of Conamara." MA thesis, Queens University Belfast.
Costello, Éamonn Seosamh. 2015. "Sean Nós Singing and Oireachtas na Gaeilge: Identity, Romantic Nationalism, and the Agency of the Gaeltacht Community Nexus." Unpublished PhD diss., The Irish World Academy of Music and Dance, University of Limerick.
Daniel, Yvonne. 1995. *Dance and Social Change in Contemporary Cuba*. Bloomington: Indiana University Press.

Dudley, Shannon. 2003. "Creativity and Control in Trinidad Carnival Competitions." *The World of Music: Journal of the Department of Ethnomusicology, Otto-Friedrich University of Bamberg* 45: 11–33.

Erlmann, Veit. 1996. *Nightsong: Performance, Power and Prctice in South Africa.* Chicago: University of Chicago Press.

Foley, Catherine E. [1988] 2012. *Irish Traditional Step Dancing in North Kerry: A Contextual and Structural Analysis* (with an accompanying DVD). Listowel: North Kerry Literary Trust.

Foley, Catherine E. 2001. "Perceptions of Irish Step Dance: National, Global and Local." *Dance Research Journal* 33(1): 34–45.

Foley, Catherine E. 2008. "Percussive Relations: An Exploration of Percussive Dance at Tráth na gCos 2002." In *Close to the Floor: Irish Dance from the Boreen to Broadway*, edited by Mick Moloney, J'aime Morrison, and Colin Quigley, 47–56. Madison, WI: Macater.

Foley, Catherine E. 2011. "The Irish *Céilí*: A Site for Constructing, Experiencing, and Negotiating a Sense of Community and Identity." *Dance Research* 29(1): 43–60.

Foley, Catherine E. 2013. *Step Dancing in Ireland: Culture and History.* Farnham, Surrey: Ashgate.

Foley, Catherine E. 2014. "Negotiating the 'Native Self' and the 'Professional Self': Ethnochoreological and Ethnomusicological Challenges in the Field." In *(Re)Searching the Field: Festschrift in Honor of Egil Bakka*, edited by Anne Margrete Fiskvik and Marit Stranden, 227–242. Bergen: Fagbokforlaget.

Hall, Frank. 2008. *Irish Competitive Step Dance: Art, Sport, Duty.* Madison, WI: Macater.

Hall, Stuart, and Paul du Gay, eds. 1996. *Questions of Cultural Identity.* London: Sage.

Larsen, Gary J. 2008. "Drag-Slides and Toe Stands: Identity, Motivation, and Change in American Clogging." In *Close to the Floor: Irish Dance from the Boreen to Broadway*, edited by Mick Moloney, J'aime Morrison, and Colin Quigley, 23–34. Madison, WI: Macater.

Ness, Sally Ann. 1992. *Body, Movement, and Culture: Kinesthetic and Visual Symbolism in a Philippine Community.* Philadelphia: University of Pennsylvania Press.

Ness, Sally Ann. 2008. "The Inscription of Gesture: Inward Migrations in Dance." In *Migrations of Gesture*, edited by Carrie Noland and Sally Ann Ness, 1–3. Minneapolis: University of Minnesota Press.

Ní Bhriain, Órfhlaith, M. 2010. "An Examination of the Creative Processes in Competitive Irish Step Dance." Unpublished PhD diss., University of Limerick.

Ó Laoire, Lillis. 1997. "Traditional Song in Ireland: Living Fossil or Dynamic Resource." In *Sharing the Voices: The Phenomenon of Singing 2. Proceedings of the International Symposium*, edited by Brian A. Roberts, 161–170. St. John's, Newfoundland: Memorial University of Newfoundland.

Ó Laoire, Lillis. 2000. "National Identity and Local Ethnicity: The Case of the Gaelic League's *Oireachtas Sean Nós* Singing Competitions." In *Sharing the Voices: The Phenomenon of Singing 2. Proceedings of the International Symposium*, edited by Brian A. Roberts and Andrea Rose, 160–169. St. John's, Newfoundland: Memorial University of Newfoundland.

Shay, Anthony, ed. 2008. *Balkan Dance: Essays on Characteristics, Performance and Teaching.* London: McFarland.

Stokes, Martin. 1994. *Ethnicity, Identity and Music: The Musical Construction of Place.* Oxford: Berg.

Turino, Thomas. 2000. *Nationalism, Cosmopolitanism, and Popular Music in Zimbabwe.* Chicago: University of Chicago Press.

CHAPTER 9

....

VISIBLE RHYTHMS

Competition in English Tap Practice

....

SALLY CRAWFORD-SHEPHERD

COMPETITION has always been a vital component of tap dance. As tap historian Constance Valis Hill writes in her book *Tap Dancing America: A Cultural History* (2010), the history of the dance form is founded on competitive rhythmic exchanges known as tap challenges. Hill (2010, 3) states that the tap challenge can be defined as "any competition, contest, breakdown, or showdown in which tap dancers compete against each other before an audience of spectators or judges." Hill (2010) later describes a scene from the 1985 film *White Knights* in which American tap dancer Gregory Hines and Russian ballet dancer Mikhail Baryshnikov engage in a showdown of their most impressive steps. During their first scene, Baryshnikov and Hines attempt to better each other through feats of speed, flexibility, and strength in the dance studio. Baryshnikov fluidly transitions between splits and jumps, while Hines responds with press-ups using his fists and martial arts kicks. As Baryshnikov balances on one leg, Hines rushes behind him with a blindingly fast alternating sidestep before breaking into a run around the studio. Baryshnikov follows and executes a sequence of leaps and effortlessly rolls to the floor. Hines adds his own touch of a side kick before copying Baryshnikov's leap and then walking out of the space, giving in to what appears to be an old injury. The scene ends without a designated "winner," but the competition spurred each dancer to rely on his ability to produce steps in response to the movement innovations of the other performer. Similarly, tap dancers use the tap challenge to demonstrate their ability to improvise rhythms by performing steps in direct response to the challenger's rhythms. However, the aforementioned scene not only captures the competitive element of the tap challenge, but also highlights the role that film and television have played in improvised tap performance. The competitive element of tap dance is restructured to contextualize the challenge scenario within a linear narrative and, although Hines and Baryshinkov appear to spontaneously select steps to out-dance each other, in actuality the scene results from multiple rehearsals and retakes.[1]

The competitive nature of televised dance shows such as *So You Think You Can Dance* and *Got to Dance* presents a comparable situation for tap dancers.[2] Tap dancers compete against dancers from a range of styles and genres; however, the format demands set choreography and the focus rests on a final performance, rather than the creative process. Competition dance shows typically remove the element of exploration that arises through improvised tap exchange and instead present a series of discrete performances. Consequently, the tap dancers must re-examine how they measure their success in competition without relying on an immediate response from another performer.

To understand how tap dancers are impacted by, and must respond to, the demands of televised competitive dance shows, I examine an English tap company the Pulse Collective (Figure 9.1). The company participated in two separate televised auditions for Sky 1's *Got to Dance 4* in 2013. While the first audition was a performance of their original choreography, the second audition performance featured choreography prepared by both the company members and additional choreographers working for the show. This second performance was judged by both the competition judges and the viewing audience, who were able to text their choice of winner. The Pulse Collective did not progress into the final round of televised performances for the competition. I interviewed founding members Kane Ricca and Eilidh Ross to learn how their time on *Got to Dance 4* shaped the company's performance and their plans for future projects. The Pulse Collective's experience in a televised dance show highlights how competition is a key factor in the creative process as well as the overall development of tap practitioners. The relationship between competition and tap dance can be traced back to the evolution of tap practice in the United States in the twentieth century and its transmission to England. This chapter explores how competition impacted theatrical

FIGURE 9.1. Kane D. Ricca and Eilidh Ross with members of the Pulse Collective in 2015.

Photography by Courtney Phillip.

performances, Hollywood films, and formal examinations with organizations such as the Imperial Society of Teachers of Dancing (ISTD) to emphasize the visual presentation of tap dance and rhythm on the small screen in the twenty-first century.

Tap Dance in England: Emerging Communities

As a tap practitioner, I grew up participating in both formal studio dance competitions and informal competitive exchanges with other dancers in the United States. The scene between Hines and Baryshinkov inspired me in my early years as a tap dancer and into my involvement with the emerging English tap dance communities of the twenty-first century. A key element of my development as a practitioner was time spent recreating this scene with friends, informally declaring a challenge to see which one of us could come up with the most rhythmically complex steps, imagining ourselves as famous dancers like Hines and Baryshnikov. Hines was my hero, a tap dancer willing to explore any musical or physical idea and incorporate it into his steps. Hill (2010, 277) states that his constantly evolving tap practice "shows us that his improvised rhythm dancing has no musical, physical, or metaphorical boundaries." Hines's endless innovation drove me to keep seeking new inspiration for my tap practice, a desire that carried over into my ethnographic investigations into English tap dance communities.[3] The more time I spent immersed in the community classes, workshops, and performances, the more I realized that I was not alone in my pursuit of new ways to interpret rhythms through my taps and my body.

The tap communities of England, formed in 2006, represent a diverse demographic, and have developed their own improvised tap practice through the exploration of a variety of music and dance styles.[4] As part of their practice, they host tap jams: informal events in which performers gather and exchange improvised tap steps to live music. The jams facilitate each community member's growth, allowing individuals to engage in improvised tap performances with live music in solos, duets, or trios as part of community events. Unlike the dramatic dance studio scene in *White Knights*, these individuals did not face off directly with one another to showcase their rhythmic discoveries. Rather, they focused on supporting each other as their tap performances grew in complexity at each tap jam.

I was surprised to uncover, within the London tap community, the Pulse Collective, a tap company created by Kane Ricca, a British man in his mid-twenties, in 2012. Ricca sent web links of the company's audition for *Got to Dance 4* to members of the community, asking individuals to watch the show and support the group. Initially, the competitive performances of the Pulse Collective appeared at odds with the supportive and social settings of the tap jams. Ricca and several members of the Pulse Collective regularly participated at the tap jams in London, where individual performances are the focus and are celebrated by the members. As I will show, however, the Pulse Collective's engagement in a televised dance competition represents a change in how these individual dancers approached their development as tap practitioners.

THE PULSE COLLECTIVE: COMPETING ON A SHOW "MADE FOR DANCERS"

As noted earlier, the Pulse Collective was founded in 2012 by Kane Ricca; in addition to his tap training, Ricca possesses a background as a hip-hop dancer and hip-hop musician. The company is defined as a "collective" of performers (Ricca 2015), which emphasizes the individual identities and contributions of each member. The dancers draw on a range of styles such as "body percussion, rhythm tap, gum-booting, hip-hop and other street inspired choreography" (Ricca 2015).

The group's first audition for *Got to Dance 4* featured choreography influenced by their diverse dance backgrounds and individual personalities. The opening shot reveals the Pulse Collective on stage against a bright blue backdrop covered with glowing stars.[5] The lights reflect on the shiny stage floor, giving the appearance that the group is dancing on starlight. Black trousers, shorts, black T-shirts, and vests were the foundation of the group costume, but each dancer added personal touches such as gold bangles, hooped earrings, or a silver tie. They perform to a track, "Bombs Away" by B.o.B, which features fast rapping mixed with electronic beats. We first glimpse the dancers balancing for a split second on one heel with their arms splayed wide before launching into a flurry of hammering flaps and heel drops. Their shoulders move in circular patterns as the dancers slightly contract forward to drop their weight onto the toe heels before their legs shoot out horizontally as they dig their heels into the floor. This is followed by rapid heel drops, accompanied by a series of quick, angular shapes with their arms. The choreography continues to highlight accents in the music as the dancers slap their torsos and clap their hands under their legs as they are lifted mid-step. Throughout the audition clip, the group executes the same tap steps, but each individual provides a personal representation of how he or she experiences the rhythm: one dancer tilts her head to the side on an accent; another drops his head quickly, only to let it pop up on the next down beat; and one dancer throws both arms straight up in the air as the dancer next to him bends both of his elbows in an angular shape. The camera occasionally zooms in from wide shots to capture the smiles or challenging stares of the dancers.

The presentation of the steps in this audition clip demonstrates the company's desire to focus on rhythmic complexity. The dancers are placed in primarily linear formations and always face the audience or judges. There are a total of five formation changes throughout the piece, with dancers arranged in simple patterns, such as two individual lines or a single curved line. Although the stage is circular, only one curved formation takes place, with the dancers briefly spreading out in a single line to the edge of the space before moving back into two straight lines. There is one change of level at the very end, when some of the dancers drop down to their knees or a crouched position in the final pose. The movement occurs almost exclusively in the sagittal and vertical planes, with a few instances of the dancers bending forward at the waist to briefly enter the horizontal plane. The dancers execute accompanying arm movements to the tap steps that feature sharp angles and straight lines. The decision to incorporate simple formation changes and clear lines in the arm movements allows the audience to focus on the lower body and feet.

In this first audition clip, the dynamics of the choreography showcase the performers' musicality. Ricca and company member Eilidh Ross described how they and the dancers selected steps that matched the tempo of the music with moments of increased speed to showcase control, as seen in the unison execution of the fast heel drops, when the group forms a half circle at the front of the stage. This is followed by a moment of silence and stillness that reflects rhythmic breaks in the music. The dancers remain in the half circle and freeze as they hold a contracted position, leaning forward with the left arm extended to the floor and the right elbow bent. Holding the pose during the break in the music, the dancers then straighten up and stand in a relaxed pose before stomping and clapping their hands as the down beat in the track resumes. This instance demonstrates the dancers' musicality, as the casual stance gives them an appearance of knowing exactly when the music will start again without having to look to each other for visual cues or hold a pose.

These moments also give the audience a chance to interact with the performers by commenting on their rhythmic choices. For instance, in the second break, American judge Kimberly Wyatt shouts, "Yeah!" as the performers strikingly halt in the forward bending pose before launching into the next step. The dancers perform the steps primarily in unison, with only one instance of a clear canon. Notably, unison tap choreography can act as a sonic amplifier for the audience, as multiple dancers executing the same step increases the volume; however, the canon allows the choreography to successively reflect the individuality of each performer without sacrificing the sound.

In many ways, the televised representation of the Pulse Collective on *Got to Dance 4* marks a striking contrast to the performances of the company members at the tap jams. The tap jams in London and Manchester occur in clubs that feature live jazz music performances. These spaces are created for intimate audiences, of often fewer than fifty people, who sit or stand in close proximity to the performers. The venues lack a full-sized stage and technical lighting equipment, thus creating performances without elaborate lighting cues. The dancers perform on a portable, wooden floor that is packed away at the end of each event in London, and a small raised stage in Manchester. Due to the size of the tap floor or stage, large ensembles are unable to fit in the space, and performances are limited to solos, duets, and trios. The live music is provided by musicians seated next to the tap floor or off to one side of the stage. The proximity of the musicians enables the tap dancers to interact directly with musicians, such as indicating tempo changes with the speed of their steps or initiating an improvised exchange of tap steps and musical phrases. Audiences at tap jams cheer, applaud, and give commentary in the form of positive affirmations, such as "Yeah!", "Go on!", and "All right!" as acknowledgment of the rhythmic discoveries of each dancer. When a dancer executes a tap step that highlights or complements the rhythms of the musicians, the audience and community members applaud. The performers and audience members understand the applause as validation of their improvisations, allowing them to measure the success of their performance in a supportive environment.

To return to *Got to Dance* 4, the second audition clip for the Pulse Collective again presents choreography that contrasts the intimate improvised performances of the tap jams. The backdrop of the stage is filled with rows of glowing, golden lights that pulse in a random pattern, and bright blue LED strobes flash in time to beats in the music. Just as the chorus starts, the camera briefly zooms out to show the entire stage, including dozens of pulsing lights in the ceiling rig, before zooming in quickly to focus on the dancers as they break out of a tight pyramid formation with two dig turn steps into a single circular line reflecting the shape of the stage. The dancers once again wear costumes that focus on individual styles, ranging in hues of gold, black, tan, and olive, with accents such as white vests. The pre-recorded music is a pop track called "I Found You" by the Wanted, and the audience claps along in time to the beat and cheers throughout the piece. The dancers perform a combination of double pirouettes and slides across the floor before finishing with a series of stomps, heel drops, digs, and shuffles in unison. The final seconds of the song feature only the singers repeating the chorus before the dancers execute their tap combinations without any music at all. The absence of the recorded music provides the dancers with an opportunity to be fully in control of the sounds produced. Although this could have been an opportunity to layer the sounds of the taps with hand claps or thigh slaps, the choreography lacks the variety of body percussion present in the first audition piece.

The choreography relies on dance vocabulary from other styles to highlight the beats of the tap steps, instead of creating audible accents with their bodies. The rhythms are visible through movement such as turns, slides across the floor, and large shifts of the torso to the side or forward on a horizontal plane. The movement in the torso presents a visual cue for the audience to see the accents in the music, instead of using movements such as slaps and claps to augment the rhythm aurally. The quality of the arm movements also demonstrates a shift in how the dancers feel the rhythm in their bodies. The clapping hands and slapping thighs and chest from the first clip are sharp, vertical, accented movements that clearly designate downbeats in the music; however, the choreography in the second clip features arm movements that swing through the space in curved pathways. This change in quality of the arm movements demonstrates how the tap dancers are now incorporating their entire bodies to find subtler ways of experiencing the music. Instead of utilizing the obvious choice of clapping their hands to keep time, the dancers use the impulse of the swing in the arm or its reverberation back through the body to accent the beat.

The use of space in the second audition piece further demonstrates a clear change in the Pulse Collective's choreography for the competition show. In the first audition, the formation changes were simple and moved the dancers through the space as an accompaniment to the tap steps. In the second clip, the formation changes are more frequent and complex, with dancers traveling through the space at different levels and timings. The performers change position in time to the music, creating another layer of visibility for the rhythms to be seen in the choreography. This is highlighted when the company splits into two dancers facing upstage, while a group of five faces the audience and simultaneously a trio slides across the space at a low level. The duet is still, the group of five executes a rhythmically complex combination of toe stands, wings, brushes, and turns, while the trio slides, creating a single accent as their taps make contact with the floor. This segmenting of the dancers into multiple groups shows the different accents in the music in multiple levels of space.

Following this formation change, all of the dancers move into a triangle formation to face the audience in time for the chorus of the song with a combination performed in unison. After the dancers break out into the single, circular line downstage, the camera zooms in for a few close-ups of the dancers' faces, making it difficult to determine the exact beginning of the next traveling step that takes them into a single line across the center of the stage. A canon starts from each end of the line as dancers come from a low *plié* and flat back position into a high toe stand before once again using turns and slides with the tap steps to split into two groups. As the group moves through space, the rhythms of the tap steps are transferred onto their bodies, transitioning through multiple planes and levels. The toe stands performed in the canon are a clear example: the shifting of the weight from a grounded and low position into a high balance on the tip of the shoe allows the audience to hear the accent in the toes and to see it in the body as it moves from a low to high level. Throughout the whole piece, the entire stage is utilized without any moments of stillness, giving the appearance of the dancers and their rhythms in constant motion.

The video clip of the first audition performance by the company demonstrates a clear emphasis on audible rhythms. Much of the choreography features movement-inspired body percussion, such as slapping the thighs and lower leg, clapping the hands, and beating the chest. The addition of body percussion emphasizes accents in the rhythms of the individual tap steps. In the second audition piece, choreographic devices such as unison and canon create visual impact, rather than rhythmic complexity. The group incorporates the use of diverse levels, different directions, and frequent formation changes choreographed in time to the music. Notably, the movement of the entire body becomes a visible representation of rhythm, rather than limiting the rhythmic production to the feet.

Ricca and Ross shed further light on the choreographic changes implemented between the first and second audition clip. During an interview, they revealed that the company was assigned a choreographer to assist in the final stages. Although they describe the process of competing on the show generally as a positive experience that allowed them to adapt their choreography for a televised audience, it undoubtedly left an impact on the group dynamic of the company:

RICCA: There were so many logistical nightmares to produce the work. . . .
ROSS: I guess they have a responsibility to make sure what is put out on the live
    shows is actually of a certain standard. So they don't actually trust the act . . . it was

good, but choreographers come to all your rehearsals from that point [after the audition] and you have so many with them . . . and I think that kind of throws a spanner in the works from that point of view, like it affects your group dynamic. . . .

RICCA: I think it's because the *Got to Dance* show is made for dancers not by dancers . . . so for the production element, hiring an additional choreographer or creative team, it allows them to kind of take control of what is seen from a visual perspective.

ROSS: Yeah, I mean don't get me wrong, they really helped us . . . because they probably made us move a lot more than in our first (audition) piece . . . you can see in the second piece there is so much pattern and direction . . . camera angles, everything that we needed help with. It was just brilliant to have them there![6]

The company members identify that the addition of the traveling steps and patterns in the group led them to reconsider how to present their rhythms for televised performance. In the first audition performance, the company drew upon their experience from the improvised performances at the tap jams. They selected tap steps that could be experienced by the audience present in the space with the performers, the accents of the steps matching the beats in the song in order to illicit an immediate reaction from the audience in the form of applause and cheers. The addition of the cameras in both audition pieces created a new temporality for the rhythms of the Pulse Collective, one that directly influenced how the audience would perceive their sound and movement. Screen dance scholar Douglas Rosenberg (2012, 29) describes the impact of the camera on an audience's experience:

> live dance unfolds in real, linear time and is intended to be consumed in a similar manner. . . . The dance made for the architecture of the camera, however, is made of individual choreographic events that exist in parallel; not intersecting, not necessarily accruing meaning, context, or linearity until recomposed in the editing process.

While Rosenberg contextualizes the disrupted linearity of live dance to screen dance, the choreographic changes required of Pulse Collective followed a similar progression: the input of technical directors and an additional choreographer selected by the show intervened in the overall choreographic process. The company had to take in to consideration what the audience would see from multiple perspectives instead of simply composing rhythms in the dance studio. Switching between cameras creates visual stimulation for television spectators, dictating where they should focus through executing fast cuts between different views of the stage. The inclusion of these techniques meant that the company members would have less creative control over how and when the aural content of the choreography would be delivered to television viewers not present in the studio audience. To ensure that the sense of rhythm and flow would not be lost during the final edit of the performance, changes in levels, floor patterns, and dynamic transitions were added to the tap choreography. The additional group formations and traveling tap steps meant that, regardless of changes in camera angles, the audience would be able to see the rhythms in the entire body as the dancers traveled through space in time to the rhythm of the music.

Competing with other dance groups within this context of televised dance performance was both exhilarating and rewarding for the members of the Pulse Collective, despite only reaching the semi-finals. Ricca and Ross did not feel that a lack of technical dance training led to their elimination after two performances; rather, their inexperience in considering the most effective approach to showcase their rhythms through mediated television performance, rather than live rhythmic improvisation, may have been a factor. Participating in the televised dance competition meant the Pulse Collective had to reconsider what they valued in their tap choreography and performance, and how it would be validated by multiple audiences. The emphasis on what an audience experiences aurally and visually had to change for the company to compete within the format of edited dance performance; consequently, the process of improvising tap steps was no longer visible, as it was not part of the competition criteria.

Moving forward as a company, Ricca and Ross advocate continued exploration in both stage and television performances to discover new ways of presenting their sounds and movement to audiences. Ricca explains this strategy by stating that innovation and competition are integral to tap dance; however, he highlights how tap practice in England differs from its origins in the United States: "the rhythm tap scene from an American perspective . . . wasn't really about performance, that isn't where it started, it was much more social than that." Ricca and Ross stated that several members of the Pulse Collective had tap training from the ISTD, which trains students in various dance styles according to a predetermined syllabus. Students must pass practical exams before progressing to the next level of training in the syllabus.

Ricca's comment suggests that American performers who originated the dance form valued the social elements of tap dance over learning tap steps to pass an examination. To understand the different values of tap competition between the United States and England, I trace the historical development of American tap practice in the twentieth century and how competition evolved between early practitioners. I follow with the transmission of American tap productions and films to English audiences, and the impact of these performances on the training of young dancers.

A History of Tap and Competition: An American Perspective

Tap challenges developed during the late nineteenth and twentieth centuries into informal performance events in the United States. The challenges evolved into events known as tap jams in New York City and became an integral part of each performer's personal practice. The tap jam provided American tap practitioners the opportunity to engage directly with other dancers off the stage and in an environment that both challenged and guided their development as performing artists. The tap jam sessions at the Hoofers Club, located in the basement of a building two doors away from the Lafayette Theater at Seventh Avenue between 131st and 132nd streets in Harlem, became one of the prominent locations for tap dancers to assemble in the 1920s and 1930s.[7] The building housed a club originally known as the Comedy Club, owned by Lonnie Hicks, an amateur pianist and tap dance enthusiast (Cullen, Hackman, and McNeilly 2007). In a small side room, no more than thirty by twenty feet, was a wooden floor and a piano. In between shows and after the night clubs closed, tap dancers gathered to improvise steps from their own repertoire, as well as creating new steps.

The members of the Hoofers Club, primarily African American men, gained entrance by an informal initiation.[8] The room was available to dancers performing in nightclubs and theaters at all times for tap dancers to rehearse, but to truly be welcomed into the "club," dancers needed to demonstrate an ability to improvise in jam sessions. Historians Jean and Marshall Stearns (1968) described how young hoofers new to the performance scene in Harlem had to be able to trade steps with seasoned professionals. These informal sessions were not open to the public, and dancers were not allowed to be in the room simply to observe without their own contribution, such as fetching drinks for older dancers or providing a newly interpreted version of another member's step in a jam session (Stearns and Stearns 1968). Individuals would seek out older tap practitioners, who took on the role of mentor for upcoming performers. A loose hierarchy was defined by age and performance experience, rather than by economic wealth or social status.[9] Working within the social structure of mentor and prodigy contributed to the competition in the tap jams, which focused on individuals rather than groups.

A frequent feature at the Hoofers Club was the tap challenge, which is also featured in performances by many American tap practitioners. The inclusion of the tap challenge for a public audience may be a conscious and creative decision, but the steps each dancer performs are improvised as a response to the rhythms of each other. The spontaneity of the tap challenge must be "perceived," Hill (2003, 90) maintains, to reinforce the improvised nature of the steps and to indicate to the audience that the exchange of rhythms was not rehearsed and will not be replicated. Hill states that the implied spontaneity of the steps also highlights the competitive element of the tap challenge: the dancers strive to constantly respond to each other's rhythmic stimulus or a referent in which

> something or someone is mocking, referring to, or commenting upon. How do you refer to it? By mimicking, repeating, copying, and deforming it through the use of humor, invective, or satire. Why refer to it? To learn it, to pay respect and admiration, to own it in a different way, to put your opponent down, to gain respect; hence it is a competition. (Hill 2003, 99)

In this context, improvisation acts as performance tool for the tap dancer to instantly distinguish her or his steps from that of another performer. As Hill notes, competition is employed in the tap challenge for entertainment. The tap dancers provide the audience with a visual and aural narrative by demonstrating a command of rhythm and movement. Characters emerge as the performers are presented as rivals competing for the audience's approval. Victory is awarded through the audience's applause and the concession of the vanquished tap dancer who is unable to produce a rhythmic response to outperform the other dancer. This could be accomplished with any creative rhythmic interpretation: increasing or decreasing tempo or volume, adding complex syncopation, or even acrobatic tricks such as flips during an accent or rest. For American tap practitioners of the early twentieth century such as John "Bubbles" or Bill "Bojangles" Robinson, improvisation in tap performance created an additional element to their performance: a reputation. These performers were known for their ability to consistently win at rhythm tap battles in buck-and-wing contests before a paying audience, or at the Hoofers Club competing with their peers (Hill 2010).[10]

Anecdotes and biographical details of the American tap practitioners provide examples of improvising together backstage at theaters or in clubs.[11] Performers worked to refine their skills to remain open and willing to reinterpret rhythms that created spontaneous responses during interactions with other tap dancers. The ability to engage in tap challenges and compete with other performers or even in informal exchanges with another member of the band became a mark of a tap dancer's identity. A tap dancer who repeatedly incorporated challenges generated excitement in his or her choreography, as it gave a chance for audiences to become more involved with the performance, waiting to see if the dancer would succeed in the creation of new rhythms to stump the challenger.

The informal environment of the Hoofers club led to the competition between young, developing performers being determined by the tap dancers themselves. A performer was acknowledged as winning a tap challenge when the other dancer could not respond with a tap step that was more rhythmically complex than that of the challenger. Anecdotal evidence demonstrates that performers valued originality, praising dancers who incorporated syncopation, extreme tempo changes, or changing the tone by utilizing different parts of the tap shoe. Hill (2010, 87) describes the dancers participating in the Hoofers club as being subjected to an "informal panel of peers, whose judgements could be cruel and mocking and were driven by an insistence on innovation." Tap practitioner and historian Rusty Frank (1990, 47) also reinforces this idea of innovation and competition in tap dance: "[t]his was just the business. Tap dancers emulated each others' steps; that is, as much as they could, and then refashioned the steps to become their own." The constant trading of steps between American tap practitioners not only led to competition between performers, but also created the need to compete with one's own repertoire. A tap dancer's ability to compete with his own creativity became essential to his development and the longevity of his performance career.

Competition between tap dancers evolved to meet the need for performers to maintain their employability in the American performance industry. The move to Broadway and other permanent theaters during the twentieth century provided tap dancers with more varied and available sources for developing their repertoire. Observing acts performed on stage offered the possibility of new steps to incorporate into their routines and highlighted a need to stand out from other performers. To maintain their individuality in performance, tap dancers would improvise to discover new ways to re-interpret the steps they gleaned from other tap dancers to bolster their own act.[12] The emphasis on individual performance style created a means for audience members to identify performers, generating marketable resources for productions.[13] The training that tap dancers received backstage and at the Hoofers Club ensured their constant employment as tap dance moved from the vaudeville stage to films in the 1930s. Tap dancers with a broader vocabulary of tap steps could continue to adapt to new show requirements and remain in employment longer. In England, competition also developed as part of tap practice, but within a very different context.

A History of Tap and Competition in England: From Hollywood to Syllabi

The transmission of tap dance from the United States in the early twentieth century to England brought a focus on the visual presentation of the dance form on theatrical stages, in films, and in the early syllabi of dance organizations such as the ISTD. English audiences witnessed individual tap performers and choruses initially through touring revue shows and later through Hollywood film musicals. Hill (2010, 51) details how the chorus girls in Ziegfield Follies of 1914 were "presented not as a tap dancing chorus but as a ranked corps of dancers . . . who made a spectacular display of tap and stepping as one of many dance specialities, to provide a visual and aural contrast in the orchestration of the choreography." The stage shows and films that inspired English viewers featured routines for chorus performers that were simple and repetitive as a necessity to maintain clarity of sound and visual movement, as seen in the work of choreographers such as Ned Wayburn.[14] Tap dancers performed highly articulated footwork that produced a range of sounds and "combined pretty poses and pirouettes with several different types of kicking steps . . . soft-shoe tap steps were inserted in unexpected places in the phrase to add a pleasing variety or sense of surprise" (Hill 2010, 83).

Hollywood musical films and theatrical productions featured tap practitioners such as Bill "Bojangles" Robinson, Fred Astaire, and Gene Kelly. Films such as *Thousands Cheer* (1943), *Singing in the Rain* (1952), and *Royal Wedding* (1951) included choreographed dance routines involving elaborate sets, costumes, and staging that presented tap dance in locations outside a traditional theater, and mixed with other dance forms such as ballet or jazz.[15] Watching performers, such as Fred Astaire dance on the ceiling, Bill "Bojangles" Robinson shuffle on a staircase, or Gene Kelly tapping in the street, created the association of tap dance with visually spectacular choreography.

The competitive element of the tap challenge became less prominent as it was contextualized within narratives and the development of the lead characters. For instance, Busby Berkeley's *Gold Diggers of 1935* integrated a spectacular tap challenge between two corps of men and women as part of the number "Lullaby of Broadway"

(Hill 2010). The women tap out rhythms and the men respond in a double-time interpretation of the steps before the corps come together in the space, creating elaborate formations spread over the stairs and ramps. The choreography incorporates the trading back and forth of rhythms observed in tap challenges, but the constant exchange between the men and women acts as a metaphor for the enticing encounters of New York City nightlife (Hill 2010). In *Singing in the Rain* (1952), Gene Kelly and Donald O'Connor engage in friendly competition during the scene where Kelly's character is practicing his diction. The actors initially attempt to one-up each other, not with tap steps, but in verbal recitation of tongue twisters such as "Moses supposes his toes are roses." The tap choreography follows after Kelly and O'Connor use the rhythms of the tongue twisters as inspiration for their steps, occasionally trading rhythms back and forth, but ultimately ending the scene by manipulating various props in time to the music and singing in unison. Here, the element of competition is used as a device to highlight how the performers must adapt to the new demands of their changing profession, rather than a demonstration of their musicality and creative responses to each other's improvised tap steps.

When situated in the context of Hollywood films or stage revues, the rhythms of the tap steps also serve as a vehicle to visually define the activities or the space that the dancers occupy. In *The Little Colonel* (1935), Bill "Bojangles" Robinson uses a staircase as inspiration for allowing his rhythms to move vertically through the space. The use of stairs was often a feature of Robinson's tap choreography, but in *The Little Colonel* it was presented as part of the film's narrative, a means for his character to interact with the child actress Shirley Temple. In *Singing in the Rain* (1952), Kelly, O'Connor, and Debbie Reynolds dance in the various rooms of a house as they sing the song "Good Morning." The tap choreography incorporates traveling steps when the performers need to change location, such as moving up or down stairs, around furniture, or over to a bar. The dancers also incorporate the props of raincoats or hats, and each performer changes his or her tap steps to reflect different dance styles, such as the can-can, Charleston, and hula dances. In films such as *42nd Street* (1933) and *Gold Diggers of 1935* (1935), Busby Berkeley's choreography is filmed from overhead, from below, and with a variety of wide shots and close-ups of the dancers' feet. The multiple angles offer the audience a compelling visual dimension as the dancers move through complex geometric formations in time to the music.

The popularity of tap dance on stage and in film created the demand to study tap dance and led to its inclusion in the syllabi of several dance societies and associations in England.[16] Various examination boards for dance emerged at the beginning of the twentieth century to meet the need for professional dance training for the stage in tap and other dance styles, such as ballet and ballroom.[17] The organizations represented the first shift in tap practice as it was incorporated into English culture. Dance scholar Stacey Prickett states that

> [a] central component of British culture is found in various boards and academies with codified approaches to artistic development and standardisation. Through

objective criteria, skill levels can be measured through the examination process, providing internationally recognised levels of achievement. (Prickett 2004, 1)

Organizations such as the ISTD were formed with the intention of creating a regulated and examinable method for improving teaching standards and providing professional training for dancers (Buckland 2007).

Tap dance was first introduced in 1932 as part of the syllabus for the Stage Branch of the ISTD (Eddleston 2002). Individuals such as ISTD Theatre Branch founder Zelia Raye and Joan Davis traveled to the United States during the 1920s to learn more about this dance form and the most efficient methods to incorporate tap dance into syllabus teaching (Eddleston 2002). Raye determined that the best method was replication of the rhythms for assessment by trained professional teachers. She seized on the opportunity to teach tap dance in this new format as a

different and more attractive form in which it is now put forward as compared with earlier interpretations. The attraction of the dance in its present form is the result of an advanced understanding of rhythm. Old-fashioned Tap Dancing in the form of steps only had its limitations, but with the introduction of syncopation and rhythm, a great change has taken place. There is perhaps very little difference in the actual technique but the study of advanced rhythm has enabled us to introduce such variations of the same steps as to make the dance appear much more attractive than formerly. (Raye 1936, 2–3)

Raye argued that the approved variations would improve the appearance of the tap steps. She claimed that the syncopation does not impact on the technique of the execution of steps, but rather would improve the visual appeal of the dance form. She did not offer any additional insight as to how this would be achieved by students and teachers. The early ISTD tap syllabi do not include any criteria for how to judge reinterpretations of rhythms, but do discuss correct alignment and posture for the torso and arms.[18]

Stressing posture and alignment implies that rhythm may be visibly represented in other parts of the body, such as changes in the position of the arms or how the entire body moves through the space in time with the music. Tap steps utilize the four surfaces of the tap shoe: two toe taps and two heel taps. When tap dancers reinterpret the rhythm to change the combination of how the toe and heel taps make contact with the floor, this often results in movement that is stationary, rather than traveling in complex patterns through the space. Raye's intention to focus on visual elements, such as arm positions, suggests that judging the student's presentation of steps using the entire body may be easier to measure objectively. If a dancer chooses to use just the feet to execute a tap step, the personal interpretation of the rhythm is limited in its visual presentation to a single area of the body.

Emphasizing the importance of the visual representation of rhythm in the examinations allows for a clear path of progression through the grades and provides a measurable way for the students to reflect on their advancement through the system.

The ISTD website supports this ideal with a page dedicated to examinations. The page features professionals touting the examination process and training as an "investment" and "structure that definitely needs to be in place for the growth of a dancer . . . syllabus work is a necessity" (ISTD 2014). The syllabus system instills students with a sense of achievement in their movement through the grades, as claimed by ISTD members Warren and Kristi Boyce, British National Ballroom Champions: "[t]he ISTD examination system is great because it provides reachable goals as opposed to dreams" (ISTD 2014). The distinction between "goals" and "dreams" suggests that value is placed on the successful and validated presentation of dance steps, rather than individual creative exploration.

The examination process in the ISTD syllabus not only codifies the form, but also sets achievement within a linear model of progression. Dance students are guided through a syllabus that designates how the steps should be performed rhythmically and visually to proceed to the next grade. Several members of the Pulse Collective participated in the ISTD training and examination system for tap dance. Both Ricca and Ross commented that this structured progression of rhythms contributed to the dancers demonstrating a solid understanding of rhythm, but also left the group with a desire to explore tap steps beyond the linear progression of examination grades.

Examining the history of tap dance's introduction to England through stage productions, film, and dance examination institutions, such as the ISTD, reveals that attention to visual elements in tap performance has always been present in English tap practice. The tap dancers in syllabi programs focused on visibly presenting the rhythm, and using the alignment of the body and how it travels through the space in order to meet competition criteria. As English tap dance emerged in new performance formats, such as televised dance shows, tap dancers encountered new challenges presenting their rhythms in competition.

English Tap Dance on the Small Screen: Measuring Success in Televised Dance Competitions

The historical overview of tap dance and competition in the United States and England demonstrates that rhythmic exploration and technical execution were valued differently in each country. In the United States, tap practitioners' success was often reflected in their employability. A key component of a tap dancers' employability was his or her ability to innovate steps and incorporate influences through competitive engagement with other dancers to generate new material for productions. American tap dancers also measured their success in their ability to keep developing material unique to their own performance identity, while paying tribute to their mentors. In England, tap dancers within dance associations, such as the ISTD, measured success through advancement of grade examinations and the ability to accurately showcase steps selected for competitions.

In televised dance competitions, dancers encounter audience applause as one indicator of success, but must consider how the performance is judged by professionals from the field of dance within the format of the show. Dance scholar Laura Robinson (2014, 314) discusses how performances within televised competition shows follow "codes and conventions" and are framed "within the wider performance of the television program." Her analysis examines how the actual dance performance is only part of the overall program, as the shows also feature backstage commentary, judges' feedback, and interviews with performers. The dancers must win over audience members on two fronts: the television studio audience and the television viewers at home. Dancers are judged not only on their performance, but also on how both audiences relate to their individual personalities offstage and their personal journey to arrive at the competition.

These additional elements meant that the Pulse Collective could not rely on its performance alone, but had to consider how to present its members to a broad audience in order to win. Despite including a backstage interview following their first audition, the members of Pulse Collective never mention tap improvisation, but rhythmic exploration is highlighted by Ricca's comments on how the company will approach the next audition.[19] The omission of improvisation was surprising, as many of the company members regularly participated in improvised performances at the tap jams.

Dance scholar Alexis Weisbrod (2014) observes how the televised dance competition show can present incomplete depictions of how dancers prepare and create choreography. Utilizing the example of *So You Think You Can Dance*, Weisbrod (2014, 331) discusses how audiences are exposed to "a whole dancing body, which is made into spectacle by the incomplete picture of its training and experience as presented by the language used by the show's judges and producers." Improvisation is not a component of televised dance competition shows, and audience members may not be familiar with the process of rhythmic exploration in tap dance. Weisbrod's analysis provides an explanation for how this key component of the tap dancer's practice is not addressed. Elements that must be factored into the overall production, such as time limitations and audience interest, mean that the focus is typically directed to the final choreographed performance.

The difference in how successful competition is measured in England is also demonstrated in the first audition clip of the Pulse Collective. Reviewing the judges' comments revealed that they all focused on visual elements of the dance. English judge Aston Merrygold's comments suggest that the piece is successful because of the "swag" and "power" of the performers, a feature he attributes to the manner in which they presented themselves on stage.[20] The judges do not discuss the rhythmic elements of the piece, nor do they offer any comment about the individual tap steps. American judge Kimberly Wyatt states that tap dance is a "traditional form of dance" and that the Pulse Collective was successful because they could "breathe new life into it."[21] She does not provide additional details on how the performers accomplished this, but by choosing music and costume that did not reflect "traditional" perceptions of tap dance the company members shared a perspective of tap dance separate from its American cultural history.

The contrasting comments of the judges in response to the first audition highlights how the element of competition continues to impact tap dance performance in England. Participating in dance competitions addresses the need to incorporate movement that is visually, as well as aurally, entertaining by allowing tap dancers such as the Pulse Collective to reflect on all of their dance inspirations, regardless of the source. Pulse Collective member Ricca frequently described how his tap practice "pays reference to what you know," citing influences from some American tap practitioners, but primarily from his background in commercial and street dance styles. Ricca addressed this need to be open to all influences in his description of the dance competition experience:

> RICCA: I think the reason why, in my opinion, why it [tap dance] hasn't been seen on such a global level is because we're giving people what they know . . . and that's great from some perspectives . . . but it's often the things that people go, "oh I didn't expect that, or that was interesting," but never would they have thought that you could do that . . . just pushing the bar up.
>
> ROSS: My opinion differs slightly. I do agree with Kane, as in I think there was a real lack of innovation for a long period of time. . . . I think the problem is people got comfortable, got lazy and there were decades in the UK where nothing moved, it was sort of static and dated. . . . I think people are looking back instead of looking forward, like "what worked last year, what won last year" . . . rather than what have we not done before? I know I'm making generalizations, there were people pushing, but maybe there just wasn't enough to have a big enough impact.
>
> RICCA: There are some amazing people in the UK doing some amazing things . . . it has inspired people to take artistic risks . . . and that's what it's all about, it's just taking an artistic and creative risk . . . that's challenging but not in any way disrespecting . . . but challenging what we're told in a syllabus.

Ricca and Ross focus on the "dated" presentations of tap dance and how to challenge the existing perceptions of the dance form in England. They argue that the recreation of material that was highly prized in syllabus organizations was seen as successful because it could be judged within the syllabus criteria. In the ISTD medal competitions, individuals are judged on how well they reproduce the material that has been choreographed to preselected music, creating limitations for dancers and their rhythmic exploration. Ricca and Ross elaborate that artistic risks are required to change the perception of tap dance in competition, include tapping to music that is not present in syllabus training, such as hip-hop or electronic dance music. The two practitioners also highlight how they will use their experience from the competition show to continue challenging perceptions of tap dance in England. In their choreography they include steps from other dance styles, such as hip-hop and other street dance practices, that are not often associated with tap dance.

During *Got to Dance 4* the members of the Pulse Collective identified a shift away from their original creative process, and state that they now consider visual elements in the arrangements of steps, as well as rhythmic choices. Changing the choreography to meet the program's requirements for more visible tap steps highlights how competition creates conflicting desires between creating new material and winning dance shows. Tap dancers respond to this challenge of how to balance complex rhythmic steps with visually dynamic movement through constant experimentation and reflection. Introducing the element of competition to their own practice may alter how the tap dancer values her or his explorative efforts, depending on where the competition occurs. This is demonstrated by the Pulse Collective's approach of continuing to incorporate diverse movement and music influences. The company draws on its competition experience and now seeks to promote its choreography as more than just a tap dance performance. The company website describes how the dancers can be employed for corporate entertainment or product endorsement.[22] This description demonstrates a change in how the company measures the success of its tap choreography: employability, as a result of their innovations, in addition to winning talent competitions or positive audience response at tap jams.

THE PULSE COLLECTIVE: CREATING TWENTY-FIRST-CENTURY TAP CHOREOGRAPHY

The analysis of the Pulse Collective audition performances led me to recall another favorite challenge scene from *White Knights* in which Hines and Baryshnikov meet again in the dance studio with the pretext of rehearsing material for Baryshnikov's upcoming show. The two engage in a duet, each executing the steps in unison to symbolize their united decision to escape the Soviet Union together. The first movement is a ball change combination focusing on just the feet, but both men are in dress shoes without taps, and their weight is low and balanced in an even fourth position, as if they were performing jazz dance. They move through a sequence of kicks and low drag turns, their feet constantly shifting between turned out and parallel positions. Hines and Baryshnikov flow through the space in a fusion of tap and ballet steps, with visible influences from martial arts and jazz dance, seen in their punches and hitch kicks. Although performed in unison, each dancer retains his individuality through the qualities of his movement: Hines is strong and grounded, his physicality evident in each step; Baryshnikov maintains the grace, fluidity, and virtuosity that distinguished him throughout his ballet career.

The evolving choreography of the Pulse Collective reflects this blending of dance styles as demonstrated by Hines and Baryshnikov. This group of dancers now uses dance competitions and employment opportunities to measure the success of its innovations, similar to the American tap practitioners of the twentieth century. The dancers reflect the development of early American tap practitioners with their reliance on influences from their past dance and musical experiences, but these evolve from genres such as hip-hop and street dance. These inspirations may not manifest as specific references to individual past practitioners, but the performers draw on the music and movement that shaped their early dance careers nonetheless. The Pulse Collective also applies the experience of its members as English tap dancers, highlighting a unique blend of improvisation from the tap jams to innovate their rhythms, along with the consideration of the visual presentation of their steps from organized competitions. While members such as Ricca and Ross express a desire to move away from the "dated" presentations of tap dance in the English dance syllabi, they acknowledge that the visual presentation of rhythm allows tap dance to compete in mediated performances such as televised dance shows. As tap dance practice and competition continue to evolve in England during the twenty-first century, it will be fascinating to witness what movement aesthetics emerge as these young performers continue to innovate their tap steps with both visual and aural influences across diverse sources.

Notes

1. A clear example of a tap challenge in a filmed context is present in the 1989 film *Tap*, directed by Nick Castle.
2. *Got to Dance* is a televised dance competition show airing in Great Britain from December 2009 to December 2014. The competition was open to all ages and styles, but participants must be considered of an amateur level and could not enter as professionals or part of a professional company. Each act auditioned for the show's producers before competing in four stages of auditions before the judges and a live audience. Judges selected the acts for the semi-final stages, and viewers voted on their favourite act to compete in the finals (Sky UK 2015).
3. As part of my doctoral research I conducted an ethnographic investigation of the tap dance communities in London and Manchester, England, from 2008 until 2011.
4. The term *tap community* is used by the tap jam organizers and participants in both Manchester and London. Participants claimed the two communities formed "organically" around the tap jams and technique classes of the two tap jam organizers, Jess Murray and Junior Laniyan. Belonging to the tap community is not determined by gender, ethnicity, or age, but by expressing a desire to explore rhythm and improvisation. The community members ranged in age from 18 to 80 years of age, and comprised a broad spectrum of ethnic and social backgrounds. These individuals participated in regular tap classes, workshops, and informal performance events organized by key members of the community.
5. Sky 1's *Got to Dance 4*: The Pulse Collective—Live Show 1 2013, (https://youtu.be/EFmk6Usf_WU, accessed February 2, 2015).
6. Author's interview with Kane Ricca and Eilidh Ross on February 15, 2015. To avoid repetition, dates of interviews will be provided the first time an interviewee is quoted but not thereafter.
7. Another location for tap dancers to meet was the back alley behind the famous Apollo Theater in New York City.

8. Members of the club were male African American performers working in theaters and clubs in Harlem and throughout New York City. Very few white performers employed in the vaudeville and Broadway shows frequented the club. Anecdotes reveal that the occasional chorus girl or female tap dancer entered the front rooms of the club, but they were not allowed into the back room with the male hoofers (Stearns and Stearns 1968, 338).

9. The majority of individuals attending the tap jams emerged from similar social classes as working performers, although a few practitioners enjoyed international fame. Most tap dancers in attendance at tap jams were not known outside the theatrical circuits.

10. "Buck-and-wing contests" often occurred on stage after theatrical shows during the early twentieth century. Tap dancers would be juried by their peers or selected theater professionals, such as directors. The contests consisted of tap dancers each executing variations on "buck" steps, flat-footed steps executed in time signatures such as 2/4 or 4/4, and "wing" steps, lateral steps in which the side of the foot is brushed on the floor as it travels horizontally through space (Hill 2010, 22).

11. Examples of these approaches are present in the works of Hill (2010), Knowles (2002), and Stearns and Stearns (1968).

12. Hill (2010, 79) claims that "hundreds" of tap steps were developed during the 1920s as tap dancers experimented offstage. These steps helped tap soloists "evolve onto a new echelon of visual and aural perfection" in their stage shows.

13. An example would be the late Bill Robinson. He was an American tap practitioner well-known for guarding his famous stair dance steps, a routine that could only be witnessed in his shows (Haskins and Mitgang 1988).

14. Dance historian Barbara Stratyner (1996) explains that the articulation of the sounds of individual steps was key in working with large numbers of dancers. Steps had to be simplified to ensure clarity of sounds. Hill (2010) credits Wayburn with the designation of the four parts of the foot (heel, toe, ball, flat foot) to be used in the simple choreography. Limiting the surfaces of the foot making contact with the floor eliminates extraneous noise in the performance of the steps.

15. Dodds (2009) explores how Fred Astaire incorporated tap dance and other dance styles in popular films such as *Daddy Long Legs* (1955).

16. The ISTD did not have information on student enrollment during the introduction of the Stage Dance and later Tap Dance Syllabi. Archival photographs showed predominately white female students, but no information was available on the specific demographics of students.

17. Organizations such as the ISTD and the International Dance Teachers Association have examinations for dance styles such as ballet, modern, and tap.

18. See Imperial Society of Teachers of Dancing (1936).

19. See the Pulse Collective's interview (https://youtu.be/IYIHeI9xMvQ, accessed July 2, 2016).

20. See the clip (https://www.youtube.com/watch?v=EFmk6Usf_WU, accessed February 2, 2014).

21. See the clip (https://www.youtube.com/watch?v=EFmk6Usf_WU, accessed February 2, 2014).

22. See the company's description of services (http://www.rhythm.army/thepulsecollective, accessed June 9, 2016).

References

Buckland, Theresa J. 2007. "Crompton's Campaign: The Professionalisation of Dance Pedagogy in Late Victorian England." *Dance Research* 25(1): 1–34.

Cullen, Frank, Florence Hackman, and Donald McNeilly. 2007. *Vaudeville Old and New: An Encyclopedia of Variety Performers in America*, Volume 1. New York: Routledge.

Dodds, Sherril. 2009. "From Busby Berkeley to Madonna: Music Video and Popular Dance." In *Ballroom, Boogie, Shimmy Sham, Shake: A Social and Popular Dance Reader*, edited by Julie Malnig, 247–260. Chicago: University of Illinois Press.

Eddleston, Pamela. 2002. *Zelia Raye and the Development of Modern Theatre Dance*. London: The Imperial Society of Teachers of Dancing.

Frank, Rusty E. 1990. *Tap! The Greatest Tap Dancing Stars and Their Stories*. New York: Da Capo.

Haskins, Jim, and N. R Mitgang. 1988. *Mr. Bojangles: The Biography of Bill Robinson*. London: Robson Books.

Hill, Constance Valis. 2003. "Stepping, Stealing, Sharing, and Daring." In *Taken by Surprise: A Dance Improvisation Reader*, edited by Ann Cooper Albright and David Gere, 89–104. Middletown, CT: Wesleyan University Press.

Hill, Constance Valis. 2010. *Tap Dancing America: A Cultural History*. New York: Oxford University Press.

The Imperial Society of Teachers of Dancing. 1936. *Syllabus of Tap Dancing for Amateurs*. London: The Imperial Society of Teachers of Dancing.

The Imperial Society of Teachers of Dancing, eds. 2004. *100 Years of Dancing*. London: The Imperial Society of Teachers of Dancing.

The Imperial Society of Teachers of Dancing. 2011. http://www.istd.org/tap-dance/about/. Accessed December 10, 2017.

The Imperial Society of Teachers of Dancing. 2014. "Competitions/Awards" Imperial Society for Teachers of Dancing. http://www.istd.org/events/competitions-awards/. Accessed September 8, 2014.

Knowles, Mark. 2002. *Tap Roots: The Early History of Tap Dancing*. Jefferson, NC: MacFarland.

Prickett, Stacy. 2004. "Techniques and Institutions: The Transformation of British Dance Tradition through South Asian Dance." *Dance Research: The Journal of the Society for Dance Research* 22(1): 1–21.

The Pulse Collective. 2013. https://www.facebook.com/ThePulseCollective. Accessed February 10, 2014.

Raye, Zelia. 1936. *American Tap Dancing*. London: Noverre.

Ricca, Kane D. 2015. *The Pulse Collective*. http://www.rhythm.army/thepulsecollective. Accessed February 8, 2015.

Robinson, Laura. 2014. "The Dance Factor: Hip-Hop, Spectacle, and Reality Television." In *The Oxford Handbook of Dance and the Popular Screen*, edited by Melissa Blanco Borelli, 304–320. New York: Oxford University Press.

Rosenberg, Douglas. 2012. *Screendance: Inscribing the Ephemeral Image*. New York: Oxford University Press.

Stearns, Marshall, and Jean Stearns. 1968. *Jazz Dance: The Story of American Vernacular Dance*. New York: Da Capo.

Stratyner, Barbara. 1996. *Ned Wayburn and the Dance Routine: From Vaudeville to the Ziegfeld Follies*. Madison: University of Wisconsin Press.

Weisbrod, Alexis. 2014. "Defining Dance, Creating Commodity: The Rhetoric of *So You Think You Can Dance*." In *The Oxford Handbook of Dance and the Popular Screen*, edited by Melissa Blanco Borelli, 320–337. New York: Oxford University Press.

Audiovisual Sources

No Maps on My Taps: The Art of Jazz Tap Dancing. 1980. Directed by George T. Nierenberg. GTN Productions: 58 minutes. DVD.

Royal Wedding. 1951. Directed by Stanley Donen. Metro-Goldwyn-Mayer Studios: 93 minutes. DVD.

Singing in the Rain. 1952. Directed by Stanley Donen and Gene Kelly. Metro-Goldwyn-Mayer Studios: 103 minutes. DVD.

Tap. 1989. Directed by Nick Castle. Tristar Pictures: 111 minutes. DVD.

Thousands Cheer. 1943. Directed by George Sidney. Metro-Goldwyn-Mayer Studios: 125 minutes. DVD.

White Knights. 1985. Directed by Taylor Hackford. Columbia Pictures: 136 minutes. DVD.

YouTube Clips

Got to Dance 4: The Pulse Collective—Live Show 1. 2013. YouTube video, 1:54. Posted by "Sky 1's Got to Dance 4," January 20. https://youtu.be/EFmk6Usf_WU. Accessed February 2, 2015.

Got to Dance 4: The Pulse Collective Backstage. 2013. YouTube video, 1:08. Posted by "Sky 1's Got to Dance 4," January 20. https://youtu.be/IYIHeI9xMvQ. Accessed July 2, 2016.

Got to Dance 4: The Pulse Collective—Live Show 2. 2013. YouTube video, 1:07. Posted by "Sky 1's Got to Dance 4," February 18. https://www.youtube.com/watch?v=V2Xc-fmnbkg. Accessed February 2, 2015.

PART III

WINNING, PARTICIPATION, AND THE NEGOTIATION OF MEANING

CHAPTER 10

THE INTERNATIONAL DANCEHALL QUEEN COMPETITION

A Discursive Space for Competing Images of Femininity

CELENA MONTEIRO

With her back to the audience, Dancehall Queen Monica[1] steps into a deep bend and lowers her upper body towards the ground. She reaches her hands between her legs to anchor her arms around her thighs. With her waist tightly scrunched into a ball and her chest squeezed between her outstretched legs, her body creates a triangle-shape with her pelvis at the tip. Adorned in an embellished g-string belt, on which gold spikes form a V-shape down her crotch, her vagina takes center stage. Still in the triangular contortion, she bends her knees forward and back, so that her hips dance at the top of her body and capture the stage's light beams glistening down from above. Peering between her legs, she looks intently at her crotch and then the audience, repeating this back-and-forth gaze eight times. Monica then re-positions herself to an upright kneel, front-on to the audience. With her head lowered and her eyes staring defiantly out at the crowd, she softly strokes her crotch with alternate hands with a sense of adoration.

—International Dancehall Queen Competition (2014)

POSITIONING THE INTERNATIONAL DANCEHALL QUEEN COMPETITION

IN this chapter I examine contemporary performance styles at the International Dancehall Queen Competition, which has taken place in Jamaica every year since

1996.[2] I focus on the performative identities presented at the competition, in relationship to issues surrounding femininity and sexuality, which, as the opening description of Monica's performance demonstrates, are key themes within the style. In examining Dancehall Queen performances, I explore how the event operates as a field dedicated to competing constructions, articulations, and renegotiations of feminine identities.

Dancehall Queen Competitions are staged performance events at which female dancers vie for the title of first prize Dancehall Queen by performing in front of an audience and set of judges. Originating in Jamaica, the Dancehall Queen has become a feminine icon within the wider music and dance culture of dancehall, which first developed in the late 1970s out of its reggae progenitor.[3] The Dancehall Queen title was first awarded to a Jamaican performer named Carlene in 1992 (Niaah 2010), who created a style of performance that was full-bodied, sensual, and centered on a movement vocabulary of precise, often slow, hip rotations and polyrhythmic articulations of the torso and buttocks. Her improvised performances, which incorporated a multitude of bodily contortions, also became known for their gymnastic style, and she wore fanciful and revealing costumes, such as leotards that used colorful mesh material to emphasize her buttocks and breasts. Carlene gained the attention of audiences across the country and beyond, and, as the first female dancer recognized as a Dancehall Queen, remains iconic within the dancehall community.

The Dancehall Queen has since developed into a title given to other prominent female dancers in the dancehall scene and, in 1996, the phenomenon of the Dancehall Queen Competition was established by Big Head Productions.[4] The competition, which takes place in Montego Bay every summer at an outdoor venue called Pier One, represents the highlight of the Dancehall Queen calendar. Like much of Kingston's nightlife, it starts notoriously late at night, and continues into the early hours of the morning. The performances take place on a large open-air stage, which includes a podium catwalk that juts into the crowd of spectators, who watch from an adjacent grassed space. The crowd, of usually about eight hundred people, mainly comprises local Jamaicans. A VIP area is placed next to the stage for a mixture of Jamaicans and non-Jamaicans, such as documentary journalists and photographers, and guests who are often supporters of a particular contestant. Typically, the DJ, situated at the side of the stage, will mix popular dancehall tracks until about midnight; around this time the judges are welcomed and seated toward the back of the stage, leaving center-stage clear for the dancers to perform. Shortly after this, the contestants take to the stage and individually introduce themselves, stating their name (usually a chosen stage name aligned to their Dancehall Queen persona) and the country they represent. Once all the dancers have spoken, the competitive solo performances finally commence.

The event remained a substantially Jamaican affair, with a majority of Jamaican contestants, until the crowning of the first non-Jamaican winner in 2002, a Japanese dancer named Junko Kudo. This formed a transitional moment in the history of the Dancehall Queen and in dancehall culture at large, because it marked a significant shift, from attracting mainly national interest to a broader international reach. Since Kudo's crowning, an increasing number of dancers from across the world are taking up Dancehall Queen identities, and today more non-Jamaican than Jamaican women commonly populate the competition. This growth in interest by international dancers has also inspired Dancehall Queen Competitions to be organized at multiple sites across the globe, including Russia, Austria, Japan, and North America.[5]

This chapter offers a concentrated examination of the International Dancehall Queen Competition, as it is a main feature within the global Dancehall Queen scene and a space particularly abundant with a wide variety of Dancehall Queen styles. It thus provides a rich object of study for an investigation into the identity politics of gender, race, and sexuality within Dancehall Queen culture as a whole and warrants a pointed inspection in and of itself. I draw on fieldwork observations and interviews conducted in Jamaica, the United Kingdom, Vienna, and online to investigate the diverse practices of feminine identities in this competition scene. I use three Dancehall Queen case studies from Jamaica, Guyana, and Italy to investigate the various ways in which Jamaican and non-Jamaican Dancehall Queens navigate the field of gender identities within this competitive performance practice.

Theoretically, I draw on postcolonial feminist theory, in particular Audre Lorde's (1978) concept of erotic power and Caribbean feminist literature that addresses the politics of the popular female dancing body (Blanco Borelli 2015; Thorington Springer 2007). In my examination of the field of feminine performance practices within the Dancehall Queen scene, I raise debate around discourses in feminist scholarship in regard to embodiment, sexuality, performance, and agency. My theoretical focus intersects between postcolonial feminist ideas engaged with the empowering potential of popular feminine black performance practices and radical feminist perspectives, which take issue with heteronormative sexualized representations of femininity (Kitzinger and Wilkinson 1994). Altogether, my examination assesses the presence of dancehall theorist Sonjah Stanley Niaah's theory of boundarylessness (2010) in relation to the discourse surrounding femininity and sexuality at the competition.

First I outline the stylistic traits identified by scholars who examine the distinctly Jamaican dancehall style, in relation to the country's postcolonial sociopolitical context. Then, in recognition of the growing international participation in the competition, I study how the postcolonial feminist discourses surrounding the form now operate in tandem with the gender politics of the developing variations in style.

FEMININE IDENTITY CONSTRUCTION AT THE INTERNATIONAL DANCEHALL QUEEN COMPETITION

During fieldwork in Jamaica in 2014, several days before the competition was due to take place, I interviewed a European Dancehall Queen named Suzie.[6] As I set up the recording equipment, she entered the room and perched on the stool provided. I looked up at her and made a mental note of her appearance; she wore a pink crop-top, with tight black "batty rider"[7] shorts, a gold-studded fanny-pack, and had a long wavy weave.[8] "This is for sure a Dancehall Queen," I thought to myself: her outlandish, self-assured, and hyper-feminine style directly signaling the archetypal Dancehall Queen image.

During the interview I asked Suzie about the performance she was preparing for and she responded,

> There's a lot of girls who think that dancehall is supposed to be a [partic-ular] way . . . sometimes it feels like restrictions. . . . Now that I've been here I've seen . . . head tops, splits, and I do all of that, . . . but I'd rather not do it because it's gonna be on the stage like ten times, over and over.

When I subsequently asked her, "What is your dancehall style about?" she reflected,

> I wanna show the tough girl, the girl that I am, . . . this is what I call dancehall, not just splits and slapping your pussy and daggering,[9] I try to censor out all that. . . . It's starting to get more and more extreme . . . that's why this year I decided to come here and show people . . . I do my splits with quality, [and] attitude like "I'm here."

Suzie's statements highlight the presence of a discourse within the scene concerning the diversity of performance styles presented at the competition, and the competing narratives they represent. Her derision of excessive displays of an "extreme" hyper-sexual style highlights the focus on female sexuality within Dancehall Queen expressive practices. Her assertion stands in contrast to the performance by Dancehall Queen Monica, described in the opening of this chapter, with its daring style and signals of veneration toward the vagina. Together, Monica's performance and Suzie's comments highlight the presence of a tension, which travels across verbal and embodied expressions, surrounding the stylistic tastes presented by the Queens. In particular, Suzie's remarks raise questions about how, through national, cultural and stylistic differences, the dancers carve out individualized Dancehall Queen identities that speak to the concepts and boundaries that surround the construction of femininity and female sexuality within the scene and beyond.

POSTCOLONIALITY, RESISTANCE, AND "BOUNDARYLESSNESS": DANCEHALL'S RELATIONSHIP TO JAMAICAN SOCIOPOLITICS

To develop a reading of the performances and constructions of feminine identities at the competition, I consider dancehall's sociopolitical and cultural underpinnings.

Several cultural and literary scholars (Cooper 1995, 2004; Hope 2006; Niaah 2010) view dancehall as a style of music and dance that represents a working-class black Jamaican positionality. These scholars convey dancehall as symptomatic of the country's current postcolonial era and perceive it as resistant to existing neocolonial power systems that operate in the region. These systems, which include imbalanced international trade agreements, poor public services, and the restricted international mobility of Jamaican citizens, developed following the country's exit from the British Empire in 1962. As a result of Jamaica's precarious geopolitical status as a postcolonial state with little international influence, declining commercial revenue, and high public debt (World Bank 2015), the country has struggled with widespread poverty since its independence.

Speaking from the perspective of the black youth who grew up in the country's poverty-stricken urban ghettos, dancehall lyrics and imagery reflect a social and political sentiment of disenfranchisement from the formal economy and power regimes in Jamaica. This sentiment is not only a manifestation of economic hardship, but also a deflated sociocultural status in a country that links skin color to class (Hope 2006). Dancehall thus expresses the oppression experienced by the black Jamaican urban youth, and their resistance to this situation. Niaah (2010, 152) discusses the resistive theme within dancehall through a theory of "boundarylessness," which she conceives as the style's transcendence of the various "categories, hierarchies, walls, states and borders" that surround it. Through its boundary-defying expressive mediums, Jamaican dancehall combats the unjust power regimes within Jamaica, which center around the vast imbalances in the country's wealth distribution and social conditions, with the aim of bettering the socioeconomic situations of the ghetto youth (Cooper 2004; Niaah 2010).

Yet conflictingly, certain aspects of the style demonstrate a concordance with mainstream and upper-class Jamaican sociocultural values. One of these, as Caribbean Studies scholar Donna Hope (2006) identifies, is dancehall's homophobic rhetoric. The emphasis on policing homosexuality in dancehall can be seen as an alignment to Jamaican society's social mores, which, driven by the country's strong commitment to Christian moral values, are committed to the celebration of heterosexuality and heteronormativity (Hope 2006). Another example of this alignment to heteronormativity is dancehall's divisive classification of "male" and "female" dance moves, which acts as a way of policing the gender performances of both male and female bodies. My observations in Jamaica suggest that female dancers tend to have more leeway and can perform both styles, although few actually do; but it is socially unacceptable for men to perform "female steps," and this is heavily policed by patrons within the scene. Male dancing bodies, just for their engagement in an embodied practice, are inherently at risk of being feminized (Hope 2010). The stakes of feminization are high and real; therefore dancers tend to abide very strictly by these gender classifications. These gendered elements highlight how dancehall has a paradoxical relationship to Jamaican moral codes, often expressing an exaggerated version of a sentiment common to the wider society's principles, while simultaneously rejecting high society's economic and political domination.

Another of the contrary issues in dancehall is its relationship to whiteness. On the one hand, dancehall fundamentally resists white beauty standards, which are often held by middle- and upper-class Jamaican society, in its celebration of black bodies and aesthetics. As cultural theorist Carolyn Cooper (2004, 86) identifies, dancehall is committed to the

> glorious celebration of full-bodied female sexuality, particularly the substantial structure of the Black working-class woman whose body image is rarely validated in the middle-class Jamaican media, where eurocentric norms of delicate female face and figure are privileged.

Yet, on the other hand, alternate trends exist within dancehall culture, such as the practice of skin bleaching by some dancehall patrons, that express compliance with the white beauty standard. Hope (2006, 45) argues that this particular practice "arises from the necessary movement away from the dark-skinned base of color-coded Jamaican society and towards the hegemonic standard of whiteness and lightness." This dual resistance to, and compliance with, Jamaican race hierarchies within dancehall positions the form as fundamentally symptomatic of its Jamaican geographic setting, and an expression of the discourse surrounding postcolonial Jamaican society. It signals dancehall's active role in Jamaican cultural practices and the participants' awareness of the stakes involved. On reflection of these dynamics, Niaah (2010, 174) contends that

> even as dancehall culture is situated in a field of boundaries, its key participants have created several unbound dancescapes and soundscapes, first through everyday street events around music and dance that transcend the street; second, through travel across geopolitical borders allowing for the articulation of an urban dancehall "transition"; and third, in the ways in which participants inaugurate and expand categories that add prestige to, and invoke long histories in support of, these spaces.

Thus, in its multilayered relationship to the Jamaican state and social politics, dancehall is continually engaged in the (re)negotiation of various explicit and implicit boundaries.

(Post) colonial Feminine Identities

In alignment with the vision of dancehall as a resistant social practice, dancehall scholars such as Cooper (2004) and Beth-Sarah Wright (2004) have positioned the boldly sexual and sensual style of Dancehall Queens, such as Carlene and Monica, described earlier, as resistant to the (post)colonial exploitation of the Jamaican woman's body for domestic and sexual labor. This argument relates the dance to the legacy of colonial depictions of black female sexuality as excessively sexual—an image produced in opposition to the "purity" of white femininity (Dyer 1997; Gilman 1985). This construction of black female sexuality has been achieved, to a large extent, through the portrayal of the black female body as "oversized" and grotesque. Propaganda surrounding the buttocks and genitalia of black women during the colonial period deemed these body parts to be out of proportion with the rest of their bodies, and their supposed inflated size was read as physical evidence of a salacious sexual essence (hooks 1997). These images continue to exist both in the Caribbean and across the Global North, as identified by English Studies scholar Jennifer Thorington Springer (2007) and black cultural theorist bell hooks (1997).

Cooper's (2004) and Wright's (2004) arguments maintain that the meanings associated with racialized female body parts can be debated and reimagined through their movement. By creating choreographies that focus on these parts of their bodies, women can signal awareness of the potency of their corporeality, and through their movement can disrupt the imposed meanings ascribed to them. This strategy often emerges within female Caribbean performance, as identified by Thorington Springer's (2007) reading of the Barbadian "wukking up" dance style and in dance theorist Melissa Blanco Borelli's (2015, 31) inquiry into the Cuban mulatta's articulation of her hips wherein she "stak[es] out space, territory, and meaning with the same body as has been used against her." The same strategy can be seen within Jamaican Dancehall Queen movement in its identifiable manipulation of the politicized body parts of the hips, buttocks, pelvis, and vagina. For instance, many popular Dancehall Queen moves involve the dancers performing a variation of a "head top." These are stylized headstands, based on a triangular base of the top of the head with two pillared hands either side. However, unlike traditional gymnastic headstands, which strive for linearity through the creation of a straight line from the head through to the toes, Dancehall Queen head tops involve a counterbalance, wherein the pelvis juts backward, out of alignment from the spine. This position increases the dancer's ability to mobilize her hip joints and, in so doing, to explore a wealth of creative movement possibilities. The vocabulary of movement created in this position focuses on balance and flexibility to create complex variations of rotations, bounces, and flicks between the hips and buttocks. The aesthetic created by the focused use of the hips, buttocks, and pelvis, as well as performance motifs such as the patting, stroking, and pointing toward the vagina, work to accentuate the mobility of the hips, highlight the dancer's control over her buttocks, and centralize the vagina as a meaning-making symbol in the style. Through this explicit focus on these sexually charged body parts, the movements actively address the politics of femininity and sexuality placed on these body parts in a Jamaican context. Thus Dancehall Queen performance, while engaging with hyper-sexual female imagery, does so with a level of embodied commitment, control, and creative ingenuity, and this imbues the dancer with symbolic power and agency.

THE BRUK OUT STYLE

At the International Dancehall Queen Competition in 2014, a Jamaican dancer named Dancehall Queen Brukker reached the top twenty in the competition. A highlight of her performance was when, in a blue, thong-shaped leotard, she perched on the stage with her back and barely covered buttocks facing the audience, and proceeded to pick up and unscrew a bottle of water, reach behind herself, and pour the water onto her vigorously shaking buttocks. The aesthetics of her freely shaking flesh, in collaboration with the water splatters, was tantalizingly erotic. Her performance also included various hyper-flexible, wide-legged bodily contortions. In these positions she patted and stroked her vaginal area, which created a visual focus on this body part and signaled her explicit intention to centralize it in the aesthetic of her style.

Watching from the crowd, I heard disdainful comments around me, such as, "That is gogo[10] dancing, not Dancehall Queen dancing," and it was perhaps due to similar scornful reactions among the competition judges that she did not make it further than the second round of the competition. Ultimately, her outlandishly erotic style remained marginal to less explicit performances. In 2015, however, she returned to the competition and remained committed to her erotic style. Wearing the same type of costume, this time a pink g-string leotard, she performed her water bottle trick once again. Her persistence was rewarded, as she won first place and was crowned the International Dancehall Queen of 2015. With this success, her previously marginal style was repositioned to become central to the Dancehall Queen image. With this adjustment, the codes of taste and value surrounding feminine identity production in the scene were challenged; the hyper-erotic became highly visible and revered in a cultural framework that, just one year earlier, had deemed a similar style by the same performer much less valuable and less deserving of recognition. It follows that Dancehall Queen Brukker, with her status as the winner of the 2015 International Dancehall Queen Competition, now has the influence to further entrench the connections between her style of feminine performance and the Dancehall Queen image.

Dancehall Queen Brukker's style was an amplified version of a contemporary style seen among some contestants, particularly Jamaicans, that centers on certain gymnastic and erotic components. I refer to this as the "bruk out" style because it epitomizes the concept of "bruk out," which is to act unruly, or to "break out." In the case of the Dancehall Queen, it means to abandon the stylistic and moral restrictions usually placed on her dancing, as expressed in Alkaline's lyrics, "Do something weh you wouldn't normally do" (Genius lyrics 2016) within the song self-titled "Gyal Bruk Out" (2013). The bruk out style generally includes the aforementioned head tops, as well as shoulder stands, handstands, various splits positions, a range of cataclysmic falls into the splits and other bodily contortions, and a multitude of gestural signals toward the vagina. The bruk out style is also identifiable for its improvisatory rough-and-ready approach, as movements are often put together with a crudeness that favors content over form. Dancers will present a collection of their strongest and most virtuosic dance moves in quick succession, with little regard for fanciful structure or patterns. With its unapologetic style and centralization of the vagina, the bruk out style takes an active role in the discourse surrounding the hyper-sexualization of the black female body. The performances, which express the dancers' awareness of their corporeal signifiers in a postcolonial context, create a power associated with women taking ownership over the symbology of their bodies. The bold nature of the style, which resists the predilection for female "delicacy" (Cooper 2004), satirically calls into question the Europeanist construction of a feminine ideal. This acts as a way of slipping through the grasp of existing exploitative forces, such as commercial enterprises looking to reap benefits from the sexual imagery involved. The style reimagines the vagina as a symbol of what Audre Lorde (1978, 89) describes as "erotic power": "an assertion of the lifeforce of women; of that creative energy empowered," and the dancers' investment in this imagery creates the opportunity to cultivate their erotic capital (Hakim 2010).

Dancehall Queen Maximum, a participant at the competition in 2014, describes the performing experience in the following way: "[there is] a fire you have inside . . . [a] feeling that you are invincible; Superwoman!"[11] Her statement suggests that there is often an intensity to the experience, which creates a sense of embodied power. During this interview, which took place on the morning after the competition, Dancehall Queen Maximum further explained, "We all have so many bruises [today] because when you dance dancehall you don't feel the pain." This statement illustrates how the intensity of the internal sensation pushed Dancehall Queens to exceed their own sense of corporeal boundaries. It is in these moments of excess, when dancers push beyond physical restrictions, that they also push beyond the notion of a fixed image of femininity. The dynamism and power that these Dancehall Queens put into their erotic performances, coupled with the unapologetically bold stylization, create an image of feminine fortitude.

Through a postcolonial feminist lens, the bruk out style reveals a demonstrated awareness of the hyper-sexualization of the black female body and the role of the hips and buttocks as the material evidence of this image; the dancer's claim to self-assertion is driven by these same body parts. By making the fetishized parts of their bodies the central focus of their choreographies, they claim space within the discourse that constitutes their bodily signifiers. In so doing, they take a subject position that assumes power by actively looking back at the colonial gaze (Bhabha 1994).[12] These corporeal strategies employed by Dancehall Queens, as with the Barbadian "wukking up" style (Thorington Springer 2007) and the "dancing mulatta" (Blanco Borelli 2015), play into a postcolonial feminist rhetoric that claims a space for alternate strategies for female empowerment, beyond the feminist theoretical canon driven in the Global North (Brooks 1997; Lewis and Mills 2003).[13] Unlike radical feminism[14] (Kitzinger and Wilkinson 1994), which seeks to denaturalize heterosexuality, the bruk out style reinforces a heterosexual and hyper-sexual image of femininity. This makes it distinct from radical feminist discourses, because it does not confront heterosexual idealism, but still resists patriarchal determination. The bruk out style of Dancehall Queen performance actually engages with the heterosexual feminine image, but does so on the dancer's terms. The principle of the dancer's own pleasure in creating the kinesthetic dialogue between her buttocks, hips, and pelvis works to undermine the emphasis on the viewer's visual pleasure. The Caribbean feminist standpoints identified by Thorington Springer (2007), Blanco Borelli (2015), and myself concerning the bruk out style, in terms of postcoloniality and the cultivation of erotic power (Lorde, 1978), are distinct in their agendas and methods of empowerment from hegemonic Euro-American feminisms. Their existence points out the need for cultural appreciation in the reading of feminine practices. As this example demonstrates, on closer inspection, supposedly oppressed women are able to cultivate their own empowerment, but through strategies specific to their environmental context, which may be alien to outsiders unaware of the nuances of their social conditions.

Whereas the rhetoric surrounding contemporary feminist performance in the Global North routinely invests in the concept of stripping away the performative falsity of womanhood as a definite and identifiable identity signifier (Butler 1990; Kitzinger and Wilkinson 1994), the Jamaican bruk out style instead affirms a particular vision of femininity. In its celebration of an idealized heterosexual femininity, the bruk out style stands out from other definitions of feminist performance that value the redefining of femininity beyond the patriarchal construct. Therefore, although Dancehall Queen performance, through its ability to create a sense of bodily awareness and ownership, resists the exploitation and abuse of the female body, it does not deny the vision of her body as a symbol of sexuality embedded within a heteronormative paradigm.

In making this claim, I am conscious that it sits in contrast to Kitzinger and Wilkinson's (1994, 447) view that

> heterosexuality is a key mechanism through which male dominance is achieved. Male dominance is "not an artificial overlay" upon heterosexuality that can somehow be stripped away to leave an uncorrupted, pure, sexual interaction; rather it is intrinsic to heterosex itself.

In this view, the bruk out style, in its conformity to heterosexual feminine imagery, is already contaminated by patriarchy and can only represent female submissiveness. This assumes that the script is already written by patriarchy and that heterosexuality cannot be reimagined beyond the dominator/subordinated roles. I concede that heterosexuality routinely exists within a patriarchal frame, but I do not accept the absolutism of Kitzinger and Wilkinson's (1994) statement, because to conceive all forms of heterosexuality to be bound to these power dynamics fails to recognize the plethora of existent examples within the heterosexual sphere of egalitarianism and matriarchy (Goettner-Abendroth 2013; Wittig 1993). The iteration of heterosexuality present in dancehall is not relieved of the power dynamics of patriarchy, but the Dancehall Queen Competition offers a vital space imbued with the opportunity for female dancers to play with and subvert said power dynamics.

THE STEPS STYLE

I mentioned earlier that, since 2002, the International Dancehall Queen Competition has become increasingly populated by non-Jamaican dancers, and this has brought stylistic shifts to the event. One of the distinctions of the trend toward internationalization arises from the expansion of the Dancehall Queen style to include movements that are categorized within the scene as "male moves." These moves use a vastly different skill set, and focus on different body parts, from the historic style of Dancehall Queen Carlene and the bruk out style. Instead of focusing on the sexually loaded body parts of the buttocks, hips, pelvis, and vagina, male moves concentrate on the feet, legs, shoulders, arms, and head. Through these body parts, the style creates sharp, angular shapes, which are commonly performed in quick succession, and this drives an aesthetic tied to alternate gender constructions associated with masculinity. For the sake of clarity, I will refer to this Dancehall Queen style, which draws from the male moves, as the "steps style." This name references the steps that draw emphasis away from movements in the torso and hips and toward the limbs, and outer extremities of the feet, hands, and head.

I now look at the second runner-up at the competition in 2015, Guyanese Dancehall Queen Martha, to present a study of this alternate styling. In so doing, I pay attention to the value implications of her positioning as runner-up to the winner, Dancehall Queen Brukker, who performed at the explicit extremity of the bruk out style. Contrastingly, the central characteristic of Martha's performance was her decidedly masculinist style of dance. She performed fast angular movements that emphasized the forearms and lower legs, coupled with dynamic turns on multiple levels, and a looseness of the neck and head. Working closely with the musical score, she performed the mechanical movements with accuracy and power, creating a sense of precision and tenacity within the style.

A European Dancehall Queen who also took part in the 2015 competition supported Martha's style by writing the following comment on Facebook:

> [She] . . . DID IT . . . 3rd place AND best choreography . . . she basically took home the 2nd runner up spot by doing what she does best and feels comfortable with . . . DANCEHALL (not DHQ). The crowd LOVED her. She deserves it. SUPERSTAR![15]

In positioning Martha's performance as "dancehall" rather than "DHQ" (an acronym for Dancehall Queen), this Dancehall Queen's comment signals Martha's use of a movement vocabulary and style that, in her view, did not fit within current definitions of Dancehall Queen movement and style. By focusing on the movements of the limbs, rather than the hips, buttocks, pelvis, and vagina, the steps style moves away from a sexualized feminine image and instead constructs a performative style of femininity that projects power through the attributes of speed, accuracy, and coordination, which are associated with masculine performativity in the scene. Further evidence of Martha's positioning in this domain is in her costume. She replaces the elaborate and erotically inclined ensembles, including revealing bras and underpants popularly worn by many Dancehall Queens, with more covered-up and simple outfits, such as plain black jeans and a leather jacket. Her style asserts power and credibility through the move away from erotic performativity as it draws capital from its alignment to patriarchal images of power.

Performances such as Martha's resonate with the radical feminist discourse, which situates female erotic performance such as the bruk out style as degrading (Kitzinger and Wilkinson 1994). This trope is present within discourses surrounding the Dancehall Queen scene, which reject the bruk out styling in favor of the newly emerging styles entering the competition: "the competition [is] just about flexibility most of the time. I think it's changing now and I think that's good, because steps are getting more and more important for the dancers as well" (European Dancehall Queen "Cher" at the European Dancehall Queen Competition 2013).[16] Comments such as this suggest that the bruk out style is seen by some non-Jamaicans as less valuable, resulting in a discourse of disenchantment toward the erotic acrobatics of the head tops and splits typical of the style. In the international circuit, many female dancers fluidly interchange between gender-prescribed moves, with some choosing to practice the male moves instead of female styles. In particular, a trend exists for female dancers to teach the steps style, with its power, speed, precision, and swagger. Focusing on this movement vocabulary enables them to perform and celebrate the dancehall style, while avoiding the sociocultural issues associated with the erotic bruk out style and its dismissal by many feminist viewers. Dancehall Queen Suzie explains: "this feminist group that represents the politicians . . . they really respect everything we do, because we are censoring like all the bad stuff, but we're still teaching the good stuff and they like that."

The privileging of the "refined" style by Suzie plays up to a narrative of class assertion through the distinction of tasteful and distasteful performances of femininity within the Dancehall Queen scene. When this discourse involves a non-Jamaican rejection of the bruk out style, geopolitics also come into discursive tension: the bruk out style symbolizes a distinctly Jamaican Dancehall Queen aesthetic taste, and the female performance of the steps style represents the "foreign," non-Jamaican development. This plays into a narrative of the non-Jamaican dancer policing the bodily expression of the Jamaican dancer, which is one of the conditions that the Dancehall Queen style resists in the first place.

Further, by producing an aesthetic that is aligned to the second wave feminist emphasis on the desexualization of the female body (Synder-Hall 2010), dancers who make the move toward male moves reinforce concepts of female sexuality as problematic. The conflation of feminine eroticism with a loss of power sits in contrast to Lorde's (1978) aforementioned theory regarding the power of the erotic as feminine life force. Pertinently, Lorde argues that the erotic has been downtrodden by patriarchy (and feminists victim to patriarchal philosophical manifestations) because it threatens patriarchal dominance. From this perspective, the steps style arguably supports a patriarchal philosophy, which silences certain aspects of feminine performance, and positions power within masculine performance codes. Thus, in its promulgation of a divergent image of femininity to the bruk out style, the steps style implicitly challenges the postcolonial feminist sentiment of erotic power (Lorde 1978).

COMPETITION BETWEEN STYLES

The differences between the respective styles of Dancehall Queen Brukker and Martha represent the wider discursive competition within which the Dancehall Queen scene is embedded, between the adherence to and rejection of social and cultural boundaries. The risqué style of those dancers who invest in the principle of unapologetic erotica retains dancehall's resistive, yet heteronormative, performative foundations. On the other hand, the steps style projects an image of the disciplined body (Foucault 1977)[17] and therefore challenges the foundation of bruk out body politics. For example, Dancehall Queen Suzie states,

> I'm making my own type of dancehall . . . [which is] . . . humble. If I'm showing the parents of my children [dance school pupils] . . . a video of a Dancehall Queen, I don't wanna show the girl doing this [grips hold of her leg to stretch it out and with her fist gestures a forward backward motion toward her vagina] . . . I wanna show them the tough girl—I wanna show them that this is what I call dancehall, not just splits and gettin' your pussy all out. . . . I try to censor out all that.

Suzie's comment suggests that dancehall is integral to her career and economic live-lihood and, as a dancehall teacher for children, is motivated to provide an alternative image of the Dancehall Queen. She is intent on creating a "clean" image, which translates as a less erotic version of femininity than the bruk out style. Her intentions are under-standable: as a teacher of children, she has a responsibility to provide them with age-appropriate dance material. Nonetheless, her motivation to censor the aspects that she deems vulgar suggests a politics of correction, which conflicts with the boundary-defying aesthetic inherent to Dancehall Queen productivity. In creating limits and presenting an image of class, she becomes a signifier of the authoritative, upper-class, and "tastefully" cultured segment of society, which is in opposition to dancehall's orig-inal motivations (Cooper 2004).

The dancers' distinctions between performance styles create a system of taste around the degrees and types of erotica within Dancehall Queen performance. Sociologist Sarah Thornton (1995, 10) predicates that "[d]istinctions are never just assertions of equal difference; they usually entail some claim to authority and presume the inferiority of others." In this way, the taste politics inscribed onto the Dancehall Queen performances by the dancers themselves work to police alternative performances of femininity, thus undermining the primary motivation within Dancehall Queen and dancehall per-formance to refuse restriction. These politics of taste situated in female performance also further entrench the way in which female bodies act as divisive symbols and active repertoires in the construction of ideologies around honor, nation, and value.

However, while the expansion of the Dancehall Queen aesthetic creates competitive frissons and frictions in the scene between the various stylistic camps, it also speaks to the fundamental emphasis on boundarylessness in the scene (Niaah 2010). In its disruption of the unified body politics of erotic power (Lorde 1978), the steps style creates a paradoxical resistance to the stability of the bruk out style. The competition's acceptance and growing celebration of the steps style, as evidenced by Martha's top three ranking, demonstrate its dedication to the plurality of feminine identity constructions in the scene; thus Martha's success highlights the non-Jamaican dancer's role in creating an increasingly flexible Dancehall Queen image.

THE CROSSOVER STYLE

In addition to Dancehall Queens who draw from either the bruk out or steps styling, there are also others, for whom it is antithetically the opportunity to betray the binary between the two styles that attracts them to participate in the competition. Instead of choosing a side, some Dancehall Queens choreograph intertextual performances, which move between and beyond a singular image of femininity. For example, an Italian dancer named Dancehall Queen Misty repeatedly produces performances at the competition that stand out for inventively drawing from, and addressing the embodied politics of, both the bruk out and steps style. In her opening performance at the 2015 competition, she strides onto the stage, wearing a block-colored, black, yellow, and pink leotard, chunky boots, suspenders, and a black leather jacket. She walks in a circle, looking out toward the audience, head tilted down, eyes straight on. Then, facing front-on to the audience, she travels forward using deep and heavy strides and, as she reaches the front of the stage, kicks her left leg in the air, before jumping on the spot and circling her arm around her head, as if waving a flag. This section is identifiable for its use of a variety of male moves and its smoothly choreographed transitions between positions. Following this, she turns to face away from the audience and bends her upper body toward the ground, while maintaining an open straight-legged position. In this triangle shape, with her pelvis at the pinnacle, she creates a repetitive rhythmic impulse in her hips, causing a ripple effect in her buttocks. She then goes on to perform a complex variation of the head top move, incorporating a bouncing motion between her hips and buttocks, and a 360-degree turn.

In drawing from a mixture of female and male moves, Misty's style deviates from both the bruk out and steps styles. Her costume, movement, and comportment reflect key components of the bruk out style. Her outfit, with its bright colors and lingerie, signals a boldly sexual feminine style. Many of her movement choices, and the quality with which she performs, are typical of Jamaican dancehall, and thus demonstrate her embodied relationship to the art form in its Jamaican context and the performance style first developed by Jamaican Dancehall Queens. However, she also performs her movement with a fast pace and creates clear lines and shapes with her body, characteristics of the alternate steps style. Her navigation between the gender-coded dancehall movement vocabulary removes the fixity of both styles' respective associations to Jamaican and non-Jamaican bodies and feminine/masculine constructs. Her style instead presents a multi-layered relationship to dancehall movement vocabulary, which honors the erotic component, while simultaneously incorporating aspects of the alternately gendered steps style.

Her use of the steps style, in addition to her white European identity, risked an implicit linkage to the concept of reformation. The push for censorship of the bruk out style, typically associated with black Dancehall Queen performances, by steps style proponents can in these cases act as a manifestation of a neocolonial corrective process, wherein Europeanness and formalization are connected to the elitist taste values of whiteness and elevated class. Instead, she debunked this association by marrying the two styles together, thus subverting the boundaries between the two taste ideologies, which effectively positioned her as a "boundary-pusher." In its dual signaling toward the style associated with Jamaican femininity and male steps, her performance alludes to her fluid relationship to these two distinct styles of dancehall. In its multifaceted style and content, Misty's performance speaks to the potential for mobile transnational feminine identity constructions in performances where the local meets the global.

CONTRADICTION AND PROVOCATION: THE CREATIVE INSTABILITY OF TRANSNATIONAL DANCEHALL QUEEN PERFORMANCE

The annual crowning of a new International Dancehall Queen creates a cultural system that is constantly in process. This is crucial to the way in which the Dancehall Queen as an identifiable icon is understood. The passing of power each year entrenches the fluidity of the form due to this transitional act being situated as the formal highlight of the Dancehall Queen year. There is a focus, within this system, on the present moment; dancers engage in the creation of new moves, and the community celebrates this creativity by involving them in other dancehall spaces. The emphasis on productivity and the engagement in transition create a state of flux wherein instability is the only constant. This is further driven by the dancers' creative emphasis on continually rebuffing the boundaries placed on the practice and the consequential redelineation of the parameters that make up the Dancehall Queen identity. The steps style, in its presentation of an alternate feminine performativity to the characteristically boundary-pushing bruk out image, challenges the heteronormative sexual imagery embedded in the bruk out style, a boundary that the bruk out style fails to reject. The instability of the Dancehall Queen positionality, caused by the constant competition for visibility between the styles, is thus a driving force for its production. This supports a creativity within the community that engages a multitude of dancers and viewers, with diverse and sometimes conflicting agendas. This instability speaks to the precariousness and uncertainty of the situation, as the Dancehall Queen icon restlessly negotiates its continued central place in Jamaican working-class feminine culture and its simultaneous inflation as a global dance, along with the subsequent politics of appropriation and redefinition that follow. As it navigates between the local and the global, the meeting points and fractures between Jamaican postcolonialism and transcultural/national expansion are laid bare, and the role of female bodies as the proponents in this discourse is revealed.

The range of stylistic traits among Dancehall Queens Brukker, Martha, and Misty demonstrates the breadth of the performances of femininity now circulating at the annual competition. The inclusion of male moves works to deconstruct the fixity of the eroticism associated with the founding Dancehall Queens, such as Carlene's provocative stylization. Other stylistic developments, such as the inclusion of transitional moves between sections to create a more choreographed style and the incorporation of alternate fashion trends to the bright, revealing costumes of the bruk out style, work to expand the aesthetics associated with the Dancehall Queen image as it becomes increasingly transnational. That the majority of dancers who include the male moves, or deviate from the erotic Dancehall Queen image in other ways, come from outside Jamaica evidences the impact that non-Jamaican dancers are having on the identity of Dancehall Queen culture as a whole. Although the International Dancehall Queen Competition grew as a postcolonial movement for self-determination by a black, female working-class Jamaican social group, the influx of alternative movements for self-assertion within the scene from non-Jamaicans situated in vastly different social contexts adds new layers of complexity to the practice. As these new voices (and bodies) enter the discourse, the space becomes even further entrenched in the politics of constructing popular femininities both within and beyond Jamaica, through the bodies that intersect these spaces.

While dancehall remains a highly gendered dance culture, the examples discussed in this chapter highlight the various competing embodied strategies for empowerment employed by women within this cultural paradigm. The active engagement in the Dancehall Queen scene by divergently situated women, producing disparate images of femininity, positions the scene as a space committed to a multitude of feminist discourses and agendas. The competition for visibility between dancers and stylizations and the support for the different styles from the crowd and judges create a diversity of imagery and style. While this creates contradictions and speaks to a politics of policing postcolonial feminist engagements, this state of flux ultimately fulfills dancehall's investment in destabilizing "categories, hierarchies, walls, states and borders" (Niaah 2010, 152). The spectrum of feminine identity constructions at the event supports and further enriches the impetus on boundarylessness to speak to a transnational and transcultural corpus of participants.

As the international Dancehall Queen scene develops, these juxtaposing elements do not cause the scene to fray or weaken, as may be expected. Instead, the thrashing out that takes place on the stage, such as the negotiation of balance in a head top, the articulation of body parts, and the generation of great amounts of energy, fuels a rich and powerful debate to take place between the dancers' bodies. As a scene dedicated to the creative impulse of its own instability, the Dancehall Queen Competition revels in contradiction and provocation as it enables the emergence of a multifaceted transnational scene.

Notes

1. All Dancehall Queens interviewed for this chapter, or who performed at the International Dancehall Competition in 2014 or 2015, have been given pseudonyms for anonymity purposes.
2. At the time of writing, it emerged that the 20th International Dancehall Queen Competition, due to take place in Montego Bay, Jamaica, would be canceled in 2016. This may be significant for future research into the competition's future activity and legacy.
3. Dancehall grew in the stead of the politically conscious musical style of reggae, which secured Jamaica's place on the global arts and culture map (Cooper, 2004).
4. Big Head Promotions, which is led by managing director Brian "Bighead" Martin, based in Montego Bay, has been responsible for organizing the International Dancehall Queen Competition in Jamaica since 1996.
5. I explore the emergence of Dancehall Queen Competitions in Europe in my PhD thesis.
6. Dancehall Queen Suzie, interview by Celena Monteiro, August 2, 2014, in Montego Bay, Jamaica.
7. The term "batty riders," drawn originally from vernacular Jamaican language, refers to a type of tightly fitting shorts that sit on (or ride) the buttocks, often revealing a part of the flesh of the "batty" (bottom or butt).
8. A "weave" is a hair piece that is "woven" onto a person's natural hair, often worn by women of African heritage. They come in various styles, but typically resemble Caucasian or Asian hair.
9. Suzie's use of the term "daggering" refers to a particular practice in dancehall, which involves a man and a woman dancing together, in a particularly vigorous fashion. It usually emphasizes the joining of the hips, coupled with jabs and gyrations, with the man standing behind the woman.
10. The go-go dancer in the Jamaican context is a woman who dances, often half or completely naked, in a club known as a go-go club.
11. Dancehall Queen Maximum, interview by Celena Monteiro, August 3, 2014, in Montego Bay, Jamaica.
12. The use of the term "colonial gaze" here refers to the postcolonial theory that examines the way in which the colonial subject is viewed through the construct of colonialism (Fanon 1967). Postcolonial theorist Homi Bhabha (1994) developed the theory of the colonial subject returning the colonizer's gaze.
13. The feminist theoretical canon of the Global North, beginning with the first wave in the late nineteenth century and the early twentieth century, and the subsequent second wave, characterized by Carol Hanisch's (1969) assertion that "the personal is political," has been criticized for having an essentialist upper-middle-class, Euro-American perspective on women's issues. The third wave, beginning around 1990, has focused on a more plural conception of feminism. However, the feminist rhetoric in the Global North is still heavily critiqued for its cultural bias toward a "Western" vision of empowerment. Postcolonial feminism is understood as an alternative body of feminist thought and practice that derives from postcolonial feminists' own voices and experiences (Lewis and Mills 2003).
14. The term "radical feminism" is used here in reference to a portion of feminist thought that works to disassociate femininity with performances of heteronormative female sexuality (Kitzinger and Wilkinson 1994).
15. Facebook status, author's identity protected.

16. Dancehall Queen Cher, interview by Celena Monteiro, November 9, 2013, at the European Dancehall Queen Competition in Vienna, Austria.
17. See Michel Foucault (1977) for an introduction to the theory of the disciplined body in relation to institutional power systems.

References

Bhabha, Homi. 1994. *The Location of Culture.* London: Routledge.

Blanco Borelli, Melissa. 2015. *She Is Cuba: A Genealogy of the Mulata Body.* Oxford: Oxford University Press.

Brooks, Ann. 1997. *Postfeminisms: Feminism, Cultural Theory, and Cultural Forms.* London: Routledge.

Butler, Judith. 1990. *Gender Trouble: Feminism and the Subversion of Identity.* London: Routledge.

Cooper, Carolyn. 1995. *Noises in the Blood: Orality, Gender and the "Vulgar" Body of Jamaican Popular Culture.* Durham, NC: Duke University Press.

Cooper, Carolyn. 2004. *Sound Clash: Jamaican Dancehall Culture at Large.* London; New York: Palgrave Macmillan.

Dyer, Richard. 1997. *White.* London: Routledge.

Fanon, Frantz. 1967. *Black Skin, White Masks.* London: Pluto.

Foucault, Michel. 1977. *Discipline and Punish: The Birth of the Prison.* New York: Knopf Doubleday.

Genius. 2016. "Gyal Bruk Out Lyrics." http://genius.com/Alkaline-gyal-bruk-out-lyrics. Accessed August 2, 2016.

Gilman, Sander. 1985. "Black Bodies, White Bodies: Toward an Iconography of Female Sexuality in Late Nineteenth-Century Art, Medicine, and Literature." In *"Race," Writing, and Difference,* edited by Henry Louis GatesJr. and Kwame Anthony Appiah, 223–261. Chicago: University of Chicago Press.

Goettner-Abendroth, Heide. 2013. *Matriarchal Societies: Studies on Indigenous Cultures across the Globe.* Oxford: Peter Lang.

Hakim, Catherine. 2010. "Erotic Capital." *European Sociological Review* 26(5): 499–518.

Hanisch, Carol. 1969. "The Personal Is Political." *The Redstockings Collection: Feminist Revolution* (March): 204–205.

hooks, bell. 1997. "Selling Hot Pussy: Representations of Black Female Sexuality in the Cultural Marketplace." In *Writing on the Body: Female Empowerment and Feminist Theory,* edited by Katie Conboy, Nadia Medina, and Sarah Stanbury, 113–128. New York: Columbia University Press.

Hope, Donna. 2006. *Inna Di Dancehall: Popular Culture and the Politics of Identity in Jamaica.* Kingston: University of West Indies Press.

Hope, Donna. 2010. *Man Vibes: Masculinities in the Jamaican Dancehall.* Kingston: Ian Randle.

Kitzinger, Celia, and Sue Wilkinson. 1994. "'Virgins and Queers: Rehabilitating Heterosexuality?" *Gender and Society* 8(3): 444–462.

Lewis, Reina, and Sara Mills. 2003. *Feminist Postcolonial Theory: A Reader.* Edinburgh: Edinburgh University Press.

Lorde, Audre. 1978. *Uses of the Erotic: The Erotic as Power.* New York: Out and Out Books.

Niaah, Sonja Stanley. 2010. *Dancehall: From Slaveship to Ghetto*. Ottowa: University of Ottowa Press.

Synder-Hall, Claire. 2010. "Third-Wave Feminism and the Defense of 'Choice.'" *Perspectives on Politics* 8(1): 255–261.

Thorington Springer, Jennifer. 2007. "'Roll It Gal': Alison Hinds, Female Empowerment, and Calypso." *Meridians: Feminism, Race, Transnationalism* 8(1): 93–129.

Thornton, Sarah. 1995. *Club Cultures: Music, Media and Subcultural Capital*. Oxford: Polity.

Wittig, Monique. 1993. "One Is Not Born a Woman." In *The Lesbian and Gay Studies Reader*, edited by Henry Abelove, Michele Aina Barale, and David M. Halperin, 103–109. New York: Routledge.

World Bank. 2015. "Jamaica Overview." http://www.worldbank.org/en/country/jamaica/overview. Accessed August 2, 2016.

Wright, Beth-Sarah. 2004. "Speaking the Unspeakable: Politics of the Vagina in Dancehall Docuvideos." *Discourses in Dance* 2(2): 45–59.

Audio Sources

Alkaline. 2013. *Gyal Bruk Out*. Notnice Records.

CHAPTER 11

CONGRATULATIONS, WE WISH YOU SUCCESS

Competition and Community Participation in Romanian Dance Festivals

LIZ MELLISH

The music steadily increased in tempo as the girls made successive pirouettes under the arms of their partners. Finally it came to a climax and the dancers stopped still, holding hands and facing the audience and the table where the judges were sitting. After taking their bow they filed off the stage in two orderly lines and stood at the side of the hall ready to listen to the judges' comments. The judges finished their discrete conversations with heads huddled and the dance judge stood up and started his commentary by saying "*Va dorim success, felicitare!*" ("Congratulations, we wish you success").

THIS short description reflects the words of encouragement given to dancers during a local competition in a city in southwestern Romania. During these competitions the main motivation of the judges is to encourage community participation, especially by the younger generation, and instill in them the same love of local dance, music, songs, and customs that they have maintained themselves throughout their dancing lives.

In this chapter I explore Romanian dancers' participation in organized dance competitions, both within Romania and abroad. I also investigate the informal competitiveness that exists between members and organizers of dance groups within the Romanian dance community. There has been little written on the role played by formal and informal competition in Romanian dancers' lives, with the exception of works concerning the renowned national competitive festival *Cântarea României* that took place biennially during the latter years of the Romanian communist period. In order to broaden this historical perspective, I first provide the reader with a historical outline of dance competitions in Romania from the mid-nineteenth century to the present, by drawing on primary and secondary historical sources as well as academic writings on *Cântarea României*.[1] I then move on to examine the contemporary competitions in which Romanian dancers participate, focusing specifically on local competitions that take place in the city of Timișoara, in the Banat region of southwestern Romania, where I have undertaken fieldwork for over ten years. I position the formal competitions that I discuss both geographically and diachronically by drawing on literature on dance competitions within southeastern Europe and beyond.[2] In this literature, a number of themes recur that I pursue in this chapter. My historical outline is themed around the connection between dance competitions and performing national versus local or regional identity.[3] In the second section of this chapter I focus more specifically on the role played by the experts who act as judges for the dance entries during dance competitions in which Romanian dancers participate. This theme frequently reoccurs in the literature on dance competitions in the adjacent countries of southern and eastern Europe and for other genres of dance as well.[4] Aspects debated include the influence of the experts' personal life history on their judgments, experiences of judging competitions during the communist period in Romania and beyond, the challenges that judges face, and the criteria that influence the placings awarded to the participating groups. The final section of this chapter explores notions of informal competitiveness within the lives of Romanian dancers and choreographers, and discusses the sense of community among the dancers and choreographers that coexists within this harmonious informal competition. Although the theme of informal competition is less prominent in works on folk genres in southeastern Europe, it emerges in studies that cover aspects of community within dance and music groups.[5] In my own work on ensemble dancers in southwestern Romania, I draw on the ethnomusicologist Thomas Turino's (2008, 25) work on participatory performance in which he suggests that the primary intention "is to involve the maximum number of people in some performance role."[6] This motivation for encouraging participatory performance is echoed in the judges' comments in the opening of this chapter, and leads me to propose that current competitions in Romania are organized with the intention of motivating participation among local communities, rather than to identify outstanding talent, ability, or training.

My research on, and practice in, Romanian dance started from the early 1990s when I joined a Romanian dance group in London that had been established by dancers from Bucharest who remained in the United Kingdom following a tour by their dance group. During the following fifteen years I often traveled to Romania, attending dance seminars in major cities and making contact with dancers from all over the country. From 2005 my doctoral research focused on the folk ensemble community and dancers' lives in the city of Timișoara in the Banat region, and their participation in cultural events and festivals within this area and beyond. Since then, by sharing my time between the United Kingdom and Timișoara, I have attended numerous cultural events and followed changes in the local cultural scene both in the local media and through being present at the events. During this time I have carried out formal and informal interviews with local dancers and key choreographers that have contributed to my ethnography in this chapter.

ROMANIAN DANCE, COMPETITIONS,
AND IDENTITY(IES)

Romanian dancing is primarily a social activity, and dancing during social events takes place either in a group or as couples, depending on the region of the country.[7] The current state of Romania covers a large area that traverses the Carpathian mountain range (Figure 11.1). North and west of these mountains, dancing in couples predominates in the region of Transylvania. South and east of the Carpathians, in the regions of Oltenia, Muntenia, and Moldova, social dancing is mainly done in a circle or open-line formation.[8] In the multi-ethnic and multi-confessional southwest region of Banat,[9] the site of my research, the local dance repertoire includes a mix of line, circle, and couple dances, and the music, song, and dance have close cross-border connections with the neighboring regions in Serbia and Hungary.[10]

Solo dancing, which can give rise to elements of competitiveness on social occasions, is rare in Romania. It can only be seen occasionally within the *căluş* ritual suite of

FIGURE 11.1. Regional map of Romania.

Map drawn by Nick Green

dances in the south and among certain men's dances in Transylvania. Therefore the participants in formal dance competitions in Romania are most often members of organized dance groups or folk ensembles,[11] and the informal competitiveness among Romanian dancers takes place mostly between these dancer groups and their members and leaders. Organized dance groups have regularly taken part in competitions either within Romania or internationally since the late nineteenth century.[12] The earliest records of dance competitions within Romania indicate that these were set up as part of the drive for Romanian nationalism in Transylvania and involved groups of Transylvanian *căluşer* dancers who met in southern Transylvanian cities (Giurchescu 1992). From the early twentieth century, competitions took place as part of the activities of newly founded culture houses that encouraged performances of dance, music, and songs in Romanian villages.[13]

In Romania, competitions involving Romanian dance, music, and song are usually termed *festivalul concurs* (competitive festivals), although many festivals do not include a competition. These competitive festivals consist of several rounds at village, district, county, regional, or national levels, depending on the event, and culminate in a gala performance and prize giving. The majority of the dance entries comprise a suite of local dances based on the cycle of dances that is included during social events,[14] or a local dance may be embedded in a short playlet that focuses on a local custom.

The short description that introduces this chapter is from a small local competitive festival that took place in the city of Timişoara in May 2011. This and similar contemporary festival competitions are not comparable to the larger scale national competitive festivals organized during the communist period in southeastern Europe that have received critical acclaim in academic works covering this period.[15] In Romania's case, this brings to mind the renowned *Cântarea României* (Song to Romania) that took place biennially from 1976 until 1989. However, it is rarely acknowledged that this festival replaced national folklore festivals that had taken place since 1948 (Frenţescu 1975; Giurchescu 1987) and, in particular, the biennial national festivals for amateur dancers (*Concurs al Formaţiilor artistice de amatori/Concursul echipelor artistice de amatori*) that were organized between 1952 and 1974.[16]

Although, as the anthropologist Katherine Verdery (1991) commented, national identity had held a central position within culture and politics in Romania from around the mid-nineteenth century, it was only from the mid-1960s that the policies of the Communist Party became strongly nationalistic (Giurchescu 2001; Oancea 2007). One manifestation of this was the competitive national festival, *Cântarea României*. This festival was set apart from previous national festivals in Romania by its scale and grandiose spectacle, and included categories of competition that covered all aspects of life, incorporating both folk and non-folk arts. The sociologist Claudiu Oancea (2007, 8) terms *Cântarea României* as a political festival; in this respect, similar to national festivals held elsewhere in Eastern Europe during the same period, it served the purpose of reinforcing notionally harmonious images of the unity of all people living within a certain nation-state "regardless of ethnicity or social origin."[17] The only factor that set

Cântarea României apart was its use by the country's dictator, Nicolae Ceauşescu, as a propaganda instrument to endorse his personality cult.

During the late 1970s and 1980s, policies pursued by Ceauşescu to reduce the Romanian national debt resulted in the living conditions of the majority of the population becoming increasingly severe, with shortages of all the basic necessities for survival, in particular food and fuel.[18] As dance scholar Anca Giurchescu (1987) discusses, the political motivation underlying the competitive elements of *Cântarea României* was to distract attention from the economic and social hardships of this period. Participation in *Cântarea României* was compulsory; hence the competitors included groups representing every town, village, factory, trade union, university and college, school, agricultural unit, and other institutions throughout Romania (Mihăilescu 2009), and the costs involved were enormous (Rădulescu 1997).

The sociologist Vintila Mihăilescu (2009) comments that it cannot be claimed that *Cântarea României* had a single strategy. This view is reflected among many of the participants that I have interviewed who were not supporters of the regime, and did not view their participation in this festival as totally negative.[19] This has revealed that, similar to the ethnomusicologist Ana Hofman's (2011) findings among participants in the "Competition of Serbian Villages" during the same period, personal experiences did not always reflect official agendas. The ethnomusicologist Speranţa Rădulescu (1997), who was a judge during the latter editions of *Cântarea României*, commented that many participants enjoyed the opportunity to escape from their daily routines, as they were given time off work and had the rare opportunity to travel around the country and stay in hotels. In addition, for those who were considered to be loyal to the regime there was, as Giurchescu (1987) reported, potential rewards that led to personal prestige and ultimately travel abroad. My interviewees also talked about the feelings of community they shared with colleagues in their dance groups that they experienced during their performance preparation, for the duration of the events and in their free time between performances.[20] These positive reactions to participation in *Cântarea României* are reflected in the number of listings of prizes won during the various editions on personal and group websites, thus indicating that these participants still feel a pride in the recognition of their achievements during this festival.

Romanian groups have also participated in international folk festivals both within Romania and abroad since the interwar years. Certain of these festivals are notionally competitive festivals, whereas others are non-competitive festivals where certificates of participation are presented to all performers.[21] The first time Romanian dancers traveled abroad to participate in an international festival was in 1935 when a group of *Căluş* dancers[22] from the southern Romanian village of Pădureţi-Argeş performed an adaptation of their ritual village *Căluş* in London at a festival organized by the English Folk Dance and Song Society. They were acclaimed as the highlight of the festival (Howes 1935),[23] winning the highest award of all the participating countries (Proca-Ciortea 1978). Although the ritual *Căluş* only exists within parts of southern Romania, the performance of this dance tradition in London illustrates how, once a competition involves dancers from more than one country, the focus shifts from dances seen by insiders as representing a local or regional identity, to the same dances now representing a national identity.[24] After World War II, Romanian dancers regularly took part in international folk festivals and festival competitions both within Romania and in other European countries. In 1957 *Căluș* dancers again won first prize at the Llangollen Eisteddfod, in Wales, this time performed by members of the railway workers folk ensemble, CFR, from the southern Romanian town of Giuleşti (Giurchescu 1957). In 1969 the report from the Romanian International Folk Music Council national committee lists the awards received by Romanian groups at twelve international festivals and competition as including first prize at the "Golden Necklace festival in Dijon, France; 'The Golden Hatchet' in Zakopane, Poland, and 'The Golden Bag-Pipe' in Erice, Italy" (IFMC 1969, 25). Within Romania, in 1969 a major international festival was held in Bucharest that was featured in the British Pathe news (Alexandru et al. 1970)[25] and several festivals held in provincial towns were founded. One of these festivals was the *Hercules* festival, located in the spa resort of Bale Herculane, in Romanian Banat (Figure 11.2). This is a

FIGURE 11.2. Map of Banat region.

Map drawn by Nick Green

competitive festival that has retained the same format during its over forty-five-year history, where, similar to local festivals, prizes are given to many categories of performers, including the youngest and the oldest.[26] I return to the difficulties of judging dance entries in a competition festival with international participation later in this chapter.

Following the period of compulsory participation, in the years after 1990 Romanian dance activity fell to a low point, and the centrally organized national competitions stopped taking place. During this time, many dance groups closed and the number of active choreographers declined as older choreographers retired or passed away, while others re-evaluated their positions and in many cases sought alternative occupations. Over the past decade, however, an increasing awareness of local and regional identity has resurfaced in Romania, parallel to the process of entry to the European Union.[27] This has given rise to the formation (or reformation) of rural and urban dance groups and amateur and professional folk ensembles throughout the country who regularly take part in a plethora of local festivals and community cultural events organized by cultural organizations in villages, towns, and cities.[28] Romanian song, music, and dance also feature prominently in the media, on national television (TVR) during several popular light entertainment shows, and in television channels specifically dedicated to this genre.[29]

As part of this renewed interest, numerous local competitive festivals that encompass multiple genres of folk arts have been set up in the various regions of Romania. The administrators of these competitions include the county cultural offices, town or village cultural centers, independent cultural organizations, and local school teachers. These competitions are usually divided into several rounds that cumulate in a gala performance in which the winners participate, together with professional dancers and singers. Each round of these competitive festivals takes place in a local venue, most often a culture house (equivalent to a village hall), and as with the majority of cultural events in Romania, the various rounds of these competitive festivals are open events that anyone can attend. The participants in these competitions can be divided into the performers/competitors who are evaluated, the experts who act as judges, and the audience, which is an integral part of the event. The competition described in the introduction to this chapter is similar to those held regularly throughout Romania in that the proceedings take place in a relaxed atmosphere before an audience of locals, including the parents, grandparents, and siblings of the performers.[30] The participants range from small children to students and adults, and the judges are local experts who are passionate about local dance, music, song, and customs. I will return to a discussion of this competition later.

As the competitions aim to involve all parts of the local community, they include many categories, encompassing all aspects of local arts, including song, dance, customs, gastronomy, and local crafts (such as embroidery and costumes). Furthermore, there are multiple categories of awards. In addition to categories for groups and individuals who perform local dance, song, and music, there are also short playlets based on a concise portrayal of a local custom, which often include a dance that would have formed part of the custom, for example, in Banat, *hora* or *brâul*.[31] The organizers do not intend to create an environment of intense competition: rather, they foster an ethos of in-clusiveness, reflected in the certificates that are awarded to all competitors, the many categories of prize winners, and the trophies or plaques given to those with the highest marks. Notably, the dance groups who take part in these competitions are mostly village or school groups, rather than the urban-based, usually larger, folk ensembles, although the choreographers from these ensembles are often among the experts who take the role of the dance judges.

In the Banat region, two of the most prominent competitive festivals are *Vetre Străbune* (ancestral homes) competitive festival for schoolchildren and the *Lada cu Zestrea* (the dowry chest) competitive festival that includes all age groups.[32] In both cases, the competitors include groups representing many of the co-located ethnicities in Banat,[33] as well as Romanian groups. The *Vetre Străbune* competitive festival is organ-ized by a teacher, who is passionate about local folklore, from one of the high schools in Timișoara. Participation in the *Vetre Străbune* competition is open to individuals or groups of local schoolchildren from schools in Timișoara and the surrounding villages, and includes categories for local song, music, poetry in the Banat dialect, short playlets based on local customs, or local dances. The *Lada cu Zestrea* competitive festival is or-ganized by the *Centrul de Cultură și Artă al Județului Timiș-CCAJT* (the County Center for Culture and Art) and has taken place annually since 2007. The competition is divided into five sections (choreography, music, and song; poetry in the local Banat dialect of Romanian language; popular theater; exhibitions of local costume or textiles; and gas-tronomy), each with many subsections. Three prizes are awarded for each section and subsection, and the village or town that receives the highest number of points is declared the winner of the trophy.[34] I have attended both festivals, and the two ethnographic snapshots that follow draw from my experiences at each.

VETRE STRĂBUNE FESTIVAL COMPETITION

One Saturday, in May 2011, I attended the final round of this competition, then in its sixth year, held in the Timișoara Municipal Culture House. I arrived at the Culture House mid-morning, by which time the foyer was full of groups of children of various ages who were dressed in local costumes. Each group was accompanied by their group coordi-nator and many anxious parents, who were busy making last-minute adjustments to the children's dress and hair, and issuing final orders and reminders for their performances. The foyer was doubling as a dressing room and waiting room, and all the chairs were ei-ther taken by parents or covered in bags and clothing, with the exception of one table to the left that was occupied by several of the local choreographers, deep in conversation over their cups of coffee.

The girls mostly wore white embroidered cotton blouses and ankle length underskirts decorated with a row of lace or embroidery just above the hem, over which they wore two matching colored aprons (one at the front and one at the back.) These were usually red or black and were embellished with horizontal rows of gold embroidery. Their hair was neatly fastened back and adorned with braided ribbons or a small wreath of flowers. The boys wore white cotton trousers and hip-length shirts that were drawn in at the waist with a fabric belt. The girls danced in black shoes and the boys wore boots. In general, each child was meticulously dressed, with the right parts of the garments tucked in, aprons straight, and not a hair out of place. The children's costumes were either made up of a mixture of older items that looked as if they had been handed down through the generations, or were simple newly made outfits in local style, in this case forming a uniform that allowed a specific group to be identified by the color of the embroidery on their blouses, the apron color or design, and their headdress or hairstyles.

Inside the main hall, chairs stood in rows facing the stage for the parents and children waiting to perform. Apart from the contestants, the stage was empty except for a mixer desk operated by one of the Culture House employees who handed out microphones to the singers or those who read poetry. Immediately in front of the stage, the four judges sat at a long table. In front of each was a listing of the groups and individuals scheduled to perform and a stack of comment sheets, one for each item. The seats behind the judges were occupied by rows of parents who jumped up with their video cameras or cell phones when their children came onto the stage, jostling to get prime positions to record their children's performances for posterity. A lady with a clipboard organized the individuals and groups into neat lines, ready for their turn to go on stage (Figure 11.3)

FIGURE 11.3. Children lining up beside the stage.

Photo taken by Nick Green

and, from time to time, went to liaise between the group leaders and the judges. Those about to perform lined up at the left side of the hall and, after each item finished and the judges had made their comments, the children filed off the stage to the right, and exited by the main door together with their parents.

Most of the dance groups performed a short suite of local dances, which followed the same order as social occasions in the Banat plain or Banat mountain regions.[35] The dancers were usually arranged with alternating boys and girls. They entered the stage dancing *hora* or *brâul*, the community chain dances that are based on synchronized walking, with the line of dancers progressing to the right in a counterclockwise direction. When the music changed into the upbeat *ardeleana*, the dancers either continued to progress gradually to the right, traveling around the performance space with small walking steps in a chain or open circle formation, or traversed into long columns with partners facing each other and holding joined hands, using small steps to move from side to side and along the dance space and back again. Finally, the music changed into the fast and virtuosic *de doi* dance, which is usually performed with couples facing each other and involves small scampering steps, which travel from side to side, with the girls turning fast pirouettes under the men's arms. As the music accelerates, the dancers match the tempo with their steps, building to a climax; as the music stops, the dancers take their ending positions and face the audience. The short playlets mostly started with the performers acting an extract of a local custom, usually with the aid of props such as a baby doll in a cradle or wreaths of corn, then ended in a *hora* circle dance that the children used to lead off from the stage.

After each performance entry, the judges (Figure 11.4) made their comments. Depending on the genre, the lead position was taken by the relevant judge. The dance

FIGURE 11.4. Judges and parents.

Photo taken by Nick Green

judge was well known to me as one of the most respected local choreographers and authorities on local dance. Beside him sat the female schoolteacher responsible for arranging this competition, who took the lead for items that included portrayals of local customs and poetry readings. The other two judges were local experts on music and song from the county *scoala de arta* (art school). Significantly, most of the time, their comments were positive and encouraging, such as "*Va dorim success, felicitare*" ("Congratulations, we wish you success"); sometimes they offered small suggestions for improvements or a response to a specific aspect of the performance. Notably, any criticism was constructive. The event continued all day, with groups and individual performances coming and going, and ended around 4 pm.

LADA CU ZESTREA 2016

In spring 2016, I attended two of the eight preliminary rounds of the *Lada cu Zestrea* competition, as well as the three days of the county round. At the beginning of each year the regulations for this competition are published on the Country Cultural Center website (http://www.ccajt.ro/). The local rounds start in March and are held in selected towns in Timiş county. In May or June the winners from the local rounds compete in the final round, which that takes place in Timişoara. The dance section includes categories for group dances, couple dances, girls' group dances, *sorocul* (the solo men's dance from the Banat Plain),[36] and dances from groups representing the local co-located ethnicities. According to the regulations, higher scores are awarded for choreographies that include dances specific to Timiş County, the accuracy of interpretation and stage posture, the authenticity of costumes, the use of local melodic lines, and compliance with the time allocated for each item.[37] The 2016 preliminary rounds took place in eight of the larger villages in the county on sunday afternoons during March and April. Each round included participants from between nine and twenty-two of the surrounding villages. I attended the rounds in the villages of Şag and Ghilad, both of which took place in the village culture house. On both occasions, coaches, mini-buses, and cars were parked on the roadside outside the culture houses, and the performers in costume, group leaders, and hangers-on were mingling in front of the doors. On arrival I was greeted by several of the village choreographers, who enthusiastically told me about their entries in the competition.

Inside, the hall was full of competitors and spectators who came and went freely over the course of the afternoon. The seats inside the hall were all occupied, with many people standing in the aisles and at the back, so the only way to get a clear view of the proceedings was to find a gap between the heads of the other spectators. As before, the groups lined up at the side of stage, ready for their performance, and the judges were seated at a table in front of stage. Each village had an allotted time slot during which they presented their entries, encompassing all categories of the festival; dance items were interspersed with poetry readings and performances by local musicians, singers, and choirs. During each performance, many parents and friends of the performers videoed the proceedings on their cell phones and as each village finished its slot, many people left the hall and others came in, taking any empty seats. The 2016 regulations for *Lada cu Zestrea* stipulated that dancers should only perform the more sedate dances from the Banat plain, rather than the Banat mountains dances described earlier. Most, but not all, of the groups followed this instruction, even though, as I was told, in some cases it meant learning new material specifically for this occasion. The only difference from *Vetre Străbune* was that the judges did not make any commentary between items, or at the end of each village's slot. They noted their commentary and scoring on sheets for each item, which they discussed among themselves after each round so that an overriding decision would be made as to which entries to put through to the county final. Once these deliberations had been made, the results were published on the website of the county office.

The final round of *Lada cu Zestrea* (Figure 11.5) took place at the County Cultural Center in Timişoara over a weekend in May, starting on Friday mid-afternoon and ending early Sunday afternoon. In contrast to the local rounds, and to *Vetre Străbune*, the performances of the three main categories of the competition, dance, music and song, and poetry took place simultaneously in three different locations within the Cultural Center. The venue for the dance section was the covered stage in the open courtyard. The stage and the tiered rows of hard plastic seats for the audience and judges were covered, although the space between them where the dancers waited for their allotted time slots was open and the weather was unseasonally inclement.

FIGURE 11.5. *Lada cu Zestrea* final round.

Photo taken by Nick Green

The organization of the proceedings was similar to *Vetre Străbune*. On arrival, the participants checked in at a table just inside the Center. They then had time to prepare for their performances. Each village was allocated a time slot during which they presented their dances for all the subsections one after another. In most cases this included entries for several age groups and dances from more than one ethnicity, solo and couple dancers, custom portrayals with dance, and groups of older dancers. The instruction was that they should nominate one person to clearly announce the name of the subsection in which they were competing before each part of their program. In general, during the county round, the audience was smaller, with the exception of certain villages where many of the local dignitaries, dressed in their sharp suits, accompanied the performers and clapped loudly at the end of each item. It was evident—both from my observations and from discussions with the group leaders, many of whom I have known for some years—that allegiance to the village took precedence over any nationalistic or ethnic allegiance, and this was also evident in the enthusiastic responses of the village dignitaries to all performances from their village. In some cases, it was obvious that the members of the dance groups were of mixed ethnicity, even though they performed dances of one ethnicity, and for the groups representing the co-located (non-Romanian) ethnicities, either the same dance group presented dances from more than one ethnicity, or the participating village had several dance groups specific to those ethnicities. In the latter cases, the dances presented nearly always had their provenance in the "homeland" (this being Serbia, Hungary, or Germany) rather than being local material. (The reason for this is that the local material from these ethnicities is either considered to be more mundane, or sparse, or else they call on choreographers from their homeland to construct their performances.) It should also be noted that the villages with the largest numbers of competitors (and the richest folklore), who had entries in most of the subsections, are not remote villages, but are villagers located on the outskirts of the city. This is not a recent trend, as these villages were also ones with a long history of participation in similar events and whose entries were commended during the communist-period festivals.

For this occasion there were three dance judges: the choreographer of the Timișoara students ensemble, a choreographer from the nearby town of Lugoj in Timiș county, and a choreographer from the adjacent county of Arad. They sat through the three long sessions on the cold, hard plastic chairs, only getting up from time to time to stretch their legs (Figure 11.6). As with the preliminary rounds, they made no commentary, instead writing long notes on the sheets of paper in front of them. The only occasion where they interjected was to reprimand the musicians for playing one melody too fast for the dancers. At the end of each session, they finally got up looking stiff and tired. As the rest of the participants were leaving, I exchanged a few words with them, asking how they were able to recollect which group was which, and what criteria they used to judge non-local material. They reassured me that they relied on the extensive notes that they wrote contemporaneously (Figure 11.7), and that their marks for the non-local material were based mainly on the stage arrangements and posture, as they were unable to award marks for the local provenance of the dances.

FIGURE 11.6. Judges at *Lada cu Zestrea* competition.

Photo taken by Nick Green

FIGURE 11.7. Judges' tools of trade.

Photo taken by Nick Green

The organization of both competitive festivals played out in the same way as similar events that I have attended: the groups of children and parents gathering outside the hall, the stage and seats for the audience in the main room, the relaxed and informal atmosphere, and the efficient administration that ensured the right groups performed at the correct time, therefore avoiding long gaps in the proceedings. The lack of separation between the competitors, the judges, and the audience meant that the children were exposed to all those present both before, during, and after the short period that they were performing (in sociologist Ervin Goffman's [1959] terms, there was no line between the front and back regions), and the audience was an integral part of the event.[38] The intermingling of all present and the social nature of these occasions form a major contribution to the air of inclusiveness. These events offer an opportunity for family gatherings and meeting friends, and in Banat this means a multi-ethnic inclusiveness where people from the local ethnicities mix freely. Participation in local dance groups gives children a sense of their local or ethnic identity from an early age,[39] and a means to embody their local history.[40] This local identity reflected in dance is strongly linked to the locality and the multi-ethnic region of Banat (Mellish 2013a), and demonstrates the manner in which locals dance during both calendar events (saints' days and other festivities) and life-cycle events (wedding and baptisms).

Competitive festivals, such as *Vetre Străbune* and *Lada cu Zestrea*, provide opportunities for performances of local identities, based on the dances of Romanians and other ethnicities living within the borders of current-day Romania. In contrast to the national festivals held prior to 1989, where the intention was to reinforce the unity of the Romanian people through nationalist performances of dance, music, and song, in contemporary competitions identities of difference are made visible during the various rounds, in the subsequent gala performances, and in media transmissions of local dance, music, and song.

JUDGES' MOTIVATION AND JUDGING CRITERIA

The judges play a major role in all the levels of Romanian dance competitions. They act as the expert authorities (Zebec 2005), the elders, or the shamans (Marion 2008); they are responsible for making judgments on matters of authenticity (or not) of the performances, and their judgments can influence the future of the performers' groups. In Banat, as elsewhere, the individuals who are selected to take the role of judges are passionate about local music, dance, and customs. They have extensive knowledge of local repertoire, gained over a long period of time, and are always interested in building on their existing knowledge.[41] The placings that they award are implicitly guided by their personal life histories, their upbringing in Romanian villages, whether they learned to dance through formal or informal methods, where they received their dance training, the field research they undertook while students and subsequently, and their long-term involvement in the genre as a dancer, instructor, or choreographer. This accumulated knowledge leads to a bundle of personal aesthetic preferences that fit within the bounds of the locally accepted cultural aesthetics (Mellish 2013a) that they draw on when making their evaluations. This stress on the local is closely linked to the pride of being from the multi-ethnic region of Banat, irrespective of ethnic heritage. The performed identity that the judges seek is a "local identity," although the judges do not necessarily always agree on the finer details (for example, the speed of the music for dancing, or the extent of the rise and fall of the dancers). These minor disagreements arise from specific differences in their personal dance knowledge and are reflected in their relative marks for the different groups. The stress on the local means that groups from the co-located ethnicities (Serbian, Hungarian, Bulgarian, Ukrainian) receive lower markings when their entry is a dance suite from their parent nation and is not based on their local material. This usually occurs when they have invited a "guest" choreographer who does not have local dance knowledge to compile their material.

On most occasions, as in the *Vetre Străbune* competition, four judges preside over the proceedings and are selected according to their expertise in local song, dance, music, and customs. The structure of the expert panel, which includes a specialist for each genre of dance or music included in the competition, is typical of similar competitions, both in Romania and beyond.[42] Several of my key informants regularly act as dance judges during competitions in Banat and take pride in their participation. As discussed, after each performance they give the participants constructive comments. Their overriding concern is to encourage participation by all, but especially the younger generation, through awarding positive feedback, thus reflecting the general ethos of inclusiveness, rather than highlighting the exceptional and inciting strong competitiveness between the groups.[43] Clearly, they value their role as judges. As an illustration of this Toma Frențescu, artistic director of the Timișoara municipal ensemble, Timișul, states on its website, "I have formed part of the jury of specialists at different competitions, at all levels, as well as at professional certifications of various professional ensembles" (www. timisul.ro 2011). Interviews with local judges reveal that they make their assessments based on adherence to local repertoire, but they also look for "new" moves, such as the introduction of dances from the latent local repertoire, or new arrangements using a custom that is specific to that locality. The artistic director of Timișul also explained that he "looks at the group's composition and interpretation, their material must be correct for the region, they should have exemplary costumes, be good dancers and have their own musicians and, even if their singers are not totally in tune, they should still sound good, but what is most important for him is that the children want to participate" (Mellish 2013a).

In practice, only a limited number of potential experts exist in any field and within a relatively limited geographical region and social network. For example, nowadays, within Banat and its neighboring regions of western Romania, there are around twenty potential "experts" in local dance. Hence the dance specialist is often also a leader or instructor of one or more local dance groups, has trained the leaders of other groups that are among the participants, or has family members in one of the groups.[44] In fact, the artistic director of Timişul noted that, when he judges, invariably 70 percent of the arrangements of dances have connection with the dance suites performed by his ensemble, as he has been responsible over the years for training many of the dance instructors who now work in the local villages and towns within the Banat region, and also across the border among the Romanian community in Serbian Banat.

Although experts sometimes come from adjacent regions (for instance, competitions in Timiş County are judged by experts from the neighboring counties in western Romania), the time and costs of travel may well prevent judges from traveling further afield. It should also be noted that, for the majority of the experts, their ethnographic authority is limited to their own region or ethnographic zone and ethnic group. This therefore places limits on their authority to judge performances from other regions or ethnic groups.[45] Furthermore, personal factors can influence the judges' decisions. The ethnochoreologist Tvrtko Zebec, drawing on his own experience as a dance judge in Croatia, observes that "many expert evaluations and decisions . . . can be characterized as the views of individual experts." He continues by saying that everyone has a personal sense of what is "appropriate" and the "degree to which this attitude will be imposed as a model or a rule that others have to respect depends on the position of the individual" (Zebec 2005, 197). Thus individuals who assume the role of expert potentially have a personal power bestowed on them based on their local standing and network of personal relationships.[46]

The structure of the judging panel is similar for international competitions; however, the partial knowledge that applies to local competitions is evident to a far greater extent where there is international participation, as the judges typically have in-depth knowledge of only the material that comes from their own area of expertise. Hence, their choice of prize winners relies upon their "criteria for local performance aesthetics and personal notions of authenticity" (Mellish 2013a, 198–199), which are frequently out of line with those who consider themselves as winners in the "informal competition" based on audience appreciation.[47] In view of these limitations on the caliber of the judging, the awards given at international festivals can be viewed more as a matter of status among colleagues, rather than an endorsement of regional authenticity. Despite this, prior to their recent participation in a prestigious international festival in Istanbul, the artistic director of the Timişul ensemble commented that "we must send the best dancers as this is a very important festival." Clearly his choice of dancers was correct, as Timişul won one of the top awards for its performances at the festival and proudly proclaimed its achievement in the local press and on its social media pages (Casa de Cultura a Municipiului Timişoara 2015).

There is a marked contrast between the role of the judges at contemporary dance competitions in Romania, who freely and independently decide upon awards, and that of the judges at the Romanian national festival *Cântarea României*, where they were obliged to award the top placings to groups who had the highest political prestige (and in some cases, their judgments were overturned before the results were announced).[48] Prior to 1989, in addition to the experts, every jury included members with political affiliations at either local or national level, with the latter always holding the authority for the final decisions.[49] Despite the strong political involvement in judging during this period, the judges were not precluded from giving encouragement and making positive comments, as was revealed to me during two separate interviews regarding the Banat regional round of the 1971 national competition. Anca Giurchescu was the dance judge, and the choreographer of the dance group from the village of Borlova in the Banat mountains was Toma Frențescu, now artistic director of Timișul ensemble. Giurchescu recalled that the Borlova group wore modern styled folk costumes during the 1969 festival, which had meant that they were awarded a lower placing, although she had commended their dancing. In 1971 she was impressed by their new set of costumes, constructed with the traditional motifs from Borlova, and this, together with their impressive dancing, meant that she awarded them first prize. Toma Frențescu's recollection of this occasion was the pride he felt from the recognition given by Anca Giurchescu; hence, in the paper that he wrote for his choreographer's qualification in 1975, he included the positive commendations that she had made.[50]

Gala Performances

Similar to most festivals, the final round of *Vetre Străbune* competitive festival was followed by a gala performance and the awarding of prizes. Gala performances are a frequent occurrence in Romania and elsewhere. These can take place after a competition, as described earlier, or else can be part of a festival or a stand-alone occasion. During summer months, galas are held on outdoor stages at venues in the city or village center and, in the case of competitive festivals, this contrasts to the earlier rounds of the competition, which take place in indoor venues. These galas often include other performers who did not participate in the rounds of the competition, such as famous local singers, who draw in a larger audience beyond the competitors' families and so provide wider visibility to those competitors selected to perform at the gala.

The judges take responsibility for the selection of groups for the gala performance. In this case, their judgments can be influenced by constraints on the number of groups that can be included and/or the blend of groups to make what they consider will be a good show that appeals to the relevant audience. Gala performances are often broadcast on local or national television, thus giving the competition prize winners visibility beyond the audience present at the event. This in turn can lead to invitations to perform at other festivals or to take part in media productions, including television shows or promotional videos for singers. For example, each year the artistic director of Timișul selects two local groups from among those he sees while judging competitions or during gala performances to take part in the Timișoara international festival, *Festivalul Inimilor* (Festival of the Hearts). Thus, when deciding on the rankings to award, the judges are endowed with a power that can affect the future of the competitors because their decisions can have further implications for the dancers in question. Zebec (2005, 197) expresses concern that, in these circumstances, the opinions of the individuals who take the role of judges are "more or less imposed" on the public. He considers that this can lead to the formation of stereotypes that are perpetuated both among the professionals and in the public sphere. However, he also reveals that there are instances when the verdict of the judges can subsequently be overturned by the aesthetic considerations of others, such as television producers. He cites the case of a Croatian group that portrayed a contemporary version of a custom in a competition and was awarded first prize, but because the participants did not wear traditional costumes for their performance, they were omitted from the subsequent television broadcast (Zebec 2005). Similar situations occur in Romania when a television company records an entire gala performance, but edits the footage to fit broadcasting slots, using criteria that are based on the anticipated television audience rather than the placements made by the judges.

The *Vetre Străbune* gala performance took place in the open air theater in *Parcul Rozelor* (the Rose Park) in central Timișoara. Before the event started, numerous rows of gold plastic cups were set out on a table on the stage (Figure 11.8). The prize giving was a lengthy ceremony, in which the participants lined up on the stage and each took their turn to come forward to receive a signed certificate from the judges and, where appropriate, one of the gold plastic cups. The audience sat in front of the stage, and the parents stood up clapping as their children received their prizes. Several of the children handed a bouquet of flowers to the female schoolteacher who was responsible for organizing the competition. Once the awarding of prizes was finally completed, the concert began. The three-hour long

FIGURE 11.8. Rows of cups at *Vetre Străbune* gala performance.

program included performances by selected prize winners, arranged in a balanced presentation of music, song, and dance. As with the final round that I had attended in the Municipal Culture House, the audience included the parents, grandparents, and siblings of the performers. However, for the gala, this was supplemented by locals who had come to the park for a relaxing summer afternoon's entertainment, and to hear the invited popular local singer that took the ultimate place in the afternoon's program.

Informal Competitiveness, Community, and Dance in Romania

Throughout the day of the final round of the *Vetre Străbune* competition, several of the local choreographers sat around a table in the foyer of the Municipal Culture House, drinking coffee while socializing and discussing the proceedings. Similarly, during the gala performance, a slightly different group of local choreographers sat beside a BBQ stall facing the stage, talking to each other while watching the performances. Other group leaders also joined them for shorter periods from time to time in between their own group's performances. These informal meetings of the "experts" and younger group leaders reflect the social nature of the occasion, when members of the local choreographic network are able to relax and socialize as well as supervise group performances and act as judges. On occasions such as these, when the choreographers gather together, the conversation often focuses on the relative merits of their groups, the new dance material that they plan to introduce into their groups' repertoires, and their future plans for performances. These conversations take place in a friendly manner, but with an underlying thread of informal competition between the choreographers to outdo each other and increase the self-ascribed ranking and visibility of their groups. During the same gala performance, the dancers from the various groups mixed together at the sides of the stage, chatting and consuming soft drinks. Such times spent socializing during shared performances lead to the creation of long-term friendships between members of groups, thus endorsing that this activity falls within what Turino (2008, 25) terms "participatory performance." This camaraderie and feeling of community among group members, coupled with informal competitiveness between dance groups and pride in being part of a group that was commended by a team of "experts," are ongoing elements of dancers' and choreographers' lives, both in Romania and elsewhere,[51] and are frequently mentioned during my fieldwork interviews.[52]

I therefore propose that the notion of competition in connection with community dance in Romania extends beyond the realms of the organized local competitions to encompass various manifestations of informal competitiveness in the lives of local dance practitioners in Romania.[53] I contend that through time, from before World War I, through the communist period and continuing into the years since 1989, formal competition and elements of informal competitiveness have coexisted among members of the extended social networks of Romanian dancers and choreographers. This informal competition serves to attract the best dancers, sustaining a strong dance repertoire, through maintaining existing key choreographies and reacting to external trends when revising or restructuring repertoire, and by endeavoring to secure the most prestigious performance opportunities. From my fieldwork and long-term contacts, I suggest that informal competitiveness is actually more often at the forefront of the minds of those involved than the status put on official placements during competitions, which is evident only in the trophies displayed in the choreographer's office, the group's curriculum vitae on their publicity leaflets and website, and during performances when the announcer introduces the groups by listing their past achievements. This prime role played by informal competitiveness does not detract from the pride taken in winning or collecting trophies from formal competitions, or displaying them in dusty cabinets in the offices of the group leaders, but these exist only as static artifacts. Conversely, the informal competitiveness between groups and their members forms an ongoing element of life as a dancer or choreographer that manifests itself in every aspect of group dynamics. Group leaders strive to out-compete each other in performance strategy and self-ascribed ranking and visibility of their ensembles, both within their locality and on a national basis (Mellish 2013a). This informal ranking is constructed from the deemed caliber of their performances, audience opinions, and the number of appearances on folk television shows and in festivals within Romania as well as international festivals, especially those in places that can be deemed more "exotic." On occasions, when they attend a festival that includes a competition, the leaders are determined that their group should receive the highest award. On the other hand, in cases where there is not a competition and diplomas of participation are given to all participants, this does not detract from informal competitiveness among the groups to gain the highest appreciation from the audience.[54]

In recent years, this informal competition between dancers and group leaders has been heightened through the increased use of visual media to view each others' performances. Group leaders strive to maximize opportunities to appear on television to increase the visibility and media profile of their group. The belief exists that increased visibility leads to increased performance opportunities. This is reinforced by the open availability of their performances on YouTube and similar video sites, posted by groups or festival organizers, or local and national television companies (Mellish 2013a).

FINAL PLACINGS: THE BLENDING OF FORMAL COMPETITION AND INFORMAL COMPETITIVENESS

I have traced three themes to explore the coexistence of formal competition and notions of informal competitiveness in Romanian dancers' lives. The first theme followed a historical trajectory on the changing importance of performances of local, regional, and national identity in dance competitions, revealing that contemporary dance competitions aim to reinforce local and/or regional identity and I observed that, today, emphasis on the performance of national identity only occurs during competitions with international participation. This contrasts with the years before 1989, when Romanian national identity was dominant during participation in competitions held within Romania as well as those abroad.

The second theme looks at the motivation and challenges faced by the experts who act as judges during formal dance competitions. The conclusions that can be drawn from this discussion indicate that in making their decisions the judges draw on their personal backgrounds and dance training, and their individual views of performance aesthetics. They hold control over the relative placings of the groups, and this can have implications on future performance opportunities for the groups. However, there are situations when their placing may be overturned by other external factors, such as political constraints prior to 1989 or, more recently, aesthetic choices for media presentations. During the local contemporary competitions that I have attended, the overriding concern of the judges is to give encouragement to all the participants, by making positive comments after each performance, in their summaries in the closing stages of each competition, and during the awarding of prizes at gala performances, offering the participants congratulations, and wishing them success for their dancing futures. This reflects the judges' desire to encourage community participation in local dance competitions and to reinforce awareness and expand knowledge of local traditions.

The final theme explores the informal competitiveness between dancers and group leaders who are also the experts, but stresses that this occurs in good spirits, as evidenced through the strong sense of community among dancers and the relationships among the participants, group leaders, and choreographers. Consequently, I propose that notions of formal competition and informal competitiveness coexist and are interrelated in the minds of both the leaders and the dancers, and that the prime motivation of the local judges in contemporary local competitions is to encourage the involvement of the maximum numbers of participants and to enhance feelings of community, rather than to identify outstanding talent, ability, or training, or to stress the exclusivity of individual participants.

NOTES

1. For more on the Romanian national competitive festival *Cântarea României*, see Giurchescu (1977, 1987, 2001), Mihăilescu (2009), Oancea (2007), Rădulescu (1997), and Vasile (2014).
2. The closest work both geographically and by genre is Jennifer Cash's research on folk ensembles in the neighboring Republic of Moldova (Cash, 2002, 2004, 2011). Cash looked at the choreographers and judges and the role played by dance in establishing a national identity following the independence of Moldova in 1991. Her fieldwork included attending several competitive festivals where she examined the relationships between the organizers, judges, and group leaders, and how this influenced the awards made during

these competitions. I also draw on Daniela Ivanova-Nyberg's study of contemporary competitions among members of the newly established *horo* clubs in neighboring Bulgaria and among Bulgarians living outside Bulgaria (Ivanova 2009; Ivanova-Nyberg 2016).

3. Works on identity and competition include Anne Margrete Fiskvik's (2013) investigation of the use of a regional dance to represent Norwegian national identity, and Helena Wulff's (2007) deliberation of whether an Irish dancer has to live in Ireland to win the most prestigious Irish dance competitions.

4. The ethnochoreologist Tvrtko Zebec (2005), who is both a dance practitioner and judge of similar competitions in Croatia, critically examines his role as a judge in dance competitions, and Anca Giurchescu, Speranta Radulescu, and Claudia Oancea all consider judging dance competitions in Romania prior to 1989. Moving out to encompass dance and competition in other genres, Helena Wulff writes on Irish dance competitions (Wulff 2007) and competition among dancers in ballet companies (Wulff 1998), and Jonathan Marion (2008) examines ballroom dance competitions. For judging during international dance competitions, see the ethnomusicologists Ivanka Vlaeva (2011) on international folk festivals in Bulgaria and Timothy Cooley (2005) on the Festival of Mountain Folklore in Poland.

5. Research on community and informal competition includes the ethnomusicologist Thomas Turino's (1989) work among the Aymara musicians in Peru, the Bulgarian ethnochoreologist Daniela Ivanova-Nyberg on community among dancers in Bulgarian folk ensembles (Ivanova 2009; Ivanova-Nyberg 2016), Helena Wulff's studies of informal competitiveness and camaraderie among ballet dancers in a dance company (Wulff 1998), and Irish dance competitions as way to socialize children and instill in them a sense of their Irish identity (Wulff 2007).

6. See also Mellish (2013a).

7. Art dance in Romania exists only in Western classical genres. In the 1930s there was some meeting of genres when ballet-trained professors introduced elements of Romanian folk dances into their productions. After World War II, the Moiseyev model for folk performance was adopted by newly formed folk ensembles in Bucharest and the main provincial cities. However, following Ceauşescu's renewed drive for nationalism from the mid-1960s, there was a move away from the Russian model to return to a performance style that could be more closely linked to Romanian nationalist ideology and hence regional folklore.

8. For a detailed account of the wide variety of Romanian dances, see Giurchescu and Bloland (1995).

9. The historical area of Banat extends beyond the border of current-day Romania into northern Serbia and southeastern Hungary. Its specific history as a multi-ethnic and multi-confessional region, due to the eighteenth-century migrations into this area, gives it a unique character that is played out in the many cultural events and festivals held in the region. Present-day Romanian Banat is divided between the two administrative counties of Timiş and Caraş-Severin. Geographically, Timiş county covers the flat Banat plain that extends into Hungary and Serbia, and the low foothills to the east, and Caraş-Severin covers mainly the Banat mountain area. The ethnographic examples in this chapter draw from my fieldwork in the county of Timiş, especially focusing on the city of Timişoara, the capital city of the Banat region.

10. This cross-border research project into dance in the Banat region is in conjunction with Selena Rakočević from the Institute of Musicology in Belgrade.

11. I use the term "dance group" to refer to a group that includes only dancers, and "ensemble" to refer to an organization that includes a folk orchestra and local singers as well as amateur

or professional dancers. The majority of Romanian folk ensembles (but not all) are urban based, whereas dance groups exist in both villages and towns and can be attached to culture houses, schools, or organized by an independent cultural organization.

12. For example, the national competition *Concurs de Dansuri national. Liceenii Dansatori "Ardeleansca" si "Pambriul"* held in 1904 (Fochi and Datcu 2002, 557). Examples of dance groups from Romania with a long history of participation in competitions and festivals, both national and international, include the groups from the village of Drăguş, near Braşov, Arcanul group from Fundu Moldovei, Suceava county, and Doina from Sânnicolau Mare, Banat.

13. Examples of interwar dance competitions in Romania include *De pe Someş* in 1934 (Hadareanu 2008), *Concurs Societăţii "Tinerimea Română"* in 1936, and *Concursul de Coruri şi Jocuri Româneşti* in 1938 (Muşlea 2003).

14. "Dance cycle" is a term used to refer to the order in which dances are played during social occasions. Anca Giurchescu sets out the dances included in the local dance cycles in the various regions of Romanian in her book *Romanian Traditional Dance: A Contextual and Structural Approach* (Giurchescu and Bloland 1995).

15. These festivals include the *Koprivshtitsa* National Festival in Bulgaria and the *Gjirokastër* Albanian National Folklore Festival, both of which have continued into the post-communist era. For more on the *Koprivshtitsa* festival, see Mellish (2013b, 2016a), and for the *Gjirokastër* festival, see Ahmedaja (2011) and Green and Mellish (Unpublished).

16. For reviews of the Romanian national festivals, see Comisel (1962), Pop (1962), Giurchescu (1964), and Frenţescu (1975).

17. For further discussions on political festivals in Eastern Europe prior to 1989, see Frank Dubinskas (1983) on Croatia; Carol Silverman (1983) on Bulgaria; and Sydel Silverman (1985) for political festivals in Italy.

18. For a detailed history of Romania in this period, see British historian Dennis Deletant (1999, 2006), and anthropologist Katherine Verdery (1991, 1996).

19. The dancers and choreographers with whom I have discussed this festival include both those who were established choreographers and those who were university students during this period.

20. Hofman's (2011, 62) work on "The Competition of Serbian Villages" similarly reported that during the preparation for this competition, the members of the local community "shared common duties, interests and goals, which provided cohesion in the rural community."

21. Timothy Cooley (2005) and Ivanka Vlaeva (2011) both discuss awards during international folk festivals in Poland and Bulgaria, respectively. As Vlaeva (2011, 132) explains, at non-competitive festivals each participating group receives a certificate or diploma of participation that "represents a 'symbolic sign' recognising festival participation." This is in contrast to placing the participating groups in a ranked order and awarding prizes.

22. The Romanian *Căluş* is a healing ritual that takes place in villages at Whitsun. For a fuller description, see Mellish (2006).

23. The Romanian dancers created a stir in London by refusing to dance until Douglas Kennedy, chairman of the English Folk Dance and Song Society, scouted London to locate fresh garlic for the ritual flag, as without this they did not consider they would have their supernatural powers (Giurchescu 2004; Mellish 2006).

24. This has parallels with Anne Margrete Fiskvik's (2013) discussion on the Norwegian *Halling* dance that originated in the Telemark region of southern Norway, but has been used through the centuries as a marker for Norwegian nationalism.

25. A video from this festival can be seen at https://www.facebook.com/276924052463097/videos/495747730580727/.

26. In contrast to the competitive *Hercules* festival, which takes place in southern Banat, the non-competitive *Festivalul Inimilor* (the Festival of the Hearts) is held every July in Timişoara. In the latter case, the festival director has stressed to me during interviews that the emphasis is on enjoyment by all the participants, and the reactions of the audience and participants are more important than the opinions of a jury.

27. This increased interest in reasserting local or regional identity associated with renewed enthusiasm for local dance, music, or customs has been identified by scholars elsewhere; for example, see the works of Eli Miloseska (2007) on the practice of mask customs in Macedonia, Barbara O'Connor (1997, 149) on Irish set dancing, who observed an increased "desire to maintain a distinctive ethnic culture" following Ireland's ascension to the European Union, and Mellish (2016b) on newly established dance groups among the Bulgarian community in London.

28. This renewed enthusiasm for local music, dance, and customs is especially relevant in Banat, as locals have a strong sense of *Bănăţeni* identity with its close links to their regional history. Within this region, local dancing, music, and song continues to form part of the majority of community calendrical and life-cycle events and local festivals.

29. Commercial television channels with dedicated broadcasts of Romanian folk song, music, and dance include Etno TV, Favorit TV, and Horo TV.

30. The relaxed, family atmosphere during these competitions in Romania is similar to that described by Wulff (2007) during Irish dance competitions.

31. *Hora*, the most widely known dance in Romania, is danced in an open circle. There are two types of Banat *hora*, known as *hora mare* (big *hora*) and *hora mica* (little *hora*). Banat *brâul* originates from the Banat mountain region but is now danced both in the plain and mountain regions. It starts as a men's line dance; then, when indicated, the women join the line to dance beside their partners.

32. The locals' sense of belonging to the geographical and ethnographic area of Banat is born out in the names chosen for the competitive festivals listed in this chapter.

33. Following the planned colonization in the eighteenth century, the region of Banat is home to groups of Serbians, Hungarians, Bulgarians, Germans, Czech, Ukrainians, and Roma, all of whom have dance groups as part of their community activities. See Djuric (2007) for more on eighteenth-century colonization and identity in Banat.

34. See http://www.pressalert.ro/2016/03/primavara-plina-de-folclor-banat-cand-va-avea-loc-spectacolul-final-al-concursului-lada-cu-zestre/.

35. Anca Giurchescu lists the dances in the dance cycle in the Banat plain region as *Hora, Sorocul, Întroarsa, Ardeleana, Pre loc (De doi)*, and in the Banat mountain cycle as *Hora, Brâul, Ardeleana, De doi* (Giurchescu and Bloland 1995). It should be noted that in the Romanian context, the term "dance cycle" is used for the dance order during social occasions (see note 14), whereas the term "dance suite," or "choreography" refers to a sequence of dances danced by an organized group for a presentational performance (see Mellish 2013a).

36. The dance *Sorocul* from the Banat Plains is both a solo dance for men that includes heel clicks, jumps, and leg rotations, and a couple dance (Giurchescu and Bloland 1995).

37. See http://www.timisoaraexpress.ro/stiri-locale-timisoara/mestesuguri-traditionale-artizani-populari-si-traditii-gastronomice-ale-banatului_17411.

38. The organization of this and comparable events in Romania is similar to many community dance competitions elsewhere, for example the Irish dance competitions described

by Helena Wulff (2007), Sherry Johnson's (2012) account of step dance competitions in Canada and Charlotte Davies' (1997) discussion on the audience involvement at the Welsh National Eisteddfod.

39. My source for this comes from an informal discussion with an ethnic Hungarian living in Timişoara with regard to his daughter's participation in the Hungarian dance group.

40. A similar point regarding Irish identity is made by Helena Wulff (2007).

41. Cash (2011) uses the term "ethnographic experience" for this cumulative knowledge in her work on competitive festivals in the Republic of Moldova.

42. A similar structure of the judges' panel is evident in the Republic of Moldova (Cash 2011) and in Croatia (Zebec 2005).

43. Zebec (2005, 194) also comments that the judges at comparable competitions in Croatia "are encouraging to the younger generation as they want them to maintain an interest in local folklore and traditions."

44. Jonathan Marion (2008) also mentions that within the ballroom dance community, the judges are also ballroom dance coaches.

45. Cash (2011, 86) also raises this point in her discussion of similar competitive festivals in the Republic of Moldova, where she claims that "[p]ersonal knowledge, however, also limits the authority of jury members." She continues by saying that when they are judging groups from areas or villages where they have not undertaken research, their personal authority "can be, and is, questioned" by the leaders of the participating groups. She particularly cites one case of the final round of a competition held in the capital city, Chisinau, when all four judges were representatives of national-level organizations who lived and worked in Chisinau at the time and whose regional expertise was limited.

46. See Mellish (2013a) for a more detailed account of power relations among local choreographers.

47. Timothy Cooley (2005) discusses the dilemmas faced by the judges during the long running international competitive Festival of Mountain Folklore in Zakopane, Poland. Note that this situation also applies when judging performances by other ethnicities at local festivals, as was confirmed to me by one of the judges at the 2016 *Lada cu Zestrea* competition.

48. Anca Giurchescu (1987) cites such a case during the national round of the 1979 *Cântarea României*. She recounts that when the final results were published in the newspapers two days after the competition, the order of the prize winners has been reversed, with the dance group from the village of Scorniceşti (Ceauşescu's natal village) being awarded first place rather than third.

49. According to an oral history interview undertaken by Oancea (2007), at the local level the jury comprised three experts, and in addition the town secretary of propaganda, and occasionally a political activist from the county capital. Speranţa Rădulescu (1997, 10–11) lists the political representation at national level as "one member of Securitatea, one representative of the army, one of the Ministry of Culture and Socialist education."

50. My source for this information was personal communications with both Toma Frenţescu and Anca Giurchescu. See also Frenţescu (1975).

51. Daniela Ivanova-Nyberg (2009, 2016) reflects on similar sentiments of community and informal competition among dancers in a Bulgarian folk dance performance group. She mentions the shared enjoyment of being part of the community and the opportunities that this offers, such as travel within their own country and abroad. Wulff (1998) observes that within ballet companies, although the dancers may compete to move up the company

ranks, there is also strong camaraderie among them, and they are always willing to encourage and assist each other.

52. The interviews with Romanian dancers and choreographers that I have made over an extended period spans those whose dancing careers commenced in the 1950s to younger dancers who only commenced dancing during the last ten years.

53. There are also times when informal competitions take place between dancers. Kligman (1981), in her account of the *Căluş* tradition, recounts that when groups of *Căluş* dancers met, a ritual fight or competition took place. Similarly, during a dance course in 1997, a local mayor and the dance teacher tried to out-dance each other using their personal selection of *Căluş* dance figures.

54. Thomas Turino (1989, 19–20) discusses informal competitiveness between music ensembles in his work among the Aymara in Peru. He explains that during large fiestas in the town of Conima, "community ensembles compete with each other for greater numbers of dancers and spectators, and for the prestige of being recognized as the best ensemble in the fiesta." This recognition is based on audience appreciation and provides a boost to community pride after the fiesta. He observes that the "informal nature of this competition, which does not involve formal judging, trophies, and the like, allows a number of communities to believe, or at least publicly to maintain, that their ensembles actually 'won.'"

References

Ahmedaja, Ardian. 2011. "The Role of the Researchers and Artists in Public Presentations of Local Music and Dance in Albania." In *Proceedings of the Second Symposium of the International Council for Traditional Music Study Group on Music and Dance in Southeastern Europe*, edited by Elsie Ivancich Dunin and Mehmet Öcal Özbilgin, 3–14. İzmir, Turkey: Ege. University State Turkish Music Conservatory.

Alexandru, Tiberiu, Andrei Bucşan, and Paul P. Petrescu. 1970. "Însemnări pe Marginea Primului Festival şi Concurs Internaţional de Folclor "România '69". *Revista de Etnografie şi Folclor* 15(1): 87–92.

C.C.A.J.T. 2015. "Lada cu Zestrea." [The dowry chest] Timişoara: Centrul de Cultură şi Artă al Judeţului Timiş. http://www.ccajt.ro/. Accessed August 25, 2015.

Casa de Cultura a Municipiului Timişoara. 2015. *Am luat premiu internaţional!!* https://www.facebook.com/culturatm/photos/a.441226692752545.1073741829.439159126292635/448603818681499/?type=1. Accessed August 23, 2015.

Cash, Jennifer. 2002. "After the Folkloric Movement: Traditional Life in Post-socialist Moldova." *Anthropology of East Europe Review* 20(2): 83–88.

Cash, Jennifer. 2004. "In Search of an Authentic Nation: Folkloric Ensembles, Ethnography, and Ethnicity in the Republic of Moldova." PhD diss., Department of Anthropology, Indiana University.

Cash, Jennifer. 2011. *Villages on Stage: Folklore and Nationalism in the Republic of Moldova.* Berlin; London: Lit Verlag.

Comisel, E. 1962. "Al II-lea Festival Folcloric al Echipelor Artistice de Amatori din Regiunea Bucureşti." *Revista de Folclor* 7(1–2): 146–147.

Cooley, Timothy J. 2005. *Making Music in the Polish Tatras: Tourists, Ethnographers and Mountain Musicians.* Bloomington: Indiana University Press.

Davies, Charlotte Aull. 1997. "A Oes Heddwch' Contesting Meanings and Identities in the Welsh National Ensteddford." In *Ritual, Performance, Media*, edited by Felicia Hughes- Freeland, 141–159. London; New York: Routledge.

Deletant, Dennis. 1999. *Romania under Communist Rule*. Iaşi, Romania; Portland, OR: Center for Romanian Studies in cooperation with the Civic Academy Foundation.

Deletant, Dennis. 2006. *Romania sub regimul comunist*. Bucureşti: Fundatia Academica Civica.

Djuric, Aleksandra. 2007. "The Cross with Four Pillars as the Centre of Religious Gathering: Discussing Micro Regional Identity." In *Region, Regional Identity and Regionalism in Southeastern Europe*, Part 1: *Ethnologia Balkanica*, edited by Klaus Roth and Ulf Brunnbauer, 171–184. Berlin: Lit Verlag.

Dubinskas, Frank A. 1983. "Leaders and Followers: Cultural Pattern and Political Symbolism in Yugoslavia." *Anthropological Quarterly* 56(2): 95–99.

Fiskvik, Anne Margrete. 2013. "*Halling* as a Tool for Nationalist Strategies." In *Bodies of Sound: Studies across Popular Music and Dance*, edited by Sherril Dodds and Susan C. Cook, 85–102. Burlington, VT: Ashgate.

Fochi, Adrian, and Iordan Datcu. 2002. *Bibliografia generală a etnografie şi folclorului Românesc II (1892–1904)*. Bucureşti: Editura Saeculum I.O.

Frenţescu, Toma. 1975. *Borlova: Centru de Referinţă al Folclorului Coreografic din Banatul de Sud*. Bucureşti: Consiliul Culturii şi Educaţiei Socialiste.

Giurchescu, Anca. 1957. "Din Realizării Folcloristicii Noastre." *Revista de Folclor* 2(4): 129–130.

Giurchescu, Anca. 1964. "Însemnări pe Marginea Celui de-ai VII-lea Concurs al Formaţiilor Artistice de Amatori." *Revista de Etnografie şi Folclor* 9(1): 639–642.

Giurchescu, Anca. 1977. "Valorificarea Folclorului în Cadrul Festivalului Naţional 'Cântarea României.'" *Revista de Etnografie şi Folclor* 21(2): 227–231.

Giurchescu, Anca. 1987. "The National Festival 'Song to Romania': Manipulation of Symbols in the Political Discourse." In *Symbols of Power: The Esthetics of Political Legitimation in the Soviet Union and Eastern Europe*, edited by Claes Ardvisson and Lars Blomqvist, 163–172. Stockholm: Almqvist & Wiksell.

Giurchescu, Anca. 1992. "A Comparative Analysis between the "Căluş" of the Danube Plain and "Căluşerul" of Transylvania (Romania)." *Studia Musicologica* 34(1–2): 31–44.

Giurchescu, Anca. 2001. "The Power of Dance and Its Social and Political Uses." *Yearbook for Traditional Music* 33: 109–121.

Giurchescu, Anca. 2004. "Căluş—Between Ritual and National Symbol." http://owe.ompom.se/calus/.

Giurchescu, Anca, and Sunni Bloland. 1995. *Romanian Traditional Dance: A Contextual and Structural Approach*. Mill Valley, CA: Wild Flower.

Goffman, Erving. 1959. *The Presentation of Self in Everyday Life*. London: Penguin Books.

Green, Nick, and Liz Mellish. Unpublished. *Reflections on the Gjirokastër Festival 2015: An Ethnographic View from Outside*.

Hadareanu, Gavril. 2008. *Zodii în Cumpăna Februarie 4, 2008: Preocupări ale intelectualita ii beiuşene pe linia promovării culturii populare, în perioada interbelică*. https://cumpana.wordpress.com/2008/02/04/preocupari-ale-intelectualitatii-beiusene-pe-linia-promovarii-culturii-populare-in-perioada-interbelica/. Accessed June 12, 2010.

Hofman, Ana R. 2011. *Staging Socialist Femininity: Gender Politics and Folklore Performance in Serbia*. Balkan Studies Library. Leiden; Boston: Brill.

Howes, Frank. 1935. "The International (European) Folk Dance Festival." *Journal of the English Folk Dance and Song Society* 2: 1–16.

IFMC. 1969. *Bulletin of the International Folk Music Council*. Vol. XXXV, October 1969. Kingston, ON: International Folk Music Council, Department of Music, Queen's University.

Ivanova, Daniela. 2009. "'Horo Se Vie, Izviva' (Observation on 'Horo Se Vie, Izviva' Festival-Competing in Dancing and on the Activities of the New-born Clubs for Traditional Dances in Bulgaria)." In *First Symposium of the ICTM Study Group on Music and Dance in Southeastern Europe*, edited by Velika Stoykova, 173–182. Struga, Macedonia: SOKOM.

Ivanova-Nyberg, Daniela. 2016. "*Rachenitsa! Try to Outdance Me!*—Competition and Improvisation the Bulgarian Way." In *Improvisation in Music and Dance of Southeastern Europe/Professionalization of Music and Dance in Southeastern Europe, Proceedings for the Fourth Symposium of the ICTM, Study Group on Music and Dance in Southeastern Europe, Petnica*, edited by Liz Mellish, Nick Green and Mirjan Zakić, 16–23. Belgrade: Institute of Musicology, Belgrade.

Johnson, Sherry. 2012. "Role of Competition in Ottawa Valley Step Dancing Contests." In *ICTM Study Group on Ethnochoreology*, conference presentation, 27th Symposium of the ICTM Study Group on Ethnochoreology. The Irish World Academy of Music and Dance, University of Limerick, Ireland, July 27.

Kligman, Gail. 1981. *Căluş: Symbolic Transformation in Romanian Ritual*. Chicago: University of Chicago Press.

Marion, Jonathan S. 2008. *Ballroom: Culture and Costume in Competitive Dance, Dress, Body, Culture*. Oxford; New York: Berg.

Mellish, Liz. 2006. "The Romanian Căluş Tradition and Its Changing Symbolism as It Travels from the Village to the Global Platform." https://www.academia.edu/31310745/The_Romanian_C%C4%83lu%C8%99_tradition_and_its_changing_symbolism_as_it_travels_from_the_village_to_the_global_platform.

Mellish, Elizabeth. 2013a. "Dancing through the City and Beyond: Lives, Movements and Performances in a Romanian Urban Folk Ensemble." PhD diss., University College London (UCL) School of Slavonic and East European Studies, London.

Mellish, Liz. 2013b. "The Koprivshtitsa Festival: From National Icon to Globalised Village Event." In *Global Villages: Rural and Urban Transformations in Contemporary Bulgaria*, edited by Ger Duijzings, 153–171. London: Anthem.

Mellish, Liz. 2016a. "Bulgarian Tracks: The Road to the Koprivshtitsa Festival (and Back Again, and Again)." *Ethnomusicology Ireland* 4: 1–10.

Mellish, Liz. 2016b "The southeast Europeans are (still) dancing: Recent dance trends in Romania and among southeast Europeans in London." In *Music and Dance in Southeastern Europe: Myth, Ritual, Post-1989, Audiovisual Ethnographies, Fifth Symposium of the ICTM Study Group on Music and Dance in Southeastern Europe 2016 South-West University "Neofit Rilski"*, edited by Liz Mellish, Ivanka Vlaeva, Lozanka Peycheva, Nick Green, Ventsislav Dimov, 189–197. Bulgaria: University Publishing House "Neofit Rilski".

Mihăilescu, Vintilă. 2009. "A New Festival for the New Man: The Socialist Market of Folk Experts during the Singing Romania National Festival." In *Studying Peoples in the People's Democracies II: Socialist Era Anthropology in South-East Europe*, edited by Vintilă Mihăilescu, Ilia Iliev, and Slobodan Naumovic, 55–80. Hamburg: Lit Verlag.

Miloseska, Eli. 2007. "Mask Customs and Identity in the Region of Southeast Europe: The Case of Macedonia." In *Region, Regional Identity and Regionalism in Southeastern Europe*, Part 1, edited by Klaus Roth and Ulf Brunnbauer, 237–256. Berlin: Lit Verlag.

Muşlea, I. 2003. *Bibliografia Folclorului Românesc 1930–1955*. Bucureşti: Editura Saeculum I.O.

O'Connor, Barbara. 1997. "Safe Sets: Women, Dance and 'Communitas.'" In *Dance in the City*, edited by Helen Thomas, 149–172. New York: St. Martin's Press.

Oancea, Claudiu. 2007. "When Forgers of Steel Became Creators of Art: The National Festival 'Song to Romania' 1976–1989." MA thesis, Central European University, Budapest.

Pop, Mihai. 1962. "Folclorul la al VI-lea Concurs al Formaţiilor Artistice de Amatori." *Revista de Folclor* 7(1–2): 126–128.

Proca-Ciortea, Vera. 1978. "The 'Căluş' Custom in Rumania—Tradition—Change—Creativity." *Dance Studies* 3: 1–43.

Rădulescu, Speranţa. 1997. "Traditional Musics and Ethnomusicology: Under Political Pressure: The Romanian Case." *Anthropology Today* 13(6): 8–12.

Silverman, Carol. 1983. "The Politics of Folklore in Bulgaria." *Anthropological Quarterly* 56(2): 55–61.

Silverman, Sydel. 1985. "Towards a Political Economy of Italian Competitive Festivals." *Ethnologia Europaea* XV(2): 95–103.

Timişul. 2011. *Timişul Ansamblul Folcloric din Timişoara.* http://www.timisul.ro/. Accessed June 1, 2011.

Turino, Thomas. 1989. "The Coherence of Social Style and Musical Creation among the Aymara in Southern Peru." *Ethnomusicology* 33(1): 1–30.

Turino, Thomas. 2008. *Music as Social Life: The Politics of Participation.* Chicago: University of Chicago Press.

Vasile, Cristian. 2014. *Viaţă Intelectulala şi Artistică în Primul Deceniu al Regimului Ceauşescu 1965–1974.* Bucureşti: Humanitas.

Verdery, Katherine. 1991. *National Ideology under Socialism.* Los Angeles: University of California Press.

Verdery, Katherine. 1996. *What Was Socialism and What Comes Next?* Princeton, NJ: Princeton University Press.

Vlaeva, Ivanka. 2011. "Strategy of the International Folk Festivals in Bulgaria in the Last Two Decades." In *Proceedings of the Second Symposium of the ICTM Study Group on Music and Dance in Southeastern Europe*, edited by Elsie Ivancich Dunin and Mehmet Öcal Özbilgin, 129–136. İzmir, Turkey: Ege University State Turkish Music Conservatory.

Wulff, Helena. 1998. *Ballet across Borders: Career and Culture in the World of Dancers.* Oxford; New York: Berg.

Wulff, Helena. 2007. *Dancing at the Crossroads: Memory and Mobility in Ireland.* New York: Berghahn Books.

Zebec, Tvrtko. 2005. "Church Kermis to Saint Roch: Contemporary Folklore on the Stage." In *Dance and Society: Dancer as a Cultural Performer: Re-appraising Our Past, Moving into the Future: 40th Anniversary of Study Group on Ethnochoreology of International Council on Traditional Music: 22nd Symposium of the ICTM Study Group on Ethnochoreology, Szeged, Hungary, 2002*, edited by Elsie Ivancich Dunin, Anne von Bibra Wharton, and László Felföldi, 192–198. Budapest: Akademiai Kiado: European Folklore Institute.

CHAPTER 12

NON-COMPETITIVE BODY STATES

Corporeal Freedom and Innovation in Contemporary Dance

NALINA WAIT AND ERIN BRANNIGAN

A 10-year old girl dances a self-authored, contemporary dance solo at a Christmas party in a backyard in Sydney to a soft-rock ballad in a leotard and flowing chiffon skirt. Her body moves fluidly with weighted limbs, swinging, sensing, and reaching into space. As the music climaxes, her arms and feet are propelled by the torque of her torso. Her movements follow her breath, and the lines of force and rebound, as she walks, turns, jumps, and reaches out from her body with soft gestures that seem to sense the space. Her thinking is visible as she makes decisions to suit the situation: adjusting the level of energy and attack to ride the momentum she has produced, and choosing steps according to the charge of the physical-emotional state she has developed while dancing. She is followed by another girl of the same age, performing her part of a group jazz routine to a top-10 dance hit in a sequined unitard. Her movements match the accents in the music, arriving sharply in poses where each limb is extended to her limit, and her splayed hands push away from her body, cutting through the space. Her legs kick high towards her torso, which pulls upwards and inwards, challenging her connection to the floor to produce a vertical line with both legs. The choreographed movements require tension in the body, each one sequentially juxtaposed against a contrasting movement or pose to meet the requirements of the intricate group choreography. Differences between the two performances regarding music choice, costume, technique, genre, quality, notions of virtuosity and expression represent, on a small scale, the dialectical manifestations of dance in contemporary Western culture as private practice and public competition. These two dance performances occupy a shared, informal theatrical space and yet the dancers operate within entirely different modes of constituting oneself as a dancing subject.

FROM the dance floor of urban clubs to our major performing arts venues, from the local dance school to professional artists, the condition of dance as (un)professional, (un) disciplined, and (un)assertive impacts upon the form's visibility and power. The status of dance in relation to degrees of power and discipline is evidenced at the level of the body, even at the micro-level: the condition of the dancers' body tissues (in particular the muscular, connective, and nervous tissues), their capacity for shifting the tonality of their muscles, and their sensitivity to kinesthesia. We find that the competition inherent in many codified dance forms, as well as the associated pursuit of an ideal against which candidates are ranked and judged, privileges specific aspirational muscle tone and impacts kinesthesia. We examine, in particular, how the tonus of a dancer's muscles both holds and produces the power effects of a given dance technology, comparing codified forms with the un-codified or *(un)disciplined* field of somatics.[1] We interrogate this binary further by considering the types of power effects that non-competitive somatic practices engender. This is important because while these approaches may be in opposition, contemporary dancers regularly negotiate between the two. This chapter returns to a debate that, at its peak in the 1990s, interrogated the structures of power embodied in dance technologies. We do this to rethink the effect that this has on the dancers that are produced today, and the philosophical and ideological means through which such structures have been, and can be, understood.

We return to the literature on philosopher Michel Foucault and his notion of *discipline*, which was part of dance studies' unprecedented attention to philosophy from the late 1980s to the first decade of the 2000s. We do so because the attention in his work to body practices and techniques resonates with dance as an art form as much now as then, particularly in the face of current threats to the discipline-specificity of dance as a site of creative innovation within the contemporary arts.[2] The public face of dance on our major stages, as well as television, cinema, and computer screens, reiterates dance as spectacle, virtuosic display, and competition. On the other hand, the knowledges, skills, and significance of the corporeal practices of contemporary dance can be made invisible through the privacy of the studio, the relatively small scale of performances, the complexities of intermedial practices, and the subtleties of physical innovations that privilege sensation over spectacle. For these reasons, we re-mobilize Foucault's work on the role of the body as both the subject and object of structures of power and knowledge, to address an opposition that persists into the twenty-first century at all levels of dance activity between competitive and non-competitive body technologies. We pursue this path because the nature of subjection remains complex for a contemporary dancer who must negotiate and reconcile diverse ontologies within the discipline.

Despite its popularity, the application of Foucault's theories of "body disciplines" and "the docile body" outlined in *Discipline and Punish* (1977) to the analysis of dance and issues of power has a problematic place in dance theory, primarily due to the absence of dance from his case studies. However, dance theorist Mark Franko (2011, 108) proposes that dance "may occupy a more integral place in Foucault's thinking than is usually acknowledged either by Foucault or by his critics." Franko eloquently examines how choreographer William Forsythe both mobilized and challenged Foucault's theories in reconfiguring the ballet lexicon beyond the "art of command," by empowering dancers with agency in his improvisation technologies. Following Franko's recalibration of the exchange between Foucault and dance, in which Forsythe challenges the limits of Foucault's theory of physical discipline through *practice*, we examine how somatics has introduced a non-competitive, resistant, critical agency into dance pedagogy and creative process that is closer to Foucault's later notion of "aesthetics of experience," but also pushes at the limits of this model of "production of the self" (Foucault 1985, 27). This involves an account of a new, contemporary body-subject, far removed from the condition of inescapable and repressive subjection that Foucault finds in his case studies of the eighteenth and nineteenth centuries, while still operating within a rigorous field of bodily practice.

If we accept that many codified forms of dance enforce subjection via competitive modalities, and that somatically informed dancers engage in degrees of self-formation through inherently non-competitive practices, then how can Foucault's models and terminology be extended to analyze such different physical disciplines of subject formation? Such a project requires attention to the work of Australian dance theorist Elizabeth Dempster (2002) and her application of Foucault's (1977) classical models of physical disciplines of subjection in her analysis of the oppositional dance techniques of ballet and ideokinesis.[3] Her work clarifies the need for a repurposing of Foucault's model when put into dialogue with the movement systems of somatics. Articulating somatics as a form of knowledge that enables a dancer to transform her own "modes of being" (Foucault 1985, 30) requires an extension of current terminology to include Nalina Wait's terms: *prohibitive* and *emancipatory self-surveillance*, and the contested notion of *anatomical truth*.[4] We argue that a somatic approach does not entirely require a rejection of discipline, as it is in fact a form of diligent labor and acquisition of knowledge and power. Instead, it assumes a discipline of another order, one that critiques Foucault's notion of self-surveillance as prohibitive by presenting the possibility of an emancipated and empowered subject.

KINESTHETIC PERCEPTION: IMITATIVE AND SOMATIC

In the case of our backyard performances, the more obvious signifiers of difference (costume, music, precision, sequencing, attack, force) can be understood in relation to fundamental, constitutive physical states shaped by the nature of the muscle tone. As has been established by dance theorists Laurence Louppe (2010), along with Elizabeth Dempster (1995–1996, 2005) and Susan Leigh Foster (1986, 2002), among others, by focusing on the observation of different muscle tones, on the shifting of weight, sensation, and breath, somatics has added another dimension to corporeal knowledge in dance as well as to choreographic and improvisational methodologies. This chapter seeks to address the body in terms of its materiality through an articulation of corporeal knowledges, without presupposing an original or neutral body, but rather in acknowledgment of the social forces through which a body is constituted. Therefore, before moving on, we briefly survey how self-formation occurs at a *kinesthetic* level in dance training.

Training in a codified form from a young age can be beneficial in that it allows dancers to map a detailed body-schema through their kinesthetic senses while they aspire to perform the correct placement, musicality, timing, effort, muscle tone, and performance quality of the form. This corporeal education constitutes many dancers' foundational approach to kinesthetic awareness while moving. Achieving professionalism in these methods is only possible via a sophisticated capacity for the kind of close imitation of form that requires comprehensive control over one's body movements. This approach to dance training is *imitative* in that it aims to eliminate any other possible corporeal habits in preference for a singular, or ostensibly correct, disciplined mode that replicates the form.

Imitative, and specifically professional, forms of dance training operate within a hierarchical model that privileges a specific kind of muscular tautness, often favoring virtuosic and extensional movements that are performed via a narrow range of muscular tone.[5] If it is predominantly through a taut and stretched effort that a dancer comes to kinesthetically understand how to maintain corporeal control while producing (mostly) extensional and exacting movements, then enacting muscular tension will be understood as the correct kinesthetic sensation associated with the achievement of technical rigor. For example, the basic movement of tracing the foot along the floor to a pointed extension known as a *tendu* translates from French as "stretched out and held tautly."[6] While this is not the only muscle tone of classical ballet, it is widely understood to epitomize the embodiment of balletic corporeal tonality. Similarly, it is through the sharpness, tension, and accuracy of the movements of the jazz dancer in the backyard performance that she kinesthetically understands her dance to be well performed, as she recognizes in the tone of her muscles that it meets the set standard for that form.

Somatic practices operate differently, by directing dancers to focus on their sensory experience as the primary source of corporeal information. This occurs via a relaxed muscle tonus that allows for greater somatosensory and kinesthetic information to be perceived. Therefore, while kinesthetic perception is at the core of all forms of dance, the way that kinesthesia operates during practices learned via imitation is radically different from its operation in somatic and released practices. This is not to suggest that a completely released muscle tone should be desired as an end in itself, replacing extensional tensility as a preferred tonality of dance, but that dancers develop the capacity to access a "shifting of tensilities" by sensing and adapting their muscle tonality along a spectrum of gradients (Louppe 2010, 117). A released muscle tonus is integral to a foundational understanding of the soft end of the tonal spectrum, where kinesthetic information is more clearly experienced. In this way, the tonal range that the muscles can engage is diversified, leading to greater freedom and choice in movement texture, quality, and scope.

However, as the sensation of taut corporeal tonality is so formatively linked to the experience of codified dance training, tensioning becomes a difficult habit to undo without considerable practice. This is, in part, due to the function of muscle memory but, more important, the difficultly arises in terms of the relationship between the psyche and the soma. The quality of deeply relaxed muscle tone, in the practice of somatics, is beyond the parameters experienced by the dancer trained in a codified regime because it requires a complete acceptance of the body-mind *as it is*, insofar as one can perceive what is, by which we mean the relinquishment of aspiration.[7] So there is no question of a neutral body released of all physical and psychological load, but rather an approach seeking clarity or honesty regarding the condition of the body in a given moment, detached from external ideals. It is only through the acceptance of *what is* that dancers can observe and notice the hidden *psychosomatic* holding, tension, or aspiration in their tissues that needs to be released for a broader range of muscle tones to be accessed (Alexander 1932; Todd 1937).[8] Mentally accepting the body-mind *as it is* is the most difficult aspect of technologies such as ideokinesis for a dancer who has been trained in an imitative, codified form because it is the antithesis of what is understood as the labor of dancing in such forms, which is to constantly aspire toward an ideal.

For example, it is often not possible to accurately perceive the weight of the arms because they are usually held up, away from the pull of gravity, as a habitual by-product of their frequent use. It is only by relaxing the muscle tone of the arms and shoulders that the true weight can be felt, giving a more accurate sense of the actual weight of that part of the anatomy. Once the true weight of the arms can be accessed, the experience of the sensation of weight can be used to qualitatively shift a dancer's movement. However, the difficulty lies in relinquishing the socialized and deeply familiar habit of controlling one's own arms. Such a process is not an end in itself in a contemporary dance context. It offers a way of coming to integrate one's psycho-soma through kinesthesia, through the use of imagery and experimentation. In this context, psychosomatic integration aims to cultivate a dancing body with a greater capacity for movement innovation via an increased diversification of muscle tone available for use in composition.

The passive activity of disengaging the musculature requires considerable self-awareness. Such self-reflexivity does not subscribe to an external, audience/teacher/mirror-based orientation, and can thus appear undisciplined, as the emphasis is less on result-focused production than on reflective-based process.[9] However, such processual work has its own claims to virtuosity, discipline, and skill, and is vital to constituting a contemporary dancer's specialized embodied knowledge, as we will demonstrate.

(Un) Disciplining Practice:
Sites of Authority

Dempster's (2005, 7) work promotes the role that "unprofessional" practices such as ideokinesis have played in recent innovations in dance practices, pedagogies, and compositions.[10] In this article, Dempster focuses on "professional" versus "creative" dance knowledges and the realities of training in the goal-oriented university context, expanding upon Mabel Ellsworth Todd's (1937, xiii) suggestion that "professionalisation may be an impediment to creative thinking" (Dempster 2005, 8). This link between technologies of the body and creative innovation is central to our argument regarding the importance of dancer agency in the larger context of dance as a contemporary art form. Importantly, Dempster raises political questions about the site(s) of authority in dance and the value of providing conditions for dance that are unregulated and non-competitive. Dempster (2002, 36) uses Foucault's (1977) concept of a docile body to describe codified dance training, which she suggests encourages obedience through competition. She later contrasts this process with the ways in which unprofessionalism in dance has historically involved the critique of those same codified body practices, resulting in a new set of political and aesthetic conditions and non-competitive modes of training a dancer in the late twentieth and early twenty-first centuries.

In describing dance as unprofessional Dempster (2005, 7) uses ideokinesis as an example of "empirical, in-body research, whose vitality is contingent upon its ongoing resistance to professionalism and regulation." She contrasts this to "professionally" orientated models of the art of dance and the kinds of techniques they mobilize:

> Dance technique has often been conceived as a means whereby personal, subjective aspects of embodiment are transmuted and put to work in service of a "higher" artistic purpose. Thus the function of dance technique in a discipline such as ballet, for example, is both positive, that is producing quantifiable skills and abilities, and also negative—reducing elements of "personality" or idiosyncratic behaviour which might detract from or otherwise present an obstacle to realisation of the choreographic idea. (Dempster 2007, 49)

A technical dancer as a conduit or vehicle for someone else's choreographic vision is set in opposition here to a *self-authoring* dance artist working in movement systems and methodologies that resist competitive modes of discipline. Thus, dance theorists of the 1990s argued that dance techniques and associated codified forms aimed at producing professionals can be aligned with institutionalization. In relation to this, as an (un)disciplined, experimental approach in which the creative authority is claimed by the dancer, ideokinesis is described by Dempster as *resistant* to professionalization, institutionalization, and disciplinary formations. She also considered it productive or generative of innovation at the level of composition or choreography.

Interestingly, as Dempster (2002, 208) points out, the focus for Todd is also still on "practice, repetition and habit formation." The methods of exercise and practice, including degrees of supervision/surveillance, remain, but an (un)disciplined practice provides alternative modes of subject formation in dance, which produces new kinds of dancing. So, in what ways does such a self-authoring, resistant dancing subject challenge the terms of Foucault's body techniques of subjection? And could we reimagine (un)disciplined modes of subjection that speak back to Foucault's theory? Furthermore, as somatics are now integral to tertiary dance education, dancers must move between both disciplined and undisciplined forms of training within the institution, which requires mobility between modes of subject authority.

Foucault, Body Disciplines, and Self-Surveillance

In the late twentieth century, the evocative language Foucault used to describe physical disciplines in *Discipline and Punish: The Birth of the Prison* caught the attention of dance theorists attempting to articulate how dancing subjects are the product and producer of systems of power and knowledge.[11] Foucault (1977, 137) illustrates this through his analysis of physical systems, or "technologies of the self," in the military, education, religion, medicine, and industry in the eighteenth and nineteenth centuries. He demonstrates how individuals are "subjected" to codes of behavior that are introduced in a detailed, organized, consistent, and serialized or evolutional way through "disciplines" that mark "the moment when an art of the human body was born."[12] Through these "technique[s] of subjection a new object was being formed":

> it is the body susceptible to specified operations, which have their order, their stages, their internal conditions, their constituent elements. In becoming the target for new mechanisms of power, the body is offered up to new forms of knowledge. (Foucault 1977, 155)

In claiming ground for "new forms of knowledge" that are corporeally derived, and speaking for the effectiveness of physical disciplines in the service of new models of power, Foucault acknowledges the central role of the body, its experiences, and subjections in the broader sociopolitical realm.[13] This is an important claim for dance, now more than ever, when dance and choreography are simultaneously being mobilized as concepts in all kinds of aesthetic, philosophical, and political fields, while disappearing as a disciplinarily distinct art from our training institutions and stages.[14] This tendency increases as avant-garde dance abandons movement in what dance scholar André Lepecki (2006) identifies as the "exhaustion" of dance. When it does appear currently, it seems to be increasingly in the service of virtuosic spectacle and competition, as already described.

Foucault (1977, 170–177) explains how, once disciplined, these trained, manipulable, useful bodies are policed through "techniques of surveillance" by "supervisors" in buildings designed for the most effective combination of visibility and segregation. It is this process of surveillance, with its associated methods such as exercises and examinations, that scaffolds the physical disciplines for Foucault and which we would like to focus on in our discussion of non-competitive models of dancing.

Dempster notes a shift in Foucault's thinking in *The History of Sexuality* from *subjection* to *subjectivation*; from the maintenance of disciplined subjects through external surveillance to what we will call *prohibitive self-surveillance* (Wait 2018).[15]

> Here the emphasis is on the forms of relations with the self, on the methods and techniques by which he works them out, on the exercises by which he makes himself an object to be known, and on the practices that enable him to transform his own mode of being. (Foucault 1985, 30)

Describing Foucault's (1985, 139) notion of surveillance here as a kind of *self-surveillance* ("the subject constitutes himself in an active fashion") offers a useful way to repurpose Foucault's theory of subject formation for dance scholarship, as it can be used to describe the self-disciplining dancing subject who internalizes the authority that was once external.[16] A further bifurcation of self-surveillance as *prohibitive* or *emancipative* will assist us, in what follows, to articulate specific modes of attention, power, and agency that operate in forms of imitative, dance pedagogy and in the methods that somatics has contributed.[17]

The use of Foucault in dance theory to discuss the disciplining of dancing bodies is extensive.[18] While Foucault's project (1977, 137) is not specifically concerned with dance, it is plain to see that classical ballet, as an "art of the human body," was born at the very moment that the other physical disciplines that Foucault describes in *Discipline and Punish* were coming into being.[19] And the attention to space, time, and movement in his findings regarding the body disciplines he studies is positively choreographic; descriptions of "rhythms," "occupations," "repetitions," "forces," and a focus of spatial and temporal organization or composition (Foucault 1977, 141–149).[20]

However, there have been some reservations regarding the suitability of Foucault's work as it has been applied to theories of dance and choreography. Dempster (2002) herself notes the problem of gender blindness in Foucault's work when applied to the heavily gendered dance technique of ballet. Others, such as dance ethnographer Sally Ann Ness (2011), have argued against leveraging Foucault's philosophy for dance-based debates because the fields of dance and somatic theory have relied on the kind of phenomenological methods that Foucault rejects.[21] While phenomenology has enjoyed broad applications within dance studies, particularly historically through validating the articulation of corporeal knowledges within the academy, we question the assumption that dance studies is so closely dependent on phenomenology as its preferred philosophical paradigm. We also argue that phenomenology in dance studies has a different purpose (to articulate a dancer's experience, in a specific time and space) rather than to propose a transcendental phenomenological subject, which is the basis of Foucault's criticism of this method.[22]

Ness's (2011, 23) other concern, that following Foucault's historical method might "foreclose inquiry into the more radically creative, emergent (and even liberatory and agentive) forms of danced experience and intelligence," is overturned in what follows.[23] In turning Foucault's historically informed tools toward the task of accounting for body disciplines that experiment at the limits of corporeal habits and conditioning in the twenty-first century, we repurpose *discipline, exercise,* and *surveillance* as terms for resistant practices that innovate the form and maintain its status as a contemporary art.

DISCIPLINE, APTITUDE, AND SUBJECTION/SUBJECTIVITY

Dempster's work reflects on the regime of dance training in ballet technique that, she argues, produces Foucauldian "docile bodies." For Dempster (2002), the external gaze of the teacher, choreographer, or audience replicates the surveillance of the state, and reinforces the ideal model to which the student should aspire. She uses Foucault's theory of the docile body to explain the political ramifications of submitting the experience of one's own functional anatomy to the effort of achieving an idealized aesthetic.[24] In addition to external powers, the docile dancing body will enact control over its own corporeality by internalizing the image of an ideal dancing body-schema, not only in form but also in quality of action. For Dempster (2002, 7–8), "the question of the individual's active engagement with her own self-constitution through dance" forms the basis for her critique of the use of codified systems for dance training, as this is where she sees such engagement lacking. She subsequently promotes somatics (and the "new dance practices" [2002, 1] associated with the same) as revolutionizing the systems of power inherent in dance practices through the degrees of agency that the dancer may access.

For the ballet student, self-surveillance repeats the gaze of the teacher through the use of the mirror. As dance pedagogue and psychologist Shona Innes (1988, 46) states, "dancers use the mirror to monitor themselves and so actively participate in the control and management of their own bodies" in pursuit of the preordained ideals established by the teacher. The key difference with ideokinetic methods is their status as "unregulated" practices; while it is practiced extensively in dance institutions worldwide, "there is no system of certification, no centralised process of accreditation; there is no academy or school of ideokinesis" (Dempster 2002,161).[25] There is, thus, no preexisting standard or basis for the serialization, examination, and competition that are essential to Foucault's disciplines of subjection. Dancers who investigate experimental forms of moving and ways of constituting themselves through somatically informed practices of dance do so without a defined image of success against which to measure their achievements. Instead, their understanding of their own body in movement occurs primarily through receptivity; each individual finds her way to move with attentiveness to the body-mind as it is in each moment, supporting the proliferation of individual experiences, rather than the reproduction of an "ideal" or codified form. They may also explore a broader range of muscle tonalities with the absence of competitive forces. The standard that ideokinesis engenders is one in which the very effort of striving, for example toward an ever-deepening state of relaxation, is at odds with the practice itself.

Importantly, a codified standard is never achievable because the form is a collection of actions that are inherently aspirational; the ideal is never fully realizable. As Foucault states in relation to exercise, which he places at the heart of disciplinary methods for the body,

> Exercise, having become an element in the political technology of the body and of duration, does not culminate in a beyond, but tends towards a subjection that has never reached its limit. (Foucault 1977, 162)[26]

This "limit" or standard is that against which a dancer measures her- or himself in order to assess her or his competitive ranking and place within a scale of "aptitudes." For example, a dancer can never be satisfied by the amount of *pointe* she has achieved because it is always in the pointing, more and further, that the activity of a *pointe* exists. Therefore, while it feels empowering to perform feats of virtuosity and striving, the act of measuring oneself against an unachievable standard is written through with failure from the beginning and promotes the kind of prohibitive self-surveillance that, according to Foucault, decreases a subject's personal power.[27]

Foucault explains how submitting to physical discipline dissociates power from the body and refers it to an external source, linking "increased aptitude with increased domination." He states,

> Discipline increases the forces of the body (in economic terms of utility) and diminishes these forces (in political terms of obedience). In short, it dissociates power from the body; on the one hand, it turns into an "aptitude," a "capacity," which it seeks to increase; on the other hand, it reverses the course of the energy, the power that might result from it, and turns it into a relation of strict subjection. (Foucault 1977, 138)

Aptitude is gained at the cost of subjection. Dempster puts this into dance terms. By privileging a codified ideal and a corresponding choreographic vision, imitative forms of dance subject a dancer's bodily power to external sources of energy that direct, diminish, and contain the dancer's proprioceptive experience. Again, aptitude is privileged over personal agency, subjection over subjectivity. In comparison, somatic systems such as ideokinesis can also be considered "disciplines which produce specific forms of knowledge and forms of the self" (Dempster 2002, 157). However, "as forms of power/knowledge, [somatic systems] function not only as critiques of dominant forms of practice but as new constructs of bodily knowledge and dance expression" (Dempster 2002,

157). The "critique" occurs at the level of authorship and control through decentralizing the supervising authority, and the "new constructs" privilege individual agency.

ANATOMICAL TRUTH

Somatic approaches to corporeal knowledge, such as ideokinesis, privilege a dancer's experience of her *anatomical truth* and support the *somatic intelligence* of the dancer.[28] The use of the term *truth* here does not imply a singular or generic universal truth, applicable for all subjects. Instead, it refers to an individual's physiological anatomy *as it is experienced*, with the understanding that this is affected by any number of social and cultural codes, along with any psychosomatic idiosyncrasies. Together, such forces produce an individual's uniquely personal experience of her physical anatomy and, therefore, resist any competitive notion in which individuals could be ranked against an ideal form.[29] Anatomical truth can be experientially understood through one's own body-mind via somatic practices that foreground the conscious awareness of the psychosomatic experience *as it is* (physiologically: its weight, density, and form), quietening cognitive ideas about how *it should be* (that are socially prescribed). It describes the state through which the effect of cultural codes on the body-mind are never completely erased, as they are constantly replenished, but existing codes can be observed and loosened to create space for other possibilities. Anatomical truth is not a fixed place or experience, but an action toward a state of being that is led by body-mind. It is an action or "truth procedure" where a certain kind of truth is constructed (Badiou 2009, 38). Badiou (2009, 53) explains that a truth procedure "is testing out the truth of what the [in this case the body-mind] is capable of achieving." This action reveals how the body-mind desires to *be*, beneath and beyond the experience of a socially constructed subjectivity. Somatics, therefore, feels like a "universal panacea" because it guides the practitioner toward the experience of fulfilling her physical-mental potential, in terms of how to *be*. Somatics pulls at the edges of socially constructed subjectivities, which allow the possibility of becoming acquainted with anatomically (physiologically) constructed subjectivity. Anatomical truth can be obfuscated through both a lack of somatic awareness (no somatic training), or by an imagined body-schema of an ideal form (training that is not somatic).

The defining feature of somatic practices is the engagement of a mindful awareness or self-reflexivity in moving. Given that somatic-based work and imitative forms of dance both involve considerable self-observation, to understand more fully how a dancer can access anatomical truth we bifurcate Foucault's model of (self-)surveillance as *prohibitive* and *emancipative*. Somatic practices have developed a very specific type of self-observation that focuses on the relation between *anatomy, efficiency*, and *imagery*. This, we will argue, results in a different type of self-surveillance from the prohibitive self-surveillance described previously and which Wait has termed *emancipatory self-surveillance*.

EMANCIPATORY SELF-SURVEILLANCE

In expanding Foucault's notion of subject formation, we follow Dempster's under-standing of the physical experiences of somatics as a type of discipline with its own practices and forms of knowledge.

> [The experience of somatics is] the outcome of a specific kind of cultural labour. It is not merely a revelation, consequent upon the clearing away of social distortions and obstacles, of a pre-existing, natural state of bodily unity. The state of integration and movement flow achieved through ideokinesis or Alexander [Technique®] is an effect of practice; it is produced within the terms of a particular form of bodily knowledge. (Dempster 2002, 157)[30]

Dempster (2002, 162) further describes that, for the role of the teacher "as an exemplar of the method, what is important is the *freedom* of movement the teacher achieves within the constraints given by her own constitution and structure."[31] Here, the teacher is mod-eling how a student can connect with her or his anatomical truth through her or his own experience, as opposed to modeling an ideal to be copied.

Ideokinesis and other somatic practices work toward a refinement of bodily move-ment that strengthens and deepens the *body-mind integrity* of the dancer. Through observation, a practitioner can be trained to move with better structural support by co-ordinating movement with her or his own functional anatomy, thereby increasing her or his body's power. Such systems utilize a process of self-surveillance to identify and relinquish any limitations to the range and quality of movement that might be produced through censorship, subjection, or competition. For this reason, we term this self-sur-veillance *emancipatory*; it critically engages the body-mind in a dialogue with sociocul-turally prescribed habits and norms through creative means. So, as stated, emancipatory self-surveillance provides a way of pulling at the edges of subjection.

In her discussion of ideokinesis, Todd describes how developing a greater kinesthetic sense of the body through observation (of what is anatomically true) gives a greater in-sight into how the *form* of anatomy supports its *function*.[32] This produces an alternative to inefficient and habitually constructed body postures based on aesthetic, moral, or so-cial values. Todd explains that

> [a] familiar response is determined by our conditional reflexes. That is, the sensory-motor chain of reactions in our nerves and muscles has been gradually modified through association of ideas derived, not from mechanical or physical considerations of what balance means or how a really straight back looks, but from moral, that is so-cial concepts. (Todd 1937, 35)

Making a distinction between what is ideal and what is anatomically true is important because, in many cases, the idealized schema of an imitative dance form does not match the capacities of the actual, individual body trying to perform it. The consequence of this disparity impacts the body-mind integrity of the dancer because replicating what is ideal requires the sublimation of the awareness of what is anatomically true (for them), causing the disintegration of a body-mind connection.[33] The dancer is *emancipated* to experience anatomical truth forged by various forces on the psycho-physiology, rather than being subjected to an anatomical self-image that is socially prescribed from the outside. Clearly, any notion of competitively increasing awareness of one's anatomical truth is an irrelevant project, as each person is constituted from an entirely different set of circumstances, physicalities, and experiences, and there is no ideal neutral or natural state to aspire to. One way that the experiential depth of anatomical truth could be assessed is via self-authored dancing, where the capacity for the dancer to engage a broader range of muscle tones and movement decisions is observable. However, there is no codified standard through which to rank this kind of virtuosity. Therefore, attentiveness to the body-mind as it is in each moment supports the proliferation of individual experiences by dissolving the competitive, hierarchical, and aspirational framework of dance.

ATTENTION AND "SENSORY ACUITY"

Dempster explains how a somatic system such as ideokinesis provides a model where the power of surveillance and artistic choice is returned to the dancer. This revolution in the "technologies of the self" pertaining to dance can be traced to *the body-mind operations* at the heart of the practice and the body-states that feed this. The benefit of knowing how to practice emancipative self-surveillance, relinquishing all aspiration to allow muscle tone to soften, is that it allows dancers to sense their anatomical truth in greater detail. This is because relaxed stillness, rather than emptying the body of sensation, actually foregrounds the awareness of kinesthesia, or *sensory acuity*; it also allows for pleasure. Dempster explains this in regard to ideokinetic and release practices:

> There is an initial renunciation, constraint and denial of the body's desire for movement and activity. This "asceticism," to borrow Sontag's term, produces not paucity, but an excess of sensation and an enormously expanded capacity for kinaesthetic pleasure. In the states of stillness and silence fostered in this work, the focus of attention is not on a neutral(ised) but a libidinised body, with all the complexity and fluidity of relations between perception, action and desire that such a notion implies. (Dempster 2002, 219)

Dempster describes the role, or use, of pleasure in ideokinesis as a labor that is a "cultural accomplishment" (particularly for women, according to her feminist argument) because it addresses "issues of repression at a cellular level" (Goldberg 1996, 55, quoted in Dempster 2002, 217).

The acceptance of *things as they are* is a form of labor that resists the subjection to external power and the related impulses toward competition. This trust in the body and its knowledges overturns some key tenets of Western thought, pedagogy, and ideology. Dempster (2002, 206) goes on to explain that "ideokinesis seeks to address a culturally pervasive fear and mistrust of bodily experience, a somatophobia that Elizabeth Grosz has defined as foundational to Western philosophical thinking." Dempster goes on to suggest that the effectiveness of ideokinesis "is dependent upon the sensory acuity, imaginative ability and desire of the student." It is also dependent upon the use of *attention*, a key constituent of ideokinesis (and other forms of somatics), which activates an experience of the agency of a body's mind. In the preceding quote, Dempster (2002, 206, 228) emphasizes that this need not be a cognitive form of thought attention, but rather a "sensory acuity."

Particularly potent sensorial information can be experienced at the threshold between passive and active muscle tone, the "stillness and silence" that Dempster points to, at the juncture of ideokinesis and improvisation. This is where an ideated image transitions from stillness to movement. The release of tensile tissue states allows for the production of non-predetermined movement arising in response to the increased kinesthetic capacity and sensitivity of the body. If this traversal from stillness to movement is motivated by the desire of the body-mind and is negotiated through *sensation*, rather than willed into being through cognition, then it is possible to see how ideation (or what Bainbridge Cohen calls "somatization") can activate a *body's mind* to dance the body (Bainbridge Cohen 1994, 1; Dempster 2002, 125).[34] In arguing for a body's mind, we are not reinstating dualism, but are asserting a multiplicity of modes of cognition, thinking, awareness and intelligence that are not tied to language-based processes (Godard and Rolnik, 2008).[35]

It is in the transition from passive to active muscle tone that the initiation of each movement can be noticed. Which muscles switch on for an action to happen, in what way do they switch on, with what force, tone, or quality? If this activity is explored without the compulsion to produce movement too soon, then the threshold between being passive and being active can be extended, allowing all the miniscule detail of this transition to be experienced as a vast journey. This exercise enriches dance and particularly improvisation practice in two ways. First, it offers a way for a dancing subject to come to understand how *sensation* motivates the body, rather than language-based thought, and how, as a corollary, these practices can enable the subject to "transform his [or her] own mode of being" through attending to the physiological body and its knowledges as a source of authority (Foucault 1985, 30). It provides a tangible method of understanding what *the mind of the body* is, and what it feels like to cultivate a desire to move from a kinesthetic stimulus.

THE MIND OF THE BODY

Through practice, it is possible to allow the mind of the dancer's body to enact its agency in the production of movement (Bainbridge Cohen 1994; Dempster 2002).

This is a deeply sophisticated practice that, like ideokinesis, cannot be willed or forced through cortical thought, but occurs via the cultivation of a context in which the dancer's desire to move is activated at the bodily level. Activation can occur through a process where each increment of flesh is observed (felt, listened to, sensed) and accepted *as it is*. This psycho-physical practice is enacted through deep respiration and becoming aware of the sensational experience of one's own functional biology: its texture, weight, the function of the body's parts and how those parts connect and rely on each other. This is a way of gathering *somatic intelligence* (Goodall 1997, 20–23). Through this practice, the tonal quality of all the bodily tissues can be perceived, including visceral, connective, and nervous. What a body experiences is remembered in the cells and is expressed in terms of that cell's qualitative state. In the transition from passive to active, a dancer can perceive how the cellular memories leave traces within the tissues, producing sensations that desire to be expressed in movement. By sublimating cognitive control over the body, it is possible to follow the sensations that give those desires expression.

A cortical mind, experienced through the internal dialogue of thought, is implicated in the process, as its mode of expression is through the sociocultural medium of language. By cultivating the agency of a body-mind, without cognitive dominance but including a physical listening, artistic choices not only can be returned to the dancer and expanded, but more specifically can be returned to the body's mind (with its memories and desires). This is similar to how a system such as ideokinesis creates a situation in which the cellular intelligence of body-mind (in the case of ideokinesis, it is predominantly neuromuscular *ideation*) is privileged in the creative process (Sweigard 1974).[36] This system can be explored further in choreographic and improvisational practices as a methodology for the dancer's body-mind to drive the compositional decision-making in a dance performance.

The invisible (un)discipline of somatics is twofold: it is the dancer's self-reflexive criticality of noticing how sociocultural forces are impacting upon her or his body-mind, and it is in the delicate work of allowing these inhibitions to slip away by continually refreshing both the attention to the anatomical truth of the body and the acceptance of that anatomy *as it is*. This is a continual process of *subjectivation* that creates space for the body's mind to emerge and enact the physical thoughts, needs, and desires of the flesh.

CORPOREAL FREEDOM AND INNOVATION

An (un)disciplined relinquishment of aspiration is the basis from which a released approach to dancing opens up a range of muscle tones and allows creative expansion of the aesthetic possibilities produced. When this primary (un)learning of emancipative self-surveillance has occurred at the level of the muscles, the progression from stillness into action can begin from an entirely different basis, and can extend the qualitative palate of available muscle tones.

The somatic work that dancers have done to experience their anatomical truth and undo their habits opens up the range of potential tonal states that the bodily tissues can be in, which produces a kind of *freedom* (Louppe 2010). Cultivation of corporeal freedom leads to innovation through the validation of movement that escapes standards of codified movement practices. What is most pertinent to the ideological tension between imitative and self-observational practices does not concern discipline per se, but the question of *where site(s) of authority exist in the dancing*. As dance theorist Glenna Baston (2009, 1) explains, it is not the issue of labor that is at the core of this schism, but that "somatic education differs first from traditional dance pedagogy in its philosophical basis—that of dismembering mind-body dualism in pursuit of personal autonomy." Particularly when a dance is improvised, the site of authority is further reconfigured from the tradition of the choreographer directing the dancer from outside the dance, to the dancer(s) directing themselves from within the dance (and in response to each other) (Banes 1983).[37] This also requires a reversal of the traditional dualistic hierarchy at the level of the individual body-mind. As the subject observes and responds to the state of her or his own tissues, rather than initiating from a cognitive basis, the movement is instigated via what a dancer is able to perceive in her or his sensorium. This allows for the cultivation of different types of sensitivities, in particular the ways in which a dancer comes to know her or his own corporeality as an object of a specific kind of attention.

Therefore, while somatics is considered an essential constituent of any contemporary dance syllabus, historically, the university system has struggled to negotiate the seemingly incongruous binary of unprofessional somatic practices that divest notions of hierarchical power, and elite, competitive, vocational training methodologies that construct an articulate but arguably docile body (Dempster 1985; Vertinsky 2010). In somatics, rather than the observed subject of Foucault's oppressive disciplines who is controlled through the documentation of examinations and surveillance, we have the self-observing subject who is witnessing her or his anatomical truth in relationship with her or his social, historical, and cultural self. This might appear to be a case of replacing one ideal, the docile body, with another ideal that is emancipated and free. However, Foucault's theory of how aesthetic, moral, or social forces became internalized through various body disciplines is founded on the political understanding that self-surveillance ultimately benefits powers external to the body. In contrast, somatic practices benefit each individual's anatomical functioning, which is *self-empowering*, and its genesis is at the level of muscle tissue tonality.

Here, we are not introducing the transcendental phenomenological subject back into dialogue with Foucault. This observing subject is not one who "places its own point of view at the origin of all historicity—which, in short, leads to a transcendental consciousness" (Foucault 1970, xiv). This is a subject who is both the product and producer (object and subject) of knowledge and power that is somatically based and operating at the perception-action nexus of the individual, not an ahistorical subject. This kind of dancing subject has emerged at a particular point in history by and through the dance practices that are widely explored in Western theater contemporary dance, where training in both somatic and codified knowledges coexist in the academy. The reason for distinguishing between prohibitive and emancipative self-surveillance here is because contemporary dance is situated across this juncture: between the control and release of the body.

The various somatic approaches are *techniques of the body* producing a very specific kind of virtuosity or aptitude: the ability to move in, out, and around their docile or subjected body in an imaginative and powerful reconstitution of their corporeal behaviors. This is technique liberated from the conditions of competition and all of its trappings. And yet, when it operates in the highly visible context of performance, it may be judged in relation to the still dominant, competitive modes of codified dance. In the suburban backyard, the jazz dancer's spectacular choreography "wins" over the unassertive expression of her friend. What is required is a new level of dance literacy that recognizes the emerging virtuosity of attention and responsiveness in the young contemporary dancer, alongside the more familiar skill of the jazz dancer as she commands her body and the space around it. It takes new spectatorial skill to see the former dancer's performance for what it is: an *aesthetics of resistance*.

Notes

1. *Somatics* was a term coined by philosopher Thomas Hanna (1928–1990) in 1976 to identify the field of philosophical inquiry that explores notions of body-mind integration in both theory and practice. The term is derived from the Greek word *soma*, meaning "the living body"; Hanna (1976; 1995, 341) extends it to mean "the body as perceived from within by first-person perception." A few examples of Western somatic practices are Feldenkrais, Idiokinesis, and the Alexander Technique*.

2. As Helen Thomas (2003, 46) notes, in Foucault's philosophical approach he "is directing attention towards the material body" and "the transformation of the body in history" in an unprecedented way.

3. While Franko observes that Foucault's notion of bodily inscription has most often been taken up to discuss choreography rather than technique, we find in Dempster's engagement with Foucault (among others) a productive focus on technique and training. Created from the root words *ideo* (imagery) and *kinesis* (movement), *ideokinesis* is the name given to an evolving practice that aims to increase the efficiency of skeletomuscular alignment through the use of imagery. This practice was developed by pioneers Mabel Elsworth Todd (1880–1956) and her mentees Barbara Clark (1889–1982) and Lulu Sweigard (1895–1974).

4. These terms have emerged from Wait's PhD thesis "Improvised Composition," University of New South Wales, 2018.

5. Some Western examples of codified forms used in (or adapted for) professional contexts are classical ballet, jazz (or jazz ballet), Graham, Cunningham, Horton, and Limon techniques. It is not that choreographers necessarily rejected softness in the process of codifying their vocabulary—quite the opposite in many cases (for example, Holm, Horton, and Hawkins)—but softness is a quality that can be lost over time in the facsimile process of imitation. A possible reason for why imitating movement can reduce its softness might

be to do with the dominance of the visual senses in the process of replicating form, rather than prioritizing somesthesia, in order to match the tone of students' body tissues to those of their teacher (which occurs in somatics via a specific kind of touch).

6. Sourced on May 5, 2016, from http://www.oxforddictionaries.com/

7. It could be argued that the reverse is also true: a somatically trained dancer may not have developed the kind of kinesthetic mapping and control of the body required of an imitative form.

8. *Psychosomatic* is a term employed by somatic pioneers Mable Elsworth Todd (1874–1956) and Frederick Matthias Alexander (1869–1955) to describe the interrelation of the body and mind. Dance scholar Michael Huxley (2011) identifies the emergence of this term, which does not presuppose an original or natural state, but refers to what might be a collection of possible, and continually changing, states of being.

9. Dempster (2005) also uses the term *(un)disciplined* to describe issues concerning the academic study of dance in the 1980s.

10. In this chapter we combine Dempster's focus on the nature of dance research in the academy as relatively *(un)disciplined* (2005), and her work on pedagogy (2002). In the former, her use of *discipline* is not connected to Foucault's use of the same term.

11. As Foucault (1977, 170) notes, "Discipline 'makes' individuals; it is the specific technique of a power that regards individuals both as objects and as instruments of its exercise."

12. As Mark Franko (2011, 98) points out, "this art is never named" by Foucault.

13. This notion of the sociopolitical function of dance has been taken up in dance studies by Randy Martin (1998) and Andrew Hewitt (2005), and later still by Lepecki (2015) in his use of William Forsythe's term "system of command" as applied to choreography.

14. The mobilization of the term *choreography* in its expanded form circulates broadly in dance, visual arts, and performance studies. It has been significantly deployed in this way by writers such as Jenn Joy in *The Choreographic* (2014, 20); "How does dance encounter other media (photography, sculpture as examples) materially and conceptually to undo notions of media specificity?" The disappearance of dancing as a part of choreography goes hand in hand with this. In the Australian context, we would cite as evidence the withdrawal of Australian contemporary dance from programming at the Sydney Opera House since 2014, the closure of more dance programs in public universities, and the increased visibility of choreography in the visual arts milieu, such as Sydney's 20th Biennale of Sydney in 2016.

15. "Subjectivation" is defined by philosopher Gilles Deleuze (1988, 104) as "the relation to oneself."

16. An extension of Foucault's theories of surveillance to include non-dancerly kinds of self-surveillance is also proposed by Paulo Vaz and Fernanda Bruno (2003).

17. Dance theorist Jill Green (2000), whose work was instrumental to the popularity of Foucault in dance studies, has also described somatic education as *emancipatory pedagogy*.

18. Jill Green (1999, 2000) analyzed somatics through a sociocultural lens using Foucault's theories of subjection; Dempster (2002, 36) notes the relevance of Foucault's theories to ballet: "Michel Foucault's elaboration of the development and effective functioning of disciplinary regimes offers a productive mode of analysis of the discipline of ballet." She draws on the unpublished thesis of Taze Yanick (1998), and an article by Shona Innes (1988). These follow Susan Leigh Foster's (1986, 1997) references to Foucault. In the former, she follows Foucault's lead in *The Order of Things* in taking a historical approach to account for epistemological breaks within a body discipline, resulting in new formations of the

(dancing) subject (Foster 1986). In the latter, she mimics Foucault's description of body techniques in her account of "the theatrical dancer" (Foster 1997, 236). On Foster's (1995) edited book, reviewer Joellen A. Meglin (1997, 92) writes, "does anyone *not* cite Foucault anymore?" Most interestingly there, Joseph Roach (Foster 1997, 150) points to the influence of Foucault on "the reigning discursive vocabulary, which enables practitioners to imagine issues of power and knowledge in corporeal terms." In *Exhausting Dance* (2006, 8), Lepecki briefly cites Foucault's theory of subjectivity and "technologies of the self" alongside Deleuze's development of the same, which he sees as well matched to the creative work of the artists he cites. And Mark Franko (2011) argues for the choreographic discourse in the theoretical, and vice versa. See also Helen Thomas (2003) for an account of Foucault's approach to the body, and Ramsay Burt (2004) on Foucault versus Judith Butler.

19. Ballet was codified in the eighteenth century, within the same classical period in which Foucault locates his research for *Discipline and Punish*. Franko (2011) also makes this connection. Foucault's radio lecture published in 2009 mentions dance in passing, and Franko takes this text up in his 2011 article.

20. On space, see "The Art of Distribution" (Foucault 1977, 141–149) and on time, "The Control of Activity" (1977, 149–156).

21. Ness (2011) also discusses the absence of dance as subject matter in Foucault's work at length.

22. Ness (2011, 21) acknowledges possible affinities between Foucault's work and concerns central to dance studies: "This absence of any heated, dance-centered, critical response to at least the very early Foucault . . . may indicate that Foucault's archeological and genealogical projects and interests somehow still are aligned, and profoundly so, with those of dance studies."

23. Ness may be referring to Foster's (1986) use of Foucault's method in *Reading Dancing*, where she focuses on canonical American artists to represent specific periods in the development of dancing subjects across the twentieth century.

24. Dempster (2002) goes into much detail regarding ballet as a system of bodily subjection in Chapter 2, "The Body of Ballet."

25. In contrast to ideokinesis, which is taught widely in an unregulated form, certifications have been established for somatic practices: Skinner Release Technique™ (SRT), Body-Mind Centering® (BMC), and Alexander Technique®, among others.

26. This has religious provenance in the fourteenth century according to Foucault (1977, 161–162): "the striving of the whole community towards salvation became the collective, permanent competition of individuals being classified in relation to one another." The instruments of this were "hierarchical observation, normalizing judgment and their combination in a procedure that is specific to it, the examination" (Foucault 1977, 170).

27. Green (1999, 89) supports this idea by suggesting that "the ideal is unattainable and destructive." We would like to emphasize that we are not proposing that codified dance is inherently *bad*, or that somatic-led dancing is necessarily *good*, because that would require a further judgment of the contexts to which these methods are contingent. More simply, we explore the relation between aptitude and subjection through these different approaches to dancing.

28. *Somatic intelligence* is the term Jane Goodall (1997, 20–23) uses to describe the somatic information that can be collected through practice. Erin Brannigan (2010, 13–14) defines *somatic intelligence* as "a model of experience that places the body at the site where feelings

or sensations are registered, feelings that may be untranslatable into language or any other medium, but which accumulate as corporeal knowledge."

29. Bonnie Bainbridge Cohen (1994, 10) describes an embodied approach to the study of anatomy as *experiential anatomy*.

30. Todd (1937) also does not suggest that there is a natural pre-discursive body that is made available via ideokinesis.

31. As Dempster (2002, 171) notes, "The inter-subjective, identificatory aspect of ideokinetic method, so pronounced in Clark's recollections of Todd's teaching, is a crucial factor in its pedagogical transmission and effectiveness."

32. Todd (1937, 35–36) explains that "to do this we must make use of the *kinaesthetic* sensations coming to the central nervous system from every bone and joint, every ligament and muscle, just as surely as and more constantly than the peripheral sensations of touch, sight or sound."

33. There is a third category offered by Foster (1997, 240) of "the perceived body," which is the distorted body image resulting from the failure to realize the ideal one.

34. Bainbridge Cohen (1994, 1) defines *somatization* as "engaging the kinesthetic experience directly, in contrast to 'visualization' which utilizes visual imagery to evoke a kinesthetic experience. Through somatization the body cells are informing the brain as well as the brain informing the cells."

35. The intention here is to articulate different kinds of mind as alternative and creatively generative states of being, without implementing a reversal of traditional dualistic hierarchy. French kinesiologist and theorist Hubert Godard's (2008) research is useful here in that he refers to neurophysiologic research that identifies two "levels of analyzers" that effect the experience of either an *objective* or *subjective* sense of self. He proposes that cortical consciousness is one that is focused in a way that can interpret language, and subcortical consciousness can access the kinds of somatic intelligence that escapes language.

36. *Ideation* is the process of using images to re-educate a neuromuscular system in ideokinesis (Sweigard 1974).

37. For a detailed account of the "democratic" performance work of the Judson Dance Theatre in the early 1960s in New York (which owed much to Anna Halprin and Margaret H'Doubler), including the emergence of improvisation as a performance form, see Banes (1983).

References

Alexander, F. Matthias. 1932. *The Use of the Self: Its Conscious Direction in Relation to Diagnosis, Functioning and the Control of Reaction*. London: Methuen.

Badiou, Alain. 2009. *In Praise of Love*, translated by Peter Bush. New York: The New Press.

Bainbridge Cohen, Bonnie. 1994. *Sensing, Feeling, and Action: The Experimental Anatomy of Body-Mind Centering*. New York: Contact Editions.

Banes, Sally. 1983. *Democracy's Body: Judson Dance Theatre, 1962–1964*. Ann Arbor, MI: UMI Research Press.

Baston, Glenna. 2009. "Somatic Studies in Dance." *International Association for Dance Medicine & Science* 1–6. www.iadms.org. Online: https://cdn.ymaws.com/www.iadms.org/resource/resmgr/imported/info/somatic_studies.pdf . Accessed May 21, 2018.

Brannigan, Erin. 2010. *Moving across Disciplines: Dance in the Twenty-First Century*. Platform Paper No. 25. Sydney: Currency House.

Bruno, Fernanda, and Paulo Vaz. 2003. "Types of Self-Surveillance: From Abnormality to Individuals 'at Risk.'" *Surveillance & Society* 1(3): 272–291.

Burt, Ramsay. 2004. "Genealogy and Dance History: Foucault, Rainer, Bausch and De Keersmaeker." In *Of the Presence of the Body: Essays on Dance and Performance Theory*, edited by André Lepecki, 29–44. Middletown, CT: Wesleyan University Press.

Deleuze, Gilles. 1988. *Foucault*, translated by Seán Hand. Minneapolis: University of Minnesota Press.

Dempster, Elizabeth. 1985. "Image Based Movement Education." *Writings on Dance: Ideokinesis and Dancemaking* 1: 13–15.

Dempster, Elizabeth. 1995–1996. "Explorations within the New Dance Aesthetic: Eva Karczag Interview." *Writings on Dance: Exploring the New Dance Aesthetic* 14: 39–52.

Dempster, Elizabeth. 2002. "An Embodied Politics: Radical Pedagogies of Contemporary Dance." PhD diss., Monash University.

Dempster, Elizabeth. 2005. "Undisciplined Subjects, Unregulated Practices: Dancing in the Academy." Published in conference proceedings for *Dance Rebooted: Initializing the Grid* by Ausdance National, Melbourne. PDF 1–11. http://ausdance.org.au/articles/details/undisciplined-subjects-unregulated-practices. Accessed September 23, 2016.

Dempster, Elizabeth. 2007. "Not Dancing under Modernism: Duncan and the Postmoderns." *Writings on Dance* 24: 49–58.

Foster, Susan Leigh. 1986. *Reading Dancing: Bodies and Subjects in Contemporary American Dance*. Berkeley: University of California Press.

Foster, Susan Leigh. 1995. *Choreographing History*. Bloomington: Indiana University Press.

Foster, Susan Leigh. 1997. "Dancing Bodies." In *Meaning in Motion: New Cultural Studies in Dance*, edited by Jane C. Desmond, 235–258. Durham, NC: Duke University Press.

Foster, Susan Leigh. 2002. *Dances That Describe Themselves: The Improvised Choreography of Richard Bull*. Middleton, CT: Wesleyan University Press.

Foucault, Michel. 1970. *The Order of Things: An Archeology of the Human Sciences*. New York: Vintage Books.

Foucault, Michel. 1977. *Discipline and Punish: The Birth of the Prison*, translated by Alan Sheridan. London: Penguin Books.

Foucault, Michel. 1985. *The History of Sexuality*, Volume 2: *The Use of Pleasure*, translated by Robert Hurley. New York: Random House.

Foucault, Michel. 2009. *Les Corps utopiques suivi de Les Hétérotopies*. Paris: Nouvelles Editions Lignes.

Franko, Mark. 2011. "Archaeological Choreographic Practices: Foucault and Forsythe." *History of the Human Sciences* 24(4): 97–112.

Godard, Hubert, and Suely Rolnik. 2008. "Blindsight." In *Peripheral Vision and Collective Body*, edited by Corinne Dissens, 178–179. Bolzano, Italy: Museion, Hatje Cantz.

Goldberg, Marianne. 1996. "Coming into Parts." *Writings on Dance* 14: 53–58.

Goodall, Jane. 1997. "Knowing What You Are Doing." *The Performance Space Quarterly* 14: 20–23.

Green, Jill. 1999. "Somatic Authority and the Myth of the Ideal Body in Dance Education." *Dance Research Journal* 31(2): 80–100.

Green, Jill. 2000. "Emancipatory Pedagogy? Women's Bodies and the Creative Process in Dance." *Frontiers: A Journal of Women Studies* 21(3): 124–140.

Grosz, Elizabeth. 1994. *Volatile Bodies: Towards a Corporeal Feminism*. Sydney: Allen & Unwin.

Hanna, Thomas. 1976. "The Field of Somatics." *Somatics* 1: 30–34.

Hanna, Thomas. 1995. "What Is Somatics?" In *Bone, Breath and Gesture: Practices of Embodiment*, edited by Don Hanlon Johnson, 341–352. Berkeley, CA: North Atlantic Books.

Hewitt, Andrew. 2005. *Social Choreography*. Durham, NC: Duke University Press.

Huxley, Michael. 2011. "F. Matthias Alexander and Mable Elsworth Todd: Proximities, Practices and the Psycho-Physical." *Journal of Dance & Somatic Practice* 3(1–2): 25–42.

Innes, Shona. 1988. "The Teaching of Ballet." *Writings on Dance* 3: 37–49.

Joy, Jenn. 2014. *The Choreographic*. Cambridge, MA: MIT Press.

Lepecki, André. 2006. *Exhausting Dance*. New York: Routledge.

Lepecki, André. 2015. "The Choreopolitical: Agency in the Age of Control." In *The Routledge Companion to Art and Politics*, edited by Randy Martin, 44–52. London: Routledge.

Louppe, Laurence. 2010. *Poetics of Contemporary Dance*, translated by Sally Gardner. London: Dance Books.

Martin, Randy. 1998. *Critical Moves: Dance Studies in Theory and Politics*. Durham, NC: Duke University Press.

Meglin, Joellen. 1997. "Review: Feminism, the Academic Moment, and Research Rigor." *Dance Chronicle* 20(1): 87–98.

Ness, Sally Ann. 2011. "Foucault's Turn from Phenomenology: Implications for Dance Studies." *Dance Research Journal* 43(2): 19–32.

Sweigard, Lulu. 1974. *Human Movement Potential: Its Ideokinetic Facilitation*. New York: Dodd, Mead.

Thomas, Helen. 2003. *The Body, Dance and Cultural Theory*. Houndmills, Basingstoke: Palgrave Macmillan.

Todd, Mabel. 1937. *The Thinking Body*. New York: Princeton Book.

Vertinsky, Patricia. 2010. "From Physical Educators to Mothers of the Dance: Margaret H'Doubler and Martha Hill." *The International Journal of the History of Sport* 27(7): 1113–1132.

Wait, Nalina. "Improvised Composition." PhD diss., University of New South Wales. In progress.

Yanick, Taze. 1998. "Choreographing the Politics of Space." PhD diss., State University of New York.

CHAPTER 13

RECLAIMING COMPETITIVE TANGO

The Rise of Argentina's Campeonato Mundial

JULIET MCMAINS

SINCE tango-mania first gripped Europe and North America in 1912, Argentine national identity has been hostage to the tango. Born in the slums and *conventillos* (immigrant tenement houses) of Buenos Aires, tango was scorned by Argentina's elite until international obsession with a dance they considered the purview of ruffians, pimps, and whores turned into Argentina's global calling card. The scandal of tango's choreography, which featured African-inspired *cortes* (cuts) and *quebradas* (breaks) in the flow of movement that sent hips swinging and thighs brushing while the dancing couple clung together in full body contact, was as distasteful to "respectable" Argentines as it was titillating to the European and North American public. The global tango craze, however, brought the relatively obscure nation of Argentina such international attention that national pride soon trumped class rivalry and racial bias. Indignation that such a low-class practice of Afro-Argentine origins had come to define the nation in the global imaginary soon gave way to attempts by Argentine elites to control that image by developing a more "refined" style of dancing tango that departed both from tango in the *arrabales* (working-class neighborhoods) of Buenos Aires and from the misappropriations of foreigners (Savigliano 1995). Although tango's association with its African origins had already faded, in part due to the surge of European immigration that reduced Argentina's black population to less than 2% by 1900 (Chasteen 2004), tango crossed class lines to become national culture due to its exoticization abroad. Tango continued to develop and flourish in Argentina, becoming the country's most popular music and dance during tango's golden age (1935–1955). Concurrently, foreign appropriations of tango were thriving, especially the English style of tango, performed in ballroom dance competitions across Europe.

The parallel trajectories of these tangos did not intersect again until the unexpected success of a 1983 Paris debut and a 1985 Broadway run of the show *Tango Argentino* ignited the twentieth century's second tango craze. The stark contrast of the Argentine style performed in the show to the ballroom tangos familiar to European and North American audiences proved to be a stimulus for the emergence of an international Argentine tango industry as well as a marketing hurdle for those forging a living through it. Teachers of the Argentine style were faced with the challenge of distinguishing their tango from ballroom versions. One of the primary points of distinction they maintained was that as an improvisational personal expression, Argentine tango could not be judged in competition. Given the extent to which competitions shaped the development of ballroom tango styles, it is not surprising that most Argentine tango dancers were dismissive and even disparaging about tango as competition. Competitions had produced ballroom tango, which many Argentines viewed as a grotesque caricature of their cultural heritage. Despite the disdain many tango dancers maintained for competitions, in 2003 the city of Buenos Aires began sponsoring an annual international tango competition, billed as the *Campeonato Mundial de Baile de Tango* (World Tango Dance Championships). This event, commonly referred to as the Mundial (World Cup), has been steadily growing in size and global status ever since, effecting significant changes in the aesthetic values, social practice, and business of Argentine tango. In 2016, I attended the Mundial in Buenos Aires and its subsidiary in San Francisco, the Argentine Tango USA Championships, in an effort to understand why Argentine tango dancers, who had disparaged competition for so long, are now entering this competition in record numbers. Based on fieldwork, interviews, media representations, and my own experience as a longtime dancer of Argentine and ballroom tango, I argue that Argentines are redefining tango competition on their own terms in ways that reclaim the dance from foreigners, while simultaneously reproducing some of the troubling consequences the competition frame has effected on ballroom tango. I invoke comparison of two broad tango traditions: that which evolved primarily inside Argentina, and that which developed outside of Argentina in ballroom dance settings. On the ballroom side, I examine English-style tango, also called international style, which, although danced in both social and competition settings, is so strongly shaped by its competition history that I address it almost exclusively as a competition form. In contrast, a vibrant social practice of Argentine tango has been maintained through the tradition of the *milongas* (public tango dances). Social Argentine tango differs markedly from the stage form, *tango escenario*, popularized through the aforementioned show *Tango Argentino*, although both social and stage Argentine tango share more in common with each other than with ballroom forms. Competitive Argentine tango has recently entered into this web of tango styles, resulting in emergence of yet another Argentine tango substyle, sometimes referred to as Mundial or *campeonato* style.

ENGLISH-STYLE COMPETITIVE BALLROOM DANCING RESHAPES TANGO

Compared side by side, major aesthetic differences between Argentine and ballroom tangos are unmistakable. Whereas Argentine tango dancers begin with their feet a few inches apart and lean forward to rest their hearts and cheeks together, international-style ballroom tango dancers maintain connection at their legs and hips while extending their chests and heads away from one another. In simplified terms, Argentine style tango dancers form an "A" shape when their two bodies meet, and ballroom tango dancers create a "V." Other discrepancies stem from these postural features. For example, in Argentine tango, dancers keep their heads and chests still while their legs and feet engage in playful hooks, wraps, and displacements. Ballroom tango dancers, on the other hand, move their legs in harmony so that dramatic effect is created through whipping actions of the head and upper spine. This contrast can, in part, be traced back to cultural mistranslation on tango's first transatlantic journey, when Europeans interpreted tango's passion as anger, failing to recognize that tango passion was more often produced through control and sublimation of desire invoked through sexual, class, and racial difference. Even more important than prudishness or displaced passion, however, ballroom dance competitions have determined ballroom tango's aesthetic values.

Evidence of ballroom tango competitions can be traced back to tango's infancy, when French dancer and impresario Camille de Rhynal modified tango to make it palatable for ballroom dancing, hosting a tango competition in Paris in 1907 (Richardson 1931). Rhynal's sanitized tango soon entered the repertoire of English ballrooms, where it was standardized alongside the waltz, foxtrot, and one step at a series of conferences convened by *The Dancing Times* in the early 1920s. Prior to the "Tango Conference" of 1922, European interpretations of tango differed so radically that some complained, "Everyone did it differently, with a result that only those who learned it together could dance together" (quoted in Richardson 1981, 40). Standardization of the steps, rhythms, and techniques not only helped popularize social tango, but facilitated the growth of ballroom dance competitions, which became the main focus of English dance teachers as their unified focus solidified after the founding of the ballroom branch of the Imperial Society of Teachers of Dancing in 1924.

Through the mid-1930s, tango practiced in European ballrooms shared with its Argentine namesake an emphasis on smooth, "cat-like and sinuous" movement (Hallewell 1991, 176). However, the sensation of competitors Eddie Camp and Alida Pasqual in the British Amateur Championships at the 1935 Blackpool Festival revolutionized the English tango. Camp's style was described by ballroom dancer Kit Hallewell as an "explosion of vigorous action from stillness." He continued, "the body stillness was itself instinct with the expectation of the next action. He had this ability to rivet the spectator's attention in this expectation, and when the action came the crowd rose to it" (quoted in Denniston 2008, 88). The juxtaposition of explosive action and controlled stillness was so visually exciting that competitors thereafter copied their approach.

The new staccato tango departed from the smooth style of both earlier ballroom interpretations and tango as practiced in Argentina. The success of the staccato tango was not based on its pleasurable physical sensations for dancers, but its power to capture the attention of spectators and judges. Camp's contemporary Monsieur Pierre, a revered authority on Latin ballroom dances, explained in a 1936 article that he could not enjoy dancing the staccato tango. Its popularity, he insisted, was based entirely on its effectiveness as a theatrical trope. "I believe that if competitions and demonstrations were to suddenly stop, the staccato Tango would not last another week!" (quoted in Denniston 2008, 89). Since the 1930s, competitions have only become more central to the ballroom dance industry, and the staccato quality of ballroom tango remains its most salient feature.

Other characteristics of international tango similarly evolved in response to the competition frame, which impacted tango's development in two ways. First, how the dance looked to judges took precedence over how the dance felt to its practitioners, drawing ballroom tango further away from its social functions based in courtship, community, and play. It is hard to imagine, for example, how head flicks commonly used in international tango steps such as the progressive link, contra check, and Spanish drag could have evolved in a social context given their potential for discomfort and even pain. I recall a day in 1995 when I woke up at 5 a.m. in excruciating pain, unable to turn my head, the day after I received a tango coaching session focused on these whiplash actions.[1] Although I never really enjoyed dancing ballroom tango, it was a requirement to participate in competitions, which highlights how the grouping of tango, waltz, foxtrot, quickstep, and Viennese waltz into a single category of competition eroded differences in technique and vocabulary between dances that in their cultures of origin shared few aesthetic qualities. Many sequences, such as the fallaway reverse slip pivot, are used so commonly across the dances that some lament that the ballroom dances are indistinguishable from one another. The posture in tango differs from that of other ballroom dances only in the placement of the woman's hand, which is suspended like a knife under her partner's triceps, thumb hooked under his armpit (Figure 13.1). Otherwise, the extreme shape of the dancers' upper spines, which spiral away from one another at a distance nearing two feet, is identical to that used in waltz, foxtrot, quickstep, and Viennese waltz. This shape is bewildering to many spectators, who imagine that, like Fred Astaire and Ginger Rogers, they would not "enjoy it half as much as dancing cheek to cheek."[2] This posture makes sense, however, in the context of competitions, which reward dancers who dominate space.

Many people assume that since tango is, after all, a Latin American dance, that it would be included in the Latin category of ballroom competitions. However, the other Latin ballroom dances (rumba, samba, cha cha cha, and paso doble) were popularized and standardized much later and were thus included together with the American swing (renamed jive) in a new category of competition called "Latin and America," later shortened to Latin (Richardson 1981). Due to this accident of timing, the tango remained in the "standard" category of ballroom competition (which, in another

FIGURE 13.1. Evgeniy Mayorov and Olga Lisovskaya competing in international style tango at the 2015 United States DanceSport Championships.

Photo by Alexander Rowan.

troubling naming convention, is the corollary to "Latin"), resulting in an English tango that shares more aesthetic values with the waltz, originating in Austria, than with the samba, a dance from Argentina's Brazilian neighbor. The Imperial Society vigorously exported English-style competitive ballroom dancing across Europe and Asia, as well as to its colonies in Australia, North America, Africa, and India. After conquering such a large percentage of the world market, English-style ballroom dancing was renamed international style in the 1960s. By the time Argentine tango recaptured the global spotlight in the 1980s and 1990s, international-style ballroom tango was deeply entrenched in most social dance markets that Argentine tango dancers entered.

THE MUNDIAL AS ARGENTINA'S NATIONAL BRAND

Following the military overthrow of Argentine populist president Juan Perón in 1955, the tango was suppressed by the new military dictatorship, which persecuted and imprisoned tango musicians, banned public gatherings, and promoted rock and roll music over the national tango that had been endorsed by Perón (Denniston 2008). Over the next thirty years, tango fell into near obscurity in Argentina, until the triumph of tango abroad once again inspired Argentines at home to reconsider its value. As *Tango Argentino* (and subsequent shows such as *Forever Tango*) stimulated the growth of Argentine tango in social dance communities throughout Europe and North America in the 1990s, demand for Argentine tango teachers rose. Economic opportunity, buoyed by a nationalist impulse to prevent another wave of tango misappropriation by foreigners, inspired many Argentines to travel abroad to work in the new Argentine tango industry. When the Argentine economic crisis of 2001 resulted in a devalued peso that transformed Argentina into a bargain basement travel destination, tango finally returned home. Cultivation of tango tourism became a key feature of government economic recovery strategies, resulting in the rapid growth of tango tourism, rising from 2.9 million to over 4 million visitors per year between 2000 and 2005 (Fitch 2015). The tourist demand for tango soon revived interest in tango among Argentines themselves, many of whom launched careers in the booming tango business.

The *Campeonato Mundial de Tango* of Buenos Aires is part of the two-week *Tango Buenos Aires Festival y Mundial* held at the end of August, which in 2016 featured over 150 concerts, performances, lectures, films, milongas, and classes, all free and open to the public. Dozens of music offerings included concerts by tango legends Walter Ríos Octeto, Horacio Salgan's Quinteto Real, Color Tango, Sexteto Mayor, Diego Schissi Quinteto, Tanghetto, and a full-length production of Piazzolla's tango-opera *María de Buenos Aires* at the Teatro Colón. Dance fans could choose from a large selection of tango stage shows and exhibitions, or could participate in workshops and social dancing. Despite the impressive lineup of 600 music and dance artists, including the greatest living legends of tango, each year the festival program showcases the dance championship as its main attraction. The festival culminates in the competition finals at Luna Park, a stadium capable of seating more than 8,000 spectators.

Not only is the competition free to watch, it is also free to enter and open to any dancer, with no differentiation by age or status as amateur or professional. The championship offers only two categories: *tango de pista* (dance floor tango) and *tango escenario* (stage tango). *Tango de pista*, which was called *tango de salon* until the category was renamed in 2013, ostensibly represents tango as it is danced socially in the milongas. Couples are permitted to do any figures in common social use, such as *giros* (turns), *barridas* (sweeps of the foot), *sacadas* (displacements of the legs), *enrosques* (corkscrew actions of the legs), and *lápices* (pencil-like drawings of the feet), as long as the couple never breaks their embrace or lifts both feet off the floor in jumps or lifts, which are explicitly prohibited. In *tango escenario*, each couple performs a choreographed duet to a song of their own choosing and can incorporate all the actions excluded from *tango de pista*, including *ganchos* (hooks), *boleos* (leg flicks), lifts, tricks, and steps that break the embrace.

The production values of the Tango Buenos Aires Festival (Tango BA) and the World Cup are exceptionally high. A fifty-six-page color program in Spanish and English detailing all festival event times, locations, and ticket procedures is widely distributed. In a city that does not even publish bus schedules, this level of centralized organization is astounding. Even more surprising, events start and end on time, which is remarkable in a culture where time is so flexible that arriving two hours late could still mean arriving early. Such punctuality is facilitated by staff members who are posted at every corner to guide and assist festival attendees. The grandeur and elegance of the festival's main venue, the Usina del Arte, a recently refurbished electric plant boasting stages and foyers of flawlessly polished wood, is a sharp contrast to the dilapidated buildings that tango dancers usually inhabit, where missing floorboards and three-inch splinters regularly threaten injury. Professional camera crews project live editing of multi-camera shots onto large screens during most festival performances, enabling audiences to enjoy close-up views of dancers' feet and violin players' bowing techniques. Lighting designers create drama and spectacle with bursts of color, not only in the theaters, but even on the exterior of the Usina building, which is illuminated in pink lights flanking a floating hologram of the Tango BA logo.

The ubiquitous Tango BA logo and its similarity to the city's BA tourism logo, which shares the same stylized "BA" letters, highlight the city's motives for investing such extensive resources in the tango festival. It is a tourism-generating machine, organized around tango as national brand. Even though festival attendees do not pay for tickets, the city is banking that out-of-town guests will liberally spend on hotels, taxis, restaurants, tango lessons, tango shoes, and tango clothes, most of which generate substantial tax revenue for the government. The festival draws Argentines from provinces and cities outside the capital, but the performance of tango as a modern, central, and well-supported feature of the city's cultural life is targeted to foreigners. The goal of promoting foreign tourism through the Mundial has been transparent since its creation. At the close of the first championship in 2003, the newspaper *Pagina 12* triumphantly reported statistics on festival-induced tourism.

> *La magnitud que alcanzó el festival hizo que comenzara a ingresar a la agenda del turismo nacional e internacional. Un 42 por ciento de los visitantes extranjeros que asistieron a los conciertos y clases llegaron motivados exclusivamente por el evento. Estos turistas gastaron un promedio de 242 pesos por día y permanecerán en la ciudad un promedio de 17 noches. El 62 por ciento compró discos y el 47 por ciento zapatos de tango, según una encuesta que hizo el gobierno de la ciudad de Buenos Aires.* (The magnitude of the festival means it will start to enter the national and international tourism agenda. Forty-two percent of the foreign visitors that attended concerts and classes came exclusively for the event. These tourists spent an average of 242 pesos a day and stayed in the city an average of 17 nights. Sixty-two percent bought CDs and 47 percent bought tango shoes, according to a survey by the city of Buenos Aires.) (Micheletto 2003)

Tourist attendance at the Mundial has been steadily growing since, especially after it was merged with the city's International Tango Festival and moved to August in 2008, just a year after right-leaning businessman Mauricio Macri became mayor. Prioritizing tourist access by rescheduling the event to coincide with European and North American summer travel seasons exemplifies Macri's approach to tango as cultural commodity for export. Macri's declaration that tango is the *soja porteña* (soybean of Buenos Aires) during the 2010 festival has been widely cited as evidence of his investment in tango as an exportable mass commodity, at the expense of its artistic growth in local communities (Gubner 2014; Luker 2016). The 2016 festival attracted record numbers of foreigners, even in the midst of a general tourism slump, accredited to inflation approaching 50% in the first half of 2016 under the economic policies of newly elected Argentine president Mauricio Macri.

In addition to its ability to stimulate tourism, the Mundial offers Argentines the opportunity to regulate, define, and control tango and its image, wresting power away from British ballroom dance societies, which have been crowning world tango champions since 1922. "Ahora sí, Argentina es campeona mundial de tango" (Now yes, Argentina is tango world champion), read one newspaper headline after the inaugural Campeonato Mundial de Baile de Tango in 2003 (Micheletto 2003). The substitution of the entire nation of Argentina for the Argentine dancers who won the competition (Enrique Usales and Gabriela Sanguinetti) reveals the extent to which Argentine national identity is conflated with the tango. This headline reflects both the indignation many Argentines felt at the theft of their dance by foreign cultures and their pride at being able to legitimize Argentine superiority in tango through the medium of competition, the very means through which British dancers have for so long justified their own tango authority. The Argentine flag has topped the scoreboard at almost every Mundial championship since, with the exception of 2009, when a Japanese couple (Hiroshi and Kyoko Yamao) won the salon category, and 2006, when a Colombian couple (Carlos Alberto Paredes and Diana Giraldo Rivera) won the stage category. Many of the competition policies appear rigged to ensure that Argentine couples continue to dominate. For instance, all judges are Argentines, and foreigners dancing with an Argentine partner must represent Argentina unless the Argentine can prove that she or he has lived for at least two years in the foreign partner's home country. Even preliminary competitions held outside Argentina, such as the Argentine Tango USA Championships at which the US national champions and representatives to the Mundial are crowned, are tightly controlled by the committee in Buenos Aires. The Office of Festivals and Central Events of the Ministry of Culture in Buenos Aires dictates not only the rules for the American branch competition, but selects the music, approves the judges, and sends an auditor to ensure adherence to all competition procedures.

The impulse for Argentines to maintain control over the Mundial, in an attempt to protect their tango from theft and desecration, is balanced by a concurrent pride in tango's growing international appeal. By 2016, Argentine tango had so securely overtaken ballroom tango in global popularity that Argentine newspaper headlines did not reflect the earlier anxiety about the foreign appropriation of tango. Rather, the media portray national pride in tango's triumph abroad, where dancers and musicians are studying the tradition seriously enough to perform at a level worthy of a Porteño audience. A *Clarin* headline from August 29, 2016, reads, "Las finales del Mundial de Tango, con muchas parejas extranjeras" (The World Tango Cup Finals, with many foreign couples). The article begins, "Furor global por el baile porteño. De las 58 que compiten, 21 son del exterior. Colombianos y rusos son los más numerosos, pero también hay de Coreo, Italia o Brasil." (Global frenzy for the dance from Buenos Aires. Of the 58 who are competing, 21 are foreigners. Colombians and Russians are the most numerous, but there are also competitors from Korea, Italy, and Brazil.) An article in *La Nación* the same day entitled "Un festival de tango verdaderamente mundial" (A truly global tango festival) brags about foreign musicians invited to play in the festival, *bandoneón* virutuosos Wu Yung-Lung from Taiwan and Ivan Talanin from Russia (Apicella 2016). This iconic tango instrument is notoriously difficult to play and is virtually unknown outside of tango circles, offering further evidence of tango's global triumph, this time on Argentina's terms. Rather than playing tango music in the ballroom style developed in England during the 1930s, when the *bandoneón* was replaced by Western snare drums, foreigners are rigorously studying the tradition as it is practiced in Argentina.

Journalists were not the only ones enamored with the presence of so many foreigners at the Mundial. When speaking about their experience competing, many Argentines identified meeting fellow competitors from all over the world as one of their favorite aspects of participating. Sitting among approximately 7,000 spectators in Luna Park for the championship finals, I witnessed enthusiastic public reception of foreign contestants. With the exception of a few other underdogs, like the elderly couple Francisco "Choclo" Allo and Olga "Coca" Albesetti competing in a field of dancers in their twenties and thirties, the foreign couples garnered the most applause at their initial appearance. It almost seemed possible that national pride engendered by so many foreigners exhibiting such dedication to Argentine tango had overtaken the corollary impulse to protect tango from foreign exploitation—almost, but not quite.

The 2016 winners of both the *tango de pista* and *tango escenario* championships were, not surprisingly, Argentine. It is hard to begrudge them this victory. After all, winners of the Mundial, who are invited to teach and perform internationally as a result of their victory, become global ambassadors for tango. For Argentines, it is a matter not only of cultural pride, but of economics. Professional tango dancers living in Buenos Aires can barely scrape together enough money to live, even when juggling multiple jobs: for example, performing at a *casa de tango* (tango house that stages tourist-oriented tango dinner shows) or Caminito (the street in La Boca where tourists flock to have their picture taken posing with a tango dancer in front of the brightly colored buildings), teaching classes at multiple tango schools and milongas, and continually cultivating new private students amidst the rapid turnover of tango tourists. Touring to teach abroad, despite its disruption to family life at home, offers such an improved standard of living that most Argentine professional tango dancers who can establish the connections and secure the visas to do so opt to tour for three to six months a year. The Mundial is the platform through which up-and-coming Argentine tango dancers launch their international touring careers. At the individual level, it may seem somewhat unfair to the many foreigners who have immigrated to Buenos Aires to pursue careers in tango, especially to those from countries like Colombia or Brazil where citizens confront similar economic hardships, that non-Argentines face a handicap in the Mundial championships. Considered in the context of tango history, however, which upholds that for three-quarters of a century tango world champions were head-whipping foxtrot dancers named by English judges, does it really seem so unreasonable that the Argentine tango world champions actually be Argentine?

Government control over the external image of tango through the Campeonato Mundial, however, extracts a heavy cost on the practice of tango within Argentina. Government resources for tango are almost exclusively dedicated to the tourist-focused Mundial, resulting not only in limited support for tango during the rest of the year, but active persecution of tango by government agencies. Ethnomusicologist Jennie Gubner (2014) describes the negative impact of then-mayor Macri's export-oriented urban development policies on local tango music communities, including permitting policies that favor mega-festivals over small, grassroots ventures and inspection sweeps that have closed neighborhood bars and community centers sponsoring tango music. Although these crackdowns are cloaked in the guise of ensuring safety, a platform on which Macri ran after the Cromañón tragedy of 2005 when nearly 200 people were killed in a nightclub fire, the inspections and bureaucracy concerning permits disproportionately impact tango nightlife. By 2015, the city government of Buenos Aires began targeting milongas for surprise inspections where minor code violations were cited as justification for closure of many of the city's most iconic milonga venues, including Sunderland Club, Salon Canning, and La Catedral (Gómez 2015; Télam 2015; Valenzuela 2015). Despite protests and media outrage, the crisis of the *clausuras* (closures) continued into 2016, resulting in widespread resentment about this government hypocrisy during the festival. While the government elevates the carefully curated and polished competition tango as a trophy for all the world to admire, it simultaneously decimates the local neighborhood milongas that have nurtured tango for one hundred years. So great was the outrage at the injustice of the *clausuras* that the Association of Milonga Organizers boycotted the 2016 festival, declaring that members of the association would not allow any festival events to transpire at their milongas. Many Argentines recognized the promise of the festival slogan *Tango, hoy y siempre* (Tango, today and always), featured on festival billboards and film clips, as a ruse to fool tourists who do not realize that "always" only lasts until the end of August. The weekend after the festival concluded, I heard reports of city inspectors appearing unannounced at milongas to scrutinize paperwork, fire exits, and bathrooms. Although the motivation behind government persecution (a word frequently invoked by victims of the *clausuras*) of tango nightlife is not well understood, I suggest it is partially due to the fact that tango in Argentina is still marked by its underclass origins. Echoing the Argentine elite's scorn of tango in the early twentieth century, *clausuras* reveal the twenty-first-century government's disdain for tango as an old-fashioned, irrelevant, and populist social practice that is inconsistent with the progressive, Western urban expansion that Macri (as mayor and later president) has championed. However, as with international tango fever 100 years prior, global tango-mania compels Argentina to publicly embrace a marginal cultural practice as symbolic of the nation, resulting in two contradictory government initiatives: one glorifying tango to the exterior, and the other eviscerating it at home.

CAKE DOLLS: EXTERNALIZING TANGO'S EMBRACE

Measuring something as subjective as dance may seem like a meaningless exercise in any genre, but the undertaking becomes particularly absurd in the case of Argentine tango. Many of its most treasured values (intimacy, sensitivity, connection, subtlety, internal sensation) are not even visible to an external viewer and are only accessible within the energetic web of the dancing couple's embrace. Traces of the quality of connection or sensitivity to a partner may be gleaned from watching, but only insofar as they offer insight into the internal state of the dancers. For example, observers will often intuit the quality of a man's embrace by the facial expression of a woman in his arms: a serene face with gently closed eyelids signaling that he has earned her trust, or a clenched jaw exposing his disregard for her comfort. Facial expressions in tango are not treated as aesthetic ideals in themselves, but rather as indexical signs of the dancers' physical and emotional sensations. Most tango dancers value how a partner makes them feel above how a partner looks, appreciating the visual insofar as it is indicative of the sensual. How, then, is a tango dancer's connection or embrace to be evaluated and scored by judges watching the interaction from the outside? It's a bit like evaluating someone's lovemaking skills by judging their performance in a pornographic film.

This paradox, the attempt to assess through observation what can only be understood through tactile and energetic sensation, is the justification that many people offer for dismissing tango competition and its winners as irrelevant to the true art of tango. Even in the midst of the Mundial's growing influence, many Argentine tango dancers, including those who participate as contestants and judges, express ambivalence and outright disgust at the folly of quantifying tango. Yet, reducing each couple's performance to a number is the task entrusted to judges on the Mundial panel. Each of the two competitions (*pista* and *escenario*) begins with two long days of preliminary rounds during which each couple is given a numeric score (between 4.0 and 8.0 in increments of one-tenth of a point) by each judge. In 2016, 404 couples competed in the preliminaries of *tango de pista* and 131 in *tango escenario*, although adding in couples who qualified directly for semifinal or final rounds brought the number of participating couples to 437 and 181. Scores from both days are averaged, and less than a quarter of the couples move onto the semifinal round, where they join winners of sanctioned championships held in various Argentine provinces and abroad throughout the year, who proceed directly to the semifinal round. In the semifinals, each of six judges grades each couple between 5.0 and 9.0, and the top-scoring forty couples in *pista* and twenty in *escenario* pass to the final rounds, which are held two consecutive evenings at the Luna Park stadium (Figure 13.2).

In the final, *tango de pista* competitors are grouped into four *rondas* (rounds) of ten couples each, where their performances are scored between 7.0 and 10.00. I heard many criticisms of this system. Even though the final placements are based on the average of the judges' scores, a single judge can have a much greater impact on the final outcome by using a wider spread than a judge who clusters marks in a narrow range. In addition, the fact that the finalists never dance side by side, nor dance to the same music, is noted by many as unfair, especially to those in the first *ronda*, who are at a disadvantage because judges score conservatively at the outset. Ballroom dance competitions, on the other hand, avoid these particular biases by whittling the finalists down to six couples who dance together in a single heat and are marked by relative rather than absolute rankings (judges rank the competitors in first through sixth place rather than giving them numeric scores).

The scoring system and the division of *rondas* are not the only nor the most commonly cited points of controversy in debates about fairness and transparency at the Mundial. Many people recognize the inherent fallibility of judges who cannot circumvent their own preconceptions, prejudices, and values. For example, the rules specifically state that costuming should not be considered in the *tango de pista* category, yet

FIGURE 13.2. Tango de pista finals in Luna Park, Buenos Aires, at the 2016 *Campeonato Mundial de Baile de Tango.*

Photo by Gabriel Gutierrez.

I heard tales that some judges admit over a glass of wine to docking points for any man not sporting cufflinks or a pocket square. I witnessed less controversy about the clothing choices of female competitors who, already used to having their appearance judged in milongas where men choose their partners as much on their beauty as their dancing skills, were exquisitely coiffed, painted, jeweled, and donned in velvet or shimmering hip-hugging dresses, with strategically designed ruching and slits accentuating buttocks and legs. Every aspect of their appearance, from the length of their dresses (upper calf to accentuate footwork) to the design of the hair (swept up in twists, braids, and curls to lengthen the neck line while maintaining a soft appearance), was calculated for its visual effect. Men too conform to a very narrow sartorial aesthetic: suits carefully fitted and pressed, ties and handkerchiefs selected to complement partners' dresses, beards shaved or tightly trimmed, and hair slicked back, thick with gel.

The contestants' meticulous attention to grooming reflects their understanding that moving social dance practice into a competition venue flips the priorities. In a social context, how the dance feels takes precedence over how it looks, but the competition setting requires that the visual trump the tactile. The rules for the competition, however, do not always take into account the way in which competition inevitably alters social dance. The first point listed on the festival website under evaluation criteria is: "Tango de pista is conceived as a social dance where the most important aspects are the musicality, embrace, and connection between the dance partners." It seems plausible to evaluate dancers' musicality by watching, but how can one evaluate the quality of their embrace or connection through visual inspection? The effort to maintain the primacy of these quintessential social tango values in a competition context has led to re-interpretation of what constitutes a good connection or embrace. Whereas most social dancers understand these skills to be based on one's ability to continually sense, react, and adapt to a partner's balance, comfort, and emotional state, Mundial competitors often strive to maintain an unchanging posture, connection, and embrace. Rather than allowing the embrace to breathe as it expands to make space for torsion required in *giros, sacadas*, and *ganchos*, many Mundial dancers hold a static position, the consistency of their posture easier to measure by eye than the sensitivity of their touch on a partner's back. This interpretation of embrace and connection has resulted in a style that many critics refer to as "stick up the butt," or, even more evocatively, *muñeca de torta* (cake doll). Like the figurines on top of wedding cakes who symbolize an idealized expression of heterosexual union, but as plastic objects are incapable of feeling or movement, Mundial competitors are ridiculed by some as dancers without souls.

The cake doll epithet also points to one of the most powerful effects of the Mundial's popularity: it decreases aesthetic diversity in tango styles. Competitions demand a standard or ideal that contestants can strive to match or beat. In the absence of universal standards, tango competitors refer to the previous year's champions as their model, resulting in a rapidly narrowing range of artistic expression. By far the most common critique of Mundial dancers is that they are all clones. Rodrigo Videla, who began dancing tango in his home province of San Luis before moving to Buenos Aires, recalls his own impulse to imitate former champions.

Yo me acuerdo cuando yo empecé a bailar, miraba en los videos de YouTube. "Ahí, este es el campeón de este año." Y lo tomaba, "O, mira ese. Mira lo que hace. Yo quisiera hacerlo." Y yo copiaba. No solo como caminar, copiaba el estilo. También, cuando gana alguien, toda la gente que esté empezando, en el mismo año que se gana, lo tomo un poco como referente. Por ahí, ese generó que ahora todo bailamos parecidos. Y no está bueno. (I remember when I started to dance, I was watching videos on YouTube. "There, this is this year's champion." And I took it, "Oh, look at this. Look at what he is doing. I would like to do that." And I copied. Not only how to walk, but I copied his style. Also, when someone wins, everyone who is starting the same year that he wins, takes him a bit as a model. This led to the situation that now we all dance alike. And that is not good.)[3]

The global reach of the digital video-sharing platform YouTube enables dancers in Russia, China, and Italy, as well as the Argentine provinces of Tucumán and Mendoza, to study and mimic the posture, steps, and embellishments of last year's Mundial champions. Whereas the philosophy of Argentine tango as personal expression that privileges originality and creativity is still maintained in discourse around the dance, the practice of Argentine tango continues to diverge from this ideal as tango dancers increasingly resemble cake dolls pressed from the same mold.

This narrowing aesthetic range not only has impacted the style of competitive tango, but also has influenced the social tango culture of Buenos Aires. When the Mundial was inaugurated in 2003, a new style of dancing called *tango nuevo* was popular at many Buenos Aires milongas. Characterized by a more open and flexible embrace, moves that take partners off-axis in counterbalance, incorporation of vocabulary from foreign dances, and liberal use of large athletic movements, *tango nuevo* was regarded by some traditionalists as an affront to tango tradition (Merritt 2012). By the time I first visited Buenos Aires in 2012, *tango nuevo* had virtually disappeared from social practice, despite its persistent popularity in Europe and North America. The decline of *tango nuevo* coincided with the rise of the Mundial, which prohibits and punishes the very skills in which *tango nuevo* dancers excel: open embrace dancing with extreme torsion and extensive use of *ganchos* (hooks) and *boleos* (leg flicks). Although *ganchos* and *boleos* have been part of tango since its golden age, *tango nuevo* dancers developed new and daring techniques for stringing together complex sequences of leg play that included *ganchos* of the waist and high linear *boleos* that some thought inappropriate for the social dance floor. Andrea Monti, organizer of the US subsidiary and former judge at the Mundial, explains the rationale for prohibiting *boleos* above the knee and *ganchos* from the *tango salon/pista* competition.

So actually the competition also teaches the dancers how to behave. Because as you cannot do ganchos, you cannot do powerful sacadas, you cannot kick, you cannot do colgadas, you cannot break the embrace, you cannot do jumps, fancy stuff, you learn how to dance correctly in a dance floor where you are going to share with other people. This is very good. This is the most important. The competition teaches people how to dance in a social dance floor, in a real milonga.[4]

Monti is speaking specifically about the American context, where open dance floors breed poor navigation skills, in contrast to Buenos Aires, where the tightly packed milongas necessitate more cooperative and judicial use of space. However, her assertion that limiting the use of certain steps in competition decreases their popularity in social dance settings reveals how the Mundial's restrictions on *tango nuevo* movements popular at the competition's inception may have curbed these tendencies in Buenos Aires as well. Although the decline of *tango nuevo* is the result of many converging factors, including foreigners' fetishization of tango as danced during its golden age, use of *ganchos*, *boleos*, and *colgadas* in Buenos Aires milongas has diminished so dramatically since the Mundial's early years that the correlation offers convincing evidence to many of the Mundial's influence over social dancing.

TANGO'S DIMINISHING AFRICANIST AESTHETICS

Several historians of early tango have documented the African origins of not only the word *tango*, but of the music/dance traditions candombe, milonga, and cayengue out of which tango emerged, suggesting that early tangos were danced by Afro-Argentines (Chasteen 2004; Savigliano 1995; Thompson 2005). As tango gained traction in whiter and higher-class Argentine communities in the early twentieth century, Africanist aesthetics of the dance started to disappear in favor of more European aesthetics. Knees and spines straightened; hip movement was minimized; and syncopated rhythms were smoothed over. Compared to mambo or salsa dancing, for example, which clearly reference their African roots in the use of flexed limbs and hips, asymmetrical and curvilinear shapes, and call-and-response improvisational structures, tango does not at first glance appear to be an Afro-disaporic dance. Closer inspection, though, reveals traces of tango's African ancestry, including polyrhythms expressed by the feet, subtle movements of the hips, and privileging of improvisation over choreography. Even the remaining Africanist aesthetics, however, are being pushed further out of tango practice as the Mundial's influence spreads. Aesthetic values that are rewarded by competition judges (straight knees, pointed toes, vertical spines, extended lines) are supplanting flat-footed, angled, and idiosyncratic tango styles on social dance floors as well.

Dance scholars have argued that the commercialization of ballroom dances in the early twentieth century contributed to the elimination of their African aesthetics in favor of whiter and more easily salable products (McMains 2006; Robinson 2015). Likewise, I suggest that intensified commercialization of tango is once again shifting tango styles away from their (albeit distant) African origins. The Mundial, as a central commercial tango player, performs a key role in validating balletic, white, European aesthetics in tango. In selecting world ambassadors for tango, racial bias may influence the judges who (perhaps unconsciously) hope to access ballet's white privilege and prestige by awarding higher rankings to tango dancers using balletic shapes of the legs and feet. This effort to elevate Argentina's national status through association with white, aristocratic, European ballet is yet another example of how concern about Argentina's external image is impacting the practice of tango inside its borders.

While, on the one hand, the influence of the Mundial brings Argentine tango aesthetics closer to Europeanized ballroom tangos, privileging verticality, unbroken lines, and static shapes, the Mundial simultaneously prioritizes other African aesthetic values that were eliminated from ballroom tangos: the interdependence of music and dance, improvisation, and individual variation. Competitive ballroom dancers perform preset choreography, rarely adapting their timing to respond to the music selected by the DJ, resulting in music becoming an accompaniment to the dancing, rather than motivation for it. Argentine *tango de pista* competitors, on the other hand, are judged on their musical improvisational acumen. Each round of competitors is required to improvise to three different tango songs (one lyrical, one rhythmical, and one dramatic), offering the judges the opportunity to evaluate how dancers interpret varying musical styles. Whereas DJs at ballroom competitions fade each song out after the first ninety seconds, the short length of tangos recorded during the golden age, limited to three minutes by the size of wax records, enables tango DJs to play each song through to its conclusion. Competitors are compared on their ability to construct a dance that complements the structure of tango music. How do the dancers respond to the entrance of the singer, to the repetition of the B section when the melody is established by the piano rather than the violins, or the speed of the *bandoneón* in the *variación*? Musicality is one of the most highly valued skills in the social practice of tango, and the Mundial maintains its centrality, sustaining tango's (tenuous) link to Africa, where music and dance are so intertwined that many African languages do not have separate words to describe them. Although Argentines will readily admit that racism makes the discussion of tango's African roots controversial (*Tango Negro* 2013), this resolve to maintain certain African aesthetic values in the dance, even as others are erased, exemplifies the tensions that Latin Americans must negotiate in global power plays. They will strategically emphasize tango's similarity to white, European dances in order to elevate its international status, while simultaneously protecting some African aesthetic values in order to shelter tango from co-option and theft.

MEDIATING MENTAL HEALTH OUTCOMES

All competitions have the potential to negatively impact the psychological health of individual competitors, whose sense of sense of self-worth is tied to the results. When dance, which might be described as self-expression, is judged in competition, the distinction between self-expression and self becomes difficult to maintain. A dancer is likely to experience a low competition result as a negative evaluation of self, rather than a critique of behavior ("I am a failure," as opposed to, "I failed to execute my *giros* smoothly"). Whereas most sports competitors have the buffer of objective measures like speed or distance to help maintain a separation between athletic performance and self, the subjective nature of judging in dance competitions proves even more problematic for dancers' self-esteem. The absence of quantifiable and transparent measures for explaining successes and failures leaves many dancers who participate in competitions vulnerable to destruction of self-worth. For example, Sidney Grant, who taught in the Dancing Classrooms ballroom dance program for New York City schoolchildren featured in the documentary *Mad Hot Ballroom* explained, "while the idea of a school from Washington Heights and Tribeca and Forrest Hills, Queens competing against one another makes a great plotline for a movie, it makes a miserable experience for the children . . . I would literally watch these kids collapse in grief, uncontrollably sobbing on the floor when they didn't win."[5] After watching competitions erode the self-esteem that the program was designed to build, Grant formed a non-competitive partner dance program for school children, Ballroom Basix.

The negative effects of competition on adults can be just as destructive. A professional ballroom dance competitor whom I will call Lisa explained, "I left ballroom because I didn't want to be a part of that world anymore, the competition. It was very superficial. There was so much pressure to have a certain type of body, to dance a certain way. After so many competitions, if we didn't get the result we wanted, my dance partner would ignore me, wouldn't talk to me. I would get so much shit, I wasn't happy. I was in a not very good place." Because status and income-earning potential are so closely tied to competition ranking in the ballroom dance industry, poor competition results can lead to eating disorders, depression, emotional abuse between partners, and cruelty between competitors. Recognizing the destructive cycle of competition, Lisa made the radical decision to abandon the ballroom dance career to which she had devoted her life and move to Argentina, where she fell in love with tango. Now a professional tango dancer, Lisa reflected on her experience competing in Argentine tango at the Mundial in the context of her career in DanceSport:

> I never felt once this pressure from him [my partner]. I felt I danced amazing because I wasn't worried about what is he going to think or what is going to be the consequence after. And the competition, it was amazing because it was not like the competitive Russians from the ballroom world that you know for years, and then the day of the competition they don't even say "hi," and they look at you strange. It was like being in the milonga, like "hey, what's up? How are you?" Backstage before we went on we were joking and laughing the whole time. . . . After the semi when we were waiting for the final results and there was nothing going on and I started joking around doing the wave . . . it took some time but I got everyone to do the wave in the Usina. Going out of it, I take more those memories and dancing and enjoying than anything else.

Such stories of camaraderie with other competitors as they waited backstage were recounted by many participants in the Mundial, contrasting sharply with the cutthroat culture of ballroom dance competitions (McMains 2006). Likewise, Lisa's insistence that she did not feel attached to the outcome of the competition was shared by many Mundial competitors, who did not express disappointment when asked how they felt about their scores. They appreciated the Mundial for the benefits it could offer, even when they failed to advance into the semifinals or the finals: a goal to focus their training, a venue to showcase their dancing, and a chance to bond with other competitors. Because tango dancers receive validation for their status as tango artists through so many other avenues (performing at milongas and in stage shows, being highly sought after as social dance partners, invitations to teach and perform abroad), the outcome of this one event, even though it is billed as the world tango championships, does not have a strong impact on their identities as dancers. Whereas it is virtually impossible for a ballroom dancer to build a high-profile career without amassing a long résumé of competition titles, tango dancers do not need competition victories to earn respect or status. In fact, some of the most highly respected tango dancers in the world have never competed and are admired precisely because of the distinctiveness of their artistic vision, which cannot be forced into the mold out of which cake dolls spring. For example, Mariano "Chico" Frumboli violates nearly all of the aesthetics venerated by Mundial champions: his elbows droop too low, his knees are too bent, his embrace opens too far, he steps too heavily onto flat feet, his unkempt long hair hangs untethered and his shirts lay open at the neck, he rarely uses *enrosques* or *lápices* to decorate his own actions, and yet few tango dancers would deny his status as one of the most brilliant tango dancers of all time. Thus, even though the Mundial brings competition to the forefront of Argentine tango culture for the month of August each year, tango competitions are still are a minor aspect of most tango professionals' careers.

Competitions are more often the springboard for careers that expand far beyond the competition frame. For example, Maria Nieves, who starred in *Tango Argentino* with her partner and the show's choreographer, Juan Carlos Copes, entered tango competitions in the early 1950s. Nieves explains that it was due to "*el éxito que tuvimos en esos concursos que nuestro nombre trascendió el mundo de los campeonatos*" (the success that we had in those contests that our name transcended the world of the championships) (Oliva 2014, 71). In other words, Copes and Nieves outgrew competitions as soon as their competition achievements produced more desirable performing jobs. So although competitions may have helped to launch their career, competitions were not the driving force behind the dance style that Nieves and Copes developed and showcased in *Tango Argentino*, which sparked the second global tango craze. Whereas ballroom dance championship titles generate increased pressure to defend the title in the next competition, a win at the Mundial ensures that the dancers never need compete again. Like well-established Argentine tango professionals, Mundial champions have nothing to gain and everything to lose by returning to the competition floor. Perhaps knowledge that so few of the industry's most well-respected professional dancers have entered the Mundial allows current competitors to laugh off low scores. Dancers choose not to take the competition too seriously because Mundial champions are only revered outside Buenos Aires. Within the tango culture of Buenos Aires, everyone knows the competition that counts is at the milongas. As one competitor exclaimed when I asked him if he thought there was rivalry during the Mundial, "the real rivalry is at La Viruta," the late-night milonga that attracts the highest number of professional dancers who, in spite of dim lighting to facilitate its main function as a site for seduction, scrutinize every step of their rivals' repertoires.

QUEERING TANGO COMPETITION

In addition to using the Mundial as a platform for launching their own careers, some competitors use the Mundial to advance social and political agendas. Argentina has been at the forefront of lesbian, gay, bisexual, transgender, and queer legislation, becoming the first country in Latin American to legalize same-sex marriage in 2010. The tango community, however, lags behind many other sectors of society in its resistance to same-sex and gender-fluid dancing. Buenos Aires boasts a vibrant queer tango scene where pioneers such as Augusto Balizano and Mariana Docampo have for over a decade hosted gay and queer milongas that attempt to rupture the link between gender and the role assumed when dancing tango (Gasió 2011). Outside these designated queer spaces, however, it is relatively rare to see same-sex dancing in the Buenos Aires milonga circuit, especially between men. For the first ten years of its existence, the Mundial promoted an exclusively heteronormative tango. In 2013, however, Mundial officials publicized that for the first time they would welcome same-sex competitors because, as Mundial artistic director Gustavo Mozzi explained in *La Nación*, "*La competencia intenta reflejar la evolución del tango y los cambios sociales*" (The competition tries to reflect the evolution of tango and social changes) (Massa 2013). Four same-sex couples entered the Mundial in 2013, garnering a flurry of international media attention (Agence France Presse, 2013). No same-sex couples advanced to the finals, however, until 2016 when Daniel Arroyo and Juan Pablo Ramírez, dressed in blacks suits and low heels, with only sequins on his lapels to mark Ramírez's position in the role danced by women in the other partnerships, became the first same-sex couple to dance in the Mundial *tango de pista* finals. By 2016, Arroyo and Ramírez, who had entered the competition four years prior, had achieved widespread respect in Buenos Aires through their expertly crafted tango performances (often in drag) at many of the city's more traditional milongas, including Salon Canning. Rather than launching their personal career, as it did for many heterosexual couples, their placement in the Mundial finals validated same-sex dancing in general, offering a stamp of public approval for work that Arroyo, Ramírez, and many other queer tango activists have been engaged in for many years.

The Argentine Tango USA Championships also welcomed their first same-sex couple into the *tango de pista* finals in 2016, Sidney Grant and Claudio Marcelo Vidal (Figure 13.3). Grant led Vidal who, wearing a neatly clipped beard, a white suit trimmed with black stitching to complement Grant's black suit, and three-inch black and white polka dotted high heels, executed with expert dexterity and finesse the steps

FIGURE 13.3. Sidney Grant and Claudio Vidal competing at the 2016 Argentine Tango USA Championships in San Francisco.

Photo by Don An.

conventionally danced by women. The conjoining of beard and high heels on Vidal's body produced even more anxiety and excitement than the sight of two men enrapt in an amorous embrace. Through his masterful control of high heels, one of the most iconic markers of femininity, Vidal troubled not only the heterosexual mandate of tango, but the category of gender itself. Vidal's long-standing use of heels is so provocative that two judges are rumored to have recused themselves from the panel when he first appeared competing in heels at the 2013 Mundial in Buenos Aires. In 2016, the American crowd was captivated by the power, elegance, and musicality of Grant and Vidal's dancing, and many were rooting for them to win, especially since Grant won the 2011 USA Tango Championships in New York dancing with female partner Gayle Madeira. Fans were disappointed, however, that after advancing to the final round, Grant and Vidal finished near the bottom of the pack of finalists in 2016. Despite hearing gossip that some of the judges expressed confusion about how to judge a same-sex partnership, Grant and Vidal did not seem troubled by the final scores given that their primary goal was to expand the visibility of same-sex dancing. The crowd's positive reception was evidence that even though they did not walk away with the trophy, the couple had succeeded in advancing their agenda of expanding acceptance for same-sex dancing. Grant recalled, "everyone was so supportive of us, every one of the competitors, and especially the audience. When we walked out there, we just got such affirmation from the crowd."[6] Although no same-sex couple has yet won the Mundial or any of its subsidiary championships, the breakthrough of Grant and Vidal making it to the finals in San Francisco, as well as Arroyo and Ramírez advancing to the finals in Buenos Aires in 2016, was cause for celebration among queer tango dancers and their allies who (much like the state of Argentina) are eager to use the Mundial as a platform for promotion and publicity of an image of tango they choose to endorse.

A View from the Stands

Despite my reservations about the effect the Mundial has on the social practice of tango, reducing diversity and creativity in social tango styles in favor of whiter and more externally focused performances, I could not resist getting caught up in the drama as I sat in the stands at Luna Park. My heart started to race as the *tango de pista* finalists were paraded out to stand wringing their hands, assembled shoulder to shoulder across the stage, and the scores of the fifth-place couple were projected onto the screen, their names withheld. A voice announced slowly, "el quinto lugar es para . . ." (fifth place goes to . . .), and another emcee took over to continue "pareja . . . numero . . ." (couple . . . number . . .). When their names were finally revealed, I felt a jolt of vicarious joy as I watched her jump into his arms. My pulse rate continued to climb as the fourth, third, and second place winners were likewise presented with their awards. As the announcers geared up to name the champions, I was in such a state of anxiety I almost felt as if I were up on stage myself waiting to hear my name called. Like other sporting events, the Mundial creates communal experiences of shared trial and triumph for the 7,000 live spectators and thousands more watching the live video stream. The drama reached a climax as champion Cristian Palomo dropped to his knees when he heard his name (Figure 13.4). Palomo remained on the floor crying until a fellow competitor lifted him to his feet so that he could embrace his partner Melissa Sacchi and claim their prize.[7] How befitting of tango, filled with songs of men publicly confessing their most intimate emotions (Savigliano 1995), that it was the male partner who claimed the center of the drama, the photo of Palomo on his knees appearing in several newspapers the next day. Fans were thrilled that Palomo, a portly young man with grace seemingly incongruent with his size, won the top prize, the departure from stereotypical dancer's body type signaling to some a rupture of the cake doll mold.

The results of the *tango escenario* championships the next night likewise revealed a promising new direction. *Tango escenario* routines are typically packed with dazzling tricks and lifts, portray an intense relationship through facial expressions bordering on constipation, and are performed to the high-drama music of Osvaldo Pugliese or Color Tango. Many people feel as if *tango escenario* is more suited for the competition format because of the athleticism required and the exclusive attention each couple receives to

FIGURE 13.4. Cristian Palomo (right) and Melisa Sacchi (center) reacting to winning the *tango de pista* championships at the 2016 *Campeonato Mundial de Baile de Tango* in Buenos Aires.

Photo by Daniel Jayo/www.malacarapress.com.

showcase their skills. However, I found it impossible to absorb twenty such routines in a row. By the fourth couple, my focus started to waver, and everything blurred into a tornado of ganchos. After nineteen expertly crafted, but overwrought escenario routines, Hugo Mastrolorenzo and Agustina Vignau (Figure 13.5) offered a radical departure from the formula with their interpretation of Astor Piazzolla's "Balada por un loco."[8] The audience exhaled into the spoken poetry and sparse music, telling the story of a *loco* in love. Mastrolorenzo, fully committed to the role in a suit thick with dust and unkempt half-shaved head of hair, tries to win over the innocent Vignau, clad in a white cloak. Central to their dance-drama is a balloon inside a birdcage, which they cleverly manipulate with their feet at select moments timed with the entrance of the bass and violin cutting over the poetry. By the time Mastrolorenzo has persuaded Vignau to adopt his worldview and she opens the cage to let the balloon float upward on the words *vení, volá, vení* (come, fly, come), it appears as if the audience too sees the world through this crazy man's eyes when they burst into applause as if she has freed an imprisoned bird. The crowd was so enthusiastic about their performance that I feared they would riot if Mastrolorenzo and Vignau were not crowned champions. Mastrolorenzo placed in the top three in 2014 and 2015 with different partners, but each year judges complained that

FIGURE 13.5. Hugo Mastrolorenzo and Agustina Vignau performing their winning *tango escenario* choreography at the 2016 *Campeonato Mundial de Baile de Tango* in Buenos Aires.

Photo by Gabriel Gutierrez.

there was not enough tango in his theatrical choreographies. In 2016, he finally hit the golden ratio of tango to theater and was rewarded with the championship title. Upon hearing the news, Mastrolorenzo jumped off the stage to hug his mother seated in the audience, the male champion again monopolizing the drama of the awards. The stadium erupted in elation. For those anxious about the homogenizing power of the Mundial, the Mastrolorenzo/Vignau win was a hopeful sign that the championships might in the future inspire innovation over imitation.

Within a week after the conclusion of the Mundial, attendance at Buenos Aires milongas dropped to half of what it had been in August, as tourists concluded their holidays and Argentines embarked on tours teaching abroad. The heightened sense of competition and social posturing that had infiltrated even the social tango circuit during the Mundial subsided with the formal adjudication process, leaving potential dance partners, lovers, rivals, and peers to judge each other, rewarding their personal champions with eye contact, jokes, smiles, and a *tanda* (set) on the dance floor. In tango nightlife, where seduction reigns as the primary organizing logic, words cannot be trusted. "No" is rarely accepted to be a refusal, and "yes" could mean anything from "I'd love to" to "I'm only saying yes to be polite but would rather roast my dog on the *parilla*." It is in this context of irony and double meaning that the paradoxes of the Mundial find home. The Mundial is *both* an exhibition of autoexoticism, Argentina performing for the Global North their displaced sexual desire, *and* Argentina's means of reclaiming tango by appropriating the ballroom competition format. The Mundial privileges European aesthetics of verticality and linearity that characterize ballroom tangos while concurrently reaffirming African aesthetic values such as idiosyncratic play and choreomusical interdependence that ballroom tangos had eschewed. The Mundial is a machine for promotion of a state-sanctioned version of tango, designed to maximize tourist revenues at the expense of local tango culture. Simultaneously, it offers local tango artists opportunities to enter into and at times alter the trajectory of tango commerce in ways that are more consistent with their artistic and social values. Undeniably, the Mundial is effecting change in the aesthetics, social practice, and business of tango, in some ways bringing it closer to the English ballroom dance model that privileges codified form over social function. However, despite its growing influence, the Mundial remains a subculture within the larger complex of Argentine tango culture, which continues to maintain improvisation, individuality, subtlety, intimate personal connection, and respect for musical tradition as tango's core values.

ACKNOWLEDGMENTS

The author would like to thank all the dancers who generously shared their insights and experiences about the Mundial, especially Julio Azorin, Florencia Curatella, Valentina Ferronti, Victor Francia, Sidney Grant, Rachel Makow, Pancho Martínez Pey, Andrea Monti, Julio Montoya, Guillermo Nieto, Glen Royce, Marina Teves, Silvio la Via, Rodrigo Videla, and Jamila Williams, none of whom necessarily share the viewpoints expressed in this chapter.

NOTES

1. I competed on the DanceSport circuit as an amateur from 1991–1997 and as a professional from 1997–2003, averaging one competition a month over twelve years.
2. Lyrics from "Cheek to Cheek," written by Irving Berlin for *Top Hat* (1935), starring Astaire and Rogers.
3. Rodrigo Videla, interview with Juliet McMains, September 4, 2016, Buenos Aires.
4. Andrea Monti, Skype interview with Juliet McMains, April 12, 2016.
5. Sidney Grant, telephone interview with Juliet McMains, April 25, 2016.
6. Sidney Grant, telephone interview with Juliet McMains, April 25, 2016.
7. https://www.youtube.com/watch?v=hSqGjlfyE6w.
8. https://www.youtube.com/watch?v=knVaQQVK4Cw.

REFERENCES

Agence France Presse. 2013. "Argentine Tango Competition Welcomes Gay Couples for the First Time." *The Huffington Post*, August 25. http://www.huffingtonpost.com/2013/08/26/argentine-tango-gay-couples_n_3814273.html. Accessed January 15, 2017.

Apicella, Mauro. 2016. "Un festival de tango verdaderamente mundial." *La Nación.* August 29. http://www.lanacion.com.ar/1931952-un-festival-de-tango-verdaderamente-mundial. Accessed January 15, 2017.

Barrionuevo, Alexei. 2010. "Argentina Approves Gay Marriage, in a First for Region." *New York Times,* July 16. https://www.nytimes.com/2010/07/16/world/americas/16argentina.html. Accessed May 9, 2018.

Chasteen, John Charles. 2004. *National Rhythms, African Roots: The Deep History of Latin American Popular Dance.* Albuquerque: University of New Mexico Press.

Clarín. 2016. "Las finales del Mundial de Tango, con muchas parejas extranjeras." August 29. https://www.clarin.com/ciudades/finales-mundial-tango-parejas-extranjeras_0_SkT6eT-i.html. Accessed July 12, 2018.

Denniston, Christine. 2008. *The Meaning of Tango: The Story of the Argentinian Dance.* London: Portico Books.

Fitch, Melissa A. 2015. *Global Tangos: Travels in the Transnational Imaginary.* Lewisburg, PA: Bucknell University Press.

Gasió, Guillermo, ed. 2011. *La historia del Tango, 21: Siglo XXI, Década 1, 2a parte.* Buenos Aires: Corregidor.

Gómez, Silvia. 2015. "Clausuran diez milongas porteñas y hay preocupación en los tangueros." *Clarín,* March 7. https://www.clarin.com/ciudades/ciudad_de_buenos_aires-milongas-clausuras_0_S1ke1nLFwQg.html. Accessed July 12, 2018.

Gubner, Jennie Meris. 2014. "Tango, Not-For-Export: Participatory Music-Making, Musical Activism, and Visual Ethnomusicology in the Neighborhood Tango Scenes of Buenos Aires." PhD diss., University of California, Los Angeles.

Hallewell, Kit. 1991. "Freddie Camp's Tango." *The Ballroom Dancing Times* 5(34): 176–177.

Luker, Morgan James. 2016. *The Tango Machine: Musical Culture in the Age of Expediency.* Chicago: University of Chicago Press.

Massa, Fernando. 2013. "Por primera vez, parejas del mismo sexo compiten en el Mundial de Tango." *La Nación,* August 25. http://www.lanacion.com.ar/1613787-por-primera-vez-parejas-del-mismo-sexo-compiten-en-el-mundial-de-tango. Accessed January 15, 2017.

McMains, Juliet. 2006. *Glamour Addiction: Inside the American Ballroom Dance Industry.* Middletown, CT: Wesleyan University Press.

Merritt, Carolyn. 2012. *Tango Nuevo.* Gainesville: University of Florida Press.

Micheletto, Karina. 2003. "Ahora sí, Argentina es campeona mundial de tango." *Página 12,* March 11. http://www.pagina12.com.ar/diario/espectaculos/6-17471-2003-03-11.html. Accessed January 15, 2017.

Oliva, María. 2014. *Soy tango: Biografía de María Nieves.* Buenos Aires: Planeta.

Richardon, Philip J. S. 1931. "The Story of the Tango: I. Pre-War." *The Dancing Times* (December): 285–288.

Richardson, Philip J. S. 1981. *A History of English Ballroom Dancing (1910–1945): The Story of the Development of the Modern English Style.* London: Herbert Jenkins.

Robinson, Danielle. 2015. *Modern Moves: Dancing Race during the Ragtime and Jazz Eras.* New York: Oxford University Press.

Savigliano, Marta E. 1995. *Tango and the Political Economy of Passion.* Boulder, CO: Westview.

Tango Buenos Aires Festival and Dance World Cup 2016. http://festivales.buenosaires.gob.ar/2016/tangofestivalymundial/en/reglamento. Accessed May 9, 2018.

Télam. 2015. "Convocan a una marcha contra la clausura de milongas en la Ciudad." June 30. http://www.telam.com.ar/notas/201506/110888-marcha-ciudad-clausura-milongas.html. Accessed January 15, 2017.

Thompson, Robert Farris. 2005. *Tango: The Art History of Love*. New York: Pantheon Books.

Valenzuela, Andrés. 2015. "Así se baila el tango para protestar." *Pagina 12*, July 4. http://www.pagina12.com.ar/diario/sociedad/3-276348-2015-07-04.html. Accessed January 15, 2017.

Audiovisual Sources

Mundial de tango, 2016, Final Pista, LA consagración de los 6 mejores y el campeón. 2016. YouTube video, 12:03. Posted by "AiresDeMilonga," August 30. https://www.youtube.com/watch?v=hSqGjlfyE6w. Accessed January 15, 2017.

"Mundial de Tango 2016 Final Final escenario, Hugo Mastrolorenzo, Agustina Vignou." 2016. YouTube video, 5:21. Posted by "AiresDeMilonga," August 31. https://www.youtube.com/watch?v=knVaQQVK4Cw. Accessed January 15, 2017.

Pedro, Dom. 2013. *Tango Negro: The African Roots of Tango*. Paris: AMA Productions. Distributed by ArtMattan Productions.

CHAPTER 14

DANCE-OFF, OR A BATTLE FOR THE FUTURE

Dance Reality Shows in India

PALLABI CHAKRAVORTY

HINDU mythology tells us that a most reasonable method of settling an argument is a dance-off. The story involves two of the most powerful Hindu deities, Shiva and Kali (who are husband and wife). Once they clashed over territorial dominance of the Thillai forest in the southern part of India. Kali was the patron goddess of the forest and the temple within it. But Shiva, following his two devotees who wanted to worship him in the temple (in the form of his abstract representation called the Shiva lingam), came to dance in the forest. This basically meant that Shiva wanted to occupy the forest and oust Kali. Kali refused to leave and challenged Shiva to enter a dance competition with her on the condition that the loser would leave the forest. Lord Vishnu presided as the judge.

Kali (the goddess of Shakti, or power, who is often shown naked in Hindu iconography, standing on the chest of her consort Shiva, prostrated beneath her) danced fearlessly. She matched Shiva's every move and every posture with ease and grace. Shiva, the cosmic dancer of the universe, danced his *tandava nritya* (the cyclic dance of creative destruction) with fierce intensity. They were unrelenting. They danced for days and nights, but no one won. Then Shiva performed a transgressive act. He cheated. He lifted one of his legs high above his head in what classical dance parlance calls *ananda tandavam* (the dance of bliss). Kali, a modest and respectable woman (despite her nakedness and unconventional lifestyle), could not follow. Thus, the story goes, she was unable to strike such a lurid posture. Shiva won the competition and Kali admitted defeat and left the forest. Thus, Shiva became the Supreme Being, the creator of the cosmos and the world we live in today.

This origin myth about the universe and about the competitive spirit that belongs to the divine or spirit world tells us that competition is also innately human. Undoubtedly, there is much to be gleaned from this tale about gender, art, justice, and power. But by narrating the tale here, I want to highlight the idea that artistic competitions are not new in India. They have long been part of Indian myth and fictional history. Here I am thinking about the famous musical duel between Tansen and Baijnath Mishra in the Mughal court, where the latter melts a marble slab with the power of his singing, popularized through the Hindi movie *Baiju Bawra* (1952). These examples remind us about the power of the performing arts and the ability of the human spirit to ascend to great heights through performance. It comes as no surprise, then, that the current incarnation of dance competitions in India is as fierce and intense, as virtuoso and transformative, as it supposedly was in the past.

In this chapter, I explore the genre of dance reality shows that are now ubiquitous on Indian television to explicate the myriad meanings of dance competitions. First, I look at the reality show *Boogie Woogie*, as it is considered one of the earliest dance competitions on Indian television. Then I shift my analysis to a more recent and popular show, *Dance India Dance*. In addition to textual analysis, this analysis includes ethnographic material from my fieldwork in India in 2011.[1] Second, I analyze the meaning of *bhakti rasa*, or aesthetic desire, in classical Indian dances and its transformation into the "remix" of Bollywood dances that are performed on reality shows. I propose that the aesthetic of "remix" represents the desire for consumption in post-liberalization India. The act of winning a dance contest on reality television is packaged with the desire for commodity and celebrity culture. Third, I show how dance reality shows shape new embodiments of femininity and masculinity in India. Through my ethnographic work, I approach questions surrounding gender and respectability and analyze how they take on new meanings through dance competitions in contemporary India. Interestingly, in these changing times, female sexuality and eroticism through dance continue to remain as controversial as they were in the mythic past.

FROM *BOOGIE WOOGIE* TO *DANCE INDIA DANCE*

Television reality shows in India began to grow in the 1990s. The liberalization of the economy, or market reforms, triggered the globalization of media, which was accompanied by a staggering multiplication of television channels. This opening to the globalization of the culture and economy created a great turbulence in the public sphere, coalescing and dismantling previous boundaries between "high" and "low" cultural forms. The momentum of change facilitated various kinds of boundary crossings among cultural forms, between classical and folk, and Indian and Western, thus breaking down received and accepted classifications. The most important aspect of this chaotic economic and cultural change was the spread of media and electronic communication. The Bollywood industry and the song-and-dance sequence of Bollywood films (which is perhaps one of the most visible products of India's new economy) spread in a rhizomatic reproduction through electronic media such as television, music videos, and YouTube

(Chakravorty 2009, 2016). Bombay film dance, or what was previously known as *filmee naach*, associated with lowbrow culture (as opposed to the classical arts) quickly transformed into a desirable, glamorous, and international product called Bollywood dance. It is important to note that there is a symbiotic relationship between Bollywood dance, the television industry, and the reality shows that are some of the building blocks of contemporary Indian celebrity culture.

One of the earliest television shows based on the format of a dance competition was *Boogie Woogie*, broadcast on the Sony cable network. It is often retrospectively called the first dance reality show on Indian television, although the term was not in circulation then. It first aired in 1997 and included contestants as young as six who danced to spicy numbers from hip-hop to classical dance genres (the show had no reference to the original "Boogie Woogie" style, other than the name). It displayed a new genre of Indian commercial dance where *filmee naach* (what is now Bollywood dance), classical, folk, hip-hop, breaking, and disco were packaged for consumption by a new generation and a new aspirational class. The judges were dancer Javed Jaffrey and celebrity personalities Naved Jaffrey and Ravi Behl. The show included special events such as child championship shows, teenage championship shows, and celebrity championship shows, where Bollywood film stars like Mithun Chakravorty and Govinda (who are excellent dancers themselves) appeared as celebrity judges. It also integrated humor, whereby the judges interacted with comedians on stage, and included a live audience. Initially, there were no cash prizes for the performers, merely enthusiastic applause from the judges and the live audience. The popularity of *Boogie Woogie* created an alternative narrative of dance in India that was for everyone, both experts and amateurs, and it released Indian dance from the more austere conventions of classicism (Chakravorty 2008).

Boogie Woogie is now considered one of the longest running dance talent or reality shows in India. It was discontinued and relaunched several times, including an international *Boogie Woogie* in 2008, which was launched by Sony Entertainment Television Asia in London. *Boogie Woogie* constantly innovated the content of the competition, which ranged from highlighting young solo dancers to group performances. In 2014, it organized an all-India show, which was promoted as "battles between gangs" to underline the intensity of the competition. The show even invited two actors/humorists from Pakistan to liven it up and offered a cash prize of eight lakh rupees to the winner. It began with Javed Jaffrey stating that *Boogie Woogie* was about to launch a "gang war" through its dance competition. The program, he claimed, was unstoppable, and that it was unique in the way it brought dance together with *mazak* (humor) to the audience. They had flown in *kalakar parindes* (artists who are like birds) from Pakistan for that particular show. Thus, in one stroke, *Boogie Woogie* was creating entertainment for a mass television audience and forging cultural diplomacy between the two archenemies Pakistan and India (although this is not unique to *Boogie Woogie*, as reality shows in India routinely feature artists and judges from Pakistan and Bangladesh). The two humorists from Pakistan, Aslam and Shakeel, worked hard to create a rapport with the audience. They admired the elaborate stage lighting design and compared it to a *mela* (kind of a *deshi* carnival or fair).

The dialogue and exchanges between the artists from Pakistan and their hosts created a humorous intertext before we saw the first "gang" on the dance floor. The tone of the exchanges highlighted that the "battles between gangs" were really about the fun of dancing among friendly performers. The first group of young male dancers, from Mumbai, spun a humorous story through their dancing and narrative. Before they launched their dance number, they shared with the audience a story about their journey from the streets of Mumbai to the stage. They said they had come from a village to Mumbai to get work and get rich, but instead had become beggars on the streets of the city. They were dressed in rags and their faces were smeared with black paint. One of the gang members/dancers was bare-chested, thin, and gaunt, emphasizing the theme of street urchins. They danced to the popular music video by Adnan Sami with these words addressed to *maula* (god): "Mujko Bhi Lift Karade, Bungla, Motor, Car Dila De" (Lift me up [maula/god] give me a bunglow, motorbike, and car, [like you have given others]). Throwing their arms around with energetic jumping and stomping, the group performed a humorous dance/theater enactment with this song. The dance included hip-hop moves, such as krumping, and tilting of the head and neck with energetic torso movements and hip thrusts. A double parody operated in their performance, as dance reality shows routinely shower their winners with fancy cars and money to buy luxury apartments; they are also considered tickets to "celebrity" for talented dancers among the struggling masses. Humorously knitting the story of coming to Mumbai from a village with the rags to riches story of reality shows, the performance underlined the everyday narrative of the influx of migrants from rural to urban India.

This group was followed by another group of young men dressed as women in Kathak costumes. They performed a gender-bending dance number to the song "Dil Cheez Kya Hai" (What Is This Thing Called Heart) from the Bombay/Bollywood film *Umrao Jaan* (1981), originally performed by the popular actress Rekha. The stage reverberated with the Kathak *bols* (rhythmic syllables) *Dha Gin Ta Dha Gin Ta Dha* as the dancers swirled around and stomped their belled feet in unison. They danced in the Kathak *mujra* style (associated with the *tawaifs*/courtesans from Islamic courts, usually performed solo by a female), rendered here in a group choreography by males. The next group performed a Ganesh *Vandana* (invocation to the Hindu god Ganesha) in Bharatanatyam style, with flexed knees and angular arm movements, set to orchestral music. This group was from Alibagh, a small town south of Mumbai, in Maharashtra.

One by one, other groups arrived on the *Boogie Woogie* stage to perform their dances, and the clash of groups or the "gang war" intensified. There were other dance styles represented in these battles and some were received with loud applause from the audience. The one that stood out for me was a jazz number performed by a group from Bangalore, dressed in outfits that looked like black and white designer body suits. The event was the second elimination round for the *Boogie Woogie* contest and whoever won was to be included in the next contest, before it went to the final battle. Throughout the episode, there was humor and good cheer, which created a certain camaraderie among the contestants, and the judges played on and subverted the rhetoric of "gang war." It reflected the show's reputation for being civil, fair, and authentic (meaning the winners were not fixed ahead of time), unlike some of the other reality shows where judges were known to fight among themselves, fix winners, or belittle contestants. *Boogie Woogie* is considered a precursor to the popular reality show on national television *Dance India Dance*, which started as *Dance Bangla Dance* on a local network, Zee Bangla.

Dance India Dance, or *DID*, premiered on Zee in 2009. It held all-India auditions in the leading metropolitan cities of India for contestants between the ages of fifteen and thirty. Those initial selections were then screened for selection into the "mega auditions" and thereafter selected for the final stage for *DID*, which was a prestigious milestone for the contestants. Once chosen for the final round, professional Bollywood choreographers trained the dancers. These final dancers had to be proficient in performing all styles of dancing from salsa, samba, and contemporary, to hip-hop, Bollywood, and Indian classical. The final round was between eighteen dancers, split up into three groups, who competed for the big prize in a fierce test of stamina and talent. The final award included the title of the "Best Dancer in India" and a cash prize of twenty lakh rupees (enough money to buy a nice apartment in a good neighborhood in almost any Indian city).

During my ethnographic fieldwork in Kolkata in 2011, I observed some of the contestants during an audition for *DID*. The auditions took place at the Swabhumi Heritage Plaza close to the Eastern Bypass. A gate had been constructed with the banner of *DID*, featuring large pictures of the three judges, Bollywood choreographers Remo D'souza, Geeta Kapoor, and Terence Lewis. The renowned *DID* judges were now household names. Terence Lewis specialized in contemporary dance and had trained in the Alvin Ailey American Dance Theater and the Martha Graham Center for Contemporary Dance in New York. Remo D'souza was not only a successful dance choreographer but later also directed the 2013 film *Any Body Can Dance* (popularly known as ABCD), which led to a sequel *ABCD 2* (2015) that featured two *DID* contestants. Remo D' Souza was self-trained and considered Michael Jackson his guru (he learned his moves from watching Jackson's videos, a methodology used by many reality show contestants). He was first noticed during an "All India Dance Competition." Geeta Kapoor's journey to stardom followed a different and more traditional route for Bollywood choreographers. She became well-known by assisting the famous choreographer Farah Khan, who used to be an assistant to the legendary Bollywood choreographer Saroj Khan. Kapoor, unlike D'souza, belonged to a Bollywood dance lineage.

At Swabhumi, I was smuggled inside by one of the crew members into the privately sealed-off space for the *DID* auditions. This was a spacious area where multiple television sets hung and various cameras panned and focused on the contestants on stage. The raised stage area had "Dance India Dance" written prominently across the backdrop. The judges sat at a distance from the stage to observe and provide comments. In the next layer sat the audience in a raised makeshift gallery. I sat with the technicians on the ground behind the audience in the last layer and quietly observed.

Framing the stage were bright lights that hung from an extensive lighting grid and steel structures of industrial design. At the outer circumference of the stage were perched several cameras that followed the dancers across space. Many men with headsets stood next to television monitors and watched the dancers closely. The judges behind these men were in an enclosed area.

A very young woman dressed in black tights, a skinny blacktop, and a short red skirt, with her hair pulled in a ponytail and a red flower clipped to the side, began to dance. She threw her right leg forward in a giant kick and then dragged the rest of her body weight forward; she extended her arms to her sides and threw her head back. She repeated the phrase again then quickly drew her legs together and crossed her palms above her head in the shape of a butterfly. She used the gesture or mudra from Bharatnatyam *tripataka* (which bends the ring finger while the palm remains flat and taut). She twirled a few times with her arms extended above her head, swung her hips, and then glided across the stage like a ballet dancer *en pointe*. The music was a fusion style with various instruments like drums, tabla, and guitar woven in, with a North Indian classical voice that sang "Jhum na na na" (the words associated with resounding anklets or bells tied around a dancer's feet). The dancer had bare feet but was not wearing any bells, despite what the song suggested. The dancer used some Bharatnatyam moves with flexed knees and stomping. She extended her hands on both sides with flower-like gestures, but then changed from the Bharatanatyam-style moves to an angular kick and a quick turn. I recognized the dance as "freestyle dancing" prevalent in Bollywood. However, some dancers I spoke to during the auditions called this style of dancing "fusion," and some even referred to the style as "contemporary dance." It became apparent to me that the label was fluid.

The next dancer was a young male who carried a long ribbon like Chinese ribbon dancers. He wore a white outfit and manipulated the ribbon with a flourish, making a circular loop around his head. Then he began pirouetting like a ballet dancer. Both the dancer and the ribbon created an elegant visual. He then performed a feathery somersault to let go of the ribbon. He continued with a mix of moves from ballet, gymnastics, and Western modern dance. This song-and-dance genre was called "lyrical contemporary." The next dancer provided a sharp contrast. He was dressed in black and he walked across the stage with the attitude of a hip-hop dancer and donned a pair of sunglasses. He then performed some breaking and popping moves. The music was a loud mechanical sound and he moved with it like a robot. He fell to the floor and did some isolation with his hands and then stood up in one swift move and continued his popping. The music changed continuously and the words were in English.

This event was like many other auditions of dance reality shows, including *Boogie Woogie*, that were regularly organized in various cities of India and abroad. *DID* was a major national reality show on Zee TV. To be seen on television as a contestant on this show was a huge accomplishment for young aspiring dancers. Many I spoke to believed that to win a *DID* contest would be a sure ticket to stardom, a ticket that they firmly believed would be theirs someday. The dancers and choreographers of reality shows such as *DID* represent the new dance embodiments and identities of an aspirational generation. Dance reality shows were their pathways to success and self-actualization. In the next section, I explore how such aspirations or desire to win shape the contemporary aesthetics of "remix." The meaning of desire associated with classical/traditional dance aesthetics of devotion (*bhakti rasa*), I argue, is transformed into a new kind of desire—a desire to win and participate in consumption in a globalizing Indian economy

EMBODIMENT OF REMIX AND COMMODITY DESIRE

The globalization of culture in India is integral to the spread of media and electronic communication; it is also associated with a culture of consumption that was sparked by liberalization. Both globalization and liberalization have created a spectacular sensory world of images, sounds, and commodities that are fueled by new desires and aspirations in an expanding economy. Anthropologist William Mazzarella associates contemporary India with "voluptuous desire" (2004). In order to analyze the new Indian dances of Bollywood and reality shows through an Indian aesthetics and experience, I look at the changing meaning of desire, as it was associated with Indian dances in the past and its present consumerist context.

Ideas of eroticism and desire have been foundational to traditional/classical Indian dances. In theories of the *bhava-rasa* emotive-aesthetic system (where *bhava* is everyday emotion and *rasa* is aesthetic emotion), desire and love have been fused to express both corporeal/sexual love and devotional love, or *bhakti*. The idea of *bhakti rasa* has encompassed a devotional desire that expresses both earthly and spiritual longings for one's beloved or god. The aesthetics are derived from the mythopoetic genres of *bhakti* and Sufi traditions. The new desires and aesthetics in dance competitions we see in reality shows are diametrically different from such idealistic concepts of love and devotion found in mythopoetic genres, but it is important to understand some of the key features associated with an older aesthetic system like *bhakti rasa*. A close examination of the traditional enables us to grasp the new desires or the aspirational aesthetics of contemporary forms that are "remixes."

Bhakti rasa is one of the key emotional/aesthetic concepts in classical Indian dances. *Bhakti*, which means "devotion," is ignited through dancing, which is also considered a form of prayer, leading to the supplication of one's ego to reach the sublime. The emotion of *bhakti* is also infused through the practice of dance pedagogy in India called *gurushishya parampara* (a student–teacher apprenticeship system), where the guru is equivalent to god and the *shishya*/student surrenders to the teacher as a *bhakta* (devotee). The immersion in classical dances through such training structures supposedly produces the spiritual/yogic bodies of the classical dancers. The training requires a long-term association and/or cohabitation with a particular teacher or guru, and knowledge is transmitted orally and through repetition. The student learns the metrical systems of *laya* and *tala* (cycles of rhythms) that are part of the movement repertoire and imbues them with kinesthetic memory and aesthetic emotions. The experience of time through the cyclical structures of *tala* are circular and continuous, and the exploration of space is both inward and outward, thus making this experience both cosmological and real. In this kind of performance experience, space and time are molded through a subjective experience rather than an objective one.

The embodiment of dance in such a spatiotemporal construct is phenomenological and differently oriented than Western choreographic conventions derived from objective scientific time/space construct.[2] The modernization of Indian dance and its related aesthetics are associated with India's political independence in 1947, when the state, especially the central government, became the official patron of culture and various regional dances were refashioned to fit the concert stage. However, the ideology of *gurushishya parampara* was instituted in state institutions and cultural centers or Akademies, and it became an important ideological device for preserving and promoting India's cultural heritage. Accordingly, the aesthetics of *bhava-rasa* became the marker of India's (invented) classical traditions.

These hegemonic ideologies of classicism perpetuated through state institutions have come unhinged due to liberalization and globalization. Now the meaning of *guru* has become diffused. Moreover, the gurus are no longer strictly associated with long dynastic lineages or elite families (like in the past), nor are the dancers immersed in a singular dance aesthetic to embody a particular regional identity that has been deemed "classical." The dancers now learn from multiple sources and embody multiple styles to create flexible bodies and hybrid identities.[3] Desire, which was once expressed through aesthetic concepts of devotion and love in Indian dances, is now expressed through the consumption of spectacular commodities. Purnima Mankekar (2004) writes about the relationship between experiencing emotion and producing/consuming commodity. Here desire and pleasure are not just about the acquisition of commodity, but gazing upon it and displaying it, that is, in consuming spectacles. She looks at the relationship between erotics and the consumption of commodities, and the reconfiguration of gender, family, caste, and nation in contemporary India. Detailing the eroticization of commodities through images, texts, billboards, television, and films in the late twentieth century, she shows how they stimulate the onlooker to desire, possess, or purchase the product. The conjunction between erotic desire and the desire to consume, she argues, is the "commodity affect" (Mankekar 2004, 408). Through this "affect," a new kind of subjectivity is produced: an active, sexual, and consuming subject full of desires. I suggest that the "item numbers" of Bollywood films (these are the song-and-dance sequences, to be elaborated in the next section) and the "item girl" and "item boy" who appear in "item numbers" embody the new consumerist desires of "remix" (much like the "commodity affect"), encoded through the aspirations of winning.

Therefore "remix," both as a practice and an embodied aesthetic, expresses the aspirational desires of consumerist modernity. Remix is usually associated with technological innovation, such as DJs mixing different musical styles. It is also an aspect of the hip-hop genre, such as "breaking," that mixes with other styles as it travels globally and morphs into new hybrid forms (Osumare 2002). This nomadic aspect of remix is now integral to Bollywood dance and music and their byproducts such as television reality shows. The remix aesthetics perpetuated by Bollywood dance fuses high and low, classical and folk, Indian and other dance styles to produce endless hybridity. Therefore remix itself implies a multitude of categories that can borrow freely from Indian classical and folk dance traditions or from non-Indian/global dance traditions. It displays an aesthetics that are no longer bounded by the classical ideology of Indian dance whereby the purity and rigidity of the form have to be upheld. The dancer's body acts as an instrument where movements are mixed through a copy-and-paste technique, producing a particular kind of hybrid disembodied embodiment.

Remix is the embodiment of pastiche that blurs the line between culture and commodity (Jameson 1991, 1998). In Bollywood films, the song-and-dance sequences (now called "item numbers") have been the platform for remixes. The song-and-dance sequences have increasingly become detached from the main narrative of the film in the 1980s and 1990s to operate as individual products (Gopal and Moorty, 2008). They circulate globally as music videos and as item numbers and are disseminated through various electronic outlets such as YouTube, Itunes, and social media such as Facebook.

The item numbers from Bollywood films are also remediated through the televisual format of dance reality shows, thus multiplying the process of circulation (Chakravorty 2016; Novak 2012). Ethnomusicologist David Novak (2012) explains remediation to be the repurposing of media from one context to another. In remix aesthetics, dance movements are uprooted from any context and remixed to produce an item number. Thus, dance reality shows use the song-and-dance sequences of Bollywood or item numbers to re-choreograph and repackage them to make a new product. The remixing and remediation produce the hybrid cosmopolitan dancing bodies of postmodernism, endowed with the new desire/emotion of aspiration. Indian dance now inhabits a world dominated by the aesthetics and bodily dispositions of remix, where experiential states once associated with the mythopoetics of *bhava-rasa* now appear as fleeting emotions of a bygone era. They create the experience of what anthropologist Arjun Appadurai (1997, 30) calls "nostalgia without memory." Dance reality shows open up the discursive space for the construction of new modes of dance that shape not only new concepts of desire, but also how these desires are expressed through new ways of being feminine and masculine. These are the hyper-sexualized item girls and item boys of Bollywood films. They shape the new gender codes of femininity and masculinity in contemporary India. In the next section, I focus on the construction of female sexuality by comparing two song-and-dance sequences from Bombay/Bollywood films to delve into the changing notions of women's sexuality.

FEMALE SEXUALITY
IN SONG-AND-DANCE SEQUENCES

The two song-and-dance sequences I analyze here are both popular hits that created new standards for dance choreography on screen. The first one, "Mohe Panghat Pe

Nandalal Cheed Gayo Re" (On My Way to the River Nandalal Teases Me), is a poetic rendition of a Thumri (a North Indian classical musical genre associated with Kathak dance) from the Bombay film *Mughal-E-Azam* (1960). The song and the dance convey the amorous love play between the Hindu deities Radha and Krishna (Nandalal is another name for Krishna). In this particular sequence, Anarkali, who is a courtesan and a dancer in Mughal emperor Akbar's court and is also the love of his son Salim, performs the dance. The story is about the transgressive love between a courtesan and a prince. The song-and-dance sequence juxtaposes the archetypal Radha and Krishna legend (also about illicit love, as Radha is a married woman) with the historical fictional story of Salim and Anarkali. The scene opens with Anarkali, played by Madhubala, seated at the center of Akbar's *darbar* (court) with her long red skirt falling around her in a circle on the floor. She slowly rises up and lifts her veil to expose her bejeweled face. She wears a large nose ring, an ornament on her forehead, and bangles that extend to her palms, with attached rings for all the fingers. She makes undulating movements, and her hand gestures frame her face to create an intimate visual transaction with the audience. The camera cuts to the faces of the king and queen and we are drawn into a simultaneous exchange of interlocking gazes. The ornate architectural arches and the luminescent lamps in the backdrop add to the richness of the scene. The swirling multicolored skirts (*ghagras*) of the dancers in the background enhance the sensory experience. Madhubala lifts her arms in the shape of a pot, with her back to the audience, and moves toward the dancers with gentle hip sways. The dancers (replicating the cowherd girls of the Radha-Krishna tale) raise their hands like Madhubala and move in circles in similar kinesthetic nuances. They all wear *ghagra cholis* (long skirts and blouses) with the transparent fabric or *churnis* that cover their exposed torso. In another shot we see women musicians playing the sitar (a stringed instrument), seated in a row by water fountains, and next we see the dancers lined up behind them, dancing with stretched arms and gentle wrist movements. The gestures, movements, and the facial expressions are drawn from Kathak repertoire, and the legendary Kathak guru Lacchu Maharaj choreographed the dance. Although the portrayal of the dancing girl in this scene (the courtesan played by Madhubala) is not of an item girl, she can be considered the precursor to what emerged as the item girl in Bollywood films after the 1980s.

The song-and-dance sequence "Sheila Ki Jawani" (2010) from *Tees Maar Khan* (He Who Killed Thirty) is the definition of an item number with the explosive dancing girl (item girl) taking center stage. Here we see Katrina Kaif (playing the role of Anya Singh, a struggling actress) sprawled in bed, covered with a white satin sheet. The song, dance, and the lyrics are all remixes in this sequence, where English words are thrown in with Hindi, such as "I am too sexy for you," "tere haath na anni" (do not let your hand touch me). The lyrics explicitly speak about the vitality of Sheila's youth; no man can satiate her sexuality. From the bedroom scene, where she is surrounded by applauding men, the shot moves to a bar where Sheila dances with full abandonment a fusion combining belly dance with Bollywood pelvic thrusts. She goes through four costume changes as the shots change to capture her seductive dancing, surrounded by men who dance around her. In most of these, she wears a short tight *choli* (blouse) and a low-rise *ghagra* or *dhoti* (skirt or pants). She wears no jewelry and her hair is open and flowing. The costumes expose a large part of her toned midriff as she gyrates energetically. She throws her arms upward and swings them freely, adhering to no particular style. The camera mostly lingers on her body parts, inviting the audience to explore the curvaceous undulations of her torso and the heaving breasts. The repeated pelvic thrusts and the jerky swaying of the hips and the arms create a wildly sexy and exuberant spectacle. In another shot, we see Katrina dressed in a white shirt with short boxers, wearing a hat, and doing MTV-like dancing moves reminiscent of Madonna's music videos, such as "Express Yourself" (1989). Not unlike that video, the item girl in this scene also exhibits excessive sexuality and is also surrounded by leering males. Both provoke a sense of forbidden and explosive sexuality. "Sheila Ki Jawani" was choreographed by Bollywood choreographer Farah Khan, became a rage, and earned her the best choreographer award that year.

No doubt, the representation of woman in this song-and-dance sequence is in sharp contrast to the previous sequence I discussed. However, both have transgressive elements that push the boundaries of idealized domesticated women of India's nationhood, which I will come to shortly. The transgressive sexuality of the courtesan in the first scene is tempered by the mythopoetic story of Radha and Krishna and the emotional *bhava-rasa* aesthetics of Kathak dance. The second scene pushes the acceptable norms of womanhood to create a controversial discourse on the excesses of women's sexuality—so much so, that the film and the song-and-dance sequence sparked a public discourse on women's sexuality and censorship before it was released. The Central Board of Film Certification in India tried to ban the film and urged the producers to delete the word "Sheila" from the lyrics. But the film was considered a comedy and a spoof and it ultimately passed the censorship board with very few changes. I delve deeper into issues of women's identity and sexuality in the next section to illustrate the challenges surrounding dance reality shows, Bollywood, and the constructions of femininity in contemporary India.

GENDERED IDENTITIES IN THE AGE OF COMMODITY

The popularity of dance reality shows and the ubiquitous item numbers that accompany them have created a public battleground for discourses surrounding women's bodies and sexuality in contemporary India. The confluence of consumerism, eroticization, and celebrity culture in dance reality shows forms an irresistible kind of desire that is constantly on display for consumption. Middle-class anxieties surrounding respectability are at the heart of this allure of the senses that is now intertwined with notions of success (to be a winner), the power of fame, and the glamor of celebrity culture. The new generation of dancers and choreographers of dance reality shows not only have replaced the past categories of embodied aesthetics, such as *bhava-rasa* derived from classical dances, but also in the process they unsettle the past notions of Indianness and idealized gender identities (Bagchi 1995; Sangari and Vaid 1990; Sinha 1996). These past gender codes were molded by Indian nationalist discourse on "respectable women." The nationalists constructed the ideal Indian women as repositories of tradition, domesticity, and spirituality (goddess/devi/domesticated mothers) (Bagchi 1995; Chatterjee 1989). It is now well accepted that classical Indian dances contributed to this ideal construction of Indian women, who were mostly Hindu and upper-caste. The selective appropriation and reconstruction of dances such as Bharatanatyam, Odissi, and Kathak shaped gender codes in modern India and produced the Sanskritized bodies of Indian dances (Chakravorty 2016; Coorlawala 2004; Meduri 1996; Soneji 2012).[4] Here, using my ethnographic research among reality show dancers and choreographers, I analyze recent debates surrounding the changing gender codes and middle-class respectability in contemporary India.

During my ethnographic research in Kolkata and Mumbai, I spoke with several dance reality show contestants and choreographers regarding their struggles and negotiations with women's respectability. The issues ranged from what kind of dance they would perform, what kind of costumes they would wear, and how they would conduct themselves during makeup and costuming, rehearsals, and shootings. A very young contestant in Kolkata explained to me in great detail the atmosphere in these competitions that created the pressure to climb the ladder of success by winning different rounds. She said getting ahead and succeeding were of utmost importance; the ultimate goal was to be the champion. I sat with her in the intimate surrounding of her living room as she showed me many medals and gold and silver ornaments, all of which she had won from dance competitions. So, when she started competing in a dance reality show on a local television channel, she was ready to face the hardest competition and win. This dance reality show was one of the first of its kind on a Bengali television channel. *Naach Dhum Machale*, the reality show in question, had the categories of Eastern and Western dance themes, along with dance and film choreographers and directors as judges. She explained that "Eastern" meant Indian folk, classical, and modern dance such as Rabindrik (the style created by poet-laureate Rabindranath Tagore) and "Western" meant Bollywood-inspired dances combining jazz, hip-hop, ballroom dancing, and other non-Indian dances.

She was disappointed from the very beginning because the choreographer designated to her was strong in Western dances and was not interested in choreographing in the styles with which she was comfortable, such as Bharatanatyam and Rabindrik. Her disappointment increased when the dances she was asked to perform also included wearing strange and revealing costumes. In a round that was called "seduction" she was dressed up like Helen, the famous Bollywood dancer, in a skimpy costume, and was asked to perform a "Western medley." But the most embarrassing and vulgar dance (according to her) was when she was dressed like a tiger in a tight tube. She was eliminated after winning several rounds and she blamed her costumes, especially the tiger one, and her discomfort with dancing in a tube dress. As she described her struggles with the costume and her dance moves, I remembered what one Bollywood choreographer had confided to me during my fieldwork in Film City Studios, Mumbai. Sunita Shetty, the assistant to the renowned Bollywood choreographer Ajay Borade, had said, "Sometimes after choreographing a piece I go home and think that what I did is much too vulgar. But what to do, the director wants it and nowadays no one wants to see Indian folk and classical forms. They only like 'Western dance' like 'item numbers.'"[5]

The general discomfort with reality shows was not confined to dancers and choreographers, but spilled over into public discourse regarding women's morality and sexuality. These discourses were often about the anxieties of westernization of Indian culture associated with globalization and Bollywoodization. I learned from some of the contestants that their schools and colleges have often been hostile and critical of students who participate in reality shows. Somehow, participating in dance reality shows marked them as promiscuous and women of low moral stature. The attitude perhaps was connected to the representation of women's bodies on screen, especially what was perpetuated by Bollywood item numbers, as some argue.

It was a subject of great concern among feminist activists and media scholars in India in general. In a recent show celebrating International Women's Day on the television network NDTV, sponsored by the cosmetics company L'Oréal, the Bollywood actress and feminist/activist Shabana Azmi pointed to the lyrics of the hit item song "Main To Tandoori Murgi Hoon Yaar, Gatkaale Saiyyan Alcohol Se" (I am a tandoori chicken, lover, gobble me with alcohol) as an example of the perpetuation of such sexual objectification of women in society. She argued that, although it was written, composed, and sponsored by a few, it was consumed by millions of Indians. Azmi added that women need autonomy on how the camera captures their bodies and that there should be self-regulation about such representation. Ravish Kumar, the journalist hosting the show, added that young children dance to these lyrics in schools every day, normalizing such sexualized portrayals of women. Of course, they are also regularly performed in dance reality shows by thousands of young men and women (and also children) and beamed from various television networks, which make them ubiquitous in contemporary India. If we take the long view, however, we recall, among other things, that this debate is not new; it was the sexually explicit lyrics in *devadasi* performances in colonial India that affronted women reformers such as Rukmini Devi and others who "cleaned up" and "purified" the form and made Bharatanatyam "classical" and oriented to worship and the divine.

In the context of this ongoing and complex social transformation in India, which looks at the new middle-class formations, sociologists Ruchira Ganguly-Scrase and Timothy Scrase (2009, 152) observe,

> The struggle to preserve middle-class culture and identity in the face of great social change highlights the way in which cultural politics is at the core of middle-class opposition to neoliberal reforms and, moreover, these cultural struggles take place as much within the relative privacy of the home, as in the public sphere of the street, the workplace or the tea shop. In other words, while neoliberal reforms have inexorably

changed social and economic life, their indirect impact through globalised-induced cultural change has also been an affront to middle-class morals, culture, and identity.

Although these debates about gender codes and representation of women's bodies on screen reflect the sentiments and judgments of a section of the middle classes, some also actively contest these sentiments and moral judgments. Many of them clearly recognize the possibility of showcasing talent and class mobility in reality shows. These attitudes were repeatedly apparent to me during my conversations not only with the contestants and choreographers, but also with producers, recruiters, and audience members. Many from the small towns saw this as an opportunity to realize their dream of buying an apartment in Kolkata or a car. This was not unlike the humorous song-and-dance sequence for the reality show *Boogie Woogie* that I described at the beginning of the chapter, where dancers pretend to enact a rags-to-riches story that mirrors the experience of winning a reality show. In this chaotic social transition in India, dance reality shows throw into relief questions of class mobility, women's sexuality, respectability, and identity within the context of liberalization and globalization. Not unlike the Kali and Shiva myth, the battleground is the performance context, whether it is the precincts of a temple or a television screen. Both are windows into relations of gender, power, and norms of respectability.

Notes

1. I conducted ethnographic fieldwork in India, mainly in Kolkata and Mumbai, during 2006–2012 for my book project *This Is How We Dance Now* on television dance reality shows and Bollywood dance.
2. See Foster (2011) regarding choreography and notation.
3. Anusha Kedar (2014) writes about the intersection of race and citizenship in the context of the flexibility of the body among diaspora South Asian performers in the United Kingdom.
4. "Sanskritization" is a complex process that, at it root, involves the transformation of "low" and "folk" to "high" and "classical." It applies to culture (music, dance, literature) and social identity ("low" and "high" castes).
5. Shetty distinguishes Bollywood dance, which uses a remix aesthetics, from earlier *filmee naach* or dance in Bombay film, which uses traditional Indian aesthetics.

References

Appadurai, Arjun. 1997. *Modernity at Large*. New Delhi: Oxford University Press.

Bagchi, Jasodhara. 1995. *Indian Women: Myth and Reality*. Hyderabad: Sangam Books.

Chakravorty, Pallabi. 2008. *Bells of Change: Kathak Dance, Women, and Modernity in India*. Calcutta: Seagull Books; Chicago: University of Chicago Press.

Chakravorty, Pallabi. 2009. "Moved to Dance: Remixed, Rasa, and a New India." *Visual Anthropology* 22(2–3): 211–228.

Chakravorty, Pallabi. 2016. "Sensory Screens, Digitized Desires: Dancing Rasa from Bombay Cinema to Reality TV." In *The Oxford Handbook on Screen Dance Studies*, edited by Douglas Rosenberg, 125–142. Oxford: Oxford University Press.

Chatterjee, Partha. 1989. "The Nationalist Resolution of the Women's Question." In *Recasting Women: Essays in Colonial History*, edited by Kumkum Sangari and Sudesh Vaid, 233–253. New Delhi: Kali for Women.

Coorlawala, Uttara A. 2004. "The Sanskritized Body." *Dance Research Journal* 36(2): 50–63.

Foster, Susan. 2011. *Choreographing Empathy: Kinesthesia in Performance*. New York: Routledge.

Ganguly-Scrase, Ruchira, and Timothy J. Scrase. 2009. *Globalisation and the Middle Classes in India*. London: Routledge.

Gopal, Sangita A., and Sujata Moorti, eds. 2008. *Global Bollywood: Travels of Hindi Song and Dance*. Minneapolis: University of Minnesota Press.

Jameson, Fredric. 1991. *Postmodernism, or The Cultural Logic of Late Capitalism*. Durham, NC: Duke University Press.

Jameson, Fredric. 1998. "Notes on Globalization as Philosophical Issue." In *The Cultures of Globalization*, edited by Fredric Jameson and Masao Miyoshi, 54–77. Durham, NC: Duke University Press.

Kedar, Anusha. 2014. "Flexibility and Its Bodily Limits: Transnational South Asian Dancers in an Age of Neoliberalism." *Dance Research Journal* 46(1): 23–40.

Mankekar, Purnima. 2004. "Dangerous Desires: Television and Erotics in Late Twentieth Century India." *Journal of Asian Studies* 63(2): 403–431.

Mazzarella, William. 2004. "Culture, Globalization, and Mediation." *Annual Review of Anthropology* 33: 345–367.

Meduri, Avanthi. 1996. "Nation, Woman, Representation: The Sutured History of the Devadasi and Her Dance." Unpublished PhD diss., New York University.

Novak, David. 2012. "Cosmopolitanism, Remediation and the Ghost World of Bollywood." *Cultural Anthropology* 25(1): 40–72.

Osumare, Halifu. 2002. "Break Dancing and the Intercultural Body." *Dance Research Journal* 34(2): 30–45.

Sangar, Kukum, and Sudesh Vaid. 1990. *Recasting Women*. New Brunswick, NJ: Rutgers University Press.

Sinha, Mrinalini. 1996. "Gender in the Critique of Colonialism and Nationalism: Locating the 'Indian Woman.'" In *Feminism and History*, edited by Joan Scott, 477–504. New York: Oxford University Press.

Soneji, Davesh. 2012. *Unfinished Gestures: Devadasis, Memory, and Modernity in South India*. Chicago: University of Chicago Press.

PART IV

JUDGING, SPECTATORSHIP, AND THE VALUES OF MOVEMENT

CHAPTER 15

....

MISS EXOTIC WORLD

Judging the Neo-Burlesque Movement

....

KAITLYN REGEHR

JUDGING AT THE BURLESQUE HALL OF FAME

IN June 2014 I arrived at the Orleans, an off-strip hotel in Las Vegas, where, as I have been told by numerous cab drivers, is "the place the locals go." As I stepped off the hot concrete of the parking lot into the smoky lobby, I moved toward the hotel's front desk, adorned in signature Mardi Gras–themed decorations. I noted the check-in line had a familiar combination of both "muggles" (a neo-burlesque term to describe the general public) and—distinguished by their vintage apparel, animal print suitcases, and various combinations of piercings, tattoos, and fake eyelashes—the Burlesque Hall of Fame (BHoF) weekenders. The BHoF reunion has been an annual tradition since 1955 when the Exotic Dancers League (EDL), one of America's earliest formal unions for women in exotic dance, held its first meeting. Today, thanks to the efforts of late EDL member Dixie Evans, also known as the "Marilyn Monroe of Burlesque," the BHoF annual reunion continues to be a gathering for former dancers. In addition, as of 1991, Evans added a competition component to the reunion, which in turn became the most prestigious pageant for the neo-burlesque movement (Figure 15.1).

Growing out of a performance art community in the 1990s, neo-burlesque has been praised by both dance and feminist scholarship as a body-positive, feminist community, which through rejuvenating and repurposing this historic form of erotic entertainment has celebrated difference, alternative lifestyle choices, and has argued for a broader spectrum of beauty, sexuality, and orientation (Baldwin 2004; Dodds 2011; Ferreday 2008; Nally 2009; Sally 2009; Urish 2004; Willson 2008). From the perspective of both an alternative performance genre and distinctive lifestyle, the neo-burlesquers' use of the term "muggle" signals their belief in, and celebration of, their difference—a foundational tenet of the neo-burlesque community and annual weekender. Since the inception of the neo-burlesque movement, performers from around the world have made

FIGURE 15.1. Crowning the Queen of Burlesque, Miss Exotic World Award Ceremony, 2014.

Matilda Temperley, 2014

the pilgrimage to the BHoF Weekender and Miss Exotic World pageant, also known as the Tournament of Tease, to be judged by a collection of erotica celebrities and Exotic Dancers League members. These contestants carry the hopes of claiming titles such as "Best Burlesque Troupe," the "Best Boylesque," and the paramount honor Miss Exotic World.

This was my third year attending the BHoF reunion and my third experience of lining up with both the mere muggles and the outright magical at the Orleans check-in. However, as I reached the front of the line, I noted that this was the first year that I was provided with a complimentary room; the first year I was scheduled for a pre-pageant information session with the headmistress of the *New York School of Burlesque*, Jo "Boobs" Weldon; and it would be the first year I was given a ribbon to distinguish me as a Tournament of Tease judge. The ribbon was baby pink, topped with a large pin depicting Miss Exotic World 2009, Kalani Kokonuts, leaning her head back in an expression of ecstasy. Feeling both a sense of gratitude and discomfort at being charged with bestowing the community's most coveted title, I closed my fist tightly around the precious object, a badge of honor for the remainder of the weekend.

The BHoF Weekender includes a variety of events such as Barecats Burlesque Bowling, where neo-burlesque teams bowl adorned in a variety of extravagant or provocative accessories; the Stitch 'n' Bitch, a burlesque-themed sewing class; and Naked Ladies Reading, which is self-explanatory. The weekend also enables the former EDL

members, or "legends," as they are now known in the community, to reconnect and rem-
inisce at the Legends' Brunch or Legends' Panel, a question and answer session where
younger neo-burlesque enthusiasts question the legends about working in the burlesque
theaters and supper clubs of the mid-twentieth century.

Although these events and activities are important social spaces of connection and
community, for most who attend the Weekender, the evening entertainment forms the
main focus. The large-scale nightly shows span the four days of the reunion. The Movers,
Shakers and Innovators Showcase opens the weekend on Thursday evening, followed by
the celebratory Annual Titans of Tease: Legends Showcase, where the legends perform
their half-century-old striptease routines, in an outright rejection of preconceptions
surrounding aging women and their bodies. Saturday evening, however, hosts the
weekend's most coveted ticket, the Tournament of Tease, or Miss Exotic World pageant.[1]

On Saturday night, we, the judges, were briskly escorted by Weldon, past the ringing
slot machines in the Orleans lobby and through the crowd of buzzing burlesquers, into
the theater, where we sat side by side in a panel. The panel comprised the following: Gina
Bon Bon, representing the Legends; Las Vegas community representative Lou Lou
Roxy; former Miss Exotic World (2005) representative Michelle L'amour; academic and
activist Dr. Judith Lynne Hanna; the host of the History Network's American Pickers,
Danielle Colby; former Playboy Bunny and reality television star Holly Madison; and
myself, a representative of the burlesque community.

It was my role as a broadcaster on a Canadian documentary series, which used burlesque as a tool for empowerment, that facilitated my foundational relationship to this
community. The role of television personality had granted me another occupation outside the role of scholar, when I began my doctoral research Exotic Dancer's League. It
was during my first meeting with Weldon that she cautioned that this community does
not need the "approval of some PhD" to tell them if they are empowered or not.[2] As
I navigated this project over the next five years, I heeded this warning and tried to play
three roles, all of which I made known to participants: the researcher; the television
personality; and, most important, the community member. It was this latter role that
I worked to strengthen over the years, as it allowed me to engage with and, most significantly, be a part of this social microcosm. As I sat at the judges' table, nestled between
scholar judge Judith Lynn Hanna and celebrity judge Holly Madison, I, the burlesque
community judge, felt pleased that at least in this representation I had achieved that.
Yet, as the pageant began and a procession of thin-bodied dancers paraded across
the stage, I was forced to enter into a different participatory world from that which
I had encountered when working with this community thus far. I struggled to reconcile years of ethnographic study, which considered issues of inclusivity and safe space,
with this abrupt transformation into the role of "judge." Furthermore, contrary to my
field experiences at smaller festivals and localized neo-burlesque communities, these
dancers did not seem overtly subversive, political, or champions of difference. Contrary
to this, in body type, costume, and performance style, the dancers complied with beauty
ideals consistent with mainstream (or dare I say "muggle") media. I wondered about the
selection process that filtered out the performers from the hundreds who had applied to

compete and, as I looked down at my judging sheet that asked me to grade the primarily female participants on a ten-point scale, it hit me that competition is incompatible with the foundational principles of the neo-burlesque movement.

The interviews in this project were conducted and transcribed over a five-year period as I attended the BHoF and engaged with both the Legend and neo-burlesque community with friend and photographer Matilda Temperley. Utilizing ethnographic methodology and oral history interviews collected during my time working with the BHoF community, this chapter examines my experience of judging the Miss Exotic World Pageant. In the first section I outline the origins of the neo-burlesque movement and the prevailing academic and popular understanding of the ethos of this counterculture community. I then examine the Tournament of Tease as a "classic burlesque" pageant, as it is termed by the community. In contrast to many of the claimed tenets of the neo-burlesque movement, "classic burlesque" often attempts to "authentically" adhere to the parameters of mid-twentieth-century burlesque (the mainstream exotic entertainment of the period), which often includes a somewhat limited spectrum of body types and representations of gender and sexuality. In the second section, I draw from my experience judging the pageant to examine factors that complicate judging the tournament, including the demographics on the judges' panel, the methods of grading and placing value on the acts, and the limited diversity represented on the tournament stage with regard to race and sexual orientation. In conclusion, I argue that attempts to "authentically" recreate this mid-twentieth-century erotic performance perpetuate narrow perspectives on beauty, sexual orientation, and race—an aesthetic profoundly at odds with the ideologies of difference, supposedly championed by the movement. Finally, I find that the process of competition, with its demand for grading, ranking, and judging, not only normalizes and regulates this supposedly inclusive, sex positive practice, but that it is incongruous with the philosophical underpinnings of the neo-burlesque community.

Reviving Burlesque: Real and Believed

Scholarship on American burlesque typically categorizes the genre into three historical periods, or what burlesque scholar Jackie Willson (2008) terms "booms." The first boom, sparked by British music hall dancer Lydia Thompson's arrival in New York, refers to the parodies of plays that flourished in the late nineteenth century (Allen 1991; Pullen 2005). Thompson's troupe, the British Blondes, sang, danced, and enacted parodies of plays, often involving the women playing male characters, such as Robinson Crusoe, while sporting form-fitting tights (Allen 1991; Pullen 2005). The second boom, often termed the golden age, reached its peak in the 1930s as burlesque transitioned into historic Broadway theaters (Zeidman 1967). This period is characterized by vaudevillian revue format, elaborate sets and costumes, famed comics such as W. C. Fields, Bob Hope, Fanny Brice, and Charlie Chaplin, and striptease dancers such as Gypsy Rose Lee.

Many versions of burlesque history then paint a dark age when theatrical burlesque died (Shteir 2004; Willson 2008) in the mid-twentieth century, which has enabled the concept of a rebirth or resurgence, hence the term *neo-burlesque*.

Neo-burlesque performances, which involve elements of performance art, circus, and striptease, mark the origin of the burlesque revival. Scholar and neo-burlesque performer Lynn Sally, however, suggests that early performers did not initially use the term "burlesque" to define the work.[3] Burlesque community member and writer Michelle Baldwin (2004) notes that World Famous *BOB* was performing numbers, in a Marilyn Monroe wig, in a gay bar in New York City, when it was suggested that she was doing burlesque. Utilizing the revue format and classic burlesque iconography, neo-burlesque performers began to create shows that operated within a recognizable cabaret or variety act structure, but then subverted some of the staples of these performance idioms as a means to question gender norms, state political views, or include marginalized body types. Burlesque revival communities began to form across the United States, Canada, and the United Kingdom. Tease-O-Rama, a convention where neo-burlesque performers from a variety of cities unite and share their work, first took place in the spring of 2000.

Most of the work performed by the foundational members of the neo-burlesque movement questioned erotic performance and, often radically, suggested that bodies could simultaneously be hyper-sexualized while also being ugly or grotesque. Miss Exotic World 2006, Julie Atlas Muz, epitomizes these beautifully ugly performances. In her act *The Hand*, performed to "I Put a Spell on You" by Screamin' Jay Hawkins, Muz acts as if her right hand is both disembodied and possessed, as it seduces and attacks Muz. The hand then strips off her clothing, leaving her in sheer underwear and red pasties,[4] and further caresses her breasts and pleasures her through simulated vaginal and anal penetration. The hand eventually becomes violent, strangling Muz and finally choking her to death. *The Hand* references a traditional striptease structure, where golden age burlesque dancers would wear a puppet on one side of their body. These puppets would often take the form of the devil or an evil monkey character that would touch, caress, and seduce the naïve dancer. *The Hand* performance, by contrast, builds upon this often simplistic, golden age structure as it becomes sexually overt and violent. The performance seems to reference issues of objectification and the possession of women and their bodies, as Hawkins growls, "I don't care if you don't want me because I'm yours. I put a spell you because you are mine." Further, the routine deals with questions surrounding unattached, dehumanized sex, and potentially emotional or physical abuse. Yet there is also levity in this performance for, "the hand" is Muz's hand, over which she ultimately has complete control. Thus, the performance also gestures toward a sense of release and surrendering to one's own physical desires.

When I first encountered Muz in 2014 at the Slipper Room[5] in New York, she was dressed in a nuclear radiation protection suit and, under black light, she systematically stripped off her costume to reveal glow-in-the-dark pasties, lipstick, wig, and nails. Utilizing large iron tongs, Muz picked up a glowing "nuclear pellet," which she swallowed. She reacted by languidly undulating her torso as if the radiation was coursing through her body, and finally a glow stick slid out of her vagina, which she promptly tossed into the audience.[6]

Both these performances, whether involving a gruesome severed hand or glow stick–ejecting vagina, offered a new perspective on the act of stripping, fusing traditional elements of erotic entertainment with subversive presentations of the female anatomy. Other neo-burlesque performances might confront Western culture's preoccupation with able bodies. For instance, at the 2012 Toronto Burlesque Festival, Kristina Nekyia, dressed in a dirty and faded white tank top, dragged her motionless legs across the floor and up onto a pair of arm braces, on which she both painfully and erotically struggled to twist and turn her lower torso.

By contrast, Nasty Canasta's performances often confront gendered binaries in an outright rejection of normative representations of femininity. In a signature routine, she wears combat boots, a welder's helmet, and a metal-plated corset on which she grinds a heavy-duty metal sander, thus creating large sparks that leap halfway across the stage. Through performances of this kind, the burlesque resurgence operates separately from the continuum of mainstream erotic entertainment and, subsequently, contemporary exotic dance. Since the early days of the neo-burlesque movement, many members have been invested in disassociating burlesque from stripping. As Baldwin states,

> The question asked most in the early days of the new burlesque was "Are you a stripper?" to which many answered emphatically "No." They were dancers, striptease artists, burlesque performers, but many wanted nothing to do with the term stripper. Many still hold this position. (2004, 49)

Theater scholar David Owen (2014, 34) concurs with Baldwin, affirming that "(neo)burlesque is not stripping" as a burlesque show is "more about the tease and the art of the reveal rather than about simple exposure." From this perspective, the neo-burlesque movement has often positioned burlesque as separate from claims of exploitation that sit at the heart of much of the discourse regarding mainstream exotic dance (Barton 2002, 2006; Barton and Hardesty 2010; Bell and Slone 1998; Egan 2006; Frank 2002; Hanna 2003; Manaster 2006; Wesley 2000, 2003) and the sexual entertainment industry at large.

For many involved in the neo-burlesque community, these performances are recreational. Although many burlesque shows offer performers financial reimbursement, generally this does not cover performers' costs. Thus, most neo-burlesque artists do not make a living from their performance work, but rather enjoy the act of performing striptease as part of a liberated lifestyle. As a result, neo-burlesque concerns personal choice rather than financial need, which becomes a unifying element of the community. As dance scholar Sherril Dodds (2013) notes, the neo-burlesque community frequently represents a space of class privilege in that performers, by way of financial and intellectual capital, are able to produce such performances. Further, as performers have less concern with commercially viable erotic entertainment, instead they have greater freedom to focus on sexual exploration, performance expression, and community engagement. For these reasons, Dodds (2013, 78) suggests that the neo-burlesque community welcomes and celebrates difference: "a multitude of physiques occupy the neo-burlesque stage. While the overt display of 'imperfections', such as sagging breasts and wobbly bellies, is embraced and applauded, the idealized and unattainable bodies of consumer capitalism are a rarity." Similarly, theater scholar Joanna Mansbridge (2014, 7) suggests that, in contrast to strip clubs, burlesque shows offer an "opportunity to gather and a stage on which to develop ideas, create personas, and make fun of our cultural fixations around sex and female bodies." Furthermore, Baldwin suggests that the presentation of bodies in the neo-burlesque scene, which sit outside societal norms of sexual attractiveness, can be seen as a political statement. In reference to the plus-sized dance troupe the Fat Bottom Review, Baldwin (2004, 57) asserts that the troupe has the power to "change perceptions about full-figured women everywhere." From the perspective of this commercially disinterested, safe space, neo-burlesque artists take the opportunity to comment on conventional framings of women's bodies and sexuality.

When I first saw Dirty Martini (Miss Exotic World 2004) perform at the BHoF Weekender, she appeared, covered in red balloons like a ripe bunch of grapes, while she smoked a cigarette in a disinterested fashion. Amidst eye rolls and irritated puffs, as if annoyed by the very presence of the audience, she comically utilized her cigarette to pop each balloon one by one. With each touch of the hot ash, the balloons exploded to slowly reveal her voluptuous figure. Similarly, when performing at the Icons and All Stars showcase in 2015, sporting a flowing purple gown and a large swan puppet, Martini endeavored to gracefully flit about the stage, but was constantly hindered by the swan, which attacked her and ripped at her costume (Figure 15.2). Once disrobed, Martini struggled to protect herself from the swan, which began to nip at her pastie until it was devoured by the angry bird, leaving her naked nipple exposed.

That same year, two days before she would judge the 2015 Tournament of Tease, I sat with Dirty Martini in the El Cortez hotel in downtown Las Vegas. I asked Martini, who wore a platinum blond wig, bubble-gum pink lipstick, and a newly purchased sundress, about the place of the Miss Exotic World competition within the neo-burlesque community. Seeming to reflect upon the question carefully, she shared the following:

> I don't think that the word "competition" should be used. It should be "exhibition." It should be "the best of the best" or "showing your best" because the word "competition" is false. It's like women are so used to having people believe that we're pitting each other against each other and that we're against each other instead of building each other up. So, I think that the word "competition" in this sense is really out-dated. I think a lot of people like to still have it and there is a big split in the whole organization. . . . But I think the semantics are off.[7]

Martini's statement notes a significant dichotomy in the neo-burlesque movement: competition as a metric of value can position members of this community (often women) against each other, perpetuating the socially constructed rhetoric of female rivalry, which the neo-burlesque movement often seeks to reject. She proposes that instead

FIGURE 15.2. Dirty Martini performs her swan routine, 2015.

Matilda Temperley, 2015

of competition, implementing an "exhibition" where one "shows" one's personal best might be more appropriate and more in line with the principles of the neo-burlesque community.

Yet this suggestion proposed by Martini brings into question what one's "best" really amounts to. When competing for Miss Exotic World, most dancers opt for subtler or less subversive routines than they might choose to perform on the neo-burlesque cabaret circuit. For example, Muz's severed hand and comedy glow stick sit in contrast to a more circumspect routine she performed to win her Miss Exotic World title. In this piece, she gracefully dances to the classic ballad *Moon River* while floating a large balloon around the stage. Muz slides her way inside the balloon and, once inside, appears like a stunning human snow globe. She floats inside until she then pops the large sphere to reveal her naked body. This performance clearly glorifies the female form, and her imaginative use of the balloon is undoubtedly creative. However, she presents a more conventional portrait of femininity than the work I have previously mentioned.

I asked Martini about the notably understated (and unpolitical) performances on display at the Tournament of Tease and the factors involved in performers' decisions regarding what to perform at the pageant. She replied,

> In its essence, it's a classic burlesque pageant because it was started by Dixie Evans. And so, I think that even the judges and the people watching . . . even though there was a big pull to be like, oh, can we just open it up and make it a little bit more performance art or whatever, I think that people know that, if they are going to win Miss Exotic World, they have to show perfect 1940s, 50s, 30s burlesque.[8]

Here Martini mentions "classic burlesque," a term often used by the neo-burlesque community to define performances that adhere to the aesthetics and movement vocabulary of golden age burlesque. As pornographic film was not accessible or legal until the late 1960s (Turner and Zito 1974; Williams 1989), "classic burlesque" was a (if not, the) predominant mode of erotic entertainment during this period.[9] Thus "classic burlesque" refers to performances that endeavor to be sexually alluring in accordance with the constructs of commercial striptease of the mid-twentieth century, which capitalized on (mainly male) sexual arousal. As a result, the dancers performing classic burlesque at the Tournament of Tease, a "classic burlesque" pageant, often have lean and toned bodies, in accordance with mainstream beauty ideals, and a notable proportion of Miss Exotic World winners have opted for breast augmentation. Thus, when Martini suggests that the pageant was formed by the late Dixie Evans as an addition to the annual reunion of the EDL, she implies that the pageant adheres to the parameters and tastes of mid-twentieth-century striptease, the predominant erotic entertainment of the period. Consequently, although the neo-burlesque community positions its work as an alternative to stripping, at its highest competitive level it turns to the codes and values of traditional stripping, a term that, as Baldwin (2004, 49) states, most neo-burlesquers "wanted nothing to do with."

MISS EXOTIC WORLD
AND METRICS OF VALUE

In the Orleans showroom, the contestants in the Best Debut category began to perform in a procession of sequins and shimmies.[10] In a stunning silver flapper ensemble, London's Bonnie Fox performed a confident Charleston routine, and Mama Ulita, the self-proclaimed "Long Legged Lady from Lapzig," bounced about with a pair of emerald green fans to the 1941 hit "Watch the Birdie."

I felt pleased to be sharing the judging panel with former Playboy bunny and seeming representative of modern-day erotica Holly Madison. The process of distinguishing the term "stripper" from "Burlesque dancer"[11] to differentiate neo-burlesque from contemporary erotic entertainment has always sat uneasily with me, as it often stigmatizes women who work professionally in these industries (Regehr and Temperley 2017). Madison's presence offered at least some acknowledgment of burlesque and this pageant's relationship to contemporary commercial exotic entertainment. Yet I was also aware that having Madison and legend Gina Bon Bon as a judges might be another reason why "classic burlesque" performances were graded so highly at the Tournament of Tease. These judges, who have made professional careers out of commercial or heteronormative erotica, might potentially value more conservative representations of bodies and sexuality in line with those on display in the exotic entertainment industry.

Neo-burlesque producer Penny Starr Jr., who is the granddaughter of legend Penny Starr Sr., provides interesting insight into both communities. In response to my question concerning differences between Starr Jr. and her grandmother's perspectives on burlesque, she comments:

> Ok . . . this is strictly generational; she [Penny Starr Sr.] has a hard time with girls who aren't traditionally pretty or thin, because she has spent her whole life being told that thin is the most important thing. So, she's like, "I don't understand how these big girls do it . . . I don't understand why they're just not on diet pills," because that's how she was brought up. I know she was on diet pills. We had a discussion one night where . . . she's seen me produce, and she knows how hard I work when I'm producing, for virtually nothing. She's like, "ugh, what you girls get paid is terrible." And I said, "yeah, but honey, if I were dancing in your day, I'd be too old, and too fat to be doing it. No one would book me and, certainly, no one would let me produce," and she's like, "that's 100% true." What we gained in our freedom, we lost in a certain financial gain.[12]

This statement adds to the discussion in two ways. First, Starr Jr. reiterates that, in contrast both to exotic dancers of the mid-twentieth century and to contemporary strippers, neo-burlesque is rarely performed for financial gain; instead, performers enjoy its potential for liberated expression, or what she terms "freedom." Second, Starr Jr. addresses the mid-twentieth-century pressures for the legends to comply to the limited spectrum of beauty in order to commoditize their bodies and performances. Consequently, Starr Jr. suggests that her legendary grandmother brings these values into her assessment of neo-burlesque performers who fail to live up to these narrow standards of a feminine ideal.[13]

I looked along the judges' panel at legend Gina Bon Bon and wondered if she felt the same way as Penny Starr Sr. did about the dancers competing. Was she also told that "thin is the most important thing" and was she subsequently confused by the multitude of body types on display at many neo-burlesque festivals? I picked up my clipboard and focused on the categories by which I was to judge Mama Ulita, whose long thin body now sported nothing but emerald pasties and black sheer underwear.

The categories against which all competitors in the BHoF Tournament of Tease are judged are "entrance," "costume," "innovation," "technical skill," and "overall impression," and we were asked to rate each of these criterion out of ten. When I was first handed my clipboard, this scoring system felt appropriate, as it seemed to offer an acceptable framework for placing value on striptease performances. Yet when I was asked to grade acts on entrance or technical skill, the performances that were graded highly by the combined scores of the judges often included other forms of dance training, acrobatics, or circus skills. Further, these trained dancers or circus performers typically had lean, athletic bodies, which conformed to a limited bodily ideal.

In the Miss Exotic World category, Midnight Martini began her routine perched atop a tall ladder. Blue silks suspended from the ceiling wrapped around her body and draped over the ladder, giving the impression of a magnificently tall skirt. Martini then proceeded to unwrap the silks to reveal her legs straddling the metal ladder on which she undulated her body, slowly pulling off her gloves and the first stocking. She removed her final stocking while hanging upside-down on the ladder, using the toes from her naked foot to strip off the remaining garment. She then climbed the silks and, with her back to the audience, remained suspended in a straddle split, proudly displaying her white leather thong (Figure 15.3). Finally, she removed the white leather bondage vest to reveal her lean, toned bare back, before sliding down the silks to display a set of silver pasties.

Although Midnight Martini did not exhibit overt personality or audience interaction in her performance, she went on to take the title of Miss Exotic World 2014. When asked to rate her entrance, technical skill, and innovation, she scored the highest on my sheet. Notably, energy or character were not categories available to me, and they were therefore not the criterion by which I was able to value the performance.

FIGURE 15.3. Midnight Martini competes for Miss Exotic World, 2014.

While some dancers might have offered stronger bids for the title Miss Exotic World by way of charisma and connection with the audience (elements that are important at both neo-burlesque festivals and within the striptease industry), I nevertheless felt thrilled with Martini's success. Her win was arguably bigger than any of the criterion printed on my judging sheet. Indeed, Martini's title was truly significant within the context of this community and American burlesque history as a whole: Martini was Asian American and became the first woman of color to be crowned Miss Exotic World in almost two decades.

Midnight Martini's win is not only important within the context of neo-burlesque, but also in the context of stripping as a whole. Racial prejudice, inequitable treatment, pay disparities between visible minority and white dancers, and segregated clubs permeate American burlesque history. Racial inequities with regard to issues of fair treatment and pay continue in the exotic dance industry today (Brooks 2010). Indeed, the historical racial tensions in burlesque form a current point of discussion in the neo-burlesque community.[14] In 2013, the BHoF showcased the exhibition "Not-So-Hidden Histories: Performers of Color in Burlesque" to examine the void in the documentation of black burlesque dancers and to confront past and present race-based binaries in exotic dance. Nevertheless, the neo-burlesque movement, an often recreational, middle-class, community, has from its inception been notably white. Thus, although the neo-burlesque community is philosophically tied to concepts of inclusion and difference, the BHoF Weekender often reflects the racial demographics of historic burlesque. That is, the aesthetic of whiteness and seeming lack of racial diversity present in the pageant is at odds with the community's supposed ideology of championing difference.

Though the lasting impacts of Martini's success are yet to be seen, 2016 winner Poison Ivory wrote on her blog,

> Until this year, in the twenty-six year history of the Miss Exotic World Pageant, the most prestigious burlesque competition in the world, only one black woman had won the coveted title. Rio Savant was crowned in 1996, in the early years of the competition. And until recently, Google only had one tiny photo, her name and a date. Perhaps by her own choosing, but like her foremothers, her contribution has been all but erased. Now in 2016, I am honored to have been crowned the first black Reigning Queen of Burlesque in 20 years. And it is my goal to see that the contributions of today's performers of color continue to get the recognition they deserve. (2016)

Yet it is not solely racial and body size diversity that lack representation at the pageant; the emphasis on classic burlesque seems also to value heteronormativity at the pageant. In 2015 Lou Henry Hoover was the first drag king to compete in the Best Boylesque category (Figure 15.4). Born Erica Mason, Lou chassèd onto the stage dressed in a sailor's uniform and signature painted-on moustache. Through a series of *jetès, chaîné* turns, and pantomime style gestures, Hoover mimed the story of love-struck naval boy who, to the tune of Cindy Lauper's "Time after Time," as the song lyric suggests, would remain "waiting, time after time."

FIGURE 15.4. Lou Henry Hoover competes in the Best Boylesque category, 2015.

Matilda Temperley, 2015

Although Hoover's presence in the Best Boylesque category was regarded as a break-through by many drag and trans performers in the neo-burlesque community, some were unimpressed, feeling the coveted Miss Exotic World category remained out of reach for non-gender-conforming performers. Participants sensed that the queering of heteronormative views on sexuality, which permeate smaller productions and festivals, are for the most part omitted from the tournament. Furthermore, the few queer performances that take place at BHoF, such as Hoover's act (which was both in-novative and technically skilled) did not typically place in their categories until 2017. As Dirty Martini stated, "in its essence, it's a classic burlesque pageant." That is to say, the Tournament of Tease is aesthetically and ideologically linked to the segregated and commercial exotic dance of the mid-twentieth century, which generally valued thin, white, women, who in turn performed for heterosexual men. From this perspective, the diverse representations of bodies, gender, and sexuality present at the smaller neo-burlesque festivals and their attendant communities are often omitted from the pageant and, in particular, the winner's circle. Nevertheless, in 2017, Lou Henry Hoover received the Best Boylesque title at the BHoF's Tournament of Tease. Arguably, a win for both Hoover and for the drag burlesque community at large.

Further, in more recent years, awards have been created to recognize talent situated outside the classic burlesque structure. The tournament offers secondary awards of "Most Innovative," "Most Classic," "Most Comedic," and, up until 2016, "Most Dazzling." These awards are not rated on a ten-point scale with assessment criteria, but evaluations are based on an overall impression. Though overall impression forms a category of the judging sheet, it only counts for one-fifth of the score. Therefore these secondary prizes allow judges to solely grade the performance on an overarching perception of or response to the act.

As I judged in 2014, Hoover and wife Kitten LaRue performed a vibrant, disco routine (Figure 15.5). The number, which involved cocktail shakers, 1970s disco moves, and Hoover stripped down to a disco ball codpiece, mocked excessive drinking and lecherous men at night clubs. The couple licked each other's faces and simulated sneaky bouts of vomiting in perfect time to the disco beat. Here, in the sprit of an overall impression, Hoover and LaRue's skills were acknowledged as they received the award for "Most Comedic."

Also within these secondary awards, neo-burlesque performers such as Aurora Galore were celebrated. Galore, who took the stage in a ringmaster's costume and garish face paint, aggressively popped and twerked[15] her clothes off with such energy and control of her curvy figure that the audience leapt to their feet in awe and celebration of her skill. Although Galore did not win the Best Debut category, or place in the Miss Exotic World category two years later, she was recognized as the "Most Innovative."

FIGURE 15.5. Kitten 'n' Lou compete in the small group category, 2014.

Matilda Temperley, 2014

"Competition Is for Athletes, not Artists"

After trophies were awarded and a new queen was crowned, I filed out of the theater with some 800 neo-burlesquers and arrived at Big Al's, an alligator-themed bar, on the Orleans casino floor. I saw Arora Galore and I offered congratulations on her "Most Innovative" win. "It was what I wanted," she responded in a matter-of-fact fashion, "[because] I knew I wasn't going to win [Best Debut]." Although she received a rare standing ovation for her performance, she understood that the value systems at play would prevent her from winning her category. Galore's reflections speak to the conflicting philosophies that exist between the neo-burlesque community and the Tournament of Tease. This tension arises from the interests of three competing ideals: those of the neo-burlesque movement, which celebrate personal expression and acceptance of difference; the historic connection of Miss Exotic World to the commercial industry of mid-twentieth-century exotic dance or "classic burlesque"; and the process of competition as a whole.

Such tensions clearly play out in my own understanding of the field. My initial introduction to the neo-burlesque community was at a local grassroots level where I was drawn to its openness and inclusivity; it engendered a performance genre that prided itself on principles of sex-positive feminism, political performance art and where gender and sexual equality could be explored in a tangible way. Within the scholarly realm, neo-burlesque is praised as a body-positive, subversive, feminist practice that encourages difference and argues for a broader spectrum of beauty, sexuality, and orientation. In my role as a judge, I found the conflicting values within the pageant difficult to reconcile, and I was left with more questions than I could answer: Was I judging dancers who best personified the ideals of the neo-burlesque movement? Was I judging the most sexually arousing striptease number? Or was I judging the best re-creation of mid-twentieth-century or classic burlesque?

Lou Henry Hoover's 2017 win shows the community's interest in answering some of these questions and reconciling the dichotomies between the goals of neo-burlesque at a grass-roots level and the realities when dancers compete to perform "authentic" re-creations of this exotic entertainment. Given that the BHoF evolved from a social club for exotic dancers from the mid-twentieth century, I understand that the Tournament of Tease performances presented through the BHoF Weekender often reflect both the tastes and social stigmas of the era with which it is closely associated. As a result, the Tournament of Tease pageant often showcases a much more limited spectrum of racial diversity, body types, and gendered representation than the neo-burlesque community that it serves. Further, in an admirable effort to include both contemporary erotic entertainers and legends on the judging panel, these judges' views might sit uneasily with neo-burlesque principals, thus limiting the potential for alternative performances to score highly.

As I walked toward the Tiki-themed bar top, I passed Jo "Boobs" Weldon and thanked her; she had undeniably run a slick and well-produced competition. I ordered a drink, and found myself standing beside Bambi La Fleur. Bambi, producer of the Florida Burlesque Festival and a Marilyn Monroe impersonator, collected a colorful drink topped with two small cocktail umbrellas. As we spoke, she explained that she does not have a competition element at the Florida Burlesque Festival. Bambi believes, "competition is for athletes, not for artists."[16] Indeed, the process of putting a numeric value on predetermined criteria made it difficult to recognize and reward performers for other skills, such as audience engagement, character, charisma, or impact. It was only within the secondary awards that I was able to select a performance based on overall impact. Consequently, the struggle within the Miss Exotic World pageant is two pronged. First, the inclusive tenets of the neo-burlesque movement sit uneasily within the aesthetics of classic burlesque—white, thin bodies impersonating yet another Marilyn. Therefore, when adhering to classic re-creations of these historic performances, narrow "muggle" views on beauty, body type, sexual orientation, and race are frequently perpetuated. And second, as I unclipped my baby pink ribbon and headed back to my Orleans hotel room that night, I reflected on how the process of competition and judging not only ranks, normalizes, and regulates the practice, but it is incongruous with the philosophical underpinnings of the neo-burlesque community. Within this structure, for the most part, the dancers who won titles did not leave me with a lasting memory of their subversive political statements, audience engagement, or creativity, but were the performances that conformed to the judging sheet, met the criteria, and stayed in the boxes.

Notes

1. For an extended description and analysis of the Burlesque Hall of Fame Weekender, see Regehr and Temperley (2017).
2. Jo Weldon, interview with author, June 23, 2013. An expanded outline of this methodology (and my relationship to it) is available in Regehr and Temperley (2017).
3. Lynn Sally, interview with author, July 22, 2012.
4. "Pasties" are a decorative form of nipple covering and are signature garments of mid-twentieth-century burlesque.
5. The Slipper Room has been the unofficial home of the New York neo-burlesque scene since opening in 1999. It was the first venue to be built specifically to showcase neo-burlesque.
6. I have also utilized these accounts of Muz's performances in *The League of Exotic Dancers: Legends from American Burlesque* (2017). I am revisiting these accounts not only because Muz's work is iconic within the community, but also because I find her work to be a clear physical embodiment of the ideals of the neo-burlesque community that are at stake in this chapter.
7. Dirty Martini, interview with author, June 4, 2015.
8. Ibid.
9. In 1967 a San Francisco sexploitation theater showed a pornographic film and suffered no repercussions, subsequently giving way to porn theaters. The final transitional factor from

the illegal into the legal golden age of feature-length narrative pornography, which made pornography, or "porno" or "porn," a household name was the release of *Deep Throat* in 1972. For more on this period, see Williams (1989) and Turner and Zito (1974).

10. The term *Best Debut* is a bit of a misnomer, for regardless of a dancer's seniority within the neo-burlesque community, no one can compete in the Miss Exotic World category without first competing for best debut. Thus, the debut in this instance is a debut on the coveted BHoF stage, not within the resurgence as a whole.

11. Connections between neo-burlesque and other forms of erotic entertainments or sex work are possible, and the boundaries of neo-burlesque can be fluid. Roxi Dlite, who was crowned Miss Exotic World in 2010, works in strip clubs in her home town of Windsor, Ontario, between neo-burlesque festivals. Similarly, some of the foundational members of the neo-burlesque community also come from a background of commercial exotic dance of the 1990s, such as Jo Weldon.

12. Penny Starr Jr, interview with author, June 12, 2014.

13. An extended version of these interviews with both Penny Starr Jr. and Penny Starr Sr. can be found in Regehr and Temperley (2017).

14. See www.burlesquehall.com/category/exhibitions/pastexhibitions.

15. Twerking refers to thrusting and gyration of the hips and gluts in a sexually provocative manner, often while positioned in a low or squatting stance.

16. An initial conversation was held with Bambi La Fleur at the BHoF. A follow-up interview was conducted on February 4, 2016, which was in turn transcribed.

References

Allen, Robert. 1991. *Horrible Prettiness: Burlesque and American Culture*. Chapel Hill: University of North Carolina Press.

Baldwin, Michelle. 2004. *Burlesque and the New Bump-n-Grind*. Golden, CO: Speck.

Barton, Bernadette. 2002. "Dancing on the Mobius Strip: Challenging the Sex War Paradigm." *Gender and Society* 16(5): 585–602.

Barton, Bernadette. 2006. *Stripped: Inside the Lives of Exotic Dancers* New York: New York University Press.

Barton, Bernadette, and Constance L. Hardesty. 2010. "Spirituality and Stripping: Exotic Dancers Narrate the Body Ekstais." *Symbolic Interaction* 33(2): 280–296.

Bell, Holly, and Lacey Slone. 1998. "Exploiter or Exploited: Topless Dancers Reflect on Their Experiences." *Journal of Women and Social Work* 13: 352–368.

Brooks, Siobhan. 2010. "Hypersexualization and the Dark Body: Race and Inequality among Black and Latina Women in the Exotic Dance Industry." *Sexuality Research and Social Policy* 7: 70–80.

Burlesque Hall of Fame. 2013. *burlesquehall.com*. www.burlesquehall.com/category/exhibitions/pastexhibitions. Accessed November 25, 2016.

Dodds, Sherril. 2011. *Dancing on the Canon: Embodiments of Value in Popular Dance*. London: Palgrave.

Dodds, Sherril. 2013. "Embodied Transformations in Neo-Burlesque Striptease." *Dance Research Journal* 45(3): 75–90.

Egan, Danielle. 2006. *Dancing for Dollars and Praying for Love: The Relationships between Exotic Dancers and Their Regulars*. New York: Palgrave Macmillan.

Ferreday, Debra. 2008. "Showing the Girl: The New Burlesque." *Feminist Theory* 9(47): 47–65.

Frank, Katherine. 2002. *G-Strings and Sympathy: Strip Club Regulars and Male Desire*. Durham, NC; London: Duke University Press.

Hanna, Judith Lynn. 2003. "Exotic Dance Adult Entertainment: Ethnography Challenges False Mythology." *City and Society* 15: 165–193.

Manaster, Shelly. 2006. "Treading Water: An Autoethnographic Account(ing) of the Lap Dance." In *Flesh for Fantasy: Producing and Consuming Exotic Dance*, edited by Danielle Egan, Katherine Frank, and Lisa Merri Johnson, 3–18. New York: Thunder's Mouth.

Mansbridge, Joanna. 2014. "In Search of a Different History: The Remains of Burlesque in Montreal." *Canadian Theatre Review* 158: 7–12.

Nally, Claire. 2009. "Grrrly Hurly Burly: Neo-Burlesque and The Performance of Gender." *Textual Practice* 23(4): 621–643.

Owen, David. 2014. "Neo-Burlesque and the Resurgence of Roller Derby: Empowerment, Play, and Community." *Canadian Theatre Review* 158(Spring): 33–38.

Ivory, Poison. 2016. *MissPoisonIvory.com*. http://www.MissPoisonIvory.com. Accessed November 16, 2016.

Pullen, Kirsten. 2005. *Actresses and Whores: On Stage and in Society*. Cambridge: Cambridge University Press.

Regehr, Kaitlyn, and Matilda Temperley. 2017. *The League of Exotic Dancers: Legends from American Burlesque*. New York: Oxford University Press.

Sally, Lynn. 2009. "'It Is the Ugly That Is So Beautiful': Performing the Monster/Beauty Continuum in American Neoburlesque." *Journal of American Drama and Theatre* 21(3): 5–24.

Shteir, Rachel. 2004. *Striptease: The Untold History of the Girly Show*. New York; Oxford: Oxford University Press.

Turner, Kenneth, and Stephan F. Zito. 1974. *Sinema: American Pornographic Films and the People Who Make Them*. New York: Praeger.

Urish, Ben. 2004. "Narrative Striptease in the Night Club Era." *The Journal of American Culture* 27(2): 157–165.

Wesley, Jennifer K. 2000. "Exotic Dancing and the Negotiation of Identity: The Multiple Uses of Body Technologies." *Journal of Contemporary Ethnography* 32(6): 643–669.

Wesley, Jennifer K. 2003. "Where Am I Going to Stop? Exotic Dancers, Fluid Boundaries, and Effects on Identity." *Deviant Behavior* 24: 483–503.

Williams, Linda. 1989. *Hard Core: Power, Pleasure, and the "Frenzy of the Visible."* Berkeley: University of California Press.

Willson, Jackie. 2008. *The Happy Stripper: Pleasures and Politics of the New Burlesque*. New York: I. B. Tauris.

Zeidman, Irving. 1967. *The American Burlesque Show*. New York: Hawthorne Books.

CHAPTER 16

RAPPER DANCE ADJUDICATION

Aesthetics, Discourse, and Decision-Making

JEREMY CARTER-GORDON

THE pub is packed around the dance floor—energy high, anticipation tangible—as the crowd awaits the next dance. Five dancers, dressed in black with skirts, leggings, and orange sashes, stride into the pit, forming a tight ring facing outward. A tenor voice rings out in song, "They dance like demons, drink like fish . . . the gin-destroying, stainless, Sheffield Steel!" A whoop goes up from the crowd, building as a fiddle and accordion take up a fast minor reel and five swords flash into motion. As each dancer grabs a handle on the point of her neighbor's sword and twirls, they form a circle, percussive stepping ringing out on the hard floor. The spectating crowd leans in as the figures become more complex, then lets out a collective whoop as the bagpipe roars into the mix, lifting the atmosphere with its rollicking major key. From their table a few feet away, the four judges scribble some notes, anxious not to miss a moment; a second's inattention and a dropped sword, wrong foot, or miscommunication could mean the difference between winning and not even placing. The team moves well, though, weaving their swords into intricate patterns, leaping over the blades, and sending members tumbling in acrobatic flips off each other's shoulders as the fiddler calls to the crowd for applause. A final sweep of the swords and the dancers spin into the center, their swords sliding inward to make a five-pointed star, which is held aloft as the final bar of the jig finishes, accented by a double stomp. Screams of approval ring out from all sides as the five dancers and three musicians leave the stage, but the judges are already sharply focused, consulting charts, calculating scores, and writing comments. It is clear that Sheffield has put in a good dance, but will it be enough? What exactly do judges perceive when they watch these performances? How is the ephemeral, aesthetic experience of a four-minute dance transformed into a concrete score and ranking? What strategies, both explicit and tacit, are employed by adjudicators to make these decisions? What can these competitions tell us about aesthetic understandings of a dance, community, or culture? These questions have led me to the basement of The Wardrobe Pub in Leeds, United Kingdom, watching the Dancing England Rapper Tournament in early March 2014.

The scholarly investigation of the phenomenon of dance competition has grown in recent years, exploring topics from hip-hop to hula, high-stakes televised spectacle to private battles, drawing also on qualitative sports competition such as ice skating and Olympic diving.[1] However, most researchers writing on the topic of dance competition have focused primarily on the perspective of, and influence on, dancers, and to a lesser extent on the spectators. A marked void occupies the literature when it comes to the role of judges in the act of adjudication, with many authors dealing with judges as an impersonal mechanism that exists to exert a disembodied influence on dancers. This scholarship on competition may tackle *what* is judged (or what the judges believe they are judging), or *why* this is judged in the prescriptive sense. Noticeably lacking is the *how*; the process by which a judge turns an aesthetic experience into a set of scores is rarely questioned, and it is these perceptions, strategies, and decisions that I examine in this chapter.

I am interested in how judges mediate these subjective evaluations through their own perception and what strategies, both explicit and tacit, judges use to evaluate these dances. I investigate specific aspects of a performance on which judges focus, what they find important, and how they perceive dancing and produce scores for competitors. While all judges use certain techniques, they also demonstrate purely personal conceptions of how rapper should be danced (and therefore evaluated). These personal conceptions are tied to the judges' background and how they relate to rapper dance as a tradition. Most important, the competition setting gives power to these personal and public conceptions of the dance form, transforming the dance tradition and competitions themselves.

In this chapter, I outline my own involvement with rapper dance, and describe the Dancing England Rapper Tournament. The reader is introduced to how the judge's perspective is accessed through a form of video-assisted interview in which judges are asked to comment on moments of aesthetic judgement of a competition dance. These comments are then time-stamped and formed into a *temporal aesthetic map*, which can be analyzed to reveal some of the underlying structure of the dance. I present these findings within a framework for understanding the process of dance adjudication and conclude with some of the specific issues of background, heritage, and personal dance history that come into play for rapper dance judges.

RAPPER DANCE AND THE RESEARCHER: MY RELATION TO THE FIELD

My first exposure to the hilt-and-point sword dance known as rapper came as a child attending a folk dance camp in Plymouth, Massachusetts, at the age of eight. The other children and I were divided into groups of five dancers and were given flexible sprung steel swords with handles at both ends, by which we could form a circle by holding the end of each other's swords. Originating as a coal miners' dance from the northeast of England, rapper is fast-paced and exciting, and I reveled in learning its twisting figure, filled with geometric patterns woven from the swords. By the time I reached high school, I had started a team with several friends, spending Sunday afternoons rehearsing the split-second coordination between dancers, percussive footwork, and acrobatic jumps and flips that the dance requires. A friend or mentor would play 6/8 jigs on fiddle, concertina, whistle, or other instruments for our dancing, and we would all get pizza afterward. While rapper was originally danced for money and community pride in pubs by working-class miners in communities around England's Newcastle-upon-Tyne, we had joined the revival movement of men, women, and children who dance rapper as a leisure activity in the United States, the United Kingdom, and Europe. In 2005, we were finally ready to show our dancing on the larger stage; therefore we headed off to the unofficial center of the rapper dancing world, the annual Dancing England Rapper Tournament.

The Dancing England Rapper Tournament, colloquially referred to as DERT, takes place annually in March, drawing teams mainly from the United Kingdom, as well as the United States, and occasionally Canada or continental Europe. Hosted by a different team each year, the event is located in different cities around England and Scotland, and runs from a Friday evening social, through workshops on Sunday morning, with the competitive section happening on Saturday. The competition is held in pubs around the host city, with between two and four judges evaluating each performance. Teams dance several times throughout the day, and their scores are averaged to produce an overall winner. These judges are drawn from a pool of respected and experienced dancers, musicians, and figures in the rapper dance community who are considered experts.

I competed twice in DERT with my high school team, winning "Best Display Dance" in 2006. Continuing this passion, I competed in the first Dancing America Rapper Tournament (DART) in 2010, and taught at dance camps and schools around the United States. I lived and practiced with several English teams preparing for DERT during a fellowship to research sword dance in 2011–2012, and when I started to investigate aesthetic perception and adjudication in dance competition, it was clear that a return to the rapper world was in order.

In this research I explore the processes by which judges are able to turn a set of subjective, aesthetic experiences into a numerical score.[2] To do so, I investigate perceptions of rapper dance by people with different dance backgrounds, how judges see dancing, and what strategies are employed by these groups to evaluate and score a performance. This process has allowed me to divide the act of adjudication into four separate processes: expectation-setting, perception, interpretation, and decision-making. These each have explicit and tacit facets and, through exploring and explaining how judges employ each process, I will propose a way of understanding rapper, dance judging, and more generally how we might experience and evaluate aesthetic experience.

RAPPER COMPETITION AND THE DANCING ENGLAND RAPPER TOURNAMENT

While the first recorded rapper dance competition was held in 1881 in Blyth, England, and was popularized in the early twentieth century as part of the folk revival spearheaded by Cecil Sharp, the Dancing England Rapper Tournament takes its roots from the Dancing England Tournament started in the 1980s.[3] It has continued as its own entity since the 1990s and as a project of the Sword Dance Union since 2005.[4] It consists of several sub-competitions, including one for children and another for traditional dances performed from old notation, which have separate rules. The Spotlight and Main competitions are conducted by several pairs of judges, each stationed at different pubs where the teams compete. During the evaluation process, each judge has a form for every team, with space for comments and a score for each category. These forms are collected after each dance, and eventually an average of each category is taken, and the results tallied. A total of 100 points is awarded in seven categories: stepping, sword handling, dance technique, presentation, buzz factor, music, and characters. Stepping is a grade of the precision, volume, uniformity of the percussive step, and the variety of stepping patterns. The shapes the swords make and how skillfully the dancers move them as a group are noted in sword handling, while dance technique encompasses how well dancers move together, in time, and with fluid movements. The team is marked on presentation, which covers appearance, costumes, and confidence, and buzz factor includes the sense of a performance as a whole and the excitement level and audience engagement. Finally, the music is scored, both on its own artistic merits and on how well it matches and complements the dancers' movements. Teams have the option of including extra characters, usually known as the Tommy or Betty, which may gain points for engaging the audience and interacting with the dancers in an optional category.

These categories each have a set of criteria, given to both dancers and judges, detailing what will be evaluated. For example, the section on stepping reads as follows:

> To get the maximum 15 marks, the team's stepping must meet all these criteria: clean, crisp stepping, in time with the music, excellent volume in stepping, sharp, light, fast walking, in time with the music, consistent stepping style between dancers and throughout dance, consistent walking style between dancers and throughout dance, starting and stopping stepping at the same time, unless intended, good jumps, in time with the music, good, consistent stepping in spins, variety of stepping (e.g. 4s, 8s, train step etc.) with interesting variations. (DERT 2012).

The criteria further state that marks will be deducted for the opposite of each of these criteria, for example poor, muffled, or out-of-time stepping. What is important to note is that these are prescriptive criteria and guidelines, and they rely on a presumed shared understanding of what such phrases as "in time with the music" or "interesting variations" mean. They neither make explicit what these aesthetic judgements delin-eate, nor, as we will see shortly, do they always correspond with how judges actually mark these categories. Far from establishing a methodology of adjudication, they simply provide a skeletal structure to which judges must employ their own strategies of adherence.

Finding the Dance Landscape: Video-Assisted Interview

During DERT 2014, I shot videos of each competing team's dance from just behind the judging table to capture the judges' perspective of watching teams compete. In addition to unstructured conversations with the judges about rapper dance, their personal his-tory, and their involvement in rapper, I also explored the process of judging with a form of video-assisted interview using these videos.[5] While these recordings are obviously not equivalent to lived experience, the videos formed a basis on which to access the in-ternal processes of dance adjudicators. Watching these videos in one-on-one sessions, I asked each judge to pause the video when he or she found something important in what he or she saw, or a memory of adjudicating on the day. Through this self-selection and commentary on important moments, I sought to access the conscious and uncon-scious ways in which judges carry out the process of adjudication.

I created situational charts of each video, tracking a number of factors over time, in-cluding movement, music, text (speech), and audience reaction, to which I added each judge's comments, aligned by their video time stamp. In addition to allowing a compar-ison between the performance and the judges' comments, this provided a basic sense of how judges were commenting in relation to each other. I could now take any moment or sequence from one of the dances and observe what dancers, musicians, and audience were doing, and what the judges were (or were not) saying about it. While individual moments could be examined effectively, I wanted to be able to identify larger patterns across an entire performance, to find the "landscape" of a rapper dance, what judges were saying about it, and when they were saying it. I annotated the video with judges' comments in real-time using a web-based tool, VideoANT, as a way to create a visual representation of the aesthetic landscape of a dance. Judges' comments are pinned to specific times within the video, serving as a real-time commentary and, by viewing the dance concurrently with the comments provided, this annotation allowed me to view the dance "through the eyes of the judges."

In this process I was able to identify four stages of the adjudication process—expectation, perception, interpretation, and decision-making—which I discuss in this chapter. I introduce each of these stages, with interludes for analysis and theorization of aspects of each of them. They provide insight into the specificity of rapper judging, as well as a heuristic device that can be used in a range of settings.

EXPECTATION SETTING

Expectation setting encompasses the cluster of processes that judges go through to determine what they think they will see. This comprises a set of expectations delineating the form; a tacit definition of what rapper dancing is or is not; as well as personal memories or social discourse about the expectations for a particular team.[6] This expectation setting, which may or may not be conscious, gives boundaries to what judges are able to see and therefore are able to evaluate and reward within a set of criteria.

In trying to understand these strategies, it has been revealing to examine how judges talk and think about their role in judging dance. In casual conversation, we often pass through many ways of expressing views on the world, and in my research I found it helpful to distinguish the different levels of discourse that affect judges at DERT to identify what actions are precipitated by different discourses.

When judges are making decisions, I call the most obvious register of language *official discourse*. This includes published competition rules, score sheets used by judges, and the scoring rubric with grading criteria (DERT, 2012). Official discourse is explicit, specific, and equally available to judges, participants, and observers, and is negotiated and agreed upon by the organizers ahead of time. *Social discourse* then comprises "common-sense" ideas about the dance, which are generally agreed upon by the majority of the community. It includes conversations between individuals, teams, and judges. Like the official discourse, the social discourse can be published, but appears in emails, online forums, or articles. The official discourse is negotiated from the social discourse and, as general opinions and values have shifted, the competition rules and structure have also changed. Individual beliefs, preferences, and ideas of each judge form a third discourse, that of the *personal*. Some judges may prefer certain kinds of figures to others, like rapper dancing that is faster or slower, or may enjoy certain styles of dance more than others. These preferences may or may not be discussed openly, but when they are, the speaker usually notes that it is a personal belief, rather than official or social guidelines.

Though I will not be dealing with it in this chapter, the subconscious biases and influences of judges comprise a fourth level of discourse. It includes the factors that affect perception of which judges are unaware. Exploring this would require a different methodological approach, but I could imagine criteria such as age or gender of the dancers, physical placement of the musicians in relation to the judges, time of day, or length of dance affecting how a performance is perceived.

In their discussion of dances, judges both acknowledge a difference between the official/social and the personal levels of discourse, and consciously separate them in their minds and scores. During our conversations, judges would sometimes make a comment that did not fall within the official rules. For example, one judge complains during a figure where a dancer does a full backflip using the shoulders of neighboring dancers as support: "I'm not a fan of women in skirts somersaulting." She pauses, watching the dance, but ten seconds later she follows up, saying, "But [I] wouldn't hold it against them.

They do them very well; they do them on time. It's accurate, they're all being very supportive." As there is no rule against this, or a guideline in the scoring rubric, she notes both that it is not her preference and that this is not a (conscious) factor in her scoring. Of course, there is probably some pressure not to indicate personal bias in the actual judging during an interview with a researcher, but in general, judges did not seem shy about stating their personal beliefs. Their personal differentiation between opinion and scoring also seemed genuine, and not prompted by any kind of need to "cover up" their actions. It appears that both the judges and the community acknowledge that personal preference is an inevitable part of the judging process, though how these preferences fit into how one should carry out adjudication is not always straightforward.

There are times when these judges acknowledge that the rules offer no place to mark a team up or down. However, usually they present this not as personal opinion, but as a failure of the rules to incorporate what they perceive as general thought, in the realm of the social discourse. One judge talked about how dancers in his youth used to have a lot of banter between the dancers in the rapper set, as well as between the Tommy (a character that serves as a combination of announcer, comedian, sports commentator, and fool) and the crowd. For him, that was how rapper should be, but the rules did not incorporate this kind of humor, therefore he could not mark it.

These moments of friction between official, social, and personal discourses lay bare an underlying push–pull within the competition, which is a factor of dance competition in general. What is ultimately at stake, more than an individual team's outcome, is the delineation and definition of the dance form itself. The official discourse is not a static framework, but rather is negotiated out of the social discourse. As general opinions and values have shifted, the competition rules and structure have also changed. A notable example is the introduction of buzz factor, a scoring category that is supposed to indicate the level of audience excitement and enjoyment—the "buzz" that is created in the room by a team's dance. Before the category was introduced, one team won the tournament by performing their dance at a radically slower pace than other teams. As the technical aspects of their dance were nearly flawless, they won the competition, but public opinion held that it was boring and "not true rapper dancing" (Rutland 2007). The competition rules were changed to "correct" this, including a buzz factor score for excitement. Many dancers felt that this had led in turn to a "buzz bubble" in which teams choreographed dance to be as exciting as possible. Teams put extra flips, new instruments, unicycles, and other flashy features into their dances, until the consensus in the social discourse decided that neither was this "true" rapper, and a correction was made again. This discussion brought up the issue of innovation and choreography in rapper, and how to both maintain traditional rapper and promote a living tradition that expands and grows. It was proposed at one point to include a category in the judging rubric that awarded points for choreography or new ideas in rapper dance, but this was ultimately not included. This decision, like every decision about official discourse in a dance competition, is both influenced by and has direct impact on how judges actually see a rapper dance.

PERCEPTION

Perception deals with which of the plethora of visual and auditory stimuli produced by a rapper dance is noticed and given prominence by judges. Influenced by the expectation-setting process, it encompasses the part of the adjudication process that is least conscious. While judges may believe that they notice the different parts of the dance equally, my work shows that not only are certain moments perceived more distinctly, but also that particular aspects of a dance are more likely to be noticed in different sections of dance.

Seeking to understand how experts within an artistic and cultural form evaluate dance, I turn to discussions of the aesthetics in dance. In her article *An Introduction to Dance Aesthetics,* dance anthropologist Adrienne Kaeppler states,

> One who attempts to evaluate a production of another society or epoch is fooling himself . . . members of different cultures simply do not react in identical ways to the same stimuli, artistic or otherwise. Canons of taste arise out of cultural values. (Kaeppler 2003, 154).

Although I was tempted to try to make explicit what specific aspects of a rapper dance performance are tacitly important to judges, the comments from the video-assisted interviews indicated that judges agree (or at least did not specifically disagree) about what was important when it was in the rules, that is to say, in the official discourse. Beyond this fairly prescriptive alignment in opinion, however, the interviews revealed substantial variance of personal opinion, often about the same figures in a single dance.

While annotating the video of the Sheffield Steel performance, I noticed something surprising: while there were certain periods of time during which no judge made a comment, other moments brought a flurry of observations, often unrelated to one another, in response to relatively short sections of the performance. I therefore wondered if there are moments in performance that hold more importance than others. I recalled Kaeppler's (2003, 154) enjoinment that the "underlying organization [of aesthetics] is more important for understanding human action (behavior plus intention) than an analysis of the content of the item itself," and reflected on how to interrogate this tacit cultural structure within which expert judges could make aesthetic sense of a rapper dance.

In his book *Time Maps* (2003), cognitive sociologist Eviatar Zerubavel discusses how cultures conceive and remember their history. He finds that while, in a strictly objective sense, the same amount of time passes every year, there are *mnemonically dense* periods in history. These periods are separated from relatively unmarked time in different ways, such as national holidays, while entire decades or millennia may pass by a country's historical memory without notice. This pattern of mnemonic density, in contrast to relatively unmarked time, is found not only in national narratives, but also in personal, corporate, and societal narratives, and is indicative of underlying structures that provide a wealth of information as to how entities discursively construct a "self."

Adapting this concept, I propose to conceive dance, as viewed from a culturally specific perspective, as having an *aesthetic density* in which moments of concentrated aesthetic judgment are contrasted with relatively unmarked time within a dance realization.[7] By simply noting the presence of a reaction, without yet needing to fully understand the content of that reaction, the researcher may establish that not every moment is equal to other moments, and may use this idea to gain an understanding of the structure of a form. These aesthetically dense moments become focal points for aesthetic judgment and, as such, form a crucial part of the underlying structure by which dance is culturally understood and evaluated. Aesthetic viewing is culturally situated and difficult to access; however, moments of *aesthetically dense* responses can be recognized and used as footholds for deeper exploration into a cultural practice. While I will explore this understanding of aesthetic density as it applies to dance, specifically rapper, it may prove to be a useful tool for anthropologists in many fields as a way to find clues to the tacit structures and understandings that constitute cultural aesthetics.

RAPPER AND TEMPORAL-AESTHETIC MAPPING

How, then, can I use the concept of aesthetic density to investigate judges' perception and evaluation of rapper dance? I already had begun to notice that judges often commented on the same moments of dance, even though they had been interviewed separately from each other, months apart. My collaborators were cultural insiders; as officially appointed judges, they clearly set the standard for skilled observers. As an English speaker and experienced rapper dancer myself, I fulfill the minimum criteria of having a basis of cultural understanding on which to conduct research. By interviewing multiple skillful viewers and asking them to identify what is important to them, I had not only collected specific opinions on what is important, but also started to identify the underlying moments of *when* is important in judging rapper dance. I decided to attempt to deconstruct the comments made by judges during our interviews, temporarily separating the textual contents from its temporal location. Taking inspiration from *Time Maps*, I set out to create a temporal-aesthetic map of my judges' experience of a rapper dance in the competition setting.

Figure 16.1 shows this first attempt to use a temporal-aesthetic map, taken from the annotation markings of the Sheffield Steel VideoANT. Each vertical black line represents a remark by a judge, and occasionally contains two or more if judges commented at exactly the same time. It presents a somewhat rudimentary map; only the existence of aesthetic features, the judges' comments, is indicated. Beyond that, the analyst must refer to the comments in the full VideoANT, or the Excel document, to re-access the text.

FIGURE 16.1. Temporal map of Sheffield Steel.

Jeremy Carter-Gordon, VideoAnt, ant2.cehd.umn.edu

This map, like any other, raises questions: What is contained at the dense points visible in Figure 16.1, and what causes the gaps? A map of an unknown territory, it shows a structure or landscape, while hiding the character of the land, with its vistas and vegetation. Yet close analysis of these maps using VideoANT revealed a wealth of information. In particular, as I looked at aesthetically dense moments, when judges all commented on the dance at once, I found that it was just as common for them to be speaking about different features of the dance as to be addressing the same issue. The gaps of aesthetic paucity tended to be figures of repetition, where judges quickly gleaned their initial impression, and relaxed their attention, relying instead on the initial take. The most fascinating discovery, however, were the patterns of aesthetic attention when it came to particular judging categories. For example, judges consistently noticed a team's stepping almost exclusively in the first ninety seconds of dancing, only commenting later for obvious mistakes. On the other hand, the presentation category is actually marked primarily before the dance starts as the team comes on, and in the first thirty seconds of movement, and then again just as the dancers finish and leave the stage, with almost no comments over the majority of the actual dance.

Some of these correlations are fairly simple, and the judges are aware that they look for certain things at certain moments; when looking for "drive" or "an edge" in dance technique, comments were concentrated heavily on one musical phrase into circular walking figures; one judge, Sarah,[8] hints as to why this may be:

> At that point look how they're leaning in; because they're faster, there's far more drive to this dance and you can tell that by the body shape there . . . you can see them leaning, you can see *drive* in that still. . . . I know we see drive with the blurriness, but they're leaning, so you can tell they're going fast around a corner . . . and that's drive straight away for you![9]

While other figures call attention to swords, the sound of stepping, or shapes of the display figures, it may be easier to evaluate the speed and drive of the dancers when they are performing a relatively simple motion without much distraction.

Most of the comments that explicitly mention sword handling occur during "show figures." In this type of move, the dancers present the swords in a complicated pattern while stepping in place, and in many cases are held stationary for only a few seconds. Comments regarding these figures occurred about a second after the figure was first displayed, and were almost entirely negative. Judges, as expert dancers and observers, are able to tell in a flash when a display figure is not aligned well, with small mistakes jumping out, even if the mistakes are visible for only a moment. The negative slant of these comments indicates that figures performed well are less likely to draw attention than those executed poorly.

Music emerged as one of the most complex and interesting categories to observe. The first type of comment cluster appears fairly straightforward; judges comment on the quality of the musicianship itself near the beginning of the dance or during tune changes. This makes sense; like the stepping, which fades into the background after a while, the tune changes are moments when the music alters that foundation, thrusting itself into the awareness of the observer. Similarly, the musicians were credited with making adjustments during jumping or flipping figures so that the dancers appeared to land on the beat.

The tacit choreomusical relationship of a performance and the judges' reaction to it proved more complicated. For example, Sheffield Steel's third tune presents an exciting moment, with a bagpipe entering for the first time and a fast-spinning basket figure that combined to receive big cheers from the crowd. Shortly after the tune started, one judge, Andrew, commented that the dancing was "good, steady," "well controlled," and "smooth,"[10] while a few seconds later Ellen said, "[the dancing is] very neat and it's very well phrased to the music."[11] Sarah added, "their movements flow well together," and Ellen chimed in again that "they hit the beat of the music with the flow of the dance." A minute later, the tune changes and the sense of a "smooth, flowing, well-coordinated" dance vanishes from the comments. Ellen seemed to note this difference obliquely, saying, "They just suddenly started to sound to me when they did these big skips over, as if they were starting to enjoy the tune more than they were enjoying to play it [to match the dancers]. But they lost one mark." While judges did not seem specifically aware of the effect of this tune, analyzing the mapped structure clearly shows its impact. As such, this may be a case where the music is not specifically credited with points, but rather influences the perception that judges had of the whole.

INTERPRETATION

Interpretation is the process of applying expert knowledge of the dance to what is perceived in the performance. Different facets of dance are delineated from each other into categories such as music, figures, stepping patterns, and so on, and judges then work to apply their own knowledge, both intellectual and physical, to form opinions on these features. The integration of aesthetic perception to the competition rules and guidelines is not an automatic function and incorporates the official, social, and personal discourse on an explicit level. A judge may notice, for example, a group's footwork and may have a conscious aesthetic reaction to it, both influenced and mediated by the criteria for stepping. The judges' conversations and shared general knowledge of the difficulty and skill of the pattern and execution will be weighed, along with their own experience of performing these actions and personal enjoyment of the figure. The process of interpretation constitutes the most conscious stage of adjudication, and during interviews judges often wished to discuss and explain their own mental activity regarding these ideas. While much of these thoughts most closely followed the official rules, some instances emerged in which tension between these layers of discourse from the expectation-setting stage resulted in interpretations that may seem to contradict the rules.

The category of buzz factor is theoretically based on audience reaction to a dance, its excitement, and the cheers, comments, and energy it produces. In my mapping, I noticed that judges primarily talk about buzz not only when the audience had big, obvious cheers, but also when the audience looks bored. Surprisingly, both of these events seem to have a negative impact on the score; cheers sometimes lead judges to decide that the "fan club was distracting" or that the team "just has a rent-a-crowd following them and pushing up the buzz," and therefore are suspicious of the audience as an indicator of buzz. Roger elaborated,

> [If a team has] a good following and they get a lot of people to follow them from pub to pub, if they are shouting and screaming while they're watching them dance, you think "Oh, they're good, you know?" So you got to, sort of, close your ears to that and just see what *you* see, what *you* like or dislike, you know, and do it that way, 'cause as I say, some, if they've got nobody with 'em, you hear no shouts or yells.[12]

In fact, contrary to the official guidelines, judges were unanimous in that they actually tried to block out the audience most of the time. For herself, Ellen says she makes a mental division between the crowd and the rapper, and asks herself, "Is it good rapper music doing it for me? Or are the crowd giving me something? I try to separate it out a little bit, as I can." The "true" buzz factor seems to be felt by judges as internal excitement. They describe it in terms of an intangible feeling that makes them "tingle," or "feel a lift," or even "want to get up and dance." Buzz factor is not a sense of the whole audience, but rather an individualized excitement that any audience member should feel at a good dance done skillfully. While judges thought that judging buzz factor based on the audience was not reasonable, none of them expressed doubt at his or her own ability to mark the category. Everyone with whom I spoke seemed confident that his or her personal experience of the dance could be used in place of the audience experience to allow an effective and fair score; this affirms that they consciously use personal experience to stand in for audience reaction.

On a similar note, all the judges appreciated when the dancers appeared to be enjoying the dance. Usually this was considered as part of the presentation score, and judges talked about enthusiasm, being "good ambassadors for the tradition," and "[showing] their excitement in a positive way." Smiling was not necessarily considered a good thing, though. Several judges mentioned a distaste for "fixed grins," with Andrew insisting that if a team "[keeps] that constant silly grin, they ain't enjoying the dance... it's like a grimace." Smiling can be seen as suspicious, and the genuine nature is to be determined by the judge.

This process of naming is an important one; as noted earlier, judges can only judge what they perceive, and they may not always be aware of the causes of these perceptions. I will add that during the process of interpretation, judges may not fully notice that which they cannot categorize or name. In competitive ice skating, judges watch official practices to get a sense of a skater's program, to identify what moves are happening at what point, and to determine which elements should be given attention. At DERT, rapper judges do not have such access, and the effect of this is evident. At no point in my interviews did judges mention new figures, or indeed innovation at all, outside the abstract. This is possibly because the judges are focused elsewhere and do not see the moment of innovation. Even if they saw and liked a new figure, no section of the judging sheet allows for points to be specifically allocated toward choreography or innovation. However, a personal anecdote can illustrate that judges notice innovation in the negative.

While attending DERT 2005, Candy Rapper, an American team, intentionally let go of their swords in the middle of a dance to perform complicated foot percussion. I later found out that a few judges gave them no score for sword handling, with the comment that "letting go of the sword was not rapper dancing." On the surface, the problem seemed to be letting go of the swords, but this is complicated, because while the rules mark teams down for "dropping swords," the only listed requirement for competing is that "the dance must be a rapper dance, performed with rapper swords." Additionally, there are several traditional figures in which dancers let go of swords. This poses the obvious question: What is a rapper dance?

Among the questions of interpretation we must answer is how to determine the essential features of rapper dance as opposed to the accidental ones, in the Aristotelian sense—that is to say, which features a rapper dance *must* have in order to be rapper, and which features it has, but *could* do without. For example, it is obvious that rapper dance has stepping, but it does not seem to be important whether the stepping is directed perpendicularly or at a 45-degree angle to the dancer. These could be considered allokinemes in Kaeppler's usage (physically distinct movements that are not distinguished culturally), though judges note that a style of stepping between members of a team is important. Teams can utilize a huge amount of variety and differentiation in how figures are performed, what figures are chosen, how music is played, or which percussive step is executed, but they have tacit limits that remain invisible to the outsider (and occasionally the insider) until they are trespassed upon (Kaeppler 1972). The tradition has proved more elastic than most would admit, incorporating everything from unicycles to flaming rapper swords, while maintaining the rapper label. Figures, variations, and other devices that were rejected in the past are now accepted and commonplace, while others that were common have disappeared. Mapping the specific boundaries of these limits is beyond the scope of this chapter, but it is clear that the limits and perspectives on this issue are unstable and changing.

Decision-Making

Finally, in the decision-making process, these aesthetic observations and categories must be compared, and a score calculated. Judges draw upon several overlapping layers of techniques with which to process their perceptions of a dance into an aesthetic judgment. Varying backgrounds and relationships to rapper dance lead to fundamental differences in the ways judges conceive and understand the form, reflected in the way judges mark competition dances.

Through the interviews, it became clear that judges who had "inherited" the dance and those who had come to the dance later in life conceived the judging process in different ways. I use the terms *heirs* and *users* for these two groups, which I borrow from ethnochoreologist Egil Bakka's *Heir, User or Researcher: Basic Attitudes within the Norwegian Revival Movement* (1992, 117–118). In this article, Bakka describes heirs as people who are "from societies where dance . . . still [has] a strong presence . . . heirs consider themselves as having inherited their dance and or costume traditions directly from their family or close neighbours . . . they feel a strongly emotional attitude to their inheritance and feel proud to be its heirs even if they do not use this term to describe it. They feel entitled to some sort of moral authority over tradition." In my case, the rapper heirs are dancers whose fathers and forefathers had been dancers, often involved in the mining industry around Newcastle before its elimination during Thatcher-era England (Corrsin 1997).[13] They dance to connect to and perpetuate their heritage of rapper dance, as well as for fun. While there are roughly equivalent numbers of male and female rapper dancers today, the majority of heirs are male, an indication of the male-dominated past of the dance.

Users, on the other hand, "are people who feel that they are not . . . heirs in any direct manner. . . . They have been fascinated by folk dance . . . as general resources and are engaged in working for their revival" (Bakka 1992, 118). Users' involvement in rapper was limited to post-revival dancing, and they had learned to dance, started teams, and continued their involvement for fun, exercise, and community. While they also feel that the heritage is worth preserving, users experience a different sort of connection. In my work with judges from both categories, I have begun to see distinctions in the methods the two groups use to score a dance. Heirs, who have links to pre-revival rapper, imagine rapper as an idealized, historicized form, and compare dances against this standard in an absolute sense. Users, who came to rapper as social and artistic activity, compare dances to each other in a relativistic way, scoring dances against each other by finding where they rank in relation to one another.

THE "PERFECT DANCE" MODEL

In the perfect dance method, a judge imagines an ideal rapper dance in their mind. This is not a specific set of figures or particulars, but rather the Platonic form of dance, evoked by a set of principles in the dance (Bar-Elli 2004). As such, every dance starts off with a perfect score. As judges are presented with a specific realization of a rapper dance, they notice when the physical reality fails to meet the expectations set by this "perfect dance." Any shortcomings are deducted from the perfect score, taking away points as the dance progresses. In their comments during our interviews, the judges rarely talked about a team gaining points, instead focusing on the problems that they demonstrated. In the Sheffield dance, Andrew commented that the "swords look a bit off there . . . a figure like that, it's very important that they are all level." His observation both delineates the ideal way of dancing and notes how the dance fails to meet this standard. Even positive comments were usually framed in terms of the dance conforming correctly to the dance standard. During a spinning figure, he comments that it is "good, steady, flat. That's a dancing spin." The phrasing "a dancing spin," along with the characteristics of what that means, suggests that this moment met expectations for the ideal dance; therefore no points would be deducted. His colleague Fred says, "I can't see anything wrong with the presentation, so that'd be maximum marks for that."[14]

The heir judges tended to use the perfect dance model. As inheritors of a tradition, much of what is important to the dance is tied directly to how the dance used to be done by their fathers, grandfathers, and the older generation. Many of our conversations about rapper dance diverged to discuss miner's guilds of the Northeast, local history, early trains, and family trees. Andrew noted that one of the biggest honors in his life was when his rapper team was given the place of honor at a huge miner's union parade, marching at the lead. He recalled, "What an honor! And the rapper dancers were at the front of it all, all these old dancers would have been proud!" Today's rapper is connected not only to rapper in the past and future, but also to the sociohistorical past of a specific place (Cawte 1981).

While they agree that change and innovation are important to the future of rapper dance, heirs often imagine a past golden age of rapper that is to be continued. Roger describes the way his grandfather's team used to dance, and talks about his own teaching as such:

Grandfather burnt it into me that it was light on the walking, on the trotting, heavy on the stepping, and there was that so when you were moving there was a nice flow. And you trotted, you didn't walk, you trotted, so the dance looked like it was moving, ya know? And I was brought up that way. I hope I got my lads to the same these days, but yeah, it was really important that.

Fred states,

I'm old-fashioned, I look for the things I feel should be there . . . some teams come on and I think, you know, you shouldn't be doing that, you really shouldn't . . . you've got to respect the tradition . . . how close is it to proper tradition?

Fred sometimes jokes, "I've been watching rapper for so long that [my] memories are all colored sepia!" With an imagined, idealized past of exceptional dancing to draw upon, it is no surprise that these judges tend to compare the dancing to the "perfect dance," deducting points where it does not meet expectations. The judges perhaps find it more useful to try to identify *what* is wrong than try to determine *how* right it is.

THE "BEST FIT" MODEL

In the second technique, judges tend to quickly decide a baseline score for the various categories, which are further refined up or down as the dance progresses. Instead of a perfect score that can only decrease with mistakes, an initial assessment is made and then modified. Judges are also more likely to talk about improvements or gaining points over the course of the performance. For example, Ellen initially complained that the Sheffield dance was "slow" and "lacked drive," meaning that the dancers did not demonstrate enough speed, force, and energy. A minute or so later, she commented that the drive had improved and that the dancers were enjoying themselves more, and also indicated that she would have increased her marks for them in the dance technique and buzz factor categories. This re-evaluation indicated a clear break from the perfect dance technique; an initial impression was formed, and while mistakes might take points away, good dancing could gain them back.

Unsurprisingly, best-fit judges also use the scoring rubrics more frequently than perfect-dance judges. These rubrics list both positive and negative attributes of the dances, sorted into various categories. In both our general discussions and in the video-assisted interviews, the judges I had categorized as users often employed language directly from the rubric, seemingly unknowingly, whereas heirs rarely intersected with this wording. This linguistic assimilation suggests that users have cognitively internalized the criteria as a way of breaking down the dance into its component parts and judging it. I do not suggest that the rubric constitutes the full extent of their judging, but rather that it has a greater effect on the users than on the heirs.

Best-fit judges arrive at their initial score range by comparing the viewed dance to specific past dances, seen either on that day or in previous competitions. This was evident, as stated explicitly in general interviews, as well as in comments that used language that compared teams to each other during the video-assisted section. Sarah watched Stone Monkey just after Sheffield Steel, and she compared them as follows: "Look how they're leaning in because they're faster, there's far more drive to this dance. . . . The girls [Sheffield Steel] were walking round; you can see [Stone Monkey] leaning, you can see drive."

By keeping track of each team's score, these judges tried to situate each scoring category as higher or lower than other teams, searching for a "best fit." Many of these judges actually wrote down the marks awarded for each team on a piece of paper, and compared the dancing team against these ranges. Of course this meant that as the competition progressed the potential points of comparison became more numerous, which my informants considered a good thing, thus making the judging easier. Hardest to judge were the first few dances of the day, as these had no reference point through which to compare. In particular, they were hesitant to score too highly in the initial dance, preferring to leave some room for subsequent teams to improve upward. Ellen expressed the desire to have the ability to revise previous scores as she saw dances later in the day, adding, "It is always hard to grade the first dances and sometimes you look back and say,

'you know, they were pretty good! Maybe I should have given them a few more points.'
But there's nothing you can do."

To compensate for this lack of comparison points at the beginning of the day, judges
relied more on the rubric, but also drew on their experiences from previous years. Some
tried to remember what high- or low-scoring dances had looked like, while others
simply said they had an instinct or a feeling. Even if previous experience is used to judge
the first dances of the current competition, this initial intuitive leap seems necessary at
some point to avoid a recursion that breaks down at the judge's first competition.

The judges who talked about searching for a best fit for teams fell into the category of
users. In their comments they both drew comparisons between rapper dance and other
kinds of performance art, including theater, ballet, and circus, discussing costumes,
movement, stagecraft, and facial expression. While they are acutely aware and appreciative of rapper's heritage, they experience rapper as a dance that relates more to
other forms of performance than to other northeast heritage, such as miner's guilds.
While heirs consider rapper vertically rooted in time and place, it may be that users see
rapper in a matrix of forms that is connected horizontally in the present day. Evidently,
rapper is a practice that can be compared to techniques used in other performances
(Theaker 2014).

Clearly, there is no single method or even set of methods that explains how all judges
make decisions in rapper. Instead, an overlapping set of mutually interconnected
models and understandings exists that makes sense of the dance and helps translate it
into a set of scores. Judges predefine the limits of the dance form, drawing on official
policy, social discourse, and personal preference to set expectations about what they
see during a dance. Their perception of a performance is therefore narrowed to looking
for, identifying, and evaluating the criteria that are included within the form. While different judges may evaluate moments of dance differently, and even directly disagree as
to their opinions, the temporal placement of these aesthetic judgments itself holds cultural value. In other words, what matters may be that *when* matters; the overall timing
of these instants of aesthetic decision-making say as much about the understanding of a
performance as the specific content of the criticism. Having watched the dances, judges
apply the standards of the competition to their perception, using the official guidelines
but also shared social convention, which can sometimes lead to processes that directly
contradict the official guidelines. Finally, while assigning scores to teams, judges from
different backgrounds construct the scoring in notably different ways, either seeing it
as a subtraction from an ideal, historicized dance, or as a process of placing each team's
performance within a matrix of other performances, finding the best fit for different
aspects of their dancing. While these conclusions are on one level specific to rapper
dance, it is my belief that they are also helpful to understanding many other forms of
dance competition, particularly of folk dance forms.

As the scholarship on dance competition judging grows, we will see how judges in
a range of formats draw upon these stages of adjudication in different ways. The specific methods used by rapper judges at DERT are unlikely to apply to a highly regulated
form such as competitive Irish dance, or to informal judging at a party, but the stages of

the process outlined can provide a framework for future investigation. The ideas surrounding perception and temporal-aesthetic mapping can be applied widely, both in dance studies, and indeed to any aesthetic experience that takes place over time. I hope that others will expand upon these theories and systems, creating a new set of tools to engage with questions of how cultures and individuals perceive, conceptualize, and make sense of dance, competition, and judging.

Notes

1. Bassett and Perskey (1994); Brennan (1999); DesJarlait (1997); Emerson and Meredith (2010); Foley (2001, 2013); Hall (2008); Khandelwal and Akkoor (2014); Looney (2003); McMains (2006); Nannyonga-Tamusuza (2003); Scales (2007); Stillman (1996); Wulff (2007).
2. I owe a debt of gratitude to my advisor Georgiana Gore and her 2007 work, "From Village to Festival: An Example of the Construction of Canons of Correct Performance," which first brought dance competition into my academic work while studying under her at the Choreomundus international MA in Dance Knowledge, Practice and Heritage.
3. Cecil Sharp (1859–1924) was a folk dance and song collector who founded the English Folk Dance Society, which later became the English Folk Dance and Song Society. He collected, promoted, and taught morris dances and later sword dances, and is considered by many to be the most important figure in any English folk revival.
4. The Sword Dance Union is an organization that serves to encourage, develop, and maintain the traditional sword dances of England. It is run by volunteers who are mostly dancers themselves, and provides both logistical and artistic support to teams, as well as maintaining an archive of sword dance.
5. I was inspired by elicitation interview (a technique developed by psychologist Pierre Vermersch that examines very specific moments of action), and self-confrontation interview (where subjects are asked to view and comment on a video of their own actions) (Bakka and Gore 2007; Rix and Lièvre 2008, 2009; Vermersch 1994; Wierre-Gore et al. 2012).
6. Findlay and Ste-Marie (2004) discuss this phenomenon in competitive figure skating.
7. While forms of dance may exist that give each moment of a performance or practice equal weight, this does not present a difficulty to the theory; rather, the uniformity of an aesthetic density throughout is a telling and important structural feature of the form.
8. Pseudonyms are used in this chapter to preserve judges' anonymity.
9. Author's interview with "Sarah" on August 17, 2014.
10. Author's interview with "Andrew" on July 15, 2014.
11. Author's interview with "Ellen" on July 25, 2014.
12. Author's interview with "Roger" on August 2, 2014.
13. The mining industry in the United Kingdom was much reduced during Margaret Thatcher's time as prime minister. Many of the mines were closed, and there were several disputes between the government and organized labor, in particular the 1984–1985 strike led by the National Union of Mineworkers, which eventually failed without gaining any concessions from the government.
14. Author's interview with "Fred" on August 16, 2014.

REFERENCES

Bakka, Egil. 1992. "Heir, User, or Researcher: Basic Attitudes within the Norwegian Revival Movement." In *Proceedings of the 17th Symposium of the Study Group on Ethnochoreology: Dance and Its Socio-Political Aspects; Dance and Costume*, edited Irene Loutzaki, 117–126. Nafplion, Greece: Peloponnesian Folklore Foundation.

Bakka, Egil, and Gore, Georgiana. 2007. "Constructing Dance Knowledge in the Field: Bridging the Gap between Realisation and Concept." Paper presented at Society for Dance History Scholars conference, cosponsored by Congress on Research in Dance. *Re-thinking Practice and Theory: Proceedings Thirtieth Annual Conference*. Centre National de la Danse, Paris, France, June 21–24.

Bar-Elli, Gilead. 2004. "Evaluating a Performance: Ideal vs. Great Performance." *Journal of Aesthetic Education* 38(2): 7.

Bassett, Gilbert W., and Joseph Persky. 1994. "Rating Skating." *Journal of the American Statistical Association* 89(427): 1075–1079.

Brennan, Helen. 1999. *The Story of Irish Dance*. Dingle, Ireland: Brandon Books.

Cawte, Edwin Christopher. 1981. "A History of the Rapper Dance." *Folk Music Journal* 4(2): 79–116.

Corrsin, Stephen D. 1997. *Sword Dancing in Europe*. Enfield Lock; Middlesex, UK: Hisarlik.

DERT. 2012. *Main Competition Rules: DERT London 2012*. http://www.DERT2012.co.uk/rules.

DesJarlait, Robert. 1997. "The Contest Powwow versus the Traditional Powwow and the Role of the Native American Community." *Wicazo Sa Review* 12(1): 115.

Emerson, John, and Silas Meredith. 2010. "Nationalistic Judging Bias in the 2000 Olympic Diving Competition." *Math Horizons* 18(3): 8–11.

Findlay, Leanne C., and Diane M. Ste-Marie. 2004. "A Reputation Bias in Figure Skating Judging." *Journal of Sport and Exercise Psychology* 26: 154–166.

Foley, Catherine. 2001. "Perceptions of Irish Step Dance: National, Global, and Local." *Dance Research Journal* 33(1): 34.

Foley, Catherine E. 2013. *Step Dancing in Ireland*. Surrey, UK: Ashgate.

Gore, Georgiana. 2007. "From Village to Festival: An Example of the Construction of Canons of Correct Performance." In *Tánchagyomány: Ataeáas És Atvétel/Dance: Tradition and Transmission. Tanulmáanyok Felföldi László Köszöntésére/Festschrift For László Felföldi*, edited by Barna Gábor, Csonka-Takács Eszter, and Varga Sándor, 153–163. Szeged: Néprajzi és Kulturális Antropológiai Tanszék.

Hall, Frank. 2008. *Competitive Irish Dancing: Art Sport Duty*. Madison, WI: Macater.

Kaeppler, Adrienne L. 1972. "Method and Theory in Analyzing Dance Structure with an Analysis of Tongan Dance." *Ethnomusicology* 16(2): 173. doi: 10.2307/849721.

Kaeppler, Adrienne L. 2003. "An Introduction to Dance Aesthetics." *Yearbook for Traditional Music* 35: 154. doi: 10.2307/4149325.

Khandelwal, Meena, and Chitra Akkoor. 2014. "Dance On! Inter-Collegiate Indian Dance Competitions as a New Cultural Form." *Cultural Dynamics* 26(3): 277–298.

Looney, Marilyn 2003. "Evaluating Judge Performance in Sport." *Journal of Applied Measurement* 5(1): 31–47.

McMains, Juliet E. 2006. *Glamour Addiction: Inside the American Ballroom Dance Industry*. Middletown, CT: Wesleyan University Press.

Nannyonga-Tamusuza, Sylvia. 2003. "Competitions in School Festivals: A Process of Reinventing Baakisimba Music and Dance of the Baganda (Uganda)." *The World of Music* 45(1): 97–118.

Rix, Geraldine, and Pascal Lièvre. 2008. "Towards a Codification of Practical Knowledge." *Knowledge Management Research & Practice* 6(3): 225–232.

Rix-Lièvre, Geraldine, and Pascal Lièvre. 2010. "An Innovative Observatory of Polar Expedition Projects: An Investigation of Organizing." *Project Management Journal* 41: 91–98. doi: 10.1002/pmj.20184.

Rutland, Vince. 2007. "Dancing Down the DERT Years." *The NUT*. http://www.the-nut.net/articles/dert_years.php.

Scales, Christopher. 2007. "Powwows, Intertribalism, and the Value of Competition." *Ethnomusicology* 51(1): 1–29.

Stillman, Amy Ku'Uleialoha. 1996. "Hawaiian Hula Competitions: Event, Repertoire, Performance, Tradition." *The Journal of American Folklore* 109(434): 357–380. doi: 10.2307/541181.

Theaker, Kev. 2014. "Rapper as Spectacle." *The Nut* (46): 9–10.

Vermersch, Piere. 1994. *L'entretien d'explicitation*. Paris: European Social Forum.

Wierre-Gore, Georgiana, Geraldine Rix-Lievre, O. Wathelet, Anne Cazemajou, et al. 2012. "Eliciting the Tacit: Interviewing to Understand Bodily Experience." In *The Interview: An Ethnographic Approach*, edited by Jonathan Skinner, 127–142. London: Bloomsbury.

Wulff, Helena. 2007. *Dancing at the Crossroads*. New York: Berghahn Books.

Zerubavel, Eviatar. 2003. *Time Maps*. Chicago: University of Chicago Press.

CHAPTER 17

DISMANTLING THE GENRE

*Reality Dance Competitions and Layers
of Affective Intensification*

ELENA BENTHAUS

In Episode 12 of Season 2 of the American television show *So You Think You Can Dance* (SYTYCD), executive producer and judge Nigel Lythgoe stated, "We are not here to make avant-garde choreography. We are here to entertain America" (SYTYCD 2006). His response was directed at a dance routine performed by dancer-contestants Dmitry Chaplin and Ashlee Nino, which was choreographed by American dancer and choreographer Brian Friedman to Fall Out Boy's punk rock song "Dance Dance." Filmed from the back of the stage, framing a figure hidden under a white cloth standing center stage and bathed in red-blue light, Dmitry runs from his position at the edge of the audience on to the stage to the opening bars of the song. While the camera circles the hidden figure and simultaneously zooms in to a medium close-up shot, Dmitry comes to a stop at the figure's back to pull off the cloth, revealing Ashlee in a freeze-frame position with slightly spread legs, a tilted upper body facing stage right, her left arm bent with hand held mouth high while the right arm is stretched out to the back with a flexed hand. Dmitry, carrying a wand, releases Ashlee from the freeze position by first circling his right hand over her head and then tapping her lightly on the leg with the wand as if casting a spell over her. The tap not only releases Ashlee from her freeze position, but it also initiates a playful manipulation of movement between both dancers. These movement sequences are marked by broken lines due to flexed hands and feet, running, and sudden stops, all of which are punctuated by athletic and virtuosic partner work; for instance, Dmitry lifts Ashlee, in a back bend with extended legs, up on his shoulder to spin her around the stage. The movements are additionally accentuated and intensified by the quick staccato beat and rhythm of the punk rock song. The routine is loud, colorful, and vibrant, thus creating an exciting and upbeat atmosphere, summed up by Lythgoe as "entertaining."

In the episode, the judges describe the style as contemporary dance, although I refer to the style as commercial contemporary dance, a labeling issue, I will return to later in the chapter. The routine, aimed at showcasing two non-contemporary dancers[1] (Nino is a locker and Chaplin a Latin ballroom dancer), played with the "puppet come to life imagery," which caused Lythgoe to reference the nineteenth-century classical ballet *Coppélia* as part of the evaluation. It is a reference that both alludes to the storyline of the ballet and visualizes *Coppélia*'s doll character in Ashlee Nino's costume, as she wears a tutu-like white tulle skirt over calf-length white leggings, topped by a blue and gold striped bodice. Lythgoe's statements thus not only encapsulate the overall premise of SYTYCD "to entertain America" and therefore connect it to a history of American popular entertainment, but by referencing another dance text it also highlights the show's inherent intertextuality. In SYTYCD, the intertextuality results from a constant citation and incorporation of references from other screen, dance, and entertainment-related texts, thus emphasizing the show's popular entertainment status.[2] It is an intertextuality that is layered and works on multiple levels: the classification of the dance routine as a contemporary dance routine; the classification of the dancers as a Latin ballroom dancer and a locker; the use of a punk rock song; and the reworking of a classical ballet narrative for a televised entertainment format.

Created by *American Idol* producers Simon Fuller and Nigel Lythgoe (who has also been the main judge on the show) and produced by 19 Entertainment and Dick Clark Productions, the premise of SYTYCD is to find "America's Favorite Dancer." To determine "America's Favorite Dancer," each season is divided into three stages: open auditions, Vegas Week, and live performance shows. During the open audition process, auditions are held in four to six different cities across the United States, which invite dancers from all possible dance styles between the ages of eighteen and thirty to perform a solo or duet in their own style in front of a panel of judges, composed of Lythgoe and two other American choreographers or dancers. The dancers who are chosen to continue to the call-back stage of the show, which is held in Las Vegas (hence referred to throughout the show as "Vegas Week"), are asked to adapt to a variety of different dance styles, usually variations of hip-hop choreography, ballroom, Broadway/jazz, and lyrical contemporary. After each style is learned and performed for the judging panel, dancers are eliminated until about forty dancers remain, from whom the Top Twenty dancers (ten males and ten females) are chosen to proceed to the third stage of the season, the live performance shows. For the live performance shows, the Top Twenty dancers are paired up to form male/female dance partnerships. Each partnership has a week to learn a choreography, the style of which is determined by chance procedure (luck-of-the-draw principle), which they then perform on stage in front of the judges, the studio audience, and broadcast for television audiences across the country. At the end of each performance show, spectators are asked to vote for their favorite couples and, from the Top Ten downward, for each individual dancer. During the "Results Show," one male and one female dancer are eliminated from the competition based on audience voting patterns until "America's Favorite Dancer" is determined and announced in the final performance show episode of the season.

As a televised dance competition, scholars have commonly referred to SYTYCD as dance reality television (Broomfield 2011), reality dance competition (Dodds 2014; Foster 2014; Weisbrod 2014), reality talent show (Redden 2010), or simply as reality television (Boyd 2012). Instead of looking at the competitive aspect of SYTYCD and its relation to the genre of reality television, I aim in this chapter to focus on the layering of the different genre cues and intertexts that are related to the historical development of American popular entertainment forms, in particular vaudeville and melodrama, to discuss how these intertexts produce what media scholar Henry Jenkins refers to as "affective immediacy" (Jenkins 1992, 61) and "affective intensification" (Jenkins 2007, 3) as part of the spectatorship experience. I suggest that vaudeville performance aesthetics (short routines that build up movement momentum by increasingly virtuosic movement sequences) and melodramatic performance modes (an overtly and exaggerated physical and emotional expression that appeals to and affects the audience) in SYTYCD shape its audience address and the creation of affective intensification in its spectators that might inspire them to become attached to and also vote for individual dancers.

I use the terms *affect, affective,* and *affectiveness* in my analysis to indicate how the different performance modes create, increase, and intensify sensation and feeling within spectators that attract them to individual dancer-contestants while creating attachment with the show as a whole. Using English literary and cultural studies scholar John Frow's work on genre as a fluid concept and its link to expressive qualities and audience responses, and dance studies scholar Janet Adshead-Lansdale's use of the concept of intertextuality in relation to dance, I examine and interpret the vaudeville and melodramatic layers of the format by analyzing two performances by Season 8's Melanie Moore. I selected Melanie Moore as an example for this chapter because she not only won the show that year, a sign that she was a beloved and celebrated dancer-contestant in that season as spectators actively voted for her to win, but also because her performances resonated with the audience beyond the scope of the show, which I examine by looking at responses from the SYTYCD fan community. These responses are important as they indicate how Melanie's performances of an athletic vaudeville corporeality and a simultaneous melodramatic expression transmitted effectively and affectively across screens, which resulted in an active expression of what it means to be affected in comments under videos of her performances on YouTube. The chapter is organized in the following way. First I discuss genre as an affective and intertextual practice to produce audience responses. Then I focus on the historical development of vaudeville and melodrama as specific genres, and show how vaudeville aesthetics and melodramatic performances modes can be traced in SYTYCD and how this is affective.

GENRE AS AFFECTIVE INTERTEXTUAL
PRACTICE

In the introduction to his book *Genre*, Frow (2006, 1) argues, "I take it that all texts are strongly shaped by their relation to one or more genres, which in turn they may modify." Taking this assumption as a starting point, he argues against the formulaic and conventional use of the term *genre*, rejecting the idea that genre applies to some texts, but not to others, without denying that the use of certain generic distinctions point to textual strategies and, more important, to audience reception and audience structures. Instead, he asserts that genre indicates a "universal notion of textuality" (Frow 2006, 2). He thus establishes genre as an organizing principle, which structures and orders texts and can be found in any object or practice that can be identified as a text. As a result, Frow opens the term *genre* for multiple and, more important, intertextual usages. He eschews a static and stable classification or identification of specific genres, and instead conceives genre as a textual as well as a social practice, which creates and shapes knowledge about the world and is intimately linked to how power is exercised within discourses (Frow 2006). This textual and social notion of genre, which does not exclude genre as an organizing principle, formulates genre as fluid, unstable, and changeable. Just as genres are neither static nor stable categories, neither are texts stable and fixed entities, associated with (or participating in) just one particular genre. The most important aspect of Frow's thinking emerges in the way texts and their generic categorizations are applied to and are used in reading practices, which creates an "economy of genres" (2006, 2). In this economy, genres are interrelated, mobile, and have relational structures. In this sense, generic structures matter because they are a central feature of the production of meaning (or meaning-making processes), as well as key features of the struggle over produced meanings, social and historical contexts, knowledge, and emotional and affective responses.

In SYTYCD, the struggle over produced and/or intentioned meanings can be examined in relation to the organization of dancer-contestants under (dance) stylistic categories. If, as I pointed out in my introductory example, dancer-contestants are identified as a locker and a Latin ballroom dancer, performing a contemporary dance routine means that these dancers perform outside the style under which they are organized. On the most basic level, spectators are either guided to be surprised about a really good performance as the dancers perform outside their styles, or spectators are left wondering about the general adaptability of the dancers to other styles if the performance was perceived as lacking in stylistic aptitude. Additionally, these organizing principles also open up the space to compare different performances and dancers with each other, reflecting on a potential knowledge of the dance style in question, or making sense of the way movement in this style works.

Frow (2006, 23) notes, "the textual event is not a member of a genre-class because it may have membership in many genres, and because it is never fully defined by 'its' genre." Within each performance of a text, a variety of performances of generic conventions occur, each elaborating on the others. As such, the relationship between texts and genres is one of elaboration instead of determination. Genre concerns the intertextual relations of texts of both a similar and dissimilar kind, and the intertextual relations within any given text, in which different generic conventions coexist, and are performed alongside each other. Genre-as-elaboration then proposes a "potential use value" (Frow 2006, 25) of the texts in question, in which "potential" can be understood as a possibility rather than a closed determination; hence, genre classification as a process, instead of a static nomenclature, acknowledges its instability and unpredictability due to the different histories, knowledge, and potential affective responses that coexist within any given text. As Frow (2006, 45) argues,

> The embedding of the logic of one genre within the logic of another takes place textually, then; and the general process of which I have been speaking could perhaps be called *citation*: that is, the shifting of text from one textual and generic context to another.

The process of citation that Frow mentions here, in the sense of shifting texts or elements of texts, from one genre into another can be applied in a dance context as well. Going back to the example at the start of this chapter, the transference of the storyline of the classical comedic ballet *Coppélia*, in which a puppet comes to life, into the context of SYTYCD as a televised dance entertainment format occurs in the form of a citation. It is a citation and shift that take place on multiple levels: medium (from theater stage to television stage and screen); dance style (from classical ballet to contemporary dance); music (from classical orchestral music to punk rock music); length (from *Coppélia* as a full-length narrative ballet to the dance routine that condenses the narrative to ninety seconds); and costume (from a classical tutu, tights, and point shoes to a modified version of a tulle skirt, leggings, and bare feet). All of these levels, or intertexts, are related to each other and to the text that is referenced and elaborated upon.

Looking more closely and specifically at the relation between intertextuality and dance, Janet Adshead-Lansdale (1999, 8) similarly argues that thinking of a dance text always involves imagining "a text as a series of traces, which endlessly multiply and for which there can be no consensus of interpretation," which means considering these traces as intrinsic and unavoidable aspects of the dance text and the relationship between them. As Adshead-Lansdale (2007, 81) further suggests, "these notions of trace, absence and flickering presence are central to the construct of intertextuality." Indeed, traces are always characterized by their absent presence,[3] considering that traces of stories, structures, personalities, characters, and other texts are not necessarily materially present, even if they implicitly shape perception and reception. Adshead-Lansdale's notion of the trace as a "flickering presence" specifically suggests that generic intertexts are similarly present and absent, making themselves seen in the way they "flicker" in the text and as a result flare up in the sensory memory of spectators—there and not there at the same time, but generating an experience of affect. Thus, the identification and experience of traces adds an affective layer to the interaction between performance, performer, and spectator, by means of the expressive qualities of these traces.

Frow (2006, 72) writes, "let us take as our starting point the assumption that all genres possess historically specific and variable *expressive qualities*: they offer frameworks for constructing meaning and value in one or another medium." The framework chosen in the construction of meaning-making depends on what Frow highlights as "expressive qualities." The expressive and hence discursive qualities relate to and are derived from the structural qualities of a specific medium, and the way that the medium organizes its material within the framework of the genre, including formal qualities, thematic qualities, certain topoi (and recurrent iconography when it comes to images), corporeality, and structures of address (Frow 2006). They are what make generic texts effectively affective for off-screen spectators.

The notion of effective affectiveness relates to how the flickering presences of different intertextual layers (as a series of effects) contribute to the expressive qualities of a certain text, its reception, its affective immediacy, and a potential emotional attachment to the text. Effective affectiveness specifically relates to the ability of intertextual layers to trigger or arouse strong feelings and emotions in spectators. They are technologies of an affective performance. As feminist, queer, and critical race scholar Sara Ahmed (2004, 30) argues, "How the feelings feel in the first place may be tied to a past history of readings, in the sense that the process of recognition (of this feeling or that feeling) is bound up with what we already know." In SYTYCD, these effects, the combination thereof, and the resulting affective responses are tied to the "corporeality" of the relationship between the on-screen dancer-contestants and the off-screen spectators (television audience). Corporeality in these instances refers to the importance of the corporeal, physical materiality of the dancers on screen and the equally important corporeal, physical materiality of the spectators in front of the screen, who are affected by the dance performance they are seeing. It similarly refers to spectators' trace memories, which are evoked by the dancers on screen within the history of the format as a whole (all its dancers and all its performances) and the history of popular entertainment, which is closely related to this.

For an analysis of SYTYCD and the notion of effective affectiveness, the consideration that the show's intertextuality enhances affective responses is specifically linked to the modes of address, or expressive qualities, of vaudeville and melodrama as specific American popular entertainment genres, which exist alongside the competitive aspect of the show. The historical roots of vaudeville and melodrama and their particular modes of audience address are discussed throughout the rest of the chapter and are linked to the expressive qualities of SYTYCD by analyzing two performances of Season 8 dancer-contestant Melanie Moore and in relation to audience responses on social media.

"WOW" ME: VAUDEVILLE AESTHETICS AND SYTYCD

As proposed earlier, the expressive qualities that contribute to the effective affectiveness of SYTYCD are produced by the format's more implicit intertextuality, or what Adshead-Lansdale describes as "traces" and "flickering presences." It is implicit because, unlike the explicit classification of the show as a serialized televised dance competition, the references to vaudeville (and melodrama) are woven into the imagery of the format, particularly the structure of the Top Twenty live performance shows.

The roots of American vaudeville are found in locally based, primarily masculine saloon culture, for example music halls, which in turn changed when the practice itself became more respectable and mainstream to appeal to a wider (bourgeois) audience between 1835 and 1868 (Allen 1991). From its existence in saloon culture came the mainly comedic and musical acts, which were then joined by so-called speciality acts, like acrobatics, dancing, and juggling. These mixed items were arranged into a specific form and order to fit the variety bill. Jenkins notes that the vaudeville show is diverse, heterogeneous, inconsistent, and spectacular, depending on the performers' unique skills. In vaudeville, all of these elements, or effects, work to create "affective intensification" (Jenkins 2007, 3) with regard to spectators and the emotional impact of the performance, which is related to an affective response to that performance. As such, the primary function of vaudeville acts is to produce an "affective immediacy" (Jenkins 1992, 61), which means to provoke and trigger an affective and potentially emotional response from the audience in the moment of the performance through spectacularity, athleticism, and virtuosity, on the one hand, and comedy and musical acts, on the other hand, the combination of which makes the performance and the variety bill effectively affective. As Jenkins observes, "the program as a whole offered no consistent message; individual acts might offer competing or conflicting messages. In the end, what vaudeville communicated was the pleasure of infinite diversity in infinite combinations" (Jenkins 1992, 63). As a result, the diverse, heterogeneous range of performers and acts within a variety program functioned to attract the widest possible audience to the show and appeal to a broad variety of tastes.

American popular culture scholar Robert C. Allen also notes this openness of combination and the varieties of different performative genres within vaudeville programs in his book *Horrible Prettiness: Burlesque and American Culture* (1991). He locates the development of vaudeville as specifically aimed at middle-class audiences, thus moving away from the male-centric entertainment of the saloon culture Jenkins mentions. Thus, the development of vaudeville is situated within a wider tradition of American popular entertainments that always tended to work with mixed theatrical bills to attract a mass audience, and featured such diverse genres and styles as comedy, tragedy,

melodrama, magicians, acrobats, music, farce, and dance (Allen 1991). Vaudeville therefore became a prototype of popular entertainment that was inclusive of a variety of art
forms and moved the variety bill of masculine concert hall culture toward a middle-
class and family audience (Allen 1991). Importantly, Allen specifically stresses the dis-
continuous and non-narrative structure of the variety bill, which, in terms of content,
features "nothing and everything" (Allen 1991, 185) and provides a platform for all things
show business.

What the heterogeneity and "nothing and everything-ness" of the vaudeville bill
have in common is that every single component of this bill is what Russian film director
and film theorist Sergei Eisenstein (Eisenstein and Gerould 1974, 78) has referred to as
"attractions" in relation to the individual components of theater, film, music hall, and
circus performances. These components are arranged to form a "montage of attractions"
(Eisenstein and Gerould 1974, 79) that increases the affectiveness of a performance.
Eisenstein and Gerould (1974, 78) argue that an attraction is "any aggressive aspect of
theatre; that is, any element of the theatre that subjects the spectator to a sensual or psychological impact, experimentally regulated and mathematically calculated to produce
in him certain emotional shocks." An attraction is thus not merely an acrobatic or athletic trick that can stand for itself, or which excludes narrative elements such as plot
and character construction, but is always an effect, or in terms of genre, an expressive
quality, resulting from the interrelationship of the performance as a whole (with its various attractions) and the affective response of the audience.

An extension of Eisenstein's concept of the montage of attractions, which in turn
connects the notion of the vaudeville attraction to the development of the cinematic
medium, is Tom Gunning's (2006, 382) notion of the "cinema of attractions." The cinema
of attractions is, as Gunning (2006, 382) argues, a cinema that has the "ability to *show*
something," which means it is based on a demonstration of what cinema can do via the
technologies of the new medium. It is not based on narrative continuity, but rather on a
series of displays and thrills that are aimed at creating a connection with the spectator.
The notion of attraction(s) in these instances refers to the specific connection between
spectator and screen, based on a corporeal, visceral reaction to the images, framed by a
loose storyline and thus mirroring vaudeville show aesthetics. Moreover, as Gunning
(2006, 385) points out, at first "film appeared as one attraction of the vaudeville program, surrounded by a mass of unrelated acts in a non-narrative and even nearly il-
logical succession of performances." The notion of "attraction" then is intrinsic to both
vaudeville and the development of screen technologies and becomes a mode of address
that is affective, as it is aimed at creating what Jenkins refers to as affective immediacy or
affective intensification in relation to vaudeville aesthetics.[4]

The vaudeville aesthetic of a mixed bill (or a montage of attractions) that features
"nothing and everything" with a specific emphasis on having an impact, or effect,
on the audience is similar to how the SYTYCD live performance stage of the show is
structured. The overall structure of the live performance show, which has remained
largely the same across all seasons, features individual partner dance routines and, in
later episodes when the number of dancer-contestants has been reduced from twenty

to twelve, group routines. The performances of these routines are loosely connected by the overarching generic structure of the televised dance competition format as dancer-contestants compete to remain and eventually win the competition. However, the competitive aspect of SYTYCD only functions as another intertextual component within the vaudeville component of the show with its mixed bill/montage/cinema of attractions, consisting of spectacular and emotional dance routines. Despite only consisting of dance performances, which Jenkins and Allen refer to as speciality acts that coexist with comedy, music, tragedy, farce, juggling, and acrobatics, the featured dance styles range from commercial lyrical contemporary, jazz, Broadway/musical theater, commercial hip-hop choreography, international standard/smooth ballroom (for example, foxtrot, quickstep, waltz), international Latin/rhythm ballroom (for example, cha-cha-cha, jive, rumba, paso doble, samba), to commercial Argentine tango, salsa, disco, lindy hop, and Bollywood.[5] These different dance styles operate as attractions within the larger frame of the format and aim to attract a vast audience and form ongoing attachments between SYTYCD (and all its individual intertextual components) and spectators as part of the effective affectiveness of the show.

All choreographies exhibit moments of virtuosity and athleticism, such as complicated partnering sequences, turns, jumps, and leg extensions, which are enhanced by the use of screen technologies such as cinematography and editing, to extract and attract a response from the audience in the form of screams, extensive clapping, gasps, and what I have referred to elsewhere as the "WOW-affect."[6] The WOW-affect is intimately linked to the expressive qualities of SYTYCD's athletic, virtuosic, and affective dancing bodies and the physical-verbal impact the (screened) dance performances have on spectating bodies; thus the WOW-affect is effective and affective at the same time. The athletic and acrobatic movements within the individual choreographies also function as a montage of attractions within the overall montage/cinema of attractions of the live performance show. The production of the WOW, or what Jenkins (2007) calls the "wow climax" in relation to vaudeville aesthetics as a montage of attractions, which is aimed at briefly stopping the show due to audience responses,[7] is an intrinsic part of the attraction and competitiveness of the SYTYCD event, and the focus on the dancer as an athlete and virtuoso is a desired and strived for aspect of the format. Performing the WOW shifts the emphasis from the effectiveness of the performance to its affectiveness, which can be considered as a response to the experience of the multiple layers of intertextual (screen) attractions, creating an excessive intensity and an experience of being affected by this type of intensification.

One particular example of the affective impact of the dance routines occurred during Episode 18 in Season 8, which was broadcast on July 27, 2011. Dancer-contestant Melanie Moore performed a highly athletic and affective lyrical jazz duet with guest dancer and former SYTYCD contestant Neil Haskell (Top 4 in Season 3), who was invited as an All Star[8] for this episode. In the pre-performance rehearsal footage, choreographer Mandy Moore framed the lyrical jazz routine by describing the premise of the routine, stating, "This dance is about being at the crossroads of a relationship. These guys have to nail the emotional highs and lows through the movements," which she also describes as "extremely athletic" (SYTYCD 2011). Incidentally, Mandy Moore choreographed this dance routine to Bonnie Tyler's iconic power ballad "Total Eclipse of the Heart." A power ballad describes a slow tempo song, building up to an intense and emotional (or affective) chorus, which is backed up by electric guitar, an intensifying drum section, and choric backing vocals, all of which results in what British sociomusicologist Simon Frith (2001, 101) calls "songs of feeling bottling up and bursting out."

"Total Eclipse" starts slowly. The opening bars of the melody are played by a single piano before the male back-up vocalist calls out "turn around," to which Tyler answers, "every now and then I get a little bit lonely and you're never coming round" (Tyler 1983), before a similar call and response is repeated three more times as part of the first verse, with only the piano accompanying the vocals. The dance routine, likewise, begins slowly. The camera starts in a high-angle long shot, giving a view of the whole stage, bathed in red-purple light, with Melanie and Neil positioned center stage. Neil faces away from the audience, shirtless, wearing white flowing pants, while Melanie, dressed in a white flowing dress, faces the audience. During the opening bars of the song, the camera moves into a medium long shot before cutting to a medium shot, framing Melanie and Neil from the waist up, with the stage and them now bathed in a blue eerie light at the start of the lyrics. On "turn," Melanie faces Neil with a pensive-questioning facial expression and simultaneously reaches out her right arm to brush him across the shoulder. This brush initiates Neil's response on "around," in which he faces her, taking hold of her with his right arm across her chest to pull her into his chest and turn around over his left shoulder to face the audience on a slight diagonal, a transition that moves from the back-up vocalist's lyrics into Tyler's responding lyrics, beginning with "every now and then." By this time, the camera has pulled further back into a medium long shot for the next movement sequence, set to the rest of Tyler's response, "I get a little bit lonely and you're never coming round."

Being centered mid-frame with the dancers' entire bodies clearly visible during this sequence, both of them move through the lyrics, with Neil gently pushing Melanie out into a balancing position on her right leg, on elevated toes, with her left leg extended forward, while her arms are in a relaxed yet elongated V-shape position. He keeps her stabilized with both hands on her hips, while Melanie moves her left leg to the back like a pendulum, which initiates her to step down from the balance and back into Neil's chest. Both of them curve over with slightly bended knees, now facing the audience, in preparation for the next movement in which Neil lightly throws Melanie up in the air. In the throw, the camera cuts further away from the couple, framing them from a left diagonal position to then circle them moving to the center and toward the right side of the stage, while Neil catches Melanie under her armpits as she lands and collapses into his hold, leaning back into his chest again.

From there, each call-and-response section in the song is mirrored by a call-and-response movement sequence, in which Melanie and Neil move into more complex balancing and partnering sequences, in conjunction with the increasing pace and rhythm of the bridge of the song and the now audible bass guitar, to then pick up the swelling intensity of the chorus, with its added musical texture, through the now audible drum section and the humming, underlying choric backing vocalists. The peak moment of the dance routine (its WOW climax) occurs in conjunction with a peak moment in the song's chorus. Accompanied by an intensifying drum section, Bonnie Tyler's (1983) throaty lyric "I really need you tonight" gives way into the melody section, vocalized by a background chorus. During "I really need you," Melanie runs straight at Neil, literally building up intensity and momentum to leap off the ground on the first syllable of "tonight" and into Neil's arms on the second. The momentum from the run into the leap has her whole body momentarily suspended in midair, flying through the stage and screen space. When Neil catches Melanie, the impact of her body hitting his and wrapping itself around his torso has him staggering backward two steps before the routine continues, giving physicality to the "bottling up and bursting out" aesthetics of the power ballad.

The choreography as a whole is effectively affective due to the virtuosity and athleticism of its dancers (they are physically strong and technically skilled commercial contemporary dancers), their recognizability (Melanie's overall performance in the season and Neil as a previous dancer-contestant, or corporeal trace), and the way that the camera captures, accelerates, and intensifies the momentum of the dance by alternating between medium close-up shots, long shots that linger over movement sequences, and counterclockwise revolving camera movement that add a sense of vertigo, all of which can be seen as individual attractions that form the attraction (that is, the dance routine) as a whole. In relation to the performance and its movement momentum, guest judge Lady Gaga (SYTYCD 2011) elaborated on her reaction to Melanie's dancing with these words: "There is something so athletic, so passionate, and so beautiful about you." This comment specifically addresses the athleticism of Melanie's performance by connecting the virtuosity of her dancing body and its expressive quality to the affective force her performance produced. Not only did Lady Gaga use the word "passion" in relation to Melanie's performance, which points to an affective and possibly emotional response transmitted through the dancing, but in the close-up of Lady Gaga's face, we see her slightly teary eyes, as well as hear a choked-up sound to her voice. Being affected is here clearly made visible and audible.

Describing the expressive quality of Melanie and Neil's performance as dynamic, judge Mary Murphy (SYTYCD 2011) notes the way that particularly Melanie "moved through [the movement], melted and dissolved the movement in an instant to take us on this little journey that weaves and bobs all over the place." Here, the expressive quality of the affective force and its intensification is again connected to the corporeality of Melanie's movement quality through space. This kinesthetic quality of the movements and its particular connection to stage (and screen) space are something that Lady Gaga comments on as well. Toward the end of her evaluation, she tells Melanie, "You know, you were the first dancer tonight that I didn't watch the monitor [there are small monitors installed in the judging table, in front of each judge]. I couldn't keep my eyes off the stage. I didn't need the cameras. I didn't need nothing. I just wanted you" (Lady Gaga, SYTYCD 2011). Her comment indicates that this particular dance routine did not require enhancing technologies to make it more attractive to spectators, but that it only needed Melanie's dancing body and its athletic, virtuosic, and passionate commitment to the movements she performed. It demonstrates that the increasing suspense of the dancing bodies (as attractions) and their excessive intensity results in a transmission of these excessive affective forces to spectating bodies. However, in contrast to Lady Gaga (and the rest of the judges and the studio audience), most spectators only see these dance routines as screen performances, and part of the attraction is based on the way that the screen technologies contribute to the intensification of the spectating experience.

Melanie and Neil's duet was uploaded to YouTube by user "Myke Baldwin" on July 31, 2011 (the same year the season was broadcast), and this clip, among the many others that are available of this performance on YouTube, has been viewed over 1.2 million times, received 6,149 likes, and generated 356 comments as of May 17, 2018.[9] Underneath the clip, the impact of the performance is reflected in the responses to the leap in particular, but also in the more general responses to the dance routine and Melanie as a dancer-contestant during the season. The comments are mostly positive, with a few negative ones either reflecting a dislike of Lady Gaga or the song, but not with the dance performance, Melanie, or All Star Neil. The leap as one of the most affective moments during the routine was mentioned in forty-eight different comments. User "RigoStarr" exclaims, "That Leap!!! O-o Wow!" which parallels the way most of the forty-eight comments describe the leap—that is, as the immediate impression of the moment of being affected and WOW-ed by its (on-screen) attraction. It is a brief showstopper. In a more elaborate, hence measured manner, user "Psychopracter" recalls, "the moment she leaped I was so overcome with emotion I started to cry. That never happened to me before." This impression of the affective (screen) force of the leap is given as an afterthought of the impact, which can be seen in the use of past tense. Yet, the affective force of the leap as an attraction is still visible and remembered enough to be recalled and to be mentioned in a comment.

To return to the notion of Gunning's cinema of attractions, which is linked to vaudeville aesthetics and early cinema, YouTube, as a screen performance platform, can also be described as a twenty-first-century manifestation of vaudeville aesthetics and a re-emergence of the cinema of attractions. Indeed, as film and media scholar Teresa Rizzo (2008, 1) argues in her article "*YouTube*: The New Cinema of Attractions," in which she specifically references the notion of the exhibitionism and showiness of the early cinema that Gunning describes as the cinema of attractions, YouTube "not only extend[s] the concept of attractions but more importantly produces a unique form of attraction specific to the medium, one that might be thought about as *YouTube attractions*." More specifically, it invites spectators not only to watch, but also to participate by commenting on YouTube videos to "show off" the affective impact of the screen performance. Or, as Rizzo (2008, 4) points out, YouTube as a platform of attractions revolves around "acts of display" closely related to on-screen corporeality and its off-screen physical impact or "affective immediacy." Though Psychopracter mentions "being overcome" with emotion, the emotion with which they were overcome is not registered as one specific qualification. It is given as neither sadness, nor happiness, but only as a flickering presence of being affected by the virtuosity, athleticism, and immediacy of the dancing (vaudeville) bodies, peaking and briefly stopping the show in the moment of the leap as an act of display.

MOVE ME: MELODRAMATIC PERFORMANCE MODES AND SYTYCD

While the expressive quality of the affective force of the athletic and "show-stopping" dancing (or vaudeville) body is an important aspect of the attraction of its vaudeville aesthetics, vaudeville (and as an extension, SYTYCD) also depends on the unique performance modalities of its performers. As many athletic skills and attractions as possible have to be executed and displayed within the short frame of a fifteen-minute vaudeville act (or the ninety seconds of the SYTYCD dance routine), and these skills also have to be performed with the utmost personality and charm, as performers aim to stand out from the crowd. Indeed, Eisenstein and Gerould (1974, 78) refer to characters' (or performers') charm as a "sensual magnetism," as "inseparable from the attraction of the specific mechanics of his movements," thus connecting personality and memorability to corporeality. As Jenkins (1992, 73) similarly observes, "vaudeville's emphasis on the performer led to a cult of personality, a fascination with the artists' power to shape spectators' emotional response." This observation on the cult of personality surrounding vaudeville performance artists and Eisenstein and Gerould's link between personal charm and corporeal movements differ considerably from Allen's argument about the individual performers. Allen (1991) claims that, within a vaudeville show, the body of the performing artist was eradicated due to the increasing institutionalization and standardization of vaudeville bills, and the effort to manipulate emotional responses from the audience. However, as the production of affective responses and emotional attachment lies in the hands of the performers and is a premise on being employable within the vaudeville circuit (or successful on SYTYCD), performers have to be creatively expressive and unique to be memorable and stand out from and compete with other acts. Therefore the less acrobatic and more comedic and musical acts, in particular, utilize a specific character to create a loose storyline for the individual act, which is another component in the intertextual montage of attractions and is related to bringing the personality, character, and emotionality of a performer to the fore (Jenkins 1992). It is a performance mode I refer to as *melodramatic*.

In "Melodrama Revised," feminist film theorist Linda Williams (1998) sets out to revise, as the title suggests, a theory of specifically American melodrama by considering it as a mode, instead of categorizing it as a specific film genre, to show how melodrama can be considered as the foundation of classic Hollywood films.[10] Emerging from nineteenth-century stage spectacles and discussed in opposition to cinematic realism, Williams (1998, 4) argues that the supposedly "realist cinematic *effects*, whether of setting, action, acting or narrative motivation, most often operate in the service of melodramatic *affects*," to evoke emotional registers and to create emotional or affective excess by means of intensification—or simply, as she puts it, "to being moved by a moving picture" (Williams 1998, 47). It is here that she turns to the most basic function of the word *melodrama* as a drama(tic) story set to music (melo), signifying a mode of storytelling that is exciting and sensational, but above all moving.[11]

Drawing on Peter Brooks's notion of the "melodramatic imagination"[12] in nineteenth-century fiction, for which he considers the origins of theatrical melodrama, Williams (1998) argues that the most important conveyer of the melodramatic mode and its melodramatic affects is any type of corporeal gesture and/or musical-corporeal action that is performed without the aid of spoken word. However, dialogue and language can, as is the case in theatrical melodrama, exist alongside the affectiveness of the physical corporeality of the performer, as the registers and tones of the spoken word are similarly directed toward creating affective responses (Brooks 1995). As Brooks (1995, 4) argues, in the melodramatic mode "nothing is spared because nothing is left unsaid; the characters stand on stage and utter the unspeakable, give voice to their deepest feelings, dramatize through their heightened and polarized words and gestures." This argument and observation resonate with the notion of "emotional shock" and "sensual impact" of Eisenstein's theory of the montage of attractions, which Williams (1998) also draws on in her revision of melodrama. The body of the performer, as has been observed in all these theories, becomes the vehicle for affective transmission between performer and spectator precisely by acting or performing outward, by making affect visible and in a sense tangible.

Hence, the relationship between melodrama and vaudeville emerges from its use of corporeal gestures (and also music) as nonverbal signs, which Brooks (1995, 62) calls "an aesthetics of muteness" as part of the melodramatic mode, in which meanings and feelings are always expressed by more than words, because words are inadequate. As he further argues, "melodrama handles feelings and ideas as plastic entities, visual and tactile models held out for all to see and to handle" (Brooks 1995, 41). Keeping this in mind, the melodramatic body in performance represents an excessive body since the melodramatic performance mode is always excessive and emotional in its tonality, similar to the WOW-ing capabilities of the athletic and virtuosic vaudeville body. As a performative mode and expressive quality, melodrama, or the melodramatic mode, is invariably linked to the body of the performer as the most important conveyer of meaning, viewing pleasures and, due to its attraction as the conveyor of meaning, provides the point of contact for an attachment between performer and spectator.

While vaudeville aesthetics are primarily and most highly visible in the live performance shows, the melodramatic mode can be found throughout any SYTYCD season and is actually what aims at laying the groundwork for viewer attachment based on affective intensification. Going back to the beginning of Melanie Moore's memorable and successful SYTYCD trajectory, in her open audition in the first episode of Season 8, Melanie performed a commercial lyrical contemporary solo to the lyrical piano piece "The Meadow" by Alexandre Desplat. The stage of the Fox Theatre in Atlanta, Georgia, where the audition is held, is bare, with a lightly colored floor, and the brick wall at the back of the stage is visible. The lights are bright. Everything is set up for the open audition with no mood lighting or backdrops to enhance the experience of the audience (both on screen and at home). Melanie, wearing black dance shorts and a black-and-white dance crop top, starts seated on the floor in a slight diagonal, with the left leg bent under and the right leg stretched out in front. Her upper body is straight, slightly tilted forward, and her arms are extended behind her back. She gazes down at the floor, her whole composure being one of concentrated, suspended stillness. This concentration is mirrored by a silent, waiting theater audience, which in the open auditions consists of other auditioning dancers and their families, all waiting for Nigel Lythgoe's (SYTYCD 2011) words "and . . . cue music" to start the music and the solo.

To the opening bars of the piano music, framed mid-center in a long shot, Melanie softly swings her right arm to the front, followed immediately by her left arm. At the full extension, she pulls both arms into her chest while her upper body curves forward, initiating a light rebound, which brings her into an upright position, her head facing the back of the stage, with the right arm reaching up over her head and the left arm tightly curved in front of her chest, resulting in a spiral position of the upper body. She continues by extending the spiral position further, reaching and extending the arm above her head and opening up the curve of the left arm, slowly turning her head toward the audience, at which point the camera cuts to a medium long shot, giving the spectator at home a better view of her pensive-concentrated facial expression. With a clearly audible exhale, Melanie dissolves the extension by curving her upper body forward, pulling her arms back into her chest, and bending her right leg to move into a leg extension on the floor, facing the back of the stage. Stretching her right leg out over her head while the left leg is bent under, she supports herself in this position with both arms on the floor. Again, she dissolves the suspended extension to levitate herself off the floor, supporting herself with her right arm while using the right leg to lift her hip up and over her right shoulder, momentarily suspending, or hovering in the air, before landing back on the floor. She continues to use this momentum to lift her upper body, now in an upright position, off the floor by rolling over the arches of her feet, creating another moment of suspension that is then dissolved into a floor roll from which she gets up into a standing position.

The rest of the solo is similarly choreographed as a series of fluid movement sequences incorporating turns, jumps, and more leg extensions, as well as additional floor work, which accentuate her athletic (vaudeville) dancing body even further. Similar to a classical *adagio*,[13] it featured a lot of moments where Melanie balances on one leg, while the other is extended outward, either to the back or to the side of her body. All of her balance and extension sequences convey a sense of dynamic stillness, or what Erin Manning (2009, 32) refers to as the "elasticity of the almost,"[14] in that they constantly move further by extending the leg to an even more extreme stretched position before dissolving the tension. One of her arabesques, for example, moves further into a *penché* (a move in which the arabesque position is inclined to vertical splits) with her upper body bending even further over her standing leg. Again, a moment of suspense and hovering occurs before the balance is dissolved into a forward roll onto the floor. As a result, her body is constantly caught between moments of suspense/hovering, and a controlled collapse of the tension that is built up in the moment of suspense/hovering, all of which is further exacerbated by the lyrical piano music she used.

The energy produced by this performance, by its intertextual layers of melodic and dramatic "corporeal" attractions, affected the on-screen audience from the start of her solo. The moment in which she lifts her body off the floor via the arches of her feet, a single "Woo"[15] is heard from the otherwise silent theater audience. After her *penché* into the forward roll onto the floor, the audience claps and more "Woo" and "Yeah!" sounds are audible as a sign of the sensual impact her performance creates within the spectating bodies. In the middle of the solo, the camera cuts to a medium shot of the judges' table, where judge Mary Murphy utters a little "WOW" while briefly looking downward and shaking her head in disbelief. Toward the end of Melanie's solo, the camera again cuts from the full shot of her dancing body to a medium shot of the judges' table, where Murphy and the other judges, executive producer Nigel Lythgoe and krumper Lil C, are captured watching Melanie's performance in concentrated silence. Murphy (SYTYCD 2011) breaks the silence, uttering, "My goodness." On the final bars of the music and Melanie's movements, one voice from the audience yells a more intensified version of the earlier "Yeah!" before the whole auditorium explosively joins in with clapping and cheers.

While all these reactions express being "WOW-ed" by the athletic corporeality of Melanie's dancing (vaudeville) body, none of these reactions is a cognitively comprehensible expression of a specific emotion, yet they speak of a potential burgeoning attachment with Melanie as a dancer and performer based on her performance's sensual impact. After the applause fades, the judges' evaluations, located within the realm of a recognized response, express affect and a potential attachment, rather than a single coherent emotion, as well. As Murphy (SYTYCD 2011) states, "in eight seasons I don't remember having this much damn fun and it's because of extraordinary dancers like yourself. It's . . . wow. I'm getting overwhelmed at this side of the . . . the desk." This resonates with her response to Melanie and Neil's duet discussed earlier and, indeed, mirrors many of her responses to Melanie's performances across the season. Similarly vague but clearly affected, Lil C (SYTYCD 2011) remarks, "that was phenomenal. I have nothing . . . I can't even clap. I, I, . . . Clapping would do it no justice." Lil C's response expresses the aesthetic of muteness, the "more-than-words" of the melodramatic mode, transmitted from Melanie's affective performing body to his own spectating body, as an instance of astonishment and awe that left him, as well as Murphy, almost speechless and overwhelmed.

In the YouTube commentary underneath one of the videos of Melanie's solo, posted by user Myke Baldwin on June 6, 2011 (over 2.6 million views, 13,774 likes, and 1,007 comments as of May 17, 2018),[16] these sentiments are reflected as well. User "jerikah carbajal" notes, "hands down melanie is such a wonderful dancer. this audition clearly shows the impact that she can create on one's heart. such a beautiful way to show off her talent. i can watch this over and over. like wow <3 [<3 stands for the heart emoji]." User "KalaChrisSognatrice" exclaims, "mesmerized! obsessed with her movement and personality." And user "HappyTofu" simply sums it up by stating, "There are dancers that make the judges scream. There are dancers that make the judges cry. And then there are dancers like Melanie that make the judges absolutely speechless because they forget who they are, and simply bask in the heaven that is this dance." All these responses are indicative of the sensual impact of Melanie's performance on spectators and express being affected by the double attractions of the WOW-ing capabilities of her athletic and virtuosic dancing body as well as her personal charm, both of which continued to WOW and thus increasingly intensified audience attachment across the entire season. In Melanie's corporeal performance, feelings and sensations are made not only visible but also tangible. As "KalaChrisSognatrice" notes, it is a result of the combination of the affective (screen) force of her dancing body, combined with her personality, which brings together the affective intensification of the vaudeville performance aesthetics (wow climax) and the melodramatic performance mode, which is embedded within the vaudeville aesthetics and tied to the notion of the cult of personality, to create attachment between performer and spectator. It is an attachment that results in votes and is thus crucial to the competitive aspect of the show.

While the YouTube video does not contain the pre-solo backstage footage that introduced Melanie to the audience in more detail at the start of the season, this footage (which in the live performance shows would include the rehearsal and backstage footage shown prior to a couple's performance) would be what Eisenstein and Gerould (1974, 79) call "representational segments." These segments can be seen as attractions in themselves and are shown with the purpose of not only familiarizing audiences with a dancer, but also potentially intensifying the experience of the dance routine by being used in the service of what Williams called "melodramatic affects." In Melanie's case, the pre-solo footage contained a highly emotional plotline, in which she recounts the death of her father when she was twelve years old and how close she is with her mother. Lyrical piano music underlies this (emotionally) dramatic segment of her narration and, in the medium close-up shots of her face interwoven with old family pictures, the emotional tonality of her quavering voice is mirrored in her slightly teary eyes. Yet a sense of positivity is maintained through her smile as an expression of her personal charm in this scene and in her explanation of how dance has served as an outlet that, in her own words, "I threw myself into and that really translated into becoming a better dancer" (Moore, SYTYCD 2011). Her athletic (vaudeville) body in the moment of the solo dance that follows her own words is here quite literally positioned as a vehicle for affect within the aesthetic of muteness of the melodramatic mode and adds a sense of tactility and materiality to her dance performance.

BEING WOW-ED BY BEING MOVED

User "Swordfishstick" remarks underneath the YouTube clip of Melanie's solo, "I watch this show off-and-on—usually I don't watch all the episodes in a season. But I watched every episode of season 8, and the reason was Melanie Moore. This is still the best audition in the show I've seen." Similar remarks can be found throughout the commentary section of the solo, but also other YouTube clips of Melanie's SYTYCD performances as she managed to simultaneously WOW and move spectators with the expressive qualities of her athletic (vaudeville) dancing body and her charming (melodramatic) personality. Hence, the melodramatic mode within the vaudeville structure of the format as a montage/cinema of attractions adds an intertexual complexity to the televised dance competition event, beyond the way in which SYTYCD is usually understood in the scholarship. It is precisely this complex interplay of different intertextual layers that appeals to audiences and results in an ongoing attachment with the show and its dancer-contestants. Looking not only at the SYTYCD text (the structure of the show, the dancer-contestants, or the dance routines), but also at concrete audience responses, offers a broader insight into how dance competitions attract audiences apart from the mere competitiveness of the event in question.

Considering Melanie Moore's performances as examples of vaudeville aesthetics and melodramatic performance modes within SYTYCD means that the effective affectiveness of every performance by every performer in every season depends on this layering of the intertexual attractions of the melodramatic performance mode and the vaudeville WOW-ing aesthetics. Being WOW-ed depends on being moved, and this in turn forms the basis for potential votes. Affective intensification is created by the flickering presence of each dancer's past performances in each of his or her new performances, and also against the flickering presences of any of the past seasons, of past performances, and of past performers.

Notes

1. I refer to both dancers as "non-contemporary dancers" in this instance, because of the way that the show labels its dancers according to the specific dance style with which they initially auditioned for SYTYCD. Dancers have to specify a dance style on the audition form they are required to complete, and the style is then announced as part of their dance persona. Although many dancers have, and are expected to, train in multiple styles, their named style is a label they have selected when entering the competition. Thus, whenever dancers perform in a style that is not the one associated with their dance personas on the show, they are seen as performing outside their own styles.
2. It should be mentioned here that *Coppélia* is a comic ballet, thus itself entertaining, which is referenced in other pop-cultural texts. For example, the British dance film *The Red Shoes* (Powell and Pressburger 1949) features a scene in which ballet dancer Vicky Page (played by real-life ballerina Moira Shearer) as Swanhilda disguises herself as Coppélia to save Franz and fool Dr. Coppelius.
3. Her thinking about absent presences is indebted to Jacques Derrida's concept of traces. In *Of Grammatology*, Derrida (1976, 61) notes that "the trace is not only the disappearance of origin—within the discourse that we sustain and according to the path that we follow it means that origin did not even disappear, that it was never constituted except reciprocally by a nonorigin, the trace, which thus becomes the origin of the origin." Reading a dance

text as a series of absent yet present traces acknowledges Derrida's argument about the erasure of the notion of a material origin, there and not there at the same time, and the way this contributes to meaning-making discourses.

4. It is important to note that the early cinema that Gunning discusses as cinema of attraction featured a lot of dance, which Laurent Guido (2006) specifically addresses in his chapter "Rhythmic Bodies/Movies: Dance as Attraction in Early Film Culture" in the anthology *The Cinema of Attractions Reloaded* and which Clare Parfitt-Brown discusses in relation to the history of the cancan in her unpublished PhD thesis, "Capturing the Cancan: Body Politics from the Enlightenment to Postmodernity" (Roehampton University, 2008). Moreover, Gunning (2006, 382) himself states that with the increasing importance of narrative films after 1906–1907, the cinema of attractions went "underground" and influenced the aesthetics of the song-and-dance numbers in musical films.

5. In labeling the dance styles, I took into account that the styles in question are commercialized variations of dance styles, created specifically for television, and they are understood, performed, and practiced differently in theatrical stage, social, vernacular, and different national contexts. For a more detailed analysis of the adaptation, appropriation, and transformation of South American social dance styles, see McMains (2006, 2009, 2010) and Fisher (2014). And for a more detailed analysis of American competitive dance styles, including the transformation of hip-hop dance styles, see Weisbrod (2010).

6. Benthaus (2015).

7. Jenkins (2007) specifically uses the term "wow climax" to describe the affectiveness of pop cultural performances, a concept he traces back to the conventions of vaudeville performances, particularly specialty acts, in which it was common to use a spectacular movement series or trick at the end of an act to leave the audience pleasurably speechless.

8. An "All Star" refers to popular, memorable, and beloved contestants (both with the judges and the audience) from past seasons who were invited back on the show to perform with Season 7's Top 11 dancer-contestants. Since its introduction into the live performance show structure in Season 7, it has been a recurring feature.

9. "SYTYCD Melanie and Neil, Season 8, Episode 18, Total Eclipse." YouTube video, 7:08, from SYTYCD, Season 8, Episode 8, televised by Fox, posted by "Myke Baldwin," July 31, 2011, https://www.youtube.com/watch?v=2hkcuFfAeeM.

10. Williams (1998).

11. Williams particularly draws on previous work on melodrama as a mode instead of genre, responding to its marginalization as excessive and a "woman's weepie," specifically the work of Christine Gledwill in *The Melodramatic Field: An Investigation* (1987) and Peter Brooks in *The Melodramatic Imagination: Balzac, Henry James, Melodrama and the Mode of Excess* (1976), who, as she points out, laid the groundwork for an understanding of melodrama as a performative mode. She ascribes it to his work with theater and literature and a complete disregard of film theory and film criticism (Williams 1998, 51).

12. Brooks (1995).

13. In classical ballet, an *adagio*, performed by a single dancer, refers to a series or sequence of slow movements, which are performed with a sense of fluidity and ease. A classical (solo) *adagio* usually consists of moves, showcasing a dancer's strength and ability to balance on one leg, which additionally draw attention to the body's symmetrical lines, and to transition fluidly from one balance into the next.

14. Erin Manning (2009, 5) describes moments of "languidly 'holding' the movement" as elastic in the sense that being suspended or expanded within the intensity of the

suspension of the movement means being in between, or almost in the next move-ment: almost but not yet. As Manning (2009, 32) argues, the "elasticity of the almost is the intensive extension of the movement, a moment when anything can happen, . . . No step has been taken, and yet in this elastic the microperception of every possible step can almost be felt." In this moment of hovering over, in, and through movement, in the potentiality of every move as not yet, hovering can be aligned with a response to the elasticity of the virtuosity as an instance of WOW, in which the WOW becomes an af-fective response, which is not quite there yet. In this gap of the elasticity of the almost, potential can be seen as a transgression of the merely spectacular, a potential for en-gagement and attachment, and a becoming of affective thought through an experience of movement.

15. SYTYCD, Season 8, Episode 1.
16. "Melanie Moore, SYTYCD, Season 8, Audition," YouTube video, 3:44, from SYTYCD, Season 8, Episode 1, televised by Fox, posted by "Myke Baldwin" June 6, 2011, https://www.youtube.com/watch?v=a438sPVlonI.

References

Adshead-Lansdale, Janet. 1999. "Creative Ambiguity: Dancing Intertexts." In *Dancing Texts: Intertextuality in Interpretation*, edited by Janet Adshead-Lansdale, 1–25. London: Dance Books.

Adshead-Lansdale, Janet. 2007. *The Struggle with the Angel: A Poetics of Lloyd Newson's Strange Fish*. Alton, Hampshire: Dance Books.

Ahmed, Sara. 2004. "Collective Feelings. Or, the Impressions Left by Others." *Theory, Culture & Society* 21(2): 25–42.

Allen, Robert C. 1991. *Horrible Prettiness: Burlesque and American Culture*. Chapel Hill; London: University of North Carolina Press.

Benthaus, Elena. 2015. "Hovering on Screen: The WOW-Affect and Fan Communities of Affective Spectatorship on *So You Think You Can Dance*." *The International Journal of Screendance* 5: 11–28.

Broomfield, Marc A. 2011. "Policing Masculinity and Dance Reality Television: What Gender Nonconformity Can Teach Us in the Classroom." *Journal of Dance Education* 11(4): 124–128.

Boyd, Jade. 2012. "Hey, We're from Canada but We're Diverse, Right?": Neoliberalism, Multiculturalism, and Identity on So You Think You Can Dance Canada." *Critical Studies in Media Communication* 29(4): 259–274.

Brooks, Peter. 1995. *The Melodramatic Imagination: Balzac, Henry James, Melodrama, and the Modes of Excess*. New Haven, CT; London: Yale University Press.

Derrida, Jacques. 1976. *Of Grammatology*. Translated by Gayatri Chakravorty Spivak. Baltimore, MD; London: John Hopkins University Press.

Dodds, Sherril. 2014. "Faces, Close-ups and Choreography: A Deleuzian Critique of *So You Think You Can Dance*." *The International Journal of Screendance* 4: 93–113.

Eisenstein, Sergei, and Daniel Gerould. 1974. "Montage of Attractions: For 'Enough Stupidity in Every Wiseman.'" *The Drama Review: TDR* 18(1): 77–85.

Fisher, Jennifer. 2014. "When Good Adjectives Go Bad: The Case of So-called Lyrical Dance." *Dance Chronicle* 37(3): 312–334.

Foster, Susan Leigh. 2014. "Performing Authenticity and the Gendered Labor of Dance." Provocation for "Fluid States: Performances of UnKnowing." Performance Studies International 2015 decentralized conference. http://www.fluidstates.org/index.php.

Frith, Simon. 2001. "Pop Music." In *The Cambridge Companion to Pop and Rock*, edited by Simon Frith, Will Straw, and John Street, 91–108. New York: Cambridge University Press.

Frow, John. 2006. *Genre*. London; New York: Routledge.

Gledhill, Christine. 1987. "The Melodramatic Field: An Investigation." In *Home Is Where the Heart Is: Studies in Melodrama and the Woman's Film*, edited by Christine Gledhill, 5–39. London: British Film Institute.

Guido, Laurent. 2006. "Rhythmic Bodies/Movies: Dance as Attraction in Early Film Culture." In *The Cinema of Attractions Reloaded*, edited by Wanda Strauven, 139–156. Amsterdam: Amsterdam University Press.

Gunning, Tom. 2006. "The Cinema of Attraction[s]: Early Film, Its Spectator and the Avant-Garde." In *The Cinema of Attractions Reloaded*, edited by Wanda Strauven, 381–388. Amsterdam: Amsterdam University Press.

Jenkins, Henry. 1992. *What Made Pistachio Nuts? Early Sound Comedy and the Vaudeville Aesthetic*. New York: Columbia University Press.

Jenkins, Henry. 2007. *The Wow Climax: Tracing the Emotional Impact of Popular Culture*. New York; London: New York University Press.

Manning, Erin. 2009. *Relationscapes: Movement, Art, Philosophy*. Cambridge, MA: MIT Press.

McMains, Juliet. 2006. *Glamour Addiction: Inside the American Ballroom Dance Industry*. Middletown, CT: Wesleyan University Press.

McMains, Juliet. 2009. "Dancing Latin/Latin Dancing: Salsa and DanceSport." In *Ballroom, Boogie, Shimmy Sham, Shake: A Social and Popular Dance Reader*, edited by Julie Malnig, 302–322. Urbana; Chicago: University of Illinois Press.

McMains, Juliet. 2010. "Reality Check: *Dancing with the Stars* and the American Dream." In *The Routledge Dance Studies Reader*, edited by Alexandra Carter and Janet O'Shea, 261–272. London; New York: Routledge.

Parfitt-Brown, Clare. 2008. "Capturing the Cancan: Body Politics from the Enlightenment to Postmodernity." PhD diss., Roehampton University. https://core.ac.uk/download/files/97/244551.pdf.

Redden, Guy. 2010. "Learning to Labour on the Reality Talent Show." *Media International Australia* 134(1): 131–140.

Rizzo, Teresa. 2008. "*YouTube*: The New Cinema of Attractions." *Scan Journal* 5(1): 1–6.

Weisbrod, Alexis. 2010. "Competition Dance: Redefining Dance in the United States." PhD diss., University of California, Riverside. ProQuest (Id. 748175845).

Weisbrod, Alexis. 2014. "Defining Dance, Creating Commodity: The Rhetoric of *So You Think You Can Dance*." In *The Oxford Handbook of Dance and the Popular Screen*, edited by Melissa Blanco Borelli, 320–334. Oxford: Oxford University Press.

Williams, Linda. 1998. "Melodrama Revised." In *Refiguring American Film Genres: History and Theory*, edited by Nick Browne, 42–88. Berkeley; Los Angeles: University of California Press.

Audiovisual Sources

Melanie Moore, SYTYCD, Season 8 Audition. 2011. YouTube video, 3:44. [From SYTYCD, Season 8, Episode 1, televised by Fox.] Posted by "Myke Baldwin," June 6. https://www.youtube.com/watch?v=a438sPVlonI. Accessed September 13, 2016.

So You Think You Can Dance. 2005–2014. Broadcast television. Fox Broadcasting.

SYTYCD, Melanie and Neil, Season 8, Episode 18, Total Eclipse. 2011. YouTube video, 7:08. [From SYTYCD, Season 8, Episode 8, televised by Fox.] Posted by "Myke Baldwin," July 31. https://www.youtube.com/watch?v=2hkcuFfAeeM. Accessed September 13, 2016.

The Red Shoes. 1949. Directed by Michael Powell and Emeric Pressburger. Archers Film Productions (Roadshow Entertainment; Carlton International Media, 2000), DVD.

Tyler, Bonnie. 1983. *Total Eclipse of the Heart.* Written by Jim Steinman. Columbia Records. Mp3.

CHAPTER 18

WHY ARE BREAKING BATTLES JUDGED?

The Rise of International Competitions

MARY FOGARTY

IN 2013 I was asked to be a member of a three-person judging panel for a breaking battle at a large, annual hip-hop festival. The battle took place at an outdoor, public square in Toronto, Canada, with the performers, DJs, and judges on a stage that was set apart from the audience. When it came time to render our verdict on the final battle of the competition, each judge made the customary gesture of hand and arm to indicate which-ever crew he or she believed had won the competition. While I gestured to the crew that I thought had won, the two other judges indicated a "tie," using the accepted ges-ture.[1] Suddenly, one of these judges indicated an abstention from the decision-making process due to a last-minute realization of a conflict of interest.[2] This meant that the winning crew had won by the slimmest of margins: my vote alone. The dancers who lost were visibly upset and refused to make eye contact or speak with me for the rest of the festival. While that was understandable, I was most surprised by the reaction of the event promoters, who looked equally disappointed and cross with me, as if I alone had somehow ruined the event. Even though the promoters select the judges, structure how the judging proceeds, and profit the most from these events, ultimately, the responsi-bility for a competition's outcome rests on the shoulders of individual judges, and none falls on the promoters. In other words, while individual judges often take the heat for unpopular judgments, the structures within which they work are not only opaque, but also dependent on decisions in which they have no say—particularly decisions made by the promoters. In this case, for example, the results may have been quite different if they had not allowed the judges to award ties, or if the promoters had been more careful in selecting judges without any conflicts of interest.

In this chapter, I explore how breaking battles are judged through an examination of the rise of international breaking competitions in a global context. I consider the actions of judges and competitors alongside the social, economic, and political structures that inform the aesthetic judgments upon which such competitions rely. This chapter draws on participant-observer and ethnographic research conducted in Toronto, Canada (2007), Berlin, Germany (2008), and Nantes, France (2008) that included interviews with dancers, promoters, DJs, audience members and judges, and attendance at hip-hop events. I also accompanied dancers as they traveled to compete in various cities and, in one instance, I trained with a local Berlin crew to compete with them in an international competition.

I have been breaking for about eighteen years and researching the dance formally since 2004. In 2007, I began to focus on international breaking competitions and how they are judged as a way to better understand shifts in the dance's aesthetic and its global contexts. My research is primarily ethnographic, although I also triangulate this work with close analysis of underground videos, competition videos, and online videos (Fogarty 2006), and my embodied knowledge as a dancer and educator. I never imagined I would be competing at breaking into my thirties, and I am certain that it is my research that has motivated this. Although I am a participant in the dance culture, and this informs my "insider" perspective, I am distinct from many dancers insofar as my purpose in participating is most often to gain insights as a researcher. Similarly, it is unlikely I would have competed in high-profile battles or on theatrical stages had I not been attempting to gain access to new crews and accepted their offers to perform with them. In all of this, I am aware that my evolving status (as fan, doctoral student, and now university professor) has changed my relationship not only to the dance's aesthetics, but also to participants who have known me over the years. My interest in breaking competitions and the criteria by which they are judged thus did not emerge directly from my own concerns as a dancer (since I did not compete internationally until after I had undertaken this research), but rather from the social consequences of conducting research into the dance cultures of hip-hop. That said, I note that not all breaking competitions require someone to act in the formal role of judge. I have seen many examples of "battles" (competition between dancers) that had no judge present other than the crowd.

In thinking through the relationship between aesthetic judgment and the social structuring of taste, I turn to sociologist Pierre Bourdieu (1984), who argues that the taste distinctions we make are closely tied to our educational, class, and familial upbringing. When it comes to public forms of aesthetic distinction making, the act of judging also becomes a type of performance. In breaking competitions, judges evaluate the aesthetic choices of competitors in front of audiences. In so doing, they enact objective evaluations of subjective phenomena, such as whose dance was most original, most dynamic, most moving, and they do this in a context that structurally privileges the tastes of judges over those of performers or crowds. This makes explicit the relationship between questions of individual taste and structures of power. Before examining the taste decisions articulated via breaking battles, I provide a brief overview of the history, aesthetics, and values of the dance.

"Going Off": Dancing to the "Break" of the Record

Breaking represents the original dance of hip-hop culture. It is traditionally performed to a repeated instrumental "break" found on particular records, rather than using the entirety of a song. The break is where the rhythm section (drums and percussion especially) is featured, and the beat inspires the dancers to "go off" (Harrison 2004). "Going off" indicates that moment when the break beat hits and thus inspires a dancer to break. Most authors locate the origins of the dance in the early 1970s, with a later explosion of media interest and development of the form happening when breaking appeared in motion pictures of the 1980s (Banes 1985). Although the form began in predominantly African American neighborhoods, various authors (Dyson 2004; Fricke and Ahearn 2002) suggest that Puerto Rican dancers began to dominate the dance by the late 1970s. Early writing locates the dance within African American dance traditions (Banes 1984; Holman 1984); however, little documentation exists about the experiences of the earliest generations of practitioners and the period before the 1980s wave of media interest. With the subsequent globalization of the dance, breaking has come to be practiced by many communities who have little in common (in terms of class, familial, ethnic, or educational backgrounds) except their shared love of the dance.

Breaking involves a number of elements or moves, including toprock (dancing in a standing position), get downs (how one drops to the floor), footwork or downrock (steps that involve hands on the ground and legs moving around the body), power moves (difficult spins that usually require momentum and technique), and freezes (where a pose is held for a few seconds, often in a difficult and unpredictable position) (Fogarty 2006). A "battle" is when two dancers or crews face off and take turns trying to outperform each other. An important distinction to note here is that a "battle" involves dancing that is explicitly marked as a competition, even in informal contexts without designated judges; this is distinct from a "cypher," in which different dancers take turns breaking in a shared space and does not necessarily entail competition or rivalry (Fogarty 2006). Furthermore, battles are not necessarily judged by those formally assigned the role of "judge," as the participants and crowd of spectators may reach a mutual consensus as to who won a battle. Given that formal judging is not an a priori element of breaking culture, this raises the question, why are breaking battles judged?

The dance originated in New York City (Schloss 2009), and grew into a global movement of international networks (Chang 2005; Fogarty 2010) that continue to expand. In the twenty-first century, hip-hop dance now encompasses many different forms and styles across the globe (Johnson 2015), and these developments have been strongly influenced by the ways that popular music has changed since the 1970s. The various forms of hip-hop dance are shaped in large part by the shifting musical tastes of influential dancers and new generations of b-boys and b-girls (Fogarty 2012b). B-boys and b-girls are participants who break, and most dancers adopt b-boy or b-girl names as aliases. The terms *b-boy* and *b-girl* are also lifestyle labels used to identify musical tastes, fashion, and affiliations.

Among the earliest pioneers of hip-hop was Bronx disc jockey Kool Herc (Chang 2005). At DJ Kool Herc's early hip-hop parties, records were played primarily for social dancing by the attendees. According to my research, for this first generation of dancers, including b-boys and b-girls such as Sister Boo, the dance parties were small-scale, local, community affairs.[3] Yet dancers attended who were self-consciously performers, as in the case of the Legendary Twins,[4] two well-known b-boys whose dancing involved choreographed routines and costumes. They were notorious for sneaking into parties at a young age and entering dance contests in their local communities. As early b-boys, their involvement in these dance contests included performing against dancers doing a range of different styles. Contests were a component of early hip-hop culture, and are one of the ways in which the pleasure of comparative judgment in popular culture is articulated (Fogarty 2014). This is especially indicative of the influence of African diasporic forms in popular culture (Gottschild 1996), in terms of the social capital placed on dancing within family and neighborhood gatherings. Contests are also one of the paths toward professionalization that have long existed for cultural laborers such as dancers, musicians, chefs, artists, and poets.

Breaking is born inside the localized hip-hop subculture of the 1970s and retains strong ties to an "underground" identity, even as hip-hop sounds have become a global musical mainstream and a key commodity for the cultural industries. Although the dance was highly commercialized by the early 1980s, dance practitioners developed networks globally via local community events and events organized by b-boys and b-girls. This resulted in a strong countercultural feeling in the breaking community, one enhanced during its retreat from media attention from the mid-1980s until the late 1990s, when it saw a resurgence in mainstream media (Fogarty 2006). In her book *Club Cultures* (1995), sociologist Sarah Thornton rejects the Birmingham School[5] reading of subcultures as necessarily opposed to mainstream media. For Thornton, dance music subcultures and their much-sought-after "subcultural capital"[6] were in fact dependent upon such mainstream media for definition, visibility, and legitimation. Moreover, various forms of media have been important to many subcultures, including hip-hop in the 1970s.

Building on this research, I argue that cultural intermediaries such as hip-hop promoters are crucial to both underground and mainstream hip-hop, and yet have remained surprisingly neglected in academic accounts. B-boy promoters have long been a part of hip-hop practice: from the earliest hip-hop events, such as DJ Kool Herc's parties, where his sister, Cindy Campbell, organized and promoted the events (Chang 2005), to the present day, where international b-boy competitions featuring cash prizes and corporate sponsors are run by promoters who wield a significant amount of social and economic power in the culture (Fogarty 2010). Promoters have been important to the dance both during its underground phases and during its newfound surge of worldwide popularity. Such intermediaries play a key role not only in the production of these twenty-first-century, large-scale, sponsored and formally judged events, but also in the historical underground culture of the dance, which continues to underpin understandings of it as an artistic movement by its practitioners and supporters (Fogarty 2006). Promoters are mediating figures who shape the evolving aesthetics of the dance through their organizational involvement and the choices they make. In other words, in the world of breaking, cultural intermediation and subcultural status are not anti-thetical. Since the political-economic dimensions of promotion affect the (sub)cultural values of breaking, I explore the experiences of the dancers in tandem with those of the promoters.

In early theoretical models addressing popular media culture, by Theodor Adorno and Max Horkheimer, the market of mass-produced goods, including popular music, was constituted in the manipulation and commodification of experiences. Breaking is a dance practice with strong subcultural or underground inheritances, but it too has long been tied to the consumption of music commodities in crucial ways. Dancers often bought records, cassettes, compact discs, and other musical products, and they were informed and influenced by shifts in style and fashion. Dancers' consumption cen-tered on tastemakers in the music industries, primarily hip-hop musical artists, but also gatekeepers such as promoters. Likewise, the styles of dance and experiments undertaken by dancers embody and address shifts in musical arrangements and structures, including expert DJs' manipulations of a variety of recorded music. Notably, some of the original hip-hop DJs were inspired by the b-boys to loop the break beats of the record. When the break would come on, the b-boys would "go off" and, in order to prolong that dance experience, the DJs extended the break via repetition. Thus breaking and DJing have operated in a symbiotic relationship since the earliest days of hip-hop (Chang 2005).

In b-boy battles, it is not the dancer but the DJ who selects the music (typically break beats), and so the dancers often do not know in advance what music will be played. This is complicated, however, by several recent developments. For example, particular b-boy songs have become canonical (Schloss 2009) and are thus known and expected. Such tracks harken back to the musical tastes of early hip-hop and b-boy generations that have thereby left an imprint on present-day breaking culture. Due to the intellectual property issues associated with online streaming of international competitions, new, copyright-free beats for dancers, which have less explicit or recognizable ties to that his-torical lineage, tend to be used to increase the profits of promoters who do not want to pay for the rights to this canonical music.[7] Thus once-foundational aspects of the culture have proved malleable due to the market forces of international competitions and the cultural intermediaries who choose which factors are key and which can be modified to suit the economic advantage of the promoters. This is just one area where the decisions of promoters have changed the aesthetic of the dance, as music underpins both the ex-perience of dance and the choices of the dancers, according to what parts of the music they accent with their bodies. Judges, too, are cultural intermediaries with the capacity to affect the dance. In the following, I consider some key international competitions, such as Battle of the Year and Hip Opsession, as well as an emerging judging system created by a Toronto-raised b-boy Karl "Dyzee" Alba, to reflect on such changes.

"Just to Get a Rep": Building Dance Reputations through Competitions

Tracing the historical trajectory of formal competitions within breaking requires a rethinking of the distinctions between art and sport, critical judgment and community belonging, mainstream and subculture.[8] B-boy/b-girl competitions constitute an area where judgment is part of the spectacle and thus rendered explicit, meaning that criteria for judgment also come into focus. These competitions are events where the reputations of dancers are established and tested. Consequently, building a reputation and accruing status in the hierarchies of international breaking culture are complex activities. There are the typical tensions, familiar to other musical worlds, such as the necessity for participants to be not only talented, but also reliable, professional, and popular among their peers. Furthermore, an uneven distribution of resources exists (Lull 1995), so that those with access to more resources are more likely to succeed. Likewise, ethnicity, class, gender, and place are key factors that affect the likelihood of dancers "making it" in various outlets of the scene. And the status and significance of a dancer's crew, or larger (social) affiliations, are also central to issues of reputation.[9]

One notable aspect of breaking culture, in comparison with other musical and art worlds, is how closely reputation is tied to formalizations of judgment. Those who are asked to judge events must not only be outstanding dancers, but must also have had this verified through winning events themselves. This development has taken place gradually over the history of breaking, as internationally practiced. Although competition has featured across art and music (Becker 1982), its significance and centrality to the meaning of breaking suggests that the ties between authority, authenticity, performance, and judgment are bound especially strongly. I explore these themes through an account of one of the principal international breaking competitions, Battle of the Year.

Developing Competition Judging Criteria

Thomas Hergenröther is the head organizer of the largest and longest running annual international b-boy/b-girl competition, held in Germany, Battle of the Year (BOTY).[10] This began as a small-scale event in 1990, but has now grown to a crowd of at least 6,000–10,000 people a year in attendance.[11] Despite its size, the organizers have successfully claimed legitimacy and loyalty to hip-hop roots through their commitment to underground affiliations and authenticity, and this was achieved for several reasons. First, Hergenröther was a b-boy who had a crew that helped to organize the event when it first began. In Germany, this was significant because it set the battle apart from events organized by social workers, which were stigmatized by b-boys at that time.[12] Second, reputable b-boys and b-girls have performed and judged at the event. And third, BOTY was one of the first events to bring together and celebrate crews from far corners of the globe, thus in keeping with the spirit of hip-hop culture as a global, underground movement, a discourse notably set up by traveling practitioners in the 1990s (Fogarty 2012a).

BOTY is structured so that each crew first does a "showcase round," a routine prepared in advance, which includes selecting and mixing their own music and sound (assistance from a DJ is permitted). Although this is not the typical structure for breaking battles, Hergenröther describes how the showcase round provides b-boys and b-girls with the structure, regulations, and deadline to construct a show that they can then perform for remuneration elsewhere. The judges then select the top four crews to compete in battles, in which two crews compete for third and fourth place, and two crews for first and second place. This battle structure provides a convention for breaking events, even though some are set up tournament style, unlike BOTY.

How then is the event judged? In BOTY, as the first showcase round demands a prepared performance, crews are judged on theatrical elements such as synchronicity, stage presence, theme, music, and choreography, as well as on their execution of toprock, footwork/legwork, freezes, and power moves. In recent years, the format has changed, as well as the transparency of judgment. For example, after the event, crews, dancers, and audience members can now access the judges' scorecards online to see who won each round, according to which judge.

The choice to include a showcase round where crews present a prepared choreography was a strategic one on the part of the organizers. Questions about the authenticity of a theatrical showcase, as identified by the event organizers, are weighed against an even heftier set of questions posed by scene participants about the intentions of event organizers regarding profits (and the suspicion that event organizers may be profiting from the scene). The following quotation from the BOTY webpage demonstrates the event's claim to authenticity and its rationalization for profits earned at the event:

> Yes we have our BOTY products we sell and yes of course we have some (authentic) sponsors who help us but this does not mean that the organizers behind everything are rich and forgot about the meaning of hip hop culture. Everybody who organized just a small event should know how much work, energy and costs it takes to put it together and at the end it is only fair if you earn some money with it if you still stick to the roots.[13]

In other words, small-scale events can be capitalist in structure (making enough cash to pay participants and provide a small income for organizers) and yet authentic if they do not "exploit" commercial opportunities and the people involved in such a way as to create a big division in wealth. The logic provided here is that the larger-scale event (the event that has grown its numbers over many years) has nonetheless maintained its authenticity to the dance by only working with "authentic" sponsors and asserting continuities with hip-hop "roots."

Such concerns relate to how an international b-boy/b-girl event needs to be considered authentic for the participants themselves through their experiences of it. Event organizers therefore intentionally seek out experiences that fulfill a sense of authenticity through community respect and accountability. In other words, just as dancers have to "get a rep," so do event organizers.

There are several ways that event organizers deal with the concerns of the community for accountability. First, if they invite and pay for good dancers or crews to attend, and then highlight these guest dancers in their promotional materials, other b-boys and b-girls will subsequently want to attend. Second, event organizers must ensure a non-competitive space in which to cypher, as b-boys and b-girls typically do not come to an event solely to compete or to watch other dancers battle on stage. Third, event organizers need to provide good music (by way of an excellent DJ). Other factors that attract serious dancers, from both local and international locations, are the after-parties and pre-parties that extend the duration of the event, and low ticket and accommodation costs. Ultimately, an "authentic" event caters to paying ticket holders (specifically the attending b-boys and b-girls) by giving them room to dance themselves. This reminds us that breaking is, at heart, a participatory culture. Events that fail to provide space to cypher are therefore perceived as inauthentic, because they are designed primarily for spectators to watch breaking, rather than for dancers to participate.

In an interview with me, Niels "Storm" Robitzky, who originally hails from Germany and is one of the most influential and well-respected b-boys internationally, explained that at the beginning of his career it was easier to judge because he knew less. Now, he has to study b-boys and b-girls from across the world and stay current with all the event footage to know what is new, original, and fresh. The wealth of information needs to be organized, filtered, and considered. For BOTY, in the beginning years, the judges who were originally selected tended to be a little older, and were not always paid; they often agreed to judge as a favor to the event organizers and for the recognition that marked status in the community.[14] As time has gone on, event organizers look for judges who are reliable; reputations must go beyond being a well-known dancer, since judges must now have reputations for being good judges as well. This has been a major shift in the culture, especially in the past ten years. When I asked about the judging system now in place at BOTY, Hergenröther replied:

> We have a judging system which more or less describes what it takes to be a complete and good b-boy including the aspect of the choreography so we are basically looking for judges that understand the dance as a whole, like really all aspects, and the general aspects of dancing to the rhythm, stage expression, stuff like this and of course the judges need to understand the different categories, like they have to know what a good power move is about, what is an easy power move, same for toprocking, downrocking, footwork, freezes, so those are the categories. So the judges need to know everything, all aspects of the b-boy/b-girl scene.

When BOTY organized its judging framework for the competition, it moved beyond the strategies of its past events, where individual b-boys and b-girls judged the competition based on their own criteria or intuitions. In this new judging system, with which the competitors are made familiar, the judges must now be accountable to the criteria listed. Having well-respected pioneers of the dance vouch for the system is another part of establishing its credibility. Thus, for BOTY, it was crucial that Storm participated in the development of judging criteria. Thus the authenticity of BOTY and its judging system rely on historical continuities with the dance's past that can include non-American dancers such as the German b-boy Storm. This points us toward shifts in the locus of authority in a globalized hip-hop culture.

JUDGING AND AUTHORITY

The way that battles between dancers are judged forms one of the most hotly contested topics within the breaking world. There is a further tension around who can be an authority since the globalization of breaking has occurred. Influential American dancers initially took the time to cosign dancers from other countries through representing and celebrating their achievements in underground videos circulating the globe and building international networks (Fogarty 2012a). In response, the cosigned dancers took considerable pleasure at the endorsements received from their childhood idols. "Cosign," hip-hop vernacular for endorsing another person on a street level, offers a generative analogy that compares the legitimacy in the straight world of finance (cosigning for a person on a document or contract) to giving a referral in everyday life, and codes of hip-hop culture. For example, an influential dancer might "cosign" a lesser-known dancer, thus putting the weight of their reputation behind that person to validate them. It also makes the better-known dancer somewhat responsible for the actions that can be expected of the lesser-known person. In the act of cosigning someone, the senior dancer retains authority, and the lesser-known person only has authority insofar as they are related to the cosigner. However, in the case of international breaking competitions, at a certain point, those that were once cosigned have subsequently become the international authorities, such as Storm. Thus b-boys and b-girls from other countries, who were originally endorsed by American dancers, no longer require that cosign, as they are considered credible authorities in their own right.

Related to the idea of cosigning, the question of *who* gets asked to judge proves contentious, as American dancers are now treated less as authorities than they were in the past, due to the contributions of dancers from other parts of the world. Furthermore, the competitive climate of sustaining a professional career in breaking now often includes judging at international events. Consequently, breakers who were once cosigned by New York City dancers have now become authorities, and have, to an extent, turned the tables on some of those original dancers in claiming more objectivity at judgment or credibility in shaping the global scene. In fact, some argue that the pioneering American b-boys are not "professional" enough, and with this shift in authority comes a change in the aesthetics of the dance to reflect this increasing professionalization of competitions and interpretation of the form within new generations of dancers globally. Some of these claims to authority involve racialized stereotyping that have consequences for participants' lives and careers. In other words, racial politics inform the globalization of the aesthetic and have impacted power shifts in international competitions.

Globalization has diversified the locus of authority in aesthetic evaluations of the dance. Event organizers at international breaking competitions have become especially concerned with developing systems of judgment that are accountable and fair. Similarly, individual b-boys have become committed to working on this project as well, most notably Canadian b-boy Karl "Dyzee" Alba. In the following section, I explore how Dyzee has begun work on more transparent systems of judgment that make evident to competitors *and audiences* the criteria of judgment on which international battles are built.

A New Judging System

Throughout the first decade of the 2000s, Toronto b-boy Karl "Dyzee" Alba began to develop a system to judge battles that aspired to provide more transparency and accuracy than the subjective and intuitive judging prior to this. This system, intended to professionalize the field, exists in some tension with existing breaking values and aesthetics. It was created to combat the inevitable investment, and therefore potential biases, that dancers had in the reputations of their peers and their style preferences, given that breaking remains strongly connected to the creative expression of one's identity, emotions, and artistic sensibilities. This system of judgment became influential when Dyzee moved to South Korea and launched it at an international battle called R16. Dyzee was a well-known b-boy internationally before he began to develop his system of judgment, and was one of the first b-boys to make his name on the Internet (Fogarty 2006). The globalization of hip-hop has been accelerated by the rise of the Internet, and so early Internet presence has also come to count as authenticating the "roots" or history of breaking

Although knowledge of roots is valued, assessments by younger b-boys about who is and who is not part of the scene, especially at international festivals, often suffer from lack of cultural memory. For example, Dyzee recently explained that a younger b-boy in Toronto told him at a practice how to do his own move "right." Unfortunately, the local b-boy did not realize that Dyzee himself was the creator of this move. Similarly, we find in the comments section under a YouTube clip of Dyzee discussing his judging system, a b-boy remarking that he had not realized that Dyzee was an authentic b-boy. Instead, he simply thought that Dyzee was an enthusiast of the dance, trying to introduce a judging system. For b-boys, history is fleeting, and older b-boys and b-girls (often those with families of their own in tow at b-boy/b-girl events nowadays) are not recognized for what they are: former participants in a scene from the past. This suggests that, despite the frequent recourse to discourses of "roots" as a means of authentication, there is uneven distribution of historical knowledge in the culture, something further exacerbated by the frequent turnover of participants and its perceived identity as a youth subculture.

Breaking competitions have also changed in recent years, informed by shifts in social media practices and the digitization of culture. Events such as the R16 in South Korea began to create more elaborate and digitized systems through which the audience and competitors could see judgment criteria in real time. This development was not without its quirks and disruptions, as b-boys would pause between rounds in a face-to-face battle to peer up at the screen to see their scores (in order to check if they were winning or losing mid-battle). This system, as it developed, also made claims to authority, as Dyzee sought counsel and endorsement by key dancers in New York City as part of the promotion and development of his system's categories of judgment.

Articulating how judgments are informed became one of the central foci, and judges soon were made to be accountable for their choices. As many b-boys explained, while it was once thought of as an honor, judging has actually became quite onerous and one of the quickest way to make enemies in the scene. One b-boy explained that he hated judging, but would never vocalize that to anyone because it represents his "bread and butter," and to refuse to judge would lower his profile in the field. Others began to take meticulous notes on every battle so they could prove their accountability when questioned by competitors after the battle. Another joked to me that there were two types of people who approach him after battles: those who wanted to know how to improve, and friends of competitors who wanted to let the judge know that their fellow dancer or friend should have won. Such anecdotes demonstrate the changes that arise as events undergo "professionalization" and generate added responsibilities for judges, including accountability to dancers, audiences, and promoters. Although accountability was always a dimension of judging, those now occupying paid positions face greater pressure to be transparent and articulate.

Dyzee has been promoting his judging system worldwide since 2007. His objective was to develop a system of judgment that is fair for international competitors. As an experienced competitor, he felt the need and demand for an accountable system that would let competitors know how judges reached their decisions. In his system, there are five judges. Each judge decides the winner of a battle based on one specific category. To win, a b-girl or b-boy must win three of the five categories as decided by the judges. Part of this system also involves computer displays so that the audience and competitors can see on a large screen the points as they accrue for each category during a battle. The categories he created for his system are: foundations, originality, dynamic, execution, and strategy. Part of Dyzee's aim has been to "sell" the ideas behind it to event organizers, and reputable b-boys in the scene. In 2010, for example, he explained to me his ideas for the system and the reasons behind it and shared his hopes of building a formal structure for "authenticating" judges so that they would be perceived to be qualified to judge in each of the different categories.

There are examples when judging systems looked very different from the conventions of the current international events, and this can still be witnessed at local events in various communities. For example, judges would often discuss among themselves who they thought had won after a battle, and would then tell the emcee and the crowd their decision. This approach is rarely used in the contemporary scene for several reasons, including a concern that judges with bigger reputations (or personalities) can be persuasive and influence other's decisions. The general procedure adopted now in battles involves the emcee counting down from three, prompting each of the judges to point with their hand at who they think should win. By doing this at the same time, each judge's individual decision is counted and peer pressure is minimized. Ideally, there are an odd number of judges (most competitions tend to have three or five) to reduce the likelihood of a tie.

Judges are often asked to give competitors feedback, after the battle, on why performers lost. B-boy Storm recalled to me that when South Korean b-boys asked for feedback one year, he provided them with some comments on what they could improve, and six months later *all* of the b-boys were not only performing the missing ingredient (in this case, dancing on beat), but had taken this to an absolute extreme (they were dancing on the beat through all of their power moves, which had been a rarity in the past). He jokingly mused, "What should I ask them to do next?" In this way, judges become architects for the scene, imagining better performances with ever-increasing standards and degrees of difficulty. And competitors, clearly, may change their aesthetics to suit the opinions of the judges. I will return to this issue later.

A glance at international crew competitions in 2017 demonstrates that crew routines (once a rarity during battles) have subsequently become the norm, as choreographed crew routines are performed back and forth, usually involving most dancers of a crew performing at the same time. At most of those same international events fifteen years ago, the normal flow would involve one dancer from one crew performing and then another dancer from the opposing crew responding, with the rare crew routine put in (usually one routine maximum per battle). In other words, the way that the issue of judging choreographed routines was dealt with, or arguably left alone, has changed the aesthetic of the dance as performed in international breaking competitions for crews. Similarly, hip-hop crews often had a popper who would come out when encouraged by a musical track. This no longer happens at international crew battles where each particular dance style competes separately, so the crew onstage consists only of people who break (not practitioners of other dance styles who happen to be in a crew together). Subsequently, there are fewer hip-hop crews today represented (with emcees, DJs, b-boys, b-girls, poppers, lockers, writers, and so on) and more "b-boy/b-girl crews" consisting only of dancers who break. In other words, breaking events are having an effect on the social formation of crews.

The Audiences' Judgment

Hip Opsession is an annual international breaking competition held in Nantes, France. Spectators play a huge role in this event, and are considered in every aspect of its organization, including the seating and the parties before and after. However, Hip Opsession is sometimes criticized for privileging spectatorship over the concerns of the local breaking community. For example, when I practiced with local French b-boys (a few of them originally from Russia) after the Hip Opsession in 2009, they commented that the promoters were not part of the local breaking scene. Although one year the local b-boys were asked for suggestions about which international crews to invite, since then, they have not been asked to contribute to the shaping of the event as much as they would like. The promoters, now part of the international circuit, currently rely on the international b-boys for recommendations, and are less concerned with the tastes of local dancers and their ability to access the community.

Hip Opsession takes place at a cultural center and is sponsored by business and local government. For the local community, beyond hip-hop culture, the event marks a special time of year to celebrate hip-hop, and then life returns to normal for the rest of the year. An American musician/b-boy at the event told me how much he appreciated the support the spectators were giving the dance and suggested that this is a better situation than in the United States, where spectator support is lacking. However, this community support represents only a once-a-year moment of appreciation.

The younger b-boys and b-girls at Hip Opsession tend to ignore those spectators who do not seem to know or express the accepted codes and conventions of the scene. Those that are clearly made up of families, those not dressed as b-boys or b-girls, and the support staff working at the event are ignored. This is one way that local and regional b-boys and b-girls deal with the issue of sharing space with outsiders, and with events that include outsiders.[15] Although the inclusion of outsiders is felt to change the experience for the b-boys and b-girls, it also contributes to the possibility of new, younger dancers being exposed to breaking, which is positive for the culture. Also, the introduction of a sign language guide, projected live on the video screen, makes the event accessible for those with hearing impairments. These are thoughtful gestures that b-boys and b-girls rarely mention or seem to appreciate; however, many spectators are attentive to such considerations, and this reflects how promoters think beyond the b-boy and b-girl experience.

Cyphers take on a special meaning in the context of formal, international competitions oriented toward non-dancing spectators. While only the top competitors make it to the finals of international competition, all b-boys and b-girls can participate in cyphers. When b-boys and b-girls lose or make an error in competition, they often head to the communal space of the cypher to reorganize their egos and remind themselves that they are indeed good dancers. Notably, many dancers who have difficulty with the additional pressures of competitions excel in cyphers. For example, those dancers who rely on the emotional expression of, and their relationship to, the accompanying music do not always excel in the formally organized contexts of international competition; instead, they perform better when they can choose at what point and to which song they dance. Cyphers clearly provide more control over these elements of preference and choice.

At Hip Opsession, one memorable moment highlights some of the key issues in contention when considering judging at international competitions. B-boy and judge Born arrived in France after a long flight from South Korea. He went directly from the airport to the venue, where he sat for six hours judging the prelims to the main event. At this point, he was suddenly "called out"[16] to battle by a French b-boy after the latter's crew lost their battle, due to the decision of Born. Born jumped up, without warm-up, and danced. Born not only "destroyed" the competitor in an informal battle, but the audience was also clearly on his side. Indeed, it appeared that the audience considered the French b-boy's call-out of a judge as inappropriate in this setting. This episode marks an exception to the rules, in which the new codes and conventions formalized by international competitions demarcate an artificial boundary between competitors, judges, and audiences—a boundary that was then transgressed by the French crew. However, Born's willing participation in the dance, accepting the call-out, and performing his best, actually honors a venerable tradition and harkens back to the roots of the dance, when b-boy battles served a social function intended to resolve conflicts within a community.[17] The French crew's disputation of Born's judgment was decisively resolved through dance. That said, calling out Born was also interpreted by the Hip Opsession audience as rule breaking, since they responded with verbal shouts that indicated the French b-boy was out of line. So while the foundational, "participatory" ethic of breaking remains in play despite its institutionalization, the attendant separation of audience from performer, and of performer from judge, now exists in some tension with breaking's vaunted "roots."

THE RISE OF PROMOTERS

Promoters have played an important role in the evolution of hip-hop culture, and this is especially true for the rise of international competitions as key venues for breaking. As cultural intermediaries (Bourdieu 1993), promoters can exert influence over the presentation of the dance, and profit economically from it. The rise of organized, publicized, and incentivized competitions has involved a coeval rise of dance competition promoters who contribute to the shaping of breaking culture. As a result, the current climate of breaking has shifted.

Although attention has focused on the quality of the judges and the objectivity of their judgments in most battle conversations, little attention is paid to the conditions that judges are asked to endure. This is due to the historical precedents of unpaid labor (by community and/or family members) that supported breaking competitions in the early days, and the growing discrepancies between participant incomes (what new promoters pay out versus the historical earnings of dancers who made their reputations in past scenes, working for free over years of physical labor, teaching, and performance). I do not intend here to naïvely separate "authentic" artists from "manipulative" promoters (the conventional way to think through the division of labor in the music industry).[18] Instead, I wish to point to the structural and cultural conditions of production that root and inform how aesthetic decisions come into play, spread, and mutate. I recently witnessed an event where judges were asked to sit for hours on end without being offered food or beverages. Nonetheless, they remained in the hot seat and let their reputations, friendships, and future employment opportunities hinge on their every decision, which clearly signals their "professionalism." Ironically, event promoters, those with the power to select the judges and thus inform how the decisions play out in crucial ways, are insulated from the responsibility and accountability for results faced by judges. Instead, their focus is on the economic success or failure of the event.

From a historical perspective, there have always been promoters in hip-hop culture. Cindy Campbell, as the first promoter of hip-hop culture in the 1970s, was credited for creating a cultural space, the party, that became the center of hip-hop as a musical and dance practice (Chang 2005). In the early 1980s, promoters were significant to the culture as well. At this time, crews such as the Rocksteady Crew also had a manager, Kool Lady Blue, who secured gigs for them to perform both locally and on tour. Indeed, she was even significant in labeling the dance "breakdancing," although the term was later rejected by some of those same dancers as they revisited their dance roots.[19]

I suggest that the increasing power and prominence of the promoter in recent years has resulted largely from the rise of formal breaking competitions. Promoters clearly profit from breaking in a way that sustains them professionally, and this presents a new development. Contemporary promoters are more likely to earn their entire living from the dance than the dancers themselves. Yet, more than ever before, b-boys and b-girls are now able to sustain professional careers, as competitors, judges, and even as announcers and emcees, because of this new circuit of international competitions.[20] This speaks to the earlier arguments about the coexistence of the underground and the mainstream— that tightknit, symbiotic relationship of subculture and media spawned by capitalism and its discontents.

A Sociological Intervention

Bourdieu (1993) is cynical about competitions in the performing arts, as they produce "docile students" in his view. He suggests that competitions breed collective training that homogenizes and produces hierarchies in which the power of original talent is blunted. What then is the logic of an art competition? He writes of

> the incredible docility that it assumes and reinforces in students who are maintained in an infantile dependency by the logic of competition and the frantic expectations it creates (the opening of the Salon gives rise to scenes of pathos), and the normalization brought by collective training in the ateliers, with their initiation rites, their hierarchies linked as much to seniority as to competence, and their curricula with strictly defined stages and programs. (Bourdieu 1993, 241)

B-boys and b-girls think about the logic of competitions differently. For example, many b-boys and b-girls suggest that the reason the scene has continued to evolve and progress is because of the centrality of battles for the culture. They have argued that battles push people to improve continually, and there is no question that the technical proficiency of breaking has accelerated rapidly with the rise of an international competition circuit. Also, b-boys and b-girls became self-conscious about the importance of judging fairly and began to raise the expectations for execution. If you made a mistake you were eliminated, and this fits in many ways with Bourdieu's observations. However, over time and with continuing debates about the judgment of battles, b-boys and b-girls are lessening the focus on errors, and the criteria are shifting again to accept competitors who take more risks. Having said that, the aesthetic of the form has been shaped by these judgments, and the performed routines of b-boys and b-girls at the international level have much cleaner endings than in the past. In other words, although breaking culture and practice consist of a group of activities governed by individuals of influence ("the architects"), the shifts in the culture also come from the collective intelligence of the group. In crew battles, tacit knowledge involves the knowledge formed among crew members over time and the ways this gets performed in the strategic and synchronous energy produced in competitive structures.

Although he is not specifically referring to competitions, sociologist Howard Becker (1982, 155) argues that aesthetic judgments are "reliable, and that reliability reflects not the mouthing of already agreed-on judgments, but the systematic application of similar standards by trained and experienced members of the art world." I argue that part of aesthetic of the dance comes from the situation of calling someone out (to battle) and "checking" your skills against your opponent. People often call out their competitors—people not from their own crew. Consequently, breaking has a social function performed across group structures. But with the rise of formality and seriousness of judgment, with the professionalization of the form, this aspect of the dance (choosing whom you want to battle and being ready at all times to battle anyone) has been transformed and displaced into the relations among judges and promoters. The element of surprise and suspense that governed club or party events has been superseded by a system in which the promoter holds inordinate amounts of control. This changes the rules of the game substantially. Time limits, round limits, and codified judging systems, for instance, take out some of that suspense and replace it with a "seriousness" that then dictates the form.

Thinking back to the story of judge Born being called out in France at Hip Opsessions, the audience responded with disdain for the French dancer who called out the judge after losing (seeing this as "improper" etiquette), even though this was once a key part of the suspense, excitement, and personal choice of the form. Moments like this indicate that a propriety, a disciplining of appropriate behavior, may now override some of breaking's original aesthetics. In this new environment of professionalization, audiences, promoters, judges, and dancers have come to expect everyone to follow a specific set of rules. Here, the choice of whom to battle, in what way, and for how long, have been trumped or at least prioritized.

In some ways, these concerns reveal a playing out of the classic sociological paradigm of structure versus agency. The history of breaking moves from street to arena, and in so doing shifts the balance toward the a privileging of structure; what is lost is part of that freedom associated with the street, the individual agency of informality and surprises; what is gained is a sense of legitimacy and economic profit, although the latter is unevenly distributed. This is not to say that breaking was without structure beforehand. As with all dance, it worked inside an embodied aesthetic system, even if that often remained intuitive or unarticulated. However, the rise to prominence and visibility of breaking in international competitions has, unsurprisingly, altered the form itself.

Even though judges (and promoters) now hold sway, previously the crowd (including fellow dancers) did so as well, meaning it was always out of the dancer's hands as to who won. As with all "bodily" competitions, athletics and dance alike, the judge is presumed, often mistakenly, to embody the will of the crowd, and controversy arises when crowd and judge differ.

The economic power and media prominence of international breaking competitions have thus contributed to shifts in the art form of breaking, through the aesthetic values they celebrate and reinforce. Among other things, these shifts have affected how competitors understand their art form, how they practice leading up to the competition, how judges perform their roles, and how everyone involved indicates their seriousness. Breaking is now a global form with aesthetic input from b-boys and b-girls from many different countries determining what the future will hold for the form, and although promoters have control, they too are informed by social and historical factors. The debates and conversations about how breaking battles are judged that happen in every city where breaking is practiced are the moments where embodied experiences are not only reflected upon, but shaped through such actions and engagements.

Notes

1. In breaking competitions, a tie is usually indicated by judges crossing their arms and forming an "X"-like cross with their wrists.
2. The judge in question was a crew member of the competing crew.
3. This information comes from a presentation by the Legendary Twins, when they spoke at York University during their invited visit to Toronto, Canada.
4. Keith and Kevin Smith.
5. The Birmingham School, which encompasses the scholarship that developed out of the Centre for Contemporary Cultural Studies, was the hub for work on subcultures. See Bennett and Kahn-Harris (2004) for a review of this literature and Dodds (2011) for a critique from a dance studies perspective on this work.

6. Sarah Thornton's notion of "subcultural capital," is a response to the theoretical work of Pierre Bourdieu in his conceptualization of "cultural capital." Thornton argues that subcultures are equally elitist, and some participants may have more capital than others within the frame.

7. Based on interviews with several international DJs and judges.

8. "Just to Get a Rep" is a song by rap group Gang Starr that represents the importance of street reputations. Although they are referencing the "stick-up" game of street life, b-boys and b-girls relate to the importance of gaining a reputation. Gang Starr was a musical influence for the pioneering Toronto hip-hop crew Bag of Trix who competed at BOTY for Canada.

9. My mentors in the dance promote building one's own name, rather than becoming part of a crew with an already established reputation. This is a powerful counter-narrative that continues to move me.

10. This international event has since moved to Montpellier, France, under new organizers and the estimated turnout for 2010 was 12,000 people.

11. The event now takes place in large-scale arenas.

12. This information comes from interviews I conducted in Berlin and Erfurt, Germany, with b-boys, including the event promoter and local practitioners.

13. http://www.battleoftheyear.de/about.html (accessed August 10, 2010; now defunct).

14. I gained this information from a 2008 interview with a b-boy who judged BOTY and was not paid.

15. Although b-boys and b-girls see themselves as "families" (Fogarty 2012b), many b-boys and b-girls are not interested in events where real families are welcome (without ties to the dancers or hip-hop culture). Yet many grassroots events cherish the involvement of families. Although catering to spectators is seen to change the dynamics of the event, an awareness of "audience" is felt to honor how breaking was performed at block parties and outdoor events in New York City in the early 1980s. Part of the culture initially involved the execution of spectacular moves to impress people who do not break, including family and friends.

16. A b-boy "call-out" is usually indicated through a gesture that a b-boy/b-girl makes in the midst of dancing that lets another dancer know that they want to compete against them. Crucially, since the decision is theirs, this sort of battle has a great deal of agency for the person doing the "calling out," and there is a lot of stake in the reputation of the other dancer who must respond (or look weak).

17. This is based on my own observations of the dance in Toronto, before I was a researcher, and interviews with b-boys in Toronto from 2007.

18. See Frith (1996).

19. Notably, this is the historical moment when the term *b-boying* emerges and takes over for a time as the dominant label for the dance. In my research, Crazy Legs was one of the major endorsers of this term that began to circulate globally, although there is more research needed on the genealogy of terms in breaking culture.

20. At this point in time, there is actually more money to be earned doing online commentary for an international b-boy battle than judging the event (because this is unionized in a way that judging is not).

REFERENCES

Banes, Sally. 1984. "Breaking Changing." *Village Voice*, June 12, 82.

Banes, Sally. 1985. "Breaking." In *Fresh: Hip Hop Don't Stop*, edited by Nelson George, Sally Banes, Susan Flinker, and Patty Romanowski, 79–89. New York: Random House.

Becker, Howard S. 1982. *Art Worlds*. Berkeley; London: University of California Press.

Bennett, Andrew, and Keith Kahn-Harris, eds. 2004. *After Subculture: Critical Studies in Contemporary Youth Culture*. Basingstoke, UK: Palgrave Macmillan.

Bourdieu, Pierre. 1984. *Distinction: A Social Critique of the Judgement of Taste*. London: Routledge & Kegan Paul.

Bourdieu, Pierre. 1993. *The Field of Cultural Production: Essays on Art and Literature*. Cambridge: Polity.

Chang, Jeff. 2005. *Can't Stop Won't Stop: A History of the Hip-Hop Generation*. New York: Picador.

Dodds, Sherril. 2011. *Dancing on the Canon: Embodiments of Value in Popular Dance*. Basingstoke: Palgrave Macmillan.

Dyson, Michael Eric. 2004. "General Introduction." In *That's the Joint: The Hip Hop Studies Reader*, edited by Murray Forman and Mark Anthony Neal, 1–22. New York: Routledge.

Fogarty, Mary. 2006. "Whatever Happened to Breakdancing?": Transnational B-Boy/B-Girl Networks, Underground Video Magazines and Imagined Affinities." Unpublished MA diss., Brock University.

Fogarty, Mary. 2010. "Dance to the Drummer's Beat: Competing Tastes in International B-Boy/B-Girl Culture." Unpublished PhD diss., University of Edinburgh.

Fogarty, Mary. 2012a. "Breaking Expectations: Imagined Affinities in Mediated Youth Cultures." *Continuum: Journal of Media and Cultural Studies* (Special issue: Mediated Youth Cultures, edited by Andy Bennett and Brady Robards) 26(3): 449–462. London: Routledge.

Fogarty, Mary. 2012b. "Each One Teach One: B-Boying and Ageing." In *Ageing and Youth Cultures: Music, Style, and Identity*, edited by Andy Bennett and Paul Hodkinson, 53–65. Oxford: Berg.

Fogarty, Mary. 2014. "Gene Kelly: The Original, Updated." In *The Oxford Handbook of Dance and the Popular Screen*, edited by Melissa Blanco Borelli, 83–97. New York: Oxford University Press.

Fricke, Jim, and Charlie Ahearn. 2002. *Yes Yes Y'all: Oral History of Hip-Hop's First Decade*. Cambridge: Experience Music Press.

Frith, Simon. 1996. *Performing Rites: On the Value of Popular Music*. Cambridge, MA: Harvard University Press.

Gottschild, Brenda Dixon. 1996. *Digging the Africanist Presence in American Performance: Dance and Other Contexts*. Westport, CT; London: Greenwood.

Holman, Michael. 1984. "Breaking: The History." In *That's the Joint: The Hip Hop Studies Reader*, edited by Murray Forman and Mark Anthony Neal, 31–40. New York: Routledge.

Johnson, Imani K. 2015. "Hip Hop Dance." In *Cambridge Companion to Hip Hop*, edited by Justin A. Williams, 22–31. Cambridge: Cambridge University Press.

Lull, James. 1995. *Media, Communication, Culture: A Global Approach*. Cambridge: Polity.

Schloss, Joseph G. 2009. *Foundation: B-Boys, B-Girls, and Hip-Hop Culture in New York*. New York: Oxford University Press.

Thornton, Sarah. 1995. *Club Cultures: Music, Media and Subcultural Capital*. Cambridge: Polity.

Audiovisual Sources

Harrison, Nate. 2004. "Can I Get an Amen?" Recording on acetate, turntable, PA system, paper documents, dimensions variable. Online video, 17: 46. http://nkhstudio.com/pages/popup_amen.html. Accessed March 21, 2017.

Video Explains the World's Most Important 6-Second Drum Loop. 2006. [Excerpt from Nate Harrison's 2004 video.] YouTube video, 18:08. Posted by "Landon Proctor," February 21. https://www.youtube.com/watch?v=5SaFTm2bcac. Accessed February 5, 2017.

CHAPTER 19

···

NOT ANOTHER DON QUIXOTE!

Negotiating China's Position on the International Ballet Stage

···

ROWAN MCLELLAND

"NOT another Don Quixote," a woman a couple of rows away muttered under her breath as the Minkus introduction to Kitri's famous third act fan variation began to play into the nearly empty auditorium.[1] It was the first native English I had heard in a while and, in addition to the language, I shared the sentiment. Three hours into the first round at the Beijing International Ballet and Choreography Competition (IBCC), I had already seen this exact variation six times. Each was danced with impeccable technical precision by a young ballet dancer in the main theater of the National Centre for the Performing Arts (NCPA), near Tiananmen Square.

It was not that I dislike the work; from the entire classical repertoire, I had chosen this same variation to dance as a graduation performance upon completing ballet school a decade earlier. In this short yet challenging solo, Kitri displays virtuosic technique with a flirtatious wave of her fan and coquettish wink of the eye. However, removed from the wider context of the ballet, danced on a bare stage to a recording of the score, even the most polished Kitri would have struggled to excite the small, scattered audience of coaches and parents. She faces an even greater challenge when the audience has already seen this solo six times in a single afternoon.

What emerges in this chapter is an ethnographic exploration of international ballet competitions, specifically their multilayered significance for aspiring Chinese dancers and the broader institution of ballet in the People's Republic of China. Taking the Third Beijing IBCC (2015) as a case study, I explore how international ballet competitions function independently, and on a transnational scale, as well as highlighting specific considerations arising from the IBCC's Chinese situation. I investigate the value found in engaging with ballet competitions in terms of physical, social, economic, and political capital,[2] and illustrate how competitions contribute to ballet as a global practice. I fore-ground how this value operates differently for individual competitors, dance teachers, training institutions, and even nations, both inside China and in the rest of the world, to indicate the significance of competitions as a contributing factor to China's growing importance to ballet as a transnational practice. During fieldwork conducted in Beijing during the summer of 2015, I attended every stage of the competition over a ten-day pe-riod, all rounds in both the ballet and choreography competition (where some dancers participating in the ballet competition also competed). During breaks over the course of the competition at the NCPA, I interviewed approximately twenty-five competitors from all over the world, and talked informally to many more, as well as their parents, teachers, coaches, and choreographers. This ethnography exposes the larger structures and functions of the ballet competition in relation to the transnational character of the field, as well as the individual experiences of competitors in order to account for the di-versity and complexity of the competitive arena.

First I describe the nature of international ballet competitions and their place in the broader ballet institution. From this, it emerges that many experts in the field are critical of competitions for reducing ballet as an artistic form to one better equated to sport, with a focus on technical virtuosity. Given this criticism, the chapter moves on to explore the value of partaking in competitions, such as the potential for increased social capital in a globalized field, and greater physical capital through improved skills and performance for the individual dancer. Following this, an investigation into competitions in an inter-national arena illuminates the way in which the dancers become metaphors for the state imbued with political capital. Finally, the chapter returns to China to problematize the issues that arise when the local ballet field is so heavily invested in competitive success at the expense of other areas of development.

Ballet, both in practice and institution, is structured by competition. The dancer must, at every moment, be competitive with herself: fighting gravity, time, space, phys-ical limitations, and the will and desires of her body, individuals are engaged in a never-ending competition. In training classrooms, dancers are competitive with one another, knowing that their relative success will be important to their future progression. Beyond training, ballet companies have hierarchical structures; the allocation of roles, awarding of opportunities, and mechanisms for promotion are, to some extent, built upon com-petition. Perhaps the most explicit example of these competitive structures are ballet competitions themselves.

The Beijing IBCC is the most recent addition to a group of International Ballet Competitions (IBC) held in rotation in several cities around the world. The Varna International Ballet Competition, founded in 1964 in Bulgaria, if not the first ballet competition (the Adeline Genée Competition has been running since 1931), was the first truly international professional competition of its kind and, since its inception, many more have emerged in this network. Moscow (founded in 1969), Tokyo (1976, later moved to Osaka), Jackson, Mississippi (1979), New York (1983), Helsinki (1984), Paris (1984), Shanghai (1995), Seoul (2005), and Cape Town (2008) have all held inter-national Olympic-like ballet competitions for students and professional dancers. Of these, perhaps Varna, Moscow, and Jackson are the most prestigious and well attended for professional dancers. Additionally, stand-alone competitions such as the Prix de Lausanne (1973), Switzerland and Youth American Grand Prix (YAGP), USA (1999), are held annually for talented students.

Sports-like competition and awarding dancers numerical value for their performances does not sit comfortably in an art form whose expressive and interpretive qualities are not easily quantifiable. Nevertheless, ballet competitions are an important part of the career and development of a great many dancers, and that of many great dancers.[3] Indeed, few principal dancers in top-tier ballet companies do not have a slew of competition prizes to their name. Awarding medals, cash prizes, and company contracts, these competitions have become integral to the workings of ballet as a transnational practice. They thrive as a spectacular yet efficient showcase for identifying emerging talents, and are scrutinized and celebrated by an international dance community. Events are televised and broadcast over the Internet, and winners emerge as minor celebrities (albeit field-specific ones). Winners become commercially viable for ballet companies, dancewear manufactures, and magazines, and are sought-after performers for galas or as guest artists on the freelance circuit.

In her ethnography of Chinese classical dancers in China, anthropologist Emily Wilcox (2011, 6) notes that dancers who were successful in competition "became celebrities of the dance world, and at times they even crossed over into mainstream celebrity status. They appear frequently performing their famous competition works on television and in major national media events including the annual CCTV (Chinese state television network) New Year gala and other performances with wide popular viewing audiences." This holds true for ballet dancers, too, and was reiterated in the gala for the opening of the Beijing competition, where several of the specially invited performers were "famous" winners of previous competitions. One such performer was the seventeen-year-old star of the documentary *First Position* (2011, dir. Bess Kargman), Miko Fogarty. Fogarty has won medals in the Moscow IBC, at the Varna IBC, the Prix de Lausanne, and the Youth American Grand Prix, and her success confers fame in the dance world. With over 15.5 million views of her YouTube channel (as of January 2017), Fogarty was also listed as one of "The Most Influential People of 2011" by *Dance Spirit Magazine*, when she was just fourteen years old. It was clear by the uproarious reaction of the Beijing audience when Fogarty entered the stage that she was a celebrity in the dance world, even before she had performed with a professional ballet company.[4]

"If I See Another Corsaire or Another Don Quixote!": Criticisms of Ballet Competitions

Many criticisms are levied at international ballet competition, and perhaps the most pressing of these concerns their prioritization of bravura technical feats at the expense of artistry.[5] The critics claim that ballet in these competitions is more like gymnastic displays, a sport rather than an art form. In one of the few scholarly contributions to the field, former Royal Ballet dancer and scholar Geraldine Morris (2008) asks if the ballet competition is antithetical to dance as art. She explores the way in which ballet competitions are judged and, following philosophers David Best (1978, 1985, 2004) and Graham McFee (1992, 2004, 2005), highlights the problems that arise in evaluating ballet using aesthetic rather than artistic judgments. In so doing, Morris echoes a fear commonly expressed by critics, teachers, and company directors: ballet competitions and their emphasis on virtuosic technique are damaging to the future of ballet as an artistic practice.

Morris (2008) highlights two ways in which ballet competitions overemphasize impressive technical feats at the expense of other elements of artistry, and as such fail to accurately represent the totality of ballet as an art form. She suggests that the nineteenth-century competition repertoire selected for participants to dance presents limitations when treated as a criterion for excellence. Morris (2008, 40) argues that "the perception of these dances as an amalgam of classroom steps can encourage display and technical bravura rather than artistic interpretation." Despite this, it is clear to see why these cornerstones of the classical ballet canon are standard competition fare.

Making the selection of competition repertoire broader might go some way to addressing the concerns over the lack of artistry. Including twentieth- and twenty-first-century choreographers whose work diverges more boldly from a series of classroom steps might allow for greater display of artistic interpretation. However, the conservative selection of competition repertoire might suggest an attempt on behalf of the event organizers to avoid favoring one training school, style, or nationality over another. The canonical nineteenth-century repertoire is performed all over the world. Few elite ballet schools and companies do not perform *Sleeping Beauty* (1890) or *Swan Lake* (1895). Of course, these ballets demonstrate their own specific historical, stylistic context and ethnicity, but their omnipresence and familiarity among competitors renders them almost "style-free." Choosing a piece of twentieth- or twenty-first-century repertoire (by choreographers such as George Balanchine, Sir Fredrick Ashton, John Cranko, or Hans Van Manen, for example) might privilege some competitors (those more familiar with a certain choreographic or national style) over others. Furthermore, it creates complications in judging. Judges would need to be expert in all styles to assess the artistic and stylistic merit of each performance. Moreover, how does one demonstrate parity when evaluating work from distinct choreographers, each with a unique movement vocabulary? Competitions with an aesthetic element in fields that lack canonical repertoire, such as gymnastics and figure skating (Arkaev and Georgievich 2004; Xu and Zhao 2007), deal with this by awarding a score based on technical difficulty and another based on execution. However, rating choreography with such diverse movement possibilities for technical difficulties seems fraught with problems, and perhaps does little to level the playing field.

The now defunct New York IBC (NYIBC closed in 2013) dealt with this conflict well. Teaching three pieces of distinct choreography to all the competitors serves two functions. First, few competitors will have experience of the diverse repertoire; therefore learning and performing a variety of choreography in a short time frame more accurately reflects life in a professional company, moving between different styles multiple times in a day or week. Second, when all competitors dance the same vocabulary, it allows judges to more easily compare and reward interpretation, musicality, and style. This sentiment is reiterated by the director of the NYIBC, Ilona Copen: "Each couple, although they are learning the same rep, each couple brings to it, their heritage, their background, their schooling, their culture, and although you see the same piece performed they all look quite different And, of course, they all bring their own personality to it" (*Beyond the Gold*, Inside New York Ballet Competition documentary).

Morris (2008, 45) also suggests that, in an attempt to present the most bravura technique, the dance lacks shading and variation: "The dance movement, as danced by the candidates, lacks subtle nuances, there is no attempt to play with the music, every arabesque is somewhere in the region of 180 degrees, and every jump is big. As a result, the performances appear remarkably similar to each other." This was a feature of the IBCC 2015, too, although not entirely surprising.

A dancer has only two or three short variations to impress the judges. Given the brevity of each performance, it is difficult for a dancer to make subtle choices. Impressive technical standards can be objectively assessed quickly during the duration of a short solo: body proportions, natural facility for ballet, and technical feats are observable and measurable. Artistic interpretation, however, is incredibly subjective. It is difficult to quantify, particularly under time pressure. How does one measure which Kitri best flirts with her fan or which Giselle most radiates the fit-to-burst excitement of first-time love? This raises the question of whether the bias toward observable technique in competition judging creates a flattening of individual subjective opinion toward what is concretely measurable when there are multiple judges, each holding an individual, subjective view of artistry. Moreover, when viewed empirically, the more anomalous scores, which are likely to occur with the subjective nature of the value placed on artistry, are insignificant outliers when multiple scores deviate toward a mean. Artistic director of the Seoul IBC and judge at the IBCC 2015, Hae Shik Kim, confirms that the tabulation center typically omits the highest and lowest scores for the final points (Kim in Wozny 2015, 35).

The importance of bravura technique was also understood by some of the competitors, who used this perception to make conscious decisions about their performances. Robin,[6] a professional dancer in a well-known company in the United States, stated "that [in a competition environment] it is easy to view ballet as, like a sport, because it's so a) physically demanding, and b) we're judged on a physical criteria, for the most part."[7]

Hungarian teacher Maria Fay (1997) suggests that impressive technical ability is a necessary but not a sufficient condition for a successful career as a professional ballet dancer. Fay (1997) argues that there is now such an emphasis on technique that for some it becomes a sufficient condition. In this view, competitions, and the media they produce with their worldwide audience, with their bias toward virtuosic technical ability, might be partially responsible for feeding this change. In his ethnography of the Royal

Ballet, London, sociologist Steven Wainwright (2004, 101) asked company ballet master Dexter about the bias toward gymnastic technique in international competitions and its place in a ballet company:

> DEXTER—Competitions, you know; they're now so incredibly big. If I see another *Corsaire* or another *Don Quixote*! You see I don't really like all that because it doesn't teach them to be *artists*, it only teaches them to do tricks. You've got to iron all that out of them, well not iron it all out, but you've got to start to make them think differently.

Company dancers are artists and athletes combined. The dancer must develop his or her artistry, musicality, and interpretation alongside his or her athletic technical ability in order to flourish as an artist in a ballet company. The focus on technical virtuosity in most ballet competitions does not necessarily contribute heavily to the development of the skills required for ballet dancers to be well-rounded artists and performers. Thus, it could be argued that while great artists can emerge from competitions, the practice itself is unlikely to produce them.

"Bridge of Aspiration": Why Take Part?

Given the criticisms levied against ballet competitions from some in the ballet establishment, why take part in a competition at all? One of the greatest incentives to partake in an international competition occurs when the student undertakes her final year or two of training. As the student progresses toward full-time professional employment in ballet, the social capital of her training institution becomes increasingly important. Whereas, in the early years of ballet training, quality tuition is paramount to build a solid foundation of technical skills, as the dancer approaches her final years of schooling and faces the reality of auditioning for a professional company contract, the worldwide status and recognition of the school itself becomes more important. Much as attending Ivy League universities in the United States or Oxford or Cambridge University in the United Kingdom indicates a certain exceptional attainment on behalf of the student, particular ballet schools worldwide hold similar symbolic status within the field. Furthermore, just as elite universities offer an extensive "old boy" network on graduation, which includes opportunities to gain work experience with influential employers, so do the top dance schools. For example, talented final-year students attending the British Royal Ballet Upper School are sometimes given the chance to perform as part of the *corps de ballet* with the Royal Ballet. They literally and metaphorically cross the "Bridge of Aspiration," which physically links the school to the company's base at the Royal Opera House in London. The experience of taking class, rehearsing, and performing with the company affords the student the opportunity to gain vocational skills and social capital, giving her an edge over similarly well-trained dancers also looking for a professional contract.

The prizes awarded at most international ballet competitions come in the form of full scholarships to top international training schools or apprenticeships with prestigious professional companies. While many of the winners of ballet competitions in Europe already train at these prestigious schools, many of the competitors from Asia and South America attend schools with less worldwide status and social capital. They are also geographically removed from the metropolitan centers[8] of the ballet world. Furthermore, the fees for these schools are often prohibitive for many of the individual competitors. Therefore, succeeding in a competition could provide the student with an opportunity to train, in his or her critical final years, in one of the most prestigious and well-connected institutions in the world. Better still, an apprenticeship with one of these professional companies is a year-long opportunity to work with a company, increasing the student's chance at a permanent contract.

As a result of their potential to springboard a professional career, international competitions attract some of the most talented students from around the world. The standard of ballet shown is exceptionally high and, in order to stand a chance of success, dancers begin competition-specific training as far as one year in advance of the competition. Most competitions require the students to learn one or two classical variations from a pre-approved list of nineteenth-century classics (even if the contemporary performance and aesthetics of these solos have radically changed since the nineteenth century). In addition to the dancers' normal training, these variations are intensively rehearsed and polished.

Several of the dancers I interviewed noted that they had been invited by a teacher, coach, or peer to enter the competition. Many Chinese participants told me with some pride that they had been selected by their teachers to enter. These tended to be top students in the advanced levels at prestigious state-funded ballet schools. For these students, being selected to compete in a competition conferred a special status among their peers. Only the most talented, hardworking students were selected to compete. They noted that entering competitions was an important stage in many of their favorite dancers' careers, and suggested that a competition was a good opportunity to work intensively on their technique with their teachers and coaches. These competitors understood the recognition that can come with being successful in a prestigious competition.

"What Doesn't Kill You Makes You Stronger": Recognizing Progression in the Competition Format

In interviews conducted during the IBCC, competitors primarily spoke about using the competition as an arena to develop their dancing. An international competition requires months of preparation outside a dancer's normal training, rehearsing, and performing schedule. To participate in the IBCC, dancers competing as individuals had to learn and rehearse between four and six variations. Competing in the semifinals, dancers were required to perform two variations from the competition's selected repertoire and a contemporary variation of their own choosing. Progressing to the final, dancers presented two further classical solos, one of which could be repeated from the previous round, and a contemporary variation, which could also be repeated. Learning and perfecting these variations are time-consuming, in addition to the already intensive schedule of a dancer. Many prominent teachers suggest that the pressure of performing in an elite competition forces the dancer to progress at an accelerated rate. Dominic Antonucci (2015, 33), ballet master and former principal dancer with Birmingham Royal Ballet, writes of the increased focus and commitment that preparations for competitions require and suggests that his own experience of competing in the USAIBC at Jackson were "a test of nerve, but also of consistency and mental fortitude. The saying goes, 'What doesn't kill you makes you stronger.' This rings very true in regards to competitions. Self-belief is vital to any dancer's success, and competing is a very practical way of building this."

During my fieldwork in China I spent many weeks observing the final-year boys' ballet classes at the prestigious Shanghai Dance School. Two students in the class had been selected to take part in the Shanghai IBC later in the year. Day after day, the two students rehearsed their solos after class, with their teacher correcting the tiniest of details. The Dragon Boat festival (*Duanwu jie* [端午节]) fell during this period, and the school was officially closed for the day to allow celebrations. The day before the festival, I was surprised to receive a message from the class teacher informing that there would be an extra class during the holiday. When I arrived at the school, the building was largely empty, except for the teacher and the two competition students, taking class without any accompaniment. The class lasted about two and half hours, an hour longer than the standard boys' class, with additional time afterward for each boy to practice his solos for the competition. The teacher focused on miniscule details of each student's performance, commenting on the tension in individual fingers and unnecessary lifts of the chin. The students and their teacher dripped with sweat when they eventually finished rehearsing, over four hours later. With such focused and individual additional training, it is clear to see why competitions are seen as a good method of accelerating normal progress.

The rhetoric of competition as a form of professional development and increased physical capital was reiterated by a female IBCC competitor currently performing in Romania. After several years dancing in the *corps de ballet*, she wanted to be challenged. Training often provides students with the opportunity to learn technically difficult repertoire danced primarily by principal dancers, and many hours are spent refining complex classroom steps. A dancer in her first few years performing with a professional company will not often be granted the opportunity to perform these roles. While performing *corps de ballet* roles presents its own unique demands, the dancer I interviewed wanted to try her hand at repertoire that offered more technical challenges:

> I don't know if fear is the right word, but I doubted whether I could do two variations, after a few years of being in a *corps de ballet*, you don't do that kind of stuff [virtuosic

soloist repertoire], and so it hadn't really been since school that I had done that. . . .
I do eventually want to get out of the corps, like most people, I'd like to do more, so
this [the competition] is like a test, like a moment of growth.[9]

The competition as a learning opportunity or chance to grow, removed from the expectations and hierarchical structures of their daily training, was a common theme
expressed by the competitors. Notably, differences in the format of international
competitions better suit this kind of motivation.

The format of the NYIBC indicated the development of the individual dancer as
the primary concern, and thus rewarded technical and artistic progression during the
competition period. Competitors in the first round were not required to pre-learn variations; instead, in an intensive, fully funded three-week workshop, they were taught
three pieces of competition repertoire by an expert coach. The repertoire selected in this
competition was, in general, outside the typical competition fare of nineteenth-century
classical variations. For example, in 2003, competitors were asked to learn repertoire as
diverse as a *pas de deux* from Marius Petipa's *La Bayadère* (1877), August Bourneville's
Kemiesse in Bruges (1851), and José Limón's *Mazurkas* (1958 [1985]). Often the subtle choreographic styles and idiomatic selections were beyond many of the competitors' current repertoire. The "foreign" repertoire and the intensive coaching experience leading
up to the competition performances provided participants with a unique development
experience. Furthermore, it ensured that there was an enriching learning opportunity
for all participants at the competition. It placed greater emphasis on the preparation
than the performance; thus even competitors who were eliminated after the first round
had a valuable experience. It also better reflected the reality of working as a professional
dancer, moving between different works, rather than expertly perfecting a few short variations for competition.

Similarly, the annual Prix de Lausanne also presents competitors with a greater opportunity to approach the competition as a learning opportunity. The competitors
come prepared with variations from pre-selected competition repertoire, learned
from an official Prix recording.[10] The dancers are coached on these variations by
teachers and choreographers during the course of the competition, some of which
is observed by the judges. The competitors are also judged while taking ballet and
contemporary classes; thus they are evaluated on a broader range of skills than the
singular focus of the on-stage variation performances at the IBCC. The narrow focus
of the IBCC format was highlighted by a competitor who was eliminated after the first
round in Beijing:

> I don't feel like I have much experience [in the competition]. The first two days there
> were no classes, and everyone was doing their own thing in the studio, so there wasn't
> much space to run anything . . . you then get ten minutes on the stage to have a re-
> hearsal. As a professional, it's really hard to put your head on the chopping block and
> it's a hard pill to swallow if you're cut early on. I didn't feel great about my perfor-
> mance and I only got to do it once on stage.[11]

As in the case of this competitor, the primary motivation for many dancers was that it offered an opportunity to challenge themselves and develop as technicians and artists. This discourse prioritizes "competing with oneself," which might be a healthy way to approach competition. Setting personal goals and devising strategies to reach those goals negate the idea of failure to win an award. Emphasis is placed on the process of learning, rather than on winning. However, this cannot be considered competing in its sense of out-performing others striving for the same reward. Philosopher John Loy (1968, 4–5) defines competition as "a struggle for supremacy between two or more opposing sides," and makes clear that competition requires actors who are consciously aiming for supremacy over other competitor(s). Education scholars John Martin Rich and Joseph DeVitis (1992) suggest that the idea of competing with oneself is

> misleading since someone can seek to perform well by attempting to attain a standard independently of others, whether self-created or created by an external authority. This is a variation once again of the misnomer "competing with oneself," as the individual is seeking privately to attain something or to improve oneself. Two or more persons are not striving for R[eward]. (in Gallops 2005, 19)

In this view, the performer who is pitted against herself is no longer competing in the traditional sense of the word. Ballet is a genre in which dancers are perpetually competing with themselves, striving for excellence; a higher *arabesque*, greater turnout, or a more fluid *ports de bras*. A dancer does not need the format of a competition to engage in self-improvement.

Furthermore, the idea of competing against oneself, striving for betterment, is negated when considering how participants select their competition repertoire. If participants understood the competition as primarily a chance to focus and work on weak areas consistently, and improve technique and artistry more generally, then it would be logical to attend a competition with a stronger focus on progression and development, and to select repertoire based on areas of weakness. However, more often variations are chosen based on their ability to showcase each individual's technical strengths. To this end, variations are frequently altered (a common strategy in classical ballet) to a greater or lesser extent to highlight particular areas of virtuosity or avoid areas of perceived weakness. Such modifications are implemented to ensure physical capital (for instance, showing the aesthetic of the body to its maximum potential through high-cut leotards to make legs seem longer) and to demonstrate technical virtuosity (for example, through pirouettes turned exclusively in one direction or bravura elements substituted for others). These strategies seem to run in opposition to the commonly suggested idea that participants were competing with themselves or using the competition as an opportunity for technical improvement.

While there is status attached to winning an international ballet competition for all participants, there is a uniquely Chinese motivation to take part in competitions for Chinese competitors. China operates a scheme of organization wherein there is a national ranking system in which artists can apply for status and privileges based on their education and professional accomplishments. Performers for high-status state-funded institutions (those considered "in the system," as opposed to privately funded institutions, "outside the system") are awarded the highest status. The NCPA, which is an important funder and the host of the IBCC in Beijing, is one such high-status institution, and confers this status upon the competition. To obtain Class A, the highest status, dancers must win many top-level awards in competitions, have extensive experience in a high-status institution, and be considered at the top of the field. Accompanying the Beijing competition was a high-profile three-day gala, beginning after the competition award ceremony, with performances from famous principal dancers from all over the world. The program for this gala listed short biographies of all performers. The entry for each performer included a long list of the prizes and awards secured at top international ballet competitions. The biography for Wang Zihan, a Chinese classical dancer, even noted Wang's status as a National Class-A Artist (gala program, NCPA, July 2015). Artists with this rank carry brand recognition and value, which in turn means they are able to demand high fees for guest appearances. For the Chinese competitors, the IBCC not only offers a chance to gain status and propel a career internationally (as the biographies of competition-winning star dancers demonstrate), it also presents an important means of gaining national recognition.

"Nation Dancing against Nation": Positioning Chinese Ballet in a Globalized Field

So far, we have seen that there are important motivators for individual dancers in China and elsewhere to compete in competitions. However, there are motivations to compete that extend beyond the individual dancer. In China, a country which has had institutionalized ballet for fewer than sixty years, holding a prestigious international competition demonstrates to the world that, aside from the growing success of individual Chinese dancers in international competitions, China itself is a major player in the field of ballet. Much like hosting an Olympic Games, a large-scale international competition of this type stands as a symbol of China's strength, cultural sensitivity, and commitment to ballet as an art form. It is a local forum in which to showcase the wealth and quality of Chinese training and talent.

In an article in the British *Observer* newspaper, ballerina Maude Lloyd and her husband Nigel Gosling (writing under the joint name of Alexander Bland) described international ballet competitions as "[n]ation dancing against nation" (Bland 1969). Reiterating this conception, although specifically writing about wrestling in a period of Hindu nationalism, anthropologist Joseph S. Alter (1994) notes how the body of the individual athlete (or dancer) is made into a symbol that represents his or her country in international competitions. Their strength, energy, self-discipline, vitality, and other virtuous qualities become political metaphors for the state.

Alter suggests that highly trained bodies are somewhat liberated from the burdens that ties the everyday workers to the economic infrastructure: the shackles of productivity. The virtuosic body, therefore, becomes a symbol of power. When an individual seems to embody mythical ideals, such as Herculean strength or knightly courage, rather than mundane labor power, then his or her strength, energy, vitality, and endurance become political metaphors rather than individual measures of value.

> Fitness can be used to invoke feelings of patriotism precisely because it is not an issue in an industrial economy where workers are chattels: the proverbial cogs in a machine. (Alter 1994, 558)

Alter and others (Bernett 1966; Brownell 1995; Riordan 1977) indicate how high-level bodily training in sports (or dance) has often been highlighted as ideological rhetoric in many examples of nationalism. The idea of the dancer as national symbol arose in discussion with my interlocutors in the Beijing competition. A young American student who had spent many years training in the Russian class at the Bolshoi School spoke about asking the permission of the school to compete in the Prix de Lausanne. Initially reluctant, eventually his Russian teachers relented, saying, "you might be an American competing, but remember, you're *our* [emphasis original] American."[12] In this case, the dancer has two symbolic national identities: that of the American, and that of the honorary Russian (as demonstrated in both the words of his teacher, and bodily through the dancer's Russian-style technique). This reveals a complex negotiation between the achievement of the individual from a national perspective, and the achievement of a nation from a transnational perspective. Justin clearly felt this negotiation as he described his dual identities as national symbols during the Prix de Lausanne:

> Coming from the Bolshoi Ballet School, I am in a unique position to represent both the USA and Russia, especially important at this time of tension between our countries. During the competition I wore my Russian Olympics jacket, as I am proud to represent both Russia and the USA.[13]

To return specifically to China, anthropologist Susan Brownell (1995), in her ethnography of sporting competitions in China, writes of the lasting legacy of Maoist thinking on the approach to the cultivation of bodily virtuosity. She proposes the notion of the "Maoist body" as a way of illuminating the link between Mao's communist state and the body of an individual. She describes how Maoist ideology was written on the bodies of individual people, and the physical strength and fitness of discrete Chinese citizens became a problem of national significance. Brownell argues that the Maoist body culture and preoccupation with the health and well-being of the nation was egalitarian, militaristic, and proletarian, formed in stark opposition to the body as conceived in the West, and to the Neo-Confucian late Qìng (1644–1912) body. Cultivation of the body under Mao suggested physical and mental strength, and an ability to transcend the everyday bodily desires of the undisciplined and to endure sacrifice and hardship to demonstrate a heartfelt commitment to the revolutionary cause. This discourse of sacrificing one's life for the revolutionary cause, to realize communist ideals, has consequences for the power and subjectivity of the individual. It is underpinned by the idea that an individual revolutionary subject does not own his or her body (Zhang 2005, 6).

Chairman Mao also stressed the link between a healthy physical body with virtue and morality. In Mao's manifesto, suggesting his vision for a new China (1917), physical cultivation and practice are inherently interrelated with the cultivation of morality. Physical cultivation embodies the ideology of revolutionary culture and inspires others to strive for physical and, by extension, moral cultivation. Using Alster's conception to understand the interplay between the individual's body and the nation-state, those with bodily virtuosity in Maoist China are embodiments of somatic nationalism. It is possible therefore to conceptualize the success of individual dancers in international ballet competitions as an outward-facing symbol of China's strength, power, cultural sensitivity, and indicator of the nation's growing importance as a center for balletic excellence.

At the IBCC, the high level of the Chinese dancers was noted by the head of the classical ballet jury, Manuel Legris. The former *étoile* at the Paris Opera and director of the Wiener Staatsballet suggested in his speech during the grand Opening Ceremony that "a ballet competition is an important and difficult stage for a dancer, and can change their destiny. . . . And it [the competition] taking place in Beijing is even more difficult. The place of Chinese ballet is a really high and professional world standard" (IBCC Opening Ceremony, NCPA, Beijing, July 9, 2015). This proved to be true when fourteen of the nineteen awards granted in IBCC 2015 went to Chinese dancers. The very high standard of Chinese training that produces large numbers of elite Chinese dancers is also seen in the success of Chinese dancers in many other competitions around the world. To select an example from another international competition, in the USAIBC 2014 and 2013, held in Jackson, Mississippi, Chinese dancers won two of eighteen, and seven of twenty-three prizes awarded, respectively (USAIBC website, 2015).[14] In 2016, two of nine prizes at the Prix De Lausanne were awarded to Chinese students.

In addition to the status a dancer brings to the nation when he or she competes, success in ballet competitions also serves to help individual institutions in China. The most prestigious ballet schools in China are state-funded institutions. Students, if they pay at all, are expected to contribute only very modest fees. During an interview with a senior boys teacher at one such university, the Shanghai Theatre Academy, Wang revealed how student success in prestigious competitions served as measurable proof to the Chinese government that the school was achieving comparably with other international institutions. He suggested that the success of future funding for the school was contingent on measurable markers of success such as these.[15]

Once the heads of the institution set a budget for the near future, they are asked to justify this budget based on previous achievement. Success at international competitions (even if it means the best Chinese students winning prizes to train elsewhere) is seen as a good way of evidencing that.

> The school makes a budget for the next year, they ask the government for money. The government will ask, what did you do this year, or the past two or three years. If you have the prize, yes, we have students who won Prix de Lausanne or the Youth American Grand Prix or other competitions, then the government will say, "yeah, okay, you did things, you have results, we give you the money." In China, they don't have a longer term plan, it's not like [a plan] for decades or two decades, no, three years or five, we give you the money, we have to see some results. Or even, I give you the money this year, you have to show me something next year. What's the most quick way to show them [governmental funding organizations] the things? The competitions.[16]

This indicates how central international competitions are as a way of measuring Chinese success against their international peers. Competitions function to concretely prove, even to a limited extent, that there is value in the economic support offered to ballet in China. Unlike more empirical endeavors, the value gained from governmental economic support cannot be easily appraised or quantified. The "slow burn" nature of ballet training means that investment does not produce a marketable product for as many as fifteen years, one that will never generate substantial economic capital. Moreover, the unwieldy nature of the art produced in performance means that achievement is highly subjective, whereas continued success in competitions provides immediate validation. This places a large responsibility on the dancer herself. Although she may not be aware of the responsibility resting on her shoulders, to an extent, she holds in her hands the future of ballet in China.

While this recognition of international excellence serves a function within China to secure the economic stability of future state funding, it is largely symbolic to the wider global ballet community. With the exception of the competitions held in China, ballet competitions offer scholarships to prestigious schools and apprenticeships with renowned companies as prizes to the winners. However, regardless of the growing reputation of Chinese training, institutions in China very seldom have international students. It is common at schools such as the Royal Ballet School to have upward of 50% international students (Royal Ballet School Annual Report 2014–2015). When I visited the top training institute in China, the Beijing Dance Academy, I was told there were few international students among the vast student body; the teacher estimated fewer than 5%, with the majority of those students being from Hong Kong or Taiwan. Thus the success of Chinese ballet schools stands only to grow a reputation largely about their ability to train exclusively Chinese students because they lack the social capital of longer established schools better located in world centers for ballet.

There are also incentives on the level of the individual teachers at Chinese academies to focus on training students for competitions. In an interview with a well-known Chinese teacher, Professor Ming, I was told that much as professional dancers must demonstrate career success to be considered for progression in the national ranking scheme, teachers also must be able to illustrate achievements in their field to be eligible for promotion. Having your student win a national or, better still, international competition highlights your skill as a teacher. Professor Ming also noted that there are, in some cases, cash payments or other rewards for particularly successful teachers.

LOOKING INWARD: THE ROLE OF THE COMPETITION WITHIN CHINA

As established, there are many incentives to strive for success in ballet competition in China. To some extent, this motivation to succeed is what powers the field. There is motivation to compete on the part of the individual dancer who is looking to springboard an international career; motivation on the part of the teacher who receives status, rewards, and future opportunity for training successful students; institutional motivation to receive future funding; and national motivation to highlight China's power and cultural sensitivity in the global arena. However, it proves problematic to have a field that is so tightly focused on only one arena of the broader practice of the art.

The tenacious drive toward competitions as one of the end goals in ballet training in China necessitates a commitment on the part of the teacher to focus nearly exclusively on the very best students. During my observations at the Beijing Dance Academy, the Shanghai Dance School, and Shanghai Theatre Academy, I was struck by how much of the teacher's attention and vocal feedback was dedicated to one or two students in each class. The most talented students in a class received many times more physical corrections and vocal feedback than did their peers. It would not be an exaggeration to suggest that the best student in the class may receive approximately six or seven times the number of corrections than any other member of the group might receive.[17] Moreover, when observing the end-of-term formal examinations, I noted that the students were arranged in space roughly according to their ability. All students were given a number, which correlated to the number of strokes in the characters in the student's name essentially a random ordering.[18] Yet they did not stand in this number order. At the barre, the most able students stood at the center of the barre in the middle of the room. The second and third students in the hierarchy stood to either side of the best student, and this was repeated around the room, with those students deemed less able at the end of the barre, furthest from the center of the room. Away from the barre during center practice, the most able student stood in the center of the first row (downstage, closest to the judging panel of school faculty and invited guests), with the next most able dancer to either side in the first row, progressing down the room with many rows of students ordered in terms of their technical ability. The hierarchical arrangement of students indicates how the organization of space in training focuses toward measurable markers of outward success. Thus, space is structured by competition. Those students in each class who secure the focus of the teacher's attention will undoubtedly be the ones who are trained for international ballet competitions. This is a somewhat circular process whereby once those students are registered for an important competition, the competition necessitates, and to an extent justifies, the individual student's disproportionate attention. The attention on a few at the expense of many students was felt by a great number of the young dancers I interviewed in China:

> I don't think that my teacher thinks I can be a dancer at all. She never looks at me or my classmates for many years. She only looks at the best one. The one thing that keeps me going is my passion inside. It's hard because my classmate is like my sister. We lived in a dormitory together for seven years, she is like my sister, but still I feel like I want to be like her. I want the teacher to look at me too.[19]

Whether or not this creates unhealthy, competitive intra-relationships between friends and classmates is perhaps outside the scope the discussion here; however, it does have ramifications for the development of ballet in China.

The training of one or two students per year at the expense of the other students in a cohort presents issues when those students are eventually successful in winning a scholarship or apprenticeship in an international competition. This is an outward-facing approach that aims to enhance China's status in a globalized ballet field. From the outside, the capital of the successful individual becomes equated with that of the state, and conclusions that reflect on the status of China are drawn. Yet successful dancers will ultimately leave China to dance abroad in companies with greater status, social capital, and opportunity. Those who remain have less physical capital and were effectively trained to lower standards than their classmates who were deemed to possess greater potential. This means that those who did not make the grade in international competitions populate China's national and regional companies. Thus, Chinese ballet companies are destined to be second tier in a globalized market. The ballet stars of the future that China produces populate the top tier companies internationally and thus bring symbolic status to China, but it does little to boost the actual standing of ballet as an institution within the country itself. In this way, ballet as an institution in China is self-limiting.

In recent years this has begun to change. Competitions held within China are making significant efforts to attract international competitors. Winning the "Grand Prix" title at the Beijing competition commands a prize of $20,000. While the Grand Prix prize was not awarded in 2015, the Senior category (ages 19–26) gold medal winners each took home $10,000. Silver medallists won $7,000, and recipients of bronze medals, $4,000. There are slightly smaller prize funds in the Junior category (ages 16–18, gold, silver, and bronze receiving $7,000, $5,000, and $3,000, respectively), and a number of other miscellaneous prizes such as the "NCPA Special Award" ($2,000) and the "Jury Special Award" ($2,000) (IBCC 2015 Rules and Regulations Booklet). While individual Chinese dancers certainly use international competitions to showcase their talents to a worldwide audience with hopes of a career outside

China, this is not encouraged by the Chinese ballet institution. Thus, despite the world-renowned international judging panel, there are no international scholarships or company contracts officially awarded at IBCC. Therefore, to attract high-caliber international competitors to a Chinese competition with a largely domestic audience (and little chance of a company contract), a high prize fund is necessary. The lack of social capital found in Chinese institutions needs to be mitigated with higher economic capital. The prize fund at the IBCC is substantially higher than all other International Ballet Competitions held worldwide.

While several international competitions provide accommodation, transfers, and a per diem, Beijing is the only international competition that also provides a generous contribution toward travel too. The competition pays up to 5,000 RMB[20] for international travel. Therefore the competition is essentially open to all, regardless of a competitor's financial situation. It is somewhat ironic that a competition rewards individual success so highly with a substantial prize fund, but employs meritocratic, socialist ideals. It seems that a nascent competition in a country with a relatively short history of institutionalized ballet requires these perks to draw international competitors.

Another indicator of China opening its arms to the global ballet community emerged when Shanghai Dance School became a Prix de Lausanne partner institution. This scholarship allows one winner of the Prix to study at the Shanghai Dance School. There is yet to be a Prix winner to accept a scholarship in China; however, with large numbers of Chinese winners in international competitions, the strong reputation for excellent training, and growing opportunities in China, it is clear that this will not be too far in the future. Partnering with institutions such as the Prix de Lausanne offers potential to grow the social capital and prominence of Chinese training schools. In investing so heavily in the Beijing competition, and receiving recognition by building partnerships with other important institutions such as the Prix de Lausanne, the Chinese ballet community indicates its commitment to development and excellence in the art form in China, and shows itself to be a serious player on the world stage.

I have explored the functions of competitions in the globalized practice of ballet. This illustrates the centrality of the competitions to the mobility of dancers internationally, and locates the arena as a mechanism by which individual dancers, institutions, and even nations are ascribed status. In a state where ballet is a relatively young practice, competitions serve to highlight to a global audience the technical excellence of ballet in China. Too great a focus on competition, however, and the quality of ballet on both an individual level (with an overemphasis on technical virtuosity in performance) and on a national level (with a focus on competition at the expense of other developments in the field) can hinder progression. As the English prima ballerina Margot Fonteyn once suggested, "Sooner or later, the focus of the ballet world will shift to mainland China if it continues its present system of ballet training, effort, and enthusiasm" (in Cheng 2000, 258). International competitions are responsible for shining a light on the achievements in ballet in China, and present the potential to open the world to new centers of excellence, and encourage more reciprocal transnationalism in the field.

NOTES

1. *Don Quixote* (1869) is a ballet choreographed by Marius Petipa to a score by Ludwig Minkus, based on episodes from *Don Quixote de la Mancha* (1605) by Miguel de Cervantes. Kitri, the ballet's heroine, is the beautiful and fiery daughter of an inn-keeper who defies her father's wishes to meet, and eventually marry, her beloved, the charismatic Basilio.
2. In using these terms, I draw on the work of French sociologist and anthropologist Pierre Bourdieu (1930–2002). In his work *In Cultural Reproduction and Social Reproduction* (1977) and *Distinction* (1984), Bourdieu notes how an individual's assets, attributes, and skills stratify society and can serve to promote social mobility. These terms are so widely used in contemporary scholarship that a fuller exploration of them and Bourdieu's theory is beyond the scope of this chapter; however, they are useful in identifying intangible motivations and rewards in the competition arena.
3. Examples of former winners in the Prix de Lausanne alone: Alessandra Ferri (1980), Miyako Yoshida (1983), Viviana Durante (1984), Darcey Bussell (1986), Julie Kent (1986), Jose Carlos Martinez (1987), Carlos Acosta (1990), Diana Visheva (1994), Gillian Murphy (1995), Alina Cojocaru (1997), Maria Kochetkova (2002), and Steven McRae (2003). https://www.prixdelausanne.org/community/prize-winners/ (accessed May 18, 2018).
4. Although Fogarty is now in the *corps de ballet* with the Birmingham Royal Ballet, at the time of this competition, Fogarty had yet to make a professional debut.
5. I appreciate that "artistry" presents an unwieldy term, although professionals in the field agree that ballet demands an artistic component further to simply demonstrating movement according to the rules dictated by the classical technique. There is an emphasis on *how* these movements are performed, and this is affected by many factors, such as particular choreographic style or idiom, a narrative or theme, interaction with the musical accompaniment or lack thereof, appropriate and specific choice to vary dynamics. A fuller articulation of the term *artistry* in classical ballet is beyond the scope of this discussion (see Glasstone 2000; McFee 1992, 2005; Morris 2008).
6. Names have been changed to protect the identity of my interviewees.
7. Interview with "Robin" (July 13, 2015).
8. Ballet is a transnational practice and can be found on a greater or lesser scale in almost every corner of the world. In global terms, the metropolitan centers of the ballet world could be considered to be large cities in western Europe and the United States, most notably, London, Paris, and New York, as well as historic centers of excellence in Russia, such as Moscow and St. Petersburg.
9. Interview with "Annie" (July 14, 2015).
10. There are many potential issues with learning dance from video recordings, but perhaps most relevant to ballet competition is that removing solos from the wider context of the ballet, and having them performed by one dancer on video, encourages imitation rather than substantial and appropriate personal artistic interpretation. What might be individual interpretation or an idiosyncratic style becomes fixed choreographic "fact" on film, to be reproduced in performance by young dancers.
11. Interview with "Annie" (July 14, 2015).
12. Interview with "Justin" (July 14, 2015).
13. Interview with Graham Spicer, www.gramilano.com (accessed January 31, 2017).
14. There are many complications in quantifying the success of dancers from any one nation. The number of entrants from each country and the types of prizes awarded must

be taken into consideration. Moreover, the way individual competitors are identified (by birthplace, country of residence, or country of training) presents further complications. However problematic, it is difficult to deny the success of Chinese dancers in international ballet competitions in recent years, and these statistics serve as a clear illustration of that.

15. Interview with teacher "Wang" (June 10, 2016).

16. Interview with teacher "Wang" (June 10, 2016).

17. While undertaking fieldwork at the Shanghai Dance School watching ballet class with the third-year girls (approximately twelve and thirteen years old), I attempted to quantify what I had perceived in my observations watching this group and their teacher over the course of many weeks. In this one class alone (and one should be cautious of generalizing this specific observation more broadly) the ratio was roughly 6:1; six comments directed toward the best student and one to another member of the same group. Of course, there are also general comments directed to the whole group, and it is good practice as a dancer to apply all corrections to your work, regardless of the specific student at which they were targeted.

18. This is similar to ordering the students alphabetically in a language, such as English, that uses phonemic orthography. Another random method of ordering students commonly used is to arrange them by height.

19. Interview with "Shi Yi" (July 11, 2014).

20. Approximately $725 as of January 31, 2017.

REFERENCES

Alter, Joseph S. 1994. "Somatic Nationalism: Indian Wrestling and Militant Hinduism." *Modern Asian Studies* 28(3): 557–588.

Antonucci, Dominic. 2015. "Who Wins Ballet Competitions?" https://www.brb.org.uk/post/dance-competitions. Accessed June 8, 2016.

Arkaev, Leonid, and Nikolaï Georgievich Suchilin. 2004. *Gymnastics: How to Create Champions*. Aachen: Meyer & Meyer Verlag.

Bernett, Hajo. 1966. *Nationalsozialistische Leibeserziehung: Eine Dokumentation ihrer Theorie und Organisation*. Schorndorf: Hofmann.

Best, David. 1978. *Philosophy and Human Movement*. London: George Allen & Unwin.

Best, David. 1985. *Feeling and Reason in the Arts*. London: George Allen & Unwin.

Best, David. 2004. "Aesthetic and Artistic: Two Separate Concepts. The Danger of Aesthetic Education." *Research in Dance Education* 5(2): 159–175.

Beijing International Ballet and Choreography Competition (IBCC). 2015. Gala Programme, NCPA, July 2015.

Bland, Alexander. 1969. "Nation Dancing against Nation." *The Observer* (London) March 23, 1969, 28.

Bourdieu, Pierre. 1977. "Cultural Reproduction and Social Reproduction." In *Power and Ideology in Education*, edited by Jerome Karabel and A. H. Halsey, 487–511. New York: Oxford University Press.

Bourdieu, Pierre. 1984. *Distinction: A Social Critique of the Judgement of Taste*. Cambridge, MAs: Harvard University Press.

Brownell, Susan. 1995. *Training the Body for China: Sports in the Moral Order of the People's Republic*. Chicago: University of Chicago Press.

Cheng, De-Hai. 2000. "The Creation and Evolvement of Chinese Ballet: Ethnic and Esthetic Concerns in Establishing a Chinese Style of Ballet in Taiwan and Mainland China (1954–1994)." PhD diss., New York University.

Fay, Maria 1997. *Mind over Body: The Development of the Dancer—The Role of the Teacher.* London: A. & C. Black.

Fogarty, Miko. 2017. "Biography." http://www.mikofogarty.com/biography/. Accessed July 14, 2015.

Gallops, Wayne. 2005. "Developing a Healthy Paradigm for Performers and Teachers." *Journal of Music Teacher Education* 15(1): 15–22.

Glasstone, Richard. 2000. "Technique, Virtuosity or Gymnastic Stunts?" *Dancing Times* 90(1079): 1001.

Helsinki International Ballet Competition. 2017. "History." http://ibchelsinki.fi/en/information/. Accessed January 27, 2017.

IBBC. 2015. *Rules and Regulations Booklet.* Property of the author.

Japan International Ballet Competition. 2017. "About." http://www.jjgp.jp/e_about.html. Accessed January 28, 2017.

Loy, John W. 1968. "The Nature of Sport: A Definitional Effort." *Quest* 10(1): 1–15.

Mao, Zedong. 1917. "A Study of Physical Education." In *Mao's Road to Power: Revolutionary Writings, 1912–49*: Vol. 1, edited by Stuart R. Schram: 152–161. London: Routledge.

McFee, Graham. 1992. *Understanding Dance.* London: Routledge.

McFee, Graham. 2004. *The Concept of Dance Education: Expanded Edition.* Eastbourne, UK: Pagentry.

McFee, Graham. 2005. "The Artistic and the Aesthetic." *British Journal of Aesthetics* 45(4): 368–387.

Morris, Geraldine. 2008. "Artistry or Mere Technique? The Value of the Ballet Competition." *Research in Dance Education* 9(1): 39–54.

Prix de Lausanne. 2017. "Prize Winners." http://www.prixdelausanne.org/community/prize-winners/. Accessed January 28, 2017.

Rich, John Martin, and Joseph L. DeVitis. 1992. *Competition in Education.* Springfield, IL: Charles C. Thomas.

Riordan, James. 1977. *Sport in Soviet Society: Development of Sport and Physical Education in Russia and the USSR.* Cambridge: Cambridge University Press

Royal Ballet School Annual Report., 2014–2015. 2015. https://www.royalballetschool.org.uk/wp-content/uploads/2016/08/Royal-Ballet-School-Annual-Report-2014-15.pdf. Accessed January 30, 2017.

Seoul International Ballet Competition. 2016. "About." http://www.sicf.or.kr/eng/html/01_about/05.html. Accessed January 29, 2017.

Shanghai International Ballet Competition. 2017. "About." http://www.shanghaiibc.cn/en/detail1.aspx?id=82. Accessed January 30, 2017.

South African International Ballet Competition. 2015. https://www.saibc.com/ AccessedMay 18 2018.

Spicer, Graham. 2015. "Julian Mackay on Entering and Winning the Prix de Lausanne 2015." http://www.gramilano.com/2015/02/julian-mackay-on-entering-and-winning-the-prix-de-lausanne-2015/. Accessed July 8, 2016.

USA International Ballet Competition. 2017. "History." https://www.usaibc.com/about-us/history/. Accessed January 28, 2017.

Wainwright, Steven P. 2004. "A Bourdieusian Ethnography of the Balletic Body." PhD diss., Kings College London.

Wilcox, Emily. 2011. "The Dialects of Virtuosity: Dance in the People's Republic of China." PhD diss., University of California, Berkeley.

Wozny, Nancy. 2015. "Dance by the Numbers." *Dance Magazine*, February: 34–35.

Xu, Zhao-xiao, and Guo-na Zhao. 2007. "Comparative Analysis of the Old and New Scoring Systems of the International Skating Union." *China Winter Sports* 4: 013.

Youth American Grand Prix. 2017. "History and Mission." http://yagp.org/?page_id=661. Accessed February 2, 2017.

Zhang, Everett Yuehong. 2005. "Rethinking Sexual Repression in Maoist China: Ideology, Structure and the Ownership of the Body." *Body & Society* 11(3): 1–25.

Audiovisual Sources

First Position. 2011. Kargman, Bess (dir.) First Position Films. UK Distribution: Artificial Eye. DVD. https://www.imdb.com/title/tt2008513/companycredits?ref_=tt_dt_co

New York International Ballet Competition. 2012. *Beyond the Gold, Inside New York Ballet Competition: Short Version*. http://www.nyibc.org/2013/beyondthegold/. Accessed July 14, 2015.

PART V

LOSING, FAILING, AND AUTO-CRITIQUE

CHAPTER 20

DANCING WITH THE ASIAN AMERICAN STARS

Margaret Cho and the Failure to Win

YUTIAN WONG

INTRODUCTION

IN 2010 Carrie Ann Inaba, Kristi Yamaguchi, Apolo Anton Ohno, and Margaret Cho appeared in Season 11 of *Dancing with the Stars*, making for a record number of Asian American dancers to appear on a reality television dance competition since Kaba Modern and Jabbawockeez's appearance on Season 1 of *America's Best Dance Crew*.[1] The number of dancing Asian American bodies appearing on the televised dance stage could be read as an opportunity to dispel cultural critic Lee Siegel's claim that Asian American absence from the stage and screen evidences Asian American reluctance or inability to assimilate into American culture (Siegel 2012); however, I am less concerned with the fact of bodily presence and more concerned with the relationship between success and failure as a marker of Asian American belonging and normalcy.[2]

This chapter examines Margaret Cho's appearance on *Dancing with the Stars* and how her failure to win is an attempt to rewrite the conditions of Asian American success and cultural belonging. Cho attempts to reconfigure the conditions of success by subverting ballroom dance choreography in order to disrupt the format of reality television dance competitions. She tries, but ultimately fails, thus becoming what literary critic Viet Nguyen refers to as the "bad subject"—the antithesis of the model minority (Nguyen 2002, 11). While the "bad subject" within the Asian American literary imagination is often celebrated as the anti-hero whose failure is politicized as a protest of model minority expectations,[3] I examine Margaret Cho's failure to win as a failed attempt to protest the conventions of how Asian Americans are represented in the media via the format of reality television dance competitions.

Margaret Cho and *Dancing*
with the Stars

Season 11 of *Dancing with the Stars* featured the comedian Margaret Cho as one of the twelve celebrity contestants on the show competing for a mirror ball trophy.[4] As one of four non-white contestants and the only Asian American cast in Season 11, Cho was not the first Asian American contestant to compete on *Dancing with the Stars*, but she was the first Korean American celebrity to appear on the show. Cho's appearance marked a notable break from the way other Asian American celebrities had been represented or presented themselves on the show. Voted off the show after the third episode, Cho's appearance was short-lived; however, the experience of being a contestant in the competition became fodder for her stand-up comedy routines. Citing *Dancing with the Stars* as her parents' favorite television show, Cho's monologues for her 2010 stand-up comedy tour *Cho Dependent* included segments about her rivalry with Bristol Palin (who gained notoriety during the 2008 US presidential campaign as then pregnant teenage daughter of Sarah Palin, the Republican vice-presidential candidate), as well as the reaction of Cho's mother to Cho's participation on *Dancing with the Stars*. Cho would impersonate her mother, focusing primarily on her mother's anxiety over Cho's performance and whether or not Margaret would do well on the show.

In an interview with Joy Behar for the now defunct *Joy Behar: Say Anything!* talk show (2009–2011) Cho, mimicking her mother and speaking in an exaggerated Korean accent, attempts to reassure her daughter that it might be possible for Margaret to do well in the competition: "Oh Asians do really well on the show . . . there was Ohhh-no and Ya-ma-gu-chi . . ." in reference to Olympic gold medalist speed skater Apolo Anton Ohno, who won the Season 4 competition in 2007, and Kristi Yamaguchi, the Olympic gold medalist figure skater, who won the Season 6 competition in 2008. Cho's impersonations emphasize that her mother's encouraging words were always betrayed by the look of unbridled fear on her face. The joke being that Cho is no Olympian and the comedian's lifelong struggle with body image, alcohol, and drug abuse, in addition to self-described sexual promiscuity, is a far cry from Ohno and Yamaguchi's squeaky-clean image of being both model minorities and America's darlings on ice.

If Ohno and Yamaguchi represent the pinnacle of (Asian) American bodily achievement on the world stage and their triumph on *Dancing with the Stars* is but a shadow to their former Olympic glory, Cho's appearance represents Asian American failure. Noted for her criticism of body image and racism in Hollywood, her advocacy for gay rights, and her infamous imitations of her mother's blunt observations performed in an over-exaggerated Korean accent, Cho's comedy routines draw upon her self-professed status as an outsider to both the mainstream Hollywood film and television industry as well as the "mainstream" Asian American community. In the context of competition, Cho's public persona consists of a series of failures: failures due to racial and gender discrimination.

In 1994 Margaret Cho sat on the brink of Hollywood stardom when she was cast in the television sitcom *All-American Girl*, which was the first American television show (since the five-episode *Mr. T. and Tina* went off the air in 1976) to feature an Asian American family.[5] Cho was cast in title role of Margaret Kim, a character based on herself from her own stand-up comedy routines. Panned by Asian American critics, *All-American Girl* was accused of pandering in Asian stereotypes to align with the expectations that white American audiences had about Asian American families. In a failed attempt to resuscitate the show's falling ratings, network executives infamously hired "Asian consultants" to teach Cho how to be less Asian when the network thought Cho was "too Asian" and more Asian when she was thought to be "not Asian enough." The show was cancelled after one season.

The cancellation of *All-American Girl* and Cho's subsequent spiral into depression and drug addiction became the premise of Cho's one-woman touring show *I'm the One That I Want* (1999), which was later released as a film (2000) and a book (2001) of the same title. Part confessional, part rant, and filled with raunchy humor, *I'm the One That I Want* was an indictment of the mainstream media and its treatment of women—in particular, women whose bodies did not meet Hollywood standards of size and beauty. One of the central narratives in the show revolves around Cho's battle with her weight during the filming of *All-American Girl.* Cho suffered kidney failure after going on a crash diet to lose thirty pounds in two weeks after being told by producers that her face was "too round" and that she needed to lose weight in order to play herself. At the end of *I'm the One That I Want*, Cho concludes the performance with a manifesto for surviving the impossible standards required of women in the Hollywood entertainment industry:

> I'm not going to die. I'm not gonna die because my sitcom got cancelled. And I am not gonna die because some producer tried to take advantage of me. And I am not gonna die because some network executive thought I was fat. It's so wrong that women are asked to live up to this skinny idea that is totally unattainable. For me to be 10 pounds thinner is a full-time job, and I'm handing in my notice and walking out the door. I'm gonna succeed as myself, and I'm gonna stay here and hog the mic until the next Korean American, fag hag, shit starter, girl comic, trash talker comes out and takes my place. (*I'm The One That I Want*, 2000)

Feminist theorists Rachel Lee and Linda Mizejewski both cite Cho's defiant performance of a queer Asian American female sexuality as the key to the comedian's outsider status (Lee 2004; Mizejewski 2014, 146–149). Cho's graphic descriptions of marginalized sexual preferences, interwoven with anti-racist critique, situate the comedian outside the boundaries of what network television can tolerate and would become a standard feature of Cho's public persona (Mizejewski 2014, 146–149).

In 2008, Cho hosted *The Cho Show* on VH-1, in which she engages in activities similar to those seen on other reality television shows where the actors do seemingly everyday practices, such as wearing overly tight clothing, getting spray tans, and being tattooed on screen. On *The Cho Show*, Cho goes a step further and tries out anal bleaching and a series of other intimate procedures in which she puts her body, in all of its transgressive glory, on display (Mizejewski 2014, 153). Despite the antagonistic relationship to the Hollywood industry that Cho described in *I'm the One That I Want*, Cho's post-*All-American Girl* career has been built on her periodic reappearance on network and cable television in comedic roles. In 2001 she appeared as a version of herself as a foul-mouthed fashion show diva on HBO's *Sex and the City*, and more recently she was a regular cast member on Lifetime's *Drop Dead Diva*, playing a legal assistant named Terri Lee. In 2012 Cho received an Emmy nomination for her impersonation of the North Korean dictator Kim Jong-il on *30 Rock*, and in 2015 Cho was panned by the mainstream media for appearing as a similar North Korean character at the 2015 Golden Globes Award show. Cho's public image as an industry outsider is what makes Cho's appearance on *Dancing with the Stars* both strange and not strange at the same time. Cho has made a career out of the premise of failure, making her a perfect foil for other dancers on *Dancing with the Stars*.

In pairing professional ballroom dancers with B-list celebrities and athletes, *Dancing with the Stars* is just one of the many televised dance competitions that has appeared on network and cable television in the past decade. For the first time since *Dance Fever* went off the air in 1987, dancing and dance competition have proven to be a viable form of entertainment deserving of its own subgenre in the pantheon of reality television. While *Dance Fever* (1979–1987) featured musical and dance performances by professional pop artists, one of the show's key features was the dance contest in which couples performed disco routines in rapid-fire succession. Celebrity judges, such as comedians and television stars, would make generally positive comments about each couples' energy and costumes, or would make note if they thought a female dancer had nice legs, giving points without too much commentary about the actual dancing itself. Dancers would simply be introduced by their name and their occupation, and the winners would be announced without any significant fanfare.

The millennial version of reality television dance competitions, such as *So You Think You Can Dance*, *America's Best Dance Crew*, *Step it Up and Dance*, *Abby's Ultimate Dance Competition*, *Dance Moms*, *Dance Wars*, and *Your Mama Don't Dance*, are but a few of the numerous show titles that focus on the drama of watching aspiring dancers try to make it as professionals in the commercial dance industry. *Dancing with the Stars* offers the opportunity to see unlikely groupings of semi-famous or has-been celebrities struggling to learn Viennese waltzes, rumbas, and tangos. The appeal of the stars themselves range from the nostalgic curiosity of seeing a beloved star who has been out of the public eye for decades to the prurient curiosity of watching a celebrity who has been in the recent media spotlight for questionable reasons.

DEMOCRATIZING THE DANCE FLOOR

As ethnic studies scholar Brian Chung has argued in his essay on Asian Americans and *America's Best Dance Crew* (*ABDC*), reality television functions as a meta-narrative for capitalist self-improvement (Chung 2016, 120). In the case of *ABDC*, the mastery of choreographed hip-hop routines is the mode through which poor urban black youth can escape the naturalized poverty and violence of the (black) inner city. Chung demonstrates how the show itself, a carefully packaged dance commodity, functions as a meritocratic shot at success within a capitalist framework. This capitalist meritocracy is supposedly neutral, thus allowing deserving bodies to be recognized by hard work. As the predecessor to *ABDC, Dancing with the Stars* models the metanarrative of self-improvement. Whereas *ABDC* offers its contestants a shot at fame, *Dancing with the Stars* offers its fallen or semi-forgotten celebrities a chance at redemption. Cho's failure on *Dancing with the Stars* disrupted the genre's presumed narrative about self-improvement, reinvention, and redemption—not because she did not win, but because she championed her failure as the fault of the structure of the show itself. Cho lost, not because she did not try her best, but because there was no possible way that she could ever win as an outsider. The demands of the dancing were not accessible as promised, even though the structure of the show requires that someone loses and leaves the show each week.

While Chung clearly situated *ABDC* within a capitalist language of entrepreneurship and the accessibility of success, the accessibility of dancing itself presents an important theme. Reality television dance competitions have generated much discussion in dance studies in regard to the role of technology in making dance accessible to larger audiences—in this case, audiences whose only exposure to dance would be via network or cable television and the Internet (Cardinal 2013; Chung 2016; Philips-Fein 2011). Positivistic discussions are often couched in the overlapping rhetoric of accessibility and hope (Catton 2016; La Rocco 2010). Arguments for accessibility are usually framed in terms of the ease and the statistics of consumption. Accessibility assumes that the practice of watching dance is transformed into a habit, thereby creating a new audience for dance (Bauknecht 2009; La Rocco 2010; Opene 2014). It is also the belief that the audience for televised dance competition will become the new audience who will support and de-marginalize dance itself, and not just the dance competition format. Since the shows are narratively structured as competitions, the format offers up hope for an increasingly diverse body of participants. Anyone trained or untrained in any dance form can audition for *So You Think You Can Dance* (*SYTYCD*) such that the possibility of hope for a professional dance career is no longer limited to the conservatory-trained dancer and the company circuit.

It is through the televised dance competition that any dancer with prodigious amounts of facility can potentially win, regardless of his or her previous training (or lack thereof). Contestants can receive the training they need from professional coaches and choreographers on the show itself. By dialing in to vote for favorite dancers, the audience is given the power to judge, such that dance criticism is no longer the purview of experts. Anyone can set the terms for critique (Enli 2009; Enli and Ihlebæk 2011; Jenkins 2009; Reynolds 2010). The show represents the possible proliferation of employment opportunity for the dancers appearing on the show as a vehicle with the potential to carry dancers toward a horizon of limitless future employment opportunities. Media scholar Christine Quail, in "Anatomy of a Format: *So You Think You Can Dance Canada* and Discourses of Commercial Nationalism," examines how the importation of the American British *SYTYCD* is framed as a boon to Canadian dancers, who no longer have to go to the United States to "make it" as a professional dancer (Quail 2015).

Reality television dance competitions also represent a new venue for a whole plethora of dance careers as judges, choreographers, coaches, and commentators. Quail looks at the Canadian context in which the policies set forth by the Canadian Radio-Television and Telecommunications Commission require Canadian television stations to broadcast 50%–60% of Canadian programming. By hiring Canadian celebrities and creating new Canadian celebrities, *SYTYCD Canada* qualifies as a Canadian program, even though the program is an American-British import. The talent show format of *SYTYCD* lends itself to be certified as Canadian since the appeal of the format is that of opportunity for local dancers who no longer need to cross the border into the United States to seek fame and fortune (Quail 2015). That this limitless horizon of potential is open to everyone forms the seductive premise of the genre. Whether the potential of the genre lies in the welcoming of multi-ethnic participants or the strategic franchising of talent-based shows to international markets, reality television dance shows are imagined as a platform of opportunity (Boyd 2012; Catton 2016; Quail 2015). Publicity for the American National Broadcasting Company's (NBC) new *World of Dance* reality television show promises dancers of any age from any country a chance to win one million dollars (Wagmeister 2016). Dancer and pop star Jennifer Lopez, who is the executive director of *World of Dance*, is quoted as describing the show as having "an immeasurable impact on the dance community, to give all dancers an enormous platform where their dreams can be realized" (quoted in Wagmeister 2016).

Criticism of reality television dance shows centers around two ideas. One, like sociologist and sports scholar Mary Louise Adams's warnings about the costs of equating dance to sports, is the argument that the proliferation of dancing on television does not actually teach audiences anything about dance or how to watch dance (Adams 2005; Jenkins 2009).[6] Much of the commentary provided by a panel of judges focuses on showmanship or whether a dancer made any obvious errors. They rarely provide commentary about the actual choreography, or how dancers interpret a role beyond obvious expressions of emotion or identifiable character roles. The second criticism focuses on the problematic ways that reality television dance shows reinforce gender stereotypes. Dance scholar Mark Broomfield (2011) observes that, in an attempt to ensure the American public that dance presents a socially "safe" activity for heterosexual men to consume, male contestants on *SYTYCD* are required to perform compulsory heterosexuality. Male contestants who are perceived by the judges as performing non-normative or ambiguous masculinity are penalized and instructed to be stronger rather than graceful for their bodies to read clearly as masculine (Broomfield 2011). Broomfield's analysis of an exchange between Anthony Bryant, a contestant auditioning for *SYTYCD*, and Nigel Lythgoe, a judge, focuses on Lythgoe's insistence that Bryant was not masculine. In this case, Lythgoe defined masculinity as being strong in the sense of projecting a dominant male persona within a heterosexual context.

Broomfield (2011) identifies the requirement to perform compulsory, heterosexual masculinity as a form of policing the risks that dancing can enact on network television. It is usually the male contestants who perform non-normative masculinity that are targeted for gender policing, which is what makes Margaret Cho's performance of non-normative Asian American femininity on *Dancing with the Stars* worth noting. On the first episode of Season 11, the viewer is introduced to Margaret Cho and her partner Louis van Amstel as they prepare and train to perform a Viennese waltz.[7] In the behind-the-scenes interview, Cho tells the viewer, "the Viennese Waltz is a very ladylike dance, but I've always had a really hard time allowing myself to feel pretty." The viewer is immediately drawn into the substance of Cho's comedic persona, grounded in her struggle to redefine her self-image. Dancing, femininity, prettiness, and weight become inextricably tied together as she tells a story from her childhood: "When I was really a little girl I did take ballet and I loved it and then one day when I was dancing someone said 'you're the fattest ballerina.' I did not dance after that again." The interview suggests that Cho is taking the opportunity to reclaim a childhood dream and recover from the memory of dancing mired in the tyranny of an idealized ballet body.

Are We Champions, Too?

For their first round of competition, Cho and van Amstel perform a Viennese waltz to a cover of Queen's *We Are the Champions*. Standing on stage, Cho wears a black, high-necked, long-sleeved, dress, decorated with floral appliqués covering the bodice and the bottom half of her skirt. Attached to the back of Cho's dress is what looks like a long, pleated, gold, cape. In contrast, van Amstel wears a plain all-black suit. The couple box step in circles, moving from one end of the stage to the opposite diagonal before executing a series of spins in an open position. As the music builds toward the chorus, Cho and van Amstel spin themselves to the center of the stage. Cho scrunches up her face into a highly exaggerated and dramatically ferocious expression before she pauses in a moment of stillness. She then wraps the gold cape around her shoulders, grabs the two sticks sewn into the outside edges of the cape, and opens up the cape à la Loie Fuller.[8] As Cho opens up her golden cape, van Amstel rips off his suit jacket to reveal a black button-down shirt covered in floral appliqués to match Cho's dress.

The ensuing performance becomes a campy parody of the Viennese waltz, as Cho's expression grows increasingly histrionic as she attempts to wave her gold cape while spinning. Cho eventually gets tangled up in the fluttering cape and her partner comes to her dramatic rescue. The dance ends with van Amstel lowering Cho in an obviously affected dip from which Cho falls onto the floor. Bent over with her backside to the audience, Cho scrambles to stand up as if the floor were slippery. Cho recovers from her exaggerated fall before hitting one last triumphant pose with her partner.

The dance was obviously choreographed for its over-the-top comedic effect, and the judges' response to the performance focused on whether or not the comedy detracted from Cho's ability as a dancer. Reponses ranged from "What the hell was that,"[9] to "I think it was pushing it too far too soon," and "the Viennese waltz is an inappropriate dance, as far as I'm concerned, to bring all that comedic stuff into, I would have liked if you just did a dance." Perhaps what was disconcerting about Cho's comedic performance was the fact that she performed as a campy diva such that her feminine persona could not be categorized within the parameters of a recognizably heteronormative femininity. Dancing to a cover of Queen's gay anthem *We Are the Champions* (a song most commonly heard at mainstream sporting events like soccer and American football),[10] Cho is not graceful, sensual, or sexually available. She performs as the overly aggressive diva who dominates and renders her male dancing partner invisible and perhaps unnecessary. Cho's purposeful failure or refusal to perform submissive and/or sexual femininity properly made visible the gendered expectation within the dance form itself.

As Len Goodman, one of the judges, asserts, "the Viennese waltz is an inappropriate dance . . . to bring all that comedic stuff into . . ." (*Dancing with the Stars*, Season 11, Week 1, 2010). The waltz is not supposed to be funny. Fellow judge Carrie Ann Inaba tells Cho that it is supposed to be an expression of "inner beauty." A Viennese waltz demands that the couple generate a feeling of constant motion as the dancers engage in a continuous rotation around the dance floor. Halfway through the choreography, Cho shifts from being another celebrity contestant trying her best to do a respectable version of a Viennese waltz to becoming a character purposefully entangled in a cumbersome ballroom dance costume.

In stark contrast to Cho's seeming earnestness about reclaiming dance in the behind-the-scenes interview, the actual dancing makes fun of the genre. Cho ridicules the costume and does the dance wrong by rejecting the aesthetic of the movement quality and the ingrained heteronormative narrative of the partnering. Judge Bruno Torioli comments that, instead of appearing as if she is being led by her partner, Cho looks like she is about to eat somebody. In her analysis of Cho's *I'm the One That I Want* in "Where's My Parade," Rachel Lee (2004) borrows queer theorist Lauren Berlant's concept of "Diva Citizenship" to understand Cho's stage persona. Lee refers to Cho's use of a diva persona within comedic performance as a way to instruct audiences about national wrongs and oppressions. In *The Queen of America Goes to Washington City*, Berlant refers to Diva Citizenship as a series of acts: acts that do not necessarily change the world but mark moments of potential for women of color to engage in political activity by drawing attention to specific issues from a different point of view (Berlant 1997). Diva Citizenship is the "dramatic coup in a public sphere" by a person who does not hold any privilege (Berlant 1997, 223). Berlant refers to Diva Citizenship as the strategy by which women of color re-narrate what is happening as it is happening.

Whereas Diva Citizenship does not change a woman of color's social position or legal standing, it presents a disruption to how the narrative about her social or legal standing is told. She reveals the mechanisms through which she has arrived at a position of subjection. Lee argues that Cho couples Diva Citizenship, the retelling of what is happening, with white camp aesthetics to create her comedic persona in performance. Lee (2004, 115) refers to Cho's performance of Diva Citizenship (as opposed to Berlant's

Diva Citizenship) as the combination of the pedagogic and aesthetic functions that allows Cho to "discoordinate." In other words, Lee believes that Cho can mix and match women-of-color feminism and queer critique to generate queer-of-color critique.

Despite the judges' less than enthusiastic response to Cho and Van Amstel's comedic version of the Viennese waltz, the couple makes it to the next round of the competition. In the second episode, the driving theme behind Cho and van Amstel's backstory is their attempt to expunge Cho's propensity for comedy in her dancing. Van Amstel instructs Cho to tone down her facial expressions and gestures, and tells the television viewer that Cho needs to stop hiding behind her comedy and just dance. To "just dance" is to empty dance and dancing of any content other than the movement itself; thus dance becomes the vehicle through which Cho can potentially discover her true self. Cho tells the viewer, "this whole thing is not just about dancing. It's showing me that I can be vulnerable and be myself." Absented of any meaning, dancing becomes a matter of mastering a physicalized form, yet also a means to access and make available one's innermost feelings.

ASIAN AMERICANIZING THE DANCE FLOOR

The backstory constitutes an essential element of reality television dance competitions, and the dramatization of each "star's" struggle to master a new skill becomes a metaphor for overcoming some inner personal demon that comes with being a celebrity. Dancing presents an opportunity to embark on a new beginning, such as recharging a stagnant career or making a media comeback. It can also signal the positive recognition of overcoming legal problems, such as surviving a high-profile divorce, coming out of drug rehabilitation, or needing to combat generally bad publicity. Competitive ballroom dancing and its wholesome representations of heteronormative sexuality offer a safe and seemingly content-free context in which fallen and forgotten stars can stage a comeback on a clean slate. Unlike appearing in a new film or a new television series, no one expects a star to be a good ballroom dancer; therefore it is forgivable when someone is sincere and tries, but dances badly. When a celebrity turns out to be coordinated and musical, it is considered an unexpected, but ultimately nice surprise.

Cho competed against celebrities such as David Hasselhoff of *Knight Rider* (1982–1986) and *Baywatch* (1989–1999) fame; Florence Henderson, who played Mrs. Brady on *The Brady Bunch* (1969–1974); Jennifer Grey from *Dirty Dancing* (1987); singers Michael Bolton, Brandy, and Kyle Massey; athletes Rick Fox and Kurt Warner; reality television personalities Mike "The Situation" Sorrentino from *Jersey Shore* and Audrina Partridge from *The Hills*; and Bristol Palin. In *Cho Dependent*, Cho's off-screen rivalry with Bristol Palin centered on Cho's assertion that the Palins were using *Dancing with the Stars* as a platform to erase the hypocrisy of conservative politics around abstinence and sexuality. *Dancing with the Stars* would be the stage upon which Bristol Palin could redirect her image from that of an immoral and unwed teen mom into a wholesome heterosexual adult woman. This redirection sits in contrast with Cho, who struggles between wanting to be successful on the show, but also trying to resist being sexually normalized by *Dancing with the Stars*.

Since much of Cho's public persona concerns her struggle with self-acceptance, *Dancing with the Stars* would be the public arena in which Cho would reclaim a lost childhood dream to be a dancer and to be skillful. Cho tells the viewer, "That's what's so amazing to discover. This whole thing that I'm actually a dancer. The goal with the jive is that I don't have to make jokes about myself. That I can truly dance." The act of dancing is loaded. On the one hand, there is a desire for dancing to just simply be dancing. As opposed to writing a show or cracking a joke, dancing is absented of any meaning and is positioned as a difficult skill that can exist unto itself in a contextual vacuum. Of course this is not the case, and if we borrow the Aristotelian concept that nature abhors a vacuum, dancing cannot remain meaningless. On the *George Lopez Show*, Cho imitates her mother telling herself (Margaret), "I've never seen you move so kickly [quickly]," suggesting that Margaret's mother usually views her own daughter as slow-moving, lazy, and physically inept. This is part of Cho's stage persona—that of the chubby girl who does not fit in. She continues, "This is the hardest thing Mommy has ever been through, this is so hard, Mommy has such hard time. I have never had such hard time. This most difficult thing Mommy has ever done . . . ah ah . . . this so hard. And . . . and . . . Mommy live through war" (*Lopez Tonight* 2011). This last phrase, delivered in a completely deadpan manner, marks the absurdity of watching someone compete on *Dancing with the Stars* as a comparable experience to surviving the Korean War.

The temporal and physical distance between the commercial context of *Dancing with the Stars* and the circumstances of the Cho family's presence in the United States is brought together and reminds the viewer that Margaret Cho is Korean American. Any investment in how well Cho dances is momentarily framed in relation to the ultimate narrative of Asian immigrant survival: surviving and escaping from a US war fought in Asia. Interestingly, Margaret Cho's backstory on the show never uses her family history as a way to generate interest, but focuses instead on her weight and her struggle to accept her own body. Perhaps the success of Yamaguchi and Ohno on earlier seasons and Carrie Ann Inaba's constant presence on the show as a judge makes Cho's Asianess less noteworthy than the fact that Cho represents an Asian body seldom acknowledged on network television.

Unlike Inaba, Cho does not look like a Hollywood starlet. Before appearing on reality television, Carrie Ann Inaba was one of the original Fly Girls who performed hip-hop routines on the sketch comedy television series *In Living Color* (1990). While the Fly Girls were notable for being an all-female multi-ethnic cast, Inaba later played a well-trod Asian female stereotype as one half of the giggling, pony-tailed, micro-skirted, backpack-wearing Japanese twins Fook Yu and Fook Mi in *Austin Powers in Goldmember* (2002). In comparison to the backstories told about Apolo Anton Ohno and Kristi Yamaguchi, which focus on the translation of the athletes' discipline and competitiveness into expressivity, Cho breaks down during rehearsal when overwhelmed by the emotional and physical demands of dance training. Inaba, Yamaguchi, and Ohno are represented as wildly successful, hard working, and perfectly normal. In Season 6, Yamaguchi is seen as living in post-Olympic domestic bliss with her husband and two children. Ohno in Season 4 finds time to joke around with his dance partner during rehearsal, all the while training for the 2008 World Championship speed skating competition, which he would go on to win. For Yamaguchi and Ohno, competing on *Dancing with the Stars* is but another opportunity to excel, another contest to win. Winning is a matter of training, discipline, focus, and putting in the number of hours required to master the required task at hand.

Not only are Yamaguchi and Ohno "normal" in their exceptionalism, but Yamaguchi in particular is the good Asian girl. In Season 6, after Yamaguchi and her partner Mark Ballas dance a tango, the judges praise the former Olympian for her technique, but criticize her for lack of emotion. Carrie Ann Inaba tells Yamaguchi, "I don't feel much when you dance," and Bruno Tonioli describes Yamaguchi's dancing as "sharp, clean, clear, precise, and always delivered to the extreme precision." Tonioli tells Yamaguchi outright that he wants to see "more lust" and tells her "I want you to be a dirty girl" (*Dancing with the Stars*, Season 6, Episode 3, 2008). The characterization of Yamaguchi as precise, but without feeling, forms the subject of American studies scholar Grace Wang's (2010) study on Asian American participation on reality television shows such as *Top Chef* and *Project Runway*, in which Asian American success is tempered with the characterization of Asian American contestants as being robot-like and lacking in creativity. Using David Morley and Kevin Robins's concept of *techno-orientalism*, Wang (2010, 407) refers to the Asian "technical robot" as a stock character on reality television.

Derived from Edward Said's (1979) work on orientalism as the simultaneous fascination and disgust with the imagined geographic space known as the Orient, techno-orientalism describes the Western management of fear over the technological advances coming out of Asia. If orientalism justified Western interventions to bring Asia out of its ahistorical past, techno-orientalism is the response to the fear that Asian technology will enable Asian economic and cultural domination over the United States. Techno-orientalism emerged as a popular theme in science fiction in the 1980s when Japan was blamed for a failing US automotive industry. During the energy crisis that began in 1979, American consumers looked to the smaller, more fuel-efficient automobiles made by Japanese companies, as opposed to the large gas guzzlers sold by American companies. Films like *Blade Runner* (1982) envisioned a technologically advanced and dystopian future in which the skyline of Los Angeles has become dominated by Asian cultural references. Closely aligned with the model minority stereotype associated with the hard-working and diligent immigrants, techno-orientalism presents the threat that the United States will be taken over by unfeeling (Asian) robot-like humans and their superior technology (Morley and Robins 1995; Roh 2015).

Hung Huynh and Chloe Dao, respective winners of *Top Chef Season 3* and *Project Runway Season 2*, were praised for their flawless technique, but they ran the risk of being too good and possessing too much technical skill, which could get in the way of being passionate and creative. For Huynh and Dao, participating in reality television would teach them to become more "American" by becoming more creative. To become more "American," one must become an individual rather than a part of a group, in this case Asian immigrants. Technique with no creativity is considered a burden, and this new-found freedom from the burden of technique is of course an obvious metaphor for the freedom and liberty offered by the capitalistic ideals of American democracy. In becoming less Asian and robot-like, one can become more American and more human. Presented as the consummate Asian woman, Yamaguchi is petite, proficient, precise, and emotionally passive. She is the good girl who will return to the competition in the following week after having worked diligently on being more expressive. Cultivating a more expressive performance style is simply another skill that Yamaguchi successfully masters as she moves through the rounds of competition. Yamaguchi's mastery of task-like skills is not unlike the way she would have advanced through the rounds of an ice-skating competition during the prime of her career.

In contrast, Cho's backstory is fraught with her desire to be a good dancer while resisting the requirement to perform heteronormative Asian femininity. Cho's task for the second week of competition is to master the jive by fighting back the urge to pout, gesticulate, and over-emote, and she must reign in her bodily excesses. With her hair styled in tastefully loose curls and her tattooed arms hidden under a loose fitting, long-sleeved, zebra print dress with pink fringe, Cho looks conventionally feminine and pretty as she and van Amstel perform a straight-forward jive. Whereas Yamaguchi was criticized for being too precise and emotionless, Cho is advised by the judges to be more "toned" and "tight" and to watch out for over-the-top facial expressions, to which Cho replies, "that's just what my face is like, I can't help it." Even though Cho is like the bad student who talks back to the judges, she and van Amstel make it through to the next round (*Dancing with the Stars*, Season 11, Week 2, 2010).

By the time Cho is interviewed for the third round of competition, she is on tour and is incorporating her experience of being on *Dancing with the Stars* into her stand-up routine. Cho's arms are covered in full-sleeve tattoos, and she is loud as she breaks down, and has a meltdown. In rehearsal Cho stumbles, gets visibly exhausted, cries, and just cannot seem to get the steps right. Incorporated into her behind-the-scenes interviews are clips from her stand-up routine, with material that foreshadows failure as a potential eventuality. The possibility of winning is too loaded with meaning because there are too many expectations and too much pressure to make winning feasible. The palpable dissonance between wanting acceptance by doing well on the show and wanting to resist the structure of the show via dancing an alternative narrative is felt most deeply when Cho is voted off the show at the end of the third episode. This is in marked contrast with Apolo Anton Ohno's apprearance on Season 4. When Ohno is told to turn out his foot or to look sexier, Ohno does it immediately without difficulty. During the season finale that features a video clip of Ohno and his partner Julian Hough's four-month journey as contestants on the show, there is no angst, conflict, or self-doubt. At the end of the video, Hough proclaims that Ohno is a dancer.

HAVING PRIDE WHILE BEING CRITICIZED

For the third week of the competition, Cho and van Amstel perform the samba to Barry Manilow's *Copacabana*. With Cho in a rainbow-colored, flapper-style, fringe dress, and a giant yellow headdress and van Amstel in a simple blue jumpsuit, the dance begins. The routine is cheerful and energetic and, most interestingly, it lacks any kind of sexual chemistry between the two dancers. When Cho does attempt to affect an appropriately sexy "come hither" look, the effect is overly exaggerated. Halfway through the dance, Cho starts to look tired and begins to lose her place in the music and the rhythm of the samba. The dance ends as Cho and van Amstel are covered in a shower of rainbow colored streamers exploding from the ceiling (*Dancing with the Stars*, Season 11, Week 3, 2010).

During the judges' comments, Len Goodman tells Cho that he could not figure out what the dance was about, to which Cho responds, "the story is about having pride while people are criticizing you." Bruno Tonioli enthuses, "Darling, I praise you for waving your rainbow flag. Keep waving it girl. Good for you." Both Tonioli and Carrie Ann Inaba tell Cho that they appreciate her energy, but that the dancing itself ultimately falls flat. Looking disappointed as she receives comments for being off the rhythm of the music, not presenting a clear narrative, and losing control, Cho responds by declaring the routine as "the gayest thing that I think has ever happened on the show. I was so exited, I could not contain myself." Cho commits the biggest televised dance competition no-no and forces audiences to acknowledge the very thing that everyone is afraid of: that dancing, and in particular ballroom dancing with its sparkly outfits, is gay.

Cho's love–hate relationship with Hollywood manifests in her repeated attempts to comment on the structure of Hollywood from Hollywood itself. In the case of *Dancing with the Stars*, Cho attempts to critique the reality television dance competition from within the show. It is clear that Cho is uncomfortable with the format of the show in which the contestants are supposed to passively accept the judges' criticism. As Cho and van Amstel await their scores, Cho tries to recuperate the dance by refocusing the viewer's attention on the content of the dance. When asked by then co-host Brooke Burke-Charvet on whether she would reprise her role as a funny girl, Cho responds, "Our story is serious. We want to celebrate pride, we wanted to show ourselves off. It's a tough time for the gay community, a lot of gay teenagers have committed suicide, and we want this to end now."

Cho's attempt to queer ballroom dancing by associating their routine with gay pride fell flat as van Amstel told the press that they had intended to tell a story based on Cho's personal experience of being bullied as a child for being overweight and surviving to become the woman that she is. In a post-show interview with popeater.com, van Amstel claims that the moment Cho's dress was singled out as a representation of gay pride, the dance lost its potential to express more complex emotions around the experience of depression and having suicidal feelings (Smith 2014). Van Amstel's objections to Cho's choice to refer to the dance routine as a literal representation of gay pride was subsequently excerpted by other sites, citing van Amstel as stating, "That was not my message. Maybe it was Margaret's message, but not mine. The minute it was about gay pride, I knew we were gone. I knew it. But if I would have said something then and there, I would have looked like [a jerk]" (Donnelly 2010). In excerpting van Amstel's comments, he comes across as either homophobic or self-loathing and closeted. Sarah Nigel of queerty.com accuses van Amstel of thinking that if one ignores homophobia and anti-gay bullying, the problem will go away (Nigel 2010).[11]

Whether or not Margaret Cho was in fact heavy-footed and off-count, as described by Bruno Tonioli, was beside the point, as Cho attempted to make a statement about the heteronormative structure of ballroom dancing and of the show itself. On the same episode, Jennifer Grey and Derek Hough's samba routine featured a story in which Hough, dressed in a schoolboy uniform, is seduced by a sexy schoolteacher played by Grey. Goodman responds to the dance by telling the couple that the story was "very very clever," while Tonioli tells Grey, "You are the sexy mistress of cougar town." In comparison to Grey and Hough's routine, Cho and van Amstel's samba was chaste and did not exhibit the kind of overt display of sexuality portrayed in Grey and Hough's explicit schoolboy-teacher fantasy. The lack of a clear heteronormative narrative in Cho and van Amstel's dancing was supplanted with what could only be its opposite: gay pride. Within the logic of the show, if the dance did not portray an explicit heterosexual coupling, it must then be gay in order to be recognizable. Van Amstel claimed that once it became clear that his and Cho's dance could not read as a story about Cho's personal journey toward self-acceptance, Cho took whatever opportunity was presented to her. Van Amstel reports that Cho told him, "You have that one moment where you can take a stand and make a message and it's powerful and it will be remembered" (Crook 2010).

In many ways, Cho's declaration sounds similar to Dan Savage's It Gets Better Project. Savage, who is most well known as the author of "Savage Love," a relationship and sex advice column, began the It Gets Better Project in which mostly white, middle-class adults and celebrities tell queer adolescents to be proud of themselves and that things will turn out OK. Critics of It Gets Better have pointed to the normalizing narratives of the project in which marginalized youth are told that they will one day achieve the same kind of economic success and social/familial acceptance that Savage and the other celebrities posting their messages on YouTube have achieved. Performance scholar Tavio Nyong'o points out that for certain groups of people who are gender non-conforming, things may not get better. Indeed, queer theorist Jaspir Puar warns that it is possible for things to get worse (Nyong'o 2010; Puar 2010).[12]

Ultimately, Cho and van Amstel receive the lowest score of all the couples and are eliminated from the competition. While Cho failed to remain in the competition, Yamaguchi and Ohno were brought back to the show as guests to celebrate the 200th episode of Dancing with the Stars. Yamaguchi and Ohno returned as team captains for the team dance competition. Responsible for motivating their respective teams and getting them into shape, Yamaguchi and Ohno are the winners who are now in the position to model the normalcy of success for the remaining contestants. In many ways, Cho's appearance on *Dancing with the Stars* marks an important moment in which an Asian American character is neither a technical superstar nor a particularly endearing failure.[13] Chaffing against her failure, Cho leaves the show in tears as she makes a self-affirming statement that she is a "real dancer." Cho's failure is all the more tragic given that she cites Yamaguchi's and Ohno's success on the show as the precedent for her own participation as an Asian American celebrity contestant.

Could it be that Cho's failure was too self-consciously politicized, in that the failure appears too orchestrated? What was supposed to be readable as Cho's individual failure becomes unreadable when she attempts to transpose the politics of her backstory to the structure of *Dancing with the Stars* itself. Cho's bad girl persona, the bad Asian American subject, falls apart as she leaves the show in tears in an awkward attempt to reclaim her status as a bad subject. Cho's attempt to queer the show with the presence of her bodily excess in the choreography, and in her resistance to the bodily discipline required by the dance, fails to read as the rebellious bad Asian American subject as she comes across as being disappointed for not winning.

Maybe, in this case, Cho is neither a good nor bad dancer but a mediocre one. The model of success and failure that sets up Asian American failure as anything less than outright winning is too limiting. Indeed, Cho has managed to parlay a series of failures into a full-fledged career as a comedian and television personality. The success of Cho's failures tells us that such narrow definitions of Asian American success, failure, and analyses that depend on reading success or failure as a direct index to a particular experience must at times give way to consideration of the image of success or failure within the material properties of the performance—whether the dance, the dance competition show, or the stand-up routine—that follows.

NOTES

1. *Dancing with the Stars* airs on ABC in the United States and CTV/CTV Two in Canada. *Dancing with the Stars (US Season 11)* premiered on September 10, 2010. See Chung (2016, 117–118).

2. For a critique of Siegel's essay, see Wong (2016).

3. Nguyen is critical of the celebration of the "bad subject" and argues that the idealization of the "bad subject" as a politically radical subject reproduces a binary in which Asian Americans are categorized as either "bad subjects" or model minorities. Nguyen's critique centers around the idea that the idealization of the bad subject forecloses the political potential of Asian American success when Asian American success is construed as model minority behavior.

4. The mirror ball trophy is literally a mirror-covered ball on top of a gold colored base with the words "Dancing with the Stars" emblazoned on the ball. All celebrity contestants are paid a $125,000 signing bonus and earn additional bonuses for each additional week that they remain on the show.

5. *Mr. T. and Tina* is an American television sitcom that premiered on ABC in 1976. Pat Morita played the main character of Taro Takahashi. The show was cancelled after the fourth episode.

6. The format of the reality television talent show is designed to generate specific feelings about products. Jenkins's analysis of *American Idol* could be applied to *America's Best Dance Crew* in which the serialization of drama is more important than the actual content of the dancing.

7. Each celebrity contestant is paired with a professional ballroom dancer. Louis van Amstel is a Dutch-American ballroom dance champion who joined the cast of *Dancing with the Stars* after retiring from competitive ballroom dancing.

8. Loie Fuller is an American dancer who pioneered the manipulation of silk fabric and light to create improvisational dances such as the *Serpentine Dance* (1891).

9. Bruno Tonioli stands up and screams "What the hell was that?" *Dancing with the Stars*, Season 11, Week 1. 2010.

10. "We Are the Champions" was originally released in 1977 and was most often heard at sporting events. Most listeners did not consider the song a gay anthem until 1992, when a group of high school students at Sacred Heart High School in Clifton, New Jersey, were denied permission by the school principal to play the song during graduation. The school principal rejected the request on the grounds that Freddie Mercury had died from an AIDS-related illness. The denial of the request prompted the students to flood local radio stations with requests to play the song. The story became national news and students from other high schools joined in the protest, making it the number one most requested song. In response, Hollywood Record re-released the single. See Phyllis Stark (1992).

11. Columnist Sarah Nigel of queerty.com objects to van Amstel's objection to Cho's pronouncement during the show that the dance was about gay pride.

12. Critics of Savage's It Gets Better Project have focused on the recurring narrative that queer youth will one day be able to enter into the American mainstream and achieve the American dream of economic success and social/familial acceptance.

13. In 2004 William Hung became an unexpected celebrity after his tone-deaf rendition of Ricky Martin's "She Bangs" for *American Idol* was televised on the Fox network. See Kristin M. Barton (2013) for a discussion of *schadenfreude*. *Schadenfreude* is joy derived from witnessing someone else's downfall or failure. Barton's empirical study of *American Idol* and *Dancing with the Stars* demonstrates that the desire to experience *schadenfreude* by watching contestants humiliate themselves plays a role in why people watch talent-based reality television shows.

References

Adams, Mary Louise. 2005. "'Death to the Prancing Prince': Effeminacy, Sport Discourse and the Salvation of Men's Dancing." *Body and Society* 11(4): 630–686.

Barton, Kristin M. 2013. "Why We Watch Them Sing and Dance: The Uses and Gratifications of Talent-Based Reality Television." *Communication Quarterly.* 61(2): 217–235.

Bauknecht, Sara. 2009. "Popularity of TV Dance Shows Inspires New Interest in Ballroom, Salsa." *Pittsburgh Post-Gazette*, November 23. http://www.post-gazette.com/pg/09327/1015578-51.stm#ixzz0YTK8VsKd. Accessed August 15, 2015.

Berlant, Lauren. 1997. "Notes on Diva Citizenship." In *The Queen of America Goes to Washington City: Essays on Sex and Citizenship*, 221–246. Durham, NC: Duke University Press.

Boyd, Jade. 2012. "'Hey, We're from Canada but We're Diverse, Right?': Neoliberalism, Multiculturalism, and Identity on *So You Think You Can Dance Canada*." *Critical Studies in Media Communication* 29(4): 259–274.

Broomfield, Mark. 2011. "Policing Masculinity and Dance Reality Television: What Gender Non-Conformity Can Teach Us in the Classroom." *Journal of Dance Education* 11(4): 124–128.

Cardinal, Marita K. 2013. "Deciphering Dance in Reality Television: The Good, the Questionable, and the Unconscionable." *Journal of Physical Education, Recreation, and Dance* 84(1): 7–10.

Catton, Pia. 2016. "TV Dance Contestants Find Their Footing on Broadway." *The Wall Street Journal*, July 18. http://www.wsj.com/articles/tv-dance-contestants-find-their-footing-on-broadway-1468888562. Accessed August 4, 2016.

Chung, Brian Su-Jen. 2016. "'Started in the Streets . . .' Criminalizing Blackness and the Performance of Asian American Entrepreneurship on *America's Best Dance Crew, Season 1*." In *Contemporary Directions in Asian American Dance*, edited by Yutian Wong, 117–142. Madison: University of Wisconsin Press.

Crook, Phillip B. 2010. "Catching Up with Louis van Amstel." *Out Magazine*, October 17. http://www.out.com/entertainment/television/2010/10/17/catching-louis-van-amstel. Accessed December 8, 2015.

Donnelly, Matt. 2010. "Louis van Amstel: Margaret Cho's Rainbow Ruined Our 'Dancing with the Stars' Parade." *Los Angeles Times*, October 15. http://latimesblogs.latimes.com/gossip/2010/10/dancing-with-the-stars-louis-van-amstel-margaret-cho-gay.html. Accessed August 1, 2014.

Enli, Gunn Sara. 2009. "Mass Communication Tapping into Participatory Culture: Exploring *Strictly Come Dancing* and *Britain's Got Talent*." *European Journal of Communication* 24(4): 481–493.

Enli, Gunn Sara, and Karoline A. Ihlebæk. 2011. "'Dancing with the Audience': Administrating Vote-Ins in Public and Commercial Broadcasting." *Media, Culture, and Society* 33: 953–962.

Jenkins, Henry. 2009. "Buying into American Idol: How We are Being Sold on Reality TV." In *Reality TV: Remaking Television Culture*, edited by Susan Murray and Laurie Ouellette, 343–362. New York: New York University Press.

La Rocco, Claudia. 2010. "TV Gives Dance a Boost, and That's Good Right?" *New York Times*, June 11. http://www.nytimes.com/2010/06/13/arts/dance/13tvdance.html. Accessed December 1, 2015.

Lee, Rachel. 2004. "Where's My Parade." *The Drama Review* 48(2): 108–132.

Mizejewski, Linda. 2014. *Pretty/Funny: Women Comedians and Body Politics*. Austin: University of Texas Press.

Morley, David, and Ken Robins. 1995. *Spaces of Identity: Global Media, Electronic Landscapes, and Cultural Boundaries*. London; New York: Routledge.

Nguyen, Viet Thahn. 2002. *Race and Resistance: Literature and Politics in Asian America*. Oxford: Oxford University Press.

Nigel, Sarah. 2010. "Dancing with the Scars: How Come *Dance with the Stars* Louis Van Amstel Has Such a Problem with Calling Out Anti-Gay Bullies." *Queerty*, October 15. http://www.queerty.com/how-come-dancings-louis-van-amstel-has-such-a-problem-with-calling-out-anti-gay-bullies-20101015. Accessed December 1, 2015.

Nyong'o, Tavia. 2010. "School Daze." *Bully Bloggers* (blog), September 30. https://bullybloggers.wordpress.com/2010/09/30/school-daze/. Accessed December 8, 2015.

Opene, Nneka. 2014. "Reality TV's Impact on the Dance World." *Atomic Ballroom,* October 28. http://www.atomicballroom.com/blog/2014/10/28/reality-tvs-impact-on-the-dance-world/. Accessed December 1, 2015.

Philips-Fein, Jesse M. 2011. "How We Dance: Helping Students Unpack the Impact of Dance Television Shows." *Journal of Dance Education* 11(4): 134–136.

Puar, Jasbir. 2010. "In the Wake of It Gets Better." *The Guardian,* November 10. http://www.theguardian.com/commentisfree/cifamerica/2010/nov/16/wake-it-gets-better-campaign. Accessed December 8, 2015.

Quail, Christine. 2015. "Anatomy of a Format: *So You Think You Can Dance Canada* and Discourses of Commercial Nationalism." *Television and New Media* 16(5): 472–489.

Roh, David. 2015. *Techno-Orientalisms: Imagining Asia in Speculative Fiction, History, and Media.* New Brunswick, NJ: Rutgers University Press.

Reynolds, Dee. 2010. "'Glitz and Glamour' or Atomic Rearrangement: What Do Dance Audiences Want?" *Dance Research* 28(1): 19–35.

Said, Edward. 1979. *Orientalism.* New York: Vintage Books.

Siegel, Lee. 2012. "Rise of the Tiger Nation." *Wall Street Journal,* October 27. http://www.wsj.com/articles/SB10001424052970204076204578076613986930932. Accessed December 6, 2015

Smith, Stacy Jenel. 2014. "Louis van Amstel on Margaret Cho's Rainbow Statement: 'I had a breakdown.'" October 14. http://www.popeater.com/2010/10/14/louis-van-amstel-margaret-cho-dancing-rainbow/. Accessed August 1, 2014.

Stark, Phyllis. 1992. "Hollywood Record Hails Older Queen Product: Brings New Audience to Classic Hits via Rereleases." *Billboard,* July 25, 8.

Wagmeister, Elizabeth. 2016. "NBC Greenlights Reality Dance Competition Series from Jennifer Lopez." *Variety,* July 19. http://variety.com/2016/tv/news/world-of-dance-jennifer-lopez-competition-reality-nbc-1201817499/. Accessed August 1, 2016.

Wang, Grace. 2010 "A Shot at Half-Exposure: Asian Americans in Reality TV Shows." *Television New Media* 11(5): 404–427.

Wong, Yutian. 2016 "Introduction: Issues in Asian American Dance Studies." In *Contemporary Directions in Asian American Dance,* edited by Yutian Wong, 3–25. Madison: University of Wisconsin Press.

Audiovisual Sources

Dancing with the Stars, Season 11, Week 1. "Margaret Cho and Louis van Amstel–Viennese Waltz. September 27, 2010. Dailymotion video, 6:02. Posted by "Codebear," November 21, 2014. http://www.dailymotion.com/video/x2ap8ma_margaret-cho-louis-van-amstel-viennese-waltz_people. Accessed December 1, 2015.

Dancing with the Stars, Season 11, Week 2. "Margaret Cho and Louis van Amstel–Jive," September 27, 2010. Dailymotion video, 5:34. Posted by "Codebear2," November 21, 2014. http://www.dailymotion.com/video/x2aqvy4_margaret-cho-louis-van-amstel-jive_people. Accessed December 1, 2015.

Dancing with the Stars, Season 6, Week 3. "Kristi Yamaguchi and Mark Ballas–Tango–Week 3," March 31, 2008. Dailymotion video, 5:51. Posted by "Codebear2," December 3, 2014. http://

www.dailymotion.com/video/x2bm643_kristi-yamaguchi-mark-ballas-tango-week-3_
people. Last Accessed December 1, 2015.

Dancing with the Stars, Season 11, Week 3. "Margaret Cho and Louis van Amstel–Samba,"
October 4, 2010. Dailymotion video, 6:42. Posted by "Codebear 2," December 14, 2014.
http://www.dailymotion.com/video/x2ci3i9_margaret-cho-louis-van-amstel-samba_
people. Accessed December 1, 2015.

I'm the One That I Want. 2001. Produced by Lorene Machdo. Directed by Lionel Coleman.
New York: Cho Taussig Productions. VHS.

Lopez Tonight. "Margaret Cho Disses Bristol and Sarah Palin on Lopez Tonight 2/8/11."
YouTube video, 8:38. Posted by "The MRGM13," February 9, 2011. https://www.youtube.
com/watch?v=DdPJQGHl9a8. Accessed March 13, 2017.

CHAPTER 21

....

LOSS OF FACE

Intimidation, Derision, and Failure in the Hip-Hop Battle

....

SHERRIL DODDS

There's people who feel so good about what they do and they're confident, they make a mistake and they get up and you can see the disappointment in their face. And then once that happens, the other person reads that. But the movement was dead on, but you just gave it away because of your face. So you know your confidence is down, that opponent knows that your confidence is now lost, so they take advantage of that.

—Viazeen[1]

ALTHOUGH hip-hop[2] battles produce "winners" who may be rewarded with cash prizes, trophies, or "bragging rights," these competitions also produce "losers" who fail to make it through to the next round or win the overall contest. As b-boy Viazeen describes, such failure plays out as a "loss of face" in the moment of defeat. A loss of face can be taken literally to mean a loss of facial control, and metaphorically to suggest a feeling of humiliation, and both coexist in the battle context. Notably, many dancers recall their early battle experiences through tales of humiliation, embarrassment, and loss:[3]

So he came at me and I was so frightened, I was so timid, I was so scared. But, he gave me my credit after the battle was over. I lost, of course, but he just educated me on what you should do in a battle: your presence in a battle, different ways and different approaches as to how to go about battling, different ethics of a battle, like burn moves. (Sk8z)[4]

When I went in, I did somethin' and I dislocated my arm, and then they had to stop the whole jam. . . . They called an ambulance and like it was super embarrassing. . . . I was like, "Alright, I need to get better, 'cause this is like my lowest point that I ever been in. So, there's no place but up." So, now when I see a battle, like I really wanna like participate in a battle, no matter what. And like now I'm just trainin' to get better. (Jonathan Gene)[5]

This had prize money, this had judges, like, experienced dancers that are battling. . . . I was feeling really nervous and doubtful of myself because, you know, I've had limited training compared to the people who were battling there. . . . Even though I didn't win, it was a victory for me I guess, 'cause I actually got to participate in a battle and, you know, show off what I can do. (Béa Martin)[6]

I'd been to this event a couple times and I'd never battled. I'd never really had the chutzpah to do it. So I finally just signed my name up and battled this guy, my good friend, and he destroyed me. But that was my first battle. And I remember it being like a very fun experience, but also the trepidation was very strong because if you haven't danced before, it's a lot about self-image until you get on the dance floor, and you realize it's more about the movement. (Steve Believe)[7]

Although these dancers reference feelings of anxiety, they also allude to matters of private pleasure, self-education, and personal victory. Yet even seasoned dancers who have won multiple contests continue to experience a degree of tension as they enter into the battle cypher:[8]

right before I know I'm going out, all this adrenaline just builds up and . . . I start sweating and I start shaking and I go out and I do my thing, you know? But still, like this anxiety still happens. (Macca)[9]

I'm nervous every single time. And there's always this thing of, "What am I gonna do? What am I gonna do? Okay. I'm gonna do these three things, or I'm gonna start with this." And then, there's a moment of somehow I'm in the middle, I don't remember doing that, and there might be a moment of clarity, like "Wow, what am I doing out here!" (Metal) (Figure 21.1)[10]

In spite of anxiety, nerves, and loss, many hip-hop dancers commit to battling as part of their dance art, and failure to win represents only a temporary condition. For example, dancer Lil' O[11] states, "Even if my opponent beat me, I was still like, 'That was awesome. That was great, let's do it again. Next time I will beat you.'" The hip-hop battle produces a complex dialectic as dancers must approach these contests with bravura, confidence, and a desire to win; yet many experience failure, loss, and error. As Viazeen observes at the beginning of this chapter, the face plays a significant role both in strategizing toward victory and in revealing loss. All-styles dancer Danzel[12] asserts, "I feel like the face reacts before the body does," and popper Sk8z comments, "The face is the number one giveaway. The face is always supposed to remain calm, or remain cool, regardless of what's goin' on."

Overall, a broad range of facial expressions appears in hip-hop battles. I have written elsewhere that specific hip-hop styles are traditionally associated with certain facial expressions (Dodds 2016). For instance, breaking tends to employ "mean mugging" and locking plays with wide eyes and goofy smiles. Yet I also identify a slippage whereby the

FIGURE 21.1. B-boy Metal at Second Sundae, November 2015.

Photography by Ed Newton.

generic delineations fail to hold (Dodds 2016). What I would note, however, is that, particularly with seasoned dancers, the face is kept in check. Indeed, experienced dancers use their faces choreographically and expressively to articulate their style and musicality, their knowledge of the dance's foundations, and their attitude to their opponent, the audience, and the judges. Thus the face is purposefully designed, held, and manipulated throughout the course of a round. Yet, as I will show, there are moments when this capacity to engineer facial expression fails and we witness a loss of face.

The importance of the face in hip-hop battles bears little surprise, given the centrality of the face in all social interactions. Within a Western paradigm, the head and face occupy a dominant position in the hierarchical organization of the body through engendering notions of morality, intellect, and leadership (Brophy 1946; Coates 2012; Magli 1989; Vigarello 1989). We come to know the social world through four of the sensory organs located on the face (sight, hearing, taste, and smell), and we breathe, consume, and verbalize through the face (McNeill 1998). Consequently, we rely on the face to read expression, emotion, and identity (Kesner 2007). Although scholars have engaged in fervent debate as to whether the face depicts innate, universal expressions (Darwin 1872; Ekman and Rosenberg 1997) or socially constructed looks and appearances

(Kemper 1981; Lutz 1986; Neu 1987), as a cultural theorist invested in dance I align my thinking with dance anthropologists Brenda Farnell (1999) and Deirdre Sklar (1991) to suggest that movement, which includes facial expression, can only be rendered meaningful by understanding the cultural context and social interactions in which it occurs.[13] I would further argue that within the field of dance, the face is not left to chance; as I have suggested in the preceding paragraph, the face moves according to the codes and conventions of different hip-hop styles. Indeed, several scholars observe how the face operates choreographically across different popular dance practices such as striptease (Liepe-Levinson 2002), the Busby Berkeley chorus line (Franko 2002), and clubbing (Jackson 2004); dance critic Wendy Perron (2002) details distinct facial expressions within specific ballet, modern, and postmodern concert dance performances.

In this chapter, I use an ethnographic study of hip-hop dancers in the Philadelphia area to examine the deployment of the face as a choreographic tool in the dance battle.[14] My intention is not to reassert the face or head, in line with Western philosophy, as the dominant corporeal regions through which to privilege thinking, communication, and understanding. Rather, I draw attention to the significance of facial movement, but which can only be read in conjunction with the rest of the dancing body and in relation to the codes and values of the hip-hop battle. Within these contests, dancers utilize the face to provoke embodied modes of intimidation and derision to support their desire to win; however, they also conceive the face as a legible marker of weakness and loss. Although I have observed a spectrum of battles that range from informal jams in which the participating crowd agrees upon a winner through verbal and gestural assent, to structured competitions with a panel of judges and monetary prizes, a sense of contest always emerges. Public health scholar Pauline Rosenau (2003) describes how a competition paradigm dominates the United States, and sociologist Francesco Duina (2011) observes an American obsession with winning. Yet while hip-hop emerged within a US context, many dancers consider the battle less in terms of competition than as a process of participation, sharing, and support. B-boy Hannibal describes this as follows:

> You're either flipping or executing something like totally crazy in competition, and the only reply you want to get back is "I will never be able to do that." But, with my aura, I get all types of comments back. . . . "Hey man, I really love to see you dance. You're so much fun to watch. You're amazing to watch. It's comical when watching you." How do you put together comedy and the joy of having fun, and also at the same time keep how competitive you are?[15]

In light of Hannibal's conundrum, I explore how dancers negotiate strategies of victory and loss specifically through their danced facial expressions, and how the dialectic of rivalry and participation forms a co-productive paradox in the battle context. I draw upon literature on competition, sport, and African American expressive arts to examine the competition frame of the hip-hop battle, and how dancers strive against a "loss of face." First I explore hip-hop as a competitive practice, and then I consider how dancers use facial expression to defeat their opponent through strategies of intimidation, and through postures of derision. I move on to discuss dancers who reveal a loss of face, and in the concluding section I reflect on how dancers negotiate the competition paradigm. For this final section, I introduce the ancient sports philosophy of "aretism" to think through how hip-hop contests balance ideas of competition and participation, individualism and community, and winning and mastery (Holowchak and Reid 2011). For now, I turn to the competitive battle arena and its "face-to-face" encounters.

EYEING UP THE COMPETITION

> So, I look you dead in your eye and say, "Okay, do you want this more than I do?" That's what it is. That's how I look at my competitor. "Do you want this as bad as I do?"
>
> —Just Sole (Figure 21.2)[16]

As dancers prepare to battle each other, standing head on, face to face in the cypher, they clearly eye each other up. To "eye up" suggests to study carefully, which dancers do as they attempt to read their opponent and make a mental note of every move performed, but it can also mean to stare at a coveted object. While this may refer to a sexual attraction, I take it in this context to convey a desire to consume, overcome, or master the

FIGURE 21.2. House dancer Just Sole at Survival of the Illest, April 2013.

Photography by Brian Mengini.

opposing dancer. Their gazes mutually fix each other as rivals. In spite of any nerves or anxiety, dancers enter the competition full of bravado. Indeed, the rhetoric that underpins their battle attitude conveys an unwavering self-confidence and desire to annihilate the opponent:

> Whether the person is my friend or not, if I don't know them at all. . . . I wouldn't really say it's kind of bullying, but it's more along the lines of, "Look, you're not gonna win. I'm gonna win. You're gonna lose." . . . the first thing that comes to mind is, "I have to win this. I have no choice. I'm not going to lose here today." (Kat)[17]

> There's been times when I've battled someone who has talked a lot of trash about me and everything, and it's really intense. Now it's personal. It's not so much of a friendly battle anymore. It's like I'm really trying to embarrass you and take you out, you know. So, the emotions are going to fly. We'll be cool at the end of the battle, but . . . until then it's like "whatever, like, I don't like you." (Kendogg)[18]

> When I get mad and I call someone out, it's like I want to in a sense kill you in dancing. You know what I'm saying? I want to destroy your character. I want to destroy your ego. I want to destroy you to the point where you're asking for help to get up and I'm just slapping your hand. That kinda sounds ruthless, but that's the mentality that I live through. And you can see it in my face. (Rukkus)[19]

The importance of competition to hip-hop cannot be underestimated. Hip-hop journalist Jeff Chang (2005, 116) describes b-boying as a "competitive bid for dominance," and ethnomusicologist Joseph Schloss (2009, 100) observes, both in relation to breaking and other vernacular dance practices, such as jazz, "the role of competition in dance has existed in New York for decades, if not centuries." In a study of 1970s hip-hop culture, sociologist Katrina Hazzard-Donald (1996, 226) describes the "competitive one-upmanship" of breaking as historically rooted in traditions of African American music, dance, and orality in which participants throw down challenges to their opponent through devices such as "toasting," "signifying," or "burning." Africana studies scholar Tricia Rose (1991, 79) explains the "competitive and confrontational" character of hip-hop as a cultural tactic for both resisting and negotiating a society that places no value on youth of color. She states, "Hip hop remains a never-ending battle for status, prestige and group adoration which is always in formation, always contested and never fully achieved" (Rose 1991, 79).

Given the competitive frame of the battle, to some extent, hip-hop sits at the intersection of sport and art. Although its practitioners frequently refer to it as an art form and reflect on its expressive aesthetics, several of the dancers likened it to a sport due to the high-level physical training, the mental preparation, and the structured contest of the battle event. For instance, Hannibal describes how he came from a sports background and therefore the competitive element of that naturally extended into the hip-hop battle arena; Viazeen talks about traits in competitive running that he likens to the physicality of outstanding hip-hop dancers; and Rukkus employs a boxing analogy to explain how dancers read their opponents' faces. As house dancer Just Sole notes, "At the end of the day, what people are trying to do is play with your mind. That's what it is, push you out your game. Just like basketball players or football players, we are athletes."

In a study of Irish dance competitions, anthropologist Frank Hall (2008) similarly likens these to a game, but one that engenders an expressive, aesthetic dimension. He describes Irish dance competitions as social rituals coordinated around the drama of a contest, but calls upon anthropologist Claude Lévi-Strauss, who observes how social gatherings typically bring together people of equal status, whereas competitions produce asymmetrical relations in the form of winners and losers (Hall 2008). Although I specifically focus on losing in hip-hop battles, I am interested in the idea of failure as a generative concept. Before coming to this discussion, I return to the face and how dancers mobilize it to create strategies of intimidation and derision, as well as its revelations of failure, humiliation, and loss.

FACIAL TACTICS OF INTIMIDATION

> With ripped muscles and skin-tight shirt, "Mercury"[20] flicks a "v" with his fingers and flashes a vicious stare at his opponent. He then throws himself into an explosive back flip and, immediately on landing, executes a lateral slicing action with both hands and glares in disgust as if to punctuate the end of his set. His scorn lingers toward his opponent as he turns his back on him to exit the cypher, but sends a playful smile to a friend in the crowd to hint that this was just a game.
>
> —King of the Ring (August 2013)

In the hip-hop battle, dancers describe a gamut of tactics or "burn moves" to intimidate and throw their opponents' game, and to ensure they lose face. They initiate crude sexual gestures, unleash imaginary arsenal, and show command over musicality and physicality, all of which are directed at the opponent and heightened through pointed facial expression; meanwhile, on their opponents' round, they yawn, look distracted, and glance away. Although many dancers recognize that such deliberate strategies of intimidation are a temporary façade for the dance floor, almost all dancers deploy these to some degree:

> You never know what course they're gonna pull out. Like it's just so unpredictable. Even behind their poker face, they never show aggression. You can see them smirk, you can see them smile just a little. And so, you don't know like, "Are you angry? Are you laughing at me because you're about to do something really great? Do you think I don't stand a chance, or are you scared?" Like, you just don't know. (Princess Di)[21]
>
> I'm stone-faced, I don't want you to see my emotion, I just need to wipe the slate clean. So, the only way you can tell how hyped I am or my emotion is by watching me move. When I start to get confident, then I start to play with the faces on purpose because I'll clown you. Like, "Oh you're a kid, dude!" So, I'll smile at you and go,

"You really think you got something here." So, when I know I have someone on the hook, I'll reel them in and then that's when I start playing with the faces on purpose. (Viazeen)

I often do very aggressive types of gestures and moves but I'm smiling the entire time because it feels good. But what it also does is, especially if I'm battling, I do want to show that I'm a powerful guy and that I have musicality, and you can't mess with me on this floor. This is my space. . . . I like to throw other people off too. They dunno how to deal with me smiling, especially when I'm doing aggressive moves. It's kinda like hitting somebody repeatedly and then smiling. (Dr. Moose) (Figure 21.3)[22]

The desire to intimidate as a strategy for unsettling an opponent clearly emerges within the history of hip-hop. Art historian Robert Farris Thompson (1996) and legendary dancer Jorge "Popmaster Fabel" Pabon (2012) both recall late 1960s and early 1970s "uprocking," a confrontational dance in which participants would enact physical combat in pairs.[23] Dance historian Sally Banes (1994) describes how hip-hop references African and African American dance traditions with its physical rhetoric of boasts and insults, and Hazzard-Donald (1996) observes that the aggressive outward display of hip-hop arose within socially marginalized and economically impoverished African American, West Indian, and Puerto Rican communities. Speaking of 1970s New York, Chang (2005) also details the aggressive posturing of breaking battles, and he turns to celebrated hip-hop dancer and choreographer Rennie Harris, who describes "steppin'"

FIGURE 21.3. B-boy Dr. Moose at For the Love, April 2015.

Photography by Ed Newton.

contests in Philadelphia as analogous to going out to fight or to war.[24] Indeed, the language of confrontation continues in contemporary battle practices. In a study of global breaking culture, dance scholar Imani Kai Johnson (2011, 1) describes the battle as a "performed warfare" and "mental zone of strategic defense in the face of any challenge."

Schloss (2009, 111) notes how the desire to intimidate, humiliate, and "trash talk" might be characterized as bad sportsmanship in some realms of cultural life; however, a different set of values operates in the hip-hop battle. To an extent, the motions of intimidation and aggression have persisted through the embodied aesthetics of the dance, particularly in the area of breaking. As b-boy Steve Believe states,

> There's an air of macho-ness to the dance that sometimes people come off very hard and it looks silly because they try and be too rough. . . . Kids are going to do that. They're naturally going to go for trying to look strong and hard, rather than who they really are. And so I think the face is actually an important indicator of how much experience they have and how they really feel about the dance. If you're relaxed and I can see that nothing is bothering you, and even if somebody says something, you're going to smile. That says a lot more than if you keep a mug the entire time. . . . Now that works for some people. But for me, I'm much better if I react and let my face kind of speak with my movement.

Indeed, other dancers also develop a nuanced approach to negotiating the complex historical evolution of the form through deploying facial expressions that reflect their sense of self, rather than enacting an anachronistic aggression that might not resonate with their contemporary context. For instance, b-boy Metal describes a change of battle tactic in response to a nemesis on the dance floor:

> All I wanted to do was beat him, and I was genuinely really mad. So I was using this anger, and everything that I did, I crashed. I did terrible. And then after the battle he came up and was like, "Yo, I beat you before you even started." And I was like, "Oh my God, like he's right," because I wasn't being myself. So the next month I called him out again, and I just hit him with a smile. And he was like, "What're you smiling for? It's not a game." . . . I'm like, this is a game to me, I enjoy this. . . . So I always say he taught me how to break because he taught me that you gotta be yourself.

Similarly, Professor Lock describes how he attempts to undercut facial tactics of intimidation, specifically in response to a hyper-aggressive face:

> People have tried to use it against me and stuff like that. Me personally, it doesn't work. It doesn't really phase me. What works for me is I'm always smilin'. Like I might have a face dependin' on what move I'm in and what movement I'm doin', but at some point, I kill it with kindness in my dance. It's hard to be mad at me because I'm not makin' faces at you that makes me look like I wanna punch you out. And, my moves are dope, probably can't copy them, and then I'm smilin' about it, you know, makin' the girls smile, shakin' hands with the fellas that are in the audience. So, it's kinda like, you know, that's my play, that's where I approach it from.

In all of these instances, dancers are setting up their faces according to their battle philosophy. Novice dancers might create faces that significantly mask who they are as people; as they mature, they might consciously replace these faces with looks that are more akin to their experience and sense of self. Thus in the complex reality of the battle event we see dancers who try to eliminate their opponents through an aggressive persona, which may be genuine or may be contrived. We see other dancers who intimidate through smiling, either as a slightly sinister tactic or as a warm reflection of their personal attitude toward the contest. Yet across all of these scenarios, they can destabilize their opponent's game, causing them to slip up, be taken unawares, and lose face.

CHOREOGRAPHING FACES OF DERISION

"Grinder" watches his opponent throw down an explosive and angry krumping round with flared nostrils, clenched teeth, and vicious eyes directed straight at him. As his round ends, Grinder fashions a tippy-toe ballet pose, with arms in fifth position, and does a series of *bourrées* towards his opponent with a pretty smile and fluttering eyelashes as if to mock his overblown aggression.

—Battle for Your Life (November 2012)

Another tactic that dancers use to undermine their opponents and provoke loss is the use of derision and, as with intimidation strategies, this also plays out through facial expression. For instance, b-boy Super Josh[25] describes facial modes of mockery that he calls upon during his dancing round in the hope that his opponent will lose face: "I use my face to do a lot of things. I'm very childlike, so I do things, like, I'll put my finger on my nose and wiggle my fingers, I'll stick my tongue out at people, I'll suck my thumb, calling them a baby or something like that. It's just the way I like to tease people and play around with them." Meanwhile, Steve Believe recalls how dancers provide a facial commentary on opponents through interactions with their friends and allies in the cypher crowd: "There's faces that just indicate we're on the same page with somebody, right? So if somebody goes out and does something funny, I'm going to have a weird face or I'm just going to have a sneer and look at somebody and make some jokes."

"Dances of derision" occupy a long history within both African and African diaspora dance practices. Farris-Thompson (2011, 6) observes how dances of derision are pervasive in West African expressive cultures, but also describes how "Puerto Rican dancers mock fatuous or eccentric dancing with cruelly accurate movements in New York City." Similarly, Schloss (2009, 111) states that "creatively insulting one's opponent is a part of many competitive traditions across the African diaspora." Specifically in reference to 1970s breaking, Pabon (2012, 58) describes how "freezes" were employed to "mock or humiliate the opponent," and in a historical study of house, dance scholar Sally Sommer

(2008, 297) states that "humor is most pointedly made by mimicking and commenting, in dance, on the other guy's style."

Mimicry and derision were central to the development of hip-hop, and Chang (2005, 138) cites Doze Green from the Rock Steady Crew to articulate this battle strategy: "Frosty and I were like the goofs of the crew, we used to just mimic people and act like a clown. . . . They were the secret weapons." At Second Sundae battle (August 9, 2015), we see how one experienced and elite dancer, who takes his craft seriously, momentarily becomes an object of ridicule. "Mike Kool," a small, slight dancer, goes up against "B-boy Rock," a big and muscular man. Rock is known for his power moves, particularly ones that show strength and stamina, such as 1990s, darkhammers, and hand hops. After Rock throws down a virtuosic and spectacular round, Kool enters the cypher full of energy and a mysterious half-smile. At one point, he turns to Rock, strikes a classic "muscle man" pose, with arms raised, fists clenched and biceps flexed, and emits a huge playful grin. The crowd laughs, seeing both the irony of Kool's puny body in comparison to Rock, along with his mocking imitation of the hulky dancer, who stands on the edge of the cypher, still pumped and taut after his power-heavy round. Until that moment, Rock's expression had been one of fixed determination, but he instantly "loses face" and smiles as Kool unsettles him with his teasing play.

While some dancers deploy pointed imitations or exaggerated commentaries with accompanying facial expression to undermine their opponents, others use dancing prowess, combined with sharp-witted facial choreography, as a corporeal mode of derision:

> One of the breakers completely messed up. He tried to do a flare and then into a ninety, and he slipped and just horribly, horribly crashed. And it showed on his face. He was just like, "Aww." And then the other dancer kinda just, you know, slowly dragged himself onstage, lookin' at the floor, mocking his [opponent's] face and his reaction. And then he did the flare and the ninety and the whole place just exploded. And then when he landed it, he looked right at him! (Dr. Moose)

> You can also do what's called flipping a move or flipping a concept. So if you're in a battle and somebody does a move, but you know that you can do it better or you can do it cleaner, you do exactly that. For instance, if I was to battle somebody doin' waves, I could do all my waves the way that I wanna do, or I can do that same exact wave that they do—but do it cleaner, do it at a different angle. . . . And at the end of that movement would be when I would use that cocky face. . . . Just let them know that, you know, I'm proficient in that style. (Sk8z) (Figure 21.4)

So far, I have looked at how dancers use their faces, both in relationship to their dancing bodies and in interaction with other dancers and spectators at the battle, to cause their opponents to lose face and lose the round. Specifically, I have described how they employ strategies of intimidation and derision, which have a long-standing history not only in hip-hop, but also in African American vernacular dance practices broadly, to attempt to secure a personal win. In the following section I consider dancers in moments of failure as they lose face.

FIGURE 21.4. Popper Sk8z at The Gathering, September 2013.

Photography by Brian Mengini.

A Loss of Face

Here's the funny thing about dance. I'm a just put it like this: dance is the most honest form of communication on this planet.... You're involved in your body. So if you mess up, you can't really hide it. There are instances where you can. And some people train to hide it. Like, I've trained that way. I've trained to fall and make a move out of it. I've trained to knock myself off balance and make a move out of it. So you can do that, but then again, is that really a mistake? So, because when I really make a mistake, you can see it, you can always see it.

—Professor Lock

As Professor Lock describes in the preceding quote, dancers must develop strategies to accommodate mistakes or failed moves in the heat of the battle. In his discussion of breaking battles, Schloss (2009, 101) suggests, "dancing in the cypher forces b-boys to instantly incorporate mistakes into a larger framework that recharacterizes them as being correct, a skill that is arguably as important as performing the move correctly in the first place." Further to this, b-boy Alien Ness also insists on the need for dancers to exercise control at all times over their dancing (interview with Schloss 2006). Yet in the battle contest, dancers take risks, improvise, and push their bodies to the absolute limit; consequently, this can lead to errors.

In hip-hop literature, scholars have tended to focus primarily on the virtuosic, mastery of and success in the dance, with little attention devoted to loss and failure. Yet as I assert at the beginning of the chapter, the majority of dancers in any battle experience defeat, and this sense of loss can visibly play out in the composure of the face. For instance, the face both signals movement errors and the dancer's feeling toward them:

> one of the guys who battled, it was in the middle of doing a move, and he fell out of it, and he had the most upset look on his face ever. It must have been one of those moves that he lands all the time, but for some reason, he fell out of it and he just, he looked upset. But even though he continued on, I seen that glance in his eyes, he was just like, "Ugh maybe next time." (Cross)

> Yeah there have been instances where I definitely gave away like me messing up where I'm just like, "ughh," a sense of defeat. Kind of like, "Oh man, I did that wrong." But most of the time, because it's a battle, you don't want your opponent to see your face, like a lotta people just like brush that off, get back into your zone, have that same confident face that you've held for the whole battle. Yeah! Well, people slip sometimes and show that defeated face. (Béa Martin)

> You can't hide it. There's, there's a look of intense fear. Like, "Oh my God, I just messed up in front of all my friends." You know? And they'll try and play it off like, but you can totally see. It happens to everybody. I don't think there's any amount of training that can prepare you for that. (Metal)

Not only do dancers fall or slip up in movement terms, but the face also falls from one of studied competence to one of failure, frustration, and distress. Another index of loss resides in the direction of the gaze; thus when dancers consistently look down, they fail to "face up to" their opponent. The direct gaze as a mode of confrontation is considered the mark of a confident and experienced dancer. B-boy Alien Ness insists, "I think it's wack that people are winning battles and don't even look at their opponent" (interview with Schloss 2006, 29). Indeed, Ness argues that the defiant gaze potentially carries more weight than flawless technique: "you got a guy who might not be good as [his opponent], but he's coming in like *this* . . . I would rather see someone going *at* somebody than doing a million dope moves" (interview with Schloss 2006, 29). This idea of facing up to the opponent resonated with many of the dancers I interviewed:

> People can tell if you're looking down it's like you're less confident in what you're doing. If you're looking up or if you're looking straight at your opponent, you know exactly what you want to do. People see that you're more confident in your movement. (CB4)[26]

> To me, if you're timid and you're not watching my eyes, you don't want to win. . . . I've had it to the point where I've gone up to someone, I'm like, if you're not

looking at me and you're not dancing, then you ain't ready for this. . . . You're not physically able to watch me and direct your moves to me, because you don't have an understanding of your body yourself, to do it where you can look at me the whole time. (Rukkus)

Overall, dancers perceive that inexperienced opponents tend to reveal faces that fail to be collected. Sometimes this is because novice dancers still have to work hard at their movement craft. As Viazeen states, "sometimes you can see people who just got something, and they do it in the club or they do it at a jam, because they're biting their lip . . . their set-up time before the movement is a little longer than usual, they might blow, make a face, you can really see them prepping themselves. The people who have been doing it for a long time, you'll see none of the prep." On other occasions, dancers fail to stay cool or nonchalant about successfully landing a difficult move. B-girl Macca observes, "I see people when they practice a certain move and they're in a battle and they finally did it, and they get excited so they start smiling, you know, in their face." At other times, the inexperienced dancer lets slip a face of exhaustion, of which dancer Kendogg comments, "you don't want to show that you're like, you know, tired. Basically, a lot of dancers do try to hide it. But at the same time that they're trying to hide it, it's like they're holding their breath inside while they're dancing. . . . By the end of the run you can see the exhaustion that's coming out."

Clearly dancers attempt to provoke, observe evidence of, and exploit moments of loss, some of which are rendered visible through the composition of the face. While dancers might attempt to keep their face in check through choreographic strategies, interactions in the battle can cause their faces to literally fall from a previously held expression and prompt their downfall in the round. Thus a loss of face can mean a loss of status. In the final section, however, I consider the paradoxical attitudes that play out in regard to the competitive arena of the hip-hop battle in relation to ideas of loss (of face) and failure.

COMPETITION VERSUS PARTICIPATION

It's always nerve-wrecking 'cause at the end of the day it's just like a performance. You love it, you care about it, you're gonna be nervous before you start. But now, I have it a little more under control. When I come in I know that this is my goal, this is my target, don't be pushed or pulled, and just be myself. . . . So, that gives me a little bit more comfort and having more confidence in my ability due to my training and my teaching, I understand that it's a process like any other and losing doesn't mean that you lost, it just means that today that person was better than you at this very moment. There will be other moments. (Just Sole)

While I have shown how dancers strategically employ the face to enter into the competition of the battle, and closely monitor their opponents' faces for signs of loss and potential defeat, as Just Sole suggests, winning is not the ultimate outcome of the battle. Although competition and one-upmanship, supported through corporeal tactics of intimidation and derision, are characteristic of African diaspora dance practices, other personal and collective factors are also at stake, rooted in ideas of participation, which override the singular intent of winning. For instance, Danzel conveys the battle as a mode of mutual sharing through movement dialogue:

> I actually watched the other opponent, because I was so impressed and in love by what they did and I was like, "Oh my God! Let me see what I can do now!" 'Cause, I think with house, it's such a community thing . . . it's like what I give to that person, they're gonna take and give something back to me, so I can take. So it's like a conversation constantly.

Popper Tony Teknik (Figure 21.5) perceives the battle as an opportunity for self-improvement:

> Because people think, when they think of battling, they're thinking "Ooh yeah, I have to go for blood." And that's not really what I take on. I used to take it on when I was younger because I didn't know any better. I didn't know about the style, the culture and everything. . . . I battle because I want to be better.

FIGURE 21.5.   Popper Tony Teknik at The Gathering, September 2013.

Photography by Brian Mengini.

And locker Glytch[27] perceives the battle as an opportunity to represent both his dance style and the hip-hop community:

> Once you understand like on a global scale how you dance and how you represent your community, you're not just going out there representing yourself, but you representing where you're from. So now when I go to these battles mentally I'm like, "I'm not worried about winning or losing, I'm worried about representing, you know, my understanding of locking" . . . So the moment I stop caring about winning or losing is the moment I actually started winning!

That dancers lay great value on the participatory components of sharing, learning, and community building within a competitive framework appears paradoxical, although recent literature in sport studies explores this generative contradiction.[28] Dance psychologist Sanna Nordin Bates (2012) identifies significant overlap in sports and the performing arts, as both artists and athletes share common traits such as passion, motivation, and demanding physical regimes. And while physical education scholar Sheryle Bergmann Drewe (2003, 209) concludes that a philosophical distinction exists between sport and art in that the latter reveals an "expressed aspect" of human experience in a way that the former does not, she acknowledges that certain sports, such as gymnastics and synchronized swimming, are rooted in aesthetic concerns.[29]

To return to ideas of competition and winning, Rosenau (2003, 9) posits that competition is not a singular phenomenon: while "zero sum competition" centers on winning as its only aim, "appropriate competition" places little emphasis on winning and instead focuses on personal well-being and community advancement. Sports psychologist Gloria Balague (2009) asserts that, although competition often involves comparing oneself to others, it also produces "interpersonal success" in the way that it can teach people about themselves. Duina (2011) also places emphasis not only on *who* wins or loses, but also on *how* competitors win and lose. He conceives this in terms of process over outcomes in which competitors show determination, optimism, and fair play as qualities valued by spectators. In terms of losers, he suggests that a person's ability to reflect critically on his or her loss as a "willingness to learn" (Duina 2011, 135) offers a potentially beneficial trait to broader society. Clearly, experiences of and attitudes to winning and losing are nuanced.

Art scholar Sarah Lewis (2014) asserts that three hurdles intervene against success and winning: adversity, failure, and plateaus. Yet, in spite of these obstacles, she argues that competitors and participants develop "grit" (Lewis 2014, 168). Grit encompasses the urge to engage in sustained effort and commitment over time irrespective of outcomes. She states, "Grit is connected to how we respond to so-called failure, about whether we see it as a comment on our identity or merely information that may help us improve" (Lewis 2014, 169). Thus the need to develop grit speaks less to the idea of short-term failure, and instead to embodied endurance, responsibility, and dedication. Gender and queer studies scholar Judith Halberstam[30] has also sought to privilege failure outside a binary model in which winning is always framed as desirable and central to success. In her book *The Queer Art of Failure* (2011), Halberstam asserts that success is conventionally understood within a heteronormative, capitalist model of economic wealth, predicated on a delusion that good people attain success and that those who fail are personally responsible. Instead, she explores failure as an opportunity to "offer more creative, more cooperative, more surprising ways of being in the world" (Halberstam 2011, 2–3). While I do not intend here to examine whether hip-hop battles might be considered a queer site of failure, I appreciate Halberstam's reframing of failure as a positive trait that sits outside the personal glory of economic accumulation.[31] Although some hip-hop battles offer monetary rewards to the winners, the economic stakes are relatively small, and even dancers who win regularly would struggle to make a living from battles alone. And given the number of dancers who do not "win" in financial terms, they clearly value other kinds of investments in the battle contest. In a move against the privileging and immediacy of winning, Lewis (2014) values the idea of "mastery" through time, over "success," which she conceives as a short-lived moment of peak performance. This sense of endurance, perseverance, and staying power resonates with those dancers who spoke about a long-term commitment to their dance, their community, and their culture.

Many of these values, which concern personal learning and community building, are evident in the hip-hop battle. Philosophy scholars Andrew Holowchak and Heather Reid (2011) provide a useful paradigm for understanding the place of personal and community values in hip-hop battles through their study of the ancient sports philosophy of "aretism." The etymology of aretism derives from the Greek term *arête*, to mean "excellence" or "virtue" of a physical nature (Holowchak and Reid 2011, ix). To understand this, they provide two contrasting models of competition: a martial-commercial model, which encompasses athletic sports sold to a consuming public; and an aesthetic-recreational model, an area of play, which depends upon self-expression and creativity. Whereas the martial-commercial model centers on a win–lose battle, victory at all costs, and individual performance, aesthetic-recreational models of sport are autotelic in that characteristics such as pleasure, enjoyment, and aesthetics override matters of competition and winning. Furthermore, aesthetic-recreational sports are competitive only in the sense of a "spirited play" (Holowchak and Reid 2011, 117); their predominant features are the need for cooperation, enthusiasm, and inclusion. For Holowchak and Reid (2011), aretism occupies a balance between the martial-commercial and aesthetic-recreational model in that it values competition, but not at all costs, and although physical excellence is a valued outcome, so too are other benefits, such as personal growth and team building.

While different hip-hop battles lean more or less toward a martial-commercial or aesthetic-recreational model, depending on size, context, emphasis, and participants, they clearly engender values of aretism in that there is always some intent to compete to the best standard, but other factors are valued aside from simply winning. Displays of dancing excellence form one of the main objectives of dance battles, and the cypher crowd is quick to show its appreciation through gestures of approval, cries of enthusiasm, and generous smiles of support. Although I have spent time in this chapter focusing on how dancers labor to maintain face, while prompting others to lose face, they also use their faces in support of their opponents. Dancers will offer a brief nod or smile to signal admiration in response to moments of dancing prowess, and when dancers perform particularly virtuosic moves, innovative combinations of material, a deep knowledge of foundations, or impressive musicality, those in the cypher crowd will model expressions of wide-eyed surprise or huge smiles of disbelief at what they have witnessed. Although personal grudges occasionally play out between opponents, at the end of their round, dancers typically look each other directly in the eye, smile, and embrace in mutual appreciation. Thus values of aretism and good sportsmanship shape the battle event.

Although hip-hop battles can encompass an intense degree of competition, experienced participants know, and novice dancers soon learn, to approach them as a good-natured movement exchange. Too much aggression is frowned upon and is carefully policed by other dancers. While a spirit of competition always remains present, it centers on matters of self-improvement, personal learning, and representing a dance community. The skills that dancers learn and hone through hip-hop battles, regarding the prioritization of participation over winning, potentially offer productive strategies in their professional and personal lives.[32] As Duina (2011) suggests, failure presents an opportunity for learning, and a "loss of face" demands that dancers negotiate a multitude of interactions at a public event in a manner that honors the codes and values of hip-hop. Throughout the chapter, dancers have recalled how losses have brought about space for education, motivation to improve, and even a sense of personal accomplishment.

In terms of loss, the face plays an important role within the battle event, as both a choreographic device and an index of failure or humiliation. Dancers strategically employ the face to succeed against the opponent, but the face can also reveal moments of error and exposure that prevent dancers from moving on. Yet a loss of face constitutes a temporary condition. Mature dancers rarely lose face even when they slip up; instead, they use both successes and failures in battles to share and come to terms with who they are as participants. Although junior dancers are more prone to a loss of face, they mine their experiences of failure to learn how to value and engage in the competition event. Consequently, a loss of face becomes an essential component of battle knowledge.

Acknowledgments

I wish to thank all of the dancers who generously agreed to be interviewed for this research, and to the broader hip-hop community in Philadelphia for making me feel so welcome at battles, classes, and sessions. Thank you also to Julie Johnson, Elisa Davis, and Whitney Weinstein, who assisted with interview transcriptions. Finally, I would like to thank Dean Robert Stroker and acknowledge the assistance of a Boyer College Vice-Provost of the Arts Research Grant toward this research.

NOTES

1. Author's interview with Viazeen on December 11, 2012. For future reference, I will include the date of the interview when I first quote a dancer.
2. I use the term "hip-hop" to encompass a range of dances that have evolved from African American and Latin American social dance practices, such as breaking, locking, popping, house, and hip-hop party dances, but can also include waacking, tutting, krumping, and other associated forms.
3. I have interviewed dancers whose collective expertise comprises breaking, locking, popping, house, and hip-hop social. Although most of the dancers have one predominant area of dance expertise, several compete in "all styles" battles and are extremely competent in more than one style.
4. Author's interview with Sk8z on September 4, 2014.
5. Author's interview with Jonathan Gene on November 3, 2014.
6. Author's interview with Béa Martin on November 6, 2014.
7. Author's interview with Steve Believe on April 9, 2013.
8. A "cypher" is a dance circle that forms the typical spatial organization of hip-hop jams and battles.
9. Author's interview with Macca on December 18, 2012.
10. Author's interview with Metal on November 17, 2014.
11. Author's interview with Lil O on December 18, 2012.
12. Author's interview with Danzel Thompson-Stout on November 4, 2013.
13. Farnell (1999) discusses the cross-cultural variability of the smile, and Sklar (1991) reminds us of anthropologist Clifford Geertz's assertion that a wink can only be understood through its specific social context.
14. I have attended sixty battles, interviewed forty-five dancers, and participated in hip-hop classes and breaking practice sessions. I regularly visit the monthly battles Second Sundae and The Gathering, but have also attended Battle for Your Life, King of the Ring, Survival of the Illest, 610 Battle, For the Love, Ladies of Hip Hop, Rhythmic Damage, Silverback Open Championship, and the hip-hop dance showcase Clutchfest. The classes and workshops I have attended are in house, popping, locking, and hip-hop social dance, and I participate in twice-weekly breaking sessions as a novice b-girl.
15. Author's interview with Hannibal on November 27, 2012.
16. Author's interview with Just Sole on February 26, 2013.
17. Author's interview with Kat on September 22, 2014.
18. Author's interview with Kendogg on October 25, 2012.
19. Author's interview with Rukkus on May 2, 2013.
20. I have changed names and employed inverted commas to anonymize dancers who have not provided consent to be part of the research study.
21. Author's interview with Princess Di on April 5, 2013.
22. Author's interview with Dr. Moose on March 17, 2015.
23. Elements of uprocking continue to be seen in contemporary breaking practices.
24. Chang (2005, 115) describes steppin' as a popular African American dance style of the 1970s in Philadelphia, which was akin to "tapdancing without taps."
25. Author's interview with Super Josh on August 14, 2013.
26. Author's interview with CB4 on October 21, 2013.
27. Author's interview with Glytch on December 10, 2014.

28. In this volume, Karen Schupp's Chapter 2, "You've Got to Sell It! Performing on the Dance Competition Stage," also examines the generative personal and social skills that emerge from participation in youth dance competitions.
29. It is worth noting here that she primarily discusses "concert dance practice," but acknowledges that social dance practices, such as jazz and folk, fall between sport and art in that the movement can be an end in itself. I would concur that hip-hop dance in its vernacular, rather than presentational or concert, form also falls into this category.
30. Although this book is published under the name of Judith Halberstam, the author also self-identifies as Jack Halberstam.
31. Elsewhere I have looked at how the hip-hop battle is generally coded as masculine and heterosexual (waacking battles are an obvious exception), although some of the dance styles included in battles have distinctly queer histories.
32. I have explored this idea in a research project called "Life Lessons in Hip Hop," which I conducted in 2015–2017 in collaboration with Steve "Believe" Lunger and Mark "Metal" Wong of Hip Hop Fundamentals. The project sought to explore the life skills that dancers develop through the practice of breaking.

REFERENCES

Balague, Gloria. 2009. "Competition." In *Performance Psychology in Action: A Casebook for Working with Athletes, Performing Artists, Business Leaders and Professionals in High-Risk Occupations*, edited by Kate F. Hays, 161–179. Washington DC: American Psychological Association.
Banes, Sally. 1994. *Writing Dancing in the Age of Postmodernism*. Hanover, NH: Wesleyan University Press.
Brophy, John. 1946. *The Human Face*. New York: Prentice Hall.
Chang, Jeff. 2005. *Can't Stop Won't Stop: A History of the Hip Hop Generation*. New York: Picador.
Coates, Paul. 2012. *Screening the Face*. Basingstoke, UK: Palgrave.
Darwin, Charles. [1872] 1998. *The Expression of the Emotions in Man and Animals*, 3rd ed. London: Harper Collins.
Dodds, Sherril. 2016. "Hip Hop Battles and Facial Intertexts." *Dance Research Journal* 34(1): 43–63.
Drewe, Sheryle Bergmann. 2003. *Why Sport? An Introduction to the Philosophy of Sport*. Toronto: Thompson Educational Publishing.
Duina, Francesco. 2011. *Winning*. Princeton, NJ: Princeton University Press.
Ekman, Paul, and Rosenberg, Erika L., eds. 1997. *What the Face Reveals: Basic and Applied Studies of Spontaneous Expression Using the Facial Action Coding System (FACS)*. New York: Oxford University Press.
Farnell, Brenda. 1999. "Moving Bodies, Acting Selves." *Annual Review of Anthropology* 28: 341–373.
Farris Thompson, Robert. 1996. "Hip Hop 101." In *Droppin' Science: Critical Essays on Rap Music and Hip Hop Culture*, edited by William E. Perkins, 211–219. Philadelphia: Temple University Press.
Farris Thompson, Robert. 2011. *Aesthetic of the Cool: Afro-Atlantic Art and Music*. New York: Periscope.

Franko, Mark. 2002. *The Work of Dance: Labor, Movement and Identity in the 1930s.* Middletown, CT: Wesleyan University Press.

Halberstam, Judith. 2011. *The Queer Art of Failure.* Durham, NC: Duke University Press.

Hall, Frank. 2008. *Competitive Irish Dance: Art, Sport, Duty.* Madison, WI: Macater Press.

Hazzard-Donald, Katrina. 1996. "Dance in Hip Hop Culture." In *Droppin' Science: Critical Essays on Rap Music and Hip Hop Culture,* edited by William E. Perkins, 220–235. Philadelphia: Temple University Press.

Holowchak, M. Andrew, and Reid, Heather L. 2011. *Aretism: An Ancient Sports Philosophy for the Modern Sports World.* Lanham, MD: Lexington.

Jackson, Phil. 2004. *Inside Clubbing: Sensual Experiments in the Art of Being Human.* Oxford: Berg.

Johnson, Imani Kai. 2011. "B-Boying and Battling in a Global Context: The Discursive Life of Difference in Hip Hop Dance." *Alif* 31: 1–23.

Kemper, Theodore L. 1981. "Social Constructionist and Positivist Approaches to the Sociology of Emotions." *American Journal of Sociology* 87(2): 336–361.

Kesner, Ladislav. 2007. "Face as Artifact in Early Chinese Art." *RES: Anthropology and Aesthetics* 51: 33–56.

Lewis, Sarah. 2014. *The Rise: Creativity, the Gift of Failure, and the Search for Mastery.* New York: Simon & Schuster.

Liepe-Levinson, Katherine. 2002. *Strip-Show: Performances of Gender and Desire.* London: Routledge.

Lutz, Catherine. 1986. "Emotion, Thought, and Estrangement: Emotion as a Cultural Category." *Cultural Anthropology* 1(3): 287–309.

Magli, Patrizia. 1989. "The Face and the Soul." In *Fragments for a History of the Human Body: Part Two,* edited by Michel Feher, 86–127. New York: Zone.

McNeill, Dan. 1998. *The Face* Boston: Little Brown.

Neu, Jerome. 1987. "A Tear Is an Intellectual Thing." *Representations* 19: 35–60.

Nordin Bates, Sanna M. 2012. "Performance Psychology." In *The Oxford Handbook of Sport and Performance,* edited by Shane M. Murphy, 81–114. New York: Oxford University Press.

Pabon, Jorge. 2012. "Physical Graffiti." In *That's the Joint: The Hip-Hop Studies Reader,* 2nd ed., edited by Murray Forman and Mark Anthony Neal, 56–62. New York: Routledge.

Perron, Wendy. 2002. "The Face Can Say as Much as the Legs." *New York Times,* January 13. http://www.nytimes.com/2002/01/13/arts/dance-the-face-can-say-as-much-as-the-legs.html?_r=0.

Rose, Tricia. 1991. "A Style Nobody Can Deal With: Politics, Style and the Postindustrial City in Hip Hop." In *Microphone Fiends: Youth Music and Youth Culture,* edited by Andrew Ross and Tricia Rose, 71–88. London: Routledge.

Rosenau, Pauline V. 2003. *The Competition Paradigm: America's Romance with Conflict, Contest and Commerce.* Lanham, MD: Rowman & Littlefield.

Schloss, Joe. 2006. "The Art of Battling: An Interview with Zulu King Alien Ness." In *Total Chaos: The Art and Aesthetics of Hip Hop,* edited by Jeff Chang, 27–32. New York: BasicCivitas.

Schloss, Joseph G. 2009. *Foundation: B-Boys, B-Girls, and Hip-Hop Culture in New York.* Oxford: Oxford University Press.

Sklar, Deirdre. 1991. "On Dance Ethnography." *Dance Research Journal* 23(1): 6–10.

Sommer, Sally. 2008. "*C'mon to My House*: Underground-House Dancing." In *Ballroom, Boogie, Shimmy Sham, Shake: A Social and Popular Dance Reader*, edited by Julie Malnig, 285–301. Urbana; Chicago: University of Illinois Press.

Vigarello, Georges. 1989. "The Upward Training of the Body from the Age of Chivalry to Courtly Civility." In *Fragments for a History of the Human Body: Part Two*, edited by Michel Feher, 148–199. New York: Zone.

CHAPTER 22

....

MAKING PLAY WORK

Competition, Spectacle, and Intersubjectivity in Hybrid Martial Arts

....

JANET O'SHEA

"Not that you won or lost, but how you played the game."
—Grantland Rice

"Winning isn't everything, it's the only thing."
—Henry Russell Sanders

It's an unseasonably hot March morning in the flatlands of the San Fernando Valley. Ten of us are training in a small, matted space behind a yoga studio. A chainlink fence surrounds the mat; a large gate swings in the occasional breeze. My instructor, Sifu[1] Alain, rents the space for classes with a small group of students. Borrowing the parlance of UFC (Ultimate Fighting Championship) and other MMA (mixed martial arts) competitions, I've taken to calling the space Alain's Cage.

We open the class with rounds of sparring. We start out light and slow, our contact barely more than a touch. I'm working with Roland, a more senior student. He's more skilled than me but gentle in nature and, even sparring light, I find I can use that as a way in. But Roland's got a good repertoire of moves; reading his actions and responding to them is hard work.

The round is long. My stamina drops, returns, and drops again.

"Dig deep," Alain says. "You guys are fighters."

In common speech, I am, indeed, a fighter: tough, bold, aggressive, and unafraid of challenging situations, including verbal and physical confrontation. Within the martial arts world, however, I am not a fighter. In martial arts parlance, a fighter is a competitor, an athlete who participates in public matches on a regular basis. What separates a fighter from a "fighter" is competition, the realized intention to take martial arts off the mat and into the ring. For a fighter, in this narrower sense, martial arts belong not only to the informal setting of the academy, dojo, or gym, but also to the performance space of sport. For someone like me, competition is an attitude, as in a competitive spirit; for a fighter, it is an action undertaken as part of an organized, possibly institutionalized event.

This chapter takes these differences as a starting point, exploring the multiple connotations of competition within the overlapping spheres of game and sport. Central to this inquiry are the differences between competitive pleasure and competitive spectacle. In line with sports sociologists and historians, I argue that sport emphasizes outcome (winning or losing), rather than process (how the game is played) (Eichberg 2013; Eitzen 2006). American sports, and American society in general, are particularly inclined to celebrate victory and disparage defeat (Duina 2011). I suggest that attention to physical, contestatory, and exploratory interactions[2] between people may offset an overemphasis on winning. An intentional reclaiming of amateurism, with its attention to experimentation (Ackerman 1999; Lewis 2014), can play a role in this process, as can a reconsideration of the significance of failure.

This chapter is part of a larger project in which I investigate the relationship of risk, failure, and play to creativity and adaptability through the example of martial arts. In this writing, I engage with the genre of ethnographic memoir,[3] reflecting on the learning process as undertaken by a fledgling, if enthusiastic, martial artist. In keeping with the phenomenological and ethnographic traditions that I draw from, I interpret out from my own experience to examine the relative weight given to winning and losing in a range of physical activities, as well as the relationship between individual mastery and intersubjective interaction in physical play. In interpreting movement practice as a means of engaging with social and political concerns, however, I draw from my knowledge of dance and dance studies,[4] even as I move outside their conventional arenas of inquiry.

GAMES AND COMPETITIVE PLEASURE

I'm sparring with Vincent. It's a small class, only four of us, and Vincent and I are the only ones with gear. I'm nervous: Vincent has an intensity level that is similar to mine but he's more skilled. He trains more than I do and he's always several steps ahead of me. And he's younger. Decades younger.

Vincent gets in a lot of shots at the beginning. He's fast and he strategizes well. He fakes me out. He keeps his head moving so he's hard to hit. His feet move with a fragmented rhythm so I have trouble gauging exactly where he is and where he's going. He lands a hard strike, I feel a surge of anger, and, before I can stop myself, I rush in, only to end up in a headlock. He takes me down with a sweep kick and gets me on the ground in side control. I'm so tired I can't get his weight off me. All I can do is control his bicep so he can't hit, can't get me into a submission.

I finally shrimp out and we're back on our feet. Eventually, I find my moment. I come at Vincent with a sweeping right hammer fist. It's big and obvious and I know he's going to evade it. It's a set-up but I haven't figured out what for. I'm hoping it'll come to me in these moments that are flying by so fast. Vincent bobs and weaves, tight and crisp, right underneath my strike.

He comes up out of the evasion just as I reverse course with a right back fist that hits him square in the face. It's a move I learned in a form, many years ago, in a traditional kung fu class. Somehow, I managed to drag it out from deep in my memory, at a moment where it fit perfectly, like a long-lost puzzle piece completing a picture.

Sparring is a training activity common to most martial arts. It is a "live" practice, in which opponents challenge each other's tactics and strategies, contesting efforts to strike, take one another down, or execute a submission. Sparring contrasts with drills, in which movements are planned and in which partners allow each other to execute their intended moves.

Sparring differs from competition fighting in that sparring is an exploratory training activity; its purpose is learning, rather than achieving a desired end.[5] The verb "to spar" carries connotations of light fighting.[6] However, actual sparring matches vary in intensity, ranging from stalking and miming strikes to lightly landing blows to hitting and kicking with a force and speed that rivals competition fighting. The most fundamental difference between sparring and competition fighting is the lack of a specific outcome and a clear, designated winner. For this reason, sparring offers a particularly compelling example through which to explore the differences between play, games, and sports.

Sparring (Figure 22.1) is a form of play in that it is a voluntary activity undertaken for its own reasons; it is, in this sense, intrinsically valuable.[7] Although sparring is used as a training exercise, it serves no specific outside purpose; like other forms of play, it is worthwhile in itself. Those of us who do not compete still spar. We do so for enjoyment, to challenge ourselves, and to improve our skills. Sparring is also a game, an activity with rules, parameters, and goals. We play to win, even though we do not acknowledge a winner. We play within the rules, for to do otherwise would not just be poor etiquette, it would mean we were no longer playing (Suits 1978, 24); we would have turned a friendly exchange into a fight.

Games typically involve a confrontation, either with another player or an obstacle (Rodriguez 2006, 2; Suits 1978, 41). As philosopher Bernard Suits suggests, games rely on intentionally inefficient means of solving a designated problem. A soccer player kicks the ball across the field, when picking it up and running with it would work just as well, if not better. Runners agree to follow a racetrack, although they would get to the finish

FIGURE 22.1. Monique and I warm up for sparring.

Photograph courtesy of Tim Becherer.

line quicker if they ran across the middle of the field (Suits 1978, 22). Martial artists circle their opponents, punching, kicking, and looking for a takedown when they could incapacitate them by smashing their tracheas or gouging their eyes. An action that makes sense in the outside world nullifies the game.

Most combat arts, traditional and modern, involve the selection of less efficient over more efficient means of fighting.[8] Although martial arts involve bringing physical force to bear upon another human being, most martial arts put limits on what happens in these confrontations with others. In sport fighting, one does more harm than necessary; there is no good reason for a sport fighter to kick or punch the opponent that appears before her. At the same time, a sport fighter in a match does less harm than possible. Sparring represents an even greater restriction of means because, in sparring, we experiment rather than play to win.

Suits argues that although all games rely upon inefficient means, they divide into open and closed games, according to their outcomes. Open games have no "inherent goal whose achievement ends the game" (Suits 1978, 133), whereas closed games have a clear objective, the achievement of which results in winning. If sport fighting is a closed game, sparring is an open one.

Sports and Winning: Work and Play

Although sparring differs from sport fighting, it echoes the competition context and, thus, evokes the sport attributes of martial arts: a striving for excellence via a contest between contenders. Sports refine but also amplify and essentialize games. While a game is about the tension between playing and winning, sport tilts the balance toward success. Sports, however, retain the inefficient means of games (Figure 22.2): pole vaulters launch themselves over bars when they could more easily walk around them; sport fighters punch and kick opponents, but they do not grab chairs out of the stands and swing them at each other.

Sports, like games, center on experience. An athlete typically experiences what psychologist Mihalyi Csikszentmihalyi (2008) has called the autotelic state, a complete immersion in the activity at hand, where the relationship to one's body, instrument, and/or tools is seamless. In order for an intense experience to feel satisfying, it requires that focus turns inward, away from outside distractions and toward the task at hand. This condition aligns with what phenomenologists call transcendence, a state in which the body operates as an extension of intention. This full absorption does not occur only

FIGURE 22.2. Inefficient means includes the use of gloves, as well as the inclusion of some strikes and the exclusion of others.

Photograph courtesy of Tim Becherer.

in the pursuit of excellence. For Maurice Merleau-Ponty and phenomenologists who followed, transcendence occurs when we are completely present in the body, which acts as a seamless extension of intention. Indeed, we know ourselves *as* selves because of this experience of mastery.

On the flip side of transcendence, this state of seamless mastery, is immanence, a sense of being stuck within a body that fails to execute our commands. Immanence, especially for cultural, sociological, or applied phenomenologists,[9] is the state in which we fail to realize our intentions and our bodies refuse to act as the effortless extension of our wills. Most phenomenologists see immanence as moments where our sense of self, our state as a subject, is threatened by failure or inadequacy. However, Greg Downey (2010) argues that immanence is necessary to the learning process, and Vivian Sobchack (2005) maintains that immanence can produce a new awareness of the body.

Just as phenomenologists focus on mastery as it constitutes a self, Csikszentmihalyi (2008, 41) investigates how the autotelic, or flow state, enables a person to become "more of a unique individual, less predictable, possessed of rarer skills." Csikszentmihalyi notes that the flow state is produced when challenges and abilities line up, producing neither the boredom of too little stimuli or the anxiety of too much. For competitive athletes, this immersive experience is channeled toward winning:[10] finishing the race ahead of other competitors, besting the opponent in the ring, accumulating the points required to succeed. Unlike less competitive players, athletes rarely cede an advantage in order to keep a game going.[11]

In addition to the relative importance of goals, the presence of viewers, especially those with a formal relationship to the event (ticket holders versus informal observers, for instance) turns an activity from a game into a sport. If no one is watching, it is just a game, even if the players compete against each other, even if their competition is fierce and they keep score, deciding on a winner at the end. Sport hinges not only on visual display but also on high and low points that determine the fate of the match. Journalist Malcolm Gladwell (2000) thus describe the live qualities of sports as constituting the "drama of athletic competition." Sociologist Francesco Duina (2011, 27) likewise compares sport to performance: "[t]he more drama we witness, the more delighted we are." This use of theatrical terms is not incidental; although all physical games share with performance an acceptance and management of risk, the presence of spectators turns a game into a show.

The more spectacularized a sport, the less the interior experience of the athlete factors in the evaluation of the event. Because watching is so important in sports, the audience's pleasure in viewing takes precedence over the enjoyment of the athletes. While athletes clearly experience competitive pleasure[12] (at least, most of them seem to), viewers care more about what they see than what athletes feel. Viewers focus on what athletes do, not on what they experience. If the goal for an athlete is to get into and remain in the zone, moving from immanence to transcendence, the goal for the audience is to see transcendence at work. A paradox exists here: the activity appears effortless, even as we see the signs of effort—the sweat and, in martial arts, the blood of competitors.

Because this emphasis on outcome orients sport toward the end goal more than the experience, sociologist and historian Henning Eichberg (2013, 126) argues that "sport is placed in a complex way between work and play." If play emphasizes process, work demands a product (Moller, quoted in Eichberg 2013, 126). Sports sociologist D. Stanley Eitzen (2006) agrees that the commercialization of sport and its emphasis on product over process turns play into work. The product, in this situation, refers specifically to a desired outcome: only winning is acceptable.

In moving between dance and sport, I am struck by the simultaneous importance and disparagement of failure in sports. In all but the most experimental forms of dance, the goal is to present an apparently flawless rendition of choreography, even if the reality is one of constant adjustment to create the effect of mastery. Dancers obscure failure just as they occlude effort. Even in modern dance, where dancers and choreographers foreground effort and its engendering relation to gravity, effort becomes honed and streamlined over time, with rough edges smoothed out so dancers contract to release, fall to recover, and drop to rise.[13]

In sport, however, where the goal, broadly speaking, is for one player to best the other, failure is front and center. Players, when they come up against each other one on one or team against team, strive to trip each other up; they project one action, only to take another. Failure is inevitable. Failure is also what makes a game interesting: the fumbled play, the ball that barely clears the net and forces the opponent to run forward and miss. In martial arts, this is even more the case: the kick that is evaded and countered; the punch that starts strong but leaves the fighter open to a return shot; the takedown that is reversed. Sports bear a complex relationship to effort: we see the athletes' sweat and the evidence of their accelerated breathing; we see the dirt that echoes the fall or the tackle; in martial arts, we see scrapes, bruises, and blood of competitors, signals of failure in the form of blows received. And, yet, competitive sports hinge on our being able to witness nearly superhuman accomplishment. The fascination that live (and on-screen) sports injuries produce arises in part from the contrast between the excellence of physical accomplishment and the frailty of the human body.

For competition to take place, one athlete, or one team, must lose and the other must win. Losing is necessary to competition; it authorizes and enables the game. Everyone participating and everyone watching know that there will be winners and losers. And, yet, losing in modern sport is often treated as shameful. We only need to think of the taunts hurled at a losing team by their crowd as evidence of this disparagement of competitive failure. Modern sport condemns failure, even though failure enables competitive play.

FINDING THE MEETING POINT

My opponent, Rodd, is a young guy, a regular attendee in kickboxing classes and an occasional competitor. At the academy, I'm a Little Dragon's mom and a professor who does research on something related to martial arts; I'm not a competition fighter. I can tell he knows this because he starts out light and moving slow, wondering, I suspect, if he will need to bring the sparring down to a teaching level. I tighten up my footwork and get my head moving. We circle, skipping around each other. I throw out a few jabs, not too aggressive because, after all, he showed me the courtesy of a wait-and-see approach and it wouldn't be fair to respond by running him down. I land a few shots, light and controlled; I'm just touching him. But it's a signal: let's go, let's bring it up. He throws out a jab, then converts it to a hook. It lands solid on my cheek. He fakes low, then lands high. I'm reminded that my defensive game is weak. He circles briskly but drops his guard. I land a cross straight to his nose. We're on; we're doing this; we're playing the game. By the end of the round, we're smiling. When we touch gloves and hug, the joy of competing is bubbling, effervescent.

I call this process of coming together through cooperative, controlled opposition finding the meeting point. Since sparring can involve anything from non-contact stalking and looking for openings without landing punches to light contact, touching the opponent at the target zones, to competition-level force, the first thing that has to happen, often nonverbally, is that partners have to decide how hard they want to play. Do they want this to be training for the ring or to feel like it? Or do they want to have the space to explore without the anxiety that comes with being hit hard in the face? (Figure 22.3)

The two partners also have to figure out how to deal with each other's energy: match it, diffuse it, or meet it with its opposite. Sometimes it is effective to meet aggression with the same, but other times countering like with like builds into a brush fire. Similarly, we need to figure out how to handle a hesitant or unskilled opponent: Do we bring intensity to the interaction to see if he is willing to play a little harder? Or do we create space, giving him an in, so he feels more confident to try something out? The negotiation happens around the skills an opponent has: we figure out whether to match an opponent's speed or to just cover and take shots until she[14] leaves the opening that allows for a Mohammed Ali–style retaliation.[15] We determine how to deal with an opponent who uses a lot of force and one who fakes us out a lot, using our force against us. Finding the meeting point entails deciphering an opponent's signature moves, preparing for her favorite attacks, and figuring out her preferred defenses. It means scanning for indications of his training (does he come from a traditional karate background, or has she practiced mostly grappling?), and determining what the traces of that training suggest (will that side kick be followed by a spinning backfist, or does that high guard and upright torso mean that hard Thai kicks will follow?)

More than that, however, finding the meeting point means acknowledging an opponent's abilities and accomplishments without jealousy, self-aggrandizement, or self-disparagement. It means attending to process even as the end goal, hitting or evading the hit, remains vital. This no-ego ideal seems antithetical to the aggressive, dynamic practice of martial arts and, yet, paradoxically, it is absolutely crucial. Attending to the "means rather than an end" (Manning 2007) takes precedence even as the end, landing the strike or getting the submission, remains crucially important.

This process of finding a meeting point and of cooperatively developing the means through which we can compete is a physical realization of what philosophers call

FIGURE 22.3. Testing Monique's guard via a strike.

Photograph courtesy of Tim Becherer.

intersubjectivity (Manning 2007). Within the Western intellectual tradition, the idea that thought creates the subject dominated debates about what it meant to be human for centuries. Phenomenologists broke from this position when they insisted that experience, specifically physical experience, is the foundation of the self (Merleau-Ponty 1962). The phenomenologist rejects "I think therefore I am" in favor of "I am because I perceive, intend, and experience."[16] Phenomenologists suggest that we know who we are through the experience of transcendence, our body's seamless execution of our will, the ability of our bodies to act as an continuation of our intention (Young 1980). Mastery makes us a self, a subject.[17]

Although some phenomenologists focus on the senses (Grosz 1994), for others, intention toward objects and the resulting movement distinguishes the self. For many phenomenologists, most notably Merleau-Ponty, we understand ourselves via the apparently effortless mastery we experience as we pick up a pencil and write down our thoughts, walk across the room to turn on a light, or hammer in a nail that has come loose. If our existence is primarily about extending ourselves into space and executing our will, however, what happens when we come into contact with another human being? Other people can foil our exercise of mastery; they rarely carry out our intentions. As martial artist Bruce Lee says in the martial arts film *Enter the Dragon*, "boards don't hit back."

This insight is, of course, not restricted to fight sports. In love and friendship, in collaborative work and physical play of all kinds, in merely moving through public space, other people exercise their will, which causes us to reappraise and refigure our tactics and our strategies. Because of this quandary created by other people's will, phenomenologists emphasize intersubjectivity as well as experience, intention, and mastery. Intersubjectivity, in its most general sense, consists of the ability to put ourselves in someone else's place (Beyer 2015). Intersubjectivity comes out of realizing that another person's basic frames of reference are similar to our own (left, right, up, down, front, back) and that they exercise their intentionality in similar ways. It also means recognizing that they do something different with this information.

Philosopher Erin Manning (2007) examines intersubjectivity through movement, taking tango as her primary example. She argues that the coming together of people through physical touch allows individuals to experiment with difference and disagreement as well as harmony. Consensus, Manning suggests, is not necessarily the same thing as agreement; consensus can entail managing and benefiting from disagreement. Cooperation does not mean that everyone is the same. It does not even mean that everyone gets along. Cooperation concerns managing difference, dissent, and opposition.

Henning Eichberg makes a related argument about games. He suggests that games erode "the dualism between object and subject" (Eichberg 2013, 115), maintaining that, when we play a game, the game plays us as well. Play, for Eichberg, unravels a subject–object boundary and dismantles the idea of an autonomous individual bending the world to his or her will. Because games, especially physical games, bring us into an interaction with another human being that is simultaneously cooperative and competitive,[18] they give us the opportunity to practice disagreement without conflict.[19]

Sparring exemplifies the opportunities offered by intersubjective interaction. Sparring brings us into confrontation with other human beings, reminding us, in direct and sometimes painful ways, that we are not simply individuals carrying out our own agenda. The oppositional force of another human being is a potent reminder that the world does not bend to our will. Likewise, we have the opportunity to remind others that we do not merely bend to their will. Indeed, following on from Eichberg's assessment, it is not just the game that plays us; our opponent plays us as well, in at least three senses: exercising a fluid, dynamic mastery; working out the game with it; and trying to best us. Similarly, we play our opponents.

Controlled opposition reminds us that we are not alone in the world.[20] Sparring teaches us that even when human interaction is not harmonious, it can still be managed, sometimes so that both sides are satisfied even if one side's weaknesses are more apparent. Coming into contact with others can be euphoric, but it can also be painful, challenging, and infuriating. Sparring illustrates the complexity of human interaction, a realization that challenges an emphasis on winning as the only desirable outcome to a competitive encounter.

An emphasis on intersubjectivity, on experience and process, can shift a balance away from winning for its own sake and back toward competitive pleasure, not just within sparring or martial arts training, but in a broader cultural context. We can value competitive pleasure as an attribute of play, for its own sake, even as we long for particular outcomes. Excellence and achievement can be measured not only in terms of wins and losses, but also in terms of a game well played. We could likewise privilege attributes of play such as unity and participation (Duina 2011, 177). We could return to the basis of sport in play, realizing that physical interaction and play are intrinsically valuable; they do not need to serve the purpose of winning.

I am not arguing that we should offer every participant in an event an award, a solution that is sometimes put forward as a corrective to excessive competition in children's sports.[21] Instead, I suggest that we acknowledge that failure in the outcome is not the same as failure in the process. The runner who crosses the finish line last has not won the race, but has still succeeded in completing the task at hand. The runner who fails to cross the finish line, but participates with full attention, sustained commitment, and honest effort, has still achieved something significant, potentially meeting or exceeded perceived limitations. The sport fighter who takes a kick (Figure 22.4) learns something about the limitations of her game.

FIGURE 22.4. Failing to evade Monique's kick.

Photograph courtesy of Tim Becherer.

Francesco Duina (2011, 168), in writing about alternatives to our current model of competition, suggests that striving, in itself, matters: "the pursuit of something, regardless of outcomes, holds meaning in and of itself." Duina maintains that the pursuit of a goal is an act of imagination.[22] He suggests that we could value competition not for its outcome, but because it provides an opportunity to envision possible futures and to pursue those possibilities (Duina 2011, 169).[23]

The relationship between competition and imagination suggests that intersubjectivity alone is not sufficient for changing our cultural obsession with winning, however. Professional athletes and the coaches who guide them have plenty of experience with intersubjective interaction and controlled opposition. In team sports, often the intersubjective experience yields camaraderie within the team, but this empathy and affection do not extend to those beyond the team. Players retain an unaltered attitude toward competition, creating situations where, for instance, winning matters more than sporting behavior or even ethics. Worse, players sometimes engage in cruel and vicious behavior toward those beyond the team, using their exalted status and their ability to work collectively to abuse others (Eitzen 2006, 63–65). Intersubjectivity in the presence of introspection, however, may offset the winning-at-all-costs mentality that feeds into the impunity with which professional and high-level amateur athletes commit acts of violence and disregard codes of ethics. One way in which introspection presents itself is through the encounter with failure.

The Politics of Losing: Failure, Introspection, and Amateurism

Sparring, like other physical, intersubjective encounters—for instance, social dance, contact improvisation, one-on-one basketball, and pick-up games of soccer—can illuminate what physical interaction reveals about difference and disagreement. Physical practices where we need to find the meeting point remind us of the physical realities of other human beings: their strengths, their strategies, but also their vulnerabilities. This creates the space for exploring oppositional intent without succumbing to anger and without giving up.

Introspection can shed light on what intersubjectivity provides us and why it is important. It includes looking to our physical interactions as metaphors and as learning experiences. It consists of asking not just what can I do better and what are the flaws as well as the strengths of my game, but also what have I learned about myself? What do these interactions teach me about how I interact with others? What do they reveal in others that surprises me?

Commentators on competition outline the detrimental effects of failure, noting that winners' views on the world are confirmed while losers are fraught with doubt (Duina 2011, 34–36). Losers are left to their own introspection. We accept losing as long as it is a learning experience, in which losers retreat from the competition to think about how they can improve (Duina 2011, 135). Alternatively, we cease to disparage losing when it represents a dip in a narrative arc that leads toward success.

Nonetheless, introspection is depicted as a negative consequence of losing. I suggest that introspection could just as easily be perceived as a positive result of failure, providing a benefit in conjunction with a disappointing outcome. Introspection combined with intersubjectivity can allow us to see beyond a dualistic win–lose model of competition and toward a greater understanding of the complexities of human interaction.

If professional sports have moved too far toward outcome and away from this kind of reflective, intersubjective practice, will shifting a balance from watching to participating rectify this? Can we support the process of playing as actively as we do the spectacle of sports? Is there a place, in other words, for amateurism?

The term *amateur* carries pejorative connotations. According to the Merriam Webster dictionary, an amateur means both someone who undertakes an activity for pleasure rather than as their job and, yet, it also means an incompetent, someone who does something poorly. Synonyms and near-synonyms for amateur include unskilled, bumbling, inexpert, dilettante, clumsy, and awkward. *Amateur* as an adjective implies "half-hearted." But amateur also means lover, someone who adores a particular activity (Ackerman 1999; Lewis 2014). Reclaiming the idea of acting (practicing, performing) from love rather than from duty is promising. So, too, is renouncing the idea that deep engagement requires orientation toward a goal.

Arts and African American Studies scholar Sarah Lewis (2014) takes this idea one step further, presenting intentional amateurism as a strategy through which unexpected insights and discoveries can emerge. To make her point, Lewis sketches out the many accomplishments of physicist Andre Geim, who, in collaboration with Konstantin Novoselov, won a Nobel Prize for the first-ever isolation of graphene, the only two-dimensional object identified on Earth. Geim and his colleagues made this and other unlikely discoveries by "graz[ing] shallow" and questioning what others "never bother to ask" (Lewis 2014, 147). Lewis compares this approach to the Zen concept of the beginner's mind, an attempt to view circumstances anew with the fresh and open perspective of the neophyte. The intentional amateur, Lewis (2014, 151) argues, taps into a "useful wonder" that urges the practitioner out of the expert's routine and, thus, opens up unforeseen discoveries. Not surprisingly, Lewis (2014, 151) links this sense of wonder, this ability to stay in the present, with play; like play, the intentional amateur's "constant now" is immersive; it is about process and not product. The possibility of failure is not a threat; it is merely one possible outcome to a process that is worthwhile in itself. The immersive state, accompanied by a whimsy that undergirds the "gravity of the conditions required for innovation (and exploration)" (Lewis 2014, 163), the ability to step out of the expert's routine, allows for the discovery of truly new terrain.

Reading about the genius of the intentional amateur, I am reminded of iconoclast Bruce Lee, who rejected training methods in martial arts that were based in secrecy, absolute devotion to a teacher, and adherence to a single system. Although Lee dismissed the traditional training protocol in which the teacher had absolute authority, he retained the importance of sustained, repeated practice. If we consider amateurs dilettantes, then Lee, with his unwavering dedication to relentless training, was anything but. However, if we envision the intentional amateur as someone who makes unlikely discoveries because he is willing to "graze shallow," drawing from a range of approaches, as well as digging deep into particular systems, then Lee fits the bill perfectly. Lee had the courage to do what we now blithely call cross-training when adherence to a single martial arts style was not merely the norm but a requirement. He convinced Wing Chun master Ip Man to teach him, although Lee's part-European ancestry excluded him from most traditional kung fu training. Lee observed Muhammad Ali's footwork and the way in which his outfighting gave him mastery over his opponents. Lee honed his own dexterity and mobility, shifting away from wing chun's grounded, inside attack, while retaining its angularity and power. Lee studied a range of martial arts, seeking to extract what was most effective in each; he drew together elements of fencing, Western boxing, wing chun, and kung fu snap kicks, and grappling from systems such as judo and Greco-Roman wrestling. He not only created a new martial art, Jun Fan kung fu, he also created a system, jeet kune do, through which practitioners "take what is useful, leave what is useless, and make it [their] own."[24]

At the Inosanto Academy of Martial Arts, I've had the privilege of training under Bruce Lee's close friend, student, and collaborator Guro Dan Inosanto. When watching Guro Inosanto, I am continually struck by the genius produced by the willingness to graze shallow as well as dig deep. In a Filipino martial arts class, for instance, Inosanto often moves swiftly between training systems, as well as between stick, blade, sword, and staff methods. And, yet, I have heard of him lingering over the nuances of the pac sao, the hand slap block that is the most rudimentary of all wing chun techniques. Inosanto's classes are often an exercise in beginner's mind, as he invokes traditional silat and modern muay Thai in back-to-back drills, all the while reminding us that we chart our own course, urging us not just to practice, but also to "figure it out."

Such strategies of the simultaneous expert and intentional amateur create space for introspection. They open the practitioner to failure, acknowledging that failure is necessary and, sometimes, informative. A celebration of whimsy and grazing shallow, as well as digging deep, can allow us to rethink risk and failure. It may even mitigate the disparagement of losing.

An overemphasis on winning aligns with an institutionalization of sport. As Eitzen (2006, 99) argues, the highly structured and organized nature of contemporary sports evacuates creativity and the playful exploration that makes sports pleasurable; playful elements in sport, such as enjoyment, self-expression, and inventiveness, diminish as sport becomes more institutionalized and more focused on "external decision making, specialization, hierarchy, and non-sport concerns such as making money and public relations." An excess of competition can curtail play. This raises the question of whether the pursuit of competitive pleasure can demand our best, while allowing for failure. Can we accept failure—celebrate it, even—alongside striving for mastery? Can we acknowledge that failure is part of accomplishment, that grazing shallow and holding onto playful and even fanciful preoccupations are necessary for creativity?

Bernard Suits suggests that societies that are more egalitarian may privilege open games that provide opportunities for exploration, while more hierarchical societies prefer closed games that privilege a goal. Divided societies may not only crave closed games but also demand a winner.[25] Success in extra-economic arenas supports capitalist narratives of victory and continual expansion.[26] Judith Halberstam, following Scott Sandage, points out that, in a capitalist society, "profit for some means certain losses for others" (2011, 88). And, yet, a neoliberal and late capitalist society makes only minimal provision for the failure that is the baseline of its system. The denial of failure results in a condition that Halberstam calls toxic positivity (2011), an insistence that success accords to all who deserve it.

This toxic positivity articulates itself through the celebration of narratives of "failing up," stories of (economic) success that arise out of apparent failure. Although failing up acknowledges both effort and apparent wrong turns, it nonetheless continues the disparagement of true loss. Our current fascination with winning and our vitriolic disparagement of losing exemplifies toxic positivity, as well as the polarization of American society that it masks. The disparagement of a losing athlete or team evokes the market fundamentalist ideology that unfettered capitalism provides equal opportunities for economic success and that, therefore, poverty arises from moral inadequacy rather than adverse circumstances.

Where there is competition, there is failure. Losing, winning, and everything in between can be handled with respect and acknowledged as part of the competitive framework. Those labeled as winners and as losers are part of the mechanism of play and work alike. Open games can create opportunities to explore dissent and contradiction without always needing to identify a winner.[27] Open games can give us opportunities to practice disagreement and to acknowledge difference without a fixation on outcome. This suggests that there are possibilities for competitive, oppositional play that are nonetheless focused on experience and not on outcome. It also means we can participate in competitive play without being ruthlessly invested in the outcome. We can recognize the value of losing, as well as of winning. After all, the ability to lose with aplomb is part of the resilience that, we hear, sport fosters. The ability to lose and take from it insight is the key to transformation and creativity. In the same way that we can, in writer and dramatist Samuel Beckett's terms, fail better, we can lose well. Failing well and losing with immersive attention can benefit us, individually and collectively.

Notes

1. It is customary, in most martial arts, to add an honorific to a teacher's name, ranging from the apparently casual English "Coach" to the more formal Tagalog "Guro" (teacher) to the Cantonese "Sifu," which connotes both father and teacher, conflating instructional and familial lineage. I first met this instructor in a jeet kune do (JKD) class. Although JKD rejects the hierarchy and obedience to authority imbedded in traditional Kung Fu, the system retains its honorifics. I therefore refer to my instructor as Sifu, although it would be equally accurate to describe him as Guro or Coach.

2. My understanding of intersubjectivity, as realized in physical interaction, draws from Erin Manning (2007).

3. I take as examples works such as Anand Prahlad's "Getting Happy: An Ethnographic Memoir" and Gene Ayres's *Inside the New China*.

4. Prior to embarking on this project, my research focused on choreographic choices as they engaged with large-scale social, political, and economic concerns. I investigated the relationship between contrasting interpretations of the Indian classical dance form bharata natyam and questions of gender, nation, region, and globalization (O'Shea 2006, 2007, 2016a). I have also investigated how contemporary choreographic inquiries and programming decisions contend with their immediate institutional and economic as well as political contexts (2011, 2016b). Although I have long held a teaching interest in phenomenology, this is my first sustained effort to incorporate its tenets into research.

5. Because of sparring's function as a teaching and learning activity and through its ability to provide object lessons, sparring invites comparison to other aspects of life. For instance, Susan Schorn (2009) analogizes sparring to marriage in that both require vulnerability, trust, the willingness to teach and to learn, and the acknowledgment of ground rules. In the larger project, from which this chapter draws, I compare sparring to friendship for similar reasons, as well as because sparring can spark emotional responses, ranging from deep affection to anger and frustration.

6. For example, the Merriam Webster online dictionary defines the verb to spar as to "a) box, *especially*: to gesture without landing a blow to draw one's opponent or create an opening; b) to engage in a practice or exhibition bout of boxing." http://beta.merriam-webster.com/dictionary/spar.

7. Suits (1978) points out that games are intrinsically valuable. Ackerman (1999) sees play's voluntary nature as central to its identity as play.

8. Traditional martial arts emphasize the "art" aspect of the practice, its association with discipline, rigor, and self-control. Modern martial arts tend to highlight sport aspects: competition, achieving a "personal best," and defeating an opponent. An exception to the deliberate selection of inefficient means might be battlefield arts, such as Ninjitsu and much of Filipino martial arts, where the practices come out of the training regimens of peasant armies going up against larger, better-equipped forces.

9. I use these terms roughly to describe phenomenologists who are concerned with how physical experience is realized in a social context and how bodily experience intersects with cultural realities. Examples include Young (1980); Sobchack (2005); Downey (2010); and Rothfield (2010).

10. Csikszentmihalyi (2008) describes how a honed sense of time becomes part of the skill set of athletes such as runners and competitive cyclists whose accomplishment is measured in terms of time.

11. Suits (1978, 77) describes the superior player who intentionally places obstacles in his own way in the process of defeating the opponent as "the reluctant victor."

12. Game theorists describe the productive tension between playing and winning as competitive pleasure (Suits 1978, 74).

13. Although the terms I use here, contract and release and fall and recover, refer to specific techniques within modern dance (Graham and Humphrey respectively), I also use them to invoke larger patterns of tension and relaxation that characterize postmodern as well as modern dance.

14. Astute readers will notice that, instead of using "s/he" or "he or she," my strategy is to suggest diversity in practice by alternating gendered pronouns. Since the scenarios I invoke

are imagined ones that echo real-life experience, the martial artist conjured may be of any gender identity. I do, however, play with expectations, imagining the timid participant to be male and the brutal in-fighter to be female.

15. Boxer Muhammad Ali was known for the sophisticated footwork, crisp head movement, and impeccable timing that enabled his outfighter method. Known as a "classy" approach to boxing, because of its emphasis on skill and reasoning, Ali used his opponent's aggression against him, encouraging him to exhaust himself through missed (and sometimes landed) strikes. The opponent's exhaustion would typically lead to failures in judgment that would set up the knockout blow.

   Ali's outfighting was, in turn, highly influential in Bruce Lee's creation of jeet kune do.

16. Phenomenologists differ as to what aspects of corporeal experience they emphasize in their understanding of the body as central to the self. For instance, Elizabeth Grosz (1994) emphasizes sensory perception as constituting the self. Sara Ahmed (2006) highlights position and facings, physical and metaphorical. Iris Marion Young (1980), Greg Downey (2005, 2010), foreground movement as crucial to self-perception and the interaction between an individual self and the outside world. I align this project with these latter scholars.

17. Philosopher Eric Anthamatten (2014), writing in the *New York Times* Opinion Pages about Little League pitcher Mo'ne Davis, extends Iris Marion Young's argument that feminine comportment is typically in industrialized, Western societies inhibited and restricted. Following Young's use of throwing as a metaphor, he argues that, because patriarchal society restricts women's movement and use of space, throwing, for girls and women, is a revolutionary gesture. Anthamatten sums up the phenomenologist's association of physical mastery with selfhood when he states, "I throw, therefore I am."

18. I draw this idea from Bernard Suits's argument about games being both cooperative and competitive in that players agree to compete but disagree as to the desired outcome.

19. That games give us these opportunities for respectful disagreement does not, of course, mean that players and/or viewers maximize these opportunities. Competitive games clearly have the potential to go awry. Violence at sports matches is one example; another is when sport fighters intentionally cause each other serious damage, using the athletic context as an opportunity to pursue a personal grievance.

20. I paraphrase Henning Eichberg's suggestion that games remind us that we are not alone.

21. Excessive competition in children's sports is currently a point of concern for educators, sports administrators, parents, and public health researchers. Children's sport has become increasingly oriented toward competition, while participation is in decline (Atkinson 2014; Rosenwald 2015). Journalist Bob Cook (2015) calls "overdone and overrated" the debate over whether every child who participates in sports should get a trophy, whereas commentator Ashley Merryman (2013) argues that the ability to "overcome setbacks" and lose graciously are important life skills that current approaches to children's participation overlook. To my mind, participation is valuable in itself, but conflating participation with winning and obscuring failure continues, rather than rectifies, the societal disparagement of losing.

22. Here, Duina (2011) makes a similar argument to Elaine Scarry's (1985) illustration of the relationship between pain, work, and imagination. Scarry argues that, if pain is a state without an object, imagination is objects without a state. For Scarry, the ability to bring an object into existence (and to have control both process and product) separates work from pain.

23. For Duina (2011), this act of imagination through pursuit seems to hinge primarily on the anticipation of success. I think his ideas can be extended to consider how the act of pursuing a goal can be enjoyable and satisfying on its own, regardless of its outcome.

24. I base my understanding of Bruce Lee's approach to fight training from my experience of jeet kune do with Sifu Yori Nakamura, Sifu Alain Rono (mentioned earlier), and Sifu Dan Inosanto as well as from Inosanto's references to Bruce Lee in his teaching of muay Thai and Filipino martial arts at the Inosanto Academy of Martial Arts. Inosanto was one of Bruce Lee's senior students, closest friends, and collaborator. Inosanto's approach aligns with Lee's jeet kune do teaching philosophy, which emphasizes a critical, analytical, and personalized approach to training in the combat arts; for Inosanto and his students, Lee's dictum "take what is useful, leave what is useless, and make it your own" is the backbone of the JKD system. Some of Lee's other students teach Jun Fan kung fu, a training system that preserves the material developed by Bruce Lee.

25. Duina (2011) points out that American sports demand a winner and that ties tend to be avoided.

26. This assertion is based on Sara Jane Bailes's claim that failure "undermines the perceived stability of mainstream capitalist ideology's preferred aspiration to achieve, succeed, or win, and the accumulation of material wealth as proof and effect arranged by those aims" (2011, 2).

27. This suggestion is inspired by Erin Manning's (2007) assertion that intersubjectivity allows space for dissent and disagreement and not only for consensus.

References

Ackerman, Diane. 1999. *Deep Play*. New York: Random House Books.

Ahmed, Sara. 2006. *Queer Phenomenology: Orientations, Objects, Others*. Durham, NC: Duke University Press.

Anthamatten, Eric. 2014. "What Does It Mean to 'Throw Like a Girl?'" *New York Times* Opinion Pages (The Stone), August 24. http://opinionator.blogs.nytimes.com/2014/08/24/what-does-it-mean-to-throw-like-a-girl/?_r=0. Accessed October 19, 2016.

Aktinson, Jay. 2014. "How Parents Are Ruining Youth Sports: Adults Should Remember What Athletics Are Really About." *The Boston Globe*, May 4. https://www.bostonglobe.com/magazine/2014/05/03/how-parents-are-ruining-youth-sports/vbRln8qYXkrrNFJcsuvNyM/story.html. Accessed October 19, 2016.

Ayres, Gene. 2010. *Inside the New China: An Ethnographic Memoir*. New Brunswick, NJ: Transaction.

Bailes, Sara Jane. 2011. *Performance Theatre and the Poetics of Failure: Forced Entertainment, Goat Island, Elevator Repair Service*. London; New York: Routledge.

Beyer, Christian. 2015. "Edmund Husserl." *The Stanford Encyclopedia of Philosophy* (Summer 2015 Edition), edited by Edward N. Zalta. http://plato.stanford.edu/archives/sum2015/entries/husserl/.

Cook, Bob. 2015. "Participation Trophies Aren't What's Wrong with Kids These Days." *Forbes*, August 18. http://www.forbes.com/sites/bobcook/2015/08/18/participation-trophies-arent-whats-wrong-with-kids-these-days/#2715e4857a0b4d5cb7a55638. Accessed October 19, 2016.

Csikszentmihalyi, Mihayli. 2008. *Flow: The Psychology of Optimal Experience*. New York: Harper Perennial.

Downey, Greg. 2005. *Learning Capoeira: Lessons in Cunning from an Afro-Brazilian Art*. Oxford; New York: Oxford University Press.

Downey, Greg. 2010. "Throwing like a Brazilian: On Ineptness and a Skill-Shaped Body." In *Anthropology of Sport and Human Movement*, edited by Robert Sands, 297–326. Lanham, MD: Lexington Books.

Duina, Francesco. 2011. *Winning: Reflections on an American Obsession*. Princeton, NJ; Oxford: Princeton University Press.

Eichberg, Henning. 2013. "Another Globality of Sport: Towards a Differential Phenomenology of Play and Laughter." *East Asian Sport Thoughts* 3: 115–137.

Eitzen, D. Stanley. 2006. *Fair and Foul: Beyond the Myths and Paradoxes of Sport*. Lanham, MD: Rowman and Littlefield.

Gladwell, Malcolm. 2000. "The Art of Failure." *The New Yorker*, August 21, 2000. http://gladwell.com/2000/08/. Accessed October 19, 2016.

Grosz, Elizabeth. 1994. *Volatile Bodies: Toward a Corporeal Feminism*. Bloomington: Indiana University Press.

Halberstam, Judith. 2011. *The Queer Art of Failure*. Durham, NC; London: Duke University Press.

Lewis, Sarah. 2014. *The Rise: Creativity, the Gift of Failure, and the Search for Mastery*. New York: Simon & Schuster.

Manning, Erin. 2007. *Politics of Touch: Sense, Movement, Sovereignty*. Minneapolis; London: The University of Minnesota Press.

Merleau-Ponty, Maurice. [1962] 2012. *The Phenomenology of Perception*. London: Routledge.

Merryman, Ashley. 2013. "Losing Is Good for You." *New York Times*, September 24. http://www.nytimes.com/2013/09/25/opinion/losing-is-good-for-you.html?_r=0. Accessed October 19, 2016.

O'Shea, Janet. 2006. "Dancing through History and Ethnography: An Inquiry into Bharata Natyam's Performance of the Past." In *Dancing from Past to Present: Nation, Cultures, Identities*, edited by Theresa Jill Buckland, 123–152. Madison: University of Wisconsin Press.

O'Shea, Janet. 2007. *At Home in the World: Bharata Natyam on the Global Stage*. Middletown, CT: Wesleyan University Press.

O'Shea, Janet. 2011. "Intercultural Collaboration? Thinking Culture beyond the Nation in the Work of Shobana Jeyasingh and Zhang Yunfeng." In *Journal of the Beijing Dance Academy*, edited by Christopher Bannerman, 85: 209–219.

O'Shea, Janet. 2016a. "From Temple to Battlefield: Bharata Natyam in Sri Lanka." In *Choreographies of 21st Century Wars*, edited by Jens Giersdorf and Gay Morris, 111–132. Oxford; New York: Oxford University Press.

O'Shea, Janet. 2016b. "Festivals and Local Identities in a Global Economy: The Festival of India and Dance Umbrella." In *Relay: Theories in Motion*, edited by Thomas F. DeFrantz and Philipa Rothfield, 85–102. London: Palgrave Macmillan.

Prahlad, Anand. 2005. "Getting Happy: An Ethnographic Memoir." *Journal of American Folklore* 118(467): 21–44.

Rodriguez, Hector. 2006. "The Playful and the Serious: An Approximation to Huizinga's *Homo Ludens*." *The International Journal of Computer Game Research* 6(1): 1–18.

Rosenwald, Michael S. 2015. "Are Parents Ruining Youth Sports? Fewer Kids Play Amid Pressure." *Washington Post*, October 4. https://www.washingtonpost.com/local/are-parents-ruining-youth-sports-fewer-kids-play-amid-pressure/2015/10/04/eb1460dc-686e-11e5-9ef3-fde182507eacstory.html. Accessed October 19, 2016.

Rothfield, Philipa. 2010. "Differentiating Phenomenology and Dance." In *The Routledge Dance Studies Reader*, edited by Alexandra Carter and Janet O'Shea, 303–318. Abingdon, UK; New York: Routledge.

Scarry, Elaine. 1985. *The Body in Pain*. New York; Oxford: Oxford University Press.

Schorn, Susan. 2009. "Column 5: Women Beware Women." *McSweeney's Internet Tendency*. http://www.mcsweeneys.net/articles/column-5-women-beware-women. Accessed October 19, 2016.

Sobchack, Vivian. 2005. "Choreography for One, Two, and Three Legs (A Phenomenological Meditation in Movements)." *Topoi: An International Review of Philosophy* 24(1): 55–66.

Suits, Bernard. 1978. *The Grasshopper: Games, Life, and Utopia*. Edinburgh: Scottish Academic Press.

Young, Iris Marion. 1980. "Throwing like a Girl: A Phenomenology of Feminine Bodily Comportment Motility and Spatiality." *Human Studies* 3(2): 137–156.

CHAPTER 23

YOU CAN'T OUTDO BLACK PEOPLE

Soul Train, *Queer Witnessing, and Pleasurable Competition*

MELISSA BLANCO BORELLI

Close-up on gold disco ball. Soul Train *logo emblazoned on the screen. "Inside You" (1981) by the Isley Brothers plays in background. Fade in to a black woman within the frame of the disco ball, which slowly bleeds out to full square television screen. Narration begins.*[1]

"C'mon babies. Yaaas! Work mother, yaaas! [A black woman in a black dress with big shoulder pads twists her torso, swings her hips and high kicks as she dances alone down the infamous *Soul Train* line] *How you do all this in shoulder pads? C'mon, pumps! I love it!*

These were the first skinnies! Do it! [A black man in jeans and red sequined top slides in freeze frame. He poses to the left/right and then does knee lifts with shoulder shimmies in the style of 1980s workout videos] *Heeeeey!! Yaaaaass! Look, the one on the left is anxious. Your time gon' come, boo. Hold up.*

[A black woman appears in unitard and struts a bit off beat while playing with her hair]. *I want this gold unitard for the summer. Ooww! C'mon, momma. Ain't been to a single dance class but got on leg warmers. I live!*

Now this is me! [A black man in leather pants appears and does cartwheels and positions his arms asymmetrically in space in synch with the music as he dances] *Leather pants, rhinestones all on the shoulder, just all kinds of good hand geometry, look at this baby. . . . Yaaaaaasss!!*

[Another black woman dances down the line doing head isolations in circles with her arms outstretched in front of her. Hairography is quite visible.] *She got that new*

Vigorol [hair relaxer], *baby. Body. Body. Bam. Head is going . . . but why these boots? She livin' for this brooch, though. I love it!*

C'mon Miss Gold Cummerbund! [A black man in a gold cummerbund does a shuffle walk with hand isolation in the style of Michael Jackson]. *Giving us Michael! Yaaaaas! Y'all gonna see some of this stuff on me this summer. I'm going to the thrift shop.*

[A black woman in cut up tunic T-shirt and headband appears and shimmies left and right] *C'mon Tina Liggins!! I love it! I'm living for this T-shirt! Oooouf!* (Sigh). *Headband. Debbie Allen realness.* [She does a layout to the back of the line]

I love Soul Train. *You can't outdo black people. I'm sorry. C'mon poppa, get it! C'mon. He was the only straight one at* Soul Train *that day so they put him on the line too.* [A black man dressed rather conservatively in shirt and trousers plays with levels and then does fancy spins with arabesque leg at about the same time when Hunt asserts his supposed heterosexuality.]

C'mon, get it! [A black woman does twists and sinks/bops down to the beat. She does one funky grapevine to the side] *These hotpants and this top and these beads, baby, giving Patrice Rushen. I love it. (Sigh) I am just in heaven, c'mon with it. I love it!*

This old sashay from side to side [A black man in white tank and black trousers does some funky box steps].

And momma was holding it down, long hair don't care. [Black Woman with hair down to her ankles struts down and poses to show off her legs through the slit of her white jumpsuit and then touches her hair sensually]. *I wonder if she ever sold that hair? I love it!* Soul Train, *baby. Uuuunh!*

I have just described Darrell J. Hunt's viral YouTube video entitled "SOUL TRAIN BABIES!! OOWWW!!"[2] where Hunt offers commentary over an episode of the US syndicated show *Soul Train*. In it, Hunt's particular queer black commentary addresses the outfits, dances, and individual expression of each dancer as he or she struts down the line. At one point he proudly states, "You can't outdo black people!" and continues to relish in the clothes, moves, and dancing personalities strutting alone down the line. I came across this video when a friend sent it to me via Facebook. Soon after, it was circulating among many of my (black, brown, and/or queer) friends. I always paused at his proud assertion and wondered, what is it that cannot be outdone? I therefore attempt to tease out the possibilities of outdoing while also considering the types of pleasures and affective expressions that emerge from the witnessing and circulation of this viral video. I link Hunt's style of commentary to the practices of audience participation and competition at vogue balls to frame the viewing of this video as a pleasurable site of competition where we can either agree or disagree with Hunt's assessments of the *Soul Train* dancers, perhaps finding ways in our own experience of watching it to outdo Hunt. Part of my discussion also addresses how such viewing communities celebrate blackness as something of value, worth collecting, and competitively viable. The comments to Hunt's videos include celebrations of black pride ("'Commoonnnn. GET IT!' LMAO. I ♥♥♥

it! All things Black and great in my life will now be filed under 'You Can't Outdo Black People.' "—Ronda Atkins); affective responses ("This video makes me smile from ear to ear, every time I watch it. Thank you so much for posting it I LOVE IT!"—Jeremiah Christopher; "This video makes me happy, but why these boots?"—katdaddimd; "this video have me in tears everytime!!![emojis of laughter with tears] i love it. . . . Yasssssssssss-" ORIGINALREADY2MIX); and black queer language ("I liieuuuve."— Baby Ethernet; "this video gives me all kinds of life"—Safia Mohammed). It is among these comments where I claim that the affective communities of feeling emerge.

Hunt's affective analysis of the black bodies dancing is particularly relevant given the recent #BlackLivesMatter movement and the continual devaluation of black bodies globally.[3] If neoliberalism celebrates competition and individuality, how does black collective pleasure, mediated through a queer aesthetic and affective lens, actually *outdo* the emotionally devastating effects of capitalism?[4] I use four frames of analysis to think through the circulation of pleasure this video produces for a black queer community of feeling: neoliberalism, attunement, black queer affect, and discourses about pleasure. What follows is my endeavor to tease out these frames further. I focus on this viral video's affective effects or mood work, its relationship to queer witnessing, vogue ball competitions and aesthetics, and neoliberalism. If, as DeFrantz (2016, 67) states, "black social dance operate[s], emphatically, outside, or in excess, of language [and it] doesn't rely on language for legitimacy," what kind of mood work happens to me and the 83,000+ YouTube viewers who have watched Hunt's video?

Neoliberalism: Deterritorialization and Identities

Dance scholar Thomas DeFrantz (2012, 135) writes that black social dance, despite its global circulation through the idea of neoliberal freedom, contains "protean abilities [which] render it less available as a whole to methodologies that could create easily owned materials of commodity." He makes this case particularly in his discussion about the American syndicated television show *Soul Train*, which aired from 1971 to 2006. In cultural studies scholar Christopher P. Lehman's book *A Critical History of Soul Train on Television*, Lehman argues that *Soul Train* was more than a showcase for music and dance. It was a " 'platform for African American political expression' (65–67), an outlet for music that expressed a feminist agenda (62), a tool in the encouragement of Afrocentric education (74), and one of the few television shows committed to presenting Rhythm and Blues music without humor as its backdrop (78)" (Lehman, quoted in Amin 2009, 302).

Soul Train dancers were initially local high school students (the show was filmed in Chicago), but with the addition of Chicago-based choreographers Clinton Ghent and later Ronald Paul Johnson came the "iconic" presence of the *Soul Train* dancers.

It was the dancers who gave the show its appeal. These dancers came from the local black Chicago community where the show was initially recorded. Through these black dancing bodies, black social dance began to circulate. What made *Soul Train* distinctive was the *Soul Train* line. In this line, DeFrantz (2012, 130) explains succinctly, "two rows of dancers faced each other to meet and form couples at one end of the space and then improvise freely across the space between the dancing witnesses." Dancers were free to interpret the song according to whatever dance was current and/or they could dance. Often, this set up a sense of competition among the dancing witnesses who may have sought to outdo one another with their embodied improvisatory skills when it was their turn to dance down the line. Audiences at home could also determine who the "best" dancer was, according to their own tastes or the memorable performance. Notice how DeFrantz uses the word "freely" to qualify how they improvised as a central component of their danced response. In the "freedom" to be individuals demonstrating their personal relationship to rhythm through physical expression, these black bodies assert a vibrant viscerality, an aliveness that forms the theme of this chapter. But the idea of freedom, as a Western idea that privileges the notion of a liberal citizen who possesses Enlightenment values of reason and humanity, does not necessarily attend to the social, historical, and cultural valences that shape the corporeality of black bodies—bodies historically subjugated and devalued. Furthermore, this Western conception of a liberal citizen versus a displaced and extraterritorial body (refugee, migrant, or someone who can never be, or has been coerced out of being, still) sets up an idealized notion of what it means to be a person. If Western personhood relies on only certain bodies having freedom to move, to be still, to resist, or to claim space, then it is urgent to decolonize this discourse.[5] This sets up a variety of parameters: Who is allowed to move, who is allowed to remain still, who can enjoy moving for pleasure, and who must move for survival? If we frame discourses from the perspective of the moving marginalized body, not only does the perspective change, but the vantage point does as well. Here is where I would like to be still in my intellectual focus for a moment, in the place of perambulating bodies—bodies that must continually move to survive and assert their viscerality, their humanity. If the protests against police brutality in Ferguson, Missouri, and Baltimore, Maryland, have taught us anything, they show that even if a black person complies with the state's request to be still and face interrogation she or he will be arrested or shot dead.[6] If both moving and staying still will bring about the same fate, what can a black body *do*? What can a black body *do* to outdo? And, how does it *outdo*?

I am particularly interested in how the push for privatization, deregulation, and free enterprise affects our feelings and our bodies. These facets of neoliberalism affect how bodily labors, such as dancing, circulate, lose cultural context, and gain new, sometimes even evacuated, meanings (which I assert as meanings outside their specific cultural context, or more specifically, the commodification of culturally specific forms into gestures, movements that become deterritorialized). In the case of *Soul Train*, the proliferation of the videos, whether through YouTube or through Japanese VHS (DVD) distribution, positions African American social dance at a crossroads between consumption and deracination, a violent type of appropriation that literally uproots a culturally specific form and evacuates its socially and culturally specific meanings. Here I echo DeFrantz's (2012, 130) claim that the spread of African American social dance to global audiences flows "with a forcefulness that evacuates their aesthetic imperatives of regularized, community-based physical expression, towards terms of engagement" that might be outside or unrelated to its initial cultural specificity. As a result, the materiality of the black body and labor of black cultural production disappears. DeFrantz (2012, 130) confirms that this process "allows it to absorb participants who have no sustained contact with the corporeal fact of black people in the world." The constant threat of cultural deterritorialization looms over African American social dance as a pleasurable and consumable form of embodied synchronicity. Cultural theorist Stuart Hall (1992, 25) defines black popular culture as a "contradictory space." It is a space that relishes in hybrid forms, parody, and pastiche that occur within the marketplace of capitalism. Although integrated within mainstream popular culture (as *Soul Train* demonstrates, particularly in the later years of its broadcasts with a more racially diverse in-studio audience), Hall (1992, 25) insists that black popular culture has "strategic contestation. But it can never be simplified or explained in terms of the simple binary oppositions that are still habitually used to map it out: high and low; resistance versus incorporation; authentic versus inauthentic; experiential versus formal; opposition versus homogenization." In other words, binary oppositions that problematically categorize black popular culture within opposing descriptors are limiting. American studies scholar Nicole Fleetwood (2011, 126) explains that black popular culture is "not a site that is solely or exclusively black; and yet it recognizes the black public sphere, diverse audiences, and the slipperiness of the category 'black' to define a cultural product." The *black* in black popular culture already presents a complex term that belies simple categorization; however, it functions as a useful frame to help tease out how the particular cultural expressions are indeed linked to articulations of "blackness." In the case of *Soul Train* and the clip produced by Darrell J. Hunt, blackness, a particular queer blackness tied to black ballroom culture, seeps through the video, and the affective registers it titillates contravenes the 1980s time/space when the video first aired.[7] In other words, by the time the original video aired in the 1980s, *Soul Train* was not exclusively within the purview of black audiences. A more racially and nationally diverse audience had emerged. Yet, Hunt's narration of the video through a queer black sensibility reminds the viewer (regardless of his or her identitarian affiliations) that blackness operates fully in this clip. It is beyond the visible black bodies dancing or even the aural environment that sets these bodies into motion. Blackness emerges through the ballroom culture style of witnessing, as narrated by Darrell J. Hunt. His narrative act functions as a way to revivify blackness through queerness, not because it was immobile or dead, but because the historical moment of this video on YouTube sets it up against the violences committed against black men from Trayvon Martin in 2012, to Eric Garner and Michael Brown in summer of 2014.[8] During a time when identity politics endures criticism as a lens through which to address differences, this video serves as a reminder that the identity marker of blackness finds ways to re-territorialize itself through affinities and shared pleasures among its YouTube audience, geographical location (Chicago/*Soul Train* and the dances that came out of there), and community-based physical expression.[9] Dancing bodies (and their witnessing/mediation) consistently highlight the stakes in eschewing identity politics altogether.[10]

Workerist philosopher Franco "Bifo" Berardi (2015, 124) explains that

> as capitalism destroys all forms of identification, it frees the individuals from the limitations of identity, but simultaneously it provokes a sense of displacement, a sort of opacity that is attributable to the loss of previous meanings and emotional roots. As a result, capitalism ultimately provokes a need for reterritorialization, and a continual return of the past in the shape of national identities, ethnic identities, sexual identities, and so on.

Berardi concedes that identity politics is necessary because of the way that capitalism operates to emphatically erase them. Hunt's video operates within this scenario, outlining a place for a re-territorializing of blackness on YouTube (in this case) that must incorporate queerness to make it literally "live." His pronouncement of "I live," when he watches and appreciates the *Soul Train* dancers, affirms a black queer articulation of joy and embodied presence. It functions as a declarative statement, not just of his pleasure in watching, but as an assertion that queer black presence is indeed alive within black popular culture. As DeFrantz (2016, 66) argues, "queer presence and queer gesture are foundational to the Black expressive arts." Before I engage with the queer affect that moves alongside the *Soul Train* dancers, I finish this section by briefly pointing out how Hunt, due to the popularity of his video, went on to become a neoliberal entrepreneur. His website[11] "Darrell J Hunt Loves You," sells his more popular comments on T-shirts ("*You Can't Out Do Black People,*" "*C'mon pumps!*" and "*C'mon Tina Liggins*"[12]). This neoliberal circulation of black social dance (*Soul Train*) to black pleasure/joy/pride (Hunt's video) to black "celebrity" (Hunt's popularity) to black commodity (his website and T-shirts) asserts a way that blackness always already moves as capital, but I wonder about generative ways of framing this, rather than simply critiquing an individual's creative endeavor to trademark and commodify his personality and sayings. Here, the rhetoric of neoliberal individualism and competition enters the discussion, but, as I posit, Hunt's assertion that black people cannot be outdone turns the language of competition on its head, for it is not a competition, but an assertion of self-love. It represents an unwillingness to engage in a competition because institutional injustice, along with physical and epistemic violence, proves otherwise. Hunt's video functions as community service. It spreads love, specifically collective black love, particularly in 2014 (and early 2015) when his video went viral. Setting this video and the joy it collects and circulates alongside the devastating deaths of Eric Garner, Michael Brown, and Trayvon Martin (among so many others) allows for queer affect to function as a trope of healing, if not as a reminder that "I live" is a political act. This contrast between black pride, joy, and value, and black dehumanization is a significant one. It complicates the mood initially set up by the video. This prompts the following questions: What type of mood work does the black queer commentary do? How might it be trying to re-attune so many misattunements within and outside the black community? What are ways in which dance practices (and their witnessing) allow for new affinities, and how does their mediation establish attunements?

ATTUNEMENTS AND MOODS

Hunt's video is rich with affect: joy, disdain, humor, love, derision, desire. Even the story behind its creation could call forth particular affective registers for queer men of color. He shares on his personal website that he was sitting around at home on Christmas and was watching old videos of *Soul Train* and decided to comment, record, and subsequently post. The image of a black queer man sitting home alone during Christmas may call forth an assortment of sentiments (compassion, empathy, sympathy, among others) for many queer men of color who might have experienced (or know someone who has experienced) the absence of familial companionship (due to their sexuality) during the holidays. He was in the mood for community outreach. Possible loneliness notwithstanding, his comments include a panoply of queer black discernment: *c'mon babies, I live, c'mon momma, yaaaaas, werk mother, do it, ooow*. He addresses his comments to an audience who speaks his language, because there is no translation involved. His laughter is infectious. His judgmental fashion and dance skill commentary contributes to the derisive humor, and his particular references to professional and amateur black performers (Debbie Allen, Patrice Rushen, Michael Jackson, and Tina Liggins) highlight the ways in which black popular culture is citational.[13] His level of discernment, more aptly called "reading," situates his commentary within African American expressive forms, specifically queer discursive culture. Performance studies scholar E. Patrick Johnson (2005, 125) explains that "reading has a number of meanings, depending on the context . . . one is serious, and the other is playful." Reading allows the reader, in this case Hunt, to make comments about another person's character, behavior, or even comments they have made. While Johnson asserts that reading need not be about a person's appearance, within a playful context (such as watching others strutting down a *Soul Train* line) reading can become about judging appearance, talent, or even questioning an individual's aesthetic choices. This can be seen if we link Hunt's readings to the greater queer cultural spaces of vogue balls (which I come to later in the chapter), where discernment over dancers' appearance and dance skill becomes *the* primary way of reading.

Hunt reminds us more than once that he loves *Soul Train*, "I love it," and most importantly for this discussion, he queers the space of *Soul Train* by focusing on a particular solo male dancer and claiming, "He was the only straight one at *Soul Train*." What strikes me about this pronouncement is how the particularly feminized gesture of the arabesque (feminized because of its association with the ballerina) counters Hunt's assertion that this dancer is straight. Undoubtedly, this highlights the contradictory elements in black queer humorous affect that produce the overall pleasurable mood of the video. Additionally, the act of queering *Soul Train* aligns Hunt with cultural studies scholar Tim Lawrence's (2001) queering of disco, particularly in the 1970s. Lawrence (2001, 231) asserts that disco "enable[d] an affective and social experience of the body that exceeded normative conceptions of straight and gay sexuality." The social space of disco transported and reinterpreted for the televisual audience into the *Soul Train* set suggests that these spaces of pleasurable embodied encounters stem from queer sociality. This is significant in how we might consider the type of mood work that Hunt's commentary does.

Without fail, when I watch that Darrell J. Hunt video it puts me in a good mood. Interestingly enough, out of the 82,600+ YouTube viewers, 1,721 gave it thumbs up, while only 9 gave it a thumbs down. Might one speculate that these audiences were in a good mood as well, or, at least, a mood of approval? A mood is a "sustained emotion state" that "attends to the world as a whole, not focusing on any particular object or situation" (Rosfort and Stanghelli 2009, 208). Here, I sit in an intellectual space alongside feminist scholar Sara Ahmed, who thinks about the sociality of emotion, affect, and moods in her work. She particularly finds interest in exploring "how we come to feel with or not with others through impressions that do not quite become clear or distinct" (Ahmed 2014, 14). The mood of Hunt's video paints a queer black world where love, pride, cultural references, and derisive humor coexist. This is particularly the case if you pay attention to how his words generate effects, even though the visuals of the dancing black people alongside his words speak more profoundly. I privilege the dancing body as a powerful text that exceeds the limit of language to explain or discursively render it.

Ahmed contends that the more certain signs circulate, the more they increase in affective value. This is certainly the case in terms of how the video circulated among my (predominantly) black and queer friends on Facebook. At the time of this writing, I have certain friends that tell me they regularly watch this video when they need to feel something. It puts them in a good mood. Additionally, there are 303 comments for the video, with the most recent one claiming, "Have to keep coming back to this. Funny ish*. Love, 'you can't out do Black People!' I died when you said it! [three laughing emojis] Better believe I'm getting me a t-shirt with that line! [wink emoji]"—Zena De Leon, December 9, 2016). Hunt tends to reply to the comments he receives, acknowledging the approval with love emojis and promising a new video (which to this date has not materialized). Nevertheless, the video continues to function as a reliable source for a good mood for those who need it.

German philosopher Martin Heidegger writes about moods, or what he calls attunements (*Stimmung*). For him, "mood is being in relation to others" (Heidegger, quoted in Ahmed 2014, 15). Ahmed (2014, 15) takes up Heidegger and further articulates that a mood is there or around. We come to inhabit the space of the mood. It has an atmosphere. Because Hunt is in a good mood, a celebratory mood, a black is beautiful mood, and definitely a queer mood, you might become infected by it. I purposely use the word "infect" as a provocation since it calls forth the historicized discourses of cleanliness, propriety, and threat that dancing black (queer) bodies continue to dance around. Yet, moods also infect. They get transmitted from bodies to bodies. We think about a body carrying an upbeat or lively atmosphere with them (as Ahmed explains) and they bring that into the room. This is particularly interesting in this video since Hunt's body is definitely absent. We only hear his voice. I am particularly concerned with the relationship between the delivery, intonation, and affective energy of his commentary and the "corporeal orature" (DeFrantz 2004, 67) of the dancers. By corporeal orature, I reference DeFrantz's engagement with the embodied eloquence and language "spoken" by black dancing bodies. Hunt's comments therefore invite us to dialogue with him somehow: to agree, disagree, laugh, scowl, frown, wonder, misunderstand, or even to be in non-attunement. They also pleasurably compete with the dancing because his comments can be so entertaining and affect our witnessing.

Ahmed (2014) explains attunement as being with, but being with in a similar way. She goes on to consider that "attunement might register *that* we are affected by what is around, but it does not necessarily decide *how* we are affected. Could misattunements be an expression of the contingency of this how?" (Ahmed 2014, 16). This proves useful in explaining the different moods the video calls forth depending on who watches it. Sometimes, one is mis-attuned to things, and the fact of not belonging or understanding highlights different spaces of affinity. It produces multiple layers of attunements, affinities, as well as mis-attunements. The video offers pleasure if the viewer can recognize the references to hair products, black entertainers, the dances, styles, and music in the video. It may still provide pleasure without this knowledge due to the performative delivery of Hunt's voice and his comments. Or, it may just be another self-indulgent fan video that adds to the YouTube archive. I also wonder if mis-attunements are set up to force us to engage with others' histories or, more specifically, others' positionality, locality, and ultimately their subjectivity. Ahmed (2014, 18) claims that "attunement might itself be an affective history, of how subjects become attuned to others over and in time," yet there is a privilege involved in choosing to not see the historicity of dancing bodies and the ways in which they dance. If someone was mis-attuned to the different affective registers happening in Hunt's video, then the video does not specifically speak to him or her. Not every performative space warrants universal habitability.

Hunt's video as a circulating object "brings a world with it" (Ahmed 2014, 20). To become attuned to it might allow us to "live" with it to get our "life" from it, just as it constantly reasserts the living, moving, breathing bodies that show off their dancing skill and joy in being alive. Ahmed (2014, 20) writes that attunement promises life, connection, empathy. I am certainly not trying to make a case here for utopic undertones in black dancing bodies, for that would problematically be reifying their bodies into magical fetishes whose joy is so excessive that it affects us all. Furthermore, I imagine Ahmed would not want her work to be used for utopic projects. Instead, I am interested in how black gay vernacular, coupled with black social dance, creates a mood, an attunement, and how both witnesses and participants in the attunement find pleasure from it.[14] It is this process of attunement or, more precisely, creating a new world to witness from or even participate in that strikes me as valuable. As performance studies scholar José Esteban Muñoz (1994, 195–196) reminds us, "world making delineates the ways in which performances—both theatrical and everyday rituals—have the ability to establish alternative views of the world. These alternative vistas are more than simply views or perspectives; they are oppositional ideologies that function as critiques of oppressive regimes of 'truth' that subjugate minoritarian people." Hunt's "SOUL TRAIN BABIES!!!! OOWWW!!!" establishes a new world through which to experience *Soul Train* that may last a little over two minutes, but its effects and affects have a much longer duration. Almost three years after its initial upload on YouTube, viewers still respond with words of love, encouragement, and appreciation. Some also imply that they will support his entrepreneurial endeavors by promising to buy one of his T-shirts with his comments emblazoned on them. Hunt reclaims *Soul Train*, ever so briefly, through a mix of black cultural nostalgia and black queer affect. In other words, he creates a new world for us to witness *Soul Train* and take pleasure in it with him.

BLACK PLEASURE AND BLACK QUEER JOY

American literary critic and black feminist scholar Hortense Spillers (2003, 165) says this about black women and the performance of song wherein the

> dance of motives, in which the motor behavior, the changes of countenance, the vocal dynamics, the calibration of gesture and nuance in relationship to a formal object— the song itself—is a precise demonstration of the subject turning in fully conscious knowledge of her own resources toward her object. In this instance of being-for-self, it does not matter that the vocalist is "entertaining" under American skies because the woman, in her particular and vivid thereness, is an unalterable and discrete moment of self-knowledge.

Although I realize Spillers is speaking about the black female body, I am interested in how she articulates black subjectivity through the being for oneself. It is an unalterable moment where agency is always already there.[15] In other words, in that moment of singing (or even any corporeal practice) the black female subject asserts herself through herself: through being still, breathing, and being in the moment. That particular moment of "being-for-self" is crucial in terms of African American subjectivity because of the historical legacy of not being considered beings, but rather being non-beings for the exclusive purpose of certain beings to be able to be. To state this simply and bring us back to the theme of this chapter, if their historical existence has depended on their doing, not their being, how then can they outdo? Here I suggest that this phrase articulates the creative labor black bodies engage in to materialize pleasure for themselves, to create what I call "communities of feeling," and it is this idea of "communities of feeling" where Hunt's creative (queer affective) labor operates.[16]

In his book about ballroom culture in Detroit, *Butch Queen Up in Pumps*, gender studies scholar Marlon M. Bailey stresses the cultural labor that black LGBT communities rely on "not only to survive but also to enhance the quality of their lives" (2013, 16). Bailey's work helps contextualize Hunt's commentary and his practices of queer commentary. Part of Hunt's queering practice of *Soul Train* can be aligned to the form and aesthetics of ballroom culture. Bailey's ethnography of Detroit vogue balls sets up many similarities in the form, aesthetics, participation, and spatial arrangements.[17] *Soul Train* has the famous *Soul Train* line; balls have the T-formation with the runway as the center of focus. *Soul Train* dancers and vogue dancers respectively perform down the line with witnesses on either side. Both involve self-fashioning: one for a possible television debut; the other for a possible victory based on successful performances of gender, fashion, and "realness."[18] *Soul Train* has its televisual audience to contend with; balls have judges. Put simply, both the runway and the *Soul Train* line are where life happens. Bailey (2013, 149) explains the significance of the runway as such: "The runway is a site where recognition and affirmation are conferred, but it is also the space in which competition and critique are vigorously enacted in the presence of many other members of the community. The runway is the focal point, the place of spectacle, that emblematizes the interrelationship among the onlookers/participants, commentator, judges, and DJ." With his understanding of the runway in ballroom culture, it is possible to see how Hunt transforms his viewing of the *Soul Train* video into a night out at the LGBT club/vogue ball. Through his commentary, Hunt's disembodied voice mimics that of a ballroom commentator, another significant feature of ballroom culture. As Bailey (2013, 157) explains, the ballroom commentator has a pivotal role "to the actual ritual performance but also to broader community traditions." Some of his or her responsibilities include recognizing and commemorating the Immortal Icons and Legends in the culture;[19] employing critiques of social inequity; and using harsh language and tone to instruct participants on the standards of ballroom performance and practice. Ultimately, the commentator is "the keeper of cultural traditions" (Bailey 2013, 159). Bailey goes on to speak about the commentator as an interlocutor and sets up the call-and-response practices of African diasporic performance cultures as part of the commentator's repertoire.

I would like to position Hunt as an interlocutor as well, yet the call-and-response exists between his comments, the televisual dancing bodies he dissects with his commentary, and his video audience. Whereas in ballroom culture the commentator uses his position to incite participation, promote energy, and drive the performers to "serve" or "slay" (perform to the best of their ability to the point of astounding the audience), Hunt's commentator role in his video cannot fully dialogue with the televisual bodies because they cannot dance in reply. However, his commentary allows for his YouTube viewers to reply via comments, share, or re-posts. The liveness of the encounter is not the same as in ballroom culture, but the possibility for engagement with a performance is still there. Furthermore, Hunt's commentary (its vocabulary and the rhythm of its delivery) as a type of improvisational practice enables new sayings (such as "C'mon Tina Liggins!" "How you do that with them shoulder pads?" or "C'mon pumps!") to emerge within gay black vernacular and eventually appear in and circulate in broader cultural contexts. Innovation is fundamental to queer world-making, a world Hunt materializes through the traffic of nostalgia, pleasure, humor, self-love, and benign competition; *you can't outdo black people*. Indeed, Hunt could be outdone by other (more) popular

YouTube videos posted by black queer men offering commentary on things ranging from Patti's pies, to a new haircut, to self-empowerment.[20] Yet, this outdoing only manifests through the new innovations in terms of what they comment upon and, more importantly, how. I call it benign competition because it does not concern winning something tangible or material; rather the winning, if you will, is in how the creative flair for commentary provides pleasure and other affective engagements to greater black (queer) communities and their allies. As such, the affective economies that arise based around queer black pleasure instantiate Ahmed's (2004, 119) claim that such economies "align individuals with communities—or bodily space with social space—through the very intensity of their attachments." Through Hunt's nostalgic and loving tribute to *Soul Train*, he invites us to partake in his pleasure. *Soul Train* nostalgia appears in many forms, and I want to briefly make a slight detour here to further link *Soul Train* with African American queerness through contemporary dance.

Choreographer Trajal Harrell's piece *Twenty Looks or Paris Is Burning at the Judson Church* (S) (2009) imagines the postmodern dance space of Judson Church and its anti-spectacularity as the site where a vogue ball might occur.[21] In this piece, the stage is set up with a runway where he will showcase his twenty looks. Part of the performance involves Harrell putting on the looks, posing, walking and/or dancing, and then removing the looks. One particular look—Look 8, called "Serving Old School Runway,"—has him wearing a sweater, trousers, and carrying a clutch bag. What is most striking is that the clutch has the *Soul Train* logo emblazoned on it and features images from the show. He wears it proudly and, most importantly, this is the first time in the performance that he actually struts down the runway. In this performative moment, the relationship between "old-school" (referring to a type of nostalgia for an African American cultural past), ballroom culture (the runway posing), and *Soul Train* solidifies neatly. Harrell's piece, particularly Look 8, functions similarly to Hunt's video in that through these intertextual performance modes, both men set up a pleasurable encounter for themselves and for those who can attune to it. This, I claim, is how black queer pleasure and the world it creates offers affective particularities that cannot be outdone.

In her astute essay on hip-hop pleasure and its fulfillment, ethnic studies scholar Jayna Brown advocates for a reclamation of black pleasure as political and compatible with a critique of capitalism. She states,

> There is no redemption, no future, no reparative practice to restore rights that were never extended to us in the first place. In this way hip hop potentially offers a powerful critique of liberal humanism and its politics of universalist inclusion. It is precisely the horror that we live in that makes pleasure and its practices, particularly sensorial experience, so political, and potently so in its collective visions. Not as restorative, but as an assertion of being alive, of living in bodies that can never fully be owned. (Brown 2013, 148)

Living in bodies. *I live. I am livin'.* This desire to assert "aliveness" helps us to think about what it means to witness black pleasure as a site of political resistance. Hunt's sassy commentary about boots that clash with a dress, a gold cummerbund, or someone's less-than-stellar dancing ability partnered with the historicity of the dancing black bodies of the *Soul Train* clip produce this "unalterable and discrete moment" that outdoes the many other moments that seek to eradicate black pleasure and the black subjects who feel it. Perhaps the outdoing lies in the ability of blackness to endure despite the many historical attempts to restrain, manage, and often obliterate it. Perhaps the outdoing is not a competition between the fictions entrenched in the conceptualization of binary opposites (white culture versus black culture), but a pleasurable competition among those who seek to outdo among their own communities of feeling for the sake of the pleasure in outdoing. Pleasure becomes its own reward. Yet, the ability for black expressive cultures to manifest and outdo for themselves alone demonstrates that perhaps black people will never be outdone in their desire to live.

Acknowledgments

I would like to thank Madison Alexander Moore and the participants at Queer @ King's College for their various questions, suggestions and discussions that helped me shape the final draft of this chapter.

Notes

1. The narration is by Darrell J. Hunt. I have italicized his narration, and my comments in square brackets describe the dancer that Hunt addresses as he makes his running commentary.
2. Darrel Hunt, "SOUL TRAIN BABIES!!! OOWWW!!!" (https://www.youtube.com/watch?v=gY1gzvkkBGQ, accessed December 16, 2016). The video was published on YouTube in January 2014, and from late 2014 to December 2016 it has had 82,625+ views.
3. Black Lives Matter is a social justice liberation movement founded in 2012 after George Zimmerman was acquitted of the death of Trayvon Martin. It seeks to assert the value of black lives despite the state violence and anti-black racism that continues to permeate globally, but particularly in the United States. The founders are Patrisse Cullors, Opal Tometi, and Alicia Garza. More information is available on their website: http://blacklivesmatter.com/ (accessed December 16, 2016).
4. David Harvey in *A Brief History of Neoliberalism* (2005, 2) argues that neoliberalism is "in the first instance a theory of political economic practices that proposes that human well-being can best be advanced by liberating individual entrepreneurial freedoms and skills within an institutional framework characterized by strong private property rights, free markets, and free trade." His thinking informs how I navigate through the broad realm of neoliberalism's materializations and effects.
5. Ideologies of freedom and Western personhood belong in a vast bibliography. The following texts address ideas of subjectivity alongside modernity and neoliberalism: Harney

and Moten (2013); Brown (2015); Martin (2002); Povinelli (2011); Quijano (2007); and Lepecki (2016).

6. These cities held protests after police shooting deaths of Michael Brown (August 2014 in Ferguson, Missouri) and Freddie Gray (April 2015 in Baltimore, Maryland).

7. I am locating the video in the 1980s due to the song "Inside You" by the Isley Brothers, which premiered in 1981.

8. Trayvon Martin was shot and killed on February 26, 2012, by George Zimmerman, who was later acquitted. Eric Garner died after being put in a chokehold by a New York City police officer on July 17, 2014. Michael Brown was shot and killed by a Ferguson, Missouri, police officer on August 9, 2014. The police officers were not indicted for their actions.

9. A recent opinion piece in the *New York Times* by Mark Lilla, a Columbia University humanities professor, called for the end of identity liberalism. See "The End of Identity Liberalism" in the *New York Times* here: http://www.nytimes.com/2016/11/20/opinion/sunday/the-end-of-identity-liberalism.html?_r=0 (accessed December 16, 2016).

10. I have elaborated a bit on the stakes of eschewing identity politics earlier in the chapter when I address issues of the evacuation of meaning from culturally specific embodied expressions. The threat of being turned into simple commodities of all cultural production by black or minoritarian subjects is one of the continuing issues permeating cultural production.

11. Darrell J. Hunt Website: http://darelljhuntlovesyou.com/ (accessed December 16, 2016).

12. His high school dance teacher.

13. Debbie Allen is a dancer, choreographer, actor who has appeared on Broadway, television, and films. She is perhaps most famous for her role as the dance teacher in the television series *Fame*. Patrice Rushen is a multi-talented musician: pianist, singer, composer, record producer, songwriter, and music director. She is known for wearing her hair in braids and accessorizing them with beads.

14. By black social dance I am working from the taxonomic distinctions developed by Brenda Dixon Gottschild and Robert Farris Thompson about black aesthetics, which highlight polycentric/polyrhythmic articulations, high affect juxtapositions, assymetry, and body isolations.

15. "Always already" stems from the work of Louis Althusser and his theory of interpellation.

16. I play here with Raymond Williams's idea of "structures of feeling" as the culture of a particular historical moment. By "communities of feelings," I imply that individuals come together through their feelings about a particular historical or cultural experience.

17. Vogue balls and voguing emerged out of 1980s Harlem culture where black and Latino queer communities gathered to compete against one another in dancing, posing, and the ability to be creative through the aesthetics set up by the luxury fashion industry.

18. Realness as defined within ballroom culture is about being as convincing as you can (in performances of gender, attitude, high fashion representation, and/or celebrity figure). In the video when Hunt says "Debbie Allen realness," he is affirming that particular *Soul Train* dancer's convincing performance of Debbie Allen and her well-known dancing skill.

19. Immortal Icons and Legends are competition categories in the Detroit ballrooms that Bailey features in his monograph.

20. I am referring to the viral Facebook and/or YouTube videos posted by James Chanel Wright (offering a real-time review of Patti Labelle's sweet potato pies, where the mere taste of the pie makes him sing like Patti Labelle, particularly her song "On My Own"), B. Scott (sharing details with his audience or "Love Muffins" about his new hairstyle),

and Lonnie Bee offering advice to his viewers (a.k.a. his "good good girlfriends") based around lyrics to different songs he has playing in the background. Each of these viral video celebrities have particular sayings associated with them, and they have achieved a certain level of notoriety or fame (within and outside of African American community) because of their videos. The videos I am referring to are the following: James Chanel Wright, https://www.youtube.com/watch?v=qq3JVAzar0A (accessed June 8, 2016); B. Scott, https://www.youtube.com/watch?v=mi5J4YhkxN8 (accessed June 8, 2016); and Lonnie Bee, https://www.youtube.com/watch?v=LX7QaS2pms4 (accessed on June 8, 2016). The style of commentary and relationship to their audience deserves more critical attention that is currently beyond the scope of this chapter, but I link these three videos to Hunt's because of the way in which they demonstrate how black queer discursive practices circulate through social media, thereby creating *more* black queer discourse.

21. The Judson Church in New York City was the site of the development of postmodern experimental dance in the 1960s. The dancers and participants there sought to distance themselves from the narrative and spectacle that characterized American modern dance throughout the mid-twentieth century.

REFERENCES

Ahmed, Sara. 2004. "Affective Economies." *Social Text* 22(2): 117–139.

Ahmed, Sara. 2014. "Not in the Mood." *New Formations: A Journal of Culture/Theory/Politics* 82: 13–28.

Bailey, Marlon M. 2013. *Butch Queen Up in Pumps: Gender, Performance, and Ballroom Culture in Detroit.* Ann Arbor: University of Michigan Press.

Berardi, Franco "Bifo." 2015. *Heroes or Mass Murder and Suicide.* London: Verso Books.

Brown, Jayna. 2013. "Hip Hop, Pleasure, and Its Fulfillment." *Palimpsest* 2(2): 147–150.

Brown, Wendy. 2015. *Undoing the Demos: Neoliberalism's Stealth Revolution.* Cambridge, MA: MIT Press.

DeFrantz, Thomas F. 2004. *Dancing Revelations: Alvin Ailey's Embodiment of African American Culture.* Oxford: Oxford University Press.

DeFrantz, Thomas F. 2012. "Unchecked Popularity: Neoliberal Circulations of Black Social Dance." In *Neoliberalism and Global Theatres: Performance Permutations*, edited by Lara Nielsen and Patricia Ybarra, 128–140. Basingstoke, UK: Palgrave McMillan.

DeFrantz, Thomas F. 2016. "Bone-Breaking, Black Social Dance, and Queer Corporeal Orature." *The Black Scholar* 46(1): 66–74.

Fleetwood, Nicole R. 2011. *Troubling Vision: Performance, Visuality, and Blackness.* Chicago; London: University of Chicago Press.

Hall, Stuart. 1992. "What Is This 'Black' in Black Popular Culture?" In *Black Popular Culture*, edited by Gina Dent, 21–33. Seattle, WA: Bay Press.

Harney, Stefano, and Fred Moten, eds. 2013. *The Undercommons: Fugitive Planning and Black Study.* Wivenhoe, NY: Minor Compositions.

Harvey, David. 2005. *A Brief History of Neoliberalism.* New York; Oxford: Oxford University Press.

Hunt, Darrell J. *Darrell J. Hunt Personal Website.* http://darelljhuntlovesyou.com/. Accessed June 8, 2016.

Johnson, E. Patrick. 2005. "Snap! Culture: A Different Kind of Reading." *Text and Performance Quarterly* 15: 122–142.

Lawrence, Tim. 2001. "Disco and the Queering of the Dance Floor." *Cultural Studies* 25(2): 230–243.

Lehman, Christopher P. 2008. *A Critical History of Soul Train on Television*. Jefferson, NC: McFarland Books.

Lepecki, André. 2016. "Introduction: Dance and the Age of Neoliberal Performance." In *Singularities: Dance in the Age of Performance*, edited by André Lepecki, 1–25. New York: Routledge.

Lilla, Mark. 2016. "The End of Identity Liberalism." *New York Times*, November 18. https://www.nytimes.com/2016/11/20/opinion/sunday/the-end-of-identity-liberalism.html?_r=0. Accessed January 20, 2017.

Martin, Randy. 2002. *Financialization of Daily Life*. Philadelphia: Temple University Press.

Muñoz, José Esteban. [1994] 1999. *Disidentifications: Queers of Color and the Performance of Politics*. Minneapolis: University of Minnesota Press.

Nur Amin, Takiyah. 2009. "The Hippest Trip in America: Remembering *Soul Train*." *Dance Chronicle* 32(2): 302–305.

Povinelli, Elizabeth. 2011. *Economies of Abandonment: Social Belonging and Endurance in Late Capitalism*. Durham, NC: Duke University Press.

Quijano, Aníbal. 2007. "Coloniality and Modernity/Rationality." *Cultural Studies* 21(2–3): 168–78.

Rosfort, René, and Giovanni Stanghellini. 2009. "The Person between Moods and Affects." *Philosophy, Psychiatry and Psychology* 16(3): 251–266.

Spillers, Hortense. 2003. "Interstices: A Small Drama of Words." In *Black, White, and in Color: Essays on American Literature and Culture*, 152–175. Chicago: University of Chicago Press.

Audiovisual Sources

Soul Train Babies !!!Oowww!!! 2014. YouTube video, 2:08. Posted by "Darrell J. Hunt," January 26. https://www.youtube.com/watch?v=gY1gzvkkBGQ. Accessed June 7, 2016.

Good Good Girlfriends. 2015. YouTube video, 3:52. Posted by "Lillian Lee," August 10. https://www.youtube.com/watch?v=vi9tj1Q6100. Accessed January 20, 2017.

B. Scott S1:190 I Went to the Doctor Today! 2008. YouTube video, 3:20. Posted by "lovebscott," August 7. https://www.youtube.com/watch?v=mi5J4YhkxN8. Accessed January 20, 2017.

PlayTime James Wright Chanel Patti LaBelle Review Part 1. 2015. YouTube video, 3:14. Posted by "Playtime Cares," November 12. https://www.youtube.com/watch?v=qq3JVAzar0A. Accessed January 20, 2017.

PART VI

HIDDEN AGENDAS AND UNSPOKEN RULES

CHAPTER 24

....

FREEDOM TO COMPETE

Neoliberal Contradictions in Gaga Intensives

....

MEGHAN QUINLAN

ALMOST 200 people are spread across the studio. We stand alert and face the center of the room, less than an arm's length away from another person in any given direction. Ohad Naharin (Figure 24.1) stands in the middle of the crowd, calmly observing everyone. Naharin is seemingly untouched by the stifling Tel Aviv heat and wears a long-sleeve shirt, long pants, and a pair of heavily worn sneakers. They squeak against someone's sweat on the floor as he starts to turn around to see the side of the studio in which I stand. His appearance is casual, but the tension in the room is palpable. We all stare at him, waiting for a cue. I feel my muscles contract as I try to appear attentive and play the role of model student and researcher, and fight the urge to turn around and see what Naharin is looking at behind me. He starts gently to undulate his spine and lift his arms, and immediately everyone across the room starts to shift their weight and explore similar small movements in their bodies. Without even speaking, he transforms the room into a sea of motion as we all begin to practice the foundation of Gaga: floating.

This memory recalls the first class at the 2013 Gaga Summer Intensive held in Tel Aviv, Israel. This was also my first of many classes with Naharin, who developed the movement language Gaga. The atmosphere of tension described in the preceding is one that rarely occurs in Gaga classrooms, but has been present in each subsequent class I have taken with Naharin.[1]

Although Naharin is not a strict teacher, he has high expectations for his students, and they work hard to meet them. His reputation often precedes him: in addition to developing Gaga, which has become an increasingly popular training method internationally over the past decade, Naharin also acts as director of the world-renowned Batsheva Dance Company. In the Gaga intensive setting, dancers often try to impress Naharin in hopes of being invited to join Batsheva—or at least gain the valuable experience of training with him and his company members. The intensive space and Naharin's classes, in particular, are fraught with tension over one's place in the dance world and the possibility of future performance opportunities in a way that contradicts the atmosphere

FIGURE 24.1. Ohad Naharin stands in the center of the studio with his back to the camera, teaching an open Gaga/people class in Studio Varda at the Suzanne Dellal Center in Tel Aviv.

Photograph by Gadi Dagon. © Gaga Movement Ltd. Reproduced by permission of Gaga Movement Ltd.

of most open Gaga classes. Rather than personal movement research, which is how Naharin and Gaga teachers often describe Gaga in their classes,[2] these events frequently turn into competitive spaces that challenge the non-competitive ethos that exists at the core of Gaga.

In this chapter, I draw on ethnographic experiences at the summer Gaga dance intensive held annually in Tel Aviv (particularly the Summer 2015 meeting) to interrogate the tension at these events between the dance practice's philosophical imperative to focus on the self and pleasure, and the desire of many dancers to impress the teachers and gain professional contacts or jobs. Although pleasure and employment are not inherently contradictory, there is a competitive element inherent in self-improvement pursued for the purpose of obtaining a job that challenges much of the self-indulgent rhetoric about Gaga. For instance, in Gaga classes, students are encouraged to move at their own pace and not compare themselves to others. These philosophies are present in the Work Instructions[3] published on the Gaga website and encouraged in the physical practice through the teachers' directions. Teachers often encourage students to "get weird" and not worry about what their movement looks like. The Gaga home page also describes the practice as an "experience of freedom" (Gaga people.dancers 2016), emphasizing the personal and internal nature of these classes and discouraging competition between participants. At the same time, Gaga intensives are attended by advanced dance students and professionals, enveloping the events in an economic framework where employment and professional development are presumed goals for its participants. As one Gaga dancer explained regarding the atmosphere of intensives,

> it's not supposed to be a competitive thing, and it's supposed to serve a purpose for the individual, and it isn't made to be a contest of any sort. Yet at the same time they hire, I mean, the company gets to know their future dancers through their workshops and all of that, so . . . *on one hand, no, they're not fostering competitiveness, but on the other hand, people who want to dance for the company are going to workshops hoping to be noticed.* So maybe . . . they're not going to outright be like, yeah, be competitive in class, but maybe in a backwards way there's some competition being fostered in that way. (Meredith Clemons, July 14, 2015)[4]

To understand this subtle atmosphere of competition that emerges at Gaga intensives, one must examine the economic framework in which it is embroiled: neoliberalism.

Neoliberalism, as both an economic practice and a discourse, emerged in the second half of the twentieth century as several major economies shifted to free market models led by governments that believed personal and financial freedom comes from a diminishment of government oversight in the market.[5] Emerging partly out of a reaction against Cold War politics and the threat of communism, neoliberal economic policies move away from government intervention to emphasize deregulation, privatization, and individual entrepreneurial freedom. All of these shifts were geared toward personal and political freedom for individuals, which was theoretically attainable if individuals had the ability to enter the market and have free will as both workers and consumers. Anthropologist Aihwa Ong explains the significance of individualism for this economic model:

> In short, the main elements of neoliberalism as a political philosophy are . . . a return to a "primitive form" of individualism: an individualism which is "competitive," "possessive," and construed often in terms of the doctrine of "consumer sovereignty." (Ong 2006, 11)

This neoliberal conception of freedom relies upon the idea of economic independence, and the ability to make choices and attain power that comes with being financially stable and self-managed. This produces a form of individualism that is also inherently competitive, because each individual is required to provide for themselves with little to no societal or governmental support.

Freedom also represents a driving force for other popular economic models, such as Marxism's interest in developing more economic freedom for workers, but the contemporary moment's insistence on freedom obtained through radical individualism and financial success in economic markets is unique. Gaga, too, privileges the idea of individuals making choices by training dancers to develop a wide range of stylistic and dynamic options from which to choose. Although neoliberal theory privileges the independent worker and the radical free market system as the ideal model for attaining individual freedom, to uphold the necessary environment for a free market to thrive, governments often have to intervene in some capacity. This need for limited oversight provides one illustration of the difficulty in applying this theory to practice. As neoliberalism continues to spread globally and technology advances to enable hyper-mobile and flexible economic practices, both scholars and private citizens are forced to grapple with questions that emerge as the theory is enacted. This has produced tensions among global and local, widespread circulation, and the sociocultural implications of relying on individualism and economic prosperity as a base model for freedom.[6] Moving beyond offering definitions of neoliberalism, recently scholars have critiqued the overwhelming dominance of neoliberal values in contemporary life as a threat to democracy (Brown 2015) and a movement that oppresses people, instigating large social movements protesting the results of neoliberalism (Hardt and Negri 2012). Neoliberalism is now seen as an influential force in many contemporary social issues and changes, which has resulted in a broad interest from humanities scholars in this economic framework.

In response to widespread academic attention in neoliberalism, dance scholars have begun to emphasize dance as an important site for investigation into neoliberalism's lived realities. Analysis of the corporeality of dancing bodies as laboring subjects in this economic framework enables a complication of theoretical models, and illuminates ways in which the neoliberal system proves ineffective or impossible to adhere to. Dance scholar Anusha Kedhar's research offers a prime example through her theorization of the "flexible bodies" of contemporary South Asian dancers as both a physical response to, and a tactic for negotiating, issues such as "the contradictions between race and citizenship in late capitalism" (Kedhar 2014, 23). Kedhar investigates the ranges of hyperflexibility and unflexibility of both physical bodies and political policies demonstrated by South Asian dancers working in the United Kingdom, and what they must do to thrive and survive in the increasingly short-term, contract-to-contract market of contemporary art economies, where visas and work permits for international travel are increasingly difficult to obtain. Her examples of not being flexible enough, demonstrated by sore and broken bodies struggling to keep up with demands, are particularly poignant in illustrating how the corporeality of dance points to the contradictions and material effects on bodies of enacting certain neoliberal ideals. Dance, then, offers much more than an analogy for understanding neoliberalism and its impacts on individuals. The corporeality of this practice not only complicates understandings and embodiments of freedom, independence, and circulation that are integral to neoliberalism, but also exposes the real-world implications and tolls that neoliberal theory takes on actual bodies.

I therefore argue that the philosophies of self-research and personal pleasure articulated in Gaga rhetoric[7] are unable to exist neatly in the competitive socioeconomic climate of the contemporary concert dance world. At the same time, I also assert that a simplistic reading of Gaga as resistant to economic pressures and neoliberal values invisibilizes the nuances of what makes Gaga so marketable to contemporary dancers. Rather, Gaga's focus on the self becomes co-opted by dancers entrenched in neoliberal economies as a professionalization tool to make them more competitive in the concert dance market. I therefore first outline the ways in which Gaga utilizes the rhetoric of freedom, and how this concept circulates in both Gaga and neoliberalism. I then look at the ways in which the structure of the Gaga intensives fosters competition between students, through its infrastructure and organization, and through the ways in which the students utilize the space. By looking at the intersection of freedom and competition as it is practiced in Gaga, I highlight issues that are becoming increasingly dominant in training for contemporary dancers today. Gaga, as a popular training method that circulates internationally, serves as a key case study for aesthetic and political shifts in regard to what is expected of dancers in the contemporary moment.

THE GAGA TOOLBOX: FREEDOM FROM/FREEDOM TO

In Gaga intensives, which last one to two weeks depending on the particular event, students take daily Gaga and Gaga methodics[8] classes, as well as learn Naharin's repertory in two-hour sessions, to deepen their personal Gaga research. This range of instruction goes beyond what is available in open Gaga classes offered internationally, as well as the occasional Gaga workshop that does not include teaching Naharin's repertory. The daily sequence of Gaga classes, followed by repertory and ending with an investigatory methodics class, offers the intensive students multiple opportunities to engage with Gaga principles and ideas in different ways.

The ideas explored in Gaga are rooted in sensation and imagery rather than form. Since being named Gaga in 2003, this practice has been marketed as a movement language rather than a dance technique, which indicates a clear rejection of the form-based techniques ranging from ballet to modern styles that often dominate professional dance training programs. Although Gaga draws on many ideas employed in these techniques, such as imagery in Graham technique and the sensation of fall and recovery in Limon classes, both of which Naharin has trained in and has recognized as influencing his movement practice (Galili 2015), it rejects the implementation of a posture-based practice predicated on mimicry of external forms. When I asked Naharin why he believed that Gaga was not a technique, he explained: "the reason it's my movement language, and not a technique, is because I feel that by calling it a movement language, it stays open for changes. Whereas a technique feels like something more finished" (Naharin, July 31, 2015).[9] Gaga classes are instead taught with an improvisatory structure in which the teachers lead the students through a series of movement prompts and suggestions that change depending on the teacher's preferences that day, allowing the individual student to physicalize their personal interpretations of the directives. A video of celebrity actress Natalie Portman on the Gaga home page shows her describing this phenomenon succinctly: "the language [Gaga] isn't like a set vocabulary that everyone has to learn; it's like a vocabulary that you are asked to create yourself, too. So it's like every person who uses this language will have their own dialect" (*Mr. Gaga* 2013). Although form is not imposed on these individual movement dialects in Gaga classes, a common style emerges as students begin to understand the dynamics and sensations being taught (Figure 24.2).

Not all students or teachers agree that a Gaga aesthetic or style exists, yet prompts such as "float," "boil like spaghetti," "taste something good in your mouth," or "imagine a ball of energy running through your body" often result in movement that looks oddly similar in spite of the open-ended instructions. For instance, the exercise of boiling like spaghetti, which makes its way into many Gaga classes, begins with students laying on the floor in stillness.

The teacher then directs the students to imagine that they are spaghetti in a pot of boiling water. The goal is to become increasingly soft and available to the movement created by the vigorous bubbles of water pushing the spaghetti-self around, which is explained by the teacher's own language within the broader prompt. At the end of the exercise, while students join the teacher in counting down from ten to mark the height of the exercise's velocity before relaxing back into stillness to observe the resonances of these actions within the body, everyone flails vigorously with their own interpretations of the prompt. Yet, as one senior scholar wisely commented after I presented this exercise at a conference, "every time I'm in the kitchen, my spaghetti all boils the same way!" I laughed at the time, but it is true. In Gaga, the dancers look almost identical in their interpretations of how to boil like spaghetti. The image is straightforward, and the way

FIGURE 24.2. Students explore their form in a Gaga/dancers class.

Photograph by Gadi Dagon. © Gaga Movement Ltd. Reproduced by permission of Gaga Movement Ltd.

the teacher describes the intended sensations behind the image make it difficult to interpret it in a way that looks very different from the others in the class. The students get to make choices, such as what part of the body is hit by an imaginary bubble and when, but it proves difficult to make conscious decisions or alter your form from those around you in the middle of this exercise. The feeling of doing the action includes a sense of release, as the intensity of the flailing takes over and the pleasurable sensation of bouncing your body off the floor with sharp percussive movements overrides any focus on organizing the movement into a particular form. Soon, everyone looks as if they are one strand in a jumble of spaghetti, each one moving in concert with the strands around them and similarly reacting to a single pot of boiling water. Arms and legs fly and occasionally support the body by landing on the ground as the torso is temporarily catapulted into the air, always attempting to protect the head from moving as vigorously as the rest of the body to avoid painful contact with the floor or nearby limbs.

This aesthetic similarity results from the students mimicking the teacher's expression of these ideas, as these students are trained to do in other dance practices. While instructions can be interpreted in a variety of ways, with many different relationships to the floor, gravity, speed, and other dynamics, common aesthetic trends emerge. If students move too vigorously while "floating," for instance, the teacher will often remind the class about paying attention to movement within the body and exploring small or invisible gestures as a way to police the style and to demonstrate a more uniform understanding of the sensation. In other prompts, such as boiling like spaghetti, small movement is discouraged in favor of vigorous shakes of the body. Yet, the Gaga style includes a wide range of movements and dynamics. Notable characteristics of this diverse style include an emphasis on asymmetry, grounded movement with many *pliés*, leg extensions that do not adhere to balletic alignment conventions, and the ability to switch between dynamics (such as soft and sharp) quickly. These improvisatory movement directives often challenge the formal impositions of other dance techniques, thus allowing students a degree of freedom from their previous training methods. Yet, while attempting to break students' movement habits by exploring "new" sensations, Gaga imposes a new set of habits that connect specific movement qualities to abstract prompts. In Gaga, these new habits are often dubbed a "toolbox" of skills related to dynamics and range that a dancer can use when improvising or performing.

This Gaga toolbox and its resulting aesthetic, although evident in every Gaga class through the teacher's example, are most prevalent in the intensive setting. The intensive event prepares dancers to perform on stage by cultivating performance skills such as dynamics and reactivity within the body, though it is also open to non-performers who practice dance at an advanced or professional level. Classes use movement vocabulary and skills from Western concert dance techniques (particularly ballet, with common references to exercises such as *tendus, penchées*, and *pliés*) alongside the imagery and sensations employed in Gaga/people classes through improvisatory movement prompts to create specific sensations (Figure 24.3).

According to the official Gaga website, this layering of Gaga with elements from other dance practices

FIGURE 24.3. Ohad Naharin leading a Gaga/dancers class to explore *tendus*.

Photograph by Gadi Dagon. © Gaga Movement Ltd. Reproduced by permission of Gaga Movement Ltd.

... presents dancers with fresh challenges, and throughout the class, teachers prompt the dancers to visit more unfamiliar places and ways of moving as well. Gaga/dancers deepens dancers' awareness of physical sensations, expands their palette of available movement options, enhances their ability to modulate their energy and engage their explosive power, and enriches their movement quality with a wide range of textures. (Gaga people.dancers 2016)

The expanded range of movement dynamics and textures that Gaga seeks to develop is intended to make dancers more adept at making choices regarding improvisation and style. This generates a particularly important skill for the contemporary concert dance world, as choreographers increasingly rely on dancers to be co-collaborators or improvise in performance works. Thus, even as Gaga is advertised as a tool for personal growth and research, these tools are also crucial to developing skills that help dancers excel in the contemporary concert dance market.

These skills are also ensconced in the Gaga style: if one is trying to please the instructor, as many intensive participants are, this creates a greater incentive to align oneself with the predominant style exhibited in the classroom to demonstrate facility and adaptability. There are also opportunities to practice Naharin's choreography, which arguably influences many of the Gaga teachers' improvisatory style because of their prolonged exposure to his work, exposing intensive participants to firsthand formal applications of Gaga within a highly stylized choreographic aesthetic. The combination of these choreographic and instructor inspirations creates a subtle, but noticeable, influence on students' improvisatory choices in the Gaga class. Though improvisations do not look uniform, the ways that Gaga challenges the conventions of popularly practiced dance forms, such as ballet's focus on symmetry and upward motion, produces similar investigations in many of the participants.

Gaga's "experience of freedom" (Gaga people.dancers 2016) of movement that is advertised on its home page, then, only creates freedom from formal dance habits, not a complete rejection of any external influence. My understanding of the term "freedom" emerges from feminist scholar Saba Mahmood, who writes that "positive freedom may be best described as the capacity for self-mastery and self-government, and negative freedom as the absence of restraints of various kinds on one's ability to act as one wants" (Mahmood 2004, 11). In the case of Gaga, positive freedom is given to the participants, but only to guide their own mastery of carefully worded prompts offered by instructors. Restraints in the form of the prompts and the need to negotiate the space with other bodies (and, for some, the pressures of the dance market outside the Gaga classroom) prevent Gaga from being a space of entirely uninhibited freedom. Dance scholar Danielle Goldman suggests that this restriction is not unique, however: in her 2010 book, *I Want to Be Ready*, which examines dance improvisation, she challenges the idea that freedom is something to be obtained, or an achievable endpoint. Goldman (2010, 4) argues that improvisation always exists in a "tight space" of constraints, and the understanding that "one could escape confinement only to enter into or become aware of another set of strictures is vital to understanding the political power of improvisation." According to this logic, because improvisation exists within a set of constraints and rules, it cannot be inherently free or natural. Though freedom is often associated with dance—improvisatory dance in particular—a critical analysis of the corporeality of improvisation challenges this concept by acknowledging the inspiration and training required to practice various styles of improvisation. Gaga constitutes an improvisatory-based practice, and thus Goldman's insights about the "tight spaces" and confinements of improvisation urge me to question Gaga's appeal to rhetorics of freedom and to analyze what strictures confine this particular form of improvisation even as its advertising infers a lack of constraints.

The rhetoric of freedom applied to Gaga is important, not just in the context of dance history (DeFrantz 2012; Goldman 2010), but also in understanding the neoliberal values that dominate contemporary society. As noted in the introduction to this chapter, this economic theory depends on the concept that free markets will enable the greatest amount of political, personal, and economic freedom for individuals. According to David Harvey (2005, 5), "[t]he founding figures of neoliberal thought took political ideals of human dignity and individual freedom as fundamental." Considering the widespread dominance of these values of freedom, as a practice marketed as offering an experience of freedom, Gaga must be considered in the framework of both dance and economic histories. In catering to this value of freedom, Gaga fits the contemporary economic model of encouraging and developing individualism. Yet, as I have shown, the contradictions between the rhetoric of freedom and the stylistic trends that limit the range of motion that occurs in Gaga classrooms illustrate a key tension in the neoliberal pursuit of individual freedom. Gaga bodies are constricted by the prompts and style that are intended to foster a specific "toolbox" of skills, which is termed freedom because it represents a shift in training methodology from form-based techniques. Economic freedom, too, is constrained: one can only make choices based on what is available or what might be profitable. Though technically everyone has freedom to make any choice, market trends and the need to fit into them to remain desirable in a workforce and thus financially independent shapes the choices one can "freely" make. The stylistic confinement of Gaga's aesthetic thus illustrates the limitations of freedom, in both dance and neoliberal economies.

The Precarity of Dancers' Employment: Creating a Climate of Competition

Gaga intensives are important sites of professionalization for dancers interested in pursuing performance careers. By developing the toolbox of skills practiced in Gaga classes, dancers expand their range and physical capabilities. These events are also important for networking, with both the teachers and fellow students. As Anusha Kedhar (2014) points out in her article on South Asian dancers working in the United Kingdom, international travel is an increasingly common requirement for dance jobs today. This travel is often predicated on preexisting relationships with choreographers due to the need for dancers to obtain visas and work permits for international work. While students may not be directly asked to perform as a result of partaking in an intensive, it offers a way to establish rapport with the Batsheva company members and make contacts that might assist in a future audition, as well as gain an insight into the physical range and style that the company may be looking for. Notably, the onus rests on the student to make contacts and go to the company to have a better chance of being seen as competitive. This indicates that the dance companies control the market, and that the individual dancers are the precarious workers who try to fit into this economy, rather than being the valued workers on whom the company depends.

The status of the dancer seeking a company to join represents a growing class in the neoliberal economic strata: the precariat.[10] Their lack of job security and the need to sell their own labor, rather than having their own means of production to hire other laborers to make a profit, places this class of workers at the mercy of employers. Though this hardly presents a new state of affairs in the dance economy (the presence of dance companies able to employ their workers full time has always been limited, and dancers frequently commit to short-term gigs for little or no pay), in neoliberal economies contract work rather than full time employment has begun to rise in other markets as well.

As Hardt and Negri argue, "[o]nce upon a time there was a mass of wage workers; today there is a multitude of precarious workers" (2012, loc 131 Kindle edition) who are often indebted to and dependent on capitalist control. A career in dance has always been precarious at best, due to both economic conditions and the possibility of injury or physical inability to execute a desired skill, thus a look at how dancers negotiate this condition in the present moment may provide some insight into strategies for other precarious workers emerging in the age of neoliberalism.

At the Gaga intensives, the participants most attuned to the underlying competitive atmosphere at the event are dance students about to graduate from university programs and unemployed dancers searching for a new company. While dancers in a range of ages attend the intensives, the predominant age range of students encompasses those in their late teens to early twenties. These dancers are often college or conservatory students who will soon graduate and enter the job market, or who have recently graduated and are looking for companies to join. Florence Pope, a second-year dance conservatory student from London, said of the 2015 Summer Intensive in Tel Aviv:

> the competitive edge is only, in my view, it's only with people that are still training and don't have jobs yet. Or, want to come here and dance. Like, it's not . . . *I feel myself do it. It's not that I'm trying to be better than other people, but there is that pressure,* like . . . there's a huge amount of pressure . . . especially because I'm coming from London and there are a lot of us, and they're like . . . some of them are the really good ones who, Batsheva people know their names, so that's a lot of pressure on someone that's also a part of that circle. (Florence Pope, August 5, 2015, emphasis added)

This need to be better than other participants, in spite of the fact that Gaga is not overtly competitive in its rhetoric or instruction style, is driven by extreme pressure and lack of job opportunities, particularly for students coming from vibrant dance communities with a high level of competition. For Pope, who is still studying and not currently on the job market, it was an underlying pressure as she endeavored to be seen as on par with her highly skilled peers, both at the intensive and back home in preparation for graduation and the future audition process. For students who are already on the job market, the intensive can be even more explicitly competitive, because it is seen as an opportunity to get a leg up and be noticed by the teachers.

Learning repertory becomes a particularly important part of the Gaga intensive, both pedagogically and for the students' opportunities to perform for their teachers. The choreography is ostensibly taught as a way to better understand and apply the Gaga principles learned in classes. Deborah Friedes Galili, currently the head of Foreign Affairs for the Gaga organization, explained that students are not always able to physicalize ideas right away, so "the repertory also is used to help you learn those tools more, and to understand . . . there are some things that you'll end up understanding, like explosive power when you're learning *Echad Mi Yodea* and some other repertory" (Deborah Friedes Galili, August 4, 2015). This reference to *Echad Mi Yodea*'s use of explosive energy signals a recurring moment in the piece where the dancers move abruptly from sitting still to a standing position, which requires a quick burst of energy that is often difficult to summon through abstract improvisation without a particular movement task or form to which to apply the energy.

In spite of this description of repertoire as a pedagogical tool for better understanding Gaga concepts, many students also use repertory classes as a tool for professionalization to give them a step up for future auditions. These students not only attempt to master the choreography, as seen in Figure 24.4, but also grab the attention of the teachers. This is particularly evident when observing the way competitive students place themselves in the space during repertoire classes. I witnessed this phenomenon at both of the intensives in which I participated, with the most competitive participants placing themselves closest to the instructors who gravitated around the sound systems at the front of the studio. While I hovered at the outer edges of the room and the back lines when performing repertory, giving myself a view of the other dancers and space to practice the movements, most of the other students tried to get into the space early and claim their spots near where they anticipated the teachers would be. Once in clear view, these dancers would exhibit strong bursts of energy, with little regard for the people around them. They did not choose to perform the choreography in the center of the space because there was a lot of room to practice, but rather because of the visibility of the position. Eventually, however, these over-zealous students commanded more space and pushed other dancers to the edges. People were even hit with the flying limbs of the dancers in the center, and these dancers occupied this highly sought after space to run through repertory full-out multiple times before others had a chance to perform it once.

FIGURE 24.4. Students in the 2015 Gaga Summer Intensive in Tel Aviv rehearse a piece of Naharin's choreography.

Photograph by Gadi Dagon. © Gaga Movement Ltd. Reproduced by permission of Gaga Movement Ltd.

For the people, such as myself, who had been pushed aside in the back lines or corners, due to the competitive students in the center, we possessed little room to practice, and spent more time marking than embodying the choreography. These competitive students were not reprimanded, and continued to compete for the instructors' attention throughout the event as the other students learned to negotiate the space and avoid potential collisions, thus allowing their efforts to take command of the space.

Being seen and making connections with Gaga teachers, particularly the ones teaching repertory, who are usually active or former members of Batsheva, is seen as advantageous to a future audition process. London-based dancer Valerie Ebuwa explained to me the difference between open classes and intensives as partially rooted in the need to learn repertory:

> The energy is just a lot different . . . especially like at Juilliard—a part of their second or third year thing is to learn a piece of rep from a company, so a lot of them are like, . . . I'm going to get rep from Batsheva, I'm going to have to do this so good, I have to ask them, they can teach me. (Valerie Ebuwa, July 6, 2015)

She explained that this knowledge of repertory forms a common interest for students. At the time of the interview she was also working with Hofesh Shechter (a former Batsheva member) in London, and explained that students at the Shechter intensives often asked her about learning other pieces of Shechter's choreography. Thus, the presence of repertory classes in the Gaga intensives heightens the unwritten rules of competition to the atmosphere as students are reminded of ways to make themselves more marketable for potential future jobs or competitive roles in upcoming school reconstructions. Although students do not have the rights to perform this repertory on a stage as a result of participation in an intensive, the acquisition of this repertory functions similarly to the acquisition of cultural capital.[11] This access to Naharin's repertory serves as more than a way to develop one's own ability to move or understand the sensations taught in Gaga. Knowledge of the choreography can be used in auditions or in school settings as a way to assert one's insider status, and can be used to one's advantage if asked to learn and perform similar (or sections of the same) choreography for an audition or a reconstruction of Naharin's work, as has happened at Juilliard.

Though each Gaga intensive offers access to Naharin's repertory and renowned Gaga instructors, the most competitive space for aspiring dancers is the bi-annual Tel Aviv intensive. These events are bigger than the ones held in Europe and North America because they have easier access to a range of studios (the intensives are held in Batsheva's studios while the company is on break) and teachers, many of whom live in Tel Aviv.[12] These teachers are almost all former or current company members, and Ohad Naharin is also present sporadically throughout the intensive. The presence of Naharin and members of the Batsheva Dance Company in the company's studios throughout the intensive serves as a constant reminder of a lucrative application of Gaga: joining the Batsheva Dance Company. There are also open improvisations after the standard day of classes, where several of the Gaga teachers observe what the students do with the information they have been learning in an open forum. These improvisation sessions mimic a dominant aspect of the auditions for the Batsheva Dance Company, and are often treated as spaces to show off, as if it were actually an audition.

I interviewed three students at different stages in their careers together at the 2015 Summer Gaga Intensive at Tel Aviv about their experiences and they explained:

> WALDMAN: I think in rep, definitely [people can get competitive] ... [and in] the improv that we're having, I think people are really ... they're very aware that Batsheva company members are watching them. And like, are thinking they're maybe scouting a little bit. Which I think they maybe are.
> POPE: Yeah, they definitely are.
> MARK: Of course they are. (Alison Waldman, Florence Pope, and Lauren Mark, August 5, 2015)

At the intensive, there was never an explicit statement from the teachers about scouting. Yet, the idea is so pervasive within the Gaga community that even dancers at other locations get the impression that attending a Tel Aviv intensive offers the best chance to be seen as a potential company member. One student who attended a New York intensive in 2014 told me that the atmosphere of that intensive was much more competitive than the open classes she had taken previously, but that

> if you want to get in [to the company] you need to go to Tel Aviv. They're not going to, in New York, scout people. Because they have, you know, they have their pick of the lot of Juilliard students, and all these people in Tel Aviv, and ... they [Batsheva] don't need to go to them [the students], I think. (Meredith Clemons, July 14, 2015)

Clemons then went on to mention a student she had met at the intensive who had bragged about knowing all of the faculty at the intensive in New York, right before saying that he would be traveling to Israel to attend the company's open audition two months later. Clemons's characterization of the need to go to Tel Aviv to gain attention from the company highlights the precarity of the dancers' position: with no guarantee of employment, non-Israeli dancers are expected to raise enough funds to travel to Tel Aviv to have a competitive shot at being scouted for the world-renowned company, whether it is through performing well at an intensive or attending an actual audition prepared with the skills learned at the intensive.

In spite of the precarity of dancers' positions, and the very slim chance that they will be noticed or scouted at an intensive, hundreds of dancers pay their own way to attend these events annually. Though dancers I have interviewed often note the competition between dancers and the desire to be scouted or otherwise noticed by the instructors (or, ideally, Naharin), they also acknowledge that the purpose of this intensive predominantly centers on the acquisition of skills. Gaga is well suited to prepare dancers for the contemporary dance market, because it cultivates many practical and aesthetic traits that are desirable today. Choreographers are increasingly working with smaller casts and utilizing improvisation as part of the creative process, collaborating with dancers and building off their unique capabilities. Some dance scholars have rightly argued that this personal approach results in part from economic shifts on the dance market: the lack of funds available for big budget companies with large casts, or the need to accommodate individual capabilities, for instance (Bales and Nettl-Fiol 2008; Foster 1997; Kedhar 2014). I argue that it may also be due to the increased focus on individualism and personal freedom as a result of the proliferation of neoliberal rhetoric. Dancers today are increasingly expected to possess strong improvisation skills and a unique approach to movement, whether set choreography or self-developed phrases. Gaga thrives in the contemporary moment because it works on the qualities that marketable dancers must excel in today: the ability to self-direct, move quickly between styles and movement dynamics, and perform highly textured improvisation.

As a tool to address these contemporary requirements for dancers to possess, I think of Gaga as a metatechnique, or a way of managing multiple techniques within the body. What dancers gain through the practice of Gaga is the ability to both switch between and blur styles on command while making strategic artistic choices, illustrating the idea that Gaga does not teach one form, but rather a metacognitive methodology to approaching multiple forms already existing within a dancer's body. This suggests a difference from the "hired body" model put forth by dance scholar Susan Leigh Foster (1997), which refers to the contemporary dancer who is required to train in multiple techniques and therefore is rendered bland and homogenized. Foster has updated this term in a 2010 essay, introducing what she terms the "regrooving body" that draws on a wide variety of international dance techniques to acknowledge that efforts are often made within this type of multi-stylistic training model to maintain cultural and aesthetic specificities rather than devolving into a homogenized style. Still, she maintains that the "regrooving body" is an exception that exists alongside the many homogenized dancers involved in ballet and industry training, similar to her earlier conception of the "hired body." In contrast, I suggest that Gaga's pedagogical structure as a metatechnique allows for a rich stylistic range, not as an exception, but as a way of creating a new approach for dancers who are trained in many dance forms and styles to avoid the homogenized bland-ness Foster critiques. In order to demonstrate this asset of stylistic flexibility, the dancers must showcase their abilities in terms of their range of movement and dynamics and the ability to contrast them. While the stated intention of Gaga is to be an internal exploration, it nevertheless exists within the framework of a larger neoliberal dance economy in which students are more frequently asked to demonstrate skills than invest in personal movement research. Thus, students often use Gaga classes as a laboratory not only for internal research, but also to play with ways of exhibiting their metacognitive knowledge about employing dynamic and stylistic range. This is particularly true in Gaga intensives, where the stakes of demonstrating this knowledge are higher for dancers on the job market, who hope to impress their teachers.

This training is explicitly acknowledged by dancers to be beneficial in preparing for the contemporary dance market. Many of the dancers I interviewed indicated the need to excel at improvisation in auditions, and praised Gaga for developing their improvisation skills. A recent college graduate currently training throughout Europe, Clemons explained that she continues doing Gaga because she finds it personally enjoyable, but also important for professional development:

> Particularly because lots of choreographers are looking for collaborative dancers, and dancers that have improvisation experience, and even though we talked about that it's actually a quite structured improvisation class, there are those moments, especially as classes get to the end, where you're just given complete freedom to play with the tools you've been given. I think I've become a much better improvisational dancer since starting Gaga, which in today's dance world is I think pretty invaluable when you're looking for work. And also, hitting back on this idea of maturity as a dancer, I think that's been really beneficial, that I now am self-motivated to find you know, if a choreographer isn't spelling out for me, like this may be deep and rich environment below the movement, to have the motivation from me to find that for myself, and to make this world that I'm in, I think that's really helpful professionally. (Meredith Clemons, July 14, 2015)

Although Gaga's contribution to the professionalization of dancers is focused on individual growth, this shift toward a neoliberal dance economy based on rampant individualism does not negate the ethos of competition that is the cornerstone of earlier dance economies.[13] While Gaga does not enforce competition between dancers in terms of excelling at particular movements that are easily judged against one another, it does support the type of individual pressure to maintain constant growth to continuously prove one's ability within a frequently shifting dance economy. This is fitting in a neoliberal context, where the prevalence of contract and short-term work encourages competition for workers to constantly demonstrate their worth and earn further employment. Although Gaga may not be designed as a neoliberal training method, it is well suited to be adopted by its participants to thrive in the demands of contemporary markets through an emphasis on personal research and self-development.

EMBRACING THE CONTRADICTIONS IN GAGA INTENSIVES

Gaga, as an increasingly popular training tool for contemporary concert dancers, teaches skills that have been deemed important by many choreographers for dancers in the current moment. Gaga's emphasis on improvisation and dynamic range are crucial for adhering to contemporary aesthetic interests and choreographic methods, and the focus on the self through the rhetoric of freedom allows dancers to utilize this individual work for professional gain. It is important to acknowledge, however, that Gaga's incorporation of the concept of freedom is not a replication of neoliberal values in an attempt to fit neatly into this economic system. Rather, it presents a continuation of dance-specific relationships to bodily freedom. Not every participant uses the Gaga intensive for professional gain. There remain some students who pursue Gaga training for its intrinsic value and internal research, employing the Gaga toolbox as a way of better understanding one's body, regardless of the status of an upcoming audition. Many of the dancers in the intensive who intend to use Gaga for furthering their careers, too, invest in Gaga at a personal level, and largely ignore the competitive aspects and sociality within the event. This is arguably in line with Gaga's intrinsic philosophy of creating an open space for internal movement research. Yet I observe this approach being followed more often by mature dancers who, regardless of age, have moved beyond a superficial interest in the virtuosity of dancing. As Einav Katan notes in her philosophical reading of Gaga, "[m]ovement research inquires into bodily perception and intensifies it for its own sake" (2016, 57). Thus, to truly engage in Gaga research, and not simply externalize an aesthetic interpretation of the prompts, one must be constantly attentive to one's practice. This is difficult for the many young dancers who are frequently pulled out of their internal focus by the pressure to show off or demonstrate eligibility for future employment. However, for mature dancers who are prepared to focus on the intent of the practice and not the goals of the dancers around them, especially ones without professional goals tied to their participation in Gaga intensives, the structure of open exploration allows for a freedom from not only their existing habits, but also many conventional dance training methods currently practiced in the Western concert dance world.

In framing the intensive space as a competitive one, I highlight the prevalence of economic pressures on dancers as they partake in Gaga. Although this movement language may not have been designed to further neoliberal agendas of personal freedom and development for economic gain, Gaga is easily subsumed in this process because of its applicability to contemporary demands in dance markets. This analysis of Gaga may prove useful for understanding the plights of the precariat and what they must do to remain competitive in today's economic markets, but it also questions the impact that economics can have on artistic practices in particular. Gaga's focus on independent research appears to align with these neoliberal values of freedom, individualism, and constant progress and competition, suggesting that artistic goals are not the only values that can be enacted through the practice of Gaga. As neoliberal economics continue to be a dominant model internationally, forcing individuals to remain competitive and economically motivated in all sectors of life, then practices such as Gaga that are used by dancers for professional development remain pressured by the need to make progress for professional development and job security in the contemporary dance market. As long as these neoliberal pressures remain, dance training such as Gaga cannot be considered as artistic practice devoid of external economic influence. In acknowledging this relationship between dance and economics, we are able to better understand how the embodiment of Gaga practice exists in tension with neoliberal values.

Notes

1. This observation is based on three years of fieldwork, attending Gaga classes in the United States (2012–2015) and Germany (summer 2015), and two summer intensives in Tel Aviv (summer 2013 and 2015).

2. The term *research* is often applied to the practice of Gaga in studios by instructors; in interviews and on the official Gaga website, however, it is often described in vaguer terms (such as a "way of gaining knowledge and self-awareness"). The use of the term *research* refers to the intrinsic value ascribed to knowledge and the agency of the students to teach themselves through self-exploration. The specific term *research* within the Gaga context has been the source of some humor to me as an academic researcher; at the 2015 Gaga summer intensive in Tel Aviv, during an open discussion with the students and Naharin, one student asked about people doing Gaga research, referring to academic studies, but it was interpreted by Naharin as referring to the research done inside the studio by the dancers on their own bodies. I, too, have had to clarify at times when speaking to potential interview subjects that my research is for a written academic project, and that it is not for my own personal movement research.

3. Work instructions include the following: never stop, listening to the body, awareness, silence, and adhering to class start times (Gaga people.dancers 2016).

4. All interviews cited in this chapter were with the author. I have included the dancers' real names when permission was granted. I have preserved the oral flow of their speaking style with minimal editing to reinforce the self-reflective and impromptu nature of these interviews and their representations of daily life as a dancer.

5. As David Harvey (2005, 3) notes, politicians such as Ronald Reagan, Margaret Thatcher, and Deng Xaioping were the leaders of this policy shift, which quickly became integrated into smaller economies and nations that were pressured into this neoliberal model by these leaders' powerful nation-states to the point that today "neoliberalism has, in short, become hegemonic as a mode of discourse."

6. Freedom, here, refers to both individual freedom (which in neoliberal theory is to be obtained by having economic freedom, which allows one to exist outside of government-initiated social programs) and the freedom of economic markets (which in theory would be completely deregulated and exist as open-market systems devoid of government oversight). For both the individual and market level, the theory is that lack of oversight allows for greatest independence in making choices about how to live life.

7. As mentioned previously, Naharin and Gaga teachers frequently refer to the practice of Gaga as "research" for the participants. Pleasure is another common element of Gaga rhetoric both in the formal work instructions for Gaga and throughout advertising materials and classroom instructions; it is pivotal to the practice of Gaga. The association of Gaga with pleasure and self-awareness is reinforced in journalistic articles about Gaga, where the authors largely mimic the advertising material that describes Gaga or the descriptions offered by Gaga management and instructors.

8. Methodics classes are similar to Gaga classes, but are slower paced and are focused on one or two themes to be explored in depth. The teacher also has the option to start and stop class to explain concepts and terminology, which is not allowed in the constant motion structure of regular Gaga classes.

9. This understanding of technique as restrictive and static is widely acknowledged, but not universally accepted. It also does not take into consideration the complex cultural and

racial politics of technique (for instance, see Monroe 2011). The question of what a technique is, in relation to dance practices, and how Gaga relates to this concept and label, is explored further by Friedes Galili (2015) and Quinlan (2016).

10. A popular definition of the precariat "is a distinctive socio-economic group" (Standing 2011, 7) that includes workers in precarious situations such as temporary employment. This growing class is unique to the emergence of globalization and neoliberal economic systems, which resulted in increasingly flexible open labor markets with decreased job security, particularly for lower-class wage workers. At the same time, economist Guy Standing points out, "it is not right to equate the precariat with the working poor or with just insecure employment, although these dimensions are correlated with it. The precariousness also implies a lack of a secure work-based identity, whereas workers in some low-income jobs may be building a career" (Standing 2011, 10). Rather, Standing defines the precariat as people who lack seven forms of labor-related security, those being: "Labour market security," "Employment security," "Job security," "Work security," "Skill reproduction security," "Income security," and "Representation security" (Standing 2011, 10). In this understanding of the term, dancers are easily classified as part of the precariat class. Though they have opportunities to develop skills, which is not usually true of the precariat, because this is primarily achieved through private time and resources, the status of the dancer as laborer remains precarious.

11. The learning and circulation of dance knowledge as a cultural commodity or ascribing value to this process in a capitalist structure has been the subject of important studies. Dance scholar Anna B. Scott (2001) acknowledged dance as having both cultural and monetary value as well as sociocultural markers, and other scholars such as anthropologists John and Jean Comaroff (2009) have similarly argued that cultural capital can be acquired not just through the commoditization of tangible goods but also by the acquisition of culturally specific knowledge, which can acquire economic value through the marketing of experiences and performances. Dance scholar Thomas DeFrantz (2012) suggests that the transfer of this cultural capital is less direct than the exchange of tangible goods; depending on the mode of transfer (in person, digital, and so on) and the context of the transfer (such as who is teaching, how immersed the student is in the culture), the quality and integrity of the product (here, the embodiment of specific bodily movements in choreographed sequences) possesses shifting values. DeFrantz, for instance, notes a "flattening" in the spread of black social dance as it circulates via digital platforms such as YouTube, which enables the learning of movements decontextualized from their origins that ultimately diminishes the authenticity and value of the performance of these dances. In the case of learning Naharin's choreography, students acquire the cultural capital of knowing choreography, but the quality and length of instruction are less than that of company members or those who have learned entire works, thus imparting only a fraction of the cultural capital of dancers who have learned and performed the full works. These students do not own the product (the choreography) and thus do not directly acquire a commodity that they can sell, but this cultural capital of bodily knowledge can be employed strategically in audition or improvisation settings to draw attention to their bodily histories and experiences.

12. Intensives are held biannually in Tel Aviv and New York City; workshops and intensives are also held on a semi-regular basis at European locations such as Torino, Italy; Barcelona, Spain; and Amsterdam, The Netherlands; in addition to one-time events held elsewhere in Europe and North America. The length and availability of Gaga intensives are currently being expanded in many locations.

13. By earlier dance economies, I refer to the predominance of form-based techniques in the early American modern dance era, and the need for dancers to outperform others in particular techniques to obtain a higher status in a hierarchically structured company. Though the hierarchical structure of companies is more prevalent in the ballet world, within early modern dance companies such as the Martha Graham Dance Company there were solos and other featured roles only granted to her favorite dancers. Though this is still prevalent in many ballet companies today, increasingly modern/contemporary dance companies have rejected hierarchical models of company structures that encourage competition among dancers in similar ranks who want to move up in the company in favor of more collaborative choreographic and performance modes.

References

Bales, Melanie, and Rebecca Nettl-Fiol, eds. 2008. *The Body Eclectic: Evolving Practices in Dance Training*. Champaign-Urbana: University of Illinois Press.

Brown, Wendy. 2015. *Undoing the Demos: Neoliberalism's Stealth Revolution*. New York: Zone Books.

Comaroff, John, and Jean Comaroff. 2009. *Ethnicity, Inc*. Chicago: University of Chicago Press.

DeFrantz, Thomas F. 2012. "Unchecked Popularity: Neoliberal Circulations of BlackSocial Dance." In *Neoliberalism and Global Theatres: Performance Permutations*, edited by Lara D. Nielsen and Patricia Ybarra, 128–142. London; New York: Palgrave Macmillan.

Foster, Susan Leigh. 1997. "Dancing Bodies." In *Meaning in Motion*, edited by Jane C. Desmond, 235–257. Durham, NC: Duke University Press.

Foster, Susan Leigh. 2010. "Dancing Bodies: An Addendum." *Theater* 40(1): 25–29.

Gaga people.dancers. 2016. *Gaga Movement Ltd*. http://gagapeople.com/english/.

Galili, Deborah Friedes. 2015. "Gaga: Moving beyond Technique with Ohad Naharin in the Twenty-First Century." *Dance Chronicle* 38(3): 360–392.

Goldman, Danielle. 2010. *I Want to Be Ready: Improvised Dance as a Practice of Freedom*. Ann Arbor: University of Michigan Press.

Hardt, Michael, and Antonio Negri. 2012. *Declaration*. Argo-Navis, Kindle Edition. https://antonionegriinenglish.files.wordpress.com/2012/05/93152857-hardt-negri-declaration-2012.pdf.

Harvey, David. 2005. *A Brief History of Neoliberalism*. New York; Oxford: Oxford University Press.

Katan, Einav. 2016. *Embodied Philosophy in Dance: Gaga and Ohad Naharin's Movement Research*. London: Palgrave Macmillan.

Kedhar, Anusha. 2014. "Flexibility and Its Bodily Limits: Transnational South Asian Dancers in an Age of Neoliberalism." *Dance Research Journal* 46(1): 23–40.

Mahmood, Saba. 2004. *Politics of Piety: The Islamic Revival and the Feminist Subject*. Princeton, NJ: Princeton University Press.

Monroe, Raquel. 2011. "'I Don't Want to Do African . . . What about My Technique?': Transforming Dancing Places into Spaces in the Academy." *The Journal of Pan African Studies* 4(6): 38–55.

Ong, Aihwa. 2006. *Neoliberalism as Exception: Mutations in Citizenship and Sovereignty*. Durham, NC: Duke University Press.

Quinlan, Meghan. 2016. "Gaga as Politics: A Case Study of Contemporary Dance Training." PhD diss., University of California, Riverside.

Scott, Anna B. 2001. "Dance." In *Culture Works: The Political Economy of Culture*, edited by Richard Maxwell, 107–130. Minneapolis: University of Minnesota Press.

Standing, Guy. 2011. *The Precariat: The New Dangerous Class*. London; New York: Bloomsbury.

Audiovisual Sources

Natalie Portman on Ohad Naharin's Movement Language Gaga—from Mr. Gaga by Tomer Heymann. 2013. YouTube video, 0:58. Posted by "Mr. Gaga: Ohad Naharin documentary by Tomer Heymann," November 25. https://www.youtube.com/watch?v=bFPx10Toobw. Accessed October 10, 2015.

CHAPTER 25

"WE'LL RUMBLE 'EM RIGHT"

Aggression and Play in the Dance-Offs
of West Side Story

YING ZHU AND DANIEL BELGRAD

WEST SIDE STORY, the dance musical conceived and choreographed by Jerome Robbins, with music by Leonard Bernstein and lyrics by Stephen Sondheim, is a classic of American musical theater. Its 1961 film version holds an even more prominent place in our historical consciousness than the original Broadway production of 1957. The film was received with critical acclaim and garnered eleven Academy Award nominations, winning ten of them, including Best Picture.

Among scholarly critics who have analyzed the film's social implications, a focus on its ethnic dimension has usually predominated. As a tragedy of interethnic rivalry, the movie offers a twentieth-century variation on the *Romeo and Juliet* story, in which the Puerto Rican Sharks and the white-ethnic Jets engage in a turf war that dooms the secret lovers, Tony and Maria. As literary scholar Frances Negrón-Muntaner (2000, 83) has written, "There is no single American cultural product that haunts Puerto Rican identity . . . more intensely than the 1961 film, *West Side Story*." Alberto Sandoval Sanchez (1999, 64) similarly emphasizes how the Puerto Rican migration to New York City in the 1940s and 1950s threatened the "semiotic spatial organization of Anglo-Americans" in his reading of the film from the vantage of the politics of space.

Dance scholars, in particular, have illuminated the manner by which the dancing body and the choreography in *West Side Story* are complicit in sustaining a problematic depiction of Puerto Ricans, framing their identity and ethnicity through Spanish-inflected body stylings, coupled with Cuban-inspired dance action (Scott 2010). In her analysis of "Dance at the Gym," one of the central dances of the film, Anna B. Scott (2010, 83) locates how the Sharks' dancing, with its "emphasis on the hips," as opposed to the Jets' emphasis on height and acrobatics, signals cultural difference between the two groups. Such a reading is further corroborated by Rachel Duerden and Bonnie Rowell (2013), who perceive, in the same dance, how the dancers' embodiment operates as an apparatus of racial differentiation. These readings underscore the manner by which ethnic difference is woven into the very physical warp of the musical's dances, in addition to driving the plot.

But a close attention to Jerome Robbins's choreography suggests that, in his imagination at least, the musical's fundamental conflict was not only between the Jets and the Sharks, but also the struggle of both gangs against the strictures of adult society. Thus the movie's spaces, in addition to providing a medium through which interethnic rivalry is enacted, function as sites in which a subversive construction of youth identity is embodied and defined. In his book *West Side Story as Cinema*, Ernesto Acevedo-Muñoz (2013) compares the film in this respect to the subgenre of folk musicals. In such coming-of-age tales, the homosocial and homoerotic bonds of youth give way to the heterosexual coupling associated with adulthood. The only difference is that in *West Side Story*, they don't (Acevedo-Muñoz 2013). Instead, the film celebrates youth and portrays adulthood as a surrender of individual vitality to the demands of socialization: a devil's bargain in which the adults have traded physical energy and meaningful action for social acceptance and power.

The adults' lack of vitality in *West Side Story* is embodied in the pusillanimity of Doc (the owner of the candy store, who employs Tony) and Glad Hand (the high school social worker). The more threatening face of adult authority is represented by Lieutenant Schrank and Officer Krupke. These enforcers of the law pretend that their social power is rooted in their acceptance of moral responsibility, while the film shows it to be based in fact on their privileged use of force. "Oh, yeah, sure, I know: 'it's a free country, an' I ain't got the right.' But I got a *badge*. Whadda *you* got?" Schrank taunts Bernardo, the leader of the Sharks, when he encounters him in parlay with Riff, the leader of the Jets, in Doc's candy store (Lehman 2003, 103–104).

The adults of *West Side Story* work persistently to force the Jets and Sharks into one of two binary categories that are discursively acceptable to them: responsible adults or victimized children. But the youths themselves make common cause in resisting and exceeding these categories, through forms of competitive play that sprawl from the playground into the streets, and beyond children's games to the brawling and balling that adult discourses of the time labelled as "juvenile delinquency." Just as Officer Krupke and Detective Schrank patrol the streets enforcing adult authority, so the Jets and Sharks claim the same streets in resistance to the constraints of normative adulthood. They dance and play through the streets and alleys of the West Side, occupying playgrounds, sidewalks, apartment building rooftops, and front stoops in the name of an oppositional youth identity.[1]

With their first dances and fistfights, the Jets and Sharks together colonize the socially ordered space of the playground for their own expansive play, only to be interrupted by Schrank and Krupke. It is Schrank's sneer, "You hoodlums don't own these streets!" that provokes the Jets to defy him by planning a rumble with the Sharks. They bitterly rehearse a litany of phrases by which the adults assert their control of living space, such as the street, the home, the park, the block, or the "here" of wherever the youth happen to be. "Keep offa da woild!" the Jet named Action fumes, then fervently proclaims, "A gang dat don' owna street is nothin'!" which prompts Riff to declare, "WE DO OWN IT!" (Lehman 2003, 11). When Bernardo shows up at the dance in the gym, the opportunity is presented to stage a rumble that will take back the streets—*from* Schrank.

The two youth gangs present a united front against adult restrictions by staging forms of competitive play (Acevedo-Muñoz 2013). When Schrank and Krupke break up the early fistfight on the playground, for example, the two gangs engage in a game of verbal sparring in which each tries to better the other's mockery of adult authority. The game is engaged when Riff and the Jets greet Schrank with ironically exaggerated politeness; Bernardo and the Sharks join in by giving Krupke the same treatment. Choreographically, the physical arrangement of bodies in the space is in the process transformed: from that of a face-off between the two gangs, to that of two adults surrounded by a gauntlet of youths. When Schrank drags Baby John toward the Sharks and asks him which of them attacked him, Riff intervenes to draw Schrank's attention away, offering, "We suspicion the job was done by a cop." When Officer Krupke responds, "Impossible!" it is Bernardo's turn, in the call-and-response structure of this competition, to riposte, "In America, *nothing* is impossible." He garners even more admiring looks from the Jets when he asks Schrank to translate his ensuing tirade into Spanish.

As this encounter demonstrates, in the context of the overarching struggle between youths and adult authority, the escalating conflict between the Jets and the Sharks takes shape as a form of competitive play that is structured by well-understood rules of engagement. As Johan Huizinga (1949) argues in *Homo Ludens*, play and competition are often synonymous, and competitive play may take the form of physical and verbal sparring. "All fighting that is bound by rules," he writes, "bears the formal characteristics of play" (Huizinga 1949, 89). In physical terms, the rules are expressed through a choreography that organizes bodily interactions in contested spaces. The social theorist Paul Goodman, a contemporary of Jerome Robbins who was, like Robbins, sympathetic to the notion of an oppositional youth culture, observed in his classic work *Growing Up Absurd* (1960, 10) that

> [o]ur social scientists have become so accustomed to the highly organized and by-and-large smoothly running society that they have begun to think that "social animal" means "harmoniously belonging." They do not like to think that fighting or dissenting are proper social functions.

But *West Side Story* imagines a broader range of acceptable social behaviors, including diverse forms of competitive play, which it celebrates the youth for exercising.

Upon closer inspection, all of the movie's scenes of the Jets and Sharks in conflict are staged to emphasize the nature of this fighting as a playful collective competition. Even the rumble that causes two deaths is presented as originating in a form of play that approximates the intimacy of a duet ("We're going to jazz it up and have a ball tonight," the Jets sing). The gangs bait and dare each other in the course of their conflicts in a manner very like the way that the Sharks and their girls taunt and tease each other in the dance number "America," down to the detail that the hand gesture used (a beckoning with the fingers) is the same in both cases. As Bernardo's girl Anita tells Maria, the boys fight like they dance: as if they "need to get rid of something fast . . . too much feeling" (Lehman 2003, 75–76). In her analysis of breakdancing, Sally Banes (2004, 14–15) has described its hyper-physical, competitive style as "a kind of serious game . . . that had urgent social significance for the dancers" as a vehicle for expressing rivalries between African American and Puerto Rican youths. This understanding of competitive dancing as "serious play" can be applied to the dances of *West Side Story* as well, for they too express a rivalry that is for the most part illegible to the adult authorities that the youths seek to elude and defy.

In analyzing the meanings of competitive dancing in the film, we employ an approach that synthesizes methods and theoretical approaches from both dance studies and cultural studies. In cultural studies today, an emerging interpretive revolution seeks to recover an embodied and affective subject as the center of meaning-making.[2] Dance studies offers methodological importance here because of dance's historical emphasis on the affective and embodied aspects of subjectivity (McCormack 2014). Exploding conventional notions of "dance" and "choreography," dance scholar David Gere (2004) posits dance to exist along a continuum of movement, where performances easily recognizable as dance reside alongside the less formal motions and postures that constitute deliberately designed actions. Our investigation of *West Side Story* participates in this orientation, as we attend both to the moves situated on the dance floor and to the more pedestrian choreographies of the streets and alleys.

West Side Story articulates a cultural position toward conflict that is similar to that which Paul Goodman (1960) proposed. It is presented as a necessary aspect of healthy behavior in a social context. But it distinguishes socially healthy forms of conflict from unhealthy ones, as Huizinga (1949) did, by the former's adherence to a level of affective discipline that is rendered choreographically (McNeill 1997). Consequently, healthy social conflict is rendered as a competition (whether friendly or not-so-friendly) with a structure that arises from commonly understood rules. Unhealthy forms of conflict, by contrast, are represented as unchoreographed outbursts of uncontrolled affect, a quality that marks them as socially pathological. It is only when the choreography of competition is interrupted that such a level of violence ensues. We examine three of the movie's dances: "America," performed by the Sharks and their girls; the "Mambo Dance-Off" in the dance at the gym; and the knife fight in the "Rumble." From this analysis, we argue that, in the world of *West Side Story*, as long as conflict is structured as a competition it remains a cooperative and ordered enterprise; but when the choreographic structure is disrupted, underlying social frustrations can erupt into fatal violence.

TAUNTING AND FLAUNTING IN "AMERICA"

The "America" dance, presented in the movie as a dance-off that pits Puerto Rican boys against Puerto Rican girls, demonstrates that *West Side Story* celebrates conflict as an expression of vitality, and that its representations of competitiveness are not restricted to scenes of interethnic rivalry. Past critical analyses of this number have understandably focused on its representation of the costs and benefits of immigration (Sandoval Sanchez 1999). But when critical attention centers on the dance choreography rather than on the song lyrics, sexual teasing emerges as the number's *primum mobile*. In this respect, the film integrates this dance more fully into its central problematic than does the original Broadway musical, which casts it as a girls-only number. In the film version, the teasing conflict between the sexes increases the emotional intensity of their play.

The specter of adulthood looms behind the defiantly playful sexuality of the "America" dance. As Bernardo and Anita climb the stairs to the roof before the dance begins, they are arguing about the differences between New York and Puerto Rico, but also, and primarily, about Bernardo's assumption of adult authority over Maria. Anita scorns Bernardo's parental pretensions, equating them with femininity and decrepitude ("*He* is the old married woman," she tells Maria), and she defends Maria's right to a wider scope of (sexual) play: "Girls here are free to have fun. She is in America now" (Lehman 2003, 35). But Bernardo resists this idea; and it is in this context that their debate about the relative merits of living in Puerto Rico versus New York begins.

Among the youths who are the film's main characters, mature adulthood is defined primarily by holding a job, and secondarily by heteronormative marriage (Lehman 2003). The protagonists, Tony and Maria, already have jobs; and when they fall in love during the dance at the gym, they are perilously close to joining the ranks of the enemy. In this respect, the film invites an alternative reading of its central romance, according to what James C. Scott (1990) calls a "hidden transcript": a subtext by which politically disempowered subjects articulate evasive critiques of the social world that they perforce inhabit.[3] In this hidden transcript, Tony and Maria's romance is marked by Jerome Robbins as dangerous, not because it causes conflict between the Jets and the Sharks, but because it threatens to cement their capitulation to adulthood, a fate that is foreshadowed by the mock wedding in which they kneel before internalized projections of their parents and God.

In this context, the "America" dance, which is staged directly following their dive into serious romance, provides an opportunity for resituating sexuality squarely back in the realm of youthful play. The affective quality of playful competition that pervades the dance is repeatedly emphasized in the choreography. As Bernardo and Anita fling open the door to the rooftop and emerge from the stairs, Anita jokingly thrusts a clenched fist at Bernardo's face. He redirects her combative gesture into one of sexual coyness by kissing her fist. In the bantering back-and-forth that ensues, they enlist the other Sharks and their girls in their lovers' quarrel, until a battle of the sexes is joined. The girls follow Anita's lead in praising America as a land of opportunity (for young women), while the boys complain of racial discrimination so as to defend their masculinity in light of their failure to achieve social mobility. Anita mocks Bernardo's familiar complaints; she signals the engagement of battle by extending her right leg and stomping twice in a flamenco-like step.

Anita's fistical flourish and foot stomps belong to the gestural vocabulary of *taunting*. Taunting is an affective interaction that marks a choreography of playful competition.

In the opening scene, the Jet named Tiger similarly flourishes his fist in Bernardo's face upon their first meeting, inviting the incipient gang rivalry. Another of these taunting gestures is the beckoning hand movement that is common to the opening scene, the "America" dance, and the rumble. Like the "trash talking" sometimes exchanged by competitive athletes, taunting functions both as a form of competition in itself and as a prelude to competition's more physical manifestations.

Anita's bare-legged stomp also constitutes, in a way that hand gestures do not, an instance of *flaunting*, a sexual display in which sexual teasing becomes a tool of taunting. In "America," the flaunting increases as the dance becomes more physical. Bernardo pursues Anita around the roof until he captures her in his arms. As he accuses her of being "brainwashed," her stance becomes confrontational, but her body motion remains coy and flirtatious. Her pretense of anger is overshadowed by a facial expression of wide-eyed coquetry, with her pouting lips pursed as if imparting a kiss.

Such playful defiance characterizes the women's choreography of flaunting in this dance. As the dance proper begins, Anita looks coquettishly back at Bernardo over her left shoulder, her arms splayed out at an angle around her hips, and walks toward the camera, her hips gently swaying. First her hands clasp to her chest in mock innocence and "devotion"; then the sentimentality of her motion transforms into mischievousness as she archly mimes Puerto Rico's sinking into the ocean. She swishes her hips as she walks back to a row of Sharks and their girls watching in fascination, then raises her arms around her head and sways her shoulders and upper torso (purportedly to mime "hurricanes blowing"). With a series of forward pelvic thrusts she enacts the moves of copulation. Then she juts out her right hip, steps her left foot over her right, and flips around, catching her skirt and swishing it to reveal the petticoats underneath. Lifting and swishing her skirt some more, she promenades across the space and back again. All this is a bodily enunciation, challenging Bernardo to "do" better—in short, taunting him by flaunting her sexual desirability.

Anita ends her peroration with a movement sequence offering a consummate fusion of taunting and flaunting. As her left hand grasps and lifts the hem of her skirt to reveal the frilly petticoat underneath, she pokes her right index finger repeatedly at Bernardo while thrusting her torso forward and popping out her left hip. Her stance is simultaneously confrontational and explicitly flirtatious, indicating that this offers both an invitation and a challenge. When she sings "put that in!" the sexual overtones of her movements infuse the lyric with sexual implications. She completes her statement by transforming her poking index finger into an arching reach overhead, as she dramatically flips her body around and performs a standing wheelbarrow turn, kicking her left leg in the air. In this way, she favors Bernardo (and the camera) with a fleeting glimpse of her cleavage.

Until now, the spectators to the competition have mainly been grouped in couples. At this point, the girls and boys form into two "teams," and their dancing takes on the call-and-response structure that typifies Robbins's choreographies of team competition. At first, the call-and-response of verbal repartee predominates. The five principal girls form a line and sing the praises of America in unison. Having provoked a response from

Bernardo, they circle together to the left, swishing their skirts and their hips before re-turning to continue the debate. The girls and boys trade verbal phrases, as the girls take turns displaying their bodies and the boys look them up and down. Then the competition takes a more physical turn. To the girls' cries of "*Olé*," Bernardo and two other boys dance in a triangle formation, with their right arms held in a curve and their left arms extended into space. Lunging and pirouetting, they show off their strength, dexterity, and balance. They rise to their toes and lift their arms straight up, making themselves very tall, and circle to the left with fancy footwork. The girls, impressed, gape and point admiringly. The boys end their statement by leaping into the air with both legs bent in a double "stag" jump. Having asserted their command, they beckon Anita and the girls back onto the dance floor. Their beckoning hand gesture simultaneously represents an overt call for the Shark girls to answer their challenge and a lewd catcall signaling sexual desire.

The girls respond by escalating the aggressiveness of their sexual play. Anita charges at the boys with the other Shark girls behind her. She wears a smile that is both joyful and teasing as she lifts her skirts and, stopping in front of her romantic partner, leans back to kick twice at his face, as her skirts fly up around her. Her kicks are followed by double turns that make her skirts swirl to reveal the lower half of her body. Then she executes another high kick, while continuing to gaze directly at Bernardo. This simulated fighting is rife with sexual teasing, constituting a flirtatious response to his call. She then turns, lifting the front of her skirt, and, thrusting her pelvis in a sexual back-and-forth mo-tion, locomotes away from him, her upper torso bouncing in response to the thrusting motion of her hips. Next, raising her right arm in the air, she sidles back toward him to perform a seductive hip wiggle in tantalizing proximity. But then she shatters her se-ductive mood, taunting him by stamping her right foot and shouting "ha! ha! ha!" while flinging her skirts up and down in a way that again suggests more of a challenge than an invitation. She concludes her call with a final twirl and a leap, casting Bernardo a last challenging look over her shoulder.

The boys respond to this call with a short pantomime demonstrating their difficulties as men in America. Four of them join hands and sing "la la la la la" while performing a simulated minuet, which suddenly devolves into a fistfight. "America!" they pro-claim, and the minuet returns, only to transform again, this time to kicks in the behind. The boys' pantomime transitions the dance back into the realm of verbal repartee. But though the boys seem to have the last word, the girls fight back by feigning a lack of interest. They stroll downstage together as the boys tag along beside them, trying un-successfully to regain their attention. Finally, when Bernardo shouts into Anita's ear, "Terrible time in America!" she ambushes him, swinging her arm out to grab his chest and declare archly, "You forget *I'm* in America."

Having scored what she and the other girls seem to consider the winning point, Anita turns toward Bernardo, and pushes him backward across the roof, claiming its space for the girls to perform a flirtatious victory dance. In this respect, "America" reproduces, in its contestation of space, the dynamics of the interethnic turf battle that lies at the root of the gang rivalry, emphasizing its playful aspect. (A similar claiming and relinquishing of dancing space marks the competition between the Jets and the Sharks in the dance at the gym.) Not yet ready to concede defeat, Bernardo attempts to renew the argument; but after two more rounds of verbal call-and-response in which Anita has the last word, the girls emphasize their victory by again demonstrating their control of the space, backing away from the boys across the rooftop, all the while subjecting them to the taunting of the familiar beckoning gesture and hooting catcalls.

The boys reassert a modicum of masculine dominance by edging around the girls and chasing them off the dance floor. This male aggression is well received, which further marks the competition for space as a playful one; Anita's face shows her glee as she runs. The boys then engage in an extended display of heteronormative masculine "surrender." Beginning with a hand gesture of appreciation for the girls' sexual attractiveness, they pantomime "falling" for them, then rise on their toes and raise their fingers to their heads to make bulls' horns, and finally mime serenading, thus acting out the paradoxical aggressiveness and vulnerability of their male sexuality. They advance on the girls with their lower arms splayed out at their sides, their hands wagging suggestively; stopping just short of touching them, they stutter step away again and with exuberance raise their lower legs and beat on their thighs like drums. Finally, they ask the girls for a reciprocal surrender by pretending to shoot them with guns; and the girls comply by "dropping dead" or swooning into each other's arms.

This restoration of power parity in terms of mutual surrender opens a way to the competition's denouement. In the last phase of the dance, both teams revert to an almost childlike innocence. The men hold hands and skip away across the rooftop; the girls skip along behind them. The boys turn to chase the girls and, when confronted, goof around like children embarrassed to be caught desiring. The two teams then form up and dance together: first clapping in unison, then, as if to emphasize their complementarity, forming near mirror images of each other. Finally, the girls leap into the boys' arms and perch on their shoulders. The competition thus ends with the opposing teams reunified in pairings that demonstrate the complementarity between the boys' strength and the girls' lightness. At the same time, the pairings are playful ones, in that the choreography leaves open the question of who has emerged dominant and triumphant. Have the boys proven stronger, or are the girls on top? The playful heterosexual taunting that is at the heart of the dance is thus emphasized in the moment that it is resolved, so that the threatening heteronormative romance between Tony and Maria is displaced by a playful sexuality.

"Mambo!"

In the same way that the "America" dance pits boys against girls in a playful "team" competition through dance, the mambo dance-off at the center of the "Dance at the Gym" number pits Sharks against Jets in an interethnic rivalry along the same lines.

Interethnic competition is of course at the heart of the musical's plot. And from the film's opening shots, a choreography of taunting is introduced as the primary means by which it is pursued. Meeting Bernardo for the first time on the streets of their neighborhood, the Jets begin this taunting ritual. Riff, the leader of the Jets, mocks Bernardo by looking him up and down and laughing dismissively. Two other Jets (Ice and Tiger) then follow Bernardo while making effeminizing whistling and kissing noises; and when he halts, Tiger grinningly brandishes a fist in his face. In the next shot, however, Bernardo is joined by two lieutenants and they begin to claim territory. Encountering two smaller Jets (A-Rab and Baby John), the three Sharks invite them with exaggerated politeness to walk in front of them, in order to subject them to whistles, kissing noises, and catcalls. When they suddenly come across a larger body of Jets loitering behind a parked truck, however, it is again the Sharks' turn to get taunted. The trading of taunts in this opening scene thus establishes the call-and-response structure that characterizes the Jets-versus-Sharks competition overall.

"Dance at the Gym," by introducing the presence of heterosexual couples into the choreography, allows the vocabulary of interethnic rivalry to expand, to include flaunting as well as taunting. The boys and girls of each ethnic group flaunt to members of the opposite sex within their own group, but in competition with the members of the rival group. The first instance of this emerges in the way that Graziella and Anita parade as they position themselves at the beginning of Glad Hand's circle dance preceding the mambo dance-off. Responding to Riff's minimalist invitation (a cock of the head) to join him on the dance floor, Graziella stares pointedly at the Sharks as she walks out, hands on hips, accompanied by appreciative murmurs from the Jets. Bernardo's invitational gesture to Anita is grander, and her walk to join him on the dance floor is proportionately more elaborate.

The movie makes a point of framing the mambo dance-off between Jets and Sharks within their larger struggle against adult authority by juxtaposing it to the circular "get-together dance" that Glad Hand attempts to impose. Glad Hand's feeble effort to enforce his authority is supported by Officer Krupke's implicit threat of force. It represents the adults' strategy for averting the disruptive expression of youthful energy that threatens to break out on the dance floor. In an effort to erase the tensions, Glad Hand proposes a dance in the form of a children's game. With everyone organized into two gender-specific rows, the girls are to move counterclockwise while the boys rotate in the opposite direction. A pause in the music will randomly assign them dance partners. Glad Hand's circle dance is a game of chance, rather than a competition. Lacking a competitive edge, it is affectless, like Glad Hand himself. With its absurdly simple music and its absence of a competitive spirit, it represents an adult-imposed mock-up of real play. In contrast, the authentic play of the mambo dance-off embodies the dual excitements of competition and sexuality. Significantly, both gangs are willing to play along with Glad Hand's dance only so long as it provides them with an opportunity for taunting and flaunting. But as soon as that possibility expires, they reject it.

The Jets and Sharks are allied in resisting the rules of play that Glad Hand attempts to inscribe onto their bodies, choosing instead to choreograph their own moves outside the bounds laid down by the adult authorities. As dance scholar Julia Foulkes (2015, 1042) observes, "not conceding to this fakery of the idea of tolerance through dance, Riff and Bernardo make it into a challenge and pull their own women to dance with them when the circle stops. Then the battle begins." As the rival factions regroup on opposite sides of the dance floor, they call and respond with shouts of "mambo!" thus mutually agreeing to a more expansive form of play.

The film shows this transition to be smoothly executed, as if to demonstrate that, contrary to Glad Hand's fears, youthful aggression need not be unruly or discordant. Although the mambo dance-off's choreography is exuberantly energetic, it adheres to rules. Physical and sexual aggressiveness are contained within a choreographic structure. As the dance-off begins, we see the two groups dancing fiercely in couples, each occupying one side of the gymnasium. With the late arrival of Tony, this choreography is replaced by a call-and-response of more intense taunting and flaunting: as in the "America" dance, a "team" competition is engaged, which includes multiple drives to claim the physical space of the dance floor (Foulkes 2015, 1042). This core of the dance-off adheres to a modern jazz structure, consisting of a 32-bar "chorus" by each group followed by the "trading" of shorter and shorter phrases: first 16-bar, then 8-bar, and finally 4-bar phrases. These progressively shorter time intervals intensify the energy of the competition.

Significantly, it is Tony's entrance into the gym that disrupts the original couples-dancing choreography and catalyzes a ramping up of the taunting and flaunting. In the same way that the "serious" romance between Tony and Maria prompts the reactively playful sexuality of the "America" dance, so here Tony's late appearance to the dance at the gym (he arrives late because he had to work, stacking crates of empties in the alley behind Doc's candy store) raises the specter of "responsible" adulthood that must be answered by energetic play.

While Riff is distracted by Tony's arrival, the Sharks take the first chorus. The Puerto Rican boys and girls knit together into an advancing front, with a line of girls flaunting in the lead. The female dancers, clad in coordinating shades of red, purple, and pink, strut forward with their right arms extended upward, palms open, and with their left arms akimbo and lifting the edges of their skirts. Anita prominently stands stage left. The line of six dancers marches forward in unison, the undulation of their hips seeming to motivate their steps. This phalanx of bodies, with its intent to occupy and control more of the dance space, recalls the procession of a military charge, albeit one in which the stakes are certainly less dire and the choreography more jubilant.

As dance scholar Anna B. Scott (2010) points out, this scene underscores Robbins's construction of ethnicity through dance, as he uses accentuated hip movement as a corporeal mark of Puerto Rican–ness. "The European Jets soar, leap and twirl, moving like a row of pistons," she writes; "[t]he Sharks, by contrast, are quick on their feet and twisted in the torso" (Scott 2010, 83). But the Sharks' hips are the equipment of taunting and flaunting, as well as markers of their ethnicity. Here, as in the "America" dance, taunting and flaunting coexist in unstable combination, with one or the other predominating at any particular moment. Thus the forward momentum of the Shark girls is suddenly complicated as they snap around to face the secondary line of male dancers. In this position, they taunt the Jets by using their backs and butts to progressively monopolize the dance space.

The girls shimmy their shoulders and elbows and sway their hips from side to side, as both lines inch their way further into contested territory. Having seized the attention of the remaining dancing Jets with this maneuver, they then flip around to face forward again, revealing facial expressions contorted into a provocative message of superiority and disdain. Their taunting facial expressions are matched by their body movements, as they dip their hips to begin a long waving motion with their left arms that ends in a dismissive tip of the head and flick of the hand. Both sexes then impudently shimmy their hips at the onlooking Jets. The Sharks' offensive concludes with the girls' turning their backs on the Jets once more, in prelude to a final hip thrust that functions (like Anita's foot stomps in the "America" dance) as an embodied challenge (in this case, a subtle "fuck you!") that has more taunt than flaunt to it, although clearly it contains elements of both.

As the Jets retreat to the far side of the gym to plan their counterattack, ceding the dance floor, the Sharks and their girls commence a victory dance that pretends to ignore the Jets entirely. The Puerto Rican boys and girls flaunt to each other with movements similar to those that they employ in the "America" dance; but here their affective quality is more cooperative than confrontational across the gender line. The girls perch their right arms, bent at the elbow, suggesting matadors holding their capes before the bullish boys, and repeatedly cock their hips while bending their knees (as if to signal, "get set! go!") as their left hands grasp and lift the folds of their skirts. The boys respond with their own act of effrontery, as they swivel their hips while pivoting on the balls of their feet. The girls then spin around, bringing their right hands over their heads and swirling their skirts. As in "America," this playful give-and-take resolves into unison and then couples dancing, as both lines of dancers extend their arms parallel to the dance floor and "dip their wings" in salute to one another before they return to dancing as couples on their newly conquered terrain.

The Jets' response to the Sharks' call contains their own distinctive versions of both taunting and flaunting. Even before the Sharks' 32-bar chorus is completed, the Jets begin to taunt them by sounding an "air raid siren," warning that they are about to barge in to retake the space. Accompanied by a change in the music, a line of male dancers surges onto the dance floor, taking a running skip-leap between the Shark couples, followed by a line of girls. Crouching athletically, they stride across to the opposite side of the dance floor to claim the entire space. As the Sharks scatter, the front line of boys crosses back to center stage; and the line of Jet girls, having in their turn reached the far side of the dance floor, taunt the Shark girls by shaking their fists in their faces before returning to center stage as well.

Having vanquished their rivals in this blitzkrieg fashion, the Jet boys and girls then proceed to flaunt for each other before the skeptical gaze of their rivals. The two lines step widely apart, spin around on one leg (which causes the girls' skirts to float up), then take small steps toward each other while rapidly jutting their heads forward, in a movement that suggests the mating dances of birds. Throwing their heads back, they twist and spin. For the next phrase the boys pass through the girls' line, rising to execute a high kick, after which they turn and kneel, facing the girls, and beckon them with both hands. The girls respond by rising on their tiptoes and advancing on the boys with raised arms and swiveling hips, only to make an about-face upon nearing them. Leaping into the air, they look back coquettishly, inviting pursuit; and the boys oblige.

With the Jets having completed their "solo chorus," at this point several Sharks run out onto the dance floor, beginning the trading of 16s. Surrounded by an admiring crowd of Puerto Ricans, Anita and Bernardo dance an exuberant duet characterized by much flaunting and little taunting. The gangs' playful competition has seemingly located its true meaning in a celebration of youthful energy and sexuality.[4] Ice pushes his way through the crowd of Puerto Ricans, opening a path for Graziella and Riff, and Riff enters spectacularly with a cartwheel and an aerial flip, which Graziella answers with a triple spin. The camera follows them as they dance back to the Jets' original portion of the dance floor, and then shows both couples dancing simultaneously and vigorously, each at the center of its own circle: the emphasis on taking over turf has been supplanted by the fun and excitement of dancing. The dance's competitive aspect is still prominent only at its margins, where Action and a Shark engage in a desultory shoving match as they stand back to back, cheering their respective champions.

Unlike Glad Hand's circle dance, the affective quality of the mambo dance-off is predominantly joyful and energetic. It is a defiantly youthful competition, framed as a response to the social imperative of adult "responsibility" and the truncations that this connotes. Its affective qualities are bestowed by its capacity to accommodate the aggressive impulses that Glad Hand disallows, and to incorporate them into a competitive structure via the strategies of taunting and flaunting. Although superficially emphasizing the rivalry between the two gangs, it ultimately subordinates their rivalry to the film's celebration of youth, by highlighting the physical prowess and sex appeal of the dancers.

"Fair Fight"

The social tensions motivating the mambo dance-off do not result in violent confrontation, as the adults fear that they will, because the dance-off structures the conflict into a choreographed competition. When the two gangs stage their "rumble" under the highway, the potential similarly exists to avoid gang violence by adhering to a choreography that structures the rumble as a playful competition. The rumble's parameters are agreed upon at a ritual "war council" between the Jets and the Sharks: a fistfight between two champions, one from each side. That the two factions give such deliberate consideration to their meeting time, location, and mode of fighting distinctly evokes the tenets of choreography, in the sense that dance scholar SanSan Kwan (2013, 4) suggests: "I understand choreography in its most current conventional use as the conscious designing of bodily movement through time and space. This usage implies a relationship in which bodies are explicit agents that, within certain parameters, shape the space around them." Drawing on this expansive understanding of choreography, the war council at Doc's candy store constitutes a choreographic process to design and plan the rumble as an event in the service of competitive play. Only when Tony persists in interrupting this agreed-upon choreography does excessive violence ensue.

If the rumble had gone as planned, it would have remained safely within the category of bodily and affective interactions that we can call *brawling*. Like flaunting, brawling evolves as a physical intensification of taunting. But while flaunting in this movie is restricted to competitions that pair boys with girls, brawling is primarily reserved for boy-on-boy interactions.[5] In the opening scene, the call-and-response between Jets and Sharks escalates gradually from taunting to brawling. On the basketball court, five Sharks are confronted by twice as many Jets, and the Sharks retreat when they are told to "beat it." But as they leave, A-Rab taunts them with cries of *"Olé, chico!"* prompting the last Shark to lag behind and surreptitiously trip Action, and afterward, to make the elaborately polite gesture that has been established in previous shots as a form of taunting. Action approaches him, offering a hand extended in acceptance of the "apology," which when he gets near enough, he turns into a punch that knocks the Shark to the ground. As Action walks away, the Shark sits up and spits at him, hitting the back of his head. Action then dives at him and they brawl, wrestling and kicking.

As this scene demonstrates, brawling deploys a call-and-response structure: it too is choreographed. In subsequent shots, the gangs chase each other through the streets, and the Sharks bait the Jets into several physical ambushes: dumping yellow paint on their heads, shoving them out of entryways, and pelting them with garbage. But the movie integrates this brawling with other movements that clearly belong within the vocabularies of dance and play, marking it as a related form of interaction and as sharing in the exuberant energy of those activities. The Jets repeatedly execute a leaping twirl with their right arms extended over their heads, and the two gangs play leapfrog at the entrance to a covered brick alleyway.

Schrank, the sinister representative of adult authority, overreacts to the brawling by menacing the Jets and Sharks with disproportionately higher levels of violence: "If I catch *any* of ya doin' any more brawling in my territory—I'm gonna personally beat the livin' crud outa each and every one of ya and see that ya go to jail and *rot* there!" (Lehman 2003, 8–10). The violence that he offers to unleash is far worse than the fighting that he pretends to be guarding against.[6] Similarly, the "war council" scene in which the rumble is planned presents another situation in which the two youth gangs ally themselves against Schrank, their real enemy. While the youths are mutually intent on staging a rumble, the elaborate rules of their parley supersede whatever ethnic animosity is present. By contrast, Schrank is revealed as the only one harboring bona fide racial hatred. When he saunters into Doc's candy store to interrupt the council, he indulges in racial slurs that offend the Jets as well as the Sharks. Bernardo lunges at him, but is restrained by two Jets, Riff and Ice. Schrank then aims more taunts at Bernardo in hopes of winning the Jets over to his side, but these earn him only resentful glares from Riff. Finally,

Schrank kicks Bernardo's chair out from under him. "Clear out, you!" he snarls, his voice rising, and invokes his badge as authorization for his unprovoked violence. As Bernardo attempts to leave while preserving his personal dignity, he and Riff exchange a meaningful glance of mutual understanding.

Correspondingly, in the five-part fugue sung immediately preceding the "Rumble" number, brawling is associated with playful sexuality as two expressions of youthful vitality, while both are opposed to the seriousness of adulthood and its emphases on work and heteronormative marriage. This fugue directly follows the "marriage" of Tony and Maria at the dress shop where Maria works. Musically, it divides the Jets and Sharks from the lovers by giving them very different melodies. The gang members anticipate the rumble while singing in a call-and-response structure like that of the mambo dance-off (including the shorter and shorter "trading" of phrases). Tony and Maria, by contrast, sing about their romance.

Significantly, Anita, who anticipates having sex with Bernardo after the fight, sings along with the Jets and the Sharks, and not with Tony and Maria, establishing that her sexuality is more akin to their youthful brawling than to what Tony and Maria are singing about. This comparison is furthered by a double entendre in the lyrics on the word, "mix," which is used interchangeably to refer to both brawling and sex. Bernardo and the Sharks sing, "Just in case they jump us, we're ready to mix"; and Anita sings, "We'll have our private little mix tonight" as she perches on a bed in her darkened bedroom and slips on pantyhose, readying herself for a post-rumble rendezvous. Furthermore, as she anticipates the "kicks" she'll get after the Jet/Shark showdown, Anita conjectures about Bernardo's post-rumble physical state, singing that her "poor dear" will arrive home "hot and tired." Her expectations suggest that the consequences of the rumble (as another form of choreographed competition) should not be particularly dire. Rather, its repercussions are expected to resemble the effects of any other kind of dancing, where the body becomes both "hot" and tired" from disciplined, physical exertion. If all goes as choreographed, Bernardo will emerge from his fight relatively unscathed.

The complementary singing of Anita, the Jets, and the Sharks in this fugue is jarringly interrupted by the singing of Tony (still at work in Doc's candy store, although it is nearly midnight) and Maria, and by a shot of Schrank and Krupke patrolling in their police car, a suture that links Tony's disruptive influence with their adult authority. Tony is similarly disruptive of the rumble's choreography. Like Glad Hand, he deals with social conflict by trying to mask or erase it. He is determined to dissolve the rumble/dance because he has promised Maria that there will be no fighting, "not even a fistfight." As Ice and Bernardo, the two chosen champions, circle each other warily (the circularity of the usage of space echoes the closing section of mambo dance-off, in which the dance concludes in two simultaneous rings), Tony scales the chain link fence that delineates the fight area, yelling, "Hold it!"

Up to this juncture, Ice and Bernardo have adhered to a choreographed fighting style, with clenched fists aimed sharply at each other. Although they create a spectacle of violence for the onlookers from both sides, the damage they are likely to inflict is minimal. In fact, the two barely make skin-to-skin contact. Riff, misunderstanding Tony's intentions and believing that he has come in support of the Jets, gestures to him, inviting him to join the other Jets where they are lined up as spectators. Ice then makes a similar inviting gesture to Bernardo, welcoming him to continue the fistfight in the wake of this minor interruption. The similarity between the two gestures invokes the social nature of their fighting.

But Tony, instead of joining the other Jets on the sidelines, proceeds to intervene between the two combatants. He lunges at Ice and shoves him to the side of the "ring." Bewildered, Riff asks, "Tony, what are you doing?" The answer is that he intends to talk the two gangs out of their conflict, insisting to Bernardo that "[t]here's nothing to fight about" (Lehman 2003, 89).

The movie shows emphatically that this will not work. In response to Tony's offer of friendship, Bernardo shoves him with such force that he stumbles to the ground. Riff responds by jumping into the ring with both arms extended, like a boxing referee, to try to re-establish the choreographed nature of the combat. "Now let's just cool it; the deal is a fair fight between you and Ice," he reminds Bernardo. But as Tony persists in his efforts to stifle the conflict, the choreographed one-to-one form of the combat breaks down, and the Sharks converge on him in a disorderly mass, taunting him verbally while delivering sharp slaps to his face and torso. Attempting to repel their assaults, Tony backs away into the crowd of Jets and finds himself screaming at Ice, who forcefully grasps him by the shoulders, trying one last time to remove him as an impediment to the rumble's choreography. At this emotionally charged juncture, Riff runs in unexpectedly and punches Bernardo on the jaw. Non-diegetic, discordant music wells up as Riff and Bernardo simultaneously, with surprise and fear registering on their faces, pull switchblades from their back pockets. Tony's disruption of the choreographed fighting has made the situation worse. Intending to stop a fistfight, he has instigated a knife fight.

But even for this, there is thankfully a choreography.[7] Ice and Tiger hold Tony on the sidelines to prevent him from disrupting it. Riff and Bernardo circle each other, feinting and jabbing with their knives. In blocking one of Riff's attempted attacks, Bernardo disarms him and drives him against the surrounding chain link fence. Splayed against the fence with his arms and legs spread-eagled, Riff nevertheless warns the others, "Keep outta this!" as both sides begin to swarm in. A moment of calm follows, in which the regulated nature of the combat has been reaffirmed. The converging gang members back away, and Bernardo playfully taunts Riff by tossing his switchblade jauntily from hand to hand. Action rearms Riff with a new switchblade and the competitive *pas de deux* continues.

Tony, however, interrupts it again, this time fatally. He drags Riff away from the fight; and when Riff escapes and runs back to re-engage, he accidentally impales himself on Bernardo's blade. Tony then loses all emotional control and, yelling inarticulately, stabs Bernardo to death. This unchoreographed violence then spreads everywhere, as the two gangs abandon the affective discipline that the choreography had instilled and engage in a free-for-all battle. The camera films the scene from an oddly tilted low angle in order to heighten the impression of chaos. This is no longer a competition or a dance; in their stead is a spectacle of unmediated violence.

DANCING WITH KNIVES

As the creator of *West Side Story*, Jerome Robbins appears to have shared the belief of his psychologist contemporary Paul Goodman that a modicum of physical aggression is socially functional. Goodman wrote of American society in the 1950s that it could benefit from tolerating more brawling than it was currently willing to allow. In the face of inevitable social tensions, in his opinion, brawling was preferable to the self-inhibition that Cold War American culture identified with "maturity." As Goodman (Perls, Hefferline, and Goodman 1994, 75, 80) wrote,

> "Maturity" . . . is conceived in the interest of an unnecessarily tight adjustment to a dubiously valuable workaday society, regimented to pay its debts and duties. . . . With regard to the adjustment of the mature person to reality, must we not ask . . . whether the "reality" is not rather closely pictured after, and in the interests of, western urban industrial society, capitalist or state-socialist? Is it the case that other cultures, gaudier in dress, greedier in physical pleasures, dirtier in manners, more disorderly in governance, more brawling and adventurous in behavior, were or are thereby less mature?

For both Robbins and Goodman (Perls, Hefferline, and Goodman 1994), youthful "delinquency" represented a healthy antidote to this excessive social repression. In this respect, *West Side Story* belongs among other texts of the period that laid the cultural groundwork for the 1960s youth counterculture by locating the true meaning of youthful play in the subversion of this restrictive "reality."

Goodman (Perls, Hefferline, and Goodman 1994), however, was unable to articulate the point at which healthy levels of aggression become antisocial. By contrast, *West Side Story* proposes the presence of choreographed competition as that dividing line. The movie displays a continuum of youthful play in which dance and choreography structure conflict as competition. Taunting, flaunting, and brawling comprise the embodied affective strategies by which the Jets and Sharks mediate their aggressions without repressing them. On his way to getting shot dead on the playground in a second round of unwanted violence following the ill-fated rumble, Tony yells at another Jet, "It's not playing any more!" emphasizing the distinction that the movie makes between playful competition and unchoreographed aggression.

In the world imagined by *West Side Story*, a choreography of competition tempers the potential violence of social conflict by instilling a modicum of affective discipline. The disruption of this choreography is what causes this rivalry to slide into fatal violence. Without rules to structure it, the aggression that the film represents as an otherwise healthy response to social tensions erupts in a riot. In fighting and dancing alike, the Jets and Sharks use agreed-upon rules of engagement, such as a call-and-response structure, to mediate their rivalry as play.

NOTES

1. In her article, "Seeing the City: The Filming of West Side Story," Julia L. Foulkes (2015, 1033) positions the film as a medium through which the discourses and efforts of New York City's postwar urban renewal projects are exposed, arguing that "*West Side Story* conveyed a new way to see the city." In conjunction with this idea, we argue that the film's spaces project an alternate construction of youth, mediated through the choreographies applied to the Jets and Sharks.
2. See, for example, Bruns (2000); Thrift (2004); and Clough (2007)
3. Robbins embraced his queer sexuality as a transcendence of social norms linked to his creative genius. But at the same time, given the social constraints of the era, he passed as heterosexual. See Vaill (2006).
4. Significantly, the musical accompaniment now no longer alternates between the two gangs' themes, but integrates them (Acevedo-Munoz 2013).
5. In this respect, Negrón-Muntaner (2000) has observed brawling's queer sexual connotations. The exception that proves the rule is Anybodys, a tomboy who brawls in efforts to be accepted as one of the boys (Lehman 2003).
6. According to social critics of the period, such official threats of excessive force suggested the skewed value system of a society in denial about the implications of its own nuclear arms race. The noted social psychologist Erich Fromm (1955, 12–17), in his book *The Sane Society*, wrote that a "schizophrenic indifference" to the possibility of nuclear annihilation had been widely accepted in mainstream American culture in the name of adjusting to reality, resulting in a "pathology of normalcy."
7. The screenplay provides stage directions for the knife fight stating, "THE FOLLOWING ACTION TAKES ON THE FORM OF A DANCE" (Lehman 2003, 90).

REFERENCES

Acevedo-Munoz, Ernesto R. 2013. *West Side Story as Cinema: The Making and Impact of an American Masterpiece*. Lawrence: University of Kansas Press.

Banes, Sally. 2004. "Breaking." In *That's the Joint! The Hip Hop Studies Reader*, edited by Murray Forman and Mark Anthony Neal, 13–20. New York: Routledge.

Bruns, John. 2000. "Laughter in the Aisles: Affect and Power in Contemporary Theoretical and Cultural Discourse." *Studies in American Humor* 3(7): 5–23.

Clough, Patricia Ticineto. 2007. "Introduction." In *The Affective Turn: Theorizing the Social*, edited by Patricia Ticineto Clough and Jean Halley, 1–33. Durham, NC: Duke University Press.

Duerden, Rachel, and Bonnie Rowell. 2013. "Hierarchical Reversals: The Interplay of Dance and Music in *West Side Story*." In *Bodies of Sound: Studies across Popular Music and Dance*, edited by Sherril Dodds and Susan C. Cook, 135–148. Farnham, UK: Ashgate.

Foulkes, Julia L. 2015. "Seeing the City: The Filming of *West Side Story*." *Journal of Urban History* 41(6): 1032–1051.

Fromm, Erich. 1955. *The Sane Society*. New York: Henry Holt.

Gere, David. 2004. *How to Make Dances in an Epidemic: Tracking Choreography in the Age of AIDS*. Madison: University of Wisconsin Press.

Goodman, Paul. 1960. *Growing Up Absurd: Problems of Our Youth in an Organized System.* New York: Random House Books.

Huizinga, Johan. 1949. *Homo Ludens: A Study in the Play-Element in Culture.* London: Routledge & Kegan Paul.

Kwan, SanSan. 2013. *Kinesthetic City: Dance and Movement in Chinese Urban Spaces.* Oxford: Oxford University Press.

Lehman, Ernest. 2003. *West Side Story: Screenplay.* Beverly Hills: MGM Home Entertainment.

McCormack, Derek. 2014. *Refrains for Moving Bodies: Experience and Experiment in Affective Spaces.* Durham, NC: Duke University Press.

McNeill, William. 1997. *Keeping Together in Time: Dance and Drill in Human History.* Cambridge, MA: Harvard University Press.

Negrón-Muntaner, Frances. 2000. "Feeling Pretty: *West Side Story* and Puerto Rican Identity Discourses." *Social Text* 18(2): 83–106.

Perls, Frederick, Ralph F. Hefferline, and Paul Goodman. 1994. *Gestalt Therapy: Excitement and Growth in the Human Personality.* Highland, NY: Gestalt Journal Press.

Sandoval-Sanchez, Alberto. 1999. *José, Can You See?: Latinos On and Off Broadway.* Madison: University of Wisconsin Press.

Scott, Anna B. 2010. "What's It Worth to Ya? Adaptation and Anachronism: Rennie Harris's Pure Movement and Shakespeare." In *The Routledge Dance Studies Reader*, 2nd edition, edited by Alexandra Carter and Janet O'Shea, 78–90. New York: Routledge.

Scott, James C. 1990. *Domination and the Arts of Resistance: Hidden Transcripts.* New Haven, CT: Yale University Press.

Thrift, Nigel. 2004. "Intensities of Feeling." *Geografiska Annaler: Series B Human Geography* 86(1): 57–58.

Vaill, Amanda. 2006. *Somewhere: The Life of Jerome Robbins.* New York: Broadway Books.

CHAPTER 26

DANCING LIKE A MAN

Competition and Gender in the New Orleans Second Line

RACHEL CARRICO

ON March 29, 2014, the First Annual Big Easy Footwork Competition debuted at the Tremé Center, a community venue located in Tremé, New Orleans. Tremé represents one of the oldest African American neighborhoods, and serves as an important locus for the city's black cultural traditions. The Center regularly hosts summer camps, after-school clubs, fundraisers, concerts, and more, but on this mild March afternoon, its cavernous hall was set up for a dance competition. Several rows of folding chairs faced the four-foot-high stage, ready to hold an audience of hundreds. The floor area directly in front of the stage had been cordoned off with orange traffic cones and caution tape, designating a dancing space for contestants. Three judges sat behind a folding table, positioned to the side of the taped-off area, and on the stage, a rotating roster of six local brass bands stood and played their instruments (trombones, trumpets, tubas, bass, and snare drums). Each contestant vied for a trophy (Figure 26.1) and a $250 cash prize by competing against other dancers in three age divisions: children under twelve, youth between thirteen and seventeen, and adults over eighteen. Even though the event was open to all dancers, most of the contestants were male; one girl entered the children's division, and one young woman entered the youth division. However, no female dancer claimed the top prize in any age bracket. As I will argue, the gendered dynamics of this particular competition mirrored the often unspoken gendered dynamics that influence footwork performances in social contexts.

The competitors displayed their best versions of second line dancing, also called second lining. Second lining is an African diaspora vernacular dance form that has accompanied brass band parades through New Orleans's city streets since the late nineteenth century. Individually executed yet collectively experienced, second lining carries paraders through the urban landscape in time with the syncopated rhythms of brass band music. Although second lining cannot be strictly reduced to footwork, which is the art of

FIGURE 26.1. This trophy was awarded to Rodrick "Scubble" Davis, the 2014 First Annual Big Easy Footwork champion in the eighteen years and older division.

Photo by Michael J. Mastrogiovanni.

executing intricate rhythmic patterns with the feet, many practitioners consider it a cornerstone of second lining's aesthetic form. For this reason, the contest was called a "footwork competition" and not a "second lining competition." Even though many dancers dedicate themselves to perfecting their footwork, on the whole, second liners are usually less concerned with *which steps* the dancer displays than with the *way* in which those steps are performed, and, at the heart of it, why the dancer is second lining in the first place. Second liners dance for many reasons: to experience joy, get some exercise, mourn the dead, and/or to achieve fame as footwork artists. Therefore, even though second lining can be described as a specific, coherent, and legible dance form that is historically rooted and aesthetically sophisticated, what it *is* matters less to dancers than what it *does*.[1] Second liners' function-over-form priorities crystallize in a commonly held definition of second lining as "do-watcha-wanna."[2] Perhaps unsurprisingly, second lining's subjective and affective performance criteria lead to difficulties and disagreements when judges quantitatively score contests such as the Big Easy Footwork Competition. This annual event moves second lining from its grassroots, outdoor social context to an indoor competitive arena and, in so doing, it creates a venue in which second liners systematically evaluate each other's formal performances. By dancing, scoring, and debating the judges' decisions, those present stake their claims on second lining's aesthetic and political priorities, including its relationship to gendered social scripts.

In this chapter, I take formal second line dance competitions as an entry point to examine the gendered biases that frame second lining's practice and reception. Competitions serve as an excellent venue in which to examine gendered discourses that surround the form because competitions provide a rare opportunity for these discourses to be made explicit. In social contexts, ideological attachments between gender and movement usually go unsaid, and are even sometimes denied. Given second liners' concern with the *why* of second lining, far beyond the *what*, such dismissals of gendered differences in formal aesthetics are understandable. The motivations for and benefits of second lining as a social practice are arguably available to all who are physically able to join a parade, regardless of gender or sexual identity. However, within competition contexts, the *what* becomes paramount as dancers' performances are ranked and rewarded by judges, audience members, and fellow competitors. As a result, dance competitions reveal that form contains and communicates meanings, even when popular discourses eschew the particulars of form as unimportant. Competitions make (more) explicit what female footwork artists already know: that criteria for excellent second lining are often coded as masculine. If they wish to compete, women must adhere to such codes. According to one female footwork artist, "If you dance like a man, like a boy, they going to know who you is."[3]

I argue that gendered discourses about second lining, which align excellent dancing with masculinity, cannot fully account for the dance tactics employed by some young women dancers today. Their performances open up new gendered terrain for evaluating second lining beyond a masculine/feminine binary, and footwork competitions provide an important frontier for charting this new terrain. I begin with an overview of the second line parading tradition, highlighting the gendered histories of competitive dance and music performances therein. With this context in mind, I offer an ethnographic account of the First Annual Big Easy Footwork Competition, which includes my first-person observations of the event and interviews with contestants, observers, and the event's producer. In the final sections, I suggest two feminist frameworks for understanding female footwork artists' dancing: first, the influence of double-dutch jump rope on second lining footwork and, second, a theoretical framework that dance scholar Imani Kai Johnson (2014) calls "badass femininity." I conclude that, with each step, female footwork artists move within and beyond a gendered terrain in which dancing well means dancing like a man.

FROM STREET TO STAGE:
SECOND LINE FOOTWORK

Contests such as the Big Easy Footwork Competition spring from the vernacular second line tradition, which originated on New Orleans's streets more than one hundred years ago and still thrives today. On most Sundays in New Orleans, these processions gather thousands of people to dance behind a brass band, winding through poor and working-class African American neighborhoods for hours, making several preplanned stops along a predetermined route. Each parade is organized, financed, and led by a different group, known as a social aid and pleasure club (SAPC). The hosting SAPC and brass band form the first or main line, and the trumpet's blare invites all within earshot to form a second line around them, giving the event its name. SAPCs grow out of a long-standing tradition of black benevolent and mutual aid societies that provided economic security and social networks for marginalized residents. For more than one hundred years, these organizations have employed black brass bands for members' funerals and for social functions, such as anniversary parades.[4] Today, each SAPC's anniversary parade is known as its second line.

The second line begins at 1:00 p.m. sharp (noon during the winter months' daylight savings time), when the brass band strikes up to accompany members of the hosting SAPC as they "come out the door." One by one, each woman, man, or child dramatically steps through the door of someone's house or a neighborhood establishment, such as a barroom or barber shop, revealing herself or himself to the awaiting public. All members dress in brightly colored, matching suits and wave feathered fans above their heads. Since membership numbers can range from two to one hundred (with ages in about the same range), this can take a little or a long time. A spirit of competitive one-upmanship is on full display during this portion of the ritual. Club members playfully challenge each other to up the ante during their individual entrances, and the entire show tacitly competes with all other clubs who will come out the door that season. People in the crowd momentarily play the roles of spectator and judge, vocally assessing the SAPC's chosen color scheme, apparel selections, and dance ability. After all club members have come out the door, they lead the crowd through the streets as a dancing collective.

As a verb, "second lining" refers to all participatory parade activity, such as walking, strutting, and chanting; but the term also names a distinct dance form showcased during the parade. Like many living vernacular expressions, second lining is not a static form. It absorbs influences from related street parading practices in the city and from each generation's popular culture. Therefore, second lining includes a range of bodily expressions under its umbrella. As long as you are (usually) moving on the beat and (generally) moving forward with the crowd, then, according to most second liners, you are second lining.[5] However, within this capacious, do-watcha-wanna definition, certain dancers carve out a space for artful expressions created according to specific aesthetics. In the words of one veteran second liner, "some people be doing what they do. And then they have some people that have *footwork* and it becomes an art. . . . If you're into the second line like that, you know what you're looking at."[6] Those who are into second lining "like that" create a spirit of competition during each parade that pushes their fellow footwork artists to new levels of energy, creativity, and showmanship.

Although a *spirit* of competition drives second liners' improvised dancing during weekly parades, dancers' informal attempts to earn respect are not formally adjudicated. As in most social dance scenarios, second liners' performances are regulated by complex and often implicit criteria. When second liners see something they like, they reward each other with voiced appreciation and demands for more: "Footwork! Feetwork! Cut up! Roll with it! Show me what you're working with!" Occasionally, two dancers face off in an impromptu battle as encircled onlookers shout their encouragements and judgments.

Second liners' competitive spirit drives performances in formally adjudicated contests. The 2014 event at the Tremé Center was dubbed the "First" Annual Big Easy Footwork Competition, but it was not the first second line dance competition in history. These kinds of contests have been produced in New Orleans for decades, and, of interest to my subject here, reflect second lining's performative attachments to masculinity.[7] In her study of masculinity and social dance, Maxine Leeds Craig (2014) notes that competition often characterizes dance forms that are popular among young men, such as b-boy battles. Dance competitions establish a pattern for homosocial interaction that fits within patriarchal norms, wherein men attempt to "dominate opponents through displays of daring, inventiveness, and physical technique" (Craig 2014, 8–9).[8] Even when second line dancing is removed from a competition context, and even when performed by women, displays of daring physicality, such as gymnastic feats, athletic stunts, and aggressive gestures, are frequently perceived as performances of masculinity. Such perceptions are made evident when female dancers are congratulated for "dancing like a dude."

"Dancing like a Dude": A Genealogy

Gendered divisions within second lining today have been formed by a long history of aesthetic and social influences. One root can be found in the African and Afro-Caribbean dances performed in New Orleans during the nineteenth century, such as the "Congo dance," in which men advanced and retreated in relation to a woman while leaping and spinning in the air. Women barely moved their feet, making slow, sustained, undulating movements with the torso and hips, sometimes while waving a handkerchief (Evans 2011, 92–93).[9] Much like those who recorded their observations of the nineteenth-century Congo dance, today's second liners often see athletic movements and elaborate footwork as qualities of dancing like a man, while women are frequently perceived as keeping their feet on the ground while showcasing hip and torso undulations. In contrast to these widespread perceptions, both men *and* women demonstrate energetic footwork, and some women can do it in heels. In a recent conversation with a woman who belongs to several SAPCs, I learned that she finds it easier to do footwork in heels, despite the increased risk of spraining an ankle, because she likes to dance on the balls of her feet. Her high-heeled footwork presents a feminine form of second lining that disrupts a binary between masculine dancing as physically daring and feminine dancing as slow and grounded.

If the Congo dance suggests that histories of second lining's masculinist imperatives are located at the level of the body, then the sociocultural contexts of brass band parades provide further insight. As Sherrie Tucker (2004) writes, the long history of military bands in New Orleans, composed of musicians of all races and ethnicities, solidified associations of brass bands with men and masculine performance. When second line parades first began to crisscross New Orleans in the late nineteenth century, they acted as performances of particular forms of *black* masculinity. The processions were organized by male-led fraternal organizations, which maintained the post–Civil War black social ideals of racial uplift (Blassingame 1973; Jacobs 1988). These ideals were embodied in the statuesque posture required of militia marches and Masonic rituals of the time, both of which influenced benevolent societies' processions.

Judged competitions have contributed to slightly different constructions of masculinity within New Orleans's Afro-Creole brass band traditions. Brass band battles known as bucking contests first gained popularity in the late nineteenth and early twentieth centuries (Bechet 1960). As jazz historian Thomas Brothers (2006) surmises, brass band musicians, who were and still are overwhelmingly male, performed heterosexual masculinity through musical dominance over other men. Still today, the jazz bandstand is recognized as "a battleground of male competition, an altar of sacrifice and initiation" (Guillory 1998, 201). Turn-of-the-century bands staked out their battlegrounds on the sidewalks during bucking contests, competing for recognition and for gigs. Musicians who played their horns louder and longer were not only awarded more work, but also performed a brand of masculinity aligned with working-class ideals of physical strength. At the same time, their abilities to invent on the spot performed a flexible and responsive masculinity that tempered brute strength with agility (Brothers 2006).[10]

If women were present during turn-of-the-century processions and bucking contests, they never participated as musicians, uniformed marchers, or as the deceased, whose life was honored by a funeral with music.[11] Women have belonged to mutual aid societies from their inception, but did not begin to join the main line until the mid- to late twentieth century. In the first half of the twentieth century, women joined brass band processions by politely marching with church groups or riding ceremonially in vehicles. Since the mid-1970s, women have begun to dance in parades as SAPC members and to lead funeral processions as grand marshals.[12] Today, a roughly equal number of women and men appear inside and outside the ropes during each second line season. However, numbers alone do not necessarily signal gender equality. Due in part to the historical development of a tradition that, until relatively recently, has been dominated by male musicians, marchers, and club members, second liners' movement choices earn approval when they are read as masculine.

Even though women dancers are aware of the masculinist frameworks in which their performances are often evaluated, these frameworks are not always explicitly acknowledged. Practitioners frequently refer to do-watcha-wanna definitions of the form that, on the surface, seem to value all movements equally. Thus, when vying for recognition and respect, female dancers must navigate through a tacit yet palpable assumption that to dance well means to dance like a man. When they take their deft footwork onto competition stages, they maneuver within and beyond second lining's implicitly gendered discourses. Ultimately, young women's competitive performances reveal that these discourses fail to account for full scope of their footwork.

THE FIRST ANNUAL BIG EASY FOOTWORK COMPETITION

When I arrived at the Tremé Center at 5:30 p.m., the children's division had just wrapped up. I learned that a young girl, who appeared to be about nine or ten years old, had tied a boy for the trophy. As I later found out, the girl's name is Nyesha Borsey, and she was the inspiration for the entire event.[13] According to the Competition's founder and producer, Leander "Shack" Brown, he first thought about producing a footwork contest when he saw Borsey dancing at a second line parade. "I thought, 'She is dancing with her soul. People around the world need to see this.' So I thought, 'I'm going to create a competition so that people around the world can see it and she can get rewarded for it.' "[14] Brown began producing the Competitions in order to give young dancers like Borsey an opportunity to receive material rewards, in addition to the admiration and compliments they receive on the street. He has big plans for the event's future: "Eventually I want that competition to go around the world." He envisions creating a performance group composed of outstanding contestants to appear on televised award shows and stages nationwide.[15]

That vision began to take shape with the First Annual Big Easy Footwork Competition in 2014. Around 6:30 p.m., Brown invited contestants in the youth division to the stage. Just two contestants came forward: a young male member of the Uptown Swingers SAPC, who identified himself by wearing a shirt embroidered with the club's name and logo, and Terrylynn Dorsey, who came ready to dance in her Air Jordan sneakers and matching T-shirt (Figure 26.2). Dorsey is widely recognized within the second line community as one of the most talented young footwork artists on the streets today. Her friend Rodrick "Scubble" Davis, an accomplished dancer who won the adult division of the Competition that year, describes her as someone who will "go down in history as one of the best female dancers you ever had in New Orleans."[16] Therefore, I was not surprised to see her enter the competition.

Several months after the event, I interviewed Dorsey and her cousin Terrinika Smith. Dorsey explained that she is aware of her status as a well-respected footwork artist. "When I'm in the streets," she said, "they be like, 'Shorty got footwork! She know how to *dance*.' " She started dancing at age seven when her mother, who parades with the Single Ladies Social and Pleasure Club, started taking her to second lines on Sundays. Dorsey's mother was her first dance coach, but in recent years, her cousin has assumed that responsibility. "Terrinika always be telling me, 'Uh uh! Don't be doing that! You can't be doing the same thing over! You got to do some new moves!' " Smith confirms: "Exactly. Shock them every time."[17]

FIGURE 26.2. Terrylynn Dorsey dances against her sole competitor in the youth division of the 2014 First Annual Big Easy Footwork Competition.

Photo by Michael J. Mastrogiovanni.

As Dorsey and her lone male competitor stood in front of the stage and waited for their round to begin, they gazed up at Leander Brown. He informed the contestants of two rules: "You have to roll," which is second liners' parlance for dancing continuously, "for at least thirty minutes. And no obscene gestures." The Young Fellas Brass Band began to play, and the two contestants started to dance behind the caution tape. I could not take my eyes off Dorsey. She always appears in total control of her body and completely in sync with the music. Furthermore, she has mastered the grounded-yet-lifted second line posture, so that her torso lifts up while her legs drive down into the earth, the top half of her body riding smoothly on top of fiercely working legs and feet. Dorsey dances with rhythmic sophistication, displays a wide variety of moves, and changes the dynamics of her movements, offsetting athletic drops and stylish spins with moments of subdued grooving. I watched as she performed a basic scissor-like footwork step while facing the band, as if giving her feet time to converse with the beat. Soon, she began to punctuate her steady heel-to-toe step with high-knee hopping, alternating from foot to foot, a move reminiscent of double-dutch jump rope. Next, she began bouncing on her left foot while lifting her right thigh to hip height. She bent her right knee at a ninety-degree angle and swung her lower leg back and forth in time with the music. With both feet back on the ground, Dorsey smoothed out the aerial bouncing of her footwork by gliding backward across the floor in a staccato, syncopated version of the moonwalk. In this moment, Brown picked up the microphone again, prompting the dancers to "knock," a term commonly used among second liners to refer to no-holds-barred dancing. He chanted in time with the beat, "Now go! Knock it off! Knock! Knock! Knock!" Upon hearing his encouraging demands, Dorsey threw her head back and laughed, letting the weight of her head carry her body into a tight circular pathway. All the while, her feet never missed a beat.

When reflecting on that moment, Dorsey recalled, "I was in my own zone. It's how I be at the second line, that's how I was up there at that thing. I was in my own little world." Second lining delivers her to a zone where nothing matters except her feet and the beat. When the tuba begins to thump, Dorsey said, "I ain't worried about nothing. The beat just in my head."[18] Since she was in her "own little zone," Dorsey possibly did not hear the shouting around her. While she and her competitor danced fervently, a woman in a pink tracksuit hovered over the caution tape and encouraged Dorsey, shouting, "Work it! Get it! Come on!" Brown spoke into the microphone: "Don't coach, please sit down." She ignored his request, and instead treated the caution tape like the rope that divides the main line from the second line during parades, leaning over it to demand more hype from the contestants.

Once the thirty-minute period ended, the band took a break and the contestants retired while the judges deliberated. After a short while, the judges delivered their verdict to Brown, who related the results to the crowd. Dorsey lost to her male competitor. She reacted to this news with shock and disbelief. "When they announced the trophy, I thought, 'There's no way! There's no way! Ain't no way I lost against him!'"[19] Dorsey was not alone in her reaction. I was also surprised by the verdict, and became curious about the judges' criteria for evaluation. Certainly both dancers had followed Brown's two requirements. What more did they need to do in order to win? I recognized one of the three judges as a teacher at a local dance studio that I regularly attended, so I introduced myself and asked about her experience as a judge. She explained that she is from Tremé, and has taught dance in New Orleans for fifty years. Doing things like this, she said, is a way to give back. In terms of criteria, she was looking for each dancer's number of turns, kicks, drops, and stunts, but admitted that the judging was very subjective. The three judges were not given a list of items for scoring.

I had assumed that this judge was preselected due to her profession as a dance teacher, but in fact, Brown explained to me that he selected the judges "randomly" right before the first contest began (and before I arrived). He announced to the crowd, "If I tap you on the shoulder, then you're a judge." At the second competition in 2015, he went a step further, recruiting a friend who is blind to do the shoulder tapping. Brown's rationale for choosing judges this way is to avoid accusations of unfair adjudication, for if he selected judges in advance, then their evaluations might be clouded by the inevitable biases and allegiances that form in a tightly knit community. This approach to judging both honors and wrestles with second lining's ethos as a grassroots practice. By refusing to codify criteria or identify expert judges, Brown's competitions mirror the communal creation of aesthetic values within second lining's organic social structure. Yet at the same time, by allowing three individuals' subjective conclusions to determine clear winners and losers, the competition's outcomes fall prey to hotly debated differences in taste.

After speaking with the judge, I headed outside to get some air and overheard the lady in the pink tracksuit complaining to a small group crowded around her. The judges were not second liners, she said. They could not do footwork themselves and did not know what to look for. The disgruntled patron was particularly bothered by the fact that one judge was a dance teacher whose knowledge of ballet did not qualify her to assess excellent second lining.[20] One reason, she argued, for disagreeing with the judges' verdict was that the winning dancer waved his arms too much, which distracted from his footwork, and belied his experience in a related, but distinct, dance practice: parading with a Mardi Gras Indian tribe. In fact, this is the main reason that Dorsey (2014) felt he should have lost: "Ain't no way I lost against him! Because he was Indian dancing."

The debates that occurred during the Competition demonstrate that, although second liners often eschew questions of "right" and "wrong" ways to second line in favor of a do-watcha-wanna approach, practitioners simultaneously hold firm ideas about which bodily repertoires fall within and outside second lining's aesthetic. These boundaries were negotiated as those present at the Competition harnessed dance technique as a relational language for communicating.[21] The movements performed by contestants served as a protocol for the judges and audience members to read dancing bodies (albeit to read them differently); for dancers to fashion their subjectivities as members of the second line community, and to insert other subjectivities, such as one's involvement in Mardi Gras Indian culture or as a seasoned jump roper; and for everyone involved to insert themselves into a history of footwork developed on New Orleans's streets. Dance became the language of group inclusion and exclusion, complicating allegiances formed by neighborhood, culture, and class, and making more explicit the subtle inclusions and exclusions that are regularly performed during weekly second lines.

One of the exclusions demonstrated during the competition was the exclusion of feminine movement and female dancers from the upper rungs of second lining's hierarchies. It is true that one young women and one girl competed in the Competition, and that a girl provided the inspiration for the Competition's existence. However, as is the case in second lining at large, the presence of female dancers does not necessarily signal gender equality, for the dancing displayed by female footwork artists needs to be read as masculine to be competitive.

Dorsey's cousin, Terrinika Smith, reached this conclusion through personal experience. In 2010, she entered a footwork competition, "Second Line Till Ya Drop," at Tipitina's, a music venue in uptown New Orleans. She recalled the final round, when all but two dancers had been eliminated.

> It got down to me and [Gerald] Platenburg with Nine Times [SAPC], and I knew that when he got on the stage he was going to tear me up! But . . . they [the judges] said, "We're going to give you the trophy and give him the money." I was like,

"Give me the trophy give him the *money*?!" I didn't understand that. And it was like, "Because you a girl." With the men, it don't go like that. We paid five dollars to get in the competition. . . . They didn't have no girls in the competition but me. So they said because they didn't have no girls they'd give me the trophy. Platenburg did give me $25, shout out to Platenburg. But I really felt like that was wrong. That's why I feel like . . . they'd rather [have] a man than a woman in the second line world.[22]

Smith's story provides a relatively low-stakes but clear example of the fact that discursive ideologies have material effects. Since, in the "second line world," performing movements coded as masculine are more valued, Smith was denied a cash prize, even though the judges symbolically rewarded her willingness to transgress gendered norms and compete as the lone female dancer.

Smith's reflection raises the question of what it means to second line like a man. Some say that it means "going hard," focusing on the feet, and doing daredevil tricks. If a second liner is too "soft," emphasizing her hips more than her feet, and refraining from gymnastic stunts, then she might be seen as dancing, as Smith puts it, "like a female." Don Robertson, a retired member of the Young Men Olympian, Jr., Benevolent Association, voiced this point of view. Robertson earned a reputation as a respected second line dancer in the 1980s, and earned cash by performing and teaching second line dancing throughout the city and beyond until the first decade of the 2000s. When he expressed admiration for Terrylynn Dorsey's dancing, he said, "They got some girls, they second line like dudes!" I asked him what it means to second line like a dude.

DR: They coming hard, they moving, they're not shaking like a lady, they're dancing. They straight up going hard. They skipping, they hopping, they jumping. Matter of fact, they got one, she's a Lady Buckjumper [a member of the Lady Buckjumper Social Aid and Pleasure Club]. If you watch her, she shake. You see what I'm saying?

RC: Kind of like the shoulders and hips, side-to-side a little bit?

DR: Yeah. . . . And when you watch that little girl [referring to Dorsey], she don't do that. You understand? So she dancing like a guy. She coming with it. I can *tell* you the difference [between the ways that men and women second line], but when you watch those two people, you can *see* the difference. Some people will say, "Oh, there's no difference!" Yes there is! There *is* a difference.[23]

Leander Brown agrees. When reflecting on men and women second liners, he observed, "Men are usually more energetic. You know, that's why when you see a young lady doing it and she's really good at it, it's really noticeable. Because you don't have a lot of women that are even, that doesn't have the confidence to go out and say, 'You know what? I could do it!' "[24] He has noticed that confident dancers develop a unique style, which works like their embodied signatures to stake their claims to second lining's aesthetic history.[25]

According to Robertson and Brown, perceptible differences exist between second lining "like a female" and "like a dude," and the differences are not regarded equally.

Taken together, these men's reflections align masculine dancing with affective characteristics such as aggression, athleticism, energy, confidence, and originality. Formally,
dancing like a dude can be identified when one privileges footwork over movements
in the hips and torso. At the same time, second liners must be able to invent unique
movements on the spot, which requires a keen ear for tracking the band's rhythms.
Thus, successful second line performances embody a kind of masculinity similar to that
performed by musicians during turn-of-the-century bucking contests: a flexible and responsiveness that tempers brute strength with agility. Female footwork artists who become recognized as excellent second liners seem to be noteworthy precisely because
they disrupt gendered expectations. Their bodies, gendered as female, do not match
their dancing, gendered as male.

Women such as Terrylynn Dorsey and Terrinika Smith, who are interested in gaining
respect as good dancers, are acutely aware of the points of view voiced by Robertson
and Brown. They have utilized various strategies to navigate gendered expectations of
their dancing, both reaffirming and contesting those expectations in the process. For
example, when Dorsey chose to move from the second line into the first line and debut,
or "come out," with a social aid and pleasure club, she chose an all-male group, the Single
Men. When I asked her why, she responded, "The men make you dance," an opinion that
she shares with Smith, who added,

> Nowadays the women's second line groups, there be too much competition with
> "Who's doing this," and they don't really be second lining because they got to
> pop and dance and all that. Even though second line is dance however you make
> it . . . but men making sure your footwork . . . they make you get into it, rather than
> women.[26]

According to Dorsey and Smith, female clubs compete with each other in the non-
dancing aspects of the parade's spectacle, such as suits, floats, and decorations. Smith
explained, "In second line world, it's really a competition. They'll talk about you if your
shoes too small your pants done ripped, your shoes don't match your shirt."[27] While the
sartorial elements are very important to each parade's overall success, clothes do not interest Dorsey and Smith nearly as much as the dancing. For example, the first year that
Dorsey paraded with the Single Men SAPC, she eschewed the club's uniform leather
dress shoes in favor of her Air Jordan sneakers so that her apparel would not hamper her
dancing. Notably, in 2016, the Single Men's ranks included two women: Dorsey and the
high-heeled dancer discussed earlier. Each woman displayed admirable footwork in her
own style, Dorsey in Converse sneakers and her fellow first liner in chunky heels. Seen
side by side, these two "single men" challenged simplistic conflations of footwork mastery and masculinity.

In Dorsey's and Smith's experiences, women's clubs do not challenge each other to
perfect their footwork. Instead, as Smith said, they often "pop," a term used to describe
a hip-hop dance characterized by percussive movements of the hips and buttocks.

Although popping, also called twerking, has become an international phenomenon, the dance holds particular associations in New Orleans. A local variety of rap music and dance, known as Bounce, features popping by female-identified, including transgender, performers.[28] Popping's emphasis on dexterous pelvic movements leads it to be coded as feminine.[29] As Smith sees it, popping falls outside second lining's aesthetic boundaries. Dorsey seems to share her cousin's assessments, choosing to join a men's club so that her fellow first liners (men and women alike) would push her to perfect the rhythmic movements of her feet more than her pelvis.

Although Robertson, Brown, Smith, and Dorsey all speak explicitly about gender differences in second lining's practice and reception, such discrepancies are not always so openly acknowledged among practitioners. Robertson admitted, "Some people will say, 'Oh, there's no difference!' " For example, Linda Porter, cofounder and president of the Original Lady Buckjumpers SAPC, rejects the notion that men dance more energetically and skillfully than women. "Oh, I don't know about that," she said. If people hold that opinion, then, according to Porter, "They don't know about that Lady Buckjumpers! Ask anybody. We getting it on, we bring everything, we going to sweat. Bust pants, lose shoes [*laughs*]. That's me, I done did all that."[30] The Lady Buckjumpers, founded in 1984, has long been well respected for its members' dancing prowess. Along with dancers like Dorsey and Smith, members of the Lady Buckjumpers are often presented as proof of second lining's gender neutrality. However, as the saying goes, the exception proves the rule, or, as Leander Brown put it, "when you see a young lady [second lining] and she's really good at it, it's really noticeable."

Given that most second liners value what second lining *does* for them and their communities far more than the particulars of aesthetics, it makes sense that conversations about *how* one dances, such as dancing in feminine or masculine ways, are often dismissed as irrelevant. The widely held definition of second lining as do-watcha-wanna values the *why* over the *what*, and the reasons why female second liners dance are significant. Girls' and women's growing involvement in second line culture has served as an important vehicle for developing leadership, forming communities, expressing self, celebrating families and neighborhoods, and accessing joyful, even spiritual, experiences through dancing. At the same time, evaluations of the form, such as those that occur during dance competitions, reveal persistent gendered hierarchies that structure women's dancing experiences, even if those hierarchies are dismissed in do-watcha-wanna discourse. Competitions acknowledge that, despite do-watcha-wanna values, there are criteria for superior second lining, and those criteria are coded as masculine. In other words, the dance form contains and communicates value systems and hierarchies that are not widely acknowledged in verbal discourse, but that become more apparent in competition contexts. Nevertheless, these gendered hierarchies cannot fully account for the dance tactics employed by some young women dancers today. Their performances open up new gendered terrain for evaluating second lining beyond a masculine/feminine binary, and footwork competitions provide an important frontier for charting this new terrain.

ALTERNATIVE GENEALOGIES
AND "BADASS FEMININITY"

In search of alternative genealogies for the dancing performed by female footwork art-ists, I look to two areas to suggest possibilities: double-dutch jump rope and b-girling.

The footwork and rhythmic chanting featured in African American girls' games, such as double-dutch jump rope, represent an important influence on the aesthetic properties of African American social dances like second lining. As ethnomusicolo-gist Kyra D. Gaunt (2006) illustrates, African American girls embody the ideals of black music-making (for instance, syncopation, polyrhythm, and call-and-response) in the games they play. Gaunt illuminates how girls use games to transmit embodied musical knowledges, arguing that their contributions to hip-hop often go unrecognized because their efforts are gendered as play. The same analysis could be applied to second line dancing, especially in the case of double-dutch. Present-day second lining can be seen as indebted, at least in part, to double-dutch jump rope. Considering this possibility opens up a space for the unique contributions of girls and women that have gone unaccredited.

One piece of embodied evidence for double-dutch's influence on second line footwork can be found in a video recording of a second line parade captured in 1975 by photog-rapher Jules Cahn, entitled, "Sister Eustis Funeral."[31] The opening frames show a group dancing outside Ruth's Cozy Corner, a landmark bar in the Tremé neighborhood. The musicians play near the building's brick wall while an intergenerational group of African American dancers fans out around the band, grooving on the sidewalk, stoops, and in the street. On the far left-hand side of the screen, two young girls face each other and hop quickly from one foot to the other, dancing in a way that looks like double-dutch without the ropes. The taller girl, who seems to be about ten or eleven years old, quickly discards that movement in favor of crisscrossing her feet, jumping them wide apart, and hopping down to a squat. Throughout, her body is constantly rebounding off the ground. The film is silent, but I can almost hear the music's pulse in her steady bounce.

This footage was captured at the dawn of what music historian Mick Burns (2006) has called the "brass band renaissance." During the 1970s and 1980s, musicians and dancers reinvented second lining's sound and movement to incorporate elements of rhythm and blues, funk, and hip-hop. Second liners' forward-moving steps became more levitated and the art of footwork took prominence within the form. These aesthetic shifts con-tinue to wield tremendous influence on second liners' contemporary practices, and we can see the beginnings of their developments in Cahn's footage. Out of everyone dancing in the 1975 scene, the young girls' jump-rope-style movements most closely resemble the footwork exhibited by the majority of dancers, regardless of sex or gender identity, parading on the streets today. All around these girls, people dance in a way that is more consistent with the footwork exhibited in footage of second lines during the 1960s and early 1970s: they keep their feet closer to the ground and rock a soulful step-touch. These girls alone appear to be at the vanguard of a new form of footwork.

I therefore tentatively propose that African American girls' games contributed to the aesthetic developments of second lining that emerged during the late twentieth century and remain popular today. Beyond teaching girls the musical knowledge needed to improvise dance moves in time with a live brass band, double-dutch also trains them to move in ways that are useful when second lining. The game requires a precise attention to rhythmic footwork: if the jumper gets off beat, the rope will hit her body and she will stop the game. It also teaches jumpers to negotiate gravity in ways that are crucial to second lining embodiment, lifting the torso up from the pelvis so that the feet can work furiously underneath. Finally, the stunts and tricks employed by daredevil jumpers closely resemble second liners' acrobatic feats, such as dropping to the ground and tuck jumping with both knees folded into the chest. When double-dutching, girls "straight up go hard," and have been doing so for decades. The notion that girls' creative labor influences the practice of second lining deserves serious attention, and detailing the links between double-dutch and footwork provides one place for future research.

The second area to which I look to chart an alternative genealogy of second lining can be found in Imani Kai Johnson's concept of "badass femininity." Johnson (2014, 20) coined this term to describe the performances of b-girls, or female-identified persons who break dance, and she defines badass femininity as "a performance that eschews notions of appropriateness, respectability, and passivity demanded of ladylike behavior in favor of confrontational" and "aggressive . . . expressions of a woman's strength." Such non-normative femininities are "born out of the margins of society" and, as such, speak back to the histories of enslavement, genocide, forced labor (sexual and otherwise), and colonial exploitation that has long "disallowed black women from claiming their subjectivities, and distorted the ways that gender was read on them" (2014, 20). Badass femininities are accessed and enter the public sphere through "the permissive space of performance" (2014, 20), such as b-boy/b-girl battles and second line footwork competitions.

Terrylynn Dorsey's and Terrinika Smith's experiences as competitive footwork artists illuminate how danced movement never occurs outside social conventions or political norms. This point has been made repeatedly by scholars of social and vernacular dance who analyze the ways in which dancers obey and break movement codes attached to gender, race, and class (Desmond 1997; Fraser Delgado and Muñoz 1997; García 2013; Goldman 2010; Savigliano 2003). As Maxine Leeds Craig (2014, 168) asserts, "vernacular dance performance has the capacity to naturalize racial and gender boundaries or to transgress them." However, the concept of badass femininity suggests that dancers not only decide whether to obey or break *existing* movement codes when they improvise in social and competitive settings, but also can sometimes create a space *beyond* familiar behavioral scripts and cause spectators to consider new ways of behaving, for example, black and/or female (Johnson 2014, 15–16). By reframing Dorsey's and Smith's dancing as performances of badass femininity, versus dancing like a dude, then we can begin to delink the ideological entanglements between second lining prowess and black masculinity. Such entanglements extend well beyond the realm of second lining to encompass a wide array of African American cultural expressions in which race, gender, and sexuality are written onto and by the dancing body.

"AIN'T NO WAY I LOST AGAINST HIM!"

After Terrylynn Dorsey and her male challenger had been dancing for thirty continuous minutes, Leander Brown motioned to Young Fellas Brass Band that it was time to
conclude. The musicians improvised an ending to their song, and the two sweaty, heavy-
breathing dancers took a seat on the lip of the stage and began gulping water from plastic
bottles. Dorsey felt convinced that she had out-danced her opponent. She had not only
knocked, rolled, and gone hard for thirty straight minutes, but had done so with periodic shifts in her dynamics that demonstrated her ability to respond to, and even pre-
cipitate, the musicians' changes in tempo, syncopation, and instrument emphasis. It
was evident that, to borrow Dorsey's phrase, the beat was in her head. She displayed
an expansive repertoire of unrepeated moves, heeding her cousin/coach's advice to
"shock them every time." She dramatically changed levels, dropping to the ground and
leaping above it at choice moments. She responded to the music with her feet, hardly
ever recruiting her pelvis, torso, or shoulders, which left no doubt about her mastery
of second lining's prized footwork. She heard the crowd's applause and left the battle
confident in the judges' reception of her performance. Overall, her performance in the
2014 Big Easy Footwork Competition (Figure 26.3) demonstrated why admirers such as

FIGURE 26.3. Another view of Terrylynn Dorsey and her lone competitor at the 2014 First
Annual Big Easy Footwork Competition.

Photo by Michael J. Mastrogiovanni.

Rodrick Davis describe her as "the closest thing you're going to see [as far as] male foot-work [performed by] a female."[32]

However, I would like to suggest that Dorsey's footwork, as she performed it at the Competition and at every dance event, does more than confirm a simplistic associa-tion between successful dancing and successful performances of masculinity. Like her cousin Terrinika Smith, the veteran Linda Porter, the young Nyesha Borsey, and other female dancers who dedicate themselves to footwork, Dorsey opens up new ter-rain on the gendered landscape of second line aesthetics. On this terrain, second lining cannot be contained within a masculine/feminine binary, and therefore, these women's performances must be read as more than successful appropriations of second-line masculinity.

I reach this conclusion in part because Dorsey's dancing at the Competition was *not* a successful performance of masculinity, for her male opponent took home the trophy and the cash. Even though Dorsey is widely considered as a dancer that will "go down in history,"[33] her performance still was not sufficient to claim first place. Did the judges reach this decision because they viewed Dorsey's performance through a masculinist frame in which superior second lining has always been and still is executed most suc-cessfully by male dancers? Or was it because they simply did not like her style, because one or more of the judges held personal relationships with the male competitor, or something else? Regardless of the particular reasons for the outcome of this competi-tion, it suggests that, even when a woman dances like a dude, she cannot always attain the same rewards as a dude.

If one views Dorsey's dancing through a feminist versus a masculinist lens, one might detect the importance of women's and girls' labor in her movements. During the Big Easy Footwork Competition, Dorsey improvised a step that I have seen her execute many times: she punctuated her steady heel-to-toe step with high-knee hop-ping, alternating from foot to foot, a move reminiscent of double-dutch jump rope. Knowing that Dorsey is a seasoned double-dutch jumper, I am not surprised that this move forms a staple of her footwork repertoire. However, when considered in context with the young dancers at Sister Eustis's 1975 funeral, Dorsey's jump-rope-style step appears to be more than an idiosyncratic expression. It raises the possibility of a long-standing yet unstated influence of girls' games on second line embodiment. When footwork shifted from a grounded strut to an elevated bounce in the 1970s, young black women and girls who jumped rope were uniquely poised to integrate, and per-haps even introduce, this way of moving into second line dancing. Delineating the precise connections requires further research, but merely opening up the possibility for this influence troubles associations between aesthetic excellence and masculine performance. With each double-dutch-style hop, Dorsey performs an embodied cri-tique of the assumption that she dances like a dude, and charts new terrain in the gendered discourses of second line embodiment.

Dance competitions present an important frontier for young women second liners to chart this terrain because these events present a unique site in which the commu-nity elevates form over function. Second liners' do-watcha-wanna approach to second lining prioritizes the *why* over the *what*, and, as such, the details of how one dances are often dismissed as less important than the social, cultural, and personal benefits gained through participating in the ritual. At the same time, second liners' bodily techniques contain and communicate meanings and histories that might go unsaid, or remain contested, in verbal discourse (Browning 1995; Hamera 2007). During dance competitions, second liners turn their focus to evaluating, debating, and interpreting technique, or the *what* of second lining. As a result, the discursive frameworks surrounding second liners' performances become more explicit. Terrylynn Dorsey was painfully reminded of this when she lost the 2014 competition, and reacted with disbelief: "Ain't no way I lost to him!"[34]

However, dance competitions provide an arena in which preexisting frameworks are confirmed *and* contested. When Dorsey and other young women go hard with their footwork, and challenge men to out-dance them, they issue embodied critiques of second lining's masculinist frameworks—critiques that could be called performances of badass femininity. These young women eschew not only passive ladylike behavior, but also the sexualized bodily display of popping, in favor of confrontational and aggressive expressions of a woman's strength (Johnson 2014, 20). Whether pounding out rhythmic steps in Air Jordan sneakers or high-heeled shoes, women second liners use their feet to speak back to histories of enslavement and exploitation that have distorted the ways in which gender is read on them. The legacies of second lining's gendered history means that passive behavior, polite marching, and hip-rolling dances such as popping are widely read as feminine ways to second line, while footwork, aerial stunts, and confrontations with other dancers are read as masculine. Today, female footwork artists move beyond this history, charting new territory in which they claim subjectivities that cannot be contained by a masculine/feminine binary. As expressions of badass femininity, their dancing rewrites the criteria for mastery as something far more complicated than dancing like a man.

Acknowledgments

Thank you to Imani Kai Johnson for reading an earlier draft of this chapter and providing invaluable feedback.

Notes

1. Second liners' concerns with form and approach are shared by practitioners of many African diaspora dance and music forms. See Gottschild (2003, 280); and DeFrantz (2004, 76).
2. This phrase comes from the title of popular song by the renowned Rebirth Brass Band (1995). For an extended discussion on "do-watcha-wanna" in relation to second lining's formal aesthetics, see Carrico (2016).
3. Terrinika Smith, interview with the author, August 8, 2014.

4. For more on black benevolent societies in New Orleans, see Walker (1937); Jacobs (1988, 22 n. 1, 32); and Malone (1996, 167–168). For more on the history of New Orleans brass bands, see Kmen (1966); Sakakeeny (2013); and White (2001).

5. During my interviews with dedicated second liners, I showed each person a montage of video clips that I filmed at various second line parades, which I selected to exhibit a wide range of bodily expressions. Interviewees consistently affirmed that any kind of dancing displayed in those videos could be labeled as "second lining," even if the dancers were off-beat and were not demonstrating a recognizable form of second lining's basic footwork. When asked why they would label this dancing as second lining, interviewees responded that second lining includes any form of dancing done to brass band music at a parade. For example, when asked this question, Rodrick Davis replied, "Yeah! Yeah, they grooving to the music, yes indeed." I asked, "But it's not footwork?" He confirmed, "No, it's not footwork. It's second lining. It's a big difference. Second lining is dancing and grooving. Footwork is—exactly what it's called, footwork." Davis, interview with the author, January 16, 2014.

6. Terry Gable, interview with the author, January 2, 2014.

7. Wellington Ratcliff, Jr., recalls such competitions occurring at clubs in the 1980s. Raticliff, interview with the author and Daniella Santoro, March 26, 2014.

8. According to Sharon R. Bird's sociological study, competitiveness constitutes one of three elements of patriarchal masculinity, along with emotional detachment and the objectification of women. She writes, "In male homosocial groups, a man risks loss of status and self-esteem unless he competes" (1996, 128).

9. John W. Blassingame gives very similar descriptions of two dances performed at slave balls and at Congo Square, called the "carabine" and the "pile chactas" (1973, 3).

10. Furthermore, musicians commonly identify brass instruments themselves as more appropriate for male musicians, unlike the piano, which is widely considered more feminine. Jazz scholars have pointed out that, in filmic and literary representations of jazz, the trumpet is often likened to a phallus. See Doubleday (2008); Gabbard (1992).

11. The involvement of women in early second line parades is an excellent area for further research. Brothers writes that women's involvement in early jazz culture was mostly limited to churches, brothels, and private homes, for any women who danced in public streets would be considered deviant (2006). Monique Guillory (1998) adds that women's sexual deviance lies at the heart of jazz's emergence, for Storyville brothels served as an important locus of the music's turn-of-the-century developments. As Sherrie Tucker's (2004) meticulous research demonstrates, women contributed to the development of jazz outside of brothels in ways that have been historically devalued: hosting lawn parties, singing and playing in church choirs, working as music teachers, and as vocalists and dancers in nightclubs. Kyle DeCoste's (2015) excellent master's thesis illuminates the work of female brass bands in contemporary New Orleans. Beyond these sources, the question of processions performed by women's societies, and attended by female second liners, at the turn of the century remains under-researched, to the best of my knowledge.

12. On women's involvement in US fraternal organizations, see Beito (2000, 2–3). Tamara Jackson recalls a time when women only rode in cars during second line parades. Jackson, interview with the author, April 21, 2014. Linda Porter remembers that, when she cofounded the Lady Buckjumpers SAPC in 1984, there were very few autonomous female clubs in existence. Porter, interview with the author, August 12, 2014. Their memories match an interview that appears in Alan Lomax's 1990 documentary film, *Jazz Parades*. When interviewing an unnamed woman about second lines in the late 1970s and early

1980s, Lomax asked, "What do the women come for?" The female interviewee replies, "A lot of reasons. The way they look, way they smile, way they dance, way they talk, way they shake. . . ." This exchange indicates that, at the time, women were rarely performing inside the ropes and more often attending to observe the male club members' parades. For example, it was not until 1975 that a female grand marshal, Ellyna Tatum, led a jazz funeral (Tucker 2004, 78).

13. Although Borsey tied for the title of children's division champion in 2014, she won the title single-handedly in 2015 ("Shack Brown and Nyesha Borsey" 2015, n.p.).

14. Leander Brown, interview with the author, December 16, 2015.

15. Brown's decision to produce an annual dance competition fits within his broad array of activities in various civic engagement and youth development initiatives. He coaches football teams and marching bands, holds a weekly engagement giving motivational speeches to incarcerated youth, produces festivals for stand-up comedians, and mounts various other projects. As a child, he attended Jerome Smith's Tambourine and Fan Club, an influential youth program that trained many of today's active musicians and social aid and pleasure club leaders in the techniques and philosophies of New Orleans's black cultural traditions. In many ways, Brown extends the impacts and spirit of Jerome Smith's influence to a new generation of youth. For more on the Tambourine and Fan Club, see Pierre (2007).

16. Davis, interview with the author, January 16, 2014.

17. Terrylynn Dorsey and Terrinika Smith, interview with the author, August 8, 2014.

18. Dorsey, interview with the author, August 8, 2014.

19. Dorsey, interview with the author, August 8, 2014.

20. In fact, Brown explained to me that this judge brought an informed eye to her role, not merely because she was a dance teacher, but because she was raised in a family that has been heavily involved in the second line culture for generations. Brown, interview with the author, December 16, 2015. Dorsey recalled that one of the judges was a member of the Sidewalk Steppers Social Aid and Pleasure Club and masks as a Mardi Gras Indian. Dorsey, interview with the author, August 8, 2014.

21. Judith Hamera (2007) defines dance technique in this way.

22. Smith, interview with the author, August 8, 2014.

23. Don Robertson, interview with the author, April 10, 2014.

24. Brown, interview with the author, December 16, 2015.

25. On the function of embodied signatures in African American vernacular dance, see Kraut (2016).

26. Dorsey and Smith, interview with the author, August 8, 2014.

27. Dorsey and Smith, interview with the author, August 8, 2014.

28. Big Freedia, a transgender, or self-identified "sissy," Bounce artist who has soared to international fame, remarks that Bounce, also called popping or twerking, "has extraordinary power. Moving it [the groin area] at lightning speed is more than sexual; it's also deeply intimate and transformative. For us sissies, who lived under such constant oppression—the violence, poverty, and homophobia—Bounce is our way to transmute that pain into joy" (Newman 2015, n.p.).

29. For an analysis of the ideological connections between blackness, femininity, and hip-rolling dances in the African diaspora, see Jones (2016).

30. Porter, interview with the author, August 12, 2014.

31. Cahn (1975).

32. Davis, interview with the author, January 16, 2014.
33. Davis, interview with the author, January 16, 2014.
34. Dorsey, interview with the author, August 8, 2014.

REFERENCES

Bechet, Sidney. 1960. *Treat It Gentle*. London: Twayne and Cassel.
Beito, David T. 2000. *From Mutual Aid to the Welfare State: Fraternal Societies and Social Services, 1890–1967*. Chapel Hill: University of North Carolina Press.
Bird, Sharon R. 1996. "Welcome to the Men's Club: Homosociality and the Maintenance of Hegemonic Masculinity." *Gender and Society* 10(2): 120–132.
Blassingame, John W. 1973. *Black New Orleans: 1860–1880*. Chicago: University of Chicago Press.
Brothers, Thomas. 2006. *Louis Armstrong's New Orleans*. New York: W. W. Norton.
Browning, Barbara. 1995. *Samba: Resistance in Motion*. Bloomington: Indiana University Press.
Burns, Mick. 2006. *Keeping the Beat on the Streets: The New Orleans Brass Band Renaissance*. Baton Rouge: Louisiana State University Press.
Carrico, Rachel. 2016. "Un/Natural Disaster and Dancing: Hurricane Katrina and Second Lining in New Orleans." *TBS: The Black Scholar* 46(1): 27–36.
Craig, Maxine Leeds. 2014. *Sorry I Don't Dance: Why Men Refuse to Move*. New York: Oxford University Press.
Evans, Freddi Williams. 2011. *Congo Square: African Roots in New Orleans*. Lafayette: University of Louisiana at Lafayette Press.
DeCoste, Kyle. 2015. "The Original Pinettes: Black Feminism in New Orleans Brass Bands." MA thesis, Tulane University.
DeFrantz, Thomas F. 2004. "The Black Beat Made Visible: Hip Hop Dance and Body Power." In *Of the Presence of the Body: Essays on Dance and Performance Theory*, edited by André Lepecki, 64–81. Middletown, CT: Wesleyan University Press.
Delgado, Celeste Fraser, and José Muñoz, eds. 1997. *Everynight Life: Culture and Dance in Latin/o America*. Durham, NC: Duke University Press.
Desmond, Jane C. 1997. "Embodying Difference: Issues in Dance and Cultural Studies." In *Meaning in Motion: New Cultural Studies of Dance*, edited by Jane C. Desmond, 29–54. Durham, NC: Duke University Press.
Doubleday, Veronica. 2008. "Sounds of Power: An Overview of Musical Instruments and Gender." *Ethnomusicology Forum* 17(1): 3–39.
Gabbard, Krin. 1992. "Signifyin(g) the Phallus: 'Mo' Better Blues' and the Representations of the Jazz Trumpet." *Cinema Journal* 32(1): 43–62.
García, Cindy. 2013. *Salsa Crossings: Dancing Latinidad in Los Angeles*. Durham, NC: Duke University Press.
Gaunt, Kyra D. 2006. *The Games Black Girls Play: Learning the Ropes from Double-Dutch to Hip-Hop*. New York: New York University Press.
Goldman, Danielle. 2010. *I Want to Be Ready: Improvised Dance as a Practice of Freedom*. Ann Arbor: University of Michigan Press.
Gottschild, Brenda Dixon. 2003. *The Black Dancing Body: A Geography from Coon to Cool*. New York: Palgrave Macmillan.

Guillory, Monique. 1998. "Black Bodies Swingin': Race, Gender, and Jazz." In *Soul: Black Power, Politics, and Pleasure*, edited by Monique Guillory and Richard C. Green, 191–215. New York: New York University Press.

Hamera, Judith. 2007. *Dancing Communities: Performance, Difference and Connection in the Global City*. New York: Palgrave Macmillan.

Jacobs, Claude. 1988. "Benevolent Societies of New Orleans Blacks during the Late Nineteenth and Early Twentieth Centuries." *Louisiana History: The Journal of the Louisiana Historical Association* 29(1): 21–33.

Johnson, Imani Kai. 2014. "From Blues Women to B-Girls: Performing Badass Femininity." *Women & Performance: A Journal of Feminist Theory* 24(1): 15–28.

Jones, Adanna Kai. 2016. "Take a Wine and Roll 'IT'!" Breaking through the Circumscriptive Politics of the Trini/Caribbean Dancing Body." PhD diss., University of California, Riverside.

Kmen, Henry A. 1966. *Music in New Orleans: The Formative Years, 1791–1841*. Baton Rouge: Louisiana State University Press.

Kraut, Anthea. 2016. *Choreographing Copyright: Race, Gender, and Intellectual Property in American Dance*. New York: Oxford University Press.

Malone, Jacqui. 1996. *Steppin' on the Blues: The Visible Rhythms of African American Dance*. Urbana: University of Illinois Press.

Newman, Jason. 2015. "Big Freedia Reflects on Miley Cyrus, Coming Out in New Memoir." *Rolling Stone* online, July 1, 2015. http://www.rollingstone.com/ music/news/big-freedia-reflects-on-miley-cyrus-coming-out-in-new-memoir-20150701. Accessed March 25, 2016.

Pierre, Towana. 2007. "Down to the River of Dryades and Claiborne Avenues (Jerome Smith)." In *The Long Ride: A Collection of Student Writings for the New Orleans Civil Rights Park*, 165. New Orleans: Students at the Center.

Sakakeeny, Matt. 2013. *Roll with It: Brass Bands in the Streets of New Orleans*. Durham, NC: Duke University Press.

Savigliano, Marta E. 2003. "Gambling Femininity: Wallflowers and Femme Fatales." In *Angora Matta: Fatal Acts of North-South Translations*, 166–190. Middletown, CT: Wesleyan University Press.

Tucker, Sherrie. 2004. "A Feminist Perspective on New Orleans Jazzwomen." *New Orleans Jazz National Park Service*. Published September 30, 2004. http://www.nps.gov/jazz/ learn/historyculture/upload/New_Orleans_Jazzwomen _ RS-2.pdf. Accessed September 29, 2015.

Walker, Harry J. 1937. "Negro Benevolent Societies in New Orleans: A Study of Their Structure, Function, and Membership." MA thesis, Fisk University.

White, Michael. 2001. "The New Orleans Brass Band: A Cultural Tradition." In *The Triumph of the Soul: Cultural and Psychological Aspects of African American Music*, edited by Ferdinand Jones and Arthur C. Jones, 69–96. Westport, CT: Praeger.

Audiovisual Sources

Cahn, Jules. 1975. "Sister Eustis Funeral." July 8 or 9. 16mm, silent. Jules Cahn Collection, 1963–1983. Historic New Orleans Collection.

Lomax, Alan, dir. 1990. *Jazz Parades: Feet Don't Fail Me Now*. New York: Association for Cultural Equity, 3/4 inch videotape: U-matic. Folkstreams. http://www.folkstreams.net/film,126. Accessed May 17, 2015.

Rebirth Brass Band. 1995. "Do Watcha Wanna." *Do Watcha Wanna*. New Orleans: Mardi Gras Records. Audio CD.

"Shack Brown and Nyesha Borsey." 2015. *The Goodnight Show with John Calhoun*. Posted May 4. http://www.thegoodnightshow.us/? p=515. Accessed September 29, 2015.

CHAPTER 27

MAN AND MONEY READY

Challenge Dancing in Antebellum America

APRIL F. MASTEN

IN June 1853, "Champion Dancer of the World" John Diamond was enjoying a successful month-long run at the Holliday Street Theatre in Baltimore, attracting large crowds with his "magnificent jigs" and winning effusive reviews in the press. "He now stands ABOVE ALL PUNY RIVALRY, as the very greatest of that class of Dancing which is PURELY AMERICAN," trumpeted the *Baltimore Sun*. Then, just as the theater renewed his contract, R. H. (Dick) Sliter opened a few blocks away at the Baltimore Museum, claiming that he, not Diamond, was champion jig dancer of the world, having bested him in a five-night trial of skill in Cincinnati for the "CHAMPION BELT." Feigning outrage over Sliter's "Cincinnati fabrication," Diamond called for a rematch: "I WILL DANCE WITH HIM AT ANY HALL IN THE CITY . . . TWO 'JIGS,' TWO 'REELS,' and a 'WALK AROUND,' the victor to receive the BELTS and the WAGER that may be decided upon." Having made his terms clear, Diamond then dared Sliter to "come up to the scratch" (1853a, 2).

Though little remembered after the Civil War, challenge dancing was an immensely popular form of entertainment in antebellum America. Countless working-class men, women, and children faced off in jig dancing competitions in private and public settings for pleasure, prestige, and profit. Their ranks included Irish Americans like Diamond and Sliter, their female counterparts Julia Morgan and Naomi Porter, and African American dancers like Master Juba and Aaron Molineaux. Celebrated as artists and athletes, these competitors acquired their dance steps and moves in the mixed neighborhoods of American seaboard cities and river towns, and emulated the practices and patter of European ballerinas and British boxers. Competitive jig dancers gained large followings as they met in local dance-houses, toured with circuses, or worked the theater circuits. Champions earned continental reputations by winning scored bouts for hefty purses, side bets, and silver belts.

Antebellum Americans challenged each other to contests in almost every style of dancing, but jigging challenges were the most common. Jigs were lively partner and solo step-dances of Irish origin. However, in the United States, people used the terms *jig dancing* and *Negro dancing* interchangeably to describe a style of dancing derived from Irish "set dancing" practice and African dance-movement practices. That style, which I refer to as *Negro jig dancing*, required the performance of recognizable "set dance" figures, integrating the "stamping, shuffling, grinding, skipping and hopping" steps of jigs, reels, and hornpipes, often in an alternating format that invited competition, with the rhythmic footwork, hip play, and upper body movements developed by African American dancers (O'Connor 2001, 51; Malone 1996).[1] Both blacks and whites were identified in newspaper articles and advertisements as performers of competitive Negro jigs.[2] This chapter traces the emergence and transformation of this hybrid local form of personal expression into a marketable profession with national, and even transnational, appeal. It recovers the practice, practitioners, and origins of challenge dancing and the processes by which challenge dancers professionalized their art and kept it popular for over two decades. Methodologically, I use the tools of social and cultural history, locating primary source materials through archival research, and analyzing those documents (words, images, music), paying particular attention to their contemporary meanings.[3] In so doing, I show that challenge dancing gained and maintained widespread appeal via its interaction with other sporting and entertainment fields of the time, in particular ballet, minstrelsy, and boxing.

THE MAKING OF CHALLENGE DANCERS

The Challenge

Trials of skill were ubiquitous in antebellum America. The speculation and competition that fueled the nation's market economy encouraged contests in almost every realm. Male and female artisans faced off in coach-making competitions and thread- and yarn-spinning marathons. Rural and urban laborers turned their work into games, holding plowing matches and newspaper-folding competitions. And entertainers, from circus performers to violinists and ballet dancers, advertised their performances as grand trials of skill.

Jig dancing trials of skill were held at the end of a night of dancing or other entertainments. At 1840s tavern matches, couples and solo dancers performed in the center of the room amid the spectators, who bet on their favorite and decided on the winner (Masten 2015). If the contestants were solo males or females, they danced in turn, rather than at the same time. Each danced for as long as he or she could, while the fiddle or banjo players moved from one tune to the next. The match might begin at ten or eleven o'clock, with the fiddle striking up a reel for the first dancer who demonstrated his or her expertise at jigging, reeling, shuffling, twisting, walking around, and beating out hornpipes. Then, after an hour or so, the dancer brought one foot down with a bang, ending the dance exactly in time with the music. After the cheers died down, the second dancer took the floor and tried to out-step the first. If they knew what they were about, they danced all the same dances in their own way, putting in a lot of fancy work and funny business, until they had beaten the first dancer's time ("The Negro Minstrels" [ca. 1875]).

Like everyone else, jig dancers announced challenges in the press to drum up work, gain celebrity, and attract a betting crowd to their matches. To instigate a match, a dancer or his friends made a challenge and specified the terms, which another dancer either accepted or countered. Anglo-American Henry Manning advertised his skills in the *New York Morning Herald* in July 1840, saying, "Whereas some interlopers and boasters have, in order to get an engagement, bragged that they could beat any man in America in a Sailor's Hornpipe, I now challenge one or all of them to meet me in public, and dance a hornpipe for a sum of $100 to $300." Manning's challenge was answered the next day by J. L. Garretts, a.k.a. the Dutchess County Plough Boy, who agreed to dance him for $100: "The money is now waiting at the Bar of Vauxhall Gardens, and he can cover it as soon as he dare, or 'draw in his horns.'" The two men faced off the following Monday. Garretts triumphed, after which he was added to Vauxhall Garden's roster of regular performers (*New York Morning Herald* 1840a, 1840b, 1840c).

Published challenges like Manning's, made in response to oral boasting, attest to the existence of a circle of amateurs who gained attention dancing in tavern matches. "As Mr. James Gibney has been talking about his dancing, and seems unable to get a match, I, Richard Callaghan, am prepared to dance him for $25, in two weeks after the first deposit, either jig or reel time, to either violin or banjo. Man and money ready at the Canadian House, corner of York and Queen streets, Toronto." Callaghan fared better than Manning; his challenge expanded into a tournament in which four young men danced in front of 1,200 people for a silver medal, with Callaghan coming off victorious (*New York Clipper* 1857a, 387; 1857c, 163).

The Challengers

Antebellum challenge dancing was dominated by young boys, and audiences in young America loved to watch precocious children perform. Most challenge dancers began competing in their teens, if not earlier, and used the title "Master" to signpost their young age (Figures 27.1 and 27.2).

Once noticed, an "astonishing" performing child turned himself into a jig dancer worthy of press coverage by making and winning challenges. Thirteen-year-old John Diamond was discovered dancing on New York's East River docks in 1839 by P. T. Barnum, who hired him to dance Negro jigs on the stage. One year later, Master Diamond challenged two white veteran dancers, New York's twenty-five-year-old R. W. Pelham and Philadelphia's twenty-six-year-old James Sanford. Diamond claimed he won both matches, and entered the circle of professionals as a champion dancer (*Spirit of the Times* 1840; *Philadelphia Public Ledger* 1840). Then, in 1844, a youngster

FIGURE 27.1. "Mas.^T Marks, the Celebrated Dancer."

Detail from cover of *Ethiopian Melodies of White's Serenaders* (New York, 1849), Sheet Music–Negro Minstrels. Courtesy of American Antiquarian Society.

FIGURE 27.2. "Boz's Juba."

Detail from Royal Vauxhall Gardens Playbill, 1848, Joseph N. Ireland scrapbook, Volume 2, TS939.5.3F, Harvard Theatre Collection, Houghton Library, Harvard University.

named Ruthven Jones challenged Master Diamond to a match at the Knickerbocker on New York's Bowery for $10 a side (Odell 1931). Presumably, Jones lost, since he disappeared from sight after the match.

It is not always possible to identify the race of challenge dancers. Contemporary observers described seeing "whites, blacks, and mulattos all dancing together" in the taverns of African- and Anglo-American proprietors, and the white managers of some entertainment venues hired black dancers to perform on their stages (Biddle 1883; Nichols 1864). In some cases, blackface makeup was applied to hide the race of the dancer from audiences. In 1840–1841, P. T. Barnum engaged an African American jig dancer to perform blacked-up as Master Rattler and to pose blacked-up as Irish-American Master Diamond at New York's Vauxhall Garden (*Sunday Flash* 1841).

Dancing matches could be found in almost every Northern city where whites and blacks lived in close proximity. New York City's black community numbered 16,000 in 1840, one of the largest in the North. Fully emancipated since 1827, they lived mostly in the same East River districts as Irish immigrants. In these unsegregated neighborhoods, poor whites and blacks rubbed shoulders in the streets, drank and danced together in public houses, rented rooms in the same buildings, and even intermarried (Harris 2003; Hodges 1997). Their encounters differed based on race and gender, while their locality made challenge dancing a common enterprise.

Challenge dancing was a precarious occupation at the best of times, and the number of professionals was never large. Perhaps three dozen male dancers competed on stage at one time or another between 1840 and 1860. At least one-quarter of these known dancers were men of color. Performing on stage was particularly precarious for African Americans, as even successful performers faced the possibility of being run off theatrical boards by whites threatened or angered by their achievements. Public announcements of the whereabouts of black performers also made them vulnerable targets for illegal seizure. This danger increased in the 1850s with the passage of the Fugitive Slave Act, which allowed slave hunters to capture people they deemed runaway slaves without a warrant and return them to slavery without a trial. Nevertheless, in the 1840s, the dancing matches that drew the most attention were between Irish-American Diamond and an African American teenager called Juba (Figure 27.2).

Master Juba's story illustrates both the typical route and the exceptional possibilities opened up by challenge dancing. Gaining fame as "young Juba," the boy's superior dancing ability was already recognized in 1842 when Charles Dickens was taken to see him dance against a female competitor at "Almack's" tavern in New York's Five Points district (Figure 27.3). After Dickens dubbed him "the greatest dancer known" in his travelogue *American Notes* (Dickens 1842), Juba's tavern appearances attracted notice in the sporting and penny press. Upon Juba's entering the room, "a purse was soon raised," reported the *Whip*, "when he took his station upon the floor, and we never saw such

FIGURE 27.3. Artist A. B. Frost's impression of the African American set dance or "break-down" Dickens saw at "Almack's" in New York City.

The Works of Charles Dickens Household Edition (London: Chapman and Hall, 1871). Personal collection.

dancing before. Why his feet were like the movements [of] a chronometer, so regular did they keep time. Talk about your Diamonds, why they are no comparison to the dancing we witnessed there" (*New York Whip* 1842, 2). Within a month the sporting community had matched up John Diamond, the champion, and Juba, the contender, at an informal bout in another Five Points barroom. According to one account, the match was judged by a mixed-race crowd of friends, dancers, gamblers, and pugilists ("The Negro Minstrels" [ca. 1875]). Diamond reputedly won that contest.

Then came the big rematch. On July 8, 1844, the *New York Herald* announced a "GREAT PUBLIC CONTEST" between "the Original JOHN DIAMOND" (to distinguish him from his many impersonators) and "the Colored Boy JUBA" for a $200 wager in the spacious Bowery Amphitheatre. Juba's friends had challenged "the world" to produce his superior in the art of breakdown dancing for $100. Diamond's friends accepted the challenge and put up another $100. The parties agreed that the contestants would dance three jigs, two reels, and the Camptown hornpipe.[4] "Five judges have been selected for their ability and knowledge of the Art, so that a fair decision will be made," assured the backers. "Each dancer will select his own Violin and the victory will be decided by the best time and the greatest number of steps." According to his subsequent playbills, Juba won this contest.

Through these public challenges, Juba took his place at the pinnacle of the profession and set up a career for himself. After defeating Diamond, he traveled with a number of blackface troupes (which I discuss later) as a champion dancer and performed at Anglo-American Charlie White's Melodeon (a minstrelsy and variety theater known for featuring top-notch dancers). In 1848 he migrated to England as the star and only black member of G. W. Pell's Ethiopian Serenaders, where he was lionized by the press and after a couple of years left Pell to form his own troupe.[5] While Juba's success was unusual for an African American performer at the time, the path he followed was required of all professional challenge dancers.

Female challenge dancers were rarely the focus of writers in the North, but they were there, too. At a lower-class dance-house in New York City, urban writer George Foster noted that "[p]robably three quarters of the women assembled here, and who frequent this place, are negresses, of various shades and colors." The other quarter were white women, the leader of the orchestra was black, and the male dancers were assorted white and black youths, rowdies, firemen, and sailors (Foster 1850). The *Whip* reporter who saw Juba dance at Almack's in 1842 informed his readers that "a purse" was raised to indicate that the dancer would be competing with another dancer for a wager. But he did not specify whether that other dancer was male or female. Dickens, on the other hand, made it clear that when he saw Juba dance a "regular break-down" in that same barroom three months earlier, his opponent was a woman. The English author was familiar with the format of the set dancing he described, only the style of the steps was new:

> Every gentleman sets as long as he likes to the opposite lady, and the opposite lady to him, and all are so long about it that the sport begins to languish, when suddenly the lively hero dashes in to the rescue. Single shuffle, double shuffle, cut and

cross-cut: snapping his fingers, rolling his eyes, turning in his knees, . . . spinning about on his toes and heels . . . when, having danced his partner off her feet, and himself too, he finishes by leaping gloriously on the bar-counter, and calling for something to drink. (Dickens 1842, 101)

Dickens's "lively hero" was not performing solo. He and his partner were in competition. He won the match by dancing the greatest variety of steps and by exceeding *her* time. Most scholarship on Juba's dancing ignores the female rival in Dickens's quote, as if competitive dance were a male prerogative. But if we want to recover the complex racial and gender borrowings that produced challenge dancing, we have to notice her. Boys, blacks, and women had different experiences, but challenge dancing could be an occupation for all.

Transatlantic Origins

Jig dancing contests were puffed to the skies in the popular press, but they did not begin as commercial entertainment. Their origins can be traced to village customs brought to North America via the centuries-long African slave trade and eighteenth-century Irish diaspora (Foster 1989; Green 1996). Thrown together in colonial America by chattel slavery and indentured servitude, these displaced peoples exchanged steps, moves, and musical accompaniments voluntarily and under duress on plantations and piers, market streets, and tavern floors. By the 1830s, their interactions had made Negro jig dancing widespread among North American slaves, free blacks, and laboring-class whites (Masten 2013).

The elements that Irish and African people brought to challenge dancing were different (Masten 2014). Both groups came to North America with a dance culture that included formalized practices (for example, individual dances, dancing formats, ritual purposes, contexts) and aesthetic physicality (for example, style, steps, moves, dynamics). Dancers from diverse regions of Africa, who lost much of their formalized practice when forcibly removed from their homelands and jumbled together as slaves, borrowed from each other and from the various dance practices they encountered in North America to create an African American dance tradition.

All of the dances performed by Anglo- and African American challenge dancers had a basis in "set dancing," as practiced in Ireland. In a set dance, four or more couples faced off and danced the same steps, or "figures," as friendly competitors. The term *set* referred to the stringing together of two or three tunes and the dances that accompanied them. These dances had roots in Europe and Britain, reflecting Ireland's colonial history. Jigs danced to tunes in 6/8 time featured high knee lifts and triple steps; reels danced to 2/2 or 4/4 time moved across the floor; and hornpipes danced to 2/4 or reel time highlighted percussive steps. By combining two or more of these tunes, sets encouraged the dancers to think in both jig and reel time, which share a duple downbeat but have syncopated internal rhythms. In most Irish counties, dancers accentuated foot and legwork, "trapping each note of the music on the floor" as if the body were weightless, while keeping the arms relaxed and upper body erect (Breathnach 1971, 53). Americans called set dancing "jig dancing." They also called hornpipes "walk-arounds" because hornpipe dancers circumnavigated the floor twice, in opposite directions, before launching into their steps "with arms crossed, or poised, or whirled" (Kennedy 1867).

Slaves and free blacks in North America adopted the Irish set dancing practice (in its entirety) into their dance culture, adding their own complexities and syncopations to the tunes and steps and incorporating an Africanist aesthetic (Szwed and Marks 1988; White and White 1998). Though every ethnic group in Africa had its own type of dancing, in most West African regions dances were performed in lines and circles. Dancers worked with gravity, moving with relaxed knees, using the body's weight to accent the rhythmic beats. The various groups emphasized different angulated postures and gestures, separating hip, chest, and shoulder moves. Dances might also feature "leaping, tumbling, shaking, stooping, stamping, squatting, and lifting" (Green 1996; Malone 1996, 13).

African American set dancers added these elements to their jigs, reels, and hornpipes. Then Anglo-American dancers adopted those changes, revising their own music and dance practice, and so on, back and forth. These North American challenge dancers combined a rapid striking of the toe on the ground forward and back, called double shuffle in Irish step-dancing, with the gliding, dragging, and shuffling steps of West African dance (Brennan 2001; Stearns and Stearns 1968). John Diamond called this flat-foot kind of jig dancing "purely American." The balance between Irish and African influences depended on the dancer. Some black and some white dancers accentuated the "Hibernian" and others the "Ethiopian" style.

While different in style and steps, Irish and African dance traditions shared two important practices: competition and mixed gender dancing. In many West African communities, dancers and musicians met in an area cleared for dancing and formed a circle, inside of which one person danced until challenged by another dancer who eventually took over, and so on, for hours on end (Green 1996). In rural Ireland, dancers and musicians met outside a public house to dance sets, at the end of which the favored couple, solo dancers, or musician and dancers moved to the center of their peers to exhibit their prowess and compete (Foley 2013). African American dancers called this competitive part of the set a "break-down" since the dancers were free to break the beat or the pattern with embellishments (Thompson 1991).

Competitive mixed-gender dancing was common to both traditions as well. Competition was a way to show off, win status or prizes, and attract mates. At country dances across Ireland, the young women often initiated the competitions (Friel 2004). Writing about his youth in the neighboring counties of Cork and Limerick in the 1820s, Irish author R. Shelton Mackenzie recalled that toward the end of an evening of set dancing

[a] joyous, light-hearted damsel would suddenly start up, while the music was playing, and, placing herself before the dancing-master, with that particular description of curtsy called "a bob," silently challenge him to dance with her. Now, under all circumstances, except actual inability to move, the gentleman so challenged has nothing to do but pick up the gauntlet, and "take the flure [floor]." Then, challenger and challenged would commence an Irish jig—a dance so violent . . . the very

recollection of it makes me feel as if the barometer was some two hundred in the shade. . . . When the damsel had pretty well tired herself, one of her fair friends would take her place, and so on until a round dozen or so had had their turn. All this time, [on point of honor] the doomed victim of a man had to continue dancing . . . until, at last, some male spectator would pityingly dash into the circle [and] take the tired man's place. (Mackenzie 1854, 299)

Irish dancers took this jigging contest to America, where slaves and free blacks combined it with their own competitive dancing practice. African American author Solomon Northup recalled playing the fiddle for a challenge dance on a Louisiana plantation in the 1850s. Among the slaves enjoying a Christmas dinner and frolic was a young woman called "Miss Lively," who was being courted by three men.

It was a victory for Sam Roberts, when, rising from the repast, she gave him her hand for the first "figure" in preference to either of his rivals. . . . [Samuel's] legs flew like drum-sticks down the outside and up the middle, by the side of his bewitching partner. The whole company cheered them vociferously, and, excited with the applause, they continued "tearing down" after all the others had become exhausted and halted a moment to recover breath. But Sam's superhuman exertions overcame him finally, leaving Lively alone, yet whirling like a top. Thereupon one of Sam's rivals, Pete Marshall, dashed in, and, with might and main leaped and shuffled and threw himself into every conceivable shape. . . . Pete's affection, however, was greater than his discretion. Such violent exercise took the breath out of him directly. . . . Then was the time for Harry Carey to try his hand; but Lively also soon out-winded him, amidst hurrahs and shouts, fully sustaining her well-earned reputation of being the "fastest gal" on the bayou. (Northup 1970, 218–219)

Like their Irish counterparts, Miss Lively's partners accepted her challenge and danced the "figures" with vigor, adding their own aesthetic touches as they struggled to out-step her (and their male rivals). Young male dancers brought these hybrid dance steps to the stage and turned them into a professional entertainment form. But to build audiences and generate lasting interest, challenge dancing had to engage with other popular entertainments.

THE PROFESSIONALIZATION
OF CHALLENGE DANCING

Enter the Danseuse

During the 1830s and 1840s, European ballet became wildly popular in the United States, and challenge dancers embraced and mocked it for their own benefit. Jig-dancing boys working in American theaters took their cues from the ballet-dancing girls working alongside them. Their first matches on the stage were travesties of competitions between ballerinas. Beginning in the 1830s, almost every white *danseuse* (famous female dancer) on the American stage debuted in the opera ballet *La Bayadere; or, The Maid of Cashmere*. The ballet's famous *pas de deux* entitled the "Grand Trial Dance," which pitted the newcomer against the current luminary, became a vehicle for gaining star status (Robert 1946). In 1837, twelve-year-old Augusta Maywood and thirteen-year-old Mary Ann Lee double debuted in *La Bayadere* at Philadelphia's Chestnut Street Theatre. Maywood, who was the step-daughter of the theater's manager, danced in the leading role as Zelica (named Zoloe in the original French version), and Lee as her rival and sister Fatima.[6] As staged in Philadelphia by Paul H. Hazard, the "Trial Dance" exploited the contrasting talents of the two young dancers. Audiences encouraged the rivalry, returning night after night to vote for their favorite with applause and showers of bouquets ("Lee" 1971). The contest launched both dancers' ballet careers, but Lee's diverse repertoire made her the more popular. Subsequently, she and a number of other *danseuses* supplemented their livings by performing *La Bayadere*'s "Trial Dance" separately from the ballet as the *entr'acte* at playhouses. Jig dancers modeled their theatrical dancing matches on these performances.

Challenge dancers incorporated women's innovations into their dances as well. Master Juba began his champion dance by running diagonally downstage on his toes in imitation of ballerinas like Marie Taglioni (Figure 27.4), who first popularized dancing on the extreme tips of the toes (*en pointe*) in the ballet *La Sylphide*. This move made his performance thrilling from the start (*New Orleans Picayune* 1891). Alternately, Master Diamond both mocked and challenged his toe dancing rivals by stepping forward on his heels. Jig dancers easily imitated ballerinas because their training overlapped. Most Anglo- and African American jig dancers learned to dance as children from family members, who had learned from local experts, who had studied with dancing masters trained in Ireland, Britain, or Europe. Among those local experts were slaves owned by master dancers and musicians (Jamison 2015; Thomas 1984). Dancing masters instructed their boy and girl pupils in the fundamental postures and attitudes of dance, as well as the steps of the most popular social dances: jigs, reels, hornpipes, waltzes, and quadrilles (Foley 2013). These were the same fundamentals and steps taught to ballerinas (Homans 2010).

Master dancers also trained their pupils to add their own and other dancers' moves to their performances. The combining of skill and wit was a competitive strategy used by all champion dancers. Imitating a known step could provoke the laughter of recognition and tilt the balance of support in a dancer's favor. White and black jig dancers adopted each other's moves and steps for that effect. A white dancer like Diamond, who combined perfectly executed Irish cross-cuts with African-style turned-in-knees, was more likely to win a match than a dancer who could only perform straight jigs and reels. Alternately, a black dancer like Juba aroused interest by combining "curious and opposite acts" (like highland flings and falling backward) with "the true, marking of the time" in his hornpipes (*Manchester Times* 1848).

America's male dancers looked on European *danseuses* as rivals with whom they competed for theater stages and audiences. The original opera *La Bayadère*

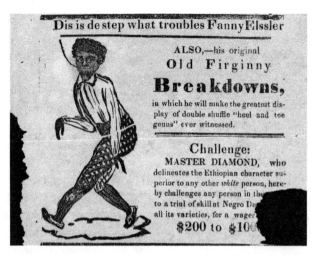

FIGURE 27.4. Marie Taglioni *en pointe.*

Marie Taglioni as Zoloe in *Le Dieu et La Bayadère,* cir. 1830, del. Alfred E. Chalon, scrit. Richard J. Lane, hand colored lithograph, published by Ackerman & Co. Victoria and Albert Museum, no. E.5046-1968.

FIGURE 27.5. Master (John) Diamond mocking renowned Viennese *danseuse* Fanny Ellsler in a sketch he called "The Black Bayadere."

Detail from New Theatre playbill, Playbill, Mobile, February 22, 1841, TS.24 o.12.1.69.F.A.Minstrels.1841, Harvard Theatre Collection, Houghton Library, Harvard University.

Amoureuse, ou, Le Dieu et La Bayadère was written by Daniel Auber for the Italian *danseuse* Marie Taglioni, who played the title role in Paris in 1830 and London in 1831. Taglioni's keenest competition was Céline Céleste, a French teenager who debuted at New York's Bowery Theatre in 1830. Céleste danced in the United States again in 1834–1837, arousing enthusiasm so great that people carried her through the streets on their shoulders. Rumor had it that President Andrew Jackson, who was an ardent admirer, adopted her as a citizen of the Union ("Céleste" 1910). The next young woman to generate such ardor was Viennese *danseuse* Fanny Elssler, who toured the United States in 1840–1841. Master Diamond contested Elssler's fame by announcing on an 1841 playbill: "Dis is de step what troubles Fanny Elssler" (Figure 27.5). He then challenged "any person in the world to a trial of skill at Negro Dancing in all its varieties for $200 to $1000" (New Theatre playbill 1841).

Another advertisement described Master Diamond's performance as a battle with all four prima ballerinas: "Diamond as the *French Danseuse,* in which he will utterly extinguish Taglioni, Augusta and Celeste, and throw the admired FANNY ELSSLER Totally, entirely, and forever in the shade" (National Theatre playbill 1840). Through these burlesques, male jig dancers drew attention to their own dancing skills and paying customers to their matches. But female dancers were right behind them. Seeing where the money was going, in 1842 Mary Ann Lee danced her own burlesque of *La Bayadere,* advertised as "Buy-It-Dear; 'Tis Made of Cashmere" (a pun that encompassed the ballet's title and its famous "Shawl Dance").

Boy dancers also cross-dressed as specific ballerinas. By default, wench dancing (blackface jig dancers who dressed as women) mocked every woman of color who presumed to dress or dance in European fashion. But its more immediate targets in the 1840s were the white *danseuses* who had come to dominate the theatrical stage. Cross-dressing performances became even more aggressive in the 1850s, after white and black women began crusading for social, legal, and political rights. Minstrel performers mocked female calls for reform by delivering parodies of women's rights speeches in black English dialect and dancing hornpipes "a la bloomer" (*Boston Herald* 1851, 3; Mahar 1999).

Female *danseuses* also danced as other wenches. In 1843, a New York journalist reported having seen a "mulatto girl playing the castanets, and imitating Elssler in what she called the *cracoveragain*," a burlesque of Ellsler's ballet *La Cracovienne*, in a cellar tavern (*Daily National Intelligencer* 1843). But unlike male wench dancers, a woman who imitated a man's dancing for humorous purposes overstepped her place and could put herself in danger. In Baltimore in 1842, "Conrad [Layman] allowed himself to get provoked by the dancing of [Mary O'Connor], which he imagined was in derision of himself, and pursued her into the house, up stairs, and there boxed her ears" (*Baltimore Sun* 1842, 1). Not until the late 1850s did female jig dancers begin cross-dressing for fun and fame. In a scene from the play *Three Fast Men* called "the Female Minstrels," two white girls disguised as white men performing in blackface demonstrated their expertise at moving and stepping as well as them. The scene was played for its broad humor, but it also became a platform for serious jig dancers like Julia Morgan, who published challenges in the sporting press and danced matches on stage while starring in the play.

Ballet's popularity offered the male jig dancer tools for gaining audiences and stage time; but his equipment did not work so well for the ballerina. By comparing and contrasting the styles of local favorites and well-known artistes, journalists encouraged rivalries between ballerinas. They also imposed a standard of femininity on female dancers. At Boston's Tremont Theater on May 9, 1842, Fanny Jones, a.k.a. "little Fanny of the Tremont," was pitted against Philadelphia's Mary Ann Lee in *La Bayadere*. "The house was crowded with their friends," Boston's *Daily Atlas* reported two days later:

> In the opening scene it was very evident that the star of the Tremont . . . would be eclipsed in brilliancy by her competitor from a sister city. . . . In the Trial Dance, act 2d, the superior physical power of Miss Lee told greatly in her favor. Her bounds seemed to take the audience by surprise. . . . But an exhibition of physical power, however surprising, produces little pleasurable effect, except when completely subordinate to grace of motion. . . . And, although much superior in this power to her juvenile rival, the dancing of Miss Lee failed to produce that pleasing effect, which in perfection would be the "poetry of motion." . . . The grace and beauty of Fanny's movements shone brighter in contrast with the greater vigor of her rival. They both received great applause from the audience, but our little Boston favorite continued the favorite still.

Lee, who also danced hornpipes on stage, possessed the physical power and dexterity needed by a challenge dancer. Yet *danseuses* with that kind of physicality were not fully respected in 1842, as they challenged notions of female frailty on which the emerging middle-class social order rested.

A number of challenge dancers, including John Diamond and Master Juba, garnered fame by imitating female dancers in the 1840s. But wench dancing was not Diamond's strong suit in 1853, when he faced off with Dick Sliter in the *Baltimore Sun*. Diamond excelled in all kinds of Negro jigs and reels, but his forte was the intricate down beats and syncopations of hornpipe walk-arounds. He therefore named those three steps in his original challenge. Sliter was also an expert Negro jig dancer, but in 1853 his specialty was wench dancing. In fact, his June 13 advertisement in the *Sun* read: "R. H. SLITER, the Champion Dancer of the World—who will imitate all the celebrated female dancers who have appeared in this country." So he countered Diamond's challenge, saying he would accept it so long as the steps "consist exclusively of Jigs, or else extend to the entire professional ability of the competitors." Diamond rejected those terms, calling them an equivocation and subterfuge meant to hide Sliter's own deficiencies. "I challenge him to Dance with me TWO 'JIGS,' TWO 'REELS,' and a 'WALK AROUND,'" Diamond repeated, "and dare him to an open and fair trial. If he is the victor, my bet is his" (*Baltimore Sun* 1853c, 2).

The Importance of Blackface

Both Diamond and Sliter were performing in Baltimore with large minstrel companies in 1853. Around 1843, quartets of white singers and musicians began to form blackface minstrel troupes that performed programs featuring their own renditions of African American music in harmony, interspersed with vulgar parodies of African American character and culture. These troupes provided another paying venue in which black and white challenge dancers could demonstrate their skills and compete with their peers. Unfortunately, the blackface minstrel mask that gave some individual dancers a means to improve their lives also "conveniently rationalized racial oppression" by inventing and commodifying degrading stereotypes "of an already enslaved, noncit izen people" (Lott 1993, 15). Minstrelsy turned blackface performance into pandering to racist curiosity and the corrupt taste of white society (Douglass 1848).

Blackface was never benign, and professional challenge dancers incorporated it from the beginning. However, blackface challenge dancing should not be conflated with minstrelsy for several reasons. Not only did competitive Negro jig dancing predate minstrelsy offstage as a casual dancing practice in laboring-class communities, blackface jig dancing preceded it on the stage. Traditionally, actors blacked-up to play "low" characters (servants, laborers, slaves, children) who transgressed their social bounds by getting one over on their betters (Cockrell 1997). This bottom-on-top humor became a prominent feature of American theater during the democratic and market revolutions of the 1830s, when young people from the countryside, manumitted slaves, and immigrants from abroad flooded Northern port cities in search of paid employment. To attract these potential audience members, theater managers (pummeled by the 1837 financial panic) reduced the price of their gallery seats (reserved for blacks, unaccompanied women and children, and the lowest classes of white men) to a shilling and engaged Negro jig dancers to perform in blackface between the plays.

For many in the gallery audience, the jig dancer's blackface makeup announced the popular origins of his dances. It acknowledged the bringing of lower-class amusements to the stage. It also signaled the non-European-ness of the dancing. Jigs, reels, and hornpipes came from Britain and Europe; everyone knew that. But when black people in America danced them, those steps became American. Challenge dancers buoyed this populist interpretation, and broadcast their particular expertise, by dancing their matches in blackface. And their "friends" (or what we might call fans) in the gallery experienced a sense of cultural importance as they watched and judged experts performing dances they felt were their own (Levine 1984; Lott 1991).

To professionalize, however, challenge dancers also had to draw in middle-class audiences. Theater managers often presented "characteristic dances" as interludes between the plays to entertain their more elite spectators. These dances were associated with common operatic groups (clowns, hunters, peasants) or were thought to express the innate character of ethnic or national groups (the Moorish "Alahambra," Spanish "Cachucha," Scottish "Highland Fling"). An eighteenth-century mainstay was the sailor's hornpipe, performed by men and women in hard shoes and distinguished by gestures and jackets found in the ethnically mixed maritime world (Bratton 1990). Often danced competitively, sailors' hornpipes appealed to seamen on leave who flocked to dockside shows, and to the new middle classes for whom hornpipe dancing was part of etiquette training.

In the late 1830s, "Ethiopian" dances surpassed sailors' hornpipes in popularity. They included Negro jigs, Virginia breakdowns, and Camptown hornpipes performed in lamp black and the garb of harlequins, street urchins, plantation slaves, and fancy-dressed women. These early blackface dances transformed the hybrid steps and competitions of challenge dancers into an art and sport that could be marketed to a range of spectators. In 1840, P. T. Barnum obtained theater engagements, including staged dancing matches, for white Negro-dancer Master Diamond by blacking his face and hands and assuring theater managers that he would draw a gallery audience and not be displeasing to other portions of the house. The dancer's blackface disguise made it safe for middle-class audiences to enjoy lower-class entertainments and was not yet alienating enough to keep gallery audiences away. It also confirmed middle-class preconceptions about blacks.

Hoping to cash in on this popular enthusiasm, blackface minstrels formed their troupes around Negro jig dancers. Each worked "in conjunction with" the other for their own benefit. Minstrel troupes relied on challenge dancers to draw audiences for them, and challenge dancers used the exposure gained by working with minstrel troupes to spread their names. Individual dancers moved from one troupe to another, exhibiting their champion steps, dancing matches after the show, and entering tournaments on the side. Minstrels followed their lead, staging banjo and singing competitions, and offering prizes for the best conundrum written by an audience member. This strategy paid off. By the late 1850s, blackface minstrelsy was a growth industry, and blackface performances had fossilized into predictable parodies of African Americans as slow-witted Southern darkies and ridiculously vain Northern dandies.

Yet even in the minstrelsy context, challenge dancing remained a trial of skill. "There were a lot of jig-dancers in those days—Inyard, Wooly Moon, Jack Diamond and others," recollected one enthusiast some decades later ("The Negro Minstrels" [ca. 1875]). To keep up with the competition, they had to keep improving. Audiences expected to see expert dancing even when minstrels performed scripted skits mocking challenge dancers. In 1857, a set piece entitled "Challenge Dance" was performed nightly by Bryant's Minstrels, an Irish-American led troupe. The characters, played by "two speaking Dancers," embody challenge dancing's mixed origins: "Ill-Count McGinnis (a Hibernian Darkie)" gets called out by "Farmyard Sam (an Ethiopian Exquisite)." The script blocks out the physical humor in the stage directions, but leaves it up to the dancers to make the competition convincing. At the climax of the sketch, the directions simply say: "new steps introduced."[7] Those new steps kept spectators who could tell the difference between counterfeit and competitive dancing in their seats.

African American abolitionist Frederick Douglass acknowledged the distinction between minstrelsy and challenge dancing when he went to see Gavitt's Original Ethiopian Minstrels in 1849. "Partly from a love of music, and partly from curiosity to see persons of color exaggerating the peculiarities of their race, we were induced last evening to hear these Serenaders," he wrote in *The North Star*. "The company is said to be composed entirely of colored people, and it may be so. We observed, however, that they too had recourse to the burnt cork and lamp black, the better to express their characters and to produce uniformity of complexion. Their lips, too, were evidently painted, and otherwise exaggerated." Douglass was not impressed by the troupe's singing, which "was but an imitation of white performers," or their "attempts at wit," the lack of which "gave their audience a very low idea of the shrewdness and sharpness of the race to which they belong." But at the risk of offending "our readers," who despise "everything that seems to feed the flame of American prejudice against colored people," he could not help but praise the dancer. "B. Richardson is an extraordinary character. His Virginia Breakdown excelled anything which we have ever seen of that description of dancing" (Douglass 1849).

Links to the Manly Art

In the 1850s, challenge dancing took on the trappings of the prizefighting ring. To entice the sporting community of middle-class men who bet on boxing, horse races, and other sports, and to distinguish their matches from their minstrelsy acts, Negro jig dancers adopted the patter of pugilists and negotiated high stakes challenges in the popular press. Contestants "socked-up" their stakes, "toed the mark," and demonstrated their "science."[8] Challenge dancers wore outfits associated with boxing, gave themselves stage names and regional affiliations ("the Albany Fat Boy," "the Boston Rattler"), held trials and exhibition tours, just as boxers traveled around re-enacting their prize bouts, competed in tournaments, and won champion belts (Figures 27.6 and 27.7).

As with boxers, skill, body type, and style made two dancers a good match-up. Some competitors invited any man or boy to batter the boards; others specified age and size. In the October 14, 1857, edition of the *New York Clipper*, Johnny West, a featherweight from Buffalo who called himself "Young America," challenged "any boy of 90 lbs in New York, to dance me a 40 stepped Jig, on time, for any amount they wish to stake."

The transformation of jig dancers into manly athletes (and marginalizing of female competitors) was aided by newspaper editors who promoted challenge dancing in their columns. Dancers representing an array of North American cities published challenges in the *New York Clipper*, a sports and entertainment periodical established in 1853. It was modeled on *Spirit of the Times: A Chronicle of the Turf, Agriculture, Field*

FIGURE 27.6. American-born prizefighter Tom Molineaux (1784–1818) wearing the boxing attire copied by challenge dancers.

Published by Robert Dighton, Spring Gardens, Jan. 1812. © National Portrait Gallery, London. [Reference Collection NPG D13314].

FIGURE 27.7. Jig-dancer Tommy Peel, wearing his dancing outfit and champion belt, posing with banjoist Frank Converse.

Minstrel Show Collection, box 4, folder 41, Performing Arts Collection, Harry Ransom Center, University of Texas at Austin.

Sports, Literature and the Stage, started in 1831, which in turn was modeled on *Bell's Life in London and Sporting Chronicle*, first published in 1822. All of these journals covered games and sports, along with theatrical news. Dance matches were not as numerous as pedestrian races or prizefights in the *Clipper*, but editor Frank Queen treated them exactly like other sports. He published challenges made by individual dancers and their sponsors in the "Challenges" section (or, if international, in the "Sports Abroad" section), publicized and covered important matches, and recorded results. Queen also "held the stakes" for competitors, answered readers' queries regarding dancers, printed letters disputing results, and denounced "humbug" or fixed dance matches.

But the connection between challenge dancing and boxing went deeper than outward appearances and newspaper coverage. Like prizefighting, challenge dancing thrived in port cities with large immigrant and black populations. Each group had its own community of dancers and boxers with their own specialties and their own audiences. These worlds of black boxers and dancers and white or Irish boxers and dancers were parallel and connected. Dancers performed for fighters' benefits, and boxers danced at sparring exhibitions. Sometimes boxers and dancers were even the same person. Black pugilist and "gymnast" Aaron Molineaux danced his "great Decanter Dance" for boxer J. E. Taylor's benefit in Boston in 1854 (*New York Clipper* 1854, 3). Johnny Golden clog danced with "Trotter Ned" of Bradford after sparring at his own benefit in New York, and champion jig dancer Ike Laws held a trial dance with Cade at the Philadelphia Sparring Association's benefit in 1858 (*Clipper* 1858b; 1858c). These connections to boxing conferred honor and manliness on the sport of challenge dancing. They also distinguished it from the competitive social dancing of men and women.

One boxing-like exchange in the *Clipper* inadvertently revealed the overlapping of these male dancing communities. In 1856, newcomer Mickey Warren challenged Dick Sliter to a match for from $100 to $500, "the dance to be a jig, straight reel, Irish reel and Irish jig. What says Sliter?" Sliter countered that "he would dance him or any other man a straight jig for from $500 to $1000, or will dance any white man (not excepting Mickey Warren) four dances he (Dick Sliter) can name" (*Clipper* 1856b, 151; 1856d, 186). By limiting the steps to jigs and reels, including Irish ones, Warren's challenge appealed to Irish dancers and spectators. Mass emigration from Ireland during the Great Famine of 1845 to 1852 augmented the ranks of jig dancers in the United States (as did German immigrants after the failed revolution of 1848). Among the newly arrived Irish would have been dancers familiar with all the steps Warren named. They might even have danced them in rural competitions back home. Warren, who may have been an immigrant himself, chose "a jig, straight reel, Irish reel and Irish jig" as his dances to drum up interest in the match and perhaps attract some challenges from the ranks of recent immigrants like "T. J. Gannon, *Champion Dancer of Ireland*," who published his own challenge in the *Clipper* on March 25, 1854. "I will dance any man or boy one Irish Jig and one Irish Reel, single, double, or treble, in public or in private, for the sum of One Thousand Dollars. Money and man ready at T. Scroggy's Segar store, 443 Vine street, Philadelphia."

But Sliter's expertise was not in Irish jigs, so he raised the stakes substantially to keep poor immigrants off the floor, then announced that he would dance *any other* man a straight jig. This exclusion of the Irish denoted the distinction between American Irish jigs and Irish Irish jigs. Apparently, Sliter believed he could dance the former better than any native-born American man (white or black) able to meet the wager. But he would only dance any *white* man the dances "he can name." Those dances would have been Negro jigs, such as his "original rattlesnake jig" or "Tar River dance." The barring of non-white men suggests that Negro jigs were considered most excellently done by African American dancers. It also tells us that Sliter knew there were champions among the black dancer community who could have raised the money and beat him.

On the other hand, challenge dancing's embrace of boxing's manliness led to the exclusion of female dancers entirely. After 1855, a sudden economic downturn and declining international economy, culminating in the Panic of 1857, stimulated a flurry of dancing challenges in American and English papers. Among those contenders were female jig dancers who knew a good thing when they saw it. Women had always danced jigs, reels, and hornpipes on and off the stage. But in the late 1850s, Nellie Howard, Kate Partington, Sally Mason, Mattie Clare, Lizzie La Grange, Clara Burton, and a host of others started billing themselves as champion dancers and advertising their own challenges in the popular press.

Like male jig dancers who took advantage of the blackface minstrelsy boom to launch professional careers, female jig dancers cashed in on the rise of concert saloons and music halls. Although these new venues commonly featured the "leg business" (such as the recently imported French can can, danced in long skirts so that petticoats, legs, and under garments were exposed during the kicks), the champion dancer's complicated steps and professional style distinguished her from the choruses of "jiggers" and "ballet-girls" with little training who made their livings alongside her (*New York Herald* 1858, 7; Logan 1869). Female challenge dancers also wore outfits that identified them as excelsior jig dancers and competed in dancing matches and tournaments (*Morning Republican* 1873).

An 1860s stock image used on theatrical playbills (Figure 27.8) and an 1870s daguerreotype of jig dancer Kitty O'Neil (Figure 27.9) present the female champion's demeanor. In both pictures, the dancer's serious face signals that she means business. She also accommodates the preference for legwork among concert saloons' male patrons by wearing short pants embellished with lace and fringe. But rather than donning the flesh-colored tights and low-cut bodice of female chorus dancers (which suggested nudity), she sports the white stockings, black pumps, and long-sleeved blouse worn by male competitors (which signified athletic skill).

During the 1860s, Civil War labor shortages encouraged women who were competitive dancers to openly pursue their desired profession. In May 1862, Julia Morgan, "the Boston Pet," challenged Tommy Peel, Dick Carroll, Hank Mason, E. Bowers, "'OR ANY OTHER MAN,' or female in the country" to dance a match for a stake of $100 to $500 in the *New York Clipper*. Naomi Porter, "the New York Favorite" accepted Morgan's challenge in the *Boston Herald*, followed by "Kate Stanton, the Invincible," who took on all comers (*Herald* 1862, 3). No men accepted Morgan's challenge, but a few brave souls did dance matches against other women. In 1863, Lotta Crabtree, Johnny Mason, and Tim Darling faced off in several matches in Comstock, Nevada, with a silver cup as the prize. Comstock audiences generally backed Lotta, according to one local paper, for the simple reason that "when a woman's toes or tongue are well trained, those of no mortal man can keep pace" (Watson 1964).

To become stars, female jig dancers had to demonstrate flawless execution of a variety of difficult steps, incorporate humor into their dances, make challenges, and win wagers, just like their male counterparts. They also had to display feminine grace and versatility, especially the ability to sing as well as dance. This "difference" would place women on a separate list of professionals in the chronicles of jig dancing. Yet for more than a decade, these female competitors reclaimed the prerogative they had enjoyed as social dancers. They challenged each other, and their erstwhile male partners, to dance them off the floor.

Although dancing matches were judged differently from boxing matches, the fact that both were competitions was key to their enduring popularity. In the 1840s, pugilists fought until one dropped or (as sometimes happened) died. Decisions at 1850s dancing matches were based on time, numerical advantage in steps, execution, and style. Three judges (one chosen by each competitor and one impartial referee) watched and listened to the dancers, counting steps and marking down (in chalk) any rhythmic mistakes. Most judges were dancers themselves, selected for their ability and knowledge of the art. Their race depended on the venue, but did not always determine the outcome. Most likely taverns patronized by blacks had black judges, while theaters dominated by whites had white judges. Audience members also took part in the judging, closely watching the dancers' steps, cheering and applauding their favorite, and assessing the chalkers' scores. Wagers ranged from $1 to $1,000. Dancers also competed for valuable prizes, such as silver cups and medals.

At a $200 championship bout in Chicago in August 1856, Joe Brown danced "fifteen minutes and one-fourth second, making ninety-nine movements, and breaking time at three different periods," while Dick Sliter danced "nineteen minutes, making one hundred and twenty-three movements, and breaking time at two different periods." Sliter danced longer than Brown. He also danced a greater number of steps while making fewer mistakes. The judges also found Sliter superior to Brown in "ease and grace of dancing" and, therefore, decided in his favor. But spectators at the match contested the decision on account of the music: "We agree, without reflecting upon the judges, with the eighteen hundred who witnessed the contest, that there was but *one brake* made, and that by Mr. Brown, in consequence of the musician misunderstanding him." Bettors also challenged decisions when the crowd got so loud a dancer could not hear the musician, or vice versa. Dancing master Mathew Kershaw complained in the *Clipper* after his pupil lost a match in Philadelphia in 1857: "as for the three chalks which were put against Edward Chew, I resolutely object to, and am prepared to swear . . . that he only missed one, and that was caused by the clapping of hands" (*New York Clipper* 1856a, 139; 1856c, 156; 1857b, 52).

FIGURE 27.8. Female jig dancer costume.

Specimens of Theatrical Cuts: Being Fac-similes, in Miniature, of Poster Cuts; Comprising Colored and Plain Designs, Suitable for Theatrical, Variety and Circus Business (Ledger Job Printing Establishment, Philadelphia, c1869), TS240.12.1.69(A)F (book 1, book 2), Harvard Theatre Collection, Houghton Library, Harvard University.

FIGURE 27.9. "Kitty O'Neil, Celebrated Jig Dancer," circa 1877.

Card Photograph Collection, box 67, Performing Arts Collection, Harry Ransom Center, University of Texas at Austin.

Disputes over victors were common in challenge dancing after 1855, when the economic downturn began closing theaters and other venues. Bets and prizes represented much-needed income to dancers. Dance matches also drew large paying crowds, which made them tempting to fake. All contests were shows, produced to draw in spectators who would spend money on entrance fees, drinks, food, or bets. What made a "trial of skill" a "match" were the risks taken by the performers and their sponsors. No challenge dancer ever admitted to throwing a match. But like boxers and other athletes, they sometimes agreed to compete for a portion of the ticket receipts, no matter who won. "Humbug" matches like these, where "not one dollar" was actually bet or staked, were "mere speculations," *Clipper* editor Frank Queen clarified. Nobody lost, so long as the show drew a big enough crowd to cover expenses (1857b, 52).

Most competitive dancers held fast to the distinction between wagers and wages. Diamond refused to consider the Cincinnati trial of skill against Sliter a real match because he was paid $50 for the five nights. "No allusion was ever made to a belt," he claimed, "or did we ever dance for one" (*Baltimore Sun* 1853a, 2). Similarly, Mickey Warren indignantly pulled out of a tournament after the organizer asked if he "would be satisfied to take $20" in lieu of the publicized prize, a gold watch (*New York Clipper* 1858a, 294). The terms of a match measured a dancer's reputation. To make a match, both dancers deposited in advance a "forfeit," or portion of the stakes, as surety. This act proved their worth. If contestants failed to put their money down, they were pronounced "blowers" or "braggers."

The need and pride that lay behind wagers were demonstrated in a series of challenges published in the *Clipper* in 1858. At the end of April, jig dancer Hank Mason (a.k.a. "Hank, the Mason") challenged "Champion Jig Dancer" Pete Lane to dance him a reel, jig, and walk-around for $200. Lane countered that four years ago he had challenged "any of the would-be-champions" to dance him one Negro jig. "This has always been my challenge, and he knows it. Now, if [Mason] means business, let him say so in your next issue; and to prevent blowing, let him deposit in your hands $25 or $50, as a forfeit, for a match for $500 or $1000, to dance for the 'Championship of Jig Dancing.'" Lane's challenge was answered on May 15 by Michael Cunningham, "better known as the Albany Fat Boy," who said that he and Lane had made a match some weeks since, but Lane had failed to put up a forfeit. "[Lane] said he had no money to make the match with," explained Cunningham, "but would meet me the following morning, which he neglected to do." Then he reiterated his offer to dance Lane for any amount of money or for free. Lane refused Cunningham's offer, calling his statement "a base lie," and accepted instead Mickey Warren's May 22 challenge to dance Lane or anyone else "a straight jig, reel, or walk around, for from $100 to $500 a side." Warren also suggested dancing for a smaller wager if the sum was too much for other competitors. These terms suited Lane, who agreed to dance Warren "*one straight jig*" and promised to send his forfeit "as soon as my *health* will warrant its *deposit*." When he still hadn't coughed up two weeks later, the *Clipper* chided him: "[Warren] left a forfeit with us two or three weeks ago. Lane promised to 'sock up,' but failed in the attempt. He now 'takes a back seat,' previous to being read out of the circle." Such trash talk was the lingua franca of boxing and other sports. But Lane never did come up to the scratch. He died a week later of consumption, aged twenty-five (*New York Clipper* 1858e).

The Saga of the Belts

Like boxers, dancers received belts, paid for by local subscribers, that designated them champion of a particular city or state. Awarded after a series of matches or at special ceremonies honoring the competitor's career, these belts were valuable (made with precious metals) and, unlike a "championship" belt, nontransferable. In other words, it was up to the individual whether or not to stake one of these belts in a bout. A national or world championship belt was distinct from a city or state champion belt in that it moved from champion to champion. For example, in 1842, when Ben Caunt wore the Champion of England belt for prizefighting, William Thompson (a.k.a. Bendigo) challenged him to a match, adding that he possessed "a belt which he will tie to the stakes against the transferable Champion's Belt, and fight Caunt for the brace of them" (*Spirit of the Times* 1842, 223).

Champion dancers adopted this boxing belt tradition. When Naomi Porter accepted Julia Morgan's $100 to $500 challenge in Boston in 1862, she proposed that instead of the wager they "dance for a SILVER CHAMPION BELT, of the value of $100," to be awarded the winner of three out of five dances. To increase revenue, she also suggested the match extend over five evenings. When the match took place, Morgan danced as "the Boston Pet" and Porter as the "New York Favorite," thereby turning it into a championship bout and rendering the belt transferable (*Boston Post* 1862a, 1862b).

No one minded that various cities claimed champion dancers, but the national title was a contentious issue. With no institution to back their claims, any number of dancers might adopt the moniker "Champion Jig Dancer of the World." And several did. Hank Mason compared the situation to that of boxers in 1858: "This championship of jig dancing reminds me of an article in the CLIPPER last winter, in relation to the championship of the manly art of self defense, between Morrissey, the Benicia Boy, and Hyer; they all three claimed the championship, but neither one had the honor of contesting for it." According to Mason, "the only man who ever wore a champion belt in this country for jig and reel dancing was Master John Diamond, who is now deceased; unless others purchased them for themselves privately" (*New York Clipper* 1858d, 23).

John Diamond received his "splendid belt, with a silver plate" at a special ceremony held at Holliday Street Theatre, the very night Sliter opened at the Baltimore Museum. The belt was paid for and awarded by the members of Baltimore's Independent Fire Company (*American and Commercial Daily Advertiser* 1853, 3). R. H. Sliter purportedly received his "*Dancer's Champion Belt*" from the citizens of Cincinnati. Both dancers claimed that his was the championship belt and the other's a local champion's belt. Therefore, Diamond proposed that they dance for the two belts and a wager, at some neutral venue in Baltimore, so that there would be no mistaking who was the national champion thereafter.

It does not look like Diamond and Sliter ever danced their 1853 match. Sliter authorized his manager, Sam Sanford, to meet with Diamond to discuss terms the following day, after which the verbal abuse turned vitriolic. When Diamond would not agree to Sliter's counter-challenge, or to dance the match at the Museum ("to fill the coffers of his manager"), Sanford wrote a card to the *Sun* accusing him of ingratitude, since Diamond had once come to him for charity. Diamond's manager John T. Ford responded by accusing Sanford of "promulgating falsehoods" and displaying "*that virtue which loses its sacredness by being trumpeted*" (*Baltimore Sun* 1853b, 1853d, 1853e, 2). And then the whole correspondence simply ended. Perhaps the rivalry had been staged from the beginning. It was certainly entertaining reading. But more likely was that the two dancers saw no professional benefit in dancing the match. In the end, each kept his own belt. Diamond wore his whenever he performed, until his death in 1857. Sliter lost his to Joe Brown at the rematch of their 1856 bout. Brown took the belt and title "Champion Dancer of the World" to England in 1857, whereupon he was immediately challenged by the Lancashire champion dancer John Booth for assuming the international title without dancing for it (*Bell's Life* 1857).

Antebellum challenge dancing was not just the sport of men like Diamond and Sliter. Challenge dancers relied on, competed with, and emulated an array of high and low cultural forms, from Irish and African American set dancing, to ballet, blackface, and boxing. The elements of their practice and competition enlarge our understanding of the world in which they danced. From them, we learn about the economic and social forces shaping cultural offerings in antebellum America, including the booms and busts of a volatile market economy that sent thousands of men, women, and children tramping to urban centers in search of freedom and prosperity. We see how challenge dancing reflected and shaped evolving racial, gender, and class formations, how its humble hybrid origins held out the promise of a more egalitarian popular culture, even as slavery divided the nation and limited democracy to white male wage earners. Challenge dancers also show us that middle-class definitions of childhood and notions of female propriety were in flux. Their contests reveal the fungibility of sports and arts, and the significance of small wagers in an era of commercial vigor, speculation, and humbuggery. But the Civil War would change all that, and when the circumstances in which people dance changes, so too does the meaning of their competition.

NOTES

1. For the origins and terminology of American jig and Negro dancing, see Brennan (2001), Foley (2013), Green (1996), Malone (1996), O'Connor (2001), and Stearns and Stearns (1968).
2. Many of the white dancers were of Irish Catholic descent, an ethnicity whose whiteness had not yet been established in the United States. For further discussion of Irishness as a racial category, see Saxton (1990), Ignatiev (1995), and Roediger (1999).
3. This chapter relies on primary source materials gathered at numerous archives: playbills and posters, sheet music, engravings, daguerreotypes, minstrelsy chronicles, and other theatrical ephemera from the Harvard Theatre Collection and Houghton Library, American Antiquarian Society, and Harry Ransom Center; nineteenth-century literature, nonfiction, and collected folklore from the Irish Traditional Music Archives, Dublin City Archives, and National Library of Ireland; private letters, memoirs, scrapbooks, theater annals, urban literature and travel guides, dancing and boxing manuals, and sporting journals from the New York Historical Society, New York Public Library, Pennsylvania Historical Society, Princeton University Archives, and other university library archives; ballet librettos, play scripts, and contemporary novels from HathiTrust Digital Library; and daily and weekly newspapers from several online sites. I have also studied with performers and scholars who specialize in Irish and African dance and music, and in historical forms and styles from the antebellum period.
4. "Camp towns" were racially mixed city suburbs that began as soldiers' camps during the Revolutionary War.
5. Personal fame and the relatively better situation of black performers in Britain (which abolished slavery throughout the Empire in 1833) and increased racial tensions in America's Northeastern states following the Fugitive Slave Act of 1850 may have influenced Juba's decision never to return to the United States.

6. A *bayadére* was an Indian temple dancer. Zoloe was an outsider, unfamiliar with the local language, who had to make her sorrows and joys known through movement.
7. Williams (n.d.).
8. At early boxing matches, wagers were literally placed in a sock or purse ("socked-up") and hung from the stakes that marked the ring. At the beginning of each round, pugilists were required to put one toe up against a line scratched in the dirt dividing the ring ("to come up to scratch" or "toe the mark") to prove they were fit enough for the bout. A boxer who relied on training rather than brute force exhibited his "science."

References

American and Commercial Daily Advertiser. 1853. "Holliday Street Theatre." June 20, 3.
Baltimore Sun. 1842. "*State vs. Conrad Layman*." July 11, 1.
Baltimore Sun. 1853a. "No Subterfuge' but Toe the Mark." June 27, 2.
Baltimore Sun. 1853b. "Challenge Accepted." June 27, 2.
Baltimore Sun. 1853c. "Truth Is Mighty and Will Prevail." June 28, 2.
Baltimore Sun. 1853d. "Card." June 28, 2.
Baltimore Sun. 1853e. "Reply to Mr. S. S. Sanford—A Card." June 29, 2.
Bell's Life in London. 1857. "A Challenge to the American Champion." August 30, 7.
Biddle, Charles. 1883. *The Autobiography of Charles Biddle*. Philadelphia: E. Claxton.
Boston Herald. 1851. "Federal Street Theatre." December 6, 3.
Boston Herald. 1862. "$500 Challenge! Miss Julia Morgan." May 29, 3.
Boston Post. 1862a. "Challenge Accepted! Arrival of the Champions." June 5, [3].
Boston Post. 1862b. "National Theatre." June 9, [3].
Bratton, J. S. 1990. "Dancing a Hornpipe in Fetters." *Folk Music Journal* 6(1): 65–82.
Breathnach, Breandán. 1971. *Folk Music and Dances of Ireland*. Cork, Ireland: Mercier.
Brennan, Helen. 2001. *The Story of Irish Dance*. Lanham, MD: Roberts Rinehart.
Brown, T. Allston. 1912. "Early History of Negro Minstrelsy, Its Rise and Progress in the United States." *The New York Clipper*. June 15, 3.
"Céleste, Madam." 1910. In *Encyclopedia Britannica*, edited by Hugh Chisholm. 11th ed., Vol. V, 599. Cambridge University Press.
Cockrell, Dale. 1997. *Demons of Disorder: Early Blackface Minstrels and Their World*. Cambridge, UK: Cambridge University Press.
Daily National Intelligencer. 1843. "From Our New York Correspondent." March 16.
Dickens, Charles. 1842. *American Notes for General Circulation*. London: Chapman & Hall.
Douglass, Frederick. 1848. "The Hutchinson Family—Hunkerism." *North Star*. October 27, 2.
Douglass, Frederick. 1849. "Gavitt's Original Ethiopian Serenaders." *North Star*. June 29, 2.
Foley, Catherine E. 2013. *Step Dancing in Ireland: Culture and History*. Surrey, UK: Ashgate.
Foster, George. 1850. *New York By Gas-Light*. New York: Dewitt & Davenport.
Foster, R. F. 1989. *Modern Ireland 1600–1972*. London: Penguin.
Friel, Mary. 2004. *Dancing as a Social Pastime in the South-east of Ireland, 1800–1897*. Dublin: Four Courts.
Green, Doris. 1996. "Traditional Dance in Africa." In *African Dance an Artistic, Historical and Philosophical Inquiry*, edited by Kariamu Welsh Asante, 13–28. Trenton, NJ: African World.

Harris, Leslie M. 2003. *In the Shadow of Slavery: African Americans in New York City, 1620–1863*. Chicago: University of Chicago Press.

Hodges, Graham. 1997. "'Desirable Companions and Lovers': Irish and African Americans in the Sixth Ward, 1830-1870." In *The New York Irish*, edited by Ronald H. Bayor and Timothy J. Meagher, 107–124. Baltimore: Johns Hopkins University Press.

Homans, Jennifer. 2010. *Apollo's Angels: A History of Ballet*. New York: Random House.

Ignatiev, Noel. 1995. *How the Irish Became White*. New York: Routledge.

Kennedy, Patrick. 1867. *The Banks of the Boro: A Chronicle of the County of Wexford* London: Simpkin, Marshall.

Jamison, Phil. 2015. *Hoedowns, Reels, and Frolics: Roots and Branches of Southern Appalachian Dance*. Chicago: University of Illinois Press.

"Lee, Mary Ann." 1971. In *Notable American Women 1607–1950: A Biographical Dictionary*, edited by Edward T. James, Janet Wilson James, and Paul S. Boyer, Vol. II G–O, 387–388. Cambridge, MA: Belnap.

Levine, Lawrence W. 1984. "William Shakespeare and the American People: A Study in Cultural Transformation." *American Historical Review* 89(1): 34–66.

Logan, Olive. 1869. "About the Leg Business." *Apropos of Women and Theatre*. New York: Carleton.

Lott, Eric. 1991. "'The Seeming Counterfeit': Racial Politics and Early Blackface Minstrelsy." *American Quarterly* 43(2): 223–254.

Lott, Eric. 1993. *Love and Theft: Blackface Minstrelsy and the American Working Class*. New York: Oxford University Press.

Mackenzie, R. Shelton. 1854. *Bits of Blarney*. New York: Redfield.

Mahar, William J. 1999. *Behind the Burnt Cork Mask: Early Blackface Minstrelsy and Antebellum American Popular Culture*. Chicago: University of Chicago Press.

Malone, Jacqui. 1996. *Steppin' on the Blues: The Visible Rhythms of African American Dance*. Urbana and Chicago: University of Illinois Press.

Manchester Times and Manchester and Salford Advertiser and Chronicle. 1848. "Juba." October 21, 5.

Masten, April F. 2013. "Partners in Time: Dancers, Musicians, and Negro Jigs in Early America." *Common-Place* 13(2). http://www.common-place.org/vol-13/no-02/masten/

Masten, April F. 2014. "The Challenge Dance: Black-Irish Exchange in Antebellum America." In *Cultures in Motion*, edited by Daniel T. Rogers, Helmut Reimitz, and Bhavani Raman, 23–59. Princeton, NJ: Princeton University Press.

Masten, April F. 2015. "Challenge Dancing in Antebellum America: Sporting Men, Vulgar Women, and Blacked-up Boys." *Journal of Social History* 48(3): 605–634.

Morning Republican. 1873. "Modern Jig Dancing." April 22, 2.

National Theatre Playbill. June 5, 1840. Folder—Diamond Minstrels and Master Diamond. Box 5 (Co-Du). Playbills—Companies/Minstrels. Harvard Theatre Collection.

"The Negro Minstrels of the Nights Gone By." [ca. 1875]. Clips Pers (Bryant, Dan). Harvard Theatre Collection.

New Orleans Daily Picayune. 1891. "Old Time Minstrels." July 5, 10.

New Theatre Playbill. February 22, 1841. Folder—Diamond Minstrels and Master Diamond. Box 5 (Co-Du). Playbills—Companies/Minstrels. Harvard Theatre Collection.

New York Clipper. 1854. "Benefit for Mr. J. E. Taylor." June 24, 3.

New York Clipper. 1856a. "Match Dance between Sliter and Brown." August 23, 139.

New York Clipper. 1856b. "To Dick Sliter." August 30, 151.

New York Clipper. 1856c. "The Match Dance—Sliter vs. Brown." September 6, 156.

New York Clipper. 1856d. "Sliter and Warren." October 4, 186.

New York Clipper. 1857a. "Dancing." March 28, 387.

New York Clipper. 1857b. "How It Was Done—The Late Dancing Match." June 6, 52.

New York Clipper. 1857c. "Dancing Match." September 12, 163.

New York Clipper. 1858a. "To the Editor of the Clipper." January 2, 294.

New York Clipper. 1858b. "Sparring and Dancing." January 20, 323.

New York Clipper. 1858c. "Philadelphia Sparring Association." February 6, 331.

New York Clipper. 1858d. "In answer to Pete Lane's remarks. . . ." May 8, 23.

New York Clipper. 1858e. April 24, 7; May 1, 15; May 15, 31; May 22, 39; May 29, 47; June 12, 63; June 19, 71.

New York Herald. 1858. "Franklin Museum." January 25, 7.

New York Morning Herald. 1840a. "Challenge." July 23.

New York Morning Herald. 1840b. "Challenge Accepted!" July 24.

New York Morning Herald. 1840c. "Vauxhall Garden." August 3.

New York Whip. 1842. "Our Eleventh Walk about Town." December 31, 2.

Nichols, Thomas L. 1864. *Forty Years of American Life.* London: J. Maxwell.

Northup, Solomon. [1853] 1970. *Twelve Years a Slave.* Mineola, NY: Dover.

O'Connor, Nuala. 2001. *Bringing It All Back Home: The Influence of Irish Music.* Dublin: Merlin.

Odell, George C. D. 1931. *Annals of the New York Stage,* Vol. V. New York: Columbia University Press.

Philadelphia Public Ledger. 1840. "The Dancing Match." March 4, 2.

Robert, Grace. 1946. *The Borzoi Book of Ballets.* New York: Knopf.

Roediger, David R. 1999. *The Wages of Whiteness.* New York. Verso.

Saxton, Alexander. 1990. *The Rise and Fall of the White Republic: Class Politics and Mass Culture in Nineteenth-Century America.* New York: Verso.

Spirit of the Times. 1840. "Things Theatrical." February 15, 600.

Spirit of the Times. 1842. "Bendigo's Benefit." July 9, 223.

Stearns, Marshall, and Jean Stearns. 1968. *Jazz Dance: The Story of American Vernacular Dance.* New York: Da Capo.

Sunday Flash. 1841. "Vauxhall Humbug Again." September 26, 2.

Szwed, John F. and Morton Marks. 1988. "The Afro-American Transformation of European Set Dances and Dance Suites." *Dance Research Journal* 20(1): 29–36.

Thomas, James. 1984. *From Tennessee Slave to St. Louis Entrepreneur: The Autobiography of James Thomas,* edited by Loren Schweninger. Columbia: University of Missouri Press.

Thompson, Robert Farris. 1991. *Dancing between Two Worlds: Kongo-Angola Culture and the Americas.* New York: Caribbean Cultural Center.

Watson, Margaret G. 1964. *Silver Theatre: Amusements of the Mining Frontier in Early Nevada, 1850–1864.* Glendale, CA: Arthur H. Clark.

White, Shane, and Graham J. White. 1998. *Stylin': African American Expressive Culture from Its Beginnings to the Zoot Suit.* Ithaca, NY: Cornell University Press.

Williams, Henry Llewellyn. [n.d.] *Challenge Dance.* London and New York: S. French.

AFTERWORD

Who Is Competing?

SUSAN LEIGH FOSTER

WHAT an abundance of dances, all considered here in terms of their relation to competition: historical dances, contemporary dances, dances of so many genres, and from a wide variety of geographical locations. Readers are presented with an arresting variety of dance types and functions, and also, with an equally diverse set of analytic perspectives. Authors invite us to consider competition in relation to intersections of categories of identity and processes of identification, such as those through which race, gender, class, ethnicity, regionality, nationality, and post-coloniality are established, as well as affiliations to the urban, the cosmopolitan, the transnational, or the global. We also learn how institutions construct or contribute to competitive environments, how competition can attract media attention and/or different audiences; and how some dance forms had meanings and functions prior to the time they entered their competitive form, while others built competition into their structure as an intrinsic contributor to their meaning from inception. We are also invited to contemplate competition's relationship to notions of virtuosity and to the experience of authenticity. And all this in relation to both predetermined or set choreography, as well as improvised choreography.

These wonderfully diverse examinations of competition analyze what is won through competition: money, honor, prestige, status, respect, adoration, celebrity, a career, or even the opportunity to deride and debunk sexist or racist stereotypes. And they also speculate about what is lost, or gained, through failure and error. They interrogate the different kinds of criteria utilized in determining winners of a competition, showing that a wide range of values is exercised when identifying a winner. These include the appropriate, the superior, the accurate, the proper or most representative, or, alternatively, that which stretches the form in new directions. Even that which is most suitable for filming sometimes wins.

The chapters also consider the personal rewards to be gained from competition: the opportunity it affords to surround oneself with others passionately committed to dancing; the ability for an individual to distinguish him- or herself from or within the group or community; or the occasion for demonstrating skills, some of which may be applicable across multiple social rubrics of engagement. Competition can promote a sense of agency or initiative; it can encourage a dancer to "put oneself out there" or to take a risk. Competition can establish a style or a sense of camaraderie. It can inculcate a feeling of belonging. Competing with oneself, against others, with others against others, against the televisual or other mediatized image of the dancing body, you try harder. Competition pushes you to places you did not imagine were possible.

Competition can enable dancers to assist in the passage of knowledge from one public to another as national patrimony, indigenous authenticity, or tourist attraction. Competition can foster a sense of participation in reviving and revitalizing a dance practice, or in corrupting it. It may encourage participation for the purposes of community affirmation, or in order to reappropriate and protect a form whose local identity had been suppressed and whose vitality co-opted. Competition can advance a political agenda, or it can provide release from the constraints of social mores and protocols.

Currently, as Sherril Dodds points out in her Introduction to this volume, competition can be found, not only in the diverse forms of dance represented here, but also in almost every aspect of our daily lives, from the most local to the most global. It permeates the everyday, the ways we cultivate the body and fashion our selves; it attaches itself to how we shop, eat, drive, and even converse with one another. Because of the assimilation of private into public space, many of these activities that were previously more resistant to competition have now been absorbed into it, or at least affected by it. Some of us have been alerted to the effects of this pervasively rampant acceleration in competitive practices through our students, whose bodies, at least in the United States, are now regularly marked by training in competition dance. And even if we do not watch them, we also have been asked by our friends and colleagues what we think of the many competition-oriented reality television shows that have glutted the networks in recent years. I confess that I, for one, have been deeply concerned by this surge in competition-oriented dance and dance training, and am fearful that it signals a large-scale co-optation of dance into a capitalist machinery of production.

The chapters in this volume provide a wonderful counterpoint to that view, by demonstrating that competition in dance has existed in so many historical periods and cultural contexts worldwide. Many of them also address the multitude of positive outcomes that competition can effect. In particular, many chapters illuminate the ways that competition forges community, sustains traditions, or even provides a refuge from hegemonic prejudices. One question I have, however, is whether, in this period of intensified focus on competition, it is possible to see clearly enough what kind of sociality competition is producing. Furthermore, is it even possible to engage in competition that is geared toward forms of social exchange outside the pervasively capitalist culture in which we are living?

Pressured by the ubiquitous drive to acquire more money, but also what Pierre Bourdieu called distinction, we find ourselves most often defined as individual agents who are maneuvering for a better position, more visibility, and a stronger network. Pressured equally by the immense precarity that global capitalism is constructing through the vast discrepancies between workers and elites, both in terms of wages and also cultural capital, it is nearly impossible not to assimilate to the ideology of the individual as an autonomous entity and of society as a network of such entities who each operate in isolation from one another.

From within that worldview, we lose a sense of the social as a structuring of obligations and supports that can literally define who we are. Instead, through mechanisms for self-representation such as Facebook and YouTube, we identify increasingly as discrete and independent, operating within a milieu of similarly singular and self-fashioning people. The social, no longer a collective understanding of the world and how we move in and through it, now merely facilitates the positioning and repositioning of the self within a network of similar selves. We start to assume that each of us is jockeying for a better position, using our contacts with others to advance, to acquire more resources, to present a better image. In short, we become entrepreneurial.

There are, seemingly, many advantages to this autonomy, not the least of which is the sense of freedom and the ease of access. Students are encouraged to choose a class that suits their needs, to design their own training regimen so as to cultivate themselves as dancers who are fulfilling their physical potential and maximizing their marketability. Teachers can devise classes that transmit clear skill sets, while also calculating how to be effective, trend-setting, challenging, or enjoyable for students. Choreographers are enabled to pick and choose from different vocabularies, to match movement phrases to the capabilities of dancers, and to devise unique and original forms of spectacle. Viewers likewise enjoy the freedom of choosing what to watch, where, how often, and for what kind of price. The ideal of freedom is thus promulgated as the discrete choice of each individual to act in a given way, acknowledging certain constraints that would infringe on others' freedom, but always with the conception, again, of the autonomous individual as central.

This free and easy access to dance also brings with it an apprehension that nothing is authentic, and that realization, in turn, produces feelings of anxiety and anomie. Because everything, literally everything, is motivated by self-interest, it is impossible to ascertain the legitimacy of personal investment in any aspect of dancing or of one's friends' alliances and allegiances to dance and to one another. Marvelously, and I write this in a voice dripping with irony, numerous strategies are being promulgated to assuage that anxiety, including the praise given to working the hardest and to doing better than ever.

Because of this intense focus on the autonomy of each individual, it becomes difficult to discern when competition is functioning as a way for dancers to honor one another or merely to advance themselves individually, or when dancers are competing in order to pay homage to the dance or in an effort to win. It becomes hard to sense when competition contributes to the very fabric of a dance's aesthetics and when it is being mobilized for personal gain. It becomes nearly impossible to assess the extent to which competition used in favor of communal affirmation actually builds community, or whether it simply gives individuals a sense of moving alongside one another, as equally motivated people, each working toward self-betterment.

Does community not depend upon a mutual sense of reciprocity and indebtedness? Wouldn't the teacher, for example, who is working to build a communal relationship with students necessarily consider how best to transmit, not skills, but knowledge about dance—its history and aesthetic values, and also the ways that any given dancer could come to understand herself as partaking in and contributing to those values? Wouldn't the student necessarily take on the responsibility of being knowledgeable about dance and the history of investments made in it? In forms of dance where there is an identified choreographer, wouldn't that person be motivated to contribute his or her thought and creativity, not for personal gain or renown, but for the vitality of the dance? And for all those who watch dance, could they give their attention to it, not to be satisfied and gratified by eye-popping virtuosity, but in order to increase their understanding of dance and what it means to be a body?

To construct community in these ways comes with its own price, one measured, not in terms of monetary values, but rather in relation to time "spent" and thought "given." It requires individuals to become vulnerable and to recognize their mutual dependence on one another. It also requires us to take a stand against the profound sense of alienation that accompanies the act of dancing purely to get ahead. In order to take such a stand, we, as scholars, teachers, choreographers, and dancers, may well want to ask, what kind of subject—isolated and autonomous, or mutually defined and dependent—is dancing?

Index